America

A CONCISE HISTORY

Volume 2
SINCE 1865

CANADA

L. Superior

Duluth

MINNESOTA

St. Paul
Minneapolis

Sioux Falls

IOWA

Des Moines

Omaha
Lincoln

WISCONSIN

Madison

Chicago

Milwaukee

MICHIGAN

L. Michigan

L. Huron

Lansing

Detroit

L. Erie

Toledo

Gary

Mississippi R.

Illinois R.

ILLINOIS

Springfield

Wabash R.

INDIANA

Indianapolis

OHIO

Columbus

Cincinnati

Cleveland

Wheeling

Pittsburgh

PENNSYLVANIA

Harrisburg

L. Ontario

NEW YORK

Buffalo

St. Lawrence R.

MAINE

Augusta

Burlington

Montpelier   VT. N.H.

Manchester   Concord

Portland

Boston

Albany   MASS.

Hartford   Providence

R.I.

CONN.

Newark   New York

Trenton   NEW JERSEY

Philadelphia

Baltimore   Dover

Washington, D.C.   Annapolis   DELAWARE

MD.

Topeka

Kansas City

Jefferson City

MISSOURI

Wichita

St. Louis

Louisville

Frankfort

KENTUCKY

Ohio R.

Cumberland R.

W. VA.

Charleston

VIRGINIA

Richmond

Roanoke R.

Norfolk

Knoxville

Nashville

Raleigh

Charlotte

NORTH CAROLINA

APPALACHIAN MOUNTAINS

Tulsa

Oklahoma City

ARKANSAS

Little Rock

Arkansas R.

Canadian R.

Memphis

TENNESSEE

Mississippi R.

Tennessee R.

SOUTH CAROLINA

Columbia

Santee R.

Charleston

Atlantic Ocean

Fort Worth

Dallas

Birmingham

ALABAMA

Atlanta

GEORGIA

Savannah

Trinity R.

Sabine R.

MISS.

Jackson

Montgomery

Oconee R.

Alabama R.

Red R.

LOUISIANA

Brazos R.

Houston

Baton Rouge

New Orleans

Mobile

Tallahassee

Jacksonville

FLORIDA

Tampa

Miami

BAHAMAS

Gulf of Mexico

Elevation

Feet	Meters
9,843	3,000
6,562	2,000
3,281	1,000
1,640	500
656	200
0	0

67°   Atlantic   66°
Ocean
San Juan

PUERTO RICO
Ponce

18°

Caribbean Sea

0   50
Miles

CUBA

0   250   500
Miles

95°   85°   80°   75°

Michael P. Conzen
University of Chicago
Advisory Editor for Cartography

America

A CONCISE HISTORY

Volume 2
SINCE 1865

James A. Henretta
University of Maryland

David Brody
University of California, Davis

Lynn Dumenil
Occidental College

Bedford/St. Martin's
Boston/New York

Executive editor: Paul Shensa
History editor: Katherine E. Kurzman
Development editor: Jennifer E. Sutherland
Production editors: Elizabeth Geller/Shuli Traub
Production supervisors: Stacey B. Alexander/Scott Lavelle
Art director: Lucy Krikorian
Text design: Design Associates
Graphic arts manager: Demetrios Zangos
Photo research: Photosearch
Cover art: *Mid-Town, New York* by Guy Wiggins. Courtesy of Owen Gallery, New York.
Cartography: Mapping Specialists, Ltd.
Composition: TSI Graphics
Printing and binding: R.R. Donnelley & Sons Company

Library of Congress Catalog Card Number: 97-62266

Manufactured in the United States of America.

4 3 2 1 0 9
f e d c b

For information, write: Bedford/St. Martin's, 75 Arlington Street, Boston, MA 02116   (617) 426-7440

ISBN: 1-57259-402-0

For Our Teachers and Students

PREFACE

*A*merica: *A Concise History* presents a succinct overview of the American experience in a handy, low-cost format while preserving the structure, balance, and inclusive vision of *America's History*, Third Edition, by James A. Henretta, W. Elliot Brownlee, David Brody, Susan Ware, and Marilynn S. Johnson. Designed as a single-column paperback, the text feels and reads less like a traditional course book and will prove more inviting to the average undergraduate.

Through an intensive development process, we've created an original text in *America: A Concise History*, narrated in a lively style and filled with new insights. Lynn Dumenil, professor of history at Occidental College, has brought her expertise as a cultural historian of twentieth-century America to the author team and has taken prime responsibility for the decades since 1914. James Henretta has rewritten all the chapters through the Civil War (Chapters 1–15), and David Brody revisits Chapters 16–22.

To write a text that would be forty percent shorter than our comprehensive survey while maintaining a strong narrative line, we decided to focus each part of *America: A Concise History* around a few themes and to link our discussions so that students could trace developments over the entire span of U. S. history. We give special emphasis to the evolution of political institutions and policies, the changing character of social groups, the increasing complexity of cultural life, and the interaction between people and their environment. This selective thematic approach provides students with a coherent overview of American history, which instructors can enrich with supplemental readings.

Most important, *America: A Concise History* presents a *balanced* narrative of our nation's past. In our discussions of government and politics, diplomacy and war, we show how they affected—and were affected by—ethnic groups and economic conditions, intellectual beliefs and social change, and religious and moral values of the times. Our text integrates social and political history, probing the lives of the rich diversity of people who have become Americans and analyzing the institutions—political, economic, and religious—that represent a common national identity.

FEATURES

To assist students while they read, *America: A Concise History* has a clear chronology and a strong conceptual framework. Every volume is divided into three parts, with each corresponding to a distinct phase of development. Every part begins at a crucial turning point, such as the Cold War, and emphasizes the dynamic forces at work. Part openers contain **Thematic Timelines** that highlight key developments and brief **Part Essays** that focus on the crucial engines of historical change that created new conditions of life. This part organization will help students understand the major themes in each period of American history, to see that bits and pieces of historical data acquire significance as part of a larger pattern of development.

Throughout the main text we have tried to mix quotations from ordinary Americans into the narrative to create a vivid account. Moving students further back into the context of the historical moment, each chapter includes two **American Voices**, first-person excerpts from letters, diaries, autobiographies, and public testimony that paint a striking picture of the social or political life of the time. These selections, virtually all newly selected and edited for *America: A Concise History*, bring history alive and remind students that the past is much more than a chronicle of the great and powerful.

Each chapter is enhanced by a selection of maps and contemporary illustrations and concludes with a **Timeline** listing important events. Finally, the Documents section reprints the Declaration of Independence and the Constitution of the United States, and the appendix lists statistical information. Also included is a comprehensive list of suggestions for further reading, organized by the headings in each chapter.

SUPPLEMENTS

Users of *America's History* have always cited the ancillary package as a key to the book's success in the classroom. We thus felt it very important to make all the materials for the big book available to adopters of *America: A Concise History*. The *Instructor's Resource Manual* provides an abundance of material to aid instructors in planning the course and enhancing student involvement, including specially commissioned Historiographic Essays and Documents Modules that focus on native Americans, African-Americans, Latino-Americans, women, and constitutional and diplomatic history. One hundred and ten full-color transparencies reproduce maps and figures from the textbook, as well as a selection of fine art and historic photographs. The *Who Built America?* CD-ROM, called "a truly exciting, high-quality electronic book" by *The Wall Street Journal*, covers the period from 1876 to World War I.

In addition, however, several key ancillaries have been specially prepared to support teaching with the concise book; the *Instructor's Resource Manual, Test Bank, Student Guides*, and *Documents Collection* have all been rewritten to take account of the important changes in coverage and approach. Finally, a new ancillary is available for people who use a brief text as a core around which to array a variety of supplements; *Using The Bedford Series in History and Culture with* America: A Concise History provides concrete suggestions for using two dozen volumes from this highly regarded series in conjunction with our text.

American History: A Concise Documents Collection, Volumes 1 and 2

by Douglas Bukowski

For instructors who like to use a variety of brief primary sources in class, a set of readings has been prepared to accompany *America: A Concise History*. For each chapter in the text, a corresponding chapter in this collection includes five to seven excerpts from important sources in political, social, economic, and cultural history. For each reading a helpful headnote gives students context on the author and selection. A series of three to five questions follow the reading to help students think critically about the source. At the end of each chapter, additional questions tie the readings together, inviting students to think about how this diverse set of pieces reflects the complex tenor of the time.

Student Guide, Volumes 1 and 2

Vol. 1 by Stephen J. Kneeshaw (College of the Ozarks); Timothy R. Mahoney (University of Nebraska–Lincoln); Linda Gies (Eastern New Mexico University); and Barbara M. Posadas (Northern Illinois University); Vol. 2 by Thomas R. Frazier (Baruch College, emeritus)

Specially prepared for *America: A Concise History*, the *Student Guide* will help conscientious students improve their performance in the course by developing better learning skills and study habits. The guide begins with an introduction by Gerald J. Goodwin (University of Houston) on how to study history, which is followed by discrete sections for each chapter that reinforce major themes and test on the book's coverage. Each chapter includes a summary of the essential facts and ideas of the text chapter, with fill-in questions; the timeline from the textbook with short explanations of the significance of each event; a glossary; skill-building exercises based on a map, table, or figure; exercises for the American Voices; and a self-test.

Instructor's Resource Manual, Volumes 1 and 2

Vol. 1 by Timothy R. Mahoney (University of Nebraska–Lincoln) and Linda Gies (Eastern New Mexico University); Vol. 2 by Thomas R. Frazier (Baruch College, emeritus), Stephen J. Kneeshaw (College of the Ozarks), and Linda Gies

The *Instructor's Resource Manual* contains materials to aid instructors in teaching *America: A Concise History* and enhance student involvement. For each chapter of the textbook the resources include a list of chapter themes, a brief summary, an annotated timeline from the textbook with additional information, lecture suggestions, class discussion starters, topics for writing assignments, and suggested topics for research. In addition, the *Instructor's Resource Manual* includes nine historiographic essays by outstanding scholars on topics like populism, a guide to writing about history by Gerald J. Goodwin (reprinted in the Student Guide), and a film and video guide by Stephen J. Kneeshaw.

Using The Bedford Series in History and Culture with *America: A Concise History*

by Scott Hovey

Recognizing that many instructors use a brief core text to provide a backbone around which to array supplements, Bedford/St. Martin's has made the Bedford series volumes available at a discount to adopters of *America: A Concise History*. This short guide by Scott Hovey gives practical suggestions for using a dozen volumes from the Bedford series with each volume of this concise text, providing links between text and supplement as well as ideas for starting discussions focused on a single primary-source volume.

Test Bank, Volumes 1 and 2

by Thomas L. Altherr and Adolph Grundman (Metropolitan State College of Denver), and James Miller

The *Test Bank* provides 80 to 110 questions for each chapter of *America: A Concise History*, including multiple-choice questions, fill-ins, and short and long essay questions. Computerized test-generation systems are also available for IBM-compatible and Macintosh platforms.

ACKNOWLEDGMENTS

The scholars and teachers who reviewed our manuscript saved us from many mistakes and made suggestions that enhanced the cogency of our interpretations. All have used concise texts in their courses, and their classroom experience has helped us create a book that will meet the needs of today's diverse students. Special thanks are due to: Thomas Blantz, University of Notre Dame; John Buenker, University of Wisconsin–Parkside; Emmett Essin, East Tennessee State University; David Huehner, University of Wisconsin–Washington County; John Johnson, University of Northern Iowa; Stephen Kneeshaw, College of the Ozarks; Chana Lee, Indiana University; Robert Martin, University of Northern Iowa; Carl Moneyhon, University of Arkansas–Little Rock; John S. Nader, State University of New York at Delhi; Steven Reiss, Northeastern Illinois University; and Kenneth Scherzer, Middle Tennessee State University.

As the authors of *America: A Concise History*, we know better than anyone else how much this book is the work of other hands and minds. We are grateful to Paul Shensa, who helped us to conceive this book, and to Jennifer Sutherland who, as always, held us to the highest scholarly standards as she masterfully edited our text. We also thank our editorial and production team for their dedicated efforts: Stacey B. Alexander, Elizabeth Geller, Lawrence Guerra, Cindy Joyce, Fernando Quinones, Shuli Traub, and Demetrios Zangos. Finally, we want to express our appreciation for the invaluable assistance of Patricia Deveneau, Lawrence Peskin, and Norman Cohen, whose work contributed in many ways to the intellectual vitality of *America: A Concise History*.

James A. Henretta
David Brody
Lynn Dumenil

CONTENTS

xvi Contents

CHAPTER 18 CAPITAL AND LABOR IN THE AGE OF ENTERPRISE, 1877–1900 **474**

Industrial Capitalism Triumphant 475
Basic Industry **475**
The Railroads **476**
Mass Markets and Large-Scale Enterprise **479**
The New South **481**

The World of Work 483
Labor Recruits **483**
Working Women **486**
Autonomous Labor **489**
Systems of Control **491**

The Labor Movement 493
Reformers and Unionists **493**
The Triumph of "Pure-and-Simple" Unionism **495**
Industrial War **497**
American Radicalism in the Making **498**

CHAPTER 19 THE POLITICS OF LATE NINETEENTH-CENTURY AMERICA **502**

The Politics of the Status Quo, 1877–1893 503
The National Scene **503**
The Ideology of Individualism **505**
The Courts **507**
Cultural Politics **508**
Organizational Politics **510**
Women's Political Culture **512**

The Crisis of American Politics: The 1890s 514
The Populist Revolt **514**
Money and Politics **518**
The Election of 1896 **520**

Race and Politics in the South 521
Biracial Politics **521**
White Reaction **523**
The Black Response **526**

CHAPTER 20 THE RISE OF THE CITY **529**

Urbanization 529
The Economic Sources of City Growth **530**
City Building **531**
The Private City **534**
A Balance Sheet: Chicago and Berlin **535**

LIST OF MAPS

ABOUT THE AUTHORS

James A. Henretta is Priscilla Alden Burke Professor of American History at the University of Maryland, College Park. He received his undergraduate education at Swarthmore College and his Ph.D. from Harvard University. He has taught at the University of Sussex, England; Princeton University; UCLA; Boston University; as a Fulbright lecturer in Australia at the University of New England; and at Oxford University as the Harmsworth Professor of American History. His publications include *The Evolution of American Society, 1700–1815: An Interdisciplinary Analysis; "Salutary Neglect": Colonial Administration under the Duke of Newcastle; Evolution and Revolution: American Society, 1600–1820; The Origins of American Capitalism*; and important articles in early American and social history. He recently completed a fellowship at the Woodrow Wilson Center working on a study of *The Transformation of the Liberal State in America, 1800–1970*.

David Brody is Professor Emeritus of History at the University of California, Davis. He received his B.A., M.A., and Ph.D. from Harvard University. He has taught at the University of Warwick in England, at Moscow State University in the former Soviet Union, and at Sydney University in Australia. He is the author of *Steelworkers in America; Workers in Industrial America: Essays on the 20th Century Struggle*; and *In Labor's Cause: Main Themes on the History of the American Worker*. He has been awarded fellowships from the Social Science Research Council, the Guggenheim Foundation, and the National Endowment for the Humanities. He is past president (1991–92) of the Pacific Coast Branch of the American Historical Association. His current research is on industrial labor during the Great Depression.

Lynn Dumenil is Professor of History at Occidental College in Los Angeles. She is a graduate of the University of Southern California and received her Ph.D. from the University of California, Berkeley. She has written *The Modern Temper: American Culture and Society in the 1920s* and *Freemasonry and American Culture: 1880–1930*. Her articles and reviews have appeared in *Journal of American History; Journal of American Ethnic History; Reviews in American History*; and *American Historical Review*. She has been a historical consultant to several documentary film projects and has served on committees of the Organization of American Historians, the American Studies Association, and the Immigration History Society. Her current work is on World War I, citizenship, and the state.

America

A CONCISE HISTORY

Volume 2
SINCE 1865

CHAPTER 16

RECONSTRUCTION, 1865–1877

- Presidential Reconstruction
- Radical Reconstruction
- Redemption

In his second inaugural address, President Abraham Lincoln spoke of the need to "bind up the nation's wounds." No one knew better than Lincoln how daunting a task that would be. Foremost, of course, were the terms for restoring the states in rebellion to the Union. But the war had opened more fundamental questions. Slavery was finished. That much was certain. But what system of labor should replace plantation slavery? What rights should the freedmen be accorded beyond emancipation itself? How far should the federal government go to settle these questions? And who should decide? the president? or the Congress?

While the war was still on, the North began to grope for answers. Relying on his wartime powers, Abraham Lincoln in December 1863 offered a general amnesty to all but high-ranking Confederates willing to pledge loyalty to the Union and accept the abolition of slavery. When 10 percent of a state's 1860 voters had taken this oath, they could organize a new government and apply for restoration to the Union. Only states under military occupation—Louisiana, Arkansas, and Tennessee—took advantage of Lincoln's generous offer, but he hoped Confederates elsewhere might also be induced to abandon the rebellion.

Although it reflected his conciliatory bent, Lincoln's Ten Percent Plan was really aimed at subverting the southern war effort. What it also did was to reveal the rocky road that lay ahead for Reconstruction. Thus, in Louisiana, sugar planters showed little remorse for the crime of slavery. On the contrary, with the aid of the occupying federal forces, they tried to regain control over the freed slaves, buttressed by oppressive curfew and vagrancy regulations. But the Louisiana freedmen fought right back. Led by the free black community of New Orleans, they began to agitate for political rights. No less than their former masters, ex-slaves intended to be actors in the savage drama of Reconstruction.

With Louisiana very much in mind, Republicans in Congress put forth a stricter substitute for Lincoln's Ten Percent Plan. The initiative came from the Radical wing of the party—those bent on a stern peace and full rights for the freedmen—but with broad support among more moderate Republicans. The Wade-Davis bill, passed on July 2, 1864, laid down, as conditions for the restoration of the rebellious states to the Union, an oath of allegiance by a majority of each state's adult white men, new state governments formed and operated only by those who had never carried arms against the Union, and permanent disfranchisement of Confederate civil and military leaders. The Wade-Davis bill served notice that the congressional Republicans were not about to hand reconstruction policy over to the president.

Lincoln was not perturbed. Rather than openly challenging Congress, he executed a "pocket" veto of the Wade-Davis bill by not signing it before Congress adjourned. At the same time he initiated informal talks with congressional leaders aimed at finding a common ground. The last speech he ever delivered, on April 11, 1865, demonstrated Lincoln's cautious realism. Reconstruction, he pleaded, had to be regarded as a practical, not a theoretical, problem. It could be solved only if Republicans remained united, even if that meant compromising, and only if the defeated South gave its consent, even if that meant forgiveness. What the speech showed, above all, was Lincoln's sense of the fluidity of events, of policy toward the South as an evolving, not a fixed, position.

What course Reconstruction might have taken had Lincoln lived is one of the great unanswered questions of American history. On April 14, 1865—five days after Lee's surrender at Appomattox—Lincoln was shot in the head at Ford's Theater in Washington by an unstable actor named John Wilkes Booth. Ironically, Lincoln might have been spared if the war had dragged on longer, for Booth and his Confederate associates had originally plotted to kidnap the president to force a negotiated settlement. Without regaining consciousness, Lincoln died on April 15.

At one stroke John Wilkes Booth had sent Lincoln to martyrdom, hardened many northerners against the South, and handed the presidency to a man utterly lacking in Lincoln's moral sense and political judgment, Vice-President Andrew Johnson.

PRESIDENTIAL RECONSTRUCTION

At the end of the Civil War, a very big constitutional question remained in dispute—whether, on seceding, the Confederate states had legally left the

Union. If so, then these states became conquered territories, and the terms of their readmission demanded the gravest consideration by the Congress. If not, if even in defeat they retained their constitutional status, the initiative for restoring them to the Union might appropriately be taken by the president. This was Andrew Johnson's view, and by an accident of timing, he was free to act on it. For, under leisurely rules that went back to the early republic, the 39th Congress elected in November 1864 was not scheduled to convene until December 1865.

Johnson's Initiative

Andrew Johnson was a self-made man and a former slaveholder from the hills of eastern Tennessee. A Jacksonian Democrat, he saw himself as the champion of the common man. He hated what he called the "bloated, corrupt aristocracy" of the Northeast, and he was just as disdainful of the southern planters, whom he blamed for the poverty of his own yeoman farmers. Johnson's political career had taken him to the U.S. Senate, where he remained when the war broke out, loyal to the Union. After federal forces captured Nashville, Johnson became Tennessee's military governor. The Republicans nominated him for vice-president in 1864 in an effort to promote wartime political unity and to court the support of southern Unionists.

In May 1865, just a month after Lincoln's death, Johnson launched his own plan for restoration. He offered amnesty to all southerners, irrespective of their part in the rebellion, who took an oath of allegiance to the Union, but excluding high-ranking Confederate officials and the wealthier planters, whom

Andrew Johnson
The president was not an easy man. This photograph of Andrew Johnson (1808–1875) conveys some of the personal qualities that contributed so centrally to his failure to reach an agreement with Republicans on a program of moderate reconstruction.

Johnson held responsible for secession. Such persons could be pardoned only by presidential order. He appointed provisional governors for the southern states, and laid down as conditions for their restoration only that they revoke their ordinances of secession, repudiate their Confederate debts, and ratify the Thirteenth Amendment, which abolished slavery. Within months all the former Confederate states had met Johnson's requirements and had functioning, elected governments.

At first Republicans responded favorably. The moderates among them were sympathetic to Johnson's states' rights argument that it was up to the states, not the federal government, to settle questions of the ballot and civil equality for the freedmen. Even the Radicals were optimistic. They liked the stern treatment of Confederate leaders, and they hoped that the new southern state governments would respond positively to Johnson's conciliatory approach and offer the vote at least to African-Americans who were literate and owned property.

Nothing of the sort happened. Instead, the newly seated southern legislatures moved to restore slavery in all but name. They enacted laws—known as Black Codes—designed to drive the freedmen back to the plantations, to restrict their freedom of movement, and to deny them equality before the law. Localities set curfews; insisted that blacks who wanted to live in town obtain white sponsors; and, in an effort to prevent political mobilization, sharply restricted rights of assembly. The new governments had mostly been formed by ex-Whigs and southern Unionists, but when it came to racist attitudes, not a lot distinguished them from the Confederates. The latter, moreover, swiftly filtered back into the corridors of power. It turned out that Johnson, despite his hard words against them, forgave ex-Confederate leaders easily, so long as he got the satisfaction of making them submit to his personal authority. His perceived indulgence of their efforts to restore white supremacy emboldened the ex-Confederates. They packed the delegations to the new Congress with old comrades—nine members of the Confederate Congress; seven former officials of Confederate state governments; four generals and four colonels; and even the vice-president of the Confederacy, Alexander Stephens.

When Congress convened in early December 1865, the Republicans refused to admit the southern delegations, effectively blocking Johnson's reconstruction program. Although relations with the president had already cooled, the Republicans assumed he would work cooperatively with them in formulating the new terms on which the South would be readmitted to Congress. To that end, a House-Senate committee—the Joint Committee on Reconstruction—was formed and began public hearings on conditions in the South. By now, the worst of the Black Codes had been rescinded, but in place of laws aimed specifically at blacks the states brought forth nonracial ordinances that accomplished the same repressive ends. On top of that, a wave of violence erupted across the South, intended to terrorize the freedmen into submission. In Tennessee, a Nashville paper reported in early 1867 that white gangs "are riding about whipping, maiming and killing all negroes who do not obey the orders of their former masters, just as if slavery existed." Listening to the vivid testimony of officials, observers, and victims, Republicans concluded the South had embarked on a concerted effort to circumvent the Thirteenth Amendment. The only possible response was for the federal government to intervene.

Back in March 1865, the previous Congress had established the Freedman's Bureau to provide emergency aid to ex-slaves and refugees during the chaotic transition from war to peace. Now, under the leadership of the moderate Republican Senator Lyman Trumbull, Congress voted to extend the Bureau's life, gave it direct funding for the first time, and authorized its agents to step into cases where blacks were being denied the "civil rights belonging to white persons."

More extraordinary was Trumbull's proposal for a civil rights bill, declaring all persons born in the United States to be citizens and granting them, without regard to race, equal rights of contract, access to the courts, and protection of person and property. Trumbull's bill nullified all state laws depriving citizens of these rights, authorized U.S. attorneys to bring enforcement suits in the federal courts, and provided for fines and imprisonment for anyone, including public officials, guilty of depriving a citizen of civil rights. In response to an unrepentant South, Republicans of the most moderate persuasion concluded that the federal government had to assume responsibility for securing the basic civil rights of the freedmen.

Acting on Freedom

While Congress debated, African-Americans as best they could acted on their own idea of freedom. News of emancipation left them exultant and hopeful. Freedom meant many things. It meant reuniting separated families, the end of punishment by the lash, the ability to move around, the opportunity to establish schools, churches, and social clubs, and, not least, the chance to engage in politics. Across the South, blacks held mass meetings, paraded, and formed organizations. In the cities, where free blacks took the lead, Union Leagues and Equal Rights Leagues worked to give the freedmen a political voice. With the encouragement of Freedmen's Bureau agents, state conventions also began to meet, invariably passing resolutions demanding equality before the law and the right to vote—"an essential and inseparable element of self-government."

First of all, however, came economic independence, which emancipated blacks believed was the basis for true freedom. During the Civil War they had acted on this assumption whenever Union armies drew near. During the final months of the war, when the Union directed its military operations against civilians, freedmen found greater opportunities to win control of land. Most visibly, General William T. Sherman reserved vast tracts of coastal lands in Georgia and South Carolina—the Sea Islands and abandoned plantations within 30 miles of the coast—for liberated slaves, and settled them on 40-acre tracts. Sherman only wanted to relieve the pressure the refugees were placing

AMERICAN VOICES

A Plea for Land

*F*ollowing is a painfully written letter by the ex-slaves of Edisto Island to President Andrew Johnson, pleading for a reversal of his order that the lands they now worked be returned to the plantation owners.

Edisto Island S.C. Oct 28th, 1865.
To the President of these United States. We the freedmen Of Edisto Island South Carolina have learned . . . with deep sorrow and Painful hearts of the possibility of government restoring These lands to the former owners. . . . Here is where secession was born and Nurtured Here is where we have toiled nearly all Our lives as slaves and were treated like dumb Driven cattle. This is our home, we have made These lands what they are. . . . Shall not we who Are freedmen and have always been true to this Union have the same rights as are enjoyed by Others? Have we broken any Law of these United States? have we forfeited our rights of property In Land?—If not then! are not our rights as A free people and good citizens of these United States To be considered before the rights of those who were Found in rebellion against this good and just Government. . . . And we who have been abused and oppressed For many long years But be subject To the will of these large Land owners? God forbid.
 . . . We the freedmen of this Island and the State of South Carolina—Do hereby petition to you as the President of these United States, that some provisions be made by which Every colored man can purchase land. and Hold as his own. We wish to have A home if It be but A few acres. . . . May God bless you in the Administration of your duties as the President Of these United States is the humble prayer Of us all.—

In behalf of the Freedmen
Henry Bram
Committee   Ishmael. Moultrie
yates. Sampson

SOURCE: Eileen Boris and Nelson Lichtenstein, eds., *Major Problems in the History of American Workers: Documents and Essays* (Lexington, MA: Heath, 1990), 137–139.

on his army as it marched across the lower South. But the freedmen assumed that Sherman's order meant that the land would be theirs.

As the war ended, resettlement became the responsibility of the Freedmen's Bureau, which was charged with distributing confiscated land to "loyal refugees and freedmen" and with regulating labor contracts between freedmen and planters. The Freedmen's Bureau also worked with the large number of northern voluntary associations that sent missionaries and teachers to the South to establish schools for former slaves.

With the encouragement of the Freedmen's Bureau, blacks across the South occupied confiscated or abandoned land, including half a million acres of "Sherman" land in Georgia and South Carolina. Many families stayed on their old plantations in the hope that they could claim some of the land after the war. When the South Carolina planter Thomas Pinckney returned home, his freed slaves told him, "We ain't going nowhere. We are going to work right here on the land where we were born and what belongs to us."

Johnson's amnesty plan, entitling pardoned Confederates to recover property seized during the war, brought these hopes to an abrupt halt. In October 1865, Johnson ordered General Oliver O. Howard, head of the Freedmen's Bureau, to tell Sea Island blacks that the land they occupied would have to be restored to the white owners. When Howard reluctantly obeyed, the dispossessed farmers protested: "Why do you take away our lands? You take them from us who have always been true, always true to the Government! You give them to our all-time enemies! That is not right!" In the Sea Islands and elsewhere, former slaves resisted efforts to remove them. Often led by black veterans of the Union army, they fought pitched battles with plantation owners and bands of ex-Confederate soldiers. In this warfare federal troops often backed the local whites, who generally prevailed in recapturing their former holdings.

As returning planters prepared for a new growing season, a great battle began to take shape over the labor system that would replace slavery. Convinced that blacks could not work without supervision, planters insisted on retaining the gang system of plantation labor, only now paying low wages instead of the food, clothing, and shelter their slaves had once received. Many freedmen voted with their feet. Thousands of families abandoned their old plantations, seeking better lives and more freedom in the towns and cities of the South. Those who remained in the countryside refused to work the cotton fields under the hated gang labor or negotiated tenaciously over the terms of their labor contracts. What was freedom all about if not to have a bit more leisure time, to work less intensely than they had as slaves, and to work for themselves and their families? Whatever system of labor finally might emerge, it was clear that the freedmen and their families would never settle for anything resembling the old plantation system.

The efforts of former slaves to control their own lives ran counter to deeply entrenched white attitudes. "The destiny of the black race," asserted one Texan, could be summarized "in one sentence—subordination to the white race." Southern whites, a Freedmen's Bureau official observed, could not "conceive of the negro having any rights at all." When freedmen resisted, white retribution was swift and often terrible. In Pine Bluff, Arkansas, "after some kind of dispute with some freedmen," whites set fire to their cabins and lynched twenty-four of the inhabitants—men, women, and children. The toll of murdered and beaten blacks mounted into untold thousands. The governments established under Johnson's plan only put the stamp of legality on the pervasive efforts to enforce white supremacy. Blacks "would be *just as well* off

Wage Labor of Ex-Slaves
This photograph, taken in South Carolina shortly after the Civil War,
shows former slaves being led from the cotton fields. Although they now
worked for wages, they were probably organized into a gang not far
removed from the earlier slave gangs. Their plug-hatted crew leader is
dressed much as his slave-driving predecessor would have been.

with no law at all or no Government," concluded a Freedmen's Bureau agent,
as with the justice they got under the restored white rule.

In this unequal struggle, blacks turned to Washington. "We stood by the
government when it wanted help," a black Mississippian wrote President
Johnson. "Now . . . will it stand by us?"

Congress versus President

Andrew Johnson was, alas, not the man to ask. In February 1866, he vetoed
the Freedmen's Bureau bill, declaring it unconstitutional because Congress
lacked authority to provide a "system for the support of indigent people" and
because the states most directly affected by its provisions were not yet represented in Congress. The Bureau, said Johnson, was an "immense patronage,"
showering benefits on blacks never granted to "our own people." A month
later, rebuffing the outraged critics of his Freedman's Bureau veto, Johnson
vetoed Trumbull's Civil Rights bill, again arguing that federal protection
of black civil rights constituted "a stride toward centralization." His racism,
hitherto muted, now blazed forth. In his view, granting blacks the privileges of

citizenship was discriminatory, operating "in favor of the colored and against the white race," and threatening all manner of evil consequences, including miscegenation.

Taken by surprise, the Republicans were galvanized into action. They failed, just barely, to override Johnson's veto of the Freedmen's Bureau bill, but in early April, they got the necessary two-thirds majorities in both houses and enacted the Civil Rights bill into law. This was a truly historic event, the first time Congress had prevailed over a presidential veto on a major piece of legislation. In July the Freedmen's Bureau was renewed over a second Johnson veto.

Anxious to consolidate their victory, Republicans moved to enshrine black civil rights in an amendment to the Constitution. They were already upset by the dividend the South had gained from emancipation: a jump in federal representation because, under the Constitution, the slave population had counted as only three-fifths, whereas as free persons blacks counted fully (even if they could not vote). Now this question was bundled with civil rights into what became the Fourteenth Amendment. Section 2 reduced a state's representation in the House of Representatives by the percentage of adult male citizens who were denied the vote. Intended to prod the South toward enfranchising the freedmen, Section 2 was quickly overtaken by events and had no lasting significance, save for the insertion of the word *male* into the Constitution, which, to the outrage of woman suffragists, cast women out from the gathering movement toward universal suffrage. The heart of the Fourteenth Amendment was Section 1, which declared that "all persons born or naturalized in the United States" were citizens. No state could abridge "the privileges or immunities of citizens of the United States," deprive "any person of life, liberty, or property, without due process of law," or deny anyone "the equal protection of the laws." These phrases were vague, intentionally so, but they established the constitutionality of the Civil Rights Act and, more important, the basis on which the courts and Congress could establish an enforceable standard of equality before the law in the states.

For the moment, however, the Fourteenth Amendment was most important for its impact on national politics. With the 1866 congressional elections approaching, Johnson somehow figured he had a winning issue in the Fourteenth Amendment. He denounced it, and urged the states not to ratify it. Months earlier, Johnson had begun to maneuver politically against the Republicans, aiming to build a coalition of white southerners, northern Democrats, and conservative Republicans under the banner of "National Union." For discredited Democrats, Johnson's scheme offered the cloak of respectability, and they eagerly seized it. Any hope of creating a new national party, however, was shattered by Johnson's intemperate behavior and by escalating violence in the South. Sympathetic Republicans and ex-Whigs backed off, a dissension-ridden National Union convention in July ended inconclusively, and Johnson's campaign against the Fourteenth Amendment became, effectively, a campaign for the Democratic party. In late August Johnson embarked

on a disastrous "swing around the circle"—a railroad tour from Washington to
Chicago and St. Louis and back. It was unprecedented for a president to campaign personally, and Johnson made matters worse by engaging in shouting
matches with hecklers and by insulting members of the hostile crowds.

The 1866 congressional elections inflicted a humiliating defeat on Johnson. The Republicans, having won a three-to-one majority in Congress, considered themselves "masters of the situation," free to proceed "entirely
regardless of [Johnson's] opinions or wishes." As a referendum on the Fourteenth Amendment, moreover, the election registered strong popular support
for the civil rights of the freedmen. The Republican Party emerged with a
new sense of unity—a unity coalescing not at the center, but on the left,
around the root-and-branch program of the Radical minority.

The Radicals represented the abolitionist strain within the Republican
party. Most of them hailed from New England, or from the area of the upper
Midwest settled by New Englanders. In the Senate, they were led by Charles
Sumner of Massachusetts; in the House, by the redoubtable Thaddeus Stevens
from Pennslyvania. For them, Reconstruction was never primarily about
restoring the Union; rather, it was about remaking southern society. "The
foundations of their institutions . . . must be broken up and relaid," declared
Stevens, "or all our blood and treasure will have been spent in vain." Only a
handful went as far as Stevens in demanding that the plantations be broken up
into small farms for the former slaves. But the Radicals had no qualms about
expanding the powers of the national government to protect the civil rights of
the freedmen and, more than that, grant them the suffrage. Radicals were aggressively partisan. They regarded the Republican party as the instrument of
the Lord, and black votes as the means by which the party could dominate the
South and bring about its regeneration.

At first, in the months after the surrender at Appomattox, few but the
Radicals themselves imagined they had any chance of putting across so extreme a program. Black suffrage especially seemed beyond reach, since the
northern states themselves (excepting in New England) denied blacks the
vote at this time. And yet, as fury mounted against the intransigent South, Republicans became ever more radicalized until, in the wake of the smashing
victory of 1866, they embraced the Radicals' vision of a reconstructed South.

RADICAL RECONSTRUCTION

Afterward, thoughtful southerners admitted that the South had brought radical Reconstruction on itself. "We had, in 1865, a white man's government in
Alabama," remarked the man who had been Johnson's provisional governor,
"but we lost it." The state's "great blunder" was not to "have at once taken the
negro right under the protection of the laws." Remarkably, the South remained defiant even after the 1866 congressional elections. Every state legislature (except, back in July, Tennessee) rejected the Fourteenth Amendment,

mostly by virtual acclamation. It was as if they could not imagine that governments installed under the presidential imprimatur and fully functioning might be swept away. But that, in fact, is just what the Republicans intended to do.

Congress Takes Command

The Reconstruction Act of 1867, enacted in March by the Republican Congress, organized the South as a conquered land, dividing it (with the exception of Tennessee) into five military districts, each under the command of a Union general. The price for reentering the Union was granting the vote to the freedmen and disfranchising the South's prewar leadership class—anyone who had taken an oath of loyalty to the Constitution as an officeholder or a commissioned officer and then had participated in the rebellion. Each military commander was ordered to register all eligible adult males, black as well as white, to supervise the election of state conventions, and to make certain that the new state constitutions contained guarantees of black suffrage. Congress would readmit a state to the Union if its voters ratified the constitution, if that document proved acceptable to Congress, and if the new state legislature approved the Fourteenth Amendment (thus ensuring the needed ratification by three-fourths of the states). Johnson vetoed the act, but Congress overrode the veto. By 1870, all ten of the ex-Confederate states had met the requirements and were readmitted to the Union.

Republicans also checkmated President Johnson. The Tenure of Office Act, a companion to the Reconstruction Act, required Senate consent for the removal of any official whose appointment had required Senate confirmation. Congress chiefly wanted to protect Secretary of War Edwin M. Stanton, a Lincoln holdover and the only member of Johnson's cabinet who favored radical Reconstruction. In his position Stanton could do much to prevent Johnson from frustrating the goals of Reconstruction. Congress also required the president to issue all orders to the army through its commanding general, Ulysses S. Grant.

Seemingly defeated, Johnson appointed generals recommended by Stanton and Grant to command the five military districts in the South. But he was just biding his time. In August 1867, after Congress had adjourned, he "suspended" Stanton and replaced him with Grant, believing that the general would act like a good soldier and follow orders. Next Johnson replaced four of the commanding generals, including Philip H. Sheridan, Grant's favorite cavalry general. Johnson, however, had misjudged Grant, who publicly registered his opposition to the president's machinations. When the Senate reconvened in the fall, it overruled Stanton's suspension. Grant, now an open enemy of Johnson's, resigned so that Stanton could resume his office.

In February 1868 Johnson dismissed Stanton. House Republicans lashed back by using the power granted them by the Constitution to impeach—to charge federal officials with "Treason, Bribery, or other high Crimes and Misdemeanors." The House overwhelmingly (128 to 47) brought eleven counts of criminal misconduct, nine of which dealt with violations of the Tenure of Office Act, against the president.

The case went to the Senate, which the Constitution empowers to act as a court in impeachment cases, presided over by Chief Justice Salmon P. Chase. After an eleven-week trial, thirty-five senators on May 15 voted for conviction, one vote short of the two-thirds majority required. Seven moderate Republicans had broken ranks, voting for acquittal along with twelve Democrats. The reluctant Republicans were overwhelmed by the drastic nature of the attack on Johnson; Congress had removed federal judges from office, but never a president. Even if Johnson had broken the law, they felt, the real issue was a political disagreement between Congress and the president. They feared that a conviction based on a policy dispute would establish a dangerous precedent and undermine the presidency, which seemed too high a price just to punish Johnson.

In any case, even without being convicted, Johnson had been defanged, and he was helpless for the remainder of his term to alter the course of Reconstruction.

The impeachment controversy made Grant, already the North's most popular war hero, a Republican hero as well, and he easily won the party's presidential nomination in 1868. In the fall campaign he supported radical Reconstruction, but he also urged reconciliation between the sections. His Democratic opponent was Horatio Seymour, a former governor of New York and a Peace Democrat who almost declined the nomination, certain that the Democrats could not overcome their identification with the disloyal South. As Seymour feared, the Republicans "waved the bloody shirt," stirring up old wartime emotions against the Democrats to great effect. Grant won about the same share of the northern vote (55 percent) that Lincoln had in 1864, and received 214 of 294 electoral votes. The Republicans also retained two-thirds majorities in both houses of Congress.

In the wake of their smashing victory, the Republicans quickly produced the last major piece of Reconstruction legislation—the Fifteenth Amendment, which forbade either the federal government or the states to deny citizens the right to vote on the basis of race, color, or "previous condition of servitude." Proponents of the amendment were aware that it left open the use of poll taxes and property or literacy tests to discourage blacks from voting. But northern states also valued such qualifications, employing them against immigrants and the "unworthy" poor. A California senator warned that in his state, with its rabidly anti-Chinese sentiment, any restriction on that power would "kill our party as dead as a stone." Despite grumbling by Radical Republicans, the amendment passed without modification in February 1869. Congress required the unreconstructed states of Virginia, Mississippi, Texas, and Georgia to ratify it before they were readmitted to the Union. A year later the Fifteenth Amendment became part of the Constitution.

If the Fifteenth Amendment troubled some proponents of black suffrage, this was nothing as compared to the outrage felt by women's rights advocates. They had fought the good fight for so many years for the abolition of slavery, only to be abandoned by their male allies when the chance finally came to get the vote for women. How could the suffrage be granted to ex-slaves, Elizabeth Cady Stanton demanded to know, but not to them? The Fifteenth Amendment opened up a schism in the ranks of the women's movement. In 1868 a group led by Lucy Stone broke with the American Equal Rights Association, which had declared against the Fifteenth Amendment, and formed the New England Woman Suffrage Association. Its goal was to maintain an alliance with the Republicans in the forlorn hope that, once Reconstruction had been settled, it would be time for woman suffrage.

The South during Radical Reconstruction

Between 1868 and 1871 all the southern states met the congressional stipulations and rejoined the Union. Protected by federal troops and encouraged by northern party leaders, state Republican organizations took hold across the South and won control of the newly established Reconstruction governments. These Republican administrations remained in power for periods ranging from a few months in Virginia to nine years in South Carolina, Louisiana, and Florida (see Map 16.1). African-Americans participated prominently in the Reconstruction governments. In Alabama, Florida, South Carolina, Mississippi,

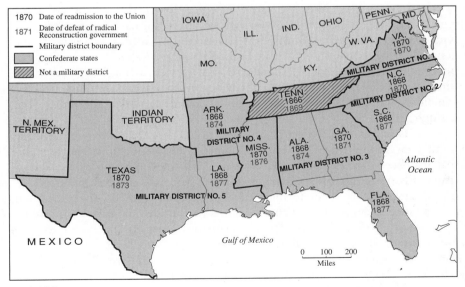

MAP 16.1

Reconstruction

The federal government organized the Confederate states into five military districts during radical Reconstruction. For each state the first date indicates when that state was readmitted to the Union; the second date shows when radical Republicans lost control of the state government. All the ex-Confederate states rejoined the Union from 1868 to 1870, but the periods of radical rule varied widely. Radicals lasted only a few months in Virginia; they held on until the end of Reconstruction in Louisiana, Florida, and South Carolina.

and Louisiana they constituted an outright majority of registered voters. They provided the votes for Republican victories in those states and in Georgia, Virginia, and North Carolina as well, where they accounted for nearly half the registered voters.

Democratic ex-Confederates mocked and scorned black Republican officeholders as ignorant field hands who could only play at politics, and they referred to whites who became Republicans as *scalawags*—an ancient Scots-Irish term for runty, worthless animals. Whites who had come from the North they denounced as *carpetbaggers*—self-seeking interlopers who carried all their belongings in cheap suitcases called carpetbags.

Actually, few southern Republicans conformed to the hostile stereotypes. Some carpetbaggers did come south for personal profit, but they also brought capital and skills. Union army veterans taken with the South—its climate, people, and economic opportunities—also figured heavily among the carpet-baggers. And interspersed with the self-seekers were many idealists anxious to advance the cause of emancipation. The scalawags were even more diverse. Some were former slaveowners, ex-Whigs and even ex-Democrats, drawn to Republicanism as the best way to attract northern capital to southern rail-roads, mines, and factories. In southwest Texas, the large population of Germans was strongly Republican. They sent to Congress Edward Degener, an immigrant and a San Antonio grocer whom Confederate authorities had imprisoned and whose sons had been executed for treason. Most numerous among the scalawags were yeomen farmers from the back-country districts who wanted to rid the South of its slaveholding aristocracy. Scalawags had generally fought against, or at least refused to support, the Confederacy; they believed that slavery had victimized whites as well as blacks. "Now is the time," a Georgia scalawag wrote, "for every man to come out and speak his principles publickly [*sic*] and vote for liberty as we have been in bondage long enough."

The Democrats' stereotypes of black political leaders were just as false. Until 1867 most African-American leaders in the South came from the elite that had been free before the Civil War. With the formation of the recon-structed Republican governments in 1867, this diverse group of ministers, artisans, shopkeepers, and former soldiers reached out to the freedmen. African-American speakers, some financed by the Republican Congressional Committee, fanned out into the old plantation districts and drew ex-slaves into political leadership. Still, few of the new leaders were field hands; most had been preachers or artisans. The literacy of one ex-slave, Thomas Allen, who was a Baptist minister and shoemaker, helped him win election to the Georgia legislature. "In my county," he recalled, "the colored people came to me for instructions, and I gave them the best instructions I could. I took the *New York Tribune* and other papers, and in that way I found out a great deal, and I told them whatever I thought was right."

Many of the African-American leaders who emerged in 1867 had been born in the North or had spent many years there. They moved south when radical Reconstruction opened up the prospect of meaningful freedom. Like

Hiram R. Revels
In 1870 Hiram R. Revels (1822–1901) was elected to the U.S. Senate from Mississippi to fill Jefferson Davis's former seat. Revels was a free black from North Carolina who had migrated to the North and attended Knox College in Illinois. He recruited blacks for the Union army and as an ordained Methodist minister served as chaplain of a black regiment in Mississippi, where he settled after the war.

white migrants, many were veterans of the Union army. Some had fought in the antislavery crusade, some were employed by the Freedmen's Bureau or northern missionary societies, and a few came from free families and had gone north for an education. Others had escaped from slavery and were returning home, like Blanche K. Bruce, who first taught school in Missouri and then in 1874 became Missisippi's second black U.S. senator.

Although never proportionate to the size of the black population, African-American officeholders held positions of importance throughout the South. In 1868 they constituted a majority in the lower house of the South Carolina legislature. They were heavily represented in the state's executive offices, elected three members of Congress, and won a seat on the state supreme court. Across the South generally, twenty African-Americans served as governor, lieutenant governor, secretary of state, treasurer, or superintendent of education, more than six hundred served as state legislators, and sixteen served in the U.S. House of Representatives. Almost all who became state executives had been free before the Civil War, but in the legislatures most black members had been slaves.

The Republicans who took office had ambitious plans for a reconstructed South. They modernized state constitutions and made more offices elective. They established hospitals, penitentiaries, and asylums for orphans and the insane. Republican governments built roads in areas where roads had never existed. They poured money into rebuilding the region's railroad network. And they did all this without federal financing. Southern Republicans fell far short of making their vision a reality, but they accomplished more than their critics gave them credit for.

To pay for their ambitious programs the Republican governments copied the taxes that northern states had relied on since the Jacksonian period. These were general property taxes applying not only to real estate but to personal wealth as well. The goal was to make planters pay their fair share of taxes and to broaden the tax base by forcing them to sell off uncultivated land. In many plantation counties, especially in South Carolina, Louisiana, and Mississippi, former slaves served as tax assessors and collectors, administering the taxation of their one-time owners.

Increasing tax revenues never managed to overtake the burgeoning obligations assumed by the Reconstruction governments. State debts mounted rapidly, and, as interest payments on bonds fell into arrears, public credit collapsed. On top of that, much of the spending was wasted, especially the aid to railroads, or ended in the pockets of state officials. Corruption was endemic to American politics, of course, present in the southern states before the Republicans came on the scene, and rampant everywhere in this era, not least in the Grant administration itself. But there was no question that, in the free-spending atmosphere of the early Republican regimes, corruption was especially luxuriant or that it was damaging to the cause of radical Reconstruction.

A Freedmen's School

An 1866 sketch from *Harper's Weekly* of a Vicksburg, Mississippi, school run by the Freedmen's Bureau illustrates the desire for education by ex-slaves of all ages. Because most southern blacks were farmers, schools often offered night classes that left students free for field work during the day.

Nothing, however, could dim the achievement in public education. Here the South had lagged woefully; only Tennessee had a system of public schooling. Republican state governments vowed to make up for lost time, viewing education as the foundation for a democratic order. African-Americans of all ages rushed to attend the newly established schools, even when they had to pay tuition. An elderly man in Mississippi explained his desire to go to school: "Ole missus used to read the good book [the Bible] to us . . . on Sunday evenin's, but she mostly read dem places where it says, 'Servants obey your masters.' . . . Now we is free, there's heaps of tings in that old book we is just suffering to learn." By 1875 about half of all the children in Florida, Mississippi, and South Carolina were enrolled in school.

Except in New Orleans, the new schools were segregated. Most African-Americans did not complain. They seemed to agree that integration was an issue for a later day; they shared Frederick Douglass's judgment that separate schools were "infinitely superior" to no schools at all.

The building of schools was part of a larger effort by African-Americans to fortify the institutions that had sustained their spirit during the days of slavery. Most important, they strengthened family life as the cornerstone of new communities. Families moved away from the slave quarters, usually building homes scattered around their old plantations (see Map 16.2, following page). Husbands, wives, and children who had been separated were reunited, sometimes after journeys of hundreds of miles. Couples stepped forward to record marriages that had not been recognized under slavery. Many women refused to work in the fields. Instead, they insisted on tending gardens, managing households, and bringing education and religion to their children. Wives asserted their independence, opening individual bank accounts, refusing responsibility for their husbands' debts at country stores, and bringing complaints of abuse and lack of child support to the Freedmen's Bureau.

Religious belief had deep roots in nineteenth-century slave society. Now, in freedom, the African-Americans buttressed their new communities by founding their own churches. They left their old white-dominated congregations, where they had been relegated to segregated balconies and denied any voice in church governance, and built churches of their own. These churches joined together to form African-American versions of the Southern Methodist and Southern Baptist denominations, including, most prominently, the National Baptist Convention and the African Methodist Episcopal Church. Everywhere the robust black churches served not only as places of worship but as schools, social centers, and political meeting halls.

Black ministers were community leaders and often held political office during Reconstruction. Charles H. Pearce, a Methodist minister in Florida, declared, "A man in this State cannot do his whole duty as a minister except he looks out for the political interests of his people." Calling for the brotherhood of man and the special destiny of the ex-slaves as the new "Children of Israel," black ministers provided a powerful religious underpinning for the Republican politics of their congregations.

MAP 16.2
The Barrow Plantation
Comparing the 1860 map of this central Georgia plantation with the 1881 map reveals the changing patterns of black residence and farming. In 1860 the slave quarters were clustered near the planter's house, which sat on a small hilltop. The free sharecroppers of 1881 built cabins along the spurs or ridges of land between the streams, scattering their community over the plantation. A black church and school were built by this date. A typical sharecropper on the plantation earned most of his income from growing cotton.

REDEMPTION

Ex-Confederates were blind to the benefits of radical Reconstruction. Indeed, no amount of achievement could have persuaded them that it was anything but an abomination, undertaken without their consent, and intended to deny them their rightful place in southern society. Led by the planters, ex-Confederates calling themselves the Redeemers staged a massive counterrevolution—one designed to "redeem" the South and restore them to political power under the banner of the Democratic party.

Counterrevolution

Insofar as they could win at the ballot box, the Democrats took that route. They worked hard to get ex-Confederates restored to the rolls of registered voters, they appealed to racial solidarity and southern patriotism, and they attacked black suffrage as a threat to white supremacy. By 1869, the Democrats had enough votes to regain office in Tennessee, and a year later, Virginia. But force was equally acceptable. Throughout the Deep South, especially where black voters were heavily concentrated, ex-Confederate planters and their supporters organized secret societies and waged campaigns of terrorism against blacks and their white allies.

The most widespread of these groups, the Ku Klux Klan, first appeared in 1866 as a Tennessee social club but quickly became a paramilitary force under the ferocious leadership of Nathan Bedford Forrest, the Confederacy's most decorated cavalry general. Forrest was notorious for a wartime incident at Fort Pillow, Tennessee, when his troops massacred African-American soldiers after they had surrendered.

By 1870 the Klan was operating almost everywhere in the South in concert with the Democratic party. The Klan murdered and whipped Republican politicians, burned black schools and churches, and attacked party gatherings. In October 1870 a group of Klansmen assaulted a Republican rally in Eutaw, Alabama, killing four African-Americans and wounding fifty-four. Such terrorist tactics enabled the Democrats to seize power in Georgia and North Carolina in 1870 and to make substantial gains elsewhere. An African-American politician in North Carolina wrote, "Our former masters are fast taking the reins of government."

Congress responded by passing a series of Enforcement Acts in 1870 and 1871, including the Ku Klux Klan Act. These laws authorized President Grant to use federal prosecutions, military force, and martial law to suppress conspiracies to deprive citizens of the rights to vote, to hold office, to serve on juries, and to enjoy equal protection of the law. Federal agents penetrated the Klan and gathered evidence that provided the basis for widespread arrests; federal grand juries indicted more than 3,000 Klansmen. In South Carolina, where the Klan was most deeply entrenched, federal troops occupied nine counties and drove as many as 2,000 Klansmen from the state.

The Grant administration's assault on the Klan raised the spirits of southern Republicans, but it also emphasized how dependent they were on the federal government. If they were to prevail over ex-Confederate terrorism, they needed what one southern Republican described as "steady, unswerving power from without."

Northern Republicans, however, had no stomach for an endless guerrilla war in the South. They grew weary of the financial costs of Reconstruction and the continuing bloodshed it seemed to produce. Although re-elected handily in 1872, Grant did not take his victory as a mandate for holding to his interventionist course. Prosecuting Klansmen under the Enforcement Acts was

White Terror

*A*lthough *Mississippi remained Republican until 1876, this letter from a party organizer attests to the stubborn white resistance to radical Reconstruction. Without federal bayonets, a town like Brandon would never be secure for the Republicans.*

Brandon, Mississippi, June 21, 1868

Dear Sir:

I came here at the most exciting time probably that this place has known since the war. The democrats had a great meeting. . . . After this I learned a paper was circulated for [the colored men] to sign, in which they promised to vote the democratic ticket, and about a 100 names were received. The colored men were induced to do this by threats of being discharged. . . . Supplies have already been stopped from those who would not promise to vote the demo-cratic ticket. One man informs me his horse and wagon, valued at $150, is to be sold to satisfy an attachment for $9, on Saturday next, if not paid before; he has owing him $100 and over from white men; none will pay, nor will the sale be stopped unless he votes democratic; but he is true steel and no signs of backing down. Several colored men have had their lives threatened, and from the best information I can get there will be a row here unless a squad of troops are sent here to keep order. There is not a white republican in town. . . .

Since writing the above, and while out about ten minutes from my room, a K.K.K. warning was put under my door. Below is a copy:

The bloody dagger is drawn; the trying hour is at hand; beware! Your steps are marked; the eye of dark chief is upon you. First he warns; then the avenging dagger flashes in the moonlight.
By order of the Grand Cyclops. . . .

Make a request of the post commander for the troops to be here on elec-tion day, or have them sent over on Wednesday, if possible.

Excuse haste, and my scribbling, mistakes, &c.

Respectfully yours,
D. S. Harrison

SOURCE: Stanley I. Kutler, ed., *Looking for America*, 2d ed. (New York: Norton, 1979), 36–37.

an uphill battle. U.S. attorneys usually faced all-white juries, and the Justice department lacked the resources to prosecute effectively. After 1872, prosecu-tions began to drop off, and many Klansmen received hasty pardons; few served significant prison terms. Moreover, the Supreme Court undercut the Enforce-ment Acts by ruling that the Fourteenth Amendment protected citizens from

Klan Portrait, 1868
Two armed Klansmen from
Alabama pose proudly in their
disguises. Northern audiences saw
a lithograph based on this photograph in *Harper's Weekly* in
December 1868.

actions by the *states*, not by other citizens, so that federal prosecution of private groups like the Klan became legally questionable.

The faltering zeal for Reconstruction in the North, however, had much broader sources. The worst depression in the nation's history struck in 1873, and the North became preoccupied with its own economic problems. North-ern business interests complained that the turmoil of Reconstruction retarded the South's economic recovery and harmed their investment opportunities. Sympathy for the freedmen also began to wane. The North was flooded with one-sided, often racist reports, such as James S. Pike's *The Prostrate State* (1873), of extravagant, corrupt Republican rule and a South in the grip of "a mass of black barbarism." In the 1874 elections, the Republicans suffered a crushing defeat, losing control of the House of Representatives for the first time since secession, and also losing seven normally Republican northern states to the Democrats. For Republican party strategists, the political costs in a disillusioned North began to outweigh their hopes for a Republican-dominated South.

In a kind of self-fulfilling prophecy, the unwillingness of the Grant admin-istration to shore up Reconstruction guaranteed that it would fail. Republican governments that were denied federal help found themselves overwhelmed by ex-Confederate politicians during the day and by terrorists at night. Democrats overthrew Republican governments in Texas in 1873, in Alabama and Arkansas in 1874, and in Mississippi in 1875.

The Mississippi campaign showed all too clearly what the Republicans were up against. As elections neared in 1875, paramilitary groups such as the Rifle Clubs and the Red Shirts operated openly. Often local Democrats paraded armed, as if they were militia companies. They identified black leaders in assassination lists called "dead-books"; broke up Republican meetings; provoked rioting that left hundreds of African-Americans dead; and threatened voters, who still lacked the protection of the secret ballot. Mississippi's Republican governor, Adelbert Ames, a Congressional Medal of Honor winner from Maine, appealed to President Grant for federal troops, but Grant refused. Ames then contemplated organizing a state militia but ultimately decided against it, believing that only blacks would join. Rather than escalate the fighting and turn it into a racial war, he conceded victory to the terrorists.

By 1877 Republican governments, backed by token U.S. military units, remained in only three states: Louisiana, South Carolina, and Florida. Elsewhere, the ex-Confederates were back in the saddle.

Sharecropping

In the meantime, the freedmen were locked in a great economic struggle with their former owners. In 1869, the Republican government of South Carolina had established a land commission empowered to buy property and resell it on easy terms to the landless. In this way about 14,000 black families acquired farms. South Carolina's land distribution plan showed what was possible, but it was the exception, not the rule. Despite a lot of rhetoric, Republican regimes elsewhere did little to help the freedmen fulfill their dreams of becoming independent farmers. Federal efforts proved equally feeble. The Southern Homestead Act of 1866 offered 80-acre grants to settlers, limited for the first year to freedmen and southern Unionists. The advantage was strictly symbolic, however, since the public land made available to homesteaders was off the beaten track in swampy, infertile parts of the lower South, and since, in any case, they lacked the resources to get started. Only about a thousand families finally succeeded. There was no reversing President Johnson's order restoring confiscated lands to ex-Confederates, even after the Radical Republicans had the power to do so. Property rights, it seemed, trumped everything else. The Freedman's Bureau, which had earlier championed the land claims of the ex-slaves, now devoted itself to teaching them how to be good agricultural laborers.

So, while they yearned for farms of their own, most freedmen started out landless, and with no option but to work for their former owners. But not, they vowed, under the conditions of slavery—no gang work, no overseers, no fines or punishments, no regulation of their private lives or personal freedom. They were willing to work for wages, provided the pay was high enough, as it

Sharecropping
This sharecropping family seems proud of its new cabin and crop of cotton, which it planted in every available bit of ground. But the presence of the white landlord in the background suggests that sharecropping was only a limited kind of economic freedom.

was, for example, on the great sugar plantations of Louisiana taken over after the war by northern investors. The problem was that cotton planters lacked the money to pay wages, at least until the crop came in, and sometimes, in lieu of a straight wage, they offered a share of the crop. As a *wage*, sharecropping was a bad deal for the freedmen, but it opened up interesting possibilities. They quickly realized that, if they could be paid in shares for their work, they could pay in those same shares to rent the land they worked. This form of land tenantry, already familiar in parts of the South among white farmers, the freedmen now seized on for the independence it offered them. Planters resisted, believing, as one wrote, that "wages are the only successful system of controlling hands." But, in a battle of wills that broke out all across the cotton South, the planters yielded to "the inveterate prejudices of the freedmen, who desire to be masters of their own time."

Thus there sprang up, quite spontaneously, a distinctively southern system of agricultural labor—*sharecropping*, in which the freedmen worked as renters, exchanging their labor for the use of land, house, implements, and sometimes seed and fertilizer. Typically they turned over between half and two-thirds of their crops to the landlord. The sharecropping system joined laborers and the owners of land and capital in a common sharing of risks and returns. But it was a very unequal relationship, given the force of southern law and custom on the white landowner's side, and given the dire economic circumstances of the sharecroppers. Starting out in poverty, they had no way of making it through the first growing season without borrowing for food and supplies.

Country storekeepers stepped in. Bankrolled by their northern suppliers, they "furnished" the sharecroppers and took as collateral *liens* on their crops. Under laws passed by the new Democratic regimes, crop liens effectively transferred the crops to the storekeeper, leaving sharecroppers only the proceeds that remained after their debts had been paid. Once indebted at one store, the sharecropper was no longer free to shop around, and became an easy target for exhorbitant prices, usurious interest rates, and crooked bookkeeping. As cotton prices declined during the 1870s, more and more sharecroppers failed to settle accounts and fell into permanent debt. And if the merchant was also the landowner, or conspired with the landowner, the debt became a pretext for forced labor, or *peonage*, although evidence now suggests that sharecroppers generally managed to pull up stakes and move on once things became hopeless. Sharecroppers always thought twice about moving, however, because part of their "capital" was being known and well-reputed in their home communities. Freedmen who lacked that local standing generally found sharecropping hard going and likely ended up in the ranks of agricultural laborers.

In the face of so much adversity, black families struggled to better themselves. By the end of Reconstruction, about one-quarter of them had managed to save enough to rent with cash payments. Land ownership was harder to achieve. In many places whites would not sell to blacks or jacked up prices exhorbitantly. For the sake of independence, however, black farmers persevered. Eventually they owned about a third of the land they cultivated, but rarely the best land and usually at a cost greater than its fertility warranted.

For the freedmen, sharecropping was not the worst choice; it certainly beat laboring for their former owners. But for southern agriculture, the costs were devastating. Sharecropping committed the South inflexibly to cotton, the one cash crop capable of satisfying the financial demands of landowners and furnishing merchants. Crop diversification declined, costing the South its self-sufficiency in grains and livestock. And with farms leased year-to-year, neither tenant nor owner had any incentive to improve the property. The crop-lien system lined merchants' pockets with unearned profits—economists estimate the excessive rate of profit at 13.5 percent—that might otherwise have gone into agricultural improvement. The result was a stagnant farm economy, blighting the South's future and condemning it to economic backwardness— a kind of retribution, in fact, for the fresh injustices visited on the people it had once enslaved.

The Political Crisis of 1877

Northerners were scarcely aware of the South's agrarian revolution. National politics had moved on, and other concerns absorbed the voter. Foremost was the stench of scandal that hung over the White House. In 1875 Grant's secretary of the treasury, Benjamin Bristow, exposed the so-called Whiskey Ring, a network of distillers and government agents who had defrauded the Treasury of millions of dollars of excise taxes on liquor. The ringleader was a Grant appointee, and Grant's own private secretary, Orville Babcock, had a hand in the scandal. The others went to prison, but Grant stood by Babcock, possibly perjuring himself to save his secretary from jail. On top of this, the economy had fallen into a severe depression after 1873. Grant's administration responded ineffectually, rebuffing the pleas of debtors for relief by increasing the money supply (see Chapter 19). Among the casualties of the depression was the Freedman's Savings and Trust Company, which had been sponsored by the Freedman's Bureau and held the small deposits of thousands of ex-slaves. When the bank failed in 1874, Congress refused to compensate the depositors, and many lost their life savings. In denying their pathetic pleas, Congress was signaling also that Reconstruction had lost its moral claim on the country.

Abandoning Grant, the Republicans in 1876 nominated Rutherford B. Hayes, governor of Ohio, a colorless figure but untainted by corruption or by strong convictions—in a word, a safe man. His Democratic opponent was Samuel J. Tilden, governor of New York, a wealthy lawyer with ties to Wall Street and a reform reputation for helping to break the grip of the thieving Tweed Ring on New York City politics. The Democrat Tilden, of course, favored "home rule" for the South but so, more discretely, did the Republican Hayes. Reconstruction actually did not figure prominently in the campaign and was mostly subsumed under broader Democratic charges of "corrupt centralism" and "incapacity, waste, and fraud." By now, Republicans had essentially written off the South, and scarcely campaigned there. Not a lot was said about the states still ruled by Reconstruction governments—Florida, South Carolina, and Louisiana.

Once the returns started coming in on election night, however, those three states began to loom very large indeed. Tilden led in the popular vote and, victorious in key northern states, seemed headed for the White House. But sleepless politicians at Republican headquarters realized that if they kept Florida, South Carolina, and Louisiana, Hayes would win by a single electoral vote. The campaigns in those states had been bitterly fought, replicating the Democratic assaults on blacks that had overturned Republican regimes everywhere else in the South. But Republicans still controlled the election machinery in those states, and, citing Democratic fraud and intimidation, they could certify Republican victories. The audacious announcement came forth from Republican headquarters: Hayes had carried the three southern states and won the election. But, of course, newly elected Democratic officials in the three states also sent in electoral votes for Tilden, and, when Congress met in early 1877, it faced two sets of electoral votes from those states.

The Constitution does not provide for this contingency. All it says is that the president of the Senate (in 1877, a Republican) opens the electoral certificates before the House (Democratic) and the Senate (Republican) and that "The votes shall then be counted." For weeks, ever since the November election, an air of crisis had gripped the country. There was wild talk of inside deals, of a new election, even of a violent coup and civil war. Just in case, the commander of the army, General William T. Sherman, deployed four artillery companies in Washington. Finally, Congress decided to appoint an electoral commission to settle the question. The commission included seven Republicans; seven Democrats; and, as the deciding member, David Davis, a Supreme Court justice not known to have fixed party loyalties. But Davis disqualified himself by accepting an Illinois seat in the Senate. He was replaced by Republican Justice Joseph P. Bradley, and by 8 to 7, the commission awarded the disputed votes to Hayes.

Outraged Democrats had one more trick up their sleeves. They controlled the House, and they set about stalling a final count of the electoral votes so as to prevent Hayes's inauguration on March 4. But a week before, secret Washington talks had begun between southern Democrats and Ohio Republicans representing Hayes. Other issues may have been on the table, but the main thing was the situation in South Carolina and Louisiana, where Republican governors physically occupied the statehouses, protected by Union troops. But for the disputed federal election, ironically, the military would not have intervened, and the ex-Confederate Redeemers would already have seized power. Exactly what deal was struck, or how involved Hayes himself was, will probably never be known, but on March 1 the House Democrats suddenly ended their filibuster, the ceremonial counting of votes went forward, and Hayes was inaugurated on schedule. He soon ordered the Union troops back to their barracks, and the Republican regimes in South Carolina and Louisiana fell. Reconstruction had ended.

In 1877 political leaders on all sides seemed ready to say that what Lincoln had called "the work" was complete. But for the freedmen, the work had only begun. Reconstruction turned out to have been a magnificent aberration, a magnum leap beyond what most white Americans actually felt was due their black fellow citizens. Redemption represented a sad falling back to the norm. Still, something real had been achieved—three rights-defining amendments to the Constitution; some elbow room to advance economically; and, not least, a stubborn confidence among blacks that, by their own efforts, they could lift themselves up. Things would, in fact, get worse before they got better, but the work of the Reconstruction was imperishable and could never be effaced.

CHAPTER 16 TIMELINE

1863	Lincoln announces his Ten Percent Plan
1864	Wade-Davis bill passed by Congress Lincoln gives Wade-Davis bill a "pocket" veto
1865	Freedmen's Bureau established Lincoln assassinated; Andrew Johnson succeeds as president Johnson implements his restoration plan
1866	Republicans fail to override Johnson's veto of Freedmen's Bureau bill Civil Rights Act passes over Johnson's veto of Freedmen's Bureau bill Johnson makes disastrous "swing around the circle" Johnson defeated in congressional elections
1867	Reconstruction Acts Tenure of Office Act
1868	Impeachment crisis Fourteenth Amendment ratified Ulysses S. Grant elected president
1870	Ku Klux Klan at peak of power Enforcement Acts passed by Congress Fifteenth Amendment ratified
1871	Ku Klux Klan Act passed by Congress
1872	Grant's re-election as president
1873	Panic of 1873 ushers in depression of 1873–1877
1874	Democrats win majority in House of Representatives
1875	Whiskey Ring scandal undermines Grant administration
1877	Congressional compromise makes Rutherford B. Hayes president after disputed election Reconstruction ends

	ECONOMY The Triumph of Industrialism	GOVERNMENT From Inaction to Progressive Reform	SOCIETY Rise of Urban Culture	DIPLOMACY An Emerging World Power
1877	Carnegie launches modern steel industry Knights of Labor becomes national movement (1878)	Election of Rutherford B. Hayes ends Reconstruction	National League founded (1876) Dwight L. Moody pioneers urban revivalism	U.S. becomes a net exporter
1880	Swift pioneers vertically integrated firm American Federation of Labor founded (1886)	Chinese Exclusion Act (1882) Civil service reform (1883)	Electrification transforms city life First *Social Register* defines high society (1888)	Diplomacy of inaction Naval buildup begins
1890	U.S. surpasses Britain in iron and steel output Economic depression (1893–97) F.W. Taylor introduces scientific management	Populist party founded (1892) McKinley defeats Bryan's free silver crusade (1896) Black disfranchisement and racial segregation in the South	Immigration from southeastern Europe rises sharply Settlement houses spread progressive ideas to cities Hearst's *New York Journal* pioneers yellow journalism	Social Darwinism and Anglo-Saxonism promote expansionism Spanish-American War (1898–99); conquest of the Philippines
1900	Great merger movement Industrial Workers of the World founded (1905)	Theodore Roosevelt attacks the trusts Hepburn Act enforces government's regulation of railroads (1906) Women take leading roles in social reform	Muckraking journalism Movies begin to overtake vaudeville	Panama cedes Canal Zone to United States (1903) Roosevelt Corollary to Monroe Doctrine (1904) Root-Takahira agreement (1908)
1910	Ford builds first automobile assembly line	Revival of the struggle for civil rights; NAACP founded (1910) New Freedom legislation creates Federal Reserve, FTC	Urban liberalism	Taft's Dollar Diplomacy promotes American business Wilson proclaims U.S. neutrality in World War I

PART 4

A MATURING INDUSTRIAL SOCIETY

1877–1914

The decade after Reconstruction marked a watershed in American life. For the first time, farmers no longer constituted a majority of the nation's work force. America's future was now linked to its industrial development. As heavy industry emerged and the railroad system was completed, nationwide firms began to dominate American enterprise. The modern labor movement emerged, and, as immigration surged, the foreign-born and their children became America's workers.

The demands of industrialism for western resources largely drove the final surge of settlement across the Great Plains and to the Pacific, in the process overwhelming the native American inhabitants, disrupting the long-established Hispanic communities of the Southwest, and attracting a multiethnic population from Europe, Asia, and Mexico. The phenomenal growth of the cities was likewise the product of industrialism. An urban way of life emerged unlike anything seen before in America.

In this era of economic expansion, there seemed little need for government intervention. The major parties were robust, but their vitality stemmed from a political culture of popular participation and the informal functions they performed as organized machines. The political status quo was upset by the rise of the Populist party during the depressed 1890s. The Republicans turned back that challenge in 1896, but they then had to contend with another economic concern—the concentration of corporate industry—that dominated the Progressive Era. In those years, the nation addressed a host of reform issues, including political corruption, urban problems, and the demands of African-Americans for equality.

Finally, the United States began to assert itself globally, warring with Spain in 1898, acquiring an overseas empire, and pressing for open markets in Latin America and Asia. As World War I approached, there would be no evading the entanglements that came with America's status as a Great Power.

CHAPTER 17

THE AMERICAN WEST

- The Great Plains
- The Far West

During the last decades of the nineteenth century, American society seemed at odds with itself. From one angle the nation looked like an advanced industrial society, with great factories and mills and enormous, crowded cities. But from another angle America still seemed to be a frontier country, with pioneers streaming onto the Great Plains, repeating the old dramas of "settlement" they had been performing ever since Europeans first set foot on the continent. Not until the census of 1890 did the federal government declare that a "frontier of settlement" no longer existed: the country's "unsettled area has been so broken into . . . that there can hardly be said to be a frontier line."

That same year, 1890, the country surpassed Great Britain in the production of iron and steel. Newspapers reported Indian wars and labor strikes in the same edition. The last tragic episode in the suppression of the Sioux, the massacre at Wounded Knee, South Dakota, occurred only eighteen months before the great Homestead steel strike of 1892. This alignment of events from the distant worlds of factory and frontier was not accidental. The final surge of settlement across the Great Plains and the Far West was powered primarily by the dynamism of American industrialism.

THE GREAT PLAINS

During the 1860s agricultural settlement reached the western margins of the high-grass prairie country. Beyond, roughly at the 98th meridian, stretched vast semiarid lands uninviting to farmers accustomed to woodlands and ample rainfall (see Map 17.1). The geologic event that created the Great Plains had occurred 60 million years before, when the Rocky Mountains had been thrust up out of the ocean covering western North America. With no outlet, the shallow inland sea to the east dried up, forming a hard pan on which sediment washing down from the mountains built up a loose, featureless surface layer. The mountain barrier also made for a dry climate, because the moisture-laden winds from the Pacific spent themselves on the western slopes. Only vegetation capable of withstanding the periodic droughts and bitter winters could take hold on the plains. The short gramma grass, the linchpin of this fragile ecosystem, matted the easily blown soil into place and sustained a rich wildlife dominated by the grazing pronghorn antelope and buffalo. What the dry short-grass country had not sustained, until Indians began migrating there in quite recent times, was human settlement.

Indians of the Great Plains

Probably a hundred thousand native Americans lived on the Great Plains at mid-nineteenth century. They were a diverse people, divided into six linguistic families and at least thirty tribal groupings. On the eastern margins and along the Missouri River, the Mandan, Arikara, and Pawnee planted maize and beans and lived in permanent villages. The ravaging smallpox and measles brought by Europeans decimated these concentrated, sedentary tribes. Less vulnerable to epidemics were the hunting tribes that had migrated to the Great Plains since the seventeenth century: Kiowa and Comanche in the southwest; Arapaho and Cheyenne on the central plains; and, to the north, Blackfeet, Crow, Cheyenne, and the great Sioux nation.

Originally the Sioux had been eastern prairie people, occupying semipermanent settlements in the lake country of northern Minnesota. With fish and game dwindling, some Sioux tribes drifted westward and around 1760 began to cross the Missouri River. These Sioux became a nomadic people, living in portable skin tepees and following the buffalo. Splendid hunters and formidable fighters, the Sioux claimed the entire Great Plains north of the Arkansas River as their hunting grounds.

The westernmost Sioux—they called themselves the Teton people, or Lakota (meaning "allies")—made up a loose confederation of seven tribes. In the winter months the tribes broke up into small bands, but each spring they assembled and prepared for the summer hunt, and for battle. Mostly, raiding parties rode forth intent on capturing ponies and taking scalps, but occasionally, long columns of warriors mounted serious territorial campaigns against rival tribes. The Sioux, it must be remembered, were an invading people who dominated the northern Great Plains by driving out or subjugating longer-settled tribes.

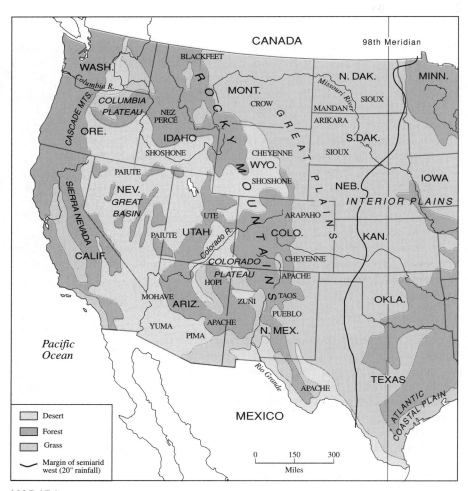

MAP 17.1

The Natural Environment of the West

As settlers pushed into the Great Plains beyond the line of semiaridity, they sensed the overwhelming power of the natural environment. In a landscape without trees for fences and barns and without adequate rainfall, ranchers and farmers had to relearn their business. The native Americans peopling the plains and mountains had learned to live in this environment, but this knowledge counted for little against the ruthless pressure of the settlers to domesticate the West.

A society that celebrates the warrior virtues is likely to define gender roles sharply. But before the Sioux acquired horses, chasing down the buffalo had involved the entire community. Women and men worked collectively to construct a "pound" and channel the herds in the right direction. With the arrival of horses, however, the hunt changed, and gender roles became more fixed. On horseback, the men became highly efficient hunters. The women stayed behind to prepare the mounting piles of buffalo skins. This was laborious, painstaking work, heavily burdening the Sioux women, but also enriching the tribe.

Living so close to nature, depending on its bounty for survival, the Sioux saw sacred meaning in every manifestation of the natural world. Unlike Europeans, they conceived of God not as a supreme being but as, in the words of the ethnologist Clark Wissler, "a controlling power or series of powers pervading the universe"—Wi, the sun; Skan, the sky; Maka, the earth; Inyan, the rock. Below these came the moon, wind, buffalo, and so on, down through a hierarchy embodying the entire natural order.

By prayer and fasting in some isolated place, Sioux prepared themselves to experience those mysterious powers. The vision, when a supplicant achieved it, attached itself to some object—a feather, the skin of an animal, or a shell—which was tied into a sacred bundle that became the person's lifelong talisman. For the tribe as a whole, Sacred Pipe bundles served as the symbolic and ceremonial core of Sioux religion. In the Sun Dance, the entire tribe engaged in the rites of coming of age, fertility, the hunt, and combat, followed by four days of fasting and dancing in supplication to Wi, the sun.

The world of the Teton Sioux was not self-contained. All along they had traded pelts and buffalo robes for the produce of the agriculturalist Indians. These exchanges expanded to the white traders who appeared on the upper Missouri River during the eighteenth century. Although the buffalo provided most of the essentials of life, the Sioux came to rely as well on the traders' pots, kettles, blankets, knives, and firearms. The trade system they entered was linked to the Euro-American market economy, yet it was also integrated into the Sioux way of life. Everything depended on the survival of the Great Plains as the Sioux had found it—wild grassland on which the antelope and buffalo ranged free.

Intruders

On first encounter, white Americans saw no better use for the Great Plains. After exploring a drought-stricken stretch in 1820, Major Stephen H. Long declared it "almost wholly unfit for cultivation, and of course uninhabitable by a people depending upon agriculture for their subsistence."

For years thereafter, maps marked the plains region as the Great American Desert. With that notion in mind, Congress formally designated the Great Plains in 1834 as permanent Indian country. Trade with the Indians would continue, but now it would be closely supervised and licensed by the federal government, with the Indian country otherwise off limits to white intrusion.

Events swiftly overtook the nation's solemn commitment to the native Americans. During the 1840s settlers began moving westward to Oregon and California. Instead of serving as a buffer against the British and Mexicans, the Indian country became a bridge to the Pacific. The first wagon train headed west for Oregon from Missouri in 1842. Soon thousands of emigrants traveled the Oregon Trail to the Willamette Valley or, cutting south beyond Fort Hall, down into California. Approaching that juncture in 1859, it seemed to Horace

Greeley as if "the white coverings of the many emigrant and transport wagons dotting the landscape" gave "the trail the appearance of a river running through great meadows, with many ships sailing on its bosom." Only these "ships" left behind not a trailing wake of foam, but a rutted landscape devoid of grass and game and littered with abandoned wagons and rotting garbage.

Talk about the need for a railroad to the Pacific soon began to be heard in Washington. How else could the distant territories formally acquired from Mexico and Britain in 1848 be firmly linked to the Union? The project languished while North and South argued over the terminus for the route to the Pacific. Meanwhile, the Indian country was crisscrossed by overland freight lines and Pony Express riders. In 1861, telegraph lines brought San Francisco into instant communication with the East. The next year, with the South in rebellion, the federal government finally moved forward with the transcontinental project.

No private company could be expected to foot the bill by itself. The construction costs were staggering, and, in the short run, not much traffic could be expected beyond the well-populated states. So the federal government awarded generous land grants along the right-of-way, plus millions of dollars in loans, to the two companies that undertook the transcontinental project.

The Union Pacific, building westward from Omaha, made little headway until the Civil War ended, but then advanced rapidly across Indian country, reaching Cheyenne, Wyoming, in November 1867. It took the Central Pacific nearly that long, moving eastward from Sacramento, to cross the crest of the Sierra Nevada. Both then worked furiously—since the government subsidy was based on miles of track laid—until, to great fanfare, the tracks met at Promontory Point, Utah, in 1869. None of the other land-grant railroads made it as far as the Rockies before the Panic of 1873 hit, throwing them into bankruptcy and bringing work to an abrupt halt.

By then, however, railroad tycoons had changed their minds about the Great Plains. No longer did they see it through the eyes of the Oregon-bound settlers, as a place to be gotten through en route to the Pacific. Rail transportation, they realized, was laying the basis for the economic exploitation of the Great Plains. This calculation spurred the railroad boom that followed the economic recovery of 1878. Construction soared. Forty thousand miles of track were laid west of the Mississippi during the 1880s, linking southern California via the Southern Pacific Railroad to New Orleans and via the Santa Fe to Kansas City, and also linking the Northwest via the Northern Pacific Railroad to St. Paul, Minnesota.

Of all the beckoning opportunities, most obvious was cattle raising. The grazing buffalo made it easy to imagine the Great Plains as cow country. But first, the buffalo had to go. A small market for buffalo robes had existed for years. Then, in the early 1870s, eastern tanneries discovered how to cure the hides, and a huge market suddenly developed. The systematic slaughter of the buffalo began. Already diminished by disease and shrinking pasturage, the great herds almost vanished within ten years. Many people spoke out against this mass killing, but no way existed to stop people bent on making a quick dollar. Besides, as General Philip H. Sheridan pointed out, exterminating the buffalo would starve the Indians into submission and open up the feeding grounds for cattle.

About 5 million head of longhorn cattle roamed south Texas in 1865, hardly worth bothering about because they could not be profitably marketed. That year, however, the Missouri Pacific Railroad reached Sedalia, Missouri. At that terminal, which connected to hungry eastern markets, a $3 longhorn might command $40. With this incentive, Texas ranchers inaugurated the famous Long Drive. Cowboys began to herd cattle hundreds of miles north to the railroads that were pushing west across Kansas.

At Abilene, Texas, and at Ellsworth and Dodge City, in Kansas, ranchers sold their cattle and trail-weary cowboys went on a binge. These wide-open cattle towns captured the nation's imagination as symbols of the Wild West. The reality was much more ordinary. The cowboys, many of them blacks and Hispanics, were in fact farmhands on horseback, working long hours under harsh conditions for small pay. Colorful though it seemed, the Long Drive was actually a makeshift means of bridging a gap in the developing transportation system. As soon as railroads reached the Texas range country during the 1870s, ranchers abandoned the hazardous and wasteful Long Drive.

The Texas ranchers owned or leased the land they used, sometimes in huge tracts. North of Texas, where the land was in the public domain, cattlemen simply helped themselves, treating the land as a free commodity for anyone who seized it and put it to use. Hopeful ranchers would spot a likely area

The Cowboy at Work
Open-range ranching, in which cattle from different ranches grazed together, gave rise to distinctive traditions. At the roundup, cowboys separated the cattle by owner and branded the calves. The cowboy, traditionally a colorful figure, was really a farmhand on horseback, with the skills to work on the range. He earned twenty-five dollars a month, plus meals and a bed in the bunkhouse, in return for long hours of grueling, lonesome work.

along a creek and claim as much land as they could qualify for as settlers under
federal homesteading laws, plus what might be added by fraudulent claims
taken out by one or two ranch hands. By a common usage that quickly became established, ranchers had a "range right" to all the adjacent land rising up
to the divide—the point where the land sloped down to the next creek.

News of easy money traveled fast. Calves were selling at $5 a head, steers at
maybe $60 on the Chicago market. Rail connections were in place or coming
in. And the grass was free. Profits of 40 percent per annum were almost ensured. The rush was on, drawing from as far away as Europe both the smart
money and the romantics (like the recent Harvard graduate Teddy Roosevelt)
eager for a taste of the Wild West. By the early 1880s the plains overflowed
with cattle, decimating the grass and trampling the water holes.

A cycle of good weather only postponed the inevitable disaster. When it
came—a hard winter in 1885, a severe drought the following summer, then
record blizzards and bitter cold—cattle died by the hundreds of thousands. An
awful scene of rotting carcasses greeted the cowhands riding out onto the
range the following spring. On top of that, beef prices plunged when hard-
pressed ranchers dumped the surviving cattle on the market. The boom collapsed and investors fled, leaving behind a more enduring ecological disaster:
the native grasses never recovered from the relentless overgrazing in the
drought cycle.

Open-range ranching came to an end. Ranchers fenced their land and planted
hay for the winter. No longer would cattle be left to fend for themselves on
the open range. Elsewhere, Hispanic grazers from New Mexico brought sheep
in to feed on the forbs and woody plants that had replaced the native grasses.
Sheep raising, previously scorned by ranchers as unmanly and resisted as a
threat to cattle, became a major enterprise in the sparser high country. Some
ranchers even sold out to the despised "nesters"—those who wanted to try
farming the Great Plains.

Homesteaders

The movement of farmers onto the plains was not exactly spontaneous. Powerful interests devoted themselves to overcoming the notion of a Great American Desert. Foremost were the railroads, eager to sell off the public land they
had been granted—180 million acres of it—and develop traffic for their
routes. They advertised aggressively, offered cut-rate tickets, and sold off their
land holdings at bargain prices. Land speculators, steamship lines, and the
western states and territories did all they could to encourage settlement of the
Great Plains. So did the federal government, with its offer under the Homestead Act (1862) of 160 acres of public land to settlers.

"Why emigrate to Kansas?" asked a testimonial in *Western Trail*, the Rock
Island Railroad's gazette. "Because it is the garden spot of the world. Because it
will grow anything that any other country will grow, and with less work. Because it rains here more than any other place, and at just the right time." As if

Preaching the Word of God

Pastor Carl Johan Nyvall of the Swedish Mission Friends describes his itinerant ministry on the Great Plains, 1876.

I heard to my surprise that some sixty or seventy Swedish immigrants, planning to settle in this vicinity [Kearney, Nebraska], were to arrive by train from the East. My friend and I met the group at the station. . . . I preached the Word of God twice for these pilgrims and it seemed that their hearts at this time were more receptive than usual. . . .

When one gets to know through firsthand contacts what pioneer life in America is like, one wonders how people can endure it. . . . Even though the settlers may have . . . sixty to eighty acres of cultivated fields, they themselves live . . . in wretched wooden sheds, in sod houses, or in dugouts. . . . A visitor is happy if he is given a place in the same bed as the family. . . . Preachers who would serve the Lord in America by seeking out the scattered immigrants must be prepared for severe privations.

But preachers got in return the warmest of welcomes, as one of Pastor Nyvall's Swedish colleagues found after the long journey to one homestead:

Some hours' sleep. I looked out the window. . . . Round about were arranged wagon seats and planks, where a large group of people had gathered. . . . When I had preached for some forty minutes, I jumped down from the box, but then a thickset man said, "You ought to know, Pastor, that we have come a long way and that we don't have meetings so often, so please, go and get up on the box again." There was nothing else to do. An equally long sermon again. Baskets and boxes were now opened. There was plenty of food. F. said, "We will go on with the meeting as soon as we have eaten." So, up on the box again. The Lord was with us. Oh, what an advantage to be able to preach for these people!

SOURCE: H. Arnold Barton, ed., *Letters from the Promised Land* (Minneapolis: University of Minnesota Press, 1975), 170–172.

to confirm the optimists, an exceptionally wet cycle occurred between 1878 and 1886. "As the plains are settled up we hear less and less of drouth, hot winds, alkali and other bugbears that used to hold back the adventurous," remarked one Nebraska man. Some settlers attributed the increased rainfall to soil cultivation and tree planting. Others credited God. As a settler on the southern plains remarked, "The Lord just knowed we needed more land an' He's gone and changed the climate."

Buffalo Chips
With no trees around for firewood, settlers on the plains had to make do with dried cow and buffalo droppings. Gathering the "buffalo chips" must have been a regular chore for Ada McColl on her homestead near Lakin, Kansas (1893).

No amount of optimism, however, could dispel the pain of migration. "That last separating word *Farewell!* sinks deeply into the heart," one pioneer woman recorded in her diary, thinking of family and friends left behind. Emigrants had always taken parting as a kind of death, with reunion unlikely "on this side of the dark river." But then came the treeless plains. "Such an air of desolation," wrote a Nebraska-bound woman; and from another woman in Texas, "such a lonely country."

For some women, this hard experience had a liberating side. Prescribed gender roles broke down as women shouldered men's work and became self-reliant in the face of danger and hardship. When husbands died or broke down, wives took up the reins and operated farms on their own. Under the Homestead Act, which accorded widows and single women the same rights as men, women filed 10 percent of the claims. "People afraid of coyotes and work and loneliness had better leave ranching alone," advised one woman homesteader. "At the same time, any woman who can stand her own company . . . will certainly succeed; will have independence, plenty to eat all the time, and a home of her own in the end."

Even with a man around, however, a woman contributed crucially to the farm enterprise. Farming might be thought of as a dual economy, in which men's labor brought in the big wage at season's end, while women's labor provisioned the family day by day and produced a steady bit of money for groceries. And if the crop failed, it was women's labor that carried the family through. No wonder farming communities placed a high premium on marriage: a mere 2.4 percent of Nebraska women in 1900 had never married.

Male or female, the vision of new land to be farmed drove people onto the plains. By the 1870s, the midwestern states had filled up, and farmers looked hungrily westward. The same excitement took hold in northern Europe. Not only Germans came, but also, for the first time, Russians, Norwegians, and Swedes. At the peak of the "American fever" in 1882, over 105,000 Scandinavians emigrated to the United States. Swedish and Norwegian became the primary languages in parts of Minnesota and the Dakotas. Roughly a third of the farmers on the northern plains were foreign-born.

The motivation for most settlers, American or European, was to better themselves economically. But for some southern blacks, Kansas briefly represented something more precious—the modern land of Canaan. In the spring of 1879, with Reconstruction over and federal protection withdrawn, black communities fearful of white vengeance were swept by religious enthusiasm for Kansas. Within a month or so, some 6,000 blacks from Mississippi and Louisiana joined the exodus, most of them with nothing more than the clothes on their backs and faith in the Lord. How many of these "Exodusters" remained is hard to say, but the 1880 census reported 40,000 blacks in Kansas—by far the largest African-American concentration in the West aside from Texas, whose expanding cotton frontier attracted hundreds of thousands of black migrants during the 1870s and 1880s.

No matter where they came from, homesteaders found the plains an alien land. A cloud of grasshoppers might descend and destroy a crop in a day; a brushfire or hailstorm could do the job in an hour. What forested land had always provided—springs for water, lumber for cabins and fencing, ample firewood—was absent. For shelter, settlers often cut dugouts into hillsides and, after a season or two, erected sod houses made of turf from the ground. The absence of trees, on other other hand, meant far less labor clearing the land. New technology and better seed overcame obstacles once thought insurmountable. Steel plows enabled homesteaders to break the tightly matted ground, and barbed wire provided cheap fencing against roaming cattle. Strains of hard-kernel wheat tolerant of the extreme temperatures of the plains came in from Europe. A homesteader would harvest good crops while the wet cycle held, and begin to anticipate the wood-frame house, deep well, and full coal bin that might make life tolerable on the plains.

Then, in the late 1880s, the dry years came and silenced such hopeful calculations. "From day to day," reported the budding novelist Stephen Crane from Nebraska, "a wind hot as an oven's fury . . . raged like a pestilence," destroying the crops and leaving farmers "helpless, with no weapon against this terrible and inscrutable wrath of nature." Land only recently settled emptied out as homesteaders fled in defeat. The Dakotas lost 50,000 settlers between 1885 and 1890, and comparable departures occurred up and down the drought-stricken plains.

Other settlers held on grimly. Stripped of the illusion that rain followed the plow, the survivors came to terms with the semiarid climate prevailing west of the 98th meridian. Mormons in the area near the Great Salt Lake (see

Chapter 13) had demonstrated how irrigation could turn a wasteland into a garden. But the Great Plains mostly lacked the surface water needed for irrigation. The answer lay in dry-farming methods, which involved deep planting to bring subsoil moisture to the roots and quick harrowing after rainfalls to turn over a dry mulch that slowed evaporation. Dry farming developed most fully on the corporate farms that covered up to 100,000 acres in the Red River Valley in North Dakota. Even family farms could not survive with less than 300 acres of cereal crops and machinery for plowing, planting, and harvesting. Dry farming was not for the unequipped homesteader.

By the turn of the century the Great Plains had fully submitted to agricultural development. About half the nation's cattle and sheep, a third of its cereal crops, and nearly three-fifths of its wheat came from the newly settled lands. In this process there was little of the "pioneering" that Americans associated with the westward movement. The railroads came before the settlers; eastern capital financed the ranching bonanza; and agriculture depended on sophisticated dry-farming techniques and modern machinery.

And where was the economic capital of the Great Plains? Far off in Chicago. There, at the hub of the nation's rail system, the wheat pit traded western grain and consigned it to world markets, and the great packing houses slaughtered western cattle and supplied the nation with sausage, bacon, and sides of beef. In return, western ranchers got lumber, barbed wire, McCormick reapers, and Sears Roebuck catalogs. Chicago was truly "nature's metropolis."

The Impact on the Indians

What of the native Americans who had inhabited the Great Plains? Basically, their fate has been told in the foregoing account of western settlement. "The white children have surrounded me and have left me nothing but an island," lamented the great Sioux chief Red Cloud in 1870, the year after the completion of the transcontinental railroad. "When we first had all this land we were strong; now we are all melting like snow on a hillside, while you are grown like spring grass."

No matter that provision for a permanent Indian country had been written into federal law and ratified by treaties with various tribes. As incursions into their lands increased from the late 1850s onward, the Indians struck back all along the frontier: the Apache in the Southwest, the Cheyenne and Arapaho in Colorado, the Sioux in the Wyoming and Dakota territories. The Indians hoped that if they resisted stubbornly enough and exacted a high enough price, the whites would tire of the struggle and leave them in peace. This reasoning seemed not altogether fanciful, given the country's exhaustion after the Civil War. But the federal government did not give up; instead, it formulated a new reservation policy for dealing with the western Indians.

Few whites questioned the necessity of moving the native Americans out of the path of settlement and into reservations. That, indeed, had been the fate of the eastern and southern tribes. Now, however, Indian removal was linked to something new: a planned approach to weaning the Indians from their tribal way of life. Under the guidance of the Office of Indian Affairs, they would be wards of the government until they learned "to walk on the white man's road."

The government set aside two extensive areas for the Indians. It allocated the southwestern quarter of the Dakota Territory—present-day South Dakota west of the Missouri River—to the Teton Sioux tribes. It assigned what is now Oklahoma to the southern Plains Indians as well as to the Five Civilized Tribes—the Choctaw, Cherokee, Chickasaw, Creek, and Seminole—who had been forceably removed there thirty years before (see Chapter 11). Scattered reservations went to the Apache, Navajo, and Ute in the Southwest and to the mountain Indians in the Rockies and beyond.

That the Indians would resist was inevitable. "You might as well expect the rivers to run backward as that any man who was born a free man should be contented when penned up and denied liberty to go where he pleases," said Chief Joseph of the Nez Percé tribe. Under the leadership of Chief Joseph, the Nez Percé undertook in 1877 a remarkable 1,500-mile march from eastern Oregon almost to Canada trying to escape confinement in a small reservation.

The U.S. Army was thinly spread, having been cut back after the Civil War to a total force of 27,000. But these were seasoned troops, including 2,000 black cavalrymen of the Ninth and Tenth regiments, whom Indians called, with grim respect, "buffalo soldiers." Technology also favored the army. Telegraph communications and railroads enabled the troopers to be quickly concentrated; repeating rifles and Gatling guns increased their firepower. As fighting intensified in the mid-1870s, a reluctant Congress appropriated funds for more western troopers. Tribal rivalries meant that the army always had Indian allies. Worst of all for the Indians, however, beyond the formidable U.S. Army or their own disunity, was the overwhelming impact of white settlement.

Resisting the reservation solution, the Indians fought on for years—in Kansas in 1868–1869; in the Red River Valley of Texas in 1874; and sporadically in New Mexico among the Apache, until the capture of Geronimo in 1886. On the northern plains the crisis came in 1875, when the Indian Office, despite a treaty guarantee, ordered the Sioux to vacate their Powder River hunting grounds and withdraw to the reservation.

Led by Sitting Bull, Sioux and Cheyenne warriors gathered on the Little Big Horn River to the west of the Powder River country. In a typical concentrating maneuver, army columns from widely separated forts converged on the Little Big Horn from three sides. The Seventh Cavalry, commanded by George A. Custer, came upon the main Sioux encampment on June 25, 1876. Disregarding orders, the reckless Custer sought out battle on his own. He attacked from three sides, hoping to capitalize on the element of surprise. But his forces were stretched too thin. The other two groups fell back with heavy losses to defensive positions, but Custer's force of 256 men was surrounded and annihilated by Crazy Horse's warriors. It was a great victory, but not a decisive one. The day of reckoning was merely postponed.

Weakened by unrelenting military pressure and increasing physical privation, the Sioux bands one by one gave up and moved onto the reservation. Last to come in were Sitting Bull's followers. They had retreated to Canada, but in 1881, after five hard years, they recrossed the border and surrendered at Fort Buford, Montana.

It was not Indian resistance but relentless white pressure that wrecked the reservation solution. In the mid-1870s prospectors began to dig gold in the Black Hills—sacred land to the Sioux and entirely inside their reservation. Unable to hold back the prospectors or buy out the Sioux, the government opened the Black Hills to gold seekers at their own risk. In 1877, after Sioux resistance had crumbled, federal agents forced the tribes to cede the western third of their Dakota reservation.

The Indian Territory of Oklahoma met the same fate. Two million acres in the heart of the territory had not been assigned to any tribe, and white homesteaders coveted that fertile land. The "Boomer" movement, stirred up initially by railroads running across the Indian Territory during the 1880s, agitated tirelessly to open this so-called Oklahoma District to settlers. In 1889 the government gave in and placed the Oklahoma District under the Homestead Act. On April 22, 1889, a horde of claimants rushed in and staked out the entire district within a few hours. Two tent cities—Guthrie with 15,000 people and Oklahoma City with 10,000—were in full swing by nightfall.

The completion of the land-grabbing process was hastened, ironically, by the avowed friends of the native Americans. The Indians had never lacked sympathizers, especially in the East. After the Civil War, reformers created the Indian Rights Association. The movement got a boost from Helen Hunt Jackson's powerful book *A Century of Dishonor* (1881), which told the story of the unjust treatment of the Indians. The reformers, however, had little sympathy for the tribal way of life. They could imagine no other future for the Indian than assimilation into white society. And they felt that defense of Indian lands against white encroachment was hopeless without granting them the property protections that Americans enjoyed as private owners.

The resulting policy was called *severalty*—the division of reservation lands into individually owned parcels. With the blessing of reformers, the Dawes Severalty Act of 1887 authorized the division of tribal lands, with 160 acres for each family head and smaller parcels for individuals. The land would be held in trust by the government for twenty-five years, and the Indians would become U.S. citizens. Remaining reservation lands would be sold off, with the proceeds placed in an Indian education fund.

The Sioux were among the first to bear the brunt of the Dawes Act. The federal government, announcing that it had gained the Sioux' approval, opened their "surplus" land to white settlement on February 10, 1887. But no surveys had been made, nor any provision for the Sioux living in the ceded

Becoming White

Zitkala-Sa, afterward the author Gertrude Simmons Bonnin, recalled in 1900 her painful transformation from Sioux child to pupil at a mission school.

The first day . . . a paleface woman, with white hair, came up after us. We were placed in a line of girls who were marching into the dining room. These were Indian girls, in stiff shoes and closely clinging dresses. The small girls wore sleeved aprons and shingled hair. As I walked noiselessly in my soft mocassins, I felt like sinking into the floor, for my blanket had been stripped from my shoulders. . . . Late in the morning, my friend Judewin gave me a terrible warning. Judewin knew a few words of English; and she had overheard the paleface woman talk about cutting our long, heavy hair. Our mothers had taught us that only unskilled warriors who were captured had their hair shingled by the enemy. Among our people, short hair was worn by mourners, and shingled hair by cowards! . . . In spite of myself, I was carried downstairs and tied fast in a chair. I cried aloud, shaking my head all the while until I felt the cold blades of the scissors against my neck, and heard them gnaw off one of my thick black braids. Then I lost my spirit. . . .

Now, as I look back upon the recent past, I see it from a distance, as a whole. I remember how, from morning till evening, many specimens of civilized peoples visited the Indian school. The city folks with canes and eyeglass, the countrymen with sunburned cheeks and clumsy feet . . . alike astounded at seeing the children of savage warriors so docile and industrious. . . .

In this fashion many have passed through the Indian schools during the last decade, afterward to boast of their charity to the North American Indian. But few there are who have paused to question whether real life or long lasting death lies beneath this semblance of civilization.

SOURCE: Linda K. Kerber and Jane De-Hart Mathews, eds., *Women's America: Refocusing the Past*, 2d ed. (New York: Oxford University Press, 1987), 254-257.

areas. On top of these signs of bad faith, drought wiped out the Indians' crops. It seemed beyond endurance. The Sioux had lost their ancestral lands. They faced a future as farmers that was alien to all their traditions. And immediately confronting them was a hard winter of starvation.

But news of salvation had also come. An Indian messiah, a holy man who called himself Wovoka, was preaching a new religion on a Paiute reservation in Nevada. In a vision, Wovoka had gone to heaven and received God's word that the world would be regenerated. The whites would disappear, all the Indians of past generations would return to earth, and life on the Great Plains would go back to the time of the roaming buffalo. All this would come to pass in the spring of 1891. Awaiting that great day, the Indians should follow Wo-

The Dead at Wounded Knee
In December 1890 U.S. soldiers massacred about 146 Sioux men, women, and children in the
Battle of Wounded Knee in South Dakota, in the last big fight on the northern plains between
Indians and whites. Black Elk, a Sioux holy man, related that "after the soldiers marched away
from their dirty work, a heavy snow began to fall . . . and it grew very cold." The body of
Yellow Bird lay frozen where it had fallen.

voka's commandments and practice the Ghost Dance. This daylong ritual of
dancing and praying sent participants into trancelike states during which their
spirits rose to heaven. As the frenzy of the Ghost Dance swept through some
Sioux encampments in the fall of 1890, resident whites became alarmed and
called for army intervention.

Among the Minneconjou, the medicine man Yellow Bird had stirred up a
fervent Ghost Dance following. But the Minneconjou chief Big Foot had
fallen desperately ill with pneumonia, and the Minneconjou had agreed to
come in under military escort to Wounded Knee Creek on December 28.
The next morning, when the soldiers attempted to disarm the Indians, a battle
exploded in the encampment. Among the U.S. troopers, 25 died; among the
Indians, 146 men, women, and children perished, many of them shot down as
they fled.

Wounded Knee was the final episode in the long war of suppression of
the Plains Indians. The process of severalty now proceeded without hindrance. On the Dakota lands the Teton Sioux fared relatively well, and many
of the younger generation settled down as small farmers and stock grazers.
Ironically, the more fortunate tribes were probably those occupying reservation lands that did not attract white settlement, and thus were bypassed by
the severalty process. The flood of whites into South Dakota and Oklahoma,
on the other hand, left the Indians as small minorities in lands once wholly
theirs—20,000 Sioux in a South Dakotan population of 400,000 in 1900,
70,000 of various tribes in a population of a million when Oklahoma became a state in 1907.

THE FAR WEST

On the western edge of the Great Plains, the Rocky Mountains rise up to form a great barrier between the flat eastern two-thirds of the country and the rugged Far West. Beyond the Rockies lie two vast plateaus: on the north side the Columbia plateau, extending into eastern Oregon and Washington; and flanking the southern Rockies, the Colorado plateau. Where they break off, the plateaus carve out the desertlike Great Basin that covers eastern Utah and all of Nevada. Separating this arid interior from the Pacific are two great mountain ranges—the Sierra Nevada and, to the north, the Cascades—beyond which lies a coastal region that is cool and rainy to the north but increasingly dry as one proceeds southward until in southern California rainfall becomes almost as sparse as in the interior.

What most impressed Americans about this far western country was its sheer inhospitability. The Far West could not be occupied in standard American fashion—that is, by a multitude of settlers moving westward along a broad front; blanketing the land; and, homestead by homestead, bringing it under cultivation. The wagon trains moving to Oregon's Willamette Valley adopted an entirely different strategy of occupation—the planting of widely scattered settlements in a vast, mostly barren landscape. This had been New Spain's strategy ever since it had sent the first contingents of settlers 700 miles northward from Mexico into the upper Rio Grande Valley in 1598. When the Southwest was taken by the United States 250 years later, major Hispanic settlements existed in New Mexico and California, and lesser settlements were scattered along the borderlands into south Texas. At that time, aside from Oregon, the only significant Anglo settlement was around the Salt Lake in Utah, where Mormons had moved to escape persecution and plant a New Zion. Fewer than 100,000 Euro-Americans—roughly 25,000 of them Anglo, the rest Hispanic—lived in the entire Far West in 1848.

The Mining Frontier

More emigrants would be coming in, certainly, but the nation's newly acquired western territory seemed unlikely to be much of a magnet. California was "hilly and mountainous," noted a U.S. naval officer in 1849, too dry for farming and surely not "susceptible of supporting a very large population." He had not taken account of the recent discovery of gold in the Sierra foothills, however. California would indeed support a very large population, drawn not by the lure of arable land but by dreams of gold.

Extraction of mineral wealth became the basis for the Far West's development (see Map 17.2, following page). This meant, first of all, explosive growth. By 1860, when the Great Plains was still Indian country, California was a booming state with 300,000 residents. There was also a burst of city building. San Francisco quickly became a bustling metropolis—it had 57,000 residents by 1860—the hub of a mining empire that stretched to the Rockies. Finally, the distinctive pattern of geographically dispersed settlement persisted, driven

MAP 17.2

The Mining Frontier
The Far West was America's gold country because of its geological history. Veins of gold and silver form when molten material from the earth's core is forced up into fissures caused by the tectonic movements that create mountain ranges, such as the ones that dominate the far western landscape. It was these veins, the product of mountain-forming activity many thousands of years earlier, that prospectors began to discover after 1848 and furiously exploit.

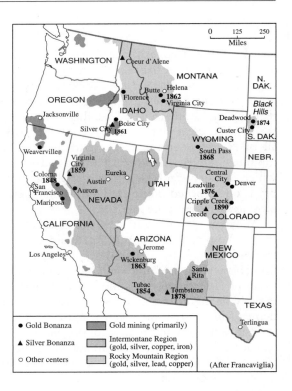

(After Francaviglia)

now, however, by a proliferation of mining sites and by people moving not from east to west, but from west to east, coming mainly from California.

By the mid-1850s, as easy pickings in the California gold country diminished, disappointed prospectors began to pull out and spread across the West in hopes of striking it rich elsewhere. Gold was discovered on the Nevada side of the Sierras, in the Colorado Rockies, and along the Fraser River in British Columbia. New strikes occurred in Montana and Wyoming during the 1860s, a decade later in the Black Hills of South Dakota, and in the Coeur d'Alene region of Idaho during the 1880s.

As the news of each gold strike spread, a wild, remote area turned almost overnight into a mob scene of prospectors, traders, gamblers, prostitutes, and saloon keepers. At least 100,000 fortune seekers flocked to the Pike's Peak area of Colorado in the spring of 1859. Trespassers on government or Indian land, the prospectors made their own law. The mining codes devised at community meetings limited the size of a mining claim to what a person could reasonably work. This kind of informal lawmaking also became an instrument for excluding or discriminating against Mexicans, Chinese, and African-Americans in the gold fields. And it turned into hangman's justice for the many outlaws who infested the mining camps.

The heyday of the prospectors was always brief. They were equipped only to skim gold from the surface of the earth and from streambeds. Extracting the metal locked in underground lodes required mine shafts and crushing mills, which took capital, technology, and business organization. The original claim holders quickly sold out after exhausting the surface gold or when a generous bidder came along. At every gold-rush site the prospector soon gave way to entrepreneurial development and large-scale mining. Rough mining camps turned into big towns.

Nevada's Virginia City started out as a bawdy, ramshackle mining camp, but after the opening of the Comstock lode in 1859, it boasted a stock exchange, ostentatious mansions for the mining kings, fancy hotels, and even Shakespearean theater. Virginia City remained a boom town nevertheless. It was a magnet for job seekers of both sexes: men labored as miners for $4 a day, and many working-class women became dance-hall entertainers and prostitutes because that was the best chance offered them by the city's bonanza economy. In 1870 men outnumbered women two to one. There were a hundred saloons, and brothels lined D Street.

In its final stage the mining frontier passed into the industrial world. At some sites gold and silver proved less important than the commoner metals—copper, lead, zinc—for which there was a huge demand in eastern manufacturing. Copper mining thrived in the Butte district of Montana. In the 1890s, Idaho's Coeur d'Alene silver district became the nation's main source of lead and zinc. Entrepreneurs raised capital, built rail connections, devised technology for treating the lower-grade copper deposits, constructed smelting facilities, and recruited a labor force.

Miners were industrial workers and, like other workers, they organized trade unions. But relations with management, once they soured during the depressed 1890s, became unusually violent. In 1892 at Coeur d'Alene, striking miners fought gun battles with company guards, sent a car of explosive powder careening into the Frisco mine, and threatened to blow up processing plants. Martial law was declared, strikers were crowded into "bullpens" (enclosed stockades), and the strike was broken. Similarly violent strikes took place at Cripple Creek, Colorado, in 1894; at Leadville, Colorado, in 1896; and again at Coeur d'Alene in 1899.

If the Far West had lacked mineral wealth, its history would certainly have been very different. Before the discovery of gold at Sutter's Mill, Oregon's Willamette Valley, not dry California, attracted most westward-bound settlers. And, were it not for the gold rush, California would likely have remained like the Willamette Valley—an economic backwater lacking markets for its products and slow to build population. In 1860, already a state, Oregon had scarcely 25,000 inhabitants, and its principal city, Portland, was little more than a village. Booming California pulled Oregon out of the doldrums by creating a market for the state's produce and timber. During the 1880s Oregon and Washington (which became a state in 1889) grew prodigiously. Where scarcely a hundred thousand settlers had lived twenty years earlier, there were nearly three-quarters of a million by 1890. Portland and, even more dramatically, Seattle had blossomed into important commercial centers, both prospering from a robust mixed economy of farming, ranching, logging, and fishing.

At a certain point, especially as railroads opened up eastern markets, this diversified growth became self-sustaining. But what had triggered it, what had provided the first markets and underwritten the service infrastructure, was the bonanza mining economy, at the hub of which, metropolis for the entire Far West, stood San Francisco.

Hispanics, Chinese, Anglos

California was the anchor of two distinct far western regions. First, it joined with Oregon and Washington to form the Pacific slope. Second, by climate and Spanish heritage, California was linked to the Southwest, which today includes Arizona, New Mexico, and Texas. There, along a 1,500-mile borderland, settlements had been planted over many years by the rulers of New Spain. Most populous and best established were the settlements along the upper Rio Grande Valley in New Mexico; the main town, Santa Fe, over 200 years old, contained 4,635 residents in 1860. At the other end, in California, a Hispanic population was spread thinly in the old presidio towns along the coast and on a patchwork of great ranchos.

The economy of this Hispanic crescent consisted primarily of cattle and sheep ranching. In south Texas there were modest-sized, family-run rancheros. Everywhere else the social order was highly stratified. At the top stood an elite—beneficiaries of royal land grants, proudly Spanish, and devoted to the traditional life of a landed aristocracy. Below them, with little in between, was a laboring population of servants, artisans, *vaqueros* (cowboys), and farm workers. New Mexico also contained a large *mestizo* population, a peasantry of mixed Hispanic and Indian blood, who were Spanish-speaking and Catholic, but who, in their village life and farming methods, were faithful to their Pueblo Indian heritage.

Pueblo Indians, although long past the golden age of their civilization, still occupied much of the Rio Grande Valley, making the New Mexico countryside a patchwork of Hispanic and Pueblo settlements. To the north a vibrant new people, the Navajo, had appeared, warriors like the Apache from whom they had sprung but also skilled craft workers and sheep raisers.

New Mexico was one place where European and native American cultures managed a successful, if uneasy, coexistence, and where the Indian inhabitants were equipped to hold their own against the Anglo challenge. In California, by contrast, the Hispanic occupation had been harder on the native hunter-gatherer peoples, undermining their tribal structure, reducing them to forced labor, and making them easy prey for the aggressive Anglo miners and settlers, who, in short order, nearly wiped out California's once numerous Indian population.

The fate of the Hispanic Southwest after its incorporation into the United States depended on the rate of Anglo immigration. In New Mexico, which remained off the beaten track even after the arrival of railroads in the 1880s, the Santa Fe elite more than held its own, incorporating the Anglo newcomers into Hispanic society through intermarriage and business partnerships. In California, on the other hand, the seizure of the great ranchos by the Anglos was relentless, even though the 1848 peace treaty with Mexico had recognized the property rights of the resident *californios* and had made them U.S. citizens. Around San Francisco the rancho system disappeared almost in a puff of smoke. Farther south, where Anglos were slow to arrive, the dons held on longer, but by the 1880s just a handful of the original families still retained their Mexican land grants.

The New Mexico peasants found themselves similarly embattled. Crucial to their livelihood was the right to graze on common lands. But this was a customary right that could not withstand legal challenge when Anglo ranchers established title and began putting up fences. The peasants responded as best they could. Traditionally, women had always raised much of the family food in small gardens, participated in the village bartering system, made the clothes, and plastered the adobe houses. With the loss of the common lands, the men began to leave the villages seasonally to work on the railroads or in the Colorado mines and sugar-beet fields, earning crucial dollars while leaving the village economy in their wives' hands.

Elsewhere, hard-pressed Hispanic peasants struck back for what they considered rightfully theirs. When Anglo ranchers began to fence in common lands in San Miguel County, the New Mexicans long settled there, *los pobres* (the poor ones), organized themselves as masked raiders and in 1889 and 1890 mounted an effective campaign of harassment against the interlopers. When Anglo farmers swarmed into south Texas after 1900, bent on exploiting new irrigation methods, the displaced *Tejanos* responded with sporadic but persistent night-riding attacks. Much of the raiding by Mexican "bandits" from across the border in the years before World War I was really a civil war waged by embittered *Tejanos* who had lived north of the Rio Grande for generations.

These *Tejanos*, however, like the New Mexico villagers who became seasonal wage laborers, could not avoid being driven into the ranks of a Mexican-American working class as the Anglo economy developed. This same development also began to attract increasing numbers of immigrants from Old Mexico.

All along the Southwest borderlands, economic activity was picking up in the late nineteenth century. Railroads were being built, copper mines were opening in Arizona, cotton and vegetable agriculture was developing in south Texas, and fruit growing was being introduced in southern California. In Texas the Hispanic population increased from about 20,000 in 1850 to 165,000 in 1900. Some Mexicans came as contract workers for railway track gangs and harvest crews; virtually all were relegated to the lowest-paying and most backbreaking work; and everywhere they were discriminated against and reviled by higher-status Anglo workers.

What stimulated the Mexican migration was the enormous demand for workers by a region undergoing explosive economic development. Hence the exceptionally high numbers of immigrants in the California population of this era: between 1860 and 1890 roughly one-third were foreign-born—more than twice the level for the country as a whole. Many came from Europe; most numerous were the Irish, followed by the Germans and British. But there was also another group that was unique to the West—the Chinese.

Attracted first by the California gold rush of 1849, 200,000 Chinese came to the United States over the next three decades. In those years they constituted a considerable minority of California's population, around 9 percent. Because virtually all Chinese were actively employed, they represented a much larger proportion of the state's labor force, probably a quarter. Elsewhere in the West, at the crest of mining activity, their presence could surge remarkably—for example, to over 25 percent of Idaho's population in 1870.

The coming of the Chinese to North America was part of a worldwide Asian migration that began in the mid-nineteenth century. Driven by poverty, Chinese went to Australia, Hawaii, and Latin America; Indians to Fiji and South Africa; and Javanese to Dutch colonies in the Caribbean. Most of these Asians migrated as indentured servants, which in effect made them the property of others. In America indentured servitude was no longer lawful, so the Chinese came as free workers. Their passage was financed by a *credit-ticket system*, by which they were able to borrow passage money from a broker while retaining their personal freedom and their right to choose their employers.

Once in America, Chinese immigrants normally entered the orbit of the Six Companies, a powerful confederation of Chinese merchants in San Francisco's Chinatown. Most of the arrivals were unattached men eager to earn a stake and return to their native Cantonese villages. The Six Companies not only acted as an employment agency but also provided new arrivals with the social and commercial services they needed to survive in an alien world. The few Chinese women—the male-female ratio was thirteen to one—worked mostly as servants or prostitutes, sad victims of the desperate poverty that drove the Chinese to America.

Until the early 1860s, when surface mining played out, Chinese men labored mainly in the California gold fields—as prospectors where the white miners permitted it, as laborers and cooks where they did not. When construction began on the transcontinental railroad, the Central Pacific hired Chinese workers. Eventually Chinese constituted four-fifths of the railroad's labor force, doing most of the pick-and-shovel labor of laying the railroad track across the Sierras. Many were recruited directly from around Canton by labor agents to work in gangs under the control of "China bosses," who not only supervised but fed, housed, paid, and often cheated them.

When the transcontinental railroad was completed in 1869, the Chinese scattered. Some continued to work in construction gangs for the railroads, while others labored on swamp-drainage projects in the Central Valley and then became agricultural workers, and if they were lucky, small farmers and

Building the Central Pacific
Chinese laborers work on the great trestle spanning the canyon at Secret-
town in the Sierra Nevada.

orchardists. The mining districts of Idaho, Montana, and Colorado also attracted large numbers of Chinese, but according to the 1880 census, nearly
three-quarters remained in California. "Wherever we put them, we found
them good," remarked Charles Crocker, one of the promoters of the Central
Pacific. "Their orderly and industrious habits make them a very desirable class
of immigrants."

White workers, however, did not share the employers' enthusiasm for Chinese labor. In other parts of the country, racism was directed against African-
Americans; in California, where there were few blacks, it found a target in the
Chinese. "They practice all the unnameable vices of the East," wrote the young
journalist Henry George. "They are utter heathens, treacherous, sensual, cowardly and cruel." Sadly, this vicious racism was intertwined with labor's republican ideals. The Chinese, argued George, would drive out free labor, "make
nabobs and princes of our capitalists, and crush our working classes into the
dust . . . substitut[ing] . . . a population of serfs and their masters for that population of intelligent freemen who are our glory and our strength." The anti-
Chinese agitation climaxed in San Francisco in the late 1870s, when mobs
ruled the streets. The fiercest agitator, an Irish teamster named Denis Kearney,
quickly became a dominant figure in the California labor movement. Under
the slogan "The Chinese Must Go!" Kearney led the Workingmen's party
against the state's major parties. Democrats and Republicans, however, jumped
on the bandwagon, joining together in 1879 to write a new state constitution
replete with anti-Chinese provisions and pressuring Washington to take up the

issue. In 1882 Congress finally passed the Chinese Exclusion Act, which barred the further entry of Chinese laborers into the country.

Chinese immigration effectively came to an end, but not the job opportunities that had attracted the Chinese in the first place. The West's agricultural development intensified the demand for cheap labor, especially in California, which was shifting from wheat, the state's first great cash crop, to fruits and vegetables. This intensive agriculture required a lot of workers—so-called "stoop labor," meagerly paid, and mostly seasonal. This was not, as one San Francisco journalist put it, "white men's work." That ugly phrase serves as a touchstone for California agricultural labor as it would thereafter develop—a kind of caste labor system, which always drew some downtrodden, footloose whites, yet was basically defined along color lines. But if not the Chinese, then who? First, Japanese immigrants, who came in increasing numbers and by the early twentieth century constituted half the state's agricultural labor force. Then, when anti-Japanese agitation closed off that population flow in 1908, Mexico became the next, essentially permanent, provider of migratory workers for California's booming commercial agriculture.

The irony of the state's social evolution is painful to behold. Here was California, a land of limitless opportunity, boastful of its democratic egalitarianism. Yet, simultaneously and from its very birth, it was a racially torn society, at once exploiting and despising the Mexican and Asian minorities whose hard labor helped make California the enviable land it was.

Golden California

Life in California contained all that the modern world of 1890 had to offer— cosmopolitan San Francisco, comfortable travel, a high living standard, colleges and universities, even resident painters and writers. Yet California was remote from the rest of America, a long journey away and, of course, differently and spectacularly endowed by nature. Location, environment, and history conspired to set California somewhat apart from the American nation. And so, in certain ways, did the Californians.

What Californians yearned for was a cultural tradition of their own. Closest to hand was the bonanza era of the Forty-Niners. California had the good fortune of attracting to its parts one Samuel Clemens. Clemens did a bit of prospecting, became a reporter in San Francisco, and adopted the pen name Mark Twain.

Listening to the old miners of Angel's Camp in 1865, Twain jotted one tale down in his notebook, as follows:

> Coleman with his jumping frog—bet stranger $50—stranger had no frog, and C. got him one:—in the meantime stranger filled C's frog full of shot and he couldn't jump. The stranger's frog won.

In Twain's hands, this fragment was transformed into a tall tale that caught the imagination of the country and made his reputation as a humorist. "The

Celebrated Jumping Frog of Calaveras County" had somehow encapsulated the entire world of make-or-break optimism in the mining camps.

In short stories such as "The Luck of Roaring Camp" and "The Outcasts of Poker Flat," Twain's fellow San Franciscan Bret Harte developed this theme in a more literary fashion and firmly implanted it in California's memory. But this bonanza past was too raw, too suggestive of the tattered beginnings of so many of the state's leading citizens—in short, too disreputable—for an up-and-coming society.

Then, in 1884, Helen Hunt Jackson published her novel *Ramona*. In this story of a half-caste girl caught between two cultures, Jackson intended to advance the cause of the Indians, but she placed her tale in the evocative context of Old California, and that rang a bell. By then, the Spanish missions—disestablished by the Mexican government back in 1833, long before the influx of Yankees—had fallen into total disrepair and the missionaries were wholly forgotten, their Indian converts scattered and in dire poverty. Now that lost world of "sun, silence and adobe" became all the rage. Sentimental novels and histories appeared in abundance. There was a movement to restore the missions. Many communities began to stage Spanish fiestas, and the mission style of architecture enjoyed a great vogue among developers.

In its Spanish past California found the cultural traditions it needed. The same kind of discovery was taking place elsewhere in the Southwest, although in the case of Santa Fe and Taos there really were live Hispanic roots to celebrate.

All this enthusiasm was, of course, strongly tinged with commercialism. And so was a second distinctive feature of California's development—the exploitation of its climate. The southern part of the state was neglected, thinly populated, and too dry for anything but grazing and some chancy wheat growing. What it did have was an abundance of sunshine. At the beginning of the 1880s there burst upon the country amazing news of the charms of southern California. "There is not any malaria, hay fever, loss of appetite, or languor in the air; nor any thunder, lightning, mad dogs . . . or cold snaps." This publicity was mostly the work of the Southern Pacific Railroad, which had reached Los Angeles in 1876 and was eager for business. When the Santa Fe Railroad arrived in 1885, a furious rate war broke out and fares from Chicago or St. Louis to Los Angeles fell to $25 or less. Thousands of people, mostly midwesterners, poured in. Los Angeles County, which had less than 3 percent of the state's population in 1870, had 12 percent by 1900. By then southern California had firmly established itself as the land of sunshine and orange groves. It had found a way to translate climate into riches.

That California was specially favored by nature some Californians knew even as the great stands of redwoods and sugar pine were being hacked down, the soil depleted by the relentless cycle of wheat crops, the streams polluted, and the hills torn apart by reckless mining techniques. Back in 1864 influential Americans who had seen the Sierras prevailed on Congress to grant to the state of California "the Cleft, or Gorge in the granite peak of the Sierra Nevada Mountain, known as Yosemite Valley," which would be reserved "for public

Kitty Tatch and Friend on Glacier Point, Yosemite
From the time the Yosemite Valley was set aside in 1864 as a place for "public pleasuring, resort, and recreation," it attracted a stream of tourists eager to experience the grandeur of the American West. As is suggested by this photograph taken sometime in the 1890s, the magic of Yosemite was enough to set even staid young ladies dancing.

pleasuring, resort, and recreation." When the young naturalist John Muir arrived in California four years later, he headed straight for Yosemite Valley. Its "grandeur . . . comes as an endless revelation," he wrote. Muir, and others like him, became devoted to studying the High Sierras and protecting them from "despoiling gain-seekers . . . eagerly trying to make everything immediately and selfishly commercial." One result was the creation of California's national parks in 1890—Yosemite, Sequoia, King's Canyon. Another was the formation in 1892 of the Sierra Club, which became a powerful voice for the defenders of California's wilderness.

Champions of California's wild lands won some battles and lost some. Advocates of water-resource development insisted that California's irrigated agriculture and thirsty cities could not grow without tapping the abundant snowpack of the Sierras. By the turn of the century, Los Angeles faced a water crisis that threatened its growth. The answer was a 238-mile aqueduct to the Owens River in the southern Sierras. A bitter controversy blew up over this immense project, driven by the objections of local residents and preservationists to the flooding of the beautiful Owens Valley. More painful was the defeat suffered by John Muir and his allies in their battle to save the Hetch Hetchy gorge, north of Yosemite National Park. In 1913, after years of controversy, the federal government approved the damming of Hetch Hetchy to serve the water needs of San Francisco.

When the stakes became high enough, nature lovers like John Muir generally came out on the short end. Even so, something original and distinctive had been added to California's heritage—the linking of a society's well-being with the preservation of its natural environment.

CHAPTER 17 TIMELINE	
1849	California Gold Rush Chinese migration begins
1862	Homestead Act
1864	Yosemite Valley reserved as public park
1865	Long Drive of Texas longhorns begins
1867	U.S. government adopts reservation policy for Plains Indians
1868	Indian treaty confirms Sioux rights to Powder River hunting grounds
1869	Union Pacific–Central Pacific transcontinental railroad completed
1874	Barbed wire invented
1875	Sioux ordered to vacate Powder River hunting grounds; war breaks out
1876	Battle of Little Big Horn
1877	San Francisco anti-Chinese riots
1879	Exoduster migration to Kansas
1882	Chinese Exclusion Act
1884	Helen Hunt Jackson's novel *Ramona*
1886	Dry cycle begins on the Great Plains
1887	Dawes Severalty Act
1889	Oklahoma opened to white settlement
1890	Indian massacre at Wounded Knee, South Dakota

CHAPTER 18

CAPITAL AND LABOR IN THE AGE OF ENTERPRISE, 1877–1900

- Industrial Capitalism Triumphant
- The World of Work
- The Labor Movement

The year that Reconstruction ended, 1877, also marked the end of the first great crisis of America's industrializing economy. In 1873, four years earlier, a severe depression had set in, bankrupting 47,000 firms and driving down wholesale prices by about 30 percent. Hundreds of thousands of workers lost their jobs, and suffering was widespread. Before long the foundations of the social order began to shake.

On July 16, 1877, railroad workers went on strike against the Baltimore and Ohio (B&O) system to protest wage cuts. In railway towns along the B&O tracks crowds cheered as the strikers attacked company property and prevented trains from running. The strike spread across the country. In Pittsburgh the Pennsylvania roundhouse went up in flames on July 21. At many rail centers rioters and looters roamed freely. Only the arrival of federal troops restored order. On August 15 President Rutherford B. Hayes wrote in his diary: "The strikers have been put down *by force.*" Never had the nation edged so close to social revolution.

And then recovery came. Within months the economy was booming again. In the next fifteen years, the output of manufactured goods increased over 150 percent. America's confidence in its industrial future rebounded. "Upon [material progress] is founded all other progress," asserted a railroad president in 1888. "Can there be any doubt that cheapening the cost of necessaries and conveniences of life is the most powerful agent of civilization and progress?"

474

INDUSTRIAL CAPITALISM TRIUMPHANT

Economic historians speak of the late nineteenth century as the age of the Great Deflation. Prices fell worldwide, not only in the United States (see Figure 18.1). Normally, falling prices signal economic stagnation: there is not enough demand for the available goods and services. For England, a mature industrial power, the Great Deflation did indeed indicate economic decline. But not for the United States; its industrial expansion went into high gear during the Great Deflation. Because of increasing manufacturing efficiencies, American firms could cut prices *and* yet earn profits that could finance still better equipment.

Basic Industry

By the 1870s, industry was long established in America. But the early factories had really been appendages of the agricultural economy. The goods they produced—textiles, shoes, paper, and furniture—were consumer goods that used familar raw materials and mostly replaced homemade or artisan-made goods (articles made by skilled workers). Gradually, however, a different kind of demand developed. This was the result of the surging economic growth of the country. Railroads needed locomotives; new factories needed machinery; and the expanding cities needed trolley lines, sanitation systems, and commercial buildings. Railroad equipment, machinery, and construction materials were *capital* goods—that is, goods that themselves added to the productive capacity of the economy.

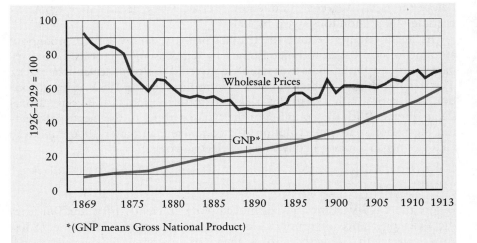

*(GNP means Gross National Product)

FIGURE 18.1
Business Activity and Wholesale Prices, 1869–1913
This graph shows the key feature concerning the performance of the late nineteenth-century economy: namely, that while output was booming, the price for goods was falling.

Central to the development of the capital-goods sector was a new technology for manufacturing steel. The country already produced large quantities of wrought iron, whose malleability made it easily worked by country blacksmiths and farmers. But wrought iron was expensive—it was produced in small batches by skilled puddlers and rollers—and did not stand up under heavy use as railway track. In 1856 the British inventor Henry Bessemer perfected a method for refining raw pig iron into an essentially new product—steel—that was harder and more durable than wrought iron. Others adopted Bessemer's process, but it was Andrew Carnegie who demonstrated its revolutionary importance.

An iron maker and former railroad man, Carnegie in 1872 erected a massive steel mill outside Pittsburgh, designed to take maximum advantage of Bessemer's method. Named the Edgar Thompson Works after Carnegie's admired boss at the Pennsylvania Railroad, his mill combined all the stages of production—smelting, refining, and rolling—into a single integrated operation. Iron ore entered the blast furnaces at one end and, with no break in operations, came out the other end as finished steel rails. The Edgar Thompson Works was hugely profitable, and became a model for the modern steel industry. Large, integrated steel plants swiftly replaced the small iron mills that had once dotted western Pennsylvania.

The technological breakthrough in steel spurred the intensive exploitation of the country's rich mineral resources. Once iron ore began to be shipped down the Great Lakes from the Mesabi range in northern Minnesota, the industry was assured of an ample supply of its primary raw material. The other key ingredient, coal, came in equal abundance from the great Appalachian field that stretched from Pennsylvaina down to Alabama. A minor enterprise before the Civil War, coal production doubled every decade after 1870, exceeding 400 million tons a year by 1910.

As steam engines became the nation's primary energy source, prodigious amounts of coal began to be consumed by railroads and factories. Earlier reliant on water power, industries rapidly converted to steam-driven machinery. The steam turbine, a further innovation introduced in the 1880s, utilized continuous rotation rather than the back-and-forth motion of the conventional steam engine. With the coupling of the steam turbine to the electric generator, the nation's energy revolution was completed, and after 1900 America's factories began a massive conversion to electric power.

The Railroads

Before the Civil War, most goods moved quite efficiently by water. But from the first appearance of primitive locomotives on iron tracks in the 1830s, Americans fell in love with railroads. They were impatient for the year-round, on-time service that canal barges and riverboats could never provide. By 1860, with a network of tracks already covering the states east of the Mississippi, the railroad clearly was on the way to being industrial America's mode of transportation (see Map 18.1).

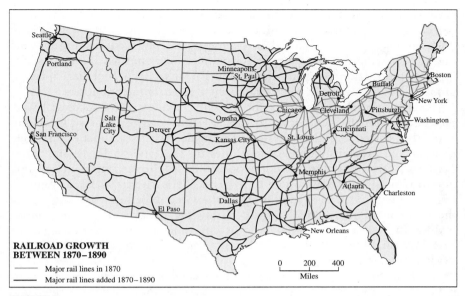

MAP 18.1

The Expansion of the Railroad System, 1870–1890

In 1870, the nation had 53,000 miles of rail track; in 1890, 167,000 miles. That burst of construction essentially completed the nation's rail network, although there would be additional expansion for the next two decades. The main areas of growth were in the South and west of the Mississippi. The Great Plains and the Far West accounted for over 40 percent of all railroad construction in this period.

The question was, who would pay for it? Railroads could be state enterprises, like the canals. Or, alternatively, they could be financed by investors trying to make money. Unlike most European countries, the United States chose to leave railroads to private enterprise. Even so, government played a big role. Many states offered financial aid, mostly by buying railroad bonds, but also, as in Maine and Texas, by offering land grants from the public domain. Land grants were the principal means by which the federal government encouraged interregional railroads; huge tracts went to the transcontinental railroads, because of the national interest in tying the Far West to the rest of the country.

The most important boost that government gave the railroads, however, was not money or land but a legal form of organization—the *corporation*—that enabled them to raise private capital in prodigious amounts. Investors who bought stock in the railroads—and thus became their legal owners—enjoyed *limited liability*: they risked only the money they had invested. A corporation also could borrow money by issuing interest-bearing bonds, which was how the railroads mostly raised the funds they needed.

The actual responsibility for railroad building generally was handed over to a construction company, which, despite the name, was really another part of the elaborate financing system. Hiring contractors and suppliers often involved persuading them to accept the railroad's bonds as payment and, when that failed, wheeling and dealing to raise cash by selling or borrowing on the bonds. Since the promoters of the railroad and the owners of the construction company were one and the same, the opportunities for plunder were enormous. The most notorious construction company, the Union Pacific's Credit Mobilier, siphoned probably half the money it paid out into the pockets of the promoters.

Railroad promotion was not for the faint of heart. Most successful were promoters with the best access to capital—their own or others'. Cornelius Vanderbilt started with the fortune he had made in the steamboat business. He consolidated previously independent lines up the Hudson River and across New York State, and ultimately developed the New York Central into a trunk line to Chicago that was rivaled only by the Pennsylvania Railroad. James J. Hill, who without federal subsidy made the Great Northern into the best of the transcontinental railroads, was certainly the nation's champion railroad builder. In contrast, Jay Gould, who at one time or another controlled the Erie, Wabash, Union Pacific, and Missouri Pacific systems, always remained a stock-market speculator at heart.

Railroad development in the United States was often sordid, fiercely competitive, and subject to boom and bust. Yet vast sums of capital were raised and a network was built exceeding that of the rest of the world combined. By 1900 virtually no corner of the country lacked rail service.

The railroads also became increasingly efficient. The early system, built by competing local companies, had been a jumble of discontinuous segments. Gauges of track—the width between the rails—varied widely, and at many points railroads were not connected. As late as 1880 goods shipped from Massachusetts to South Carolina had to be unloaded eight times and physically moved to new freight cars across a river or at the other side of a city.

Beginning with the Civil War years, however, pressure increased for a better-organized rail system. In 1883 the railroads rebelled against the jumble of local times that made scheduling a nightmare, and acting on their own, divided the country into the four standard time zones that we still use. By the end of the 1880s a standard track gauge (4 feet, 8½ inches) had been adopted across the country. Fast-freight firms and standard accounting procedures enabled shippers to use the railroad network as if it were a single unit, moving their goods without breaks in transit, transfers between cars, or the other delays that had once bedeviled them.

At the same time, railroad technology was advancing. Durable steel rails permitted heavier traffic. Locomotives became more powerful and capable of pulling more freight cars. To control the greater mass being hauled, the inventor George Westinghouse perfected the automatic coupler, the air brake, and the friction gear for starting and stopping a long line of cars. Costs per ton-mile fell by 50 percent between 1870 and 1890, resulting in a steady drop in freight rates for shippers.

The railroads brilliantly met the transportation needs of the maturing industrial economy. However, this achievement did not stem from any orderly plan; it sprang from the competitive energy of a freewheeling market economy. For the railroads, the costs of unrestrained growth were painfully high. On many routes there were too many railroads, and competitors fought for the available traffic by cutting rates to the bone. Many were saddled with huge bonded debt from the extravagant construction years; about a fifth of these bonds failed to pay interest, even in a pretty good year like 1889. When the economy turned bad, as it did in 1893, the weaker roads inevitably went under; a third of the industry (by track mileage) declared bankruptcy.

Out of the rubble came a major railroad reorganization. This was primarily the handiwork of Wall Street. Investment banks such as J. P. Morgan & Co. had sprung up to market the stocks and bonds issued by railroads. And when railroads fell into bankruptcy the investment bankers stepped in to pick up the pieces. They persuaded investors to help out by accepting lower interest rates or by putting up more money. And they eased the competitive pressures on the railroads by consolidating rivals. By the early twentieth century, half a dozen great regional systems had emerged and the nerve center of American railroading had shifted to Wall Street.

Mass Markets and Large-Scale Enterprise

The railroads sparked a revolution in how goods were marketed. Until well into the industrial age, all but a few manufacturers operated on a small scale, producing mainly for nearby markets. And they left distribution to wholesale merchants and commission agents. Then, after the Civil War, the scale of economic activity began to grow dramatically. "Combinations of capital on a scale hitherto wholly unprecedented constitute one of the remarkable features of modern business methods," the economist David A. Wells wrote in 1889. He could see "no other way in which the work of production and distribution can be prosecuted." What was there about the nation's economic activity that led to Wells's sense of inevitability?

The key to large-scale enterprise lay in the American market. Immigration and a very high birthrate swelled the population from 40 million in 1870 to over 60 million in 1890. People flocked to the cities. The railroads brought these dense consuming markets within the reach of distant producers. The telegraph, fully operational by the Civil War, speeded communications. Unlike Europe, America was not carved up into many national markets; no political frontiers impeded the flow of goods across the continent. Nowhere else did manufacturers have so vast and accessible an internal market for their products.

How they took advantage of that opportunity is perhaps best seen in the case of the meat-packing industry. With the opening of the Union Stock Yards in 1865, Chicago became the cattle market for the country. Cattle came in by rail from the Great Plains; were auctioned off at the Chicago stockyards; and then were shipped to eastern cities, where, as before, they were slaughtered in local "butchertowns." Such an arrangement—with distribution nationalized but processing still local—adequately met the demand of an exploding urban population and could have done so indefinitely. In Europe no further development ever did occur.

But Gustavus F. Swift, a shrewd Chicago cattle dealer from Massachusetts, saw the future differently. He objected that livestock deteriorated en route to the East, and that local slaughterhouses were too small to use waste by-products and cut labor costs. If dressed beef could be kept fresh in transit, Swift realized, he could concentrate the processing in Chicago. Once his engineers developed an effective cooling system, Swift invested in a fleet of refrigerator cars and constructed an immense beef-processing plant at the Chicago stockyards.

This was only the beginning of Swift's innovations. Since no refrigerated warehouses existed in the cities to which he shipped his chilled beef, Swift built his own network of branch houses. Next, he established a fleet of wagons to distribute his products to retail butcher shops. Swift constructed additional facilities to process the fertilizer, chemicals, and other usable by-products from his slaughtering operations. He also began to handle other perishable goods, so that he could fully utilize his refrigerator cars and branch houses. As demand grew, Swift built more packing houses in other stockyard centers, including Kansas City, Kansas; Fort Worth, Texas; and Omaha, Nebraska.

Step by step, Swift created a new kind of enterprise, the *vertically integrated* firm—a national company capable of handling within its own structure all the functions of an industry. In effect, Swift & Co. replaced a large number of small, specialized firms with one multifunctional national firm. Swift's lead was followed by several big Chicago packers who had already built big processsing plants that produced preserved pork products. By 1900 five firms, all of them nationally organized and vertically integrated, produced nearly 90 percent of the meat shipped in interstate commerce.

In most other fields, no single innovation was so decisive as Swift's refrigerator car. But others did share Swift's insight that the essential step was to identify a mass market and then develop a national enterprise capable of serving it. In the petroleum industry, John D. Rockefeller built the Standard Oil Company partly by taking over rival firms, but he also developed a national distribution system to reach the enormous market for kerosene as a fuel for lighting and heating homes. The Singer Sewing Machine Company formed its own sales organization, using both retail stores and door-to-door salesmen. Through such distribution systems, manufacturers provided technical information, credit, and repair facilities for their products.

American society prepared its citizens to be consumers of the standardized goods produced by national manufacturers and sold by mass marketers. The high rate of geographic mobility broke down the local loyalties that were so strong in Europe. Social class in America, though by no means absent, was blurred at the edges and did not, for example, call for class-specific ways of dressing. Foreign visitors often noted that ready-made clothing made it difficult to tell salesgirls from debutantes on city streets.

The American consumer's receptivity to standardized goods should not be exaggerated. Gustavus Swift, for example, encountered great resistance to his Chicago beef. How could it be wholesome weeks later in Boston or Philadelphia? Cheap prices helped, but advertising mattered more. Modern advertising was born in the late nineteenth century, bringing brand names and a billboard-cluttered urban landscape. By 1900 companies spent over $90 million a year for space in newspapers and magazines. Advertisements urged readers to bathe with Pears' soap, eat Uneeda biscuits, sew on a Singer machine, and snap pictures with a Kodak camera. The active molding of demand for brand names became a major function of American business.

The New South

For the South, catching up with the industrial North was no easy task. The antebellum (prewar) plantation economy had strongly impeded industrial development. The slave states had few cities, a primitive distribution system, and not much manufacturing. This modest infrastructure was quickly restored after the Civil War. And then, in 1877, with both Reconstruction and economic depression ended, a railroad boom developed. Track mileage doubled in the next decade and, at least by that measure, the South became nearly competitive with the rest of the country.

But the South remained overwhelmingly agricultural. The sharecropping system, which required a cash crop (see Chapter 16), committed the South to cotton despite soil depletion, low productivity, and unprofitable prices. Wages for southern farm labor fell steadily, dropping to scarcely half the national average by the 1890s—roughly 75 cents a day without board, for a farm laborer.

From this low agricultural wage, surprisingly, sprang the South's hopes for industrialization. Consider, for example, how southern textile mills got started in the Piedmont upcountry of North Carolina, South Carolina, and Georgia in the mid-1870s. The mills recruited workers from the surrounding hill farms, where people struggled to make ends meet. To attract them, mill wages had to be higher than farm earnings, but not much higher. Paying rock-bottom wages, the new mills had a big competitive advantage over the long-established New England industry.

The labor system that evolved likewise reflected southern rural society. To begin with, it was a family system. "Papa decided he would come because he didn't have nothing much but girls and they had to get out and work like men," recalled one woman. It was not Papa, in fact, but his girls whom the mills wanted, for work as spinners and loom tenders. Only they could not be recruited individually: no right-thinking parent would have permitted that. There was, on the other hand, no objection to hiring by families; after all, everyone had been expected to work on the farm. And so the family system of mill labor developed, in which half or more of the operatives were women and the work force was very young. In the 1880s, a quarter of all southern textile workers were under fifteen years of age.

The hours were long—twelve hours a day was the norm—but life in the mill villages was, in the words of one historian, "like a family." Employers tended to be highly paternalistic, providing company housing and a variety of services. The mill workers themselves built close-knit, supportive communities, but for whites only. Although blacks sometimes worked as day laborers and janitors, they hardly ever got production jobs in the cotton mills.

Cheap, abundant labor might have been termed the South's most valuable natural resource. But the region was blessed with other natural resources as well (see Map 18.2). From its rich soil came tobacco, the South's second cash crop. When cigarettes became fashionable in the 1880s, the young North Carolina entrepreneur James B. Duke seized the new market by taking advantage of a southern invention—James A. Bonsack's machine for producing cigarettes automatically. Blacks stemmed and stripped the leaf as they always had, but Duke followed the textile example and restricted machine-tending to white women.

Lumbering, by contrast, was largely integrated, with a labor force evenly divided between black and white men. The extensive pine forests of the South were rapidly—heedlessly is perhaps the better word—exploited in these years.

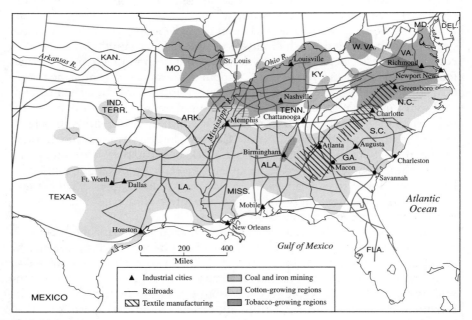

MAP 18.2
The New South, 1900
The economy of the Old South focused on raising staple crops, especially cotton and tobacco. In the New South staple agriculture continued to dominate but there was marked industrial development as well. Industrial regions developed, producing textiles, coal and iron, and wood products. By 1900 the South's industrial pattern was well defined.

Alabama's coal and iron ore deposits also attracted investors; by 1890 the Birmingham district was producing nearly a million tons of iron and steel a year.

Despite the South's high hopes, this burst of industrial development did not lift the region out of poverty. In 1900 two-thirds of all southerners made their living from the soil, just as they had in 1870. Moreover, the industries that did develop were either extractive, as with forestry and mining, or engaged in low-end processing of coarse products. Industry by industry, the key statistic—the value added by manufacturing—showed the South consistently lagging behind the North.

Southerners tended to blame the North: the South was a "colonial" economy controlled by New York and Chicago. There was some truth to this charge. Much of the capital—by no means all—did come from the North. And the integrating processes of the economy did subordinate regional to national interests. When the railway network moved to a uniform gauge in 1886, the southern railroads converted to the northern standard. Nor did northern interests hesitate to use their muscle to maintain the interregional status quo. Railroads, for example, varied freight rates so that it was cheap for southern cotton and timber to flow out and for northern manufactured goods to flow in.

Yet in the end the South's economic backwardness was mostly of its own making. The crowning irony was that the great advantage of the South—its cheap labor—also kept it from becoming a more technologically advanced economy. First, low wages discouraged employers from replacing workers with machinery. Second, low wages attracted labor-intensive industry, such as textiles. Third, a cheap labor market discouraged investment in education because of the likelihood that better-educated workers would flee to higher-wage markets.

What distinguished the southern labor market was that racially rooted barriers *insulated* it from the rest of the country: the normal flow of workers back and forth did not occur and wage differences did not narrow. So long as this condition persisted, the South would remain a tributary economy, a supplier on unequal terms to the advanced industrial heartland of the North.

THE WORLD OF WORK

In a free-enterprise system, profit drives business. But the industrial order is not populated only by profit makers. It includes—in vastly larger numbers—wage earners. What is done for profit always affects those who work for wages, but never so drastically as in the late nineteenth century.

Labor Recruits

Wherever it took hold, industrialism set people in motion. Artisans moved into factories. Farm folk migrated to the cities. An industrial labor force emerged. This happened in the United States just as it did in European countries, but with a difference: the United States could not rely primarily on its native-born population for a supply of workers.

Except in the South, native-born white Americans no longer wanted factory work. Rural Americans were highly mobile in the late nineteenth century, and of those who moved, about half ended up in cities. But the jobs they took were as white-collar workers in offices and retail stores. Rural blacks would certainly have opted for factory jobs had they been given the chance. Modest numbers—280,000—did migrate to northern cities between 1870 and 1910, but they were restricted to casual labor, janitorial work, and, for the women, domestic service. Employers turned black applicants away from the factory gates because immigrant workers already supplied them with as much cheap labor as they needed.

The great migration from the Old World had started in the 1840s, when over a million Irish peasants fled the potato famine. In the following years, as European agriculture became increasingly commercialized, peasant populations grew and outstripped the available land. The peasant economy failed first in Germany and Scandinavia and then, later in the nineteenth century, across Austria-Hungary, Russia, Italy, and the Balkans. Although the majority of migrants to America had always been drawn from Europe's peasant villages, large

Immigrant Workers
Many native-born Americans resented the influx of peasant immigrants from eastern and southern Europe that began in the 1880s. In fact, the newcomers, more than any other group, operated the machines, laid the railroad tracks, and performed the heavy construction labor that built the nation's cities. They were Europe's gift—its most vigorous and hardworking people.

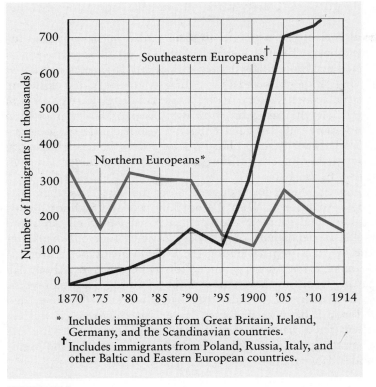

* Includes immigrants from Great Britain, Ireland, Germany, and the Scandinavian countries.
† Includes immigrants from Poland, Russia, Italy, and other Baltic and Eastern European countries.

FIGURE 18.2

American Immigration, 1870–1914

This graph shows the surge of European immigration in the late nineteenth century. While northern Europe continued to send substantial numbers, it was overshadowed after 1895 by southern Europeans pouring into America to work in mines and factories.

numbers of seasoned workers also came, attracted by the higher wages or cut loose by economic disruptions in Europe.

Ethnic origin largely determined the kind of work that the immigrants found in America. Skilled workers generally sought the same types of jobs they had held in the Old World. The Welsh worked as tin-plate workers, the English as miners, the Germans as machinists and traditional artisans, the Belgians as glassworkers, and the Scandinavians as seamen on Great Lakes boats. For common labor, employers had long counted on the brawn of Irish rural immigrants. As industrialization advanced, the demand for unskilled workers increased, helping to stimulate the heavy migration from southern and eastern Europe that began in the 1880s (see Figure 18.2). Italian and Slavic immigrants without industrial skills flooded into American factories. Heavy, low-paid labor became the domain of the recent immigrants. Blast-furnace jobs, one investigator heard, were "Hunky work," not suitable for him or any other American.

Not only skill determined where immigrants ended up in American industry. The newcomers, although generally traveling on their own, moved within well-defined networks, following relatives or fellow villagers already in America and relying on them to land a job. A high degree of ethnic clustering resulted, even within a single factory. At the Jones and Laughlin steelworks in Pittsburgh, for example, the carpentry shop was German, the hammer shop Polish, and the blooming mill Serbian. Immigrants also had different job preferences. Men from Italy, for example, liked outdoor work better than factory labor. And, already accustomed to it, they worked in gangs under a *padrone* (boss), much as they had in Italy.

Immigrants entered a modern industrial order, but they saw their surroundings through peasant eyes. With the disruption of the traditional rural economies of eastern and southern Europe, many had lost their lands and fallen into the class of dependent, propertyless servants. To avoid that bitter fate—to find the means to remain among the landed—many peasant immigrants came to America. They never intended to stay permanently. About half did return, departing from America in great numbers during depression years. No one knows how many left because they had saved enough money and how many left for lack of work. For their American employers, it scarcely mattered. What mattered was that they willingly took the worst jobs, and melted away when the jobs dried up. For the new industrial order, the immigrants made an ideal labor supply.

Working Women

Between 1870 and 1900 the number of wage-earning women jumped by almost two-thirds. Women made up a quarter of the labor force in 1900, and had become essential to America's industrial economy. The opportunities they found were shaped by gender—by the fact that they were women. Contemporary beliefs about womanhood largely determined which women took jobs and how they were treated once they became wage earners.

Wives were not supposed to work outside the home, and in fact fewer than 5 percent did so in 1890. The typical working woman at that time was under twenty-four and unmarried. Only among African-Americans did married women work for wages, in numbers that ranged over 30 percent. When older white women worked, remarked one observer, it "was usually a sign that something had gone wrong"—that they were widows or alone for other reasons.

Since women were held to be inherently different from men, it followed that they should not be permitted to do "men's work." Nor, regardless of the value of their labor, could they be paid a man's wage. A woman did not require a "living wage" because, as one investigator reported, "it is expected that she has men to support her." At the turn of the century the weekly wage of women factory workers came to roughly $7, or $3 less than that of unskilled men and $5 below the average for all industrial workers.

Women's work fell into three categories. One of every three women worked as a maid or in some other type of domestic service. Another third held "female" white-collar jobs in teaching, nursing, sales, and office work. The remaining third worked in industry, heavily concentrated in the garment trades and textile mills, but present also in many other industries as inspectors, packers, and assemblers and in other "light" occupations. Few worked as supervisors, fewer in the crafts, and nearly none as day laborers.

Just how jobs came to be defined as male or female—in sociological lingo, the "sex-typing" of occupations—is not easy to explain. The jobs of telephone operator and store clerk, originally held by men, had by the 1890s been taken over by women. Wherever an occupation became female-dominated, it was redefined as having feminine qualities, even though very similar or even identical work elsewhere was done by men. Once a job was identified as women's work, it became unsuitable for men. There were no male telephone operators by 1900.

Switchboard Operators
When the first telephone exchange was set up in Boston in 1878, it was operated by teenage boys, which followed the practice set in the telegraph industry. During the 1880s, however, young women increasingly replaced the boys, and by 1900 switchboard operation was defined strictly as women's work. In this photograph of a telephone exchange in Columbus, Ohio, in 1907, the older woman at left has risen to the position of supervisor, but it is the two men in the picture who are clearly in charge.

Getting Organized

R*ose Schneiderman (1882–1972) typified the young Jewish garment workers who became the firebrands of their industry. Schneiderman went on to an illustrious career as a unionist and reformer.*

We had no idea that there was a union in our industry and that women could join it. Nor did we have a full realization of the hardships we were needlessly undergoing. There was the necessity of owning a sewing machine before you could work. Then you had to buy your own thread. But the worst of it was the incredibly inefficient way in which work was distributed. Because we were all pieceworkers, any time lost during the season was a real hardship. . . .

We formed a committee composed of my friend Bessie Mannis, who worked with me, myself, and a third girl. Bravely we ventured into the office of the United Cloth Hat and Cap Makers Union. . . . We were told that we would have to have at least twenty-five women. . . . We waited at the doors of factories and, as the girls were leaving for the day, we would approach them and speak our piece. . . . Within days we had the necessary number, and in January 1903 we were chartered as Local 23, and I was elected secretary. . . .

The only cloud in the picture was mother's attitude toward my becoming a trade unionist. She kept saying I'd never get married because I was so busy—a prophecy which came true. . . .

That June we decided to put our strength to the test. . . . On Saturdays . . . we women had to hang around until three or four o'clock before getting our pay. I headed a committee which informed Mr. Fox that we wanted to be paid at the same time as the men. . . . He didn't say outright that he agreed; he wouldn't give us that much satisfaction. But on the first Saturday in July, when we went for our pay at twelve noon, there it was ready for us.

SOURCE: Rose Schneiderman, *All for One* (1967), reprinted in Irving Howe and Kenneth Libo, eds., *How We Lived* (New York: New American Library, 1979), 139–41.

As with men's work, ethnicity played a big part in the distribution of women's jobs among particular groups. White-collar jobs were reserved for the native-born, increasingly including, however, the second-generation daughters of immigrants. And as with men, ethnicity created clustering patterns in women's jobs; in the case of Italian families, for instance, it restricted women to subcontracted tasks, such as sewing, that could be done at home.

But if ethnicity mattered at the workplace, gender mattered at least as much. Women's identity gave their work distinctive meaning. Department store clerks, for example, developed a work culture and language just as robust as that of any male craft group. The most important fact about wage-earning women was their youth. For many, their first job freed them from family discipline. It was an opportunity to be independent; to form friendships with other young women; and to experience, however briefly, a fun-loving time of nice clothes, dancing, and other "cheap amusements."

To some degree, their youthful preoccupations made it easier for working women to accept the miserable terms under which they labored. But this did not mean that they lacked a sense of group solidarity and self-respect. Nice clothes might appear frivolous to the casual observer, but they also conveyed the message that the working girl considered herself as good as anyone. Rebellious youth culture sometimes united with job grievances to produce astonishing strike movements, as, for example, by the Jewish garment workers of New York and the Irish-American telephone operators of Boston.

Disapproval of job-holding wives, although expressed in sentimental and moral terms, was based on solid necessity. From the standpoint of the labor market, the basic economic unit was the individual employee. For workers, however, the family was the economic unit, to which the wife contributed crucially. Cooking, cleaning, and tending the children were not income-producing activities and were not reckoned in terms of money. But everyone knew that the family economy depended on the wife's household contribution. Therefore, her place was in the home.

Except among the high-paid crafts, however, working-class families found the going hard on a single income. The rockiest period came during a family's child-bearing years, when there were many mouths to feed and only the earnings of the father to provide the food. Thereafter, as the children grew up, the family income began to increase. Not only unmarried sons and daughters but the younger children as well contributed their share. In 1900 one of every five children under sixteen worked. "When the people own houses," remarked a printer from Fall River, "you will generally find that it is a large family all working together."

By the 1890s all the northern industrial states had passed laws prohibiting child labor and limiting work-hours for teenagers. Most of these states also required school attendance for a certain number of weeks each year. Working-class families continued to rely on second incomes, but this money came more and more from the wives. After 1890 the proportion of working married women crept steadily upward. About a fifth of the wives of unskilled and semiskilled men in Chicago held jobs in 1920. Wage-earning wives and mothers were on their way to becoming a primary part of America's labor force.

Autonomous Labor

No one supervised the nineteenth-century coal miner. He was a tonnage worker, paid for the amount of coal he produced. He provided his own tools, worked at his own pace, and knocked off early when he chose. Such autonomous craft workers—almost all of them men—flourished in many branches of nineteenth-century industry. They were mule spinners in cotton

AMERICAN VOICES

A Miner's Son

John Brophy (1883–1963), an important mine union official in the twentieth century, recalls what mining was like in his boyhood.

I got a thrill at the thought of having an opportunity to go and work in the mine, to go and work along side my father. . . . It was a great satisfaction to me that my father was a skilled, clean workman with everything kept in shape, and the timbering done well. . . . It's plain that the individual miner in those early days had considerable freedom of judgment. I think that was one of the great satisfactions that a miner had—that he was his own boss within his workplace. . . .

The miner is always aware of danger, that he lived under dangerous conditions in the workplace. . . . Then there is the further fact that the miner by and large lived in purely mining communities which were often isolated. They developed a group loyalty under all these circumstances. They were both individualists and they were group conscious. . . . You find time and again miners, in an effort to rescue their fellow workers, taking chances which quite often meant death for thmeselves. . . .

Along with that is a sense of justice. There was the very fact the miner was a tonnage worker and that he could be short weighed and cheated in various ways, and that the only safeguard against it was organization. . . . The miner in my day in the United States was aware that all knowledge didn't start with his generation. . . . At least on one side of my family there are at least four generations of [British] miners, and I say this with a sense of pride; very much so. I'm very proud of the fact that there is this long tradition of miners who have struggled with the elements.

SOURCE: Jerold S. Auerbach, ed., *American Labor: The Twentieth Century* (Indianapolis: Bobbs-Merrill, 1969), 44–48.

mills; puddlers and rollers in iron works; molders in stove making; and machinists, glassblowers, and skilled workers of many other types.

In the shop they abided by the *stint*, a limit they themselves placed on the amount they would produce each day. This informal system of limiting output infuriated efficiency-minded engineers. But to the worker it signified personal dignity and "unselfish brotherhood" with fellow employees. The male craft worker took pride in maintaining a "manly" bearing, toward both his fellows and the boss. One day a shop in Lowell, Massachusetts, posted regulations requiring all employees to be at their posts in work clothes at the opening bell and to remain, with the shop door locked, until the dismissal bell. A machinist promptly packed his tools and quit, declaring that he had not "been brought up under such a system of slavery."

Underlying this ethical code was a keen sense of the craft group, each with its own history and customs. Hatters, masters of the art of applying fur felting to top hats and bowlers, had a language of their own. When a hatter was hired, he was "shopped"; if fired, he was "bagged"; when he quit work, he "cried off"; and when he took an apprentice, the boy was "under teach." The hatters, most of whom worked in Danbury, Connecticut, or Orange, New Jersey, formed a distinctive, self-contained community.

The craft worker's skills were crucial to nineteenth-century production. He was valued also for the responsibilities he assumed. He hired his own helpers, supervised their work, and paid them from his earnings. In an era when the scale of production was expanding, autonomous craft workers relieved their employers of the burden of shop-floor management. Many factory managers deliberately shifted this responsibility to employees. A system of inside contracting developed in metal-fabricating firms that did precise machining and complex assembling. Contractor-employees hired and paid their own men and supervised them.

Dispersal of authority was thus characteristic of nineteenth-century industry. The aristocracy of the workers—the craftsmen, inside contractors, and foremen—enjoyed a high degree of autonomy. However, their subordinates often paid dearly for that independence. The opportunities for abuse were endless. Any worker who paid his helpers from his own pocket might be tempted to exploit them. In the Pittsburgh area, foremen were known as "pushers," notorious for driving their gangs mercilessly. On the other hand, industrial labor in the nineteenth century remained on a human scale. People dealt with each other face to face, and often developed cohesive ties within the shop. Striking craft workers commonly received the support of helpers and laborers, and labor gangs sometimes walked out on behalf of a popular foreman.

Systems of Control

As technology advanced and modern management emerged, workers increasingly lost the proud independence that had characterized nineteenth-century craft work.

One source of this de-skilling process was a new system of production—Henry Ford called it "mass production"—that lent itself to mechanization. Agricultural implements, typewriters, bicycles, and, after 1900, automobiles were assembled from standardized parts. The machine tools that cut, drilled, and ground these metal parts had originally been manned by skilled machinists. But because they produced long runs of a single item, these machine tools became more specialized; they became *dedicated* machines—machines set up to do the same job over and over—and the need for skilled operatives disappeared. In the manufacture of sewing machines, one machinist complained in 1883, "the trade is so subdivided that a man is not considered a machinist at all. One man may make just a particular part of a machine and may not know anything whatever about another part of the same machine." Such a worker, noted an observer, "cannot be master of a craft, but only master of a fragment."

Employers were attracted to dedicated machinery because it increased output; the impact on workers was not uppermost in their minds. They recognized that mechanization made it easier to discipline their workers, but that was only an incidental benefit. Gradually, however, the idea took hold that managing workers might itself be a way to reduce the cost of production.

The pioneer in this field was Frederick W. Taylor. An expert on metal-cutting methods, Taylor believed that the same engineer's approach might be applied to managing workers, hence the name for his method: *scientific management*. In order to get the maximum work from the individual worker, Taylor suggested two basic reforms. The first would eliminate the brain work from manual labor. Managers would assume "the burden of gathering together all of the traditional knowledge which in the past has been possessed by the workmen and then of classifying, tabulating, and reducing this knowledge to rules, laws, and formulae." The second reform, a logical consequence of the first, would deprive workers of the authority they had exercised on the shop floor. Workers would "do what they are told promptly and without asking questions or making suggestions. . . . The duty of enforcing . . . rests with the management alone."

Once they had the knowledge and the power, managers would put labor on a "scientific" basis. This meant subjecting each task to a *time-and-motion study*, in which an engineer analyzed and timed each job with a stopwatch. Workers would be paid at a *differential rate*—that is, a certain amount if they met the stopwatch standard, and a higher rate for additional output. Taylor claimed that his techniques would guarantee optimum worker efficiency. His assumption was that only money mattered to workers and that they would automatically respond to the lure of higher earnings.

Scientific management was not, in practice, a roaring success. Implementing it proved very expensive, and workers stubbornly resisted the job-analysis method. "It looks to me like slavery to have a man stand over you with a stopwatch," complained one iron molder. A union leader insisted that "this system is wrong, because we want our heads left on us." Far from solving the labor problem, as Taylor claimed it would, scientific management embittered relations on the shop floor.

Yet Taylor achieved something of fundamental importance. He was a brilliant publicist, and his teachings spread throughout American industry. Taylor's disciples moved beyond his simplistic economic psychology, creating the new professions of personnel administration and industrial psychology, which claimed to know how to get more and better labor from workers. A threshold had been crossed into the modern era of labor management.

So the circle closed on American workers. With each advance, the quest for efficiency cut deeper into their cherished autonomy. The process occurred unevenly. For textile workers the loss had come early. Miners and iron workers felt it much more slowly. Others, such as construction workers, escaped the process almost entirely. But increasing numbers of workers found themselves in an environment that crushed any sense of mastery or even understanding.

THE LABOR MOVEMENT

Wherever industrialization has taken hold, workers have organized and formed labor unions. However, the movements they built have varied from one industrial society to another. In the United States, workers were especially uncertain about the path they wanted to take. Only in the 1880s did the American labor movement settle into a fixed course.

Reformers and Unionists

Thomas B. McGuire, a New York wagon driver, was ambitious. He had saved $300 from his wages "so that I might become something of a capitalist eventually." But his venture as a cab driver in the early 1880s soon failed:

> Corporations usually take that business themselves. They can manage to get men, at starvation wages, and put them on a hack, and put a livery on them with a gold band and brass buttons, to show that they are slaves—I beg pardon; I did not intend to use the word slaves; there are no slaves in this country now—to show that they are merely servants.

Slave or liveried servant, the symbolic meaning was the same to McGuire. He was speaking of the crushed aspirations of the independent American worker.

What would satisfy the Thomas McGuires of the nineteenth century? Only the establishment of an *egalitarian society*, one in which every citizen might hope to become independent. This republican goal did not mean returning to the agrarian past, but rather moving beyond the existing industrial order to a juster system that did not distinguish between capitalists and workers. All would be "producers" laboring together in what was commonly called the "cooperative commonwealth." This was the ideal that inspired the Noble and Holy Order of the Knights of Labor.

Founded in 1869 as a secret society in Philadelphia, the Knights of Labor spread to other cities, and by 1878 had become a national movement. The Order's elaborate ritual and ceremony gave nineteenth-century workers a sense of belonging very much like that offered by the fraternalism of the Masons or Odd Fellows. For the Knights, however, fraternalism was harnessed to labor-reform advocacy. The goal was to "give voice to that grand undercurrent of mighty thought, which is today [1880] crystallizing in the hearts of men, and urging them on to perfect organization through which to gain the power to make labor emancipation possible."

But how was "emancipation" to be achieved? Through cooperation, the Knights argued. Funds would be raised to set up cooperative factories and shops owned and run by the employees. As these cooperatives flourished and spread, American society would be transformed into a cooperative commonwealth. But little was actually done. Instead, the Knights devoted themselves to "education." The Knights's leader, Grand Master Workman Terence V. Powderly, regarded the organization as a vast educational society that ought to be open to almost anyone (excluding lawyers and saloonkeepers). The cooperative commonwealth would arrive in some mysterious way as more and more "producers" became members and learned the group's message from lectures, discussions, and publications. Social evil would not end in a day, but "must await the gradual development of educational enlightenment."

The labor reformers expressed the higher aspirations of American workers. Another kind of organization—the trade union—tended to their day-to-day needs. Unions had long been central in the lives of craft workers. Apprenticeship rules regulated entry into a trade, and the *closed shop*—by reserving all jobs for union members—kept out lower-wage and incompetent workers. Union rules specified the terms of work, sometimes in minute detail. The trade union also expressed the social identity of the craft. A Birmingham iron worker claimed that his union's "main object was to educate mechanics up to a standard of morality and temperance, and good workmanship." Some unions emphasized mutual aid. Because operating trains was a high-risk occupation, the railroad brotherhoods provided accident and death benefits and encouraged members to assist one another. On the job and off, the unions played a big part in the lives of craft workers.

The earliest unions organized locally workers in the same craft, sometimes limited, especially among German workers, to a single ethnic group. As expanding markets broke down their insularity, these unions began to form national organizations, starting with the International Typographical Union in 1852. By the 1870s molders, ironworkers, bricklayers, and about thirty other trades had formed national unions.

The practical job interests they espoused might have seemed a far cry from the reform ideals of the Knights of Labor. But both kinds of motives arose from a single workers' culture. Seeing no conflict, many workers carried membership cards in both the Knights of Labor and a trade union. The careers of many labor leaders, including Powderly, likewise embraced both kinds of activity. For many years even the functional lines were indistinct. At the local level, little separated a trade assembly of the Knights from a local trade union; both engaged in fraternal and job-oriented activities.

Trade unions generally barred women, and so did the Knights until, in 1881, women shoe workers in Philadelphia struck in support of their male co-workers, and won the right to form their own local assembly. By 1886 probably 50,000 women belonged to the Knights of Labor. Their courage on the picket line prompted Powderly's rueful remark that women "are the best men in the Order." For a handful of women, such as the hosiery worker Leonora M. Barry, the Knights provided a rare chance to take up leadership roles as organizers and officials. Similarly, the Knights of Labor grudgingly expanded the opportunity for black workers to join out of the need for solidarity and, just as important, in deference to the Order's egalitarian principles. The Knights could rightly boast that their "great work has been to organize labor which was previously unorganized."

Samuel Gompers
This is a photograph of the labor leader in his forties taken when he was visiting striking miners in West Virginia, an area where mine operators resisted unions with special fierceness. The photograph was taken by a company detective.

The Triumph of "Pure and Simple" Unionism

In the early 1880s the Knights began to rival the trade unions. Boycott campaigns against the products of "unfair" employers achieved impressive results. With the economy booming and workers in short supply, the Knights began to win strikes, including a major victory against Jay Gould's Southwestern railway system in 1885. Workers flocked into the organization, and its membership jumped from 100,000 to perhaps 700,000 in less than a year. For a brief time the Knights stood poised as a potential industrial-union movement capable of bringing all workers into its fold.

Frightened by this success, the national trade unions began to insist on a clear separation of roles, with the Knights confined to the field of labor reform. This was partly a battle over turf, but it also reflected deepening divergence of labor philosophies.

The ideological assault on the Knights was led by Samuel Gompers, a union cigar maker from New York City. Gompers hammered out the philosophical position that would become known as "pure and simple" unionism. His starting point was that grand theories and schemes such as those that excited the labor reformers should be avoided like the plague. Unions, Gompers thought, should focus instead strictly on concrete, achievable gains, and they should organize workers not as an undifferentiated mass of "producers," but by craft and occupation. The battleground should be where workers could mobilize their power, which was where they worked, not in the quicksands of politics. While the Knights dreamt of a cooperative commonwealth, pure-and-simple unionists concerned themselves strictly with the here-and-now. "No matter how just," Gompers pronounced, "unless the cause is backed up with power to enforce it, it is going to be crushed and annihilated."

The struggle for the eight-hour day that began in 1886 crystallized the tensions between the rival movements. Both, of course, favored a shorter workday, but for different reasons. For the Knights, it was desirable because workers had duties "to perform as American citizens and members of society." Trade unionists took a more hard-boiled view of the eight-hour day: it would spread the available jobs among more workers, protect them against overwork, and (like higher wages) make life easier for them. When the trade unions set May 1, 1886, as the deadline for achieving the eight-hour day, the leadership of Knights objected. But workers everywhere responded enthusiastically, and as the deadline approached, a wave of strikes and demonstrations broke out.

In Chicago four strikers died on May 3 in a battle at the McCormick agricultural-implement works. German-American anarchists, revolutionary advocates of a stateless society, called a protest meeting the next evening at Haymarket Square. When police moved in to break it up, someone threw a bomb that killed and wounded several of the police. With no proof of their involvement, the anarchists were tried and found guilty of criminal conspiracy. Four were executed, one committed suicide, and the others received long prison sentences. They were victims of one of the great miscarriages of American justice.

The antiunion hysteria set off by the Haymarket affair enabled employers to take the offensive against the campaign for an eight-hour day. They broke strikes violently, compiled blacklists of strikers, and forced others to sign so-called *yellow-dog contracts* guaranteeing that as a condition of employment, they would not join a labor organization. If trade unionists needed any further confirmation of the tough world in which they lived, they found it in Haymarket and its aftermath.

In December 1886, having failed to persuade the Knights of Labor to desist from union activity, the national trade unions formed the American Federation of Labor (AFL), with Samuel Gompers as president. The AFL in effect locked into place the trade-union structure as it had evolved by the 1880s. Underlying this structure was the conviction that workers had to take the world as it was, not as they dreamed it might be.

The Knights of Labor never recovered from the employer counteroffensive after the Haymarket affair. Powderly retreated to the rhetoric of labor reform, but wage earners had lost interest, and he was unable to formulate a workable new strategy. By the mid-1890s, the Knights of Labor had faded away.

Industrial War

The trade unions were conservative, in that they accepted the economic order; all they wanted was a larger share for working people. But it was precisely that claim against their profits that made American employers so opposed to collective bargaining. In the 1890s they unleashed a fierce counterattack on the trade-union movement.

In Homestead, Pennsylvania, site of one of Carnegie's great steel mills, the skilled workers thought themselves safe from that threat. Mostly homeowners, they elected fellow workers to public office and considered the town very much their community. And they had faith in Andrew Carnegie, who had advocated in a famous magazine article the right of workers to combine, and also of a property right in their jobs that forbade the use of strikebreakers by employers.

Espousing high-toned principles made Carnegie feel good; but, alas, the bottom line made him feel even better. Carnegie decided that collective bargaining had become too expensive. With the new machinery he was installing, Carnegie was confident that his skilled workers could be replaced, and the union broken. Lacking the stomach for the hard battle ahead, Carnegie hid himself in his remote castle in Scotland. But he left behind a second-in-command eminently qualified for the job. This was Henry Clay Frick, a former coal baron and a veteran of labor wars in the coal fields.

After some perfunctory bargaining Frick announced that, effective July 1, 1892, the company would no longer deal with the Amalgamated Association of Iron and Steel Workers. The plant had already been fortified so that strikebreakers could be brought in to resume operations. At stake for Carnegie's employees now were not just wage cuts but the defense of a way of life. Town authorities turned away the county sheriff when he tried to take possession of the plant. The entire community—women no less than men—mobilized in defense of the union.

Behind hastily erected barricades, the strikers opened fire on barge loads of Pinkertons trying to approach the plant at dawn on July 6. When the Pinkertons surrendered after a bloody battle, they were mercilessly pummeled by the enraged women of Homestead as they were herded to the railway station. Frick appealed to the governor of Pennsylvania, who called out the state militia and placed Homestead under martial law. The great steelworks was taken over and opened to strikebreakers, while union leaders and town officials were arrested on charges of riot, murder, and treason.

The Homestead strike ushered in a decade of strife in which working people faced not only the great power of corporate industry, but the even greater power of their own government. The fullest demonstration of that hard reality came at a place that seemed an even less likely site for class warfare than Homestead. Pullman, Illinois, was a model factory town built by George M. Pullman, inventor of the sleeping car, which brought comfort and luxury to railway travel. When the Panic of 1893 struck, business fell off and Pullman cut wages, but not the rents for company housing. When a workers' committee finally complained to him in May 1894, Pullman responded that he saw no connection between his roles as employer and landlord. As for the committee members, they were fired.

The strike that ensued would have been only a footnote in American labor history, but for the fact that the Pullman workers belonged to the American Railway Union (ARU), a rapidly growing industrial union of railroad workers. Its leader, Eugene V. Debs, directed ARU members not to handle Pullman sleeping cars, which, although operated by the railroads, were owned and serviced by the Pullman Company. This was a *labor boycott*, in which force was applied at a secondary point (the railroads) to bring pressure on the primary target (Pullman). Since the railroads insisted on running the Pullman cars, a far-flung strike soon spread across the country, threatening the entire economy.

Quite deliberately, the railroads maneuvered to bring the federal government into the dispute. Their hook was the U.S. mail cars, which they attached to every train hauling Pullman cars. When strikers stopped these trains, the railroads appealed to President Grover Cleveland to protect the U.S. mail. It so happened that the attorney-general, Richard Olney, was a former railroad lawyer who unabashedly sided with his former employers. When federal troops failed to get the trains running again, Olney obtained court orders forbidding the ARU leaders to conduct the strike. Debs refused to obey; he was held in contempt of court and jailed. Now leaderless and uncoordinated, the strike quickly fell apart. No one could doubt why the great Pullman boycott had failed: it had been crushed by the naked use of government power on behalf of the railroad companies.

American Radicalism in the Making

No one who had known him as a young man would have thought that one day Eugene Debs would become the nation's leading socialist. A native of Terre Haute, Indiana, a prosperous railroad town, Debs grew up believing in the essential goodness of American society. A popular young man-about-town, Debs considered a career in politics or business, but instead got involved in the local labor movement. In 1880, at the age of twenty-five, he was elected national secretary-treasurer of the Brotherhood of Locomotive Firemen, one of the craft unions representing the skilled operating trades on the railroads. Increasingly bothered by his union's indifference to the welfare of low-paid track and yard laborers, Debs unexpectedly resigned from his comfortable post to devote himself to a new organization, the

The Pullman Strike
Chicago was the hub of the railwork network and the strategic center of the battle between the Pullman boycotters and the trunk line railroads. For the strikers, the crucial thing was to prevent those trains with Pullman cars attached from running; for the railroads, it was to get the trains through at any cost. The arrival of federal troops meant that the trains would move and that the strikers would be defeated.

American Railway Union, that would organize all railroad workers irrespective of skill—that is, an *industrial union.*

The Pullman strike visibly changed Debs. Sentenced to six months in the federal penitentiary, Debs came out of jail an avowed radical, committed to a lifelong struggle against a system that enabled employers to enlist the powers of government to beat down working people. Initially Debs identified himself as a Populist, but he quickly gravitated toward the socialist camp.

German refugees had brought the ideas of Karl Marx, the radical German philosopher, to America after the failed 1848 revolutions in Europe. Little noticed by most Americans, Marxist socialism struck deep roots in the growing German-American communities of Chicago and New York. In 1877 the Socialist Labor party was formed, and from that time onward Marxist socialism maintained a continuing, if narrowly based, presence in American politics.

When Eugene Debs appeared in their midst in 1897, the socialists were in a state of crisis. Despite the economic upheaval just ending, they had failed to make much headway. Many blamed the party head, Daniel De Leon, an ideological purist not greatly interested in attracting voters. Debs joined in the revolt against the dogmatic De Leon. When the rival Socialist Party of America was formed in 1901, it was with the aim of building a broad-based political movement.

A spellbinding campaigner, Debs talked socialism in an American idiom, making Marxism understandable and persuasive to many ordinary Americans. Under him the new party began to break down ethnic barriers and attract American-born voters. In Texas, Oklahoma, and Minnesota, socialism exerted a powerful appeal among cotton and wheat farmers. The party was also highly successful at attracting women activists. Inside of a decade, with a national network of branches and state organizations, the Socialist party had become a force to be reckoned with in American politics.

For some radical unionists, especially veterans of the fierce labor wars in the West (see Chapter 17), electoral politics seemed too tame. Led by Ed Boyce and "Big Bill" Haywood, the Western Federation of Miners joined with left-wing socialists in 1905 to create a new movement, the Industrial Workers of the World (IWW). The *Wobblies*, as IWW members were called, fervently supported the Marxist class struggle—but strictly in the industrial field. By action at the point of production and by an unending struggle against employers—ultimately by means of a general strike—they believed that the workers themselves would bring about a revolution. A workers' society would emerge, run directly by the workers through their industrial unions. The term *syndicalism* describes this brand of workers' radicalism.

In both its major forms—the politically oriented Socialist party and the syndicalist IWW—American radicalism flourished after the crisis of the 1890s, but only on a limited basis. Socialists and Wobblies lived, in a sense, on the tolerance of society. They would later be crushed without ceremony. Nevertheless, they served a larger purpose. American radicalism, by its sheer vitality, bore witness to what was exploitative and unjust in the new industrial order.

CHAPTER 18 TIMELINE

1869	Knights of Labor founded in Philadelphia First transcontinental railroad completed
1872	Montgomery Ward, first mail-order house, founded Andrew Carnegie starts construction of Edgar Thompson steelworks near Pittsburgh
1873	Panic of 1873 ushers in economic depression
1875	John Wanamaker establishes first department store in Philadelphia
1877	Baltimore and Ohio workers initiate nationwide railroad strike
1878	Gustavus Swift introduces refrigerator car
1883	Railroads establish national time zones
1886	Haymarket Square bombing in Chicago American Federation of Labor (AFL) founded
1890	U.S. surpasses Britain in producing iron and steel
1892	Homestead steel strike crushed
1893	Panic of 1893 starts depression of the 1890s Wave of railroad bankruptcies; reorganization by investment bankers begins
1894	President Cleveland sends troops to break Pullman boycott
1895	Frederick W. Taylor expounds scientific management Southeastern European immigration exceeds northern European immigration for the first time
1901	Eugene V. Debs helps found Socialist party
1905	Industrial Workers of the World (IWW) launched

CHAPTER 19

THE POLITICS OF LATE NINETEENTH-CENTURY AMERICA

- The Politics of the Status Quo, 1877–1893
- The Crisis of American Politics: The 1890s
- Race and Politics in the South

Ever since the founding of the Republic, foreign visitors had been coming to America to study its political system. Most famous of the early observers was Alexis de Tocqueville, the author of *Democracy in America* (1832). When an equally brilliant visitor, the Englishman James Bryce, sat down to write his own account fifty years later, he decided that Tocqueville's great book could not serve as his model. For Tocqueville, Bryce noted, "America was primarily a democracy, the ideal democracy, fraught with lessons for Europe." In his own book, *The American Commonwealth* (1888), Bryce was much less rhapsodic. Tocqueville's robust democracy had devolved over the next half-century into the dreary machine politics of post–Civil War America.

Bryce was anxious that his European readers not misunderstand him. Europeans needed to be aware of "the existence in the American people of a reserve of force and patriotism more than sufficient to sweep away all the evils now tolerated, and to make a politics of the country worthy of its material grandeur and of the private virtues of its inhabitants." Bryce was ultimately an optimist: "A hundred times in writing this book have I been disheartened by the facts I was stating: a hundred times has the recollection of the abounding strength and vitality of the nation chased away these tremours."

Just what it was that Bryce found so disheartening in the practice of American politics is this chapter's first subject; the second is the underlying vitality that Bryce sensed, and how it re-emerged and began to reinvigorate the nation's politics by the century's end.

THE POLITICS OF THE STATUS QUO, 1877–1893

In times of national ferment, as a rule, public life becomes magnified. Leaders emerge. Electoral campaigns debate great issues. The powers of government expand. In the Civil War era, the nation's public institutions had been severely tested, not least by the contested presidential election of 1876. In 1877, with the Republican Rutherford B. Hayes safely settled in the White House, the era of sectional strife finally ended.

Political life went on, but drained of its earlier drama. In the 1880s there were no Lincolns, no great national debates. There remained an irreducible core of public functions and even, as on the question of railroad regulation, grudging acceptance of new governmental involvement. But the dominant rhetoric celebrated that government which governed least, and as compared to the Civil War era, American government did govern less.

The National Scene

There were five presidents from 1877 to 1893: Rutherford B. Hayes (Republican, 1877–1881), James A. Garfield (Republican, 1881), Chester A. Arthur (Republican, 1881–1885), Grover Cleveland (Democrat, 1885–1889), and Benjamin Harrison (Republican, 1889–1893). All were estimable men. Hayes,

Grover Cleveland
In the years after Reconstruction, Americans did not look for charismatic personalities or dramatic leadership in their presidents. They preferred men who accepted the limits of executive power, men of "sound conservatism." Grover Cleveland fitted the bill to perfection. For political reformers, Cleveland had the additional virtues of independence and personal integrity. He best represented the late nineteenth-century ideal of the American president.

Garfield, and Harrison boasted distinguished war records. Hayes had served effectively as governor of Ohio for three terms, and Garfield had done well as a congressional leader. Arthur, despite his reputation as a machine politician, had demonstrated fine administrative skills as head of the New York customs house. Cleveland had made his mark as reform mayor of Buffalo and governor of New York. None was a charismatic leader, but circumstances, more than personal qualities, explain why none of these presidents made a larger mark on history.

The president's most demanding job was to dispense political patronage. Under the spoils system, government jobs were treated as rewards for those who had served the winning party. Reform of this system became urgent after President Garfield was shot in 1881. His assassin, Charles Guiteau, was a deranged religious fanatic, but advocates of civil-service reform blamed his death on the poisonous atmosphere of the spoils system. The resulting Pendleton Act of 1883 created a list of jobs to be filled on the basis of examinations administered by the new Civil Service Commission. The list originally covered only a small percentage of federal appointments, however, and patronage remained a preoccupation in the White House. Though standards of public administration did rise, there was no American counterpart to the elite professional civil services taking shape in Britain and Germany in these years.

The functions of the executive branch were, in any event, very modest. Of the 100,000 federal employees in 1880, fully 56 percent worked for the U.S. Post Office. During the 1880s the important government departments— Treasury, State, War, Navy, Interior—were sleepy places carrying on largely routine duties. Virtually all federal funding came from customs duties and excise taxes on liquor and tobacco. These sources produced more money than the government spent. The question of how to reduce the federal *surplus* ranked as one of the most troublesome issues of the 1880s.

On matters of national policy the presidents took a back seat to Congress. But Congress functioned badly. Party discipline was weak, and procedural rules frequently blocked legislative business. The Democrats favored states' rights, while the Republicans were heirs to the Whig enthusiasm for federally assisted economic development. After Reconstruction, however, the Republicans backed away from that activist position and, in truth, party differences became muddy. On most leading issues of the day—civil-service reform, the currency, and regulation of the railroads—the divisions occurred within the parties, not between them.

Only the tariff remained a potent partisan issue. From Lincoln's administration onward, high duties had protected American industry from imported goods. The Democrats, free traders by tradition, regularly attacked Republican protectionism. In practice, however, the tariff was a negotiable issue like any other. Congressmen voted their constituents' interests, regardless of party rhetoric. As a result, every tariff bill was a patchwork of bargains among special interests.

Issues were treated gingerly partly because the parties were so equally balanced. The Democrats, in retreat immediately after the Civil War, quickly regrouped, and by the end of Reconstruction stood on virtually equal terms with the Republicans. Every presidential election from 1876 to 1892 was decided by a thin margin, and neither party gained permanent command of Congress. Political caution seemed wise; any false move on national issues might tip the scales to the other side.

The weakening of principled politics was evident in the Republicans' retreat from their Civil War legacy. The major unfinished business after 1877 involved the plight of the former slaves. The Republican agenda called for federal funding to combat illiteracy and, even more threatening to the South, federal protection for black voters in southern congressional elections. Neither measure managed to make it through Congress, however. The Republicans back-pedaled on the race issue and gradually abandoned the blacks to their fate.

That did not stop Republican orators from "waving the bloody shirt" against the Democrats. Service in the Union army gave candidates a strong claim to public office, and veterans' benefits always stood high on the Republican agenda. The Democrats played the same game in the South as the defenders of the Lost Cause.

Alternatively, campaigns could descend into comedy. In the hard-fought election of 1884, for example, the Democrat Grover Cleveland burst on the scene as a reformer, fresh from his victories over corrupt machine politics as Buffalo mayor and New York governor. But years earlier Cleveland, a bachelor, had fathered an illegitimate child, and throughout the campaign he was dogged by the ditty, "Maw, Maw, where's Paw? He's in the White House, haw-haw-haw." His opponent, James G. Blaine, got tangled up in the scandalous charge by a too ardent Republican supporter that the Democrats were the party of "Rum, Romanism and Rebellion." In the midst of all the mudslinging, the issues got lost.

The Ideology of Individualism

The characteristics of public life in the 1880s—the inactivity of the federal government, the evasiveness of the political parties, and the absorption in politics for its own sake—derived ultimately from the conviction that little was at stake in public affairs. In 1887 Cleveland vetoed a small appropriation for drought-stricken Texas farmers with the remark that "though the people support the Government, the Government should not support the people." Governmental activity was itself considered a bad thing. All that the state could do, said Republican Senator Roscoe Conkling, was "to clear the way of impediments and dangers, and leave every class and every individual free and safe in the exertions and pursuits of life." Conkling was expressing the political corollary to the doctrine of *laissez faire*—the belief that that government was best which governed least.

A flood of popular writings trumpeted the individualist creed, from the rags-to-riches tales of Horatio Alger to the stream of success manuals with

Facing the World
The cover of this Horatio Alger novel (1893) captures the myth of opportunity. Our hero "Harry Vane" is a poor but earnest lad, valise packed, ready to make his way in the world and, despite the many obstacles thrown in his path, sure to succeed. In some 135 books Horatio Alger repeated this story, with minor variations, for an eager reading public that numbered in the millions.

such titles as *Thoughts for the Young Men of America, or a Few Practical Words of Advice to those Born in Poverty and Destined to be Reared in Orphanages* (1871). It was a lesson celebrated in the lives of such self-made men as Andrew Carnegie, whose book *Triumphant Democracy* (1886) paid homage to a nation that had enabled a penniless Scottish child to rise from bobbin boy to steel magnate.

From the pulpit came the assurances of the Episcopal bishop William Lawrence of Massachusetts that "Godliness is in league with riches." Bishop Lawrence was voicing a tradition in American Protestantism that went back to the Puritans: success in one's earthly calling signified the promise of eternal salvation. It was all too easy for a conservative ministry to make morally reassuring the furious acquisitiveness of industrial America. "To secure wealth is an honorable ambition," intoned the Baptist minister Russell H. Conwell in his lecture "Acres of Diamonds," a text for what became known as the Gospel of Wealth.

American individualism drew strong intellectual support from science. In *The Origin of Species* (1859) the British naturalist Charles Darwin had developed a bold hypothesis to explain the evolution of plants and animals. In nature, Darwin wrote, all living things struggle and compete. Individual members of a species are born with characteristics that better enable them to survive in their particular environment: camouflage coloring for a bird, for example, or resistance to thirst in a desert animal. These survival characteristics, since they are heritable, become dominant in future generations, and the species evolves. This process of evolution, which Darwin called *natural selection*, created a revolution in biological science.

Drawing on Darwin, the British philosopher Herbert Spencer developed an elaborate analysis of how human society had evolved through competition and "survival of the fittest." Social Darwinism, as Spencer's ideas became known, was championed in America by William Graham Sumner, a sociology professor at Yale. Competition, said Sumner, is a law of nature that "can no more be done away with than gravitation." And who are the fittest? "The millionaires. . . . They may fairly be regarded as the naturally selected agents of society. They get high wages and live in luxury, but the bargain is a good one for society."

Social Darwinists argued against any interference with social processes. "The great stream of time and earthly things will sweep on just the same in spite of us," Sumner wrote in a famous essay, "The Absurd Attempt to Make the World Over" (1894). As for the government, it had "at bottom . . . two chief things . . . with which to deal. They are the property of men and the honor of women. These it has to defend against crime."

The Courts

Suspicion of government not only paralyzed political initiative; it also shifted power away from the executive and legislative branches. "The task of constitutional government," declared Sumner, "is to devise institutions which shall come into play at critical periods to prevent the abusive control of the powers of a state by the controlling classes in it." Sumner meant the judiciary. From the 1870s onward the courts increasingly accepted the role that he assigned to them, becoming the guardians of the rights of private property.

Under the federal system as it was understood in the late nineteenth century, the states retained primary responsibility for social welfare and economic regulation. The basis for this authority was the *police powers* of the states to ensure the health, safety, and morals of their citizens. How to strike a balance between the general welfare and the liberty of individuals to pursue their private interests was the dominant legal issue of the era. Most states, caught up in the conservative ethos of the day, were themselves cutting back on expenditures and public services. Even so, there were more than enough state initiatives to alarm vigilant judges. Thus, in the landmark case *In Re Jacobs* (1885) the New York Supreme Court struck down a state law prohibiting cigar manufacturing in tenements on the grounds that such regulation exceeded the police powers of the state.

For the U.S. Supreme Court, the crucial weapon was the Fourteenth Amendment (1868), which prohibited the states from depriving "any person of life, liberty, or property, without due process of law." The due-process clause had been adopted during Reconstruction to protect the civil rights of the former slaves. But due process protected the property rights and contractual liberty of any "person," and corporations counted as persons. So interpreted, the Fourteenth Amendment became by the turn of the century a powerful means of restraining the states in the use of their police powers to regulate private business.

The Supreme Court erected similar barriers against the federal government through a narrow reading of the Constitution. In 1895 the Court ruled that the federal power to regulate interstate commerce did not cover manufacturing, and struck down a federal income tax law. And over matters where federal power was undeniable—such as the regulation of railroads—the Supreme Court watched like a hawk for undue interferences with the rights of property.

Power conferred status. The law, not politics, attracted the ablest people and held the public's esteem. A Wisconsin judge boasted: "The bench symbolizes on earth the throne of divine justice. . . . Law in its highest sense is the will of God." Judicial supremacy reflected how dominant the ideology of individualism had become in industrial America, and also how low American politicians had fallen in the esteem of their countrymen.

Cultural Politics

Yet for all the criticism leveled against it, politics figured centrally in the nation's life. Proportionately more voters turned out in presidential elections from 1876 to 1892 than at any other time in American history. People voted Democratic or Republican for a lifetime. National conventions attracted huge crowds. "The excitement, the mental and physical strains," remarked an Indiana Republican after the 1888 convention, "are surpassed only by prolonged battle in actual warfare, as I have been told by officers of the Civil War who latter engaged in convention struggles." The convention he described had nominated the colorless Benjamin Harrison on a routine platform. What was all the excitement about?

For one thing, politics was a lively part of the nation's culture. During the election season the party faithful marched in impressive torchlight parades. Party paraphernalia flooded the country—handkerchiefs, mugs, posters, and buttons imprinted with the Democratic donkey or the Republican elephant, symbols that had been adopted in the 1870s. In 1888 the presidential hopefuls were pictured on cards, like baseball players, packed into Honest Long Cut tobacco. Campaigns had the suspense of baseball pennant races, plus the excitement of the circus coming to town. In an age before movies and radio, politics ranked as one of the great American forms of mass entertainment.

Party loyalty was a deadly serious matter, however. Long after the Civil War, emotions remained high. Among family friends in Cleveland, recalled the urban reformer Brand Whitlock, the Republican party was "a synonym for patriotism, another name for the nation. It was inconceivable that any self-respecting person should be a Democrat." Or, in the South, that any self-respecting person could be a Republican.

Beyond these sectional differences, the most important determinants of party loyalty were religion and ethnicity. Statistically, northern Democrats tended to be foreign-born and Catholic, while Republicans tended to be native-born and Protestant. Among Protestants, the more *pietistic* a person's faith—that is, the more personal and direct the believer's relationship to God—the more likely he or she was to be a Republican, and to favor using the powers of the state to regulate individual behavior.

During the 1880s ethnic tensions began to build up in many cities. One issue was the place of foreign languages in the schools. Immigrant groups, especially the Germans, wanted their children taught in their own languages. In

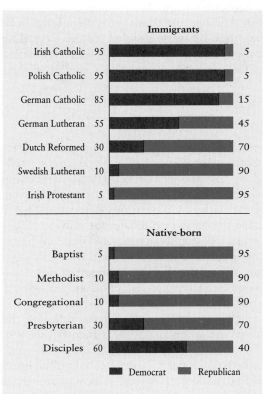

FIGURE 19.1

Ethnocultural Voting Patterns in the Midwest, 1870–1892

These figures demonstrate how voting patterns among midwesterners reflected ethnicity and religion in the late nineteenth century. Especially striking is the overwhelming preference by immigrant Catholics for the Democratic party. Among Protestants there was an equally strong preference for the Republican party by certain groups of immigrants (Swedish Lutherans and Irish Protestants) and native-born (Free Will Baptists, Methodists, and Congregationalist), but other Protestant groups were more evenly divided in their party preferences.

response, native-born Americans passed laws making English the language of instruction. Religion was an even more explosive educational issue. Catholics fought a losing battle over public aid for parochial schools. By 1900 such aid had been prohibited by twenty-three states. In Boston a furious controversy broke out in 1888 over the use of an anti-Catholic history textbook. When the school board withdrew the offending book, angry Protestants mounted a campaign to throw the moderates off the board and return the text to the curriculum.

Then there was the question of public morals. In many states so-called blue laws restricted activity on Sundays. When Nebraska banned Sunday baseball, the state supreme court approved the law as a blow struck in "the contest between Christianity and wrong." But German and Irish Catholics, who saw nothing evil in a bit of fun on Sunday, considered blue laws a violation of their personal freedom. Ethnocultural conflict also flared over the liquor question. Many states adopted strict licensing and local-option laws governing the sale and consumption of alcoholic beverages. Indiana permitted drinking, but only joylessly in rooms containing "no devices for amusement or music . . . of any kind."

Because the hottest ethnocultural issues of the day—education, the liquor question, and observance of the Sabbath—were also party issues, they lent deep significance to party affiliation. And because these issues were fought out mostly at the state and local level, they hit very close to home. Crusading Methodists thought of Republicans as the party of morality. For embattled Irish and German Catholics the Democratic party was the defender of their freedoms.

Organizational Politics

Political life was also important because of the remarkable organizational activity it generated. By the 1870s both major parties had evolved formal, well-organized structures. At the base lay the precinct or ward, whose meetings could be attended by all party members. County, state, and national committees ran the ongoing business of the parties. Conventions determined party rules, adopted platforms, and selected the party's candidates for public office.

Party administration seemed, on its face, highly democratic, since in theory all power derived from the party members in the precincts and wards. In practice, however, the parties were run by unofficial internal organizations—*machines*—which consisted of insiders willing to accept discipline and do work in exchange for getting on the public payroll, or pocketing bribes and other forms of "graft." The machines tended toward one-man rule, although the "boss" ruled more by the consent of the secondary leaders than by his own absolute power.

Absorbed in the tasks of power brokerage, party bosses treated public issues as somewhat irrelevant. And the high stakes of money, jobs, and influence made for intense factionalism. After Ulysses S. Grant left the White House in

The Levi P. Morton Association
The top-hatted gentlemen in this photograph constituted the local Republican party organization of Newport, Rhode Island, named in honor of Levi P. Morton, Benjamin Harrison's vice president. The maleness of party politics leaps from the photograph and asserts more clearly than a thousand words why the suffragist demand for the right to vote was met with ridicule and disbelief.

1877, the Republican party divided into two warring factions—the Stalwarts, who followed Senator Roscoe Conkling of New York, and the Halfbreeds, led by James G. Blaine of Maine. The split was sparked by a personal feud between Conkling and Blaine, but it persisted because of a furious struggle over patronage. The Halfbreeds represented a newer Republican generation that was more inclined to pay lip service to political reform, and less committed to the shopworn Civil War issues. But issues were secondary in the war between Stalwarts and Halfbreeds. These factions were really fighting over the spoils of party politics.

And yet the record was not wholly negative. Machine politics raised the standards of governance in certain ways. Disciplined professionals, veterans of machine politics, improved the performance of state legislatures and the Congress. More important, party machines filled a void in the nation's public life. They did informally much of what the governmental system left undone, especially in the cities (see Chapter 20).

But machine politics never managed to win public legitimacy. Many of the nation's social elite—intellectuals, well-to-do businessmen, and old-line families—resented a politics that excluded people like themselves, the "best men." There was, too, a genuine clash of values. Political reformers called for

"disinterestedness" and "independence"—the opposite of the self-serving ca-
reerism and party regularity fostered by the machine system. Many of them
had earned their spurs as Liberal Republicans who had broken from the party
and fought President Grant's reelection in 1872.

In 1884 Carl Schurz, Edwin L. Godkin, and Charles Francis Adams, Jr.,
again left the Republican party because they associated its presidential candidate, James G. Blaine, with corrupt politics. Mainly from New York and Massachusetts, these Republicans became known as Mugwumps—a derisive bit of
contemporary slang, supposedly of Indian origin, referring to pompous or
self-important persons. The Mugwumps threw their support to the Democrat
Grover Cleveland, and may have ensured his victory by providing the margin
for him in New York State.

After the 1884 election, the enthusiasm for reform spilled over into local
politics, spawning good-government campaigns across the country. Although
they won some municipal victories, the Mugwumps were more effective at
molding public opinion. Controlling the respectable newspapers and journals
and strategically placed in the urban world, the Mugwumps defined the terms
of political debate and denied the machine system public legitimacy.

The Mugwumps were reformers, but not on behalf of social justice. The
problems of working people did not evoke their sympathy, nor did they favor
using the powers of the state to ease the suffering of the poor. As far as the
Mugwumps were concerned, that government was best that governed least.
Theirs was the brand of "reform" perfectly in keeping with a politics of the
status quo.

Women's Political Culture

The young Theodore Roosevelt, an up-and-coming Republican state politician in 1884, referred to the Mugwumps contemptuously as "man-milliners"
(makers of ladies' hats). The sexual slur was not accidental. In attacking organizational politics, the Mugwumps were challenging one of the bastions of male
society. At party meetings and conventions, men carried on not only the business of politics, but also the satisfying rituals of male sociability amid cigar
smoke and whiskey. Politics was identified with manliness. It was competitive.
It dealt in the commerce of power. It was frankly self-aggrandizing. Party politics, in short, was no place for a woman.

So, naturally, the woman suffrage movement met fierce opposition in
these years. Blocked in their efforts to get a constitutional amendment, suffragists concentrated on state campaigns. But except in Wyoming, Idaho,
Colorado, and Utah, the most they could win was women's right to vote for
school boards or on tax issues. "Men are ordained to govern in all forceful
and material things, *because they are men*," asserted an antisuffrage resolution,
"while women, by the same decree of God and nature, are equally fitted to
bear rule in a higher and more spiritual realm"—that is to say, not in
politics.

Yet this invocation of the doctrine of "separate spheres" did open a channel for women to enter public life. "Women's place is Home," acknowledged the journalist Retha Childe Dorr. "But Home is not contained within the four walls of an individual house. Home is the community. The city full of people is the Family. . . . And badly do the Home and Family need their mother." So believing, women had since the early nineteenth century engaged in charitable and reform activities. Women's organizations fought prostitution, assisted the poor, agitated for the reform of women's prisons, and tried to expand educational and job opportunities for women. Since many of these goals required state intervention, women's organizations of necessity became politically active, but not, they stressed, out of any desire to participate in partisan politics or to gain the ballot. Quite the contrary: women were bent on creating their own political sphere.

No issue joined home and politics more poignantly than did the liquor question. Just before Christmas in 1873 the women of Hillsboro, Ohio, began to hold vigils in front of the town's saloons, pleading with the owners to close down and end the suffering of families of hard-drinking fathers. Thus began a spontaneous uprising of women that spread across the country and closed an estimated 3,000 saloons. From this agitation came the Woman's Christian Temperance Union (WCTU), which after its formation in 1874 rapidly blossomed into the largest organization of women in the country.

Because it excluded men, the WCTU was the spawning ground for a new generation of women leaders. Under the guidance of Frances Willard, who became president in 1879, the WCTU moved beyond temperance and adopted a "Do-Everything" policy. Alcoholism, women recognized, was not simply a personal failing; it stemmed from larger social problems in American society. Willard also wanted to attract women who had no particular interest in the liquor question. By 1889 the WCTU had thirty-nine departments concerned with labor, social purity, health, and international peace as well as temperance.

Most important, the WCTU was drawn to woman suffrage. This was necessary, Willard argued, "because the liquor traffic is entrenched in law, and law grows out of the will of majorities, and majorities of women are against the liquor traffic." Women needed the vote, said Willard, to fulfill their social responsibilities *as women*. This was very different from the claim made by the suffragists—that the ballot was an inherent right of all citizens *as individuals*—and was less threatening to masculine pride.

Not much changed in the short run. But by linking women's social concerns to women's political participation, the WCTU helped lay the groundwork for a fresh attack on male electoral politics in the early twentieth century. And in the meantime, even without the vote, the WCTU demonstrated how potent a voice women could find in the public arena, and how energetic a political culture they could build.

THE CRISIS OF AMERICAN POLITICS: THE 1890s

Ever since the end of Reconstruction in 1877 national politics had been stalemated by two evenly balanced parties. This equilibrium finally began to break down late in the 1880s. Benjamin Harrison's election to the presidency in 1888 was the last of the cliff-hanger victories: the Democratic candidate, Grover Cleveland, actually got a larger popular vote. Thereafter, the tide went heavily against the Republicans. In 1890 Democrats took the House of Representatives decisively, capturing 235 seats to the Republicans' 88, and won a number of governorships in normally Republican states. In 1892 Cleveland regained the presidency by the largest margin in twenty years.

Had everything else remained equal, the events of 1890 and 1892 might have opened a long period of Democratic supremacy. But everything else did not remain equal. By the time of Cleveland's inauguration, rising farm foreclosures and railroad bankruptcies signaled economic trouble. On May 3, 1893, the stock market crashed. In Chicago 100,000 jobless workers walked the streets; nationwide, the unemployment rate soared to over 20 percent. As always in hard times, suffering and unrest mounted alarmingly.

As the economic crisis of the 1890s set in, which party would prevail, and on what platform, became an open question. The first challenge arrived from the West and the South, where the grievances of farmers had begun to crystallize into the radical program of the Populist party.

The Populist Revolt

Farmers were of necessity joiners. They needed organization to overcome their social isolation and to obtain crucial economic services—hence the enormous appeal of the Granger movement, which had spread across the Midwest after 1867, and, after its decline, of the farmers' alliances that began to spring up among southern and western farmers. From scattered organizational beginnings, two dominant organizations emerged. One was the Farmers' Alliance of the Northwest, which was confined mainly to the midwestern states. More dynamic was the National (or Southern) Farmers' Alliance, which in the mid-1880s spread rapidly from Texas onto the Great Plains and eastward into the cotton South, as "travelling lecturers" extolled the virtues of cooperative activity and reminded farmers of "their obligation to stand as a great conservative body against the encroachments of monopolies and . . . the growing corruption of wealth and power." While thus recapitulating Granger resentment against railroads and merchants that had fueled earlier third-party movements, the alliances conceived of themselves as agents of social and economic reform, rather than as new political parties.

The Texas Alliance established a massive cooperative, the Texas Exchange, that marketed the crops of cotton farmers and provided them with cheap

En Route to a Populist Rally, Dickinson County, Kansas
Farm people traveled miles to rallies and meetings for the chance to voice their grievances and socialize with like-minded folks. This tradition infused Populism with a special fervor. Gatherings such as the one these Kansans were heading for were a visible sign of what Populism meant—a movement of the "people."

credit. When cotton prices fell sharply in 1891, the Texas Exchange failed. The Texas Alliance then proposed a new scheme: a *subtreasury system* that would enable farmers to store their crops in public warehouses. Farmers would be able to borrow against those crops from a federally supplied fund at low interest rates until prices rose enough so their cotton could be profitably marketed. The subtreasury plan would provide the same credit and marketing functions as had the defunct Texas Exchange, but with a crucial difference: the federal government would play the key role. When the subtreasury plan was rejected by the Democratic party as too radical, the Texas Alliance decided to strike out in politics independently.

These events in Texas revealed, with special clarity, a process of politicization that went on throughout the Alliance movement. Across the South and the West, as state alliances grew stronger and more impatient, they began to field independent slates. In 1890 third parties won control of the Nebraska and Kansas legislatures and in the South captured several governorships and eight state legislatures. These successes led to the formation of the national People's (Populist) party in 1892. In the elections that year, with the veteran third-party campaigner James B. Weaver as their presidential candidate, the Populists captured a million votes and carried four western states

AMERICAN VOICES

Angry Farmers

*I*n his testimony Datus E. Meyer, a Minnesota farmer, details the farmers' griev-
*ances against the railroads. But underlying is his sense of the farmers as victims
of powers beyond their control—hence the demand for government intervention that
was one of the hallmarks of Populism.*

St. Paul, Minnesota, June 25 1885

Mr. Meyer. There is very great discontent among the smaller farmers of
the State in regard to [the railroads]. . . . I can produce for you freight
receipts that will show where car-loads of stuff have been brought from
Springfield, Ohio, to Saint Paul at a charge of $65, a distance of about
800 miles, and carried to Saint Vincent, a distance of about 400 miles,
and charged $155. . . . Then there were discriminations proved [that]
they absolutely refused to allow a small farmer to have a car at all, in
which to load his corn and ship it away, unless he put it through that elevator system . . . on account of having given the exclusive privilege to
those elevator lines. . . .

You know how hard farmers are to organize; and yet there are over
three hundred secret organizations in this State, organized for the purpose of obtaining redress. . . .

The Chairman. They have a right now to go into court and sue if they
are charged an unreasonable rate?

Mr. Meyer. That is true. But suppose a farmer sues under the common
law. The railroads have their attorneys hired and paid for all the time,
and they can carry that suit on until an ordinary farmer is ruined. He
cannot contend with the railroads.

The Chairman. What would you have done?

Mr. Meyer. I would put a commission between the farmer and the
railroads that would see that he obtains justice. That is what I would
have done, and what the farmers desire shall be done. You can depend
on that.

SOURCE: U.S. Senate, Select Committee on Interestate Commerce, *Report*, 49 Cong., 1 Sess. (1886), Part 2, 1335–1337,
reprinted in Stanley I. Kutler, ed., *Looking for America* (2d ed., New York: W. W. Norton, 1975), II, 171–174.

(see Map 19.1). For the first time agrarian protest truly challenged the national two-party system.

The challenge was driven as much by ideology as by the quest for political
power. Populism contained a strong radical bent. The problems afflicting farmers, Populists felt, could stem only from some basic evil. They identified this evil
as the "money power" that controlled the levers of the economic system. "There

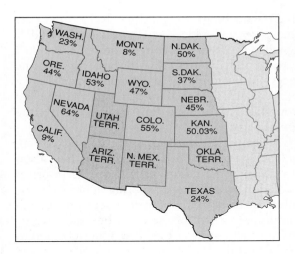

MAP 19.1

The Heyday of Western Populism, 1892

This map shows the percentage of the popular vote won by James B. Weaver, the People's party candidate, in the presidential election of 1892. Except for California and Montana, the Populists won broad support across the West and genuinely threatened the established parties in that region.

are but two sides," proclaimed a Populist manifesto. "On the one side are the allied hosts of monopolies, the money power, great trusts and railroad corporations. . . . On the other are the farmers, laborers, merchants and all the people who produce wealth. . . . Between these two there is no middle ground."

By this reasoning, farmers and workers formed a single producer class. Thus the Texas-based alliance renamed itself in 1889 the National Farmers' Alliance and Industrial Union. The title was not merely empty rhetoric. Organized in Knights of Labor assemblies, Texas railroad workers and Colorado miners cooperated with the farmers' alliances, got their support in strikes, and actively participated in forming state Populist parties. In its explicit class appeal—in recognizing that "the irrepressible conflict between capital and labor is upon us"—Populism parted company from the two mainstream parties.

Populism was distinguished also by the many women in the movement. In the established parties, the grass-roots organizations—the local political clubs—were for men only. Populism, on the other hand, arose from a network of suballiances that had formed for largely social purposes and that welcomed women. Although women were active as speakers and lecturers, few of them achieved high office in the alliances, and their role diminished with the formation of the Populist party. In deference to the southern wing, the party platform was silent on woman suffrage. Still, neither Democrats nor Republicans would have countenanced a spokeswoman such as the fiery Mary Elizabeth Lease, who became famous for calling on farmers "to raise less corn and more hell." Lease insisted just as strenuously on Populism's "grand and holy mission . . . to place the mothers of this nation on an equality with the fathers."

In an age dominated by laissez-faire doctrine, what most distinguished Populism from the major parties was its positive attitude toward the state. The Populist program declared: "We believe that the powers of government—in other words, of the people—should be expanded as rapidly and as far as the good sense of an intelligent people and the teachings of experience shall justify, to the end that oppression, injustice and poverty should eventually cease in the land."

The Omaha platform, adopted at the founding convention in 1892, called for nationalization of the railroads and communications; protection of the land, including natural resources, from monopoly and foreign ownership; a graduated income tax; the Texas Alliance's subtreasury plan; and the free and unlimited coinage of silver. From this array of issues, free silver emerged as the overriding demand of the Populist party.

In the early 1890s rock-bottom prices wreaked havoc among cotton, wheat, and corn growers. Under this pressure, farmers turned to free silver, which they hoped would, by increasing the money supply, raise farm prices and give them some relief. In addition, free silver would bring in hefty contributions from silver-mining interests. These mine operators, scornful though they might be of Populist radicalism, yearned for the day when the government would buy at a premium price all the silver they could produce, and to that end they were prepared to support the Populists.

Free silver was opposed by urban social democrats such as Henry Demarest Lloyd of Chicago and by agrarian radicals such as Georgia's Tom Watson. They pleaded that free silver not be made the leading party issue because it would undercut the broader Populist program and drive away wage earners, who had no enthusiasm for inflationary measures. Any chance of a farmer-labor alliance that might transform Populism into an American version of a social-democratic party would be doomed. As Lloyd complained, free silver was "the cowbird of reform," stealing in and taking over the nest that others had built.

Although fiercely debated within the party, the outcome was never in doubt: the political appeal of free silver was simply too great. But once Populists made that choice, they had fatally compromised their party's capacity to maintain an independent existence. For free silver was not an issue over which the Populists held a monopoly. Free silver was, on the contrary, a question at the very center of mainstream politics in the 1890s.

Money and Politics

In a rapidly developing economy, such as nineteenth-century America's, the money supply is bound to be a big political issue. Money has to increase rapidly enough to meet the economy's needs, or growth will be stifled. How fast the money supply should grow, however, is a question that creates sharp divisions. Debtors and producers of goods want a larger money supply: more money in circulation inflates prices and reduces the real cost of borrowing. The "sound-money" people—creditors, individuals on fixed incomes, people in the slower-growing sectors of the economy—have an opposite interest.

Civil War policies had very much magnified the money question. Before the war, the main source of the nation's money supply had been the banknotes issued by several thousand state banks. The Banking Act of 1863, however, sharply curtailed the freedom of these banks to create money. The economic impact of this nationalizing action was not immediately felt because the Lincoln administration itself was printing large amounts of paper money—greenbacks, so-called—to finance the Civil War. Afterward, however, the sound money interests lobbied powerfully for a return to the bimetallic policy prevailing ever since the founding of the Republic, which was to base the federal currency on the amount of *specie*—gold and silver—held by the U.S. Treasury. The issue was hotly contested for a decade, but in 1875 the inflationists were defeated, and the circulation of greenbacks as legal tender—that is, backed by nothing more than the good faith of the federal government—came to an end. With the state banknotes also in short supply, the country entered an era of chronic deflation and tight credit.

This was the context out of which the silver question emerged. The country had always operated on a bimetallic standard, but the supply of silver had gradually tightened and, as it became more valuable as metal than as money, silver disappeared from circulation. In 1873 silver was officially dropped as a medium of exchange. Soon afterward, great silver discoveries occurred in the West; silver prices fell. Inflationists began to agitate for a resumption of the traditional bimetallic policy: at the ratio of sixteen to one, silver would flow into the Treasury and greatly expand the volume of currency.

With so much at stake for so many people, the currency question became one of the staples of post-Reconstruction politics. Twice the prosilver coalition in Congress won modest victories. First, under the Bland-Allison Act of 1878, the U.S. Treasury was required to purchase and coin between $2 million and $4 million worth of silver each month. Then, in the more sweeping Sherman Silver Purchase Act of 1890, an additional 4.5 million ounces of silver bullion was to be purchased monthly, to serve as the basis for new issues of U.S. Treasury notes.

These legislative battles, although hard-fought, cut across party lines in the characteristic fashion of post-Reconstruction politics. In the early 1890s, silver suddenly became a defining issue between the parties; in particular, it had a radicalizing effect on the Democratic party.

When the crash of 1893 hit, the Democrats held power in Washington. The party in office usually gets blamed if the economy falters, but President Cleveland made things worse for the Democrats. When jobless marchers arrived in Washington in 1894 to appeal for federal relief, Cleveland's response was to disperse them forcibly and arrest their leader, Jacob S. Coxey. Cleveland's brutal handling of the Pullman strike further alienated the labor vote. Nor was he able to deliver on his campaign promise for tariff reform. He lost control of the battle when the unpopular McKinley Tariff of 1890 came up for revision in Congress. The resulting Wilson-Gorman Tariff of 1894, which he allowed to pass into law without his signature, caved in to special interests and left the most important rates largely unchanged.

Most disastrous, however, was Cleveland's rigidity on the silver question. Cleveland was a committed sound-money man. Nothing that happened after the depression set in—not collapsing prices, not the suffering of farmers, not the groundswell of support for free silver within his own party—budged Cleveland.

The Election of 1896

At their national convention in Chicago in 1896, the Democrats repudiated Cleveland and turned left. The leader of the triumphant silver Democrats was William Jennings Bryan of Nebraska. Bryan was a political phenomenon. Only thirty-six years old, he had already served two terms in Congress and become a passionate advocate of free silver. He was a skilled politician, and no less important, an inspiring public speaker. Bryan, remarked the journalist Frederic Howe, was "pre-eminently an evangelist . . . the *vox ex cathedra* of the Western self-righteous missionary mind." With biblical fervor, Bryan swept up his audiences when he joined the debate on free silver at the Democratic convention. He locked up the presidential nomination with a stirring attack on the gold standard: "You shall not press down upon the brow of labor this crown of thorns, you shall not crucify mankind on a cross of gold."

Bryan's nomination meant that the Democrats had become the party of free silver; his "cross of gold" speech meant that the money question would turn into a national crusade. No one could be neutral on this defining issue. Silver Republicans bolted their party; gold Democrats went for a splinter Democratic ticket or supported the Republican party. Even the Prohibition party split into gold and silver wings. The Populists, meeting after the Democratic convention, accepted Bryan as their candidate. The free-silver issue had become so vital that they could not do otherwise. Although they nominated their own vice-presidential candidate, the Georgian Tom Watson, the Populists found themselves for all practical purposes absorbed into the Democratic silver crusade.

The Republicans took up the challenge. Their key party leader was Mark Hanna, a wealthy Cleveland ironmaker, a brilliant political manager, and an exponent of the new industrial capitalism. Hanna orchestrated an unprecedented money-raising campaign among America's corporate interests. His candidate, William McKinley of Ohio, personified the virtues of Republicanism, standing solidly for high tariffs, honest money, and prosperity. While Bryan broke with tradition and crisscrossed the country in a furious whistle-stop campaign, the dignified McKinley received delegations at his home in Canton, Ohio. Bryan orated with moral fervor; McKinley talked of industrial progress and a full dinner pail.

Not since 1860 had the United States witnessed such a hard-fought election over such high stakes. For the middle class, sound money stood symbolically for the soundness of the social order. With jobless workers tramping the streets and bankrupt farmers up in arms, Bryan's fervent assault on the gold standard struck fear in many hearts. Republicans denounced the Democratic platform as "revolutionary and anarchistic," and Bryan's supporters as "social misfits who have almost nothing in common but opposition to the existing order and institutions."

McKinley won handily, with 271 electoral votes to Bryan's 176. He kept the ground Republicans had regained in the 1894 midterm elections and pushed into Democratic strongholds, especially in the cities. Boston, New York, Chicago, and Minneapolis, all taken by Cleveland in 1892, went for

McKinley in 1896. Bryan ran strongly only in the South, in silver-mining states, and in the Populist West. But the gains his evangelical style brought him in some Republican rural areas did not compensate for his losses in traditionally Democratic urban districts.

The paralyzing equilibrium of American politics ended in 1896. The Republicans had skillfuly handled both the economic and the cultural challenges. They persuaded the nation that they were the party of prosperity and shifted some of the burdens of morality politics onto the Democrats. The Republicans had become the nation's majority party. In 1896, too, electoral politics regained its place as an arena for national debate, setting the stage for the reform politics of the Progressive Era.

RACE AND POLITICS IN THE SOUTH

When Reconstruction ended in 1877, so did the hopes of African-Americans that they would enjoy the equal rights of citizenship promised them by the Fourteenth and Fifteenth amendments. Schools were strictly segregated. Access to jobs, to justice, and to social welfare was racially determined and unequal. But segregation in public accommodations was not yet legally required, and practices varied a good deal across the South. Only on railroads, as travel became more common, did whites begin to demand that blacks be excluded from first-class cars, with the result that southern railroads became after 1887 the first public accommodation subject to segregation laws.

In politics, the situation was even more fluid. Blacks had not been driven from politics. On the contrary, their turnout at elections was not far from that of whites. But blacks did not participate on equal terms with whites. In the Black Belt areas, where African-Americans sometimes outnumbered whites, voting districts were gerrymandered (redivided) to ensure that while blacks got some offices, political control remained in white hands. Blacks, moreover, were routinely intimidated during political campaigns. Even so, an impressive majority remained staunchly Republican, refusing, as the last black Congressman from Mississippi told his House colleagues in 1882, "to surrender their honest convictions, even upon the altar of their personal necessities."

Whatever hope blacks entertained for better days, however, faded during the 1880s and then, in the next decade, expired in a terrible burst of racist terrorism.

Biracial Politics

No democratic society can survive if it does not enable competing economic and social interests to be heard. In the United States the two-party system performs that role. The Civil War crisis severely tested the two-party system, because, in both the North and the South, political opposition came to be seen as treasonous. In the victorious North, despite the best efforts of the Republicans, the Democrats shed their disgrace and reclaimed their status as a major party. In the defeated South, however, the scars of war cut deep, and

Reconstruction cut even deeper. The struggle for "home rule" empowered southern Democrats. They had "redeemed" the South from Republican domination, hence the name they adopted: Redeemers. Cloaked in the mantle of the Lost Cause, the Redeemers claimed a monopoly on political legitimacy.

The Republican party did not fold up, however. On the contrary, it soldiered on, sustained by strong black loyalty, by a hard core of white support, by patronage from Republican national administrations, and by a key Democrat weakness. This was the gap between the universality the Democrats claimed as the party of Redemption and the reality that the party was controlled by an economic elite indifferent to the plight of poor whites.

Class antagonism, although often muted by sectional patriotism, was never absent from southern society. The Civil War had brought out long-smoldering differences between hill-country farmers and planters. Fresh sources of conflict now arose from the sharecropping system—which increasingly included whites as well as blacks—and from an emerging industrial working class. In the late 1880s, agrarian discontent boiled over, welling out of the farmers' alliances that sprang up across the South and spawning a formidable Populist challenge to Redeemer rule.

What distinguished the South was not that it experienced intense agrarian protest—so did the West—but that this agrarian challenge provoked a crisis in the South's one-party system. Refusing to accept any opposition as legitimate, the ruling Democrats stuffed ballot boxes, intimidated black voters, murdered opponents, and stirred up racial hatred by shouting "Negro domination!"

But Populists were themselves uneasy about black participation. Racism cut through southern white society and, so some thought, most infected the lowest rungs. "The white laboring classes here," wrote an Alabaman in 1886, "are separated from the Negroes, working all day side by side with them, by an innate consciousness of race superiority," which "excites a sentiment of sympathy and equality with the classes above them, and in this way becomes a healthy social leaven." Yet when times got bad enough, hard-pressed whites could also see blacks as fellow victims. "They are in the ditch just like we are," asserted one white Texan. Southern Populists never fully reconciled these contradictory impulses. They never questioned the conventions of social inequality. But once agrarian protest turned political, the logic of racial solidarity became hard to deny.

Kept out of the Southern Alliance, black farmers had organized separately into the Colored Farmers' Alliance, gaining thereby a certain amount of leverage with the emerging Populist movement. The realities of partisan politics, once the alliances turned against the conservative Democrats, clinched the argument for interracial unity. Where the Populists fused with the Republican party, as in North Carolina and Tennessee, they automatically became allies of black leaders and gained a black constituency. Where fusion did not happen and the Populists fielded independent tickets, they needed to appeal to black voters. "The accident of color can make no difference in the interest of farmers, croppers, and laborers," argued the Georgian Tom Watson. "You are kept apart that you may be separately fleeced of your earnings." By making this interracial appeal, even if not always wholeheartedly, the Populists put at risk the foundations of conservative southern politics.

White Reaction

The conservative Democrats played the race card to the hilt, parading as the "white man's party" while denouncing the Populists for courting "Negro rule." Yet they shamelessly competed for the black vote. In this, they had many advantages: money; control of the local power structures; a paternalistic relationship to the black community. When all else failed, mischief at the polls enabled the Democrats to beat back the Populists. Thus the Mississippian Frank Burkitt's bitter attack on the conservatives: they were "a class of corrupt office-seekers" who had "hypocritically raised the howl of white supremacy while they debauched the ballot boxes . . . disregarded the rights of the blacks . . . and actually dominated the will of the white people through the instrumentality of the stolen negro vote."

In the midst of these deadly struggles the Democrats decided to settle matters once and for all. An effort to disfranchise the blacks, hitherto hesitant, now turned into a potent section-wide movement (see Map 19.2). In 1890

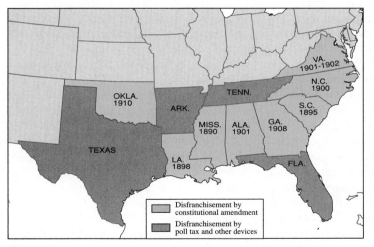

MAP 19.2

Disfranchisement in the South
In the midst of the Populist challenge to Democratic rule in the South, a movement to deprive blacks of the right to vote spread across the South. By 1910 every southern state except Tennessee, Arkansas, Texas, and Florida had made constitutional changes designed to prevent blacks from voting, and these four states accomplished much the same result through other methods. For the next half century the political process in the South would be for whites only.

Mississippi adopted a literacy test that effectively drove blacks out of politics. The motives behind it were cynical, but the literacy test could be dressed up as a reform for Mississippians tired of electoral fraud and violence. Their children and grandchildren, argued one influential figure, should not be left "with shotguns in their hands, a lie in their mouths and perjury on their lips in order to defeat the negroes." This logic even persuaded some weary Populists: Frank Burkitt, for example, was arguing *for* the Mississippi literacy test in the words quoted in the previous paragraph.

The race issue had helped to bring down the Populists; now it helped reconcile them to defeat. Embittered poor whites, deeply ambivalent all along about interracial cooperation, turned their fury on the blacks. Insofar as disfranchising measures asserted militant white supremacy, poor whites approved. It was important, of course, that they themselves be partially protected by lenient enforcement and by exemptions. But poor whites were not protected from property and poll-tax requirements, and many stopped voting.

Poor whites might have objected more had their spokesmen not been given a voice within the Democratic party. A new brand of southern politician came forward to speak for them. Tom Watson, the fiery Georgia Populist, rebuilt his political career as a brilliant practitioner of race baiting. Starting in the early 1900s, he and other racial demagogues thrived throughout the South.

The color line, hitherto incomplete, became rigid and comprehensive. Segregated seating in trains, widely adopted in the late 1880s, provided a precedent for the legal separation of the races. The enforcing legislation, known as Jim Crow laws, soon applied to every type of public facility—restaurants, hotels, streetcars, even cemeteries. In the 1890s the South became for the first time a society fully segregated by law.

The U.S. Supreme Court soon ratified the South's decision. In the case of *Plessy v. Ferguson* (1896) the Court ruled that segregation was not *discriminatory*—that is, it did not violate black civil rights under the Fourteenth Amendment—provided that blacks received accommodations equal to those of whites. The "separate but equal" doctrine of course had little regard for the realities of southern life: segregated facilities were rarely if ever "equal" in any material sense, and segregation was itself intended to underscore the inferiority of blacks. With a similar disregard for reality, the Supreme Court in *Williams v. Mississippi* (1898) validated the disfranchising devices of the southern states: so long as race was not a specified criterion for disfranchisement, the Fifteenth Amendment was not being violated even though the practical effect was the virtual exclusion of blacks from politics in the South.

Race hatred became an accepted part of southern life, manifested in a wave of lynchings and race riots and in the public abuse of blacks. For example, Benjamin R. Tillman, governor of South Carolina and after 1895 a U.S. senator, denounced blacks as "an ignorant and debased and debauched race." This ugly racism came from several sources, including job competition between whites

When C. H. Johnson, a porter at an auction house, spoke up before a visiting Senate committtee in 1883, the movement for a segregated South was just gathering steam. But even then, Johnson makes clear, southern blacks were not deceived about the fraudulence of "separate but equal."

Columbus, Ga., November 20, 1883

Question. Do you feel as though your people have had a fair chance to be heard by the committee?

Answer. I do. . . .

Q. And you think they have said all they want to say?

A. Well, I won't say that they did that. . . . It is just like as it was in the time of slavery . . . and they have got the same feelings now, a great many of them, and they want to say things, but they are afraid of the white people. . . .

Q. What do you mean by social equality?

A. . . . If I get on the cars to ride from here to Montgomery, or to Atlanta, although I pay the same fare that you pay—they make me do that—I do not have the same accommodations.

Q. Suppose you have a car just as good as the one white folks have, but are not allowed to go into their car, will that be satisfactory?

A. But that is not going to be done. They are not going to make a law of that kind. . . .

Q. That would be a different case. I am supposing a case where the accommodations provided for the two races are just the same.

A. . . . I would be satisfied. But don't allow a man to come in over my wife, or any other lady that respects herself as a lady, swearing and spitting and cursing around. . . . I do not want to kick up a fuss with any one, or with white people about getting in amongst them . . . but if a colored man comes along and pays the same fare that the white man pays, he has the same rights as the white man. . . .

SOURCE: U.S. Senate, Committee on the Relations between Capital and Labor, Report (1885), IV, 635–638, reprinted in Stanley I. Kutler, ed., Looking for America (2d ed., New York: W.W. Norton, 1979), II, 234–238.

and blacks during the depressed 1890s, and white anger against a less submissive black generation born after slavery.

But what had triggered the antiblack offensive was the political crisis in the South over Populism. From then on, white supremacy propped up the one-party system that the Redeemers had been fighting for ever since Reconstruction. If the southern elite had to share political power with demagogic poor

white leaders such as Tom Watson, it would be on terms agreeable to them—
the exclusion from the political arena of any serious challenge to the economic
status quo.

The Black Response

Southern blacks in many places resisted white oppression as best they could.
When Georgia adopted the first Jim Crow law applying to streetcars in 1891,
Atlanta blacks declared a boycott, and over the next fifteen years blacks boy-
cotted segregated streetcars in at least twenty-five cities. "Do not trample on our
pride by being 'jim crowed,'" the Savannah *Tribune* urged its readers: "Walk!" Ida
Wells-Barnett emerged as the most outspoken black crusader against lynching,
so enraging the Memphis white community by the editorials in her newspaper
Free Speech that she was forced to leave the city in 1892. Some blacks were
drawn to the Back-to-Africa movement, despairing of ever finding justice in
America. But emigration was not a real choice, and African-Americans everywhere had to bend to the raging forces of racism, and find a way to survive.

Booker T. Washington, the foremost black leader of his day, marked out the
path in a famous speech in Atlanta in 1895. Washington retreated from the
defiant stand of an older generation of black abolitionists exemplified by Frederick Douglass, who died the same year that the Atlanta speech launched
Washington into national prominence. Washington was conciliatory toward
the South; it was a society that blacks understood and loved. He considered
"the agitation of the question of social equality the extremest folly." Washington accepted segregation, provided that blacks had equal facilities. He accepted literacy tests and property qualifications for the vote, provided that
they applied equally to blacks and whites.

Washington's doctrine came to be known as the Atlanta Compromise. His
approach was "accommodationist," in the sense that it avoided a direct assault
on white supremacy. Despite the humble face he put on before white audiences, however, Washington did not concede the struggle. Behind the scenes
he did his best to resist Jim Crow laws and disfranchisement. More important,
his Atlanta Compromise, while abandoning the field of political protest,
opened up a second front of economic struggle.

Booker T. Washington sought to capitalize on a southern dilemma about
the economic role of the black population. Racist dogma dictated that blacks
be kept down, effectively reinforcing their image as lazy, shiftless workers. But
for the South to prosper, it needed an efficient labor force. Washington made
this need the target of his efforts. As founder of the Tuskegee Institute in Alabama in 1881, Washington advocated *industrial education*—manual and agricultural training. He preached the virtues of thrift, hard work, and property
ownership. Washington's industrial education program won generous support
from northern philanthropists and businessmen.

Washington assumed that black economic progress would be the key to
winning political and civil rights. He regarded members of the white southern

Booker T. Washington
In an age of severe racial oppression, Washington emerged as the acknowledged leader of blacks in the United States. He was remarkable both as spokesman to white Americans and for his deep understanding of the aspirations of black Americans. Born a slave, Washington suffered the indignities experienced by all blacks. But he also understood what it took to gain white support—and to maneuver around white hostility—in the black struggle for equality.

elite as crucial allies, because ultimately only they had the power to change the South. More important, they could see "the close connection between labor, industry, education, and political institutions." When it was in their economic interest, when they had grown dependent on black labor and black enterprise, white men of business and property would recognize the justice of black rights. As Washington put it, "There is little race prejudice in the American dollar."

For twenty years after his Atlanta address Booker T. Washington dominated the organized African-American community. In an age of severe racial oppression, no black dealt more skillfully with the elite of white America or wielded greater political influence. Black leaders knew Washington as a hard taskmaster. Intensely jealous of his authority, he did not regard opposition kindly. Black politicians, educators, and editors stood up to him at their peril.

Even so, opposition surfaced after 1900, especially among younger, educated blacks. They thought Washington was conceding too much. He instilled black pride, but of a narrowly middle-class and utilitarian kind. What about the special genius of blacks that W. E. B. Du Bois celebrated in his collection of essays, *The Souls of Black Folk* (1903)? And what of the "talented tenth" of the black population, whose promise could only be stifled by manual education? Blacks also became increasingly impatient with Washington's silence on segregation and lynching. By the time of his death in 1915, Washington's approach had been superseded by a strategy that relied on the courts and political leverage, not on black self-help and accommodation.

CHAPTER 19 TIMELINE

1874	Woman's Christian Temperance Union founded
1877	Rutherford B. Hayes inaugurated; end of Reconstruction
1881	President James A. Garfield assassinated
1883	Pendleton Civil Service Act
1884	Mugwump reformers bolt the Republican party to support Grover Cleveland, first Democrat elected president since 1856
1887	Interstate Commerce Act creates the Interstate Commerce Commission to regulate railroads Florida adopts first law segregating railroad travel
1888	James Bryce's *The American Commonwealth*
1890	The McKinley Tariff Democrats sweep Congressional elections, inaugurating brief era of Democratic party dominance Mississippi becomes first state to adopt literacy test to disfranchise blacks
1892	People's (Populist) Party founded
1893	Panic of 1893 leads to national depression Repeal of Sherman Silver Purchase Act (1890)
1894	Coxey's Army
1895	Booker T. Washington sets out Atlanta Compromise
1896	Election of William McKinley; free-silver campaign crushed *Plessy v. Ferguson* upholds constitutionality of "separate-but-equal" facilities
1897	Economic depression ends

CHAPTER 20

THE RISE OF THE CITY

- Urbanization
- City People
- Upper Class/Middle Class

In 1820 America was a land of farmers. Barely 5 percent of
the people lived in towns or cities. But after that, decade by decade, the urban
population swelled until, by 1900, one of every five Americans lived in cities
of over 100,000 residents. Nearly a tenth of the nation—6.5 million persons—lived in just three great cities: New York, Chicago, and Philadelphia.

The city was the arena of the nation's vibrant economic life. Here the factories went up, and here the new immigrants settled, constituting in 1900
about a third of the residents of major American cities. Here, too, lived the
millionaires and a growing white-collar middle class. For all these people, the
city was more than a place to make a living. It provided the setting for an
urban culture unlike anything seen before in the United States. City people,
although differing vastly among themselves, became distinctively and recog-
nizably urban.

URBANIZATION

The march to the cities seemed inevitable to nineteenth-century Americans.
"The greater part of our population must live in cities," declared the Congre-
gational minister Josiah Strong. "In due time we shall be a nation of cities."
Urbanization became inevitable because of its link to another inevitability of
American life—industrialism.

The Economic Sources of City Growth

Until the Civil War, cities had been centers of commerce, not industry. They were the places where merchants bought and sold goods for distribution into the interior or shipment out to the world market. Early industry, on the other hand, was largely rural because factories needed water power from streams, access to fuel and raw materials, and workers recruited from the countryside.

After midcentury, industry began to move into the city. Once steam engines came along, mill operators no longer needed to locate along streams. In the iron industry coal replaced charcoal as the primary fuel, so iron makers did not have to be near forests. Improved transportation, especially the railroads, enabled businesses to select the best sites in relation to supplies and markets. The result was a geographic concentration of industry. Iron makers gravitated to Pittsburgh because of its access not only to coal and iron ore, but also to markets for iron and steel products. Chicago, ideally located between livestock suppliers and consuming markets, became a great meat-packing center in the 1870s.

As factories became bigger, their size contributed to urban growth. A plant that employed thousands of workers instantly created a small city in its vicinity, sometimes a company town like Aliquippa, Pennsylvania, which became body and soul the property of the Jones and Laughlin Steel Company. Many firms set up their plants near a large city so they could draw on its labor supply and transportation facilities, as George Pullman did when he

TABLE 20.1

Ten Largest Cities by Population, 1870 and 1910

1870		1910	
City	Population	City	Population
1. New York	942,292	New York	4,766,883
2. Philadelphia	674,022	Chicago	2,185,283
3. Brooklyn★	419,921	Philadelphia	1,549,008
4. St. Louis	310,864	St. Louis	687,029
5. Chicago	298,977	Boston	670,585
6. Baltimore	267,354	Cleveland	560,663
7. Boston	250,526	Baltimore	558,485
8. Cincinnati	216,239	Pittsburgh	533,905
9. New Orleans	191,418	Detroit	465,766
10. San Francisco	149,473	Buffalo	423,715

★Brooklyn was consolidated with New York in 1898.
SOURCE: U.S. Census data.

located his sleeping-car works southwest of Chicago. Sometimes these outlying industrial towns were absorbed into the nearby metropolis, as happened to Pullman.

The established commercial cities also became more industrial. Warehouse districts could readily be converted to small-scale manufacturing; a distribution network and transportation facilities were right at hand. In addition, as gateways for immigrants, port cities offered abundant cheap labor. Boston, Philadelphia, Baltimore, and San Francisco became hives of small-scale, labor-intensive industrial activity. New York's enormous pool of immigrant workers made that city a magnet for the garment trades, cigar making, and light industry. New York was, in fact, the nation's largest producer of manufactured goods.

City Building

The commercial cities of the early nineteenth century had been compact places, densely settled around a harbor or along a river. As late as 1850, when it had 565,000 people, greater Philadelphia covered only 10 square miles. From the foot of Chestnut Street on the Delaware River a person could walk to almost anywhere in the city within forty-five minutes. Thereafter, as it developed, Philadelphia spilled out and, like American cities everywhere, engulfed the surrounding countryside.

A downtown area emerged, usually in what had been the original commercial city. Downtown in turn broke up into shopping, financial, warehousing, manufacturing, hotel and entertainment, and red-light districts. Although somewhat fluid at their edges, all these districts were well-defined areas of specialized activity. Moving out from the center, industrial development tended to follow the arteries of transportation—railroads, canals, and rivers—and, at the city's outskirts, to create concentrations of heavy industry.

While highly congested at the center, American cities actually had lower densities than European cities: 22 persons per acre for fifteen American cities in 1890, for example, versus 157.6 per acre for a comparable group of German cities. Given this difference, the development of efficient urban transportation had a much higher priority in the United States than in Europe.

The first innovation, dating back to the 1820s, was the omnibus, an elongated version of the horse-drawn carriage. Much more efficient was the horsecar. The key thing was that it ran on iron tracks, so that the car could carry more passengers, move them at a faster clip through congested city streets, and reach out into the suburbs. From the 1840s onward, horsecars were the mainstay of urban transit across America.

Then came the electric trolley car. Its development was the work primarily of Frank J. Sprague, an engineer once employed by Thomas A. Edison. In 1887 Sprague designed an electricity-driven system for Richmond, Virginia: a "trolley" carriage running along an overhead power line was attached by cable to streetcars equipped with an electric motor—hence the name trolley car.

Traffic Jam in Downtown Chicago, 1905
The purpose of urban transit systems was to move masses of people rapidly
and efficiently through the city. However, better transportation brought
more congestion as well, as this scene of gridlock at Randolf and Dearborn
streets in Chicago shows.

After Sprague's success, the trolley swiftly displaced the horsecar and became
the primary means of public transportation for most American cities.

In the great metropolitan centers, however, mounting congestion called
for the removal of public transit from the streets. In 1879 the first elevated
lines went into operation on Sixth and Ninth avenues in New York City.
Powered at first by steam engines, the "els" converted to electricity following
Sprague's success with the trolley. Chicago developed elevated transit most
fully. New York, on the other hand, turned to the subway. Although Boston
opened a short underground line in 1897, it was the completion in 1904 of a
subway running the length of Manhattan that demonstrated the full potential
of the high-speed underground train. Mass transit had become *rapid* transit.

Equally remarkable was the architectural revolution sweeping metropolitan business districts. With steel girders, durable plate glass, and the passenger
elevator available by the 1880s, a wholly new way of construction opened up.
A steel skeleton would support the building, and the walls, previously weight-
bearing, would serve as curtains enclosing the structure; the sky, so to speak,
became the limit.

The first "skyscraper" to be built on this principle was the ten-story Home
Insurance Building (1885) in Chicago. Although this pioneering effort was itself conventional in appearance—it looked just like the other commercial
buildings in the downtown district—its steel-girdered technology liberated

the aesthetic perceptions of American architects. A Chicago school sprang up, dedicated to the design of buildings whose form expressed, rather than masked, their structure and function. The masterpiece of the Chicago school was Louis Sullivan's Carson, Pirie, Scott and Company department store (1904). Chicago pioneered skyscraper construction, but New York, with its unrelenting need for prime downtown space, took the lead after the mid-1890s. Completed in 1913, the fifty-five-story Woolworth Building marked the beginning of the modern Manhattan skyline.

For ordinary citizens, the electric lights that dispelled the gloom of the city at night probably offered the most dramatic evidence that times had changed. The mainstay of city lighting since the early nineteenth century had been gaslight—illuminating gas produced from coal—but, at 12 candlepower, gaslight was too dim to brighten the downtown streets and the city's public spaces. The first use of electricity, when generating technology made it commercially feasible in the 1870s, was for arc lights that illuminated the city streets and public buildings. Electric lighting then entered the American home thanks to Thomas Edison's invention of a serviceable light bulb in 1879. Edison's motto—"Let there be light!"—truly described the experience of the modern city.

Manhattan's First Skyscraper
The Tower Building at 50 Broadway was completed in 1889. To the modern eye, this first New York skyscraper seems modest and old-fashioned. Compared with its squat neighbors, however, it was a revolutionary building based on new principles of slender, soaring architecture.

Before it had any significant effect on industry, electricity gave the city its modern tempo, lifting and lowering elevators, powering streetcars and subway trains, turning night into day. Meanwhile, Alexander Graham Bell's telephone (1876) speeded up communication beyond anything imagined previously. By 1900, 1.5 million telephones were in use, linking urban people into a network of instant communication.

The Private City

City building was very much an exercise in private enterprise. The lure of profit spurred the great innovations—the trolley car, electric lighting, the sky-scraper, the elevator, the telephone—and drove urban real-estate development. The investment opportunities looked so tempting that new cities sprang up almost overnight from the ruins of the Chicago fire of 1871 and the San Francisco earthquake of 1906. Real-estate interests, eager to develop subdivisions, often were instrumental in pushing streetcar lines outward from the central districts of cities.

America produced what the urban historian Sam Bass Warner has called the "private city"—a city shaped primarily by the actions of many private individuals, all pursuing their own goals and bent on making money. The prevailing belief was that the sum of such private activity would far exceed what the community could accomplish through public effort. This meant that the city itself handled only functions that could not be undertaken efficiently or profitably by private enterprise.

Despite that limitation, American cities actually compiled an impressive record in the late nineteenth century. Though by no means free of the corruption and wastefulness of earlier days, city governments became more centralized, better administered, and above all, more expansive in the functions they undertook. Nowhere in the world were there more massive public projects: water aqueducts, sewage systems, street paving, bridge building, extensive park systems.

Yet streets, mainly a matter of convenience for the people, were often filthy. "Three or four days of warm spring weather," remarked a New York journalist, would turn Manhattan's garbage-strewn, snow-clogged streets into "veritable mud rivers." The environment likewise suffered. A visitor to Pittsburgh noted "the heavy pall of smoke which constantly overhangs her . . . until the very sun looks coppery through the sooty haze." As for the lovely hills rising from the rivers, "they have been leveled down, cut into, sliced off, and ruthlessly marred and mutilated." Pittsburgh presented "all that is unsightly and forbidding in appearance, the original beauties of nature having been ruthlessly sacrificed to utility."

It was not that America lacked an urban vision. On the contrary, an abiding rural ideal had exerted a powerful influence on American cities for many years. Frederick Law Olmsted, who designed New York's Central Park before the Civil War and many other city parks in later years, wanted cities that exposed people to the beauties of nature. One of Olmsted's projects, the

Chicago World's Fair of 1893, gave rise to the influential "City Beautiful" movement. The results included larger park systems; broad boulevards and parkways; and, after the turn of the century, zoning laws and planned suburbs.

But cities usually heeded urban planners too little and far too late. "Fifteen or twenty years ago a plan might have been adopted that would have made this one of the most beautiful cities in the world," Kansas City's park commissioners reported in 1893. At that time, "such a policy could not be fully appreciated." Nor, even if Kansas City had foreseen its future, would it have shouldered the "heavy burden" of trying to shape its development. The American city had placed its faith in the dynamics of the marketplace, not the restraints of a planned future.

Hardest hit by urban growth were the poor. In earlier times low-income city residents had lived in makeshift wooden structures in the alleys and back streets and, increasingly, in the subdivided homes of more prosperous families that had fled to better neighborhoods. When rising land values after the Civil War made this practice unprofitable, speculators began to build housing specifically designed for the urban masses. In New York City, the dreadful result was five- or six-story tenements housing twenty or more families in cramped, airless apartments. In New York's Eleventh Ward an average of 986 persons occupied each acre, a density matched only in Bombay, India.

Reformers recognized the problem but seemed unable to solve it. Some favored model tenements financed by public-spirited citizens willing to accept a limited return on their investment. When private philanthropy failed to make much of a dent in the problem, cities turned to housing codes. The most advanced of these was New York's Tenement House Law of 1901, which required interior courts, indoor toilets, and fire safeguards for new structures, but did little for existing housing stock. Commercial development had pushed up land values in downtown areas. Only high-density, cheaply built housing could earn a sufficient profit for the landlords of the poor. This economic fact defied nineteenth-century solutions.

A Balance Sheet: Chicago and Berlin

Chicago and Berlin had virtually equal populations in 1900. Their histories were, however, profoundly different. Seventy years earlier, when Chicago was just a muddy frontier outpost, Berlin was a city of 250,000, and the royal seat of the Hohenzollerns of Prussia.

With German unification in 1871, the imperial authorities rebuilt Berlin on a grander scale. "A capital city is essential for the state, to act as a pivot for its culture," proclaimed the Prussian historian Heinrich von Treitschke. Berlin served that national purpose—as "a center where Germany's political, intellectual, and material life is concentrated, and its people can feel united." Chicago had no such pretensions. It was strictly a place of business, made great by virtue of its strategic grip on the commerce of America's industrial heartland. Nothing in Chicago evoked the grandeur of Berlin's boulevards or its monumental palaces and public buildings, nor were Chicagoans ever witness to anything like the pomp and ceremony of Berlin's imperial parades up broad, tree-lined Unter den Linden to the national cathedral.

Yet as a functioning city Chicago was in many ways superior to Berlin. Chicago's waterworks pumped 500 million gallons of water a day, or 139 gallons of water per person, while Berliners had to make do with 18 gallons. Flush toilets, a rarity in Berlin in 1900, could be found in 60 percent of Chicago's homes. Chicago's streets were lit by electricity, while Berlin still relied mostly on gaslight. Chicago had a much bigger streetcar system, twice as much acreage devoted to parks, and a public library containing many more volumes. And Chicago had just completed an amazing sanitation project, reversing the course of the Chicago River so that its waters—and the city's sewage—would flow away from the lake, and southward down into the Illinois and Mississippi rivers.

Giant sanitation projects were one thing; an inspiring urban environment was something else. For well-traveled Americans admiring of things European, the sense of inferiority was palpable. "We are enormously rich," admitted the journalist Edwin L. Godkin, "but . . . what have we got to show? Almost nothing. Ugliness from an artistic point of view is the mark of all our cities." Thus the balance sheet: an urban infrastructure that was superb by nineteenth-century standards, but "no municipal splendors of any description, nothing but population and hotels."

CITY PEOPLE

When the budding writer Hamlin Garland and his brother arrived in Chicago from rural Iowa in 1881, they knew immediately that they had entered a new world: "Everything interested us. . . . Nothing was commonplace, nothing was ugly to us." In one way or another every city-bound migrant, whether from the American countryside or from a foreign land, experienced something of this exhilaration and wonder.

But with the opportunity and boundless variety came disorder and uncertainty. The urban world was utterly unlike the rural communities the newcomers had left. In the countryside every person had been known to his or her neighbors. Mark Twain found New York "a splendid desert, where a stranger is lonely in the midst of a million of his race. . . . Every man rushes, rushes, rushes, and never has time to be companionable [or] to fool away on matters which do not involve dollars and duty and business." If rural roles and obligations had been well understood, in the city the only predictable relationships were those dictated by the marketplace.

The newcomers could never re-create in the city the worlds they had left behind. But they found ways to gain a sense of belonging, they built a multitude of new institutions, and they learned how to function in an impersonal, heterogeneous environment. An urban culture emerged, and through it there developed a new breed of American who was entirely at home in the modern city.

Newcomers

At the turn of the century, upward of 30 percent of the residents of New York, Chicago, Boston, Cleveland, Minneapolis, and San Francisco were foreign-born. The biggest ethnic group in Boston was Irish; in Minneapolis, Swedish; in most other northern cities, German. But by 1910 the influx from southern and Eastern Europe had changed the ethnic complexion of many of these cities. In Chicago, Poles took the lead; in New York, Eastern European Jews; in San Francisco, Italians.

All these immigrants—old and new—brought with them experiences and customs from the homeland that shaped their lives in the New World. But as the older "walking cities" disappeared, so did the opportunities for intermingling with the older populations. The later arrivals from southern and Eastern Europe had little choice about where they lived; they needed to be near their jobs and to find cheap housing. Some gravitated to the outlying factory districts; others settled in the congested downtown ghettos. The immigrants did not settle randomly in these districts, however. In New York, Italians crowded into the Irish neighborhoods west of Broadway, and Russian and Polish Jews pushed the Germans out of the Lower East Side. A colony of Hungarians lived around Houston Street, and Bohemians occupied the Upper East Side between Fiftieth and Seventy-sixth streets.

Capitalizing on the fellow feeling that drew ethnic groups together, a variety of institutions sprang up to meet the immigrants' needs. Wherever substantial numbers lived, newspapers appeared. In 1911 the 20,000 Poles in Buffalo, New York, supported two Polish-language daily papers. Immigrants throughout the country avidly read *Il Progresso Italo-Americano* and the Yiddish-language *Jewish Daily Forward*, both published in New York City. Companionship could always be found on street corners, in barbershops and club rooms, and in saloons. Italians marched in saint's day parades, Bohemians gathered in singing societies, and New York Jews patronized a lively Yiddish theater. To provide help in times of sickness and death, the immigrants organized mutual-aid societies. The Italians of Chicago had sixty-six of these organizations in 1903, composed mainly of people from particular provinces and towns. Immigrants built a rich and functional institutional life in urban America, to an extent unimagined in their native villages.

The great African-American migration to northern cities was just beginning at the turn of the century. The black population of New York increased by 30,000 between 1900 and 1910, making New York second only to Washington, D.C., as a black urban center, but the 91,000 blacks in New York in 1910 represented fewer than 2 percent of the population, and that was true of Chicago and Cleveland as well.

Despite their relatively small numbers, urban blacks could not escape discrimination. They retreated from the scattered black neighborhoods of older times into concentrated ghettos—Chicago's Black Belt on the south side, for example, or the early outlines of New York's Harlem. In employment, race prejudice cut down job opportunities. While 26 percent of Cleveland's blacks had been skilled workers in 1870, only 12 percent were by 1890, and entire occupations such as barbering (except for a black clientele) disappeared. Two-thirds of Cleveland's blacks in 1910 worked as domestics and day laborers, with little hope of moving up the job ladder.

In the face of pervasive discrimination, urban blacks built their own communities. They created a flourishing press; fraternal orders; a vast array of women's organizations; and a middle class of doctors, lawyers, and small business owners. Above all, there were the black churches—twenty-five in Chicago in 1905, mainly Methodist and Baptist. More than any other institution, remarked one scholar in 1913, it was the church "which the Negro may call his own.... A new church may be built ... and ... all the machinery set in motion without ever consulting any white person.... [It] more than anything else represents the real life of the race." As in the southern countryside, the church was the central institution for city blacks, and the preacher the most important local citizen. Manhattan's Union Baptist Church, housed like many others in a storefront, attracted the "very recent residents of this new, disturbing city" and, ringing with spirituals and fervent prayer, made Christianity come "alive Sunday mornings."

Ward Politics

Race and ethnicity tended to divide the newcomers and turn them in on themselves. Politics, on the contrary, acted as a powerful instrument for integrating them into the larger urban society. Every migrant to an American city automatically became a ward resident, and by living on a particular street, immediately acquired a spokesman at city hall in the form of an alderman. Immigrants learned very quickly that if they needed anything from city hall, the alderman was the person to see. That was how streets got paved, or water mains extended, or variances granted—so that, for example, in 1888 Vito Fortounescere could "place and keep a stand for the sale of fruit, inside the stoop-line, in front of the northeast corner of Twenty-eighth Street and Fourth Avenue" in Manhattan, or the parishioners of Saint Maria of Mount Carmel could set off fireworks at their Fourth of July picnic.

Machine control of political parties, although present at every level, flourished most luxuriantly in the big cities. Urban machines depended on a loyal grass-roots constituency. So each ward was divided into election districts of a few blocks, with a district captain who reported to the ward boss (who might also be the alderman). The main jobs of these functionaries were to be accessible and, as best they could, to serve the needs of the party faithful.

The machine similarly served the business community. Contractors sought city business; gas companies and streetcar lines wanted licenses and privileges; manufacturers needed services and not-too-nosy inspectors; and the liquor trade and numbers racket relied on a tolerant police force. All of them turned to the machine boss and his lieutenants. In addition to these everyday functions, the machine continuously mediated among conflicting interests and oiled the wheels of city government.

Of course, the machine exacted a price for these services. The tenement dweller gave his vote. The businessman wrote a check. Corruption permeated this informal system. Some of the money that changed hands inevitably ended in the pockets of machine politicans. This "boodle" could take the form of outright corruption—kickbacks by contractors; protection money from gamblers, saloonkeepers, and prostitutes; payoffs from gas and trolley companies. The Tammany ward boss George Washington Plunkitt, however, insisted that he had no need for kickbacks and bribes. He favored what he called "honest graft," the easy profits that came to savvy insiders. Plunkitt made most of his money building wharves on Manhattan's waterfront. One way or another, legally or otherwise, machine politics rewarded its supporters.

For the young and ambitious, this was reason enough to favor the machine system. In the mid-1870s, over half Chicago's forty aldermen were foreign-born, sixteen of them Irish immigrants. The first Italian was elected to the board in 1885, the first Pole in 1888. Blacks did not manage to get on Chicago's board of aldermen until after 1900, but Baltimore's Eleventh Ward elected an African-American in 1890 and Philadelphia had three black aldermen by 1899. As a ladder for social mobility, machine politics (like professional sports, entertainment, and organized crime) was the most democratic of American institutions.

For the ordinary tenement dweller, however, the machine had a more modest value. It acted as a rough-and-ready social service agency, providing jobs for the jobless, a helping hand for a bereaved family, and an ally against an unfeeling city bureaucracy. The Tammany ward boss Plunkitt had a "regular system" when fires broke out in his district. He arranged for housing for burned-out families, to "fix them up till they get things runnin' again. It's philanthropy, but it's politics, too—mighty good politics."

Plunkitt was an Irishman, and so were most of the ward politicians controlling Tammany Hall. But by the 1890s Plunkitt's Fifteenth District was filling up with Italians and Eastern European Jews. In general the New York Irish had no love for these newer immigrants, but Plunkitt played no favorites. On any given day (as recorded in a diary) he might attend an Italian funeral in the afternoon and a Jewish wedding in the evening, and at each he probably paid his respects with a few Italian words or a bit of Yiddish.

In an era when so many forces acted to isolate ghetto communities, politics served an *integrating* function, cutting across ethnic lines and giving immigrants and blacks a stake in the larger urban order.

Religion and Ethnicity

For most immigrants, religion was an abiding concern and was so intertwined with their ethnic identity as to be inseparable from the story of how they adapted to American life.

AMERICAN VOICES

Bintel Brief

T*he Yiddish phrase* bintel brief *means "bundle of letters." That was the name of the famous column of the* Jewish Daily Forward *devoted to letters from immigrant readers about their trials and tribulations in America.*

I was born in a small town in Russia, and until I was sixteen I studied in *Talmud Torahs* and *yeshivas*, but when I came to America I developed spiritually and became a freethinker. Yet every year when the time of *Rosh Hashana* and *Yom Kippur* comes around I become very gloomy. . . . So strong are my feelings that I enter the synagogue, not in order to pray to God but to heal and refresh my aching soul by sitting among *landsleit* [countrymen] and listening to the cantor's sweet melodies. The members of my Progressive Society don't understand. They say I am a hypocrite. . . . What do you think? *Answer:* No one can tell another what to do with himself on *Yom Kippur.*

I am a Russian revolutionist and a freethinker. Here in America I became acquainted with a girl who is also a freethinker. We decided to marry, but the problem is that she has Orthodox parents, and if we refuse a religious ceremony we will be cut off from them forever. I don't know what to do. Therefore, I ask you to advise me how to act. *Answer:* There are times when it is better to be kind in order not to grieve old parents.

I am a young man of twenty-five, and I recently met a fine girl. She has a flaw, however—a dimple in her chin. It is said that people who have this lose their first husband or wife. I love her very much. But I'm afraid to marry her lest I die because of the dimple. *Answer:* The tragedy is not that the girl has a dimple in her chin but that some people have a screw loose in their heads.

SOURCE: Irving Howe and Kenneth Libo, eds., *How We Lived* (New York: New American Library, 1979), 88–90.

About 250,000 Jews, mostly of German origin, were living in America when the Eastern European Jews began to arrive in the 1880s. The German Jews, well established and prosperous, had embraced Reform Judaism, abandoning religious practices "not adapted to the views and habits of modern civilization." Anxious to preserve their traditional piety, the Yiddish-speaking immigrants from Eastern Europe founded their own Orthodox synagogues, often in vacant stores and ramshackle buildings, and practiced Judaism in the old way.

In the villages of Eastern Europe, however, Judaism had stood not only for worship and belief, but for an entire way of life. Insular though it might be, ghetto life in the American city could not re-create the communal environment on which strict religious observance depended. "The very clothes I wore and the very food I ate had a fatal effect on my religious habits," confessed the hero of Abraham Cahan's novel *The Rise of David Levinsky* (1917). "If you . . . attempt to bend your religion to the spirit of your surroundings, it breaks. It falls to pieces." Levinsky shaved off his beard and plunged into the Manhattan clothing business. Orthodox Judaism survived this shattering of faith, but only by sharply reducing its claims on the lives of the faithful.

Catholics faced much the same problem. The issue, explicitly defined within the Roman Catholic Church as "Americanism," turned on how far Catholicism should respond to American society. Should Catholic children attend parochial or public schools? Should they intermarry with non-Catholics? Should the traditional education for the clergy be changed? Bishop John Ireland of St. Paul, Minnesota, felt that "the principles of the Church are in harmony with the interests of the Republic." But traditionalists, led by Archbishop Michael A. Corrigan of New York, denied the possibility of such harmony and argued in effect for insulating the Church from the pluralistic American environment.

Immigrant Catholics generally supported the Church's conservative wing, because they wanted to preserve their religion as they had known it in Europe. But their concerns were not purely religious; church life also had to

Immaculate Heart of Mary Church, 1908
In crowded immigrant neighborhoods the church rose from undistinguished surroundings to assert the centrality of religious belief in the life of the community. This photograph is a view of Immaculate Heart of Mary Church taken from Polish Hill in Pittsburgh in 1908.

express their ethnic identities. Newly arrived Catholics wanted their own parishes where they could celebrate their own customs, speak their own languages, and establish their own parochial schools. When they became numerous enough, they also demanded their own bishops.

The severity of the challenge depended partly on the religious convictions of each ethnic group. Italian men, for example, were known for religious apathy. Many Italians, moreover, harbored strong anticlerical feelings, much strengthened by the papacy's opposition to the unification of Italy. On the other hand, the church played so important a part in the lives of Polish immigrants that they resented any interference by the Catholic hierarchy. In 1907 fifty parishes formed the Polish National Catholic Church of America, which adhered to Catholic ritual without recognizing the pope's authority.

On the whole, however, the Church managed to satisfy the immigrant faithful. It met the demand for representation in the hierarchy by appointing immigrant priests as auxiliary bishops within existing dioceses. And ethnic parishes also flourished. Before World War I, American Catholics worshiped in more than 2,000 foreign-language churches, and many others were bilingual. Not without strain, the Catholic Church made itself a central institution for the expression of ethnic identity in urban America.

For the Protestant churches, the city posed different but not easier challenges. With each wave of immigration, the Protestant population in the cities lost ground. Seventeen Protestant churches moved out of lower Manhattan during the twenty years after 1868, as the area below Fourteenth Street filled up with immigrants.

Every major city retained great downtown churches where wealthy Protestants worshiped. Some of these churches, richly endowed, took pride in nationally prominent pastors, including Henry Ward Beecher of Plymouth Congregational Church in Brooklyn and Phillips Brooks of Trinity Episcopal Church in Boston. But the eminence of these churches, with their fashionable congregations and imposing edifices, could not disguise the growing remoteness of Protestantism from much of its urban constituency. "Where is the city in which the Sabbath day is not losing ground?" lamented a minister in 1887. The families of businessmen, lawyers, and doctors could be seen in any church on Sunday morning, he noted, "but the workingmen and their families are not there."

To counter this decline, the Protestant churches responded in two ways. They evangelized among the unchurched and the indifferent, for example, through the Sunday-school movement. Protestants also made their churches instruments of social uplift. Starting in the 1880s, many city churches provided such facilities as reading rooms, day nurseries, clubhouses, and vocational classes. Sometimes the churches linked evangelism and social uplift. The Salvation Army, which arrived from Great Britain in 1879, spread the gospel of repentance among the urban poor and built an assistance program that ranged from soup kitchens to homes for former prostitutes. When all else failed, the down-and-outers of American cities knew they could count on the Salvation Army.

The social meaning that people sought in religion explained the enormous popularity of a book called *In His Steps* (1896). The author, the Congregational minister Charles M. Sheldon, told the story of a congregation that resolved to live by Christ's precepts for one year. "If the church members were all doing as Jesus would do," Sheldon asked, "could it remain true that armies of men would walk the streets for jobs, and hundreds of them curse the church, and thousands of them find in the saloon their best friend?"

The most potent form of urban evangelism—revivalism—said little about social uplift. From their origins in the eighteenth century, revival movements had steadfastly focused on individual redemption. The defeat of earthly problems, revivalists believed, would follow the conversion of the people to Christ. Beginning in the mid-1870s, revival meetings swept through the cities.

The pioneering figure was Dwight L. Moody, a former Chicago shoe salesman and YMCA official. After preaching in Britain for two years, Moody returned to America in 1875. With his talented choir leader and hymn writer, Ira D. Sankey, Moody staged revival meetings that drew thousands. He preached an optimistic, uncomplicated, nondenominational message. Eternal life could be had for the asking, Moody shouted as he held up his Bible. His listeners needed only "to come forward and take, TAKE!"

Many other preachers followed in Moody's path. The most notable was Billy (William Ashley) Sunday, a hard-drinking former outfielder for the Chicago White Stockings who had mended his ways and found religion. Like Moody and other city revivalists, Sunday was a farm boy. His rip-snorting cries against "Charlotte-russe Christians" and the "booze traffic" carried the ring of rustic America. By realizing that many people remained villagers at heart, revivalists found a key for bringing city dwellers back into the church.

Leisure in the City

City people compartmentalized life's activities, setting workplace apart from home and working time apart from free time. "Going out" became a necessity, demanded not only as relief from a day of hard work but as proof that life was better in the new world than in the old. "He who can enjoy and does not enjoy commits a sin," a Yiddish-language paper told its readers. And enjoyment now meant buying a ticket and being entertained.

Amusement parks went up at the end of trolley lines in cities across the country. Most glittering was Luna Park at New York's Coney Island—"an enchanted, storybook land of trellises, columns, domes, minarets, lagoons, and lofty aerial flights. . . . It was a world removed—shut away from the sordid clatter and turmoil of the streets." In fact, that escape from everyday urban life explains the appeal of amusement parks. The creators of Luna Park intended it to be "a different world—a dream world . . . where all is bizarre and fantastic . . . gayer and more different from the every-day world."

The theater likewise attracted huge audiences. Chicago had six vaudeville houses in 1896 and twenty-two in 1910. Originating in cheap variety and minstrel shows, vaudeville cleaned up its routines, making them suitable for the entire family, and turned itself into thoroughly professional entertainment handled by national booking agencies. With its standard program of nine singing, dancing, and comedy acts, vaudeville attained enormous popularity just as the movies arrived. The first primitive films, a minute or so of humor or glimpses of famous people, appeared in 1896 in penny arcades and as filler in vaudeville shows. Within a decade, millions of city people were watching narrative films of increasing length and artistry at nickelodeons (named after the 5-cent admission charge) across the country.

For young unmarried workers, the cheap amusements of the city created a new social space. "I want a good time," a New York clothing operator told an investigator. "And there is no . . . way a girl can get it on $8 a week. I guess if anyone wants to take me to a dance he won't have to ask me twice." Hence the widespread ritual among the urban working class of "treating." The girls spent what money they had on dressing up; their beaus were expected to pay for the fun. Parental control over courtship broke down, and amid the bright lights and lively music of the dance hall and the amusement park, working-class youth forged a more easygoing culture of sexual interaction and pleasure seeking.

The geography of the big city reserved ample space for commercialized sex. Prostitution was not new to urban life, but in the late nineteenth century it became less hidden and ghettoized. New York's Tenderloin, running northward from Twenty-third Street between Fifth and Eighth avenues and eventually up to Times Square and beyond, was also the locale of the city's fanciest restaurants, the best hotels, and the theater district. On the side streets many of the brownstones, abandoned by their well-to-do owners for more fashionable parts of town, were taken over by brothels. The nearby concert saloons—the forerunners of the nightclub—featured not only stage shows and bars but also well-dressed prostitutes working the premises.

The Tenderloin and the Bowery were also the sites of a robust gay subculture. The long-held notion that homosexual life was covert—"in the closet"—in Victorian America appears not to be true, at least not in the country's premier city. Homosexuality was illegal, but as with prostitution, the law was mostly a dead letter. In certain corners of the city a gay world flourished, with a full array of saloons, meeting places, and drag balls, which were widely known and often patronized by uptown "slummers."

Of all forms of male diversion, none was more specific to the city, nor so spectacularly successful, than professional baseball. The game's promoters decreed that baseball had been created in 1839 by Abner Doubleday in the village of Cooperstown, New York. Actually, baseball was neither of American origin—it developed from the British game of rounders—nor a product of rural life.

Organized play began in the early 1840s in New York City, where a group of gentlemen enthusiasts competed on an empty lot. During the next twenty years the aristocratic tone of baseball disappeared. Clubs sprang up across the country, and intercity competition developed on a scheduled basis. In 1868 baseball became openly professional, as other teams followed the lead of the Cincinnati Red Stockings in signing players to contracts at a negotiated salary for the season.

Big-time commercial baseball came into its own with the launching of the National League in 1876. The team owners were profit-minded businessmen who carefully shaped the sport to please the fans. Wooden grandstands gave way to the concrete and steel stadiums of the early twentieth century, such as Fenway Park in Boston, Forbes Field in Pittsburgh, and Shibe Park in Philadelphia.

For the urban multitudes baseball grew into something more than an occasional afternoon at the ballpark. By rooting for the home team, fans found a way of identifying with the city they lived in. Amid the diversity and anonymity of urban life, baseball acted as a bridge among strangers.

Most efficient at this task, however, was the newspaper. James Gordon Bennett, founder of the *New York Herald* in 1835, wanted "to record the facts . . . for the great masses of the community." The news was whatever interested city readers, starting with crime, scandal, and sensational events. After the Civil War Charles A. Dana of the *New York Sun* added the human-interest story, which made news of ordinary, insignificant happenings. Newspapers also targeted specific audiences. A women's page offered recipes and fashion news, separate sections covered sports and high society, and the Sunday supplement helped fill the weekend hours.

Joseph Pulitzer, Publisher
Pulitzer (1847–1911) left Hungary at seventeen because he wanted to be a soldier, and his best chance was with the Union army in America. He was the greatest newspaper publisher of the century, extraordinary for his insight into what an urban reading public wanted from a newspaper and because he came to this task as a foreigner, without English as his mother tongue and without roots in American society.

When Joseph Pulitzer, the owner of the *St. Louis Post-Dispatch*, invaded New York in 1883 by buying the *World*, a furious circulation war broke out. In 1895 William Randolph Hearst, who owned the *San Francisco Examiner*, bought the *New York Journal* and challenged the *World*. Hearst developed a sensational style of newspaper reporting that became known as *yellow journalism*. The term, linked to the first comic strip to appear in color, "The Yellow Kid" (1895), referred to a type of reporting that treated accuracy as secondary to a good story.

"He who is without a newspaper," said the great showman P. T. Barnum, "is cut off from his species." Barnum was speaking of city people and their hunger for information. By meeting this need, newspapers revealed their sensitivity to the public they served.

The Higher Culture

In the midst of this popular ferment, new institutions of higher culture were taking shape in America's cities. A hunger for the cultivated life was not, of course, specifically urban. Before the Civil War the lyceum movement had sent lecturers to the remotest towns, bearing messages of culture and learning. The Chautauqua movement, founded in upstate New York in 1874, carried on this work of cultural dissemination. However, large cultural institutions such as museums, public libraries, opera companies, and symphony orchestras could flourish only in metropolitan centers.

The first major art museum, the Corcoran Gallery of Art, opened in Washington, D.C., in 1869. New York's Metropolitan Museum of Art, started in rented quarters two years later, moved in 1880 to its permanent site in Central Park and launched an ambitious program of art acquisition. When J. P. Morgan became chairman of the board in 1905, the Metropolitan's preeminence was assured. The Boston Museum of Fine Arts was founded in 1876, and Chicago's Art Institute in 1879.

Top-flight orchestras also appeared, first in New York under the conductors Theodore Thomas and Leopold Damrosch in the 1870s and then in Boston and Chicago during the next decade. National tours by these leading orchestras planted the seeds for orchestral societies in many other cities. Public libraries grew from modest collections (in 1870 only seven had as many as 50,000 books) into major urban institutions. The greatest library benefactor was Andrew Carnegie, who announced in 1881 that he would build a library in any city that was prepared to maintain it. By 1907 Carnegie had spent more than $32.7 million to establish about a thousand libraries throughout the country.

The late nineteenth century was the great age not only of money making but also of money *giving*. The new millionaires patronized the arts partly as a civic duty, and partly to help establish themselves in society. But museums and opera houses also received generous support out of a sense of national pride.

"In America there is no culture," pronounced the English critic G. Lowes Dickinson in 1909. Science and the practical arts, yes, "every possible application of life to purposes and ends," but "no life for life's sake." Such condescending remarks received a respectful hearing because of a deep sense of cultural inferiority to the Old World. In 1873 Mark Twain and Charles Dudley Warner published a novel, *The Gilded Age*, satirizing America as a land of money-grubbers and speculators. This enormously popular book touched a nerve in the American psyche. Its title has in fact been appropriated by historians to characterize the late nineteenth century—America's "Gilded Age"—as an age of materialism and cultural shallowness.

Some members of the upper class, like the novelist Henry James, despaired of the country and moved to Europe. But the more common response was to try to raise the nation's cultural level. The newly rich had a hard time of it. They did not have much opportunity to cultivate a taste for art, and a great deal of what they collected was mediocre and garish. On the other hand, George W. Vanderbilt, grandson of the rough-hewn Cornelius Vanderbilt, was an early champion of French Impressionism, and the coal and steel baron Henry Clay Frick built a brilliant art collection that is still housed, as a public museum, in his mansion in New York City. The enthusiasm of moneyed Americans—not always well directed—largely fueled the great cultural institutions that sprang up during the Gilded Age.

A deeply conservative idea of culture sustained this generous patronage. The aim was to embellish life, not to probe or reveal its meaning. "Art," says the hero of the Reverend Henry Ward Beecher's sentimental novel *Norwood* (1867), "attempts to work out its end solely by the use of the beautiful, and the artist is to select out only such things as are beautiful." The idea of culture also took on an elitist cast: Shakespeare, once a staple of popular stage entertainment (in various bowdlerized versions), was appropriated into the domain of "serious" theater. And simultaneously, the world of culture became feminized. "Husbands or sons rarely share those interests," noted one observer. In American life, remarked the clergyman Horace Bushnell, men represented the "force principle," women the "beauty principle."

UPPER CLASS/MIDDLE CLASS

In the compact city of the early nineteenth century, class distinctions had been expressed by the way men and women dressed, how they behaved, and the deference they demanded from or granted to others. As the industrial city grew, these interpersonal marks of class began to lose their force. In the anonymity of a large city, recognition and deference no longer served as mechanisms for conferring status. Instead, people began to rely on external signs: conspicuous display of wealth; membership in exclusive clubs and organizations; and above all, choice of neighborhood.

For the poor, place of residence depended, as it always had, on the location of their work. But for higher-income urbanites, where to live became a matter of personal means and social preference.

The Urban Elite

As early as the 1840s Boston merchants had taken advantage of the new railway service to escape the congested central city for the rural life of Milton, Newton, and other outlying towns. By 1848 roughly 20 percent of Boston's businessmen were making the long trip by train from the countryside to their downtown offices. Ferries that plied the harbor between Manhattan and Brooklyn or New Jersey served the same purpose for New Yorkers. As commercial development engulfed downtown residential areas, the exodus from cities by the well-to-do spread across America. In Cincinnati wealthy families settled on the scenic hills rimming the crowded, humid tableland that ran down to the Ohio River. On those hillsides, a traveler noted in 1883, "the homes of Cincinnati's merchant princes and millionaires are found . . . elegant cottages, tasteful villas, and substantial mansions, surrounded by a paradise of grass, gardens, lawns, and tree-shaded roads."

Despite the temptations of country life, many of the very richest people preferred the heart of the city. Chicago boasted its Gold Coast; San Francisco, Nob Hill; Denver, Quality Hill; and Manhattan, Fifth Avenue. The New York novelist Edith Wharton recalled how the comfortable midcentury brownstones gave way to the "'new' millionaire houses," which spread northward beyond Fifty-ninth Street and up Fifth Avenue along Central Park. By carving out fashionable areas in the heart of a city, the rich visibly demonstrated their capacity to assert their will over the larger society.

But great fortunes did not automatically confer high social standing. An established elite stood astride the social heights, even in such relatively raw cities as San Francisco and Denver. It had taken only a generation—and sometimes less—for money made in commerce or real estate to shed its tarnish and become "old" and genteel. In older cities such as Boston, wealth passed intact through several generations, creating a closely knit tribe of Brahmin families that kept moneyed newcomers at bay. Elsewhere urban elites tended to be more open, but only to the socially ambitious who were prepared to make visible and energetic use of their money.

The richest and most successful people gravitated to New York. The tycoon Frank Cowperwood, in Theodore Dreiser's novel *The Titan* (1914), reassured his unhappy wife that if Chicago society would not accept them, "there are other cities. Money will arrange matters in New York—that I know. We can build a real place there, and go in on equal terms, if we have money enough." New York thus came to be a magnet for millionaires. The city attracted them not only because of its importance as a financial center, but for the opportunities it offered for display and social recognition.

This infusion of wealth shattered the older elite society of New York. Seeking to be assimilated into the upper class, the flood of moneyed newcomers simply overwhelmed it. There followed a curious process of reconstruction, a deliberate effort to define the rules of conduct and identify those who properly "belonged" in New York society.

The key figure in this process was Ward McAllister, a southern-born lawyer who made a quick fortune in gold-rush San Francisco before devoting himself to a second career as the arbiter of New York society. In 1888 McAllister compiled the first *Social Register*, which would serve as a "record of society, comprising an accurate and careful list" of all those deemed eligible for New York society. McAllister instructed the socially ambitious on how to select guests, set a proper table, arrange a ball, and launch a young lady into society. To top things off, McAllister got the idea of "the Four Hundred"—the true cream of New York society. His list corresponded to those invited to Mrs. William Astor's great ball of February 1, 1892.

Americans were adept at making money, remarked the journalist Edwin L. Godkin in 1896, but they lacked the European traditions for spending it. "Great wealth has not yet entered our manners," Godkin remarked. "No rules have yet been drawn to guide wealthy Americans in their manner of life." In their struggle to find the rules and establish the manners, the moneyed elite made an indelible mark on urban life. If there was magnificence in the American city, that was mainly their handiwork. And if there was conspicuous waste and display, that too was their doing.

The Suburban World

The middle class left a smaller imprint on the public and cultural faces of urban society. Its members, unlike the rich, preferred privacy and retreated into the domesticity of suburban comfort and family life.

The emerging corporate economy spawned a new middle class. Bureaucratic organizations required managers, accountants, and clerks. Industry called for engineers, chemists, and designers, while the distribution system needed salesmen, advertising executives, and buyers. These salaried ranks increased sevenfold between 1870 and 1910, at a much faster rate than any other occupational group. Nearly 9 million people held white-collar jobs in 1910, more than a fourth of all employed Americans.

The salaried middle class was overwhelmingly urban. Some of its members lived within the city, in the row houses of Baltimore and Boston or the comfortable apartment buildings of New York City. But far more preferred to escape from the clamor and congestion of the city. They were attracted by a persisting "rural ideal." They agreed with the landscape architect Andrew Jackson Downing, who thought that "nature and domestic life are better than the society and manners of town." With the extension of trolley service from the city center, middle-class Americans followed the wealthy into the countryside. All sought what a Chicago developer promised for his North Shore subdivision in 1875—"qualities of which the city is in a large degree bereft, namely, its pure air, peacefulness, quietude, and natural scenery."

No major American city escaped rapid suburbanization during the last third of the nineteenth century. City limits everywhere expanded rapidly. By

1900 more than half Boston's people lived in "streetcar suburbs" outside the original city. The U.S. Census of 1910 reported that nationwide about 25 percent of the urban population lived in suburbs beyond the city limits.

The geography of the suburbs was truly a map of class structure in America, because where a family lived told where it ranked. The farther the distance from the center of the city, the finer the houses and the larger the lots. The affluent had the leisure and flexible schedules to travel the long distance into town. People closer in wanted direct transit lines convenient to home and office. Working-class suburbanites were more likely to have more than one wage earner in the family, less secure employment, and jobs requiring movement around the city. They needed easy access to crosstown transit lines, which ran closer in to the city center.

Divisions within suburbs, although always a precise measure of economic ranking, never became rigid. People in the city center who wanted to better their lives moved to the cheapest suburbs. Those already settled there fled from these newcomers, in turn pushing the next higher group farther out in search of space and greenery. Suburbanization was the sum of countless individual decisions. Each move represented an advance in living standards—not only more light, air, and quiet, but better housing than the city afforded. Suburban houses typically had more space and better design, as well as indoor toilets; hot water; central heating; and, by the turn of the century, electricity.

The suburbs also restored a basic opportunity that had seemed sacrificed by rural Americans when they moved to the city. In the suburbs, home ownership again became the norm. "A man is not really a true man until he owns his home," propounded the Reverend Russell H. Conwell in "Acres of Diamonds," his famous sermon on the virtues of making money.

The small town of the rural past had fostered community life. Not so the suburbs. The grid street pattern, while efficient for laying out lots and providing utilities, offered no natural focus for group life. Nor did the stores and services that lay scattered along the trolley-car lines. Suburban development conformed to the economics of real estate and transportation, and so did the thinking of middle-class home seekers entering the suburbs. They wanted a house that gave them good value and convenience to the trolley line.

The need for community had lost some of its force for middle-class Americans. Two other attachments assumed greater importance: work and family.

Middle-Class Families

In the preindustrial economy farmers, merchants, and artisans had carried on their work within family units, which counted as members not only blood relatives, but all others living and working in the household. As industrialism progressed, economic activity moved out of the household, especially for the middle class. The father left the home to earn a living, and children spent more years in school. Clothing was bought ready-made, food came increasingly in cans and packages. Middle-class families became smaller, excluding all

Middle-Class Domesticity
For middle-class Americans the home was a place of nurture, a refuge from the world of competitive commerce. Perhaps that explains why their residences were so heavily draped and cluttered with bric-a-brac, every space filled with overstuffed furniture. All of it emphasized privacy and pride of possession. The young woman shown playing the piano symbolizes another theme of American domesticity—wives and daughters as ornaments and as bearers of culture and refinement.

but nuclear members, typically consisting by 1900 of husband, wife, and three children.

Within this family circle, relationships became intense and affectionate. "Home was the most expressive experience in life," recalled the literary critic Henry Seidel Canby of his growing up in the 1890s. "Though the family might quarrel and nag, the home held them all, protecting them against the outside world." In a sense, the family served as a refuge from the competitive, impersonal business world. The quiet, tree-lined streets created a domestic place insulated from the hurly-burly of commerce and enterprise.

The burdens of this domesticity fell heavily on the wife. It was nearly unheard of for her to seek an outside career. Her job was to manage the household. "The woman who could not make a home, like the man who could not support one, was condemned," Canby remembered. But with fewer children, the wife's workload declined. Moreover, servants still played an important part in middle-class households. In 1910 there were about 2 million domestic servants, the largest job category for women.

"We Did Not Know Whether . . . Women's Health Could Stand the Strain of Higher Education"

M. *Carey Thomas (1857–1935), president of Bryn Mawr College for many years, recalls her dreams of college as a girl growing up in Baltimore in the 1870s.*

The passionate desire of women of my generation for higher education was accompanied thruout its course by the awful doubt, felt by women themselves as well as by men, as to whether women as a sex were physically and mentally fit for it. . . . I often remember praying about it, and begging God that if it were true that because I was a girl I could not successfully master Greek and go to college and understand things to kill me at once, as I could not bear to live in such an unjust world. . . .

We did not know when we began whether women's health could stand the strain of college education. We were haunted in those early days by the clanging chains of that gloomy little specter, Dr. Edward H. Clarke's *Sex in Education.* With trepidation of spirit I made my mother read it, and was much cheered by her remark that, as neither she, nor any of the women she knew, had ever seen girls or women of the kind described in Dr. Clarke's book, we might as well act as if they did not exist. . . .

When . . . I went to Leipzig to study after graduating from Cornell, my mother used to write me that my name was never mentioned to her by the women of her acquaintance. I was thought by them to be as much a disgrace to my family as if I had eloped with the coachman. . . .

We are now [1908] living in the midst of great and, I believe on the whole beneficent, social changes which are preparing the way for the coming economic independence of women. . . . The passionate desire of the women of my generation for a college education seems, as we study it now in the light of coming events, to have been part of this greater movement.

SOURCE: Linda K. Kerber and Jane De Hart-Mathews, eds., *Women's America: Refocusing the Past* (2d ed., New York: Oxford University Press, 1987), 263–265.

As household work eased, higher-quality homemaking became the new ideal. This was the message of Catharine Beecher's best-selling book *The American Woman's Home* (1869) and of such magazines as the *Ladies' Home Journal* and *Good Housekeeping*, which first appeared during the 1880s. In addition to her domestic duties, the wife had the higher calling of bringing sensibility, beauty, and love to the household. "We owe to women the charm and beauty of life," wrote one educator. "For the love that rests, strengthens and inspires, we look to women." In this idealized view, the wife made the home a refuge for her husband and a place of nurture for their children.

Womanly virtue, even if a happy marriage depended on it, by no means put wives on equal terms with their husbands. Although the legal status of married women—the right to own property, control separate earnings, make contracts, and get a divorce—improved markedly during the nineteenth century, sufficient legal discrimination remained to establish their subordinate role within the family. More important, custom dictated a wife's submission to her husband. She relied on his ability as the family breadwinner, and despite her superior virtues and graces, she ranked as his inferior in vigor and intellect. Her mind could be employed "but little and in trivial matters," wrote one prominent physician, and her proper place was as "the companion or ornamental appendage to man."

No wonder bright, independent-minded women rebelled against marriage. The marriage rate in the United States fell to its lowest point during the last forty years of the nineteenth century. More than 10 percent of women of marriageable age remained single, and the rate was much higher among college graduates and professionals. Married life, remarked the writer Vida Scudder, "looks to me often as I watch it terribly impoverished, for women."

Around 1890 a change set in. Although the birth rate continued to decline, more young people married, and at an earlier age. These developments reflected the beginnings of a sexual revolution in the American middle-class family. Experts began to abandon the notion, put forth by one popular medical text, that "the majority of women (happily for society) are not very much troubled by sexual feeling of any kind." In succeeding editions of his book *Plain Home Talk on Love, Marriage, and Parentage*, the physician Edward Bliss Foote began to favor a healthy sexuality that gave pleasure to both women and men.

During the 1890s the artist Charles Dana Gibson created the image of the "new woman" in his drawings for *Life* magazine. The Gibson girl was tall, spirited, athletic, and chastely sexual. She eshewed bustles, hoop skirts, and hourglass corsets, preferring shirtwaists and other natural styles that did not hide or disguise her female form. In the city, women's sphere began to take on a more public character. Among the new urban institutions catering to women, the most important was the department store, which became a temple for women's emerging role as consumers.

The children of the middle class went through their own revolution. In the past, American children had been regarded as an economic asset—added hands for the family farm, shop, or countinghouse. That no longer held true for the urban middle class. Parents stopped treating their children as working members of the family. There was such a thing as "the juvenile mind," lectured Jacob Abbott in his book *Gentle Measures in the Management and Training of the Young* (1871). The family was responsible for providing a nurturing environment in which the young personality could grow and mature.

Preparation for adulthood became increasingly linked to formal education. School enrollment went up 150 percent between 1870 and 1900. High school attendance, while still encompassing only a small percentage of teenagers, increased at the fastest rate. As the years between childhood and adulthood began to stretch out, a new stage of life—adolescence—emerged. While rooted in a lengthening period of family dependency, adolescence shifted much of the socializing role from parents to peer group. A youth culture—one of the hallmarks of American life in the twentieth century—was starting to take shape.

CHAPTER 20 TIMELINE

1869	Corcoran Art Gallery opens in Washington, D.C.
1871	Chicago fire
1873	Mark Twain and Charles Dudley Warner publish *The Gilded Age*
1875	Dwight L. Moody launches urban revivalist movement
1876	Alexander Graham Bell patents the telephone National Baseball League founded
1878	Electric arc-light system installed in Philadelphia
1879	Thomas Edison's incandescent light bulb Salvation Army arrives from Britain
1881	Carnegie offers to build libraries for every American city
1883	Brooklyn Bridge opens Joseph Pulitzer purchases the *New York World*
1885	William Jenney builds first steel-frame structure, Chicago's Home Insurance Building
1888	First electric trolley line constructed in Richmond, Virginia
1893	Chicago World's Fair "City Beautiful" movement
1895	William Randolph Hearst enters New York journalism The comic strip "The Yellow Kid" appears
1897	Boston builds first American subway
1901	New York Tenement House Reform Law
1904	New York subway system opens
1906	San Francisco earthquake
1913	Woolworth Building, New York City

CHAPTER 21

THE PROGRESSIVE ERA

- The Course of Reform
- Progressivism and National Politics

On the face of it, the political ferment of the 1890s ended with the election of 1896. After the bitter struggle over free silver, the victorious Republicans had no stomach for political crusades. William McKinley's administration devoted itself to maintaining business confidence: sound money and high tariffs were the order of the day. The main thing, as party chief Mark Hanna said, was to "stand pat and continue Republican prosperity."

Yet beneath the surface a deep uneasiness was taking hold of the country. For more than half a century Americans had been absorbed in developing their nation. At the beginning of the twentieth century they paused, looked around, and began to add up the costs—a frightening concentration of corporate power, a restless working class, misery in the cities, corrupt machine politics. The heritage of an earlier America seemed to be giving way to the demands of the new industrial order.

Now, with the crisis of the 1890s over, reform became an absorbing concern for many Americans. It was as if social awareness had reached a critical mass around 1900, and set reform activity going as a major, self-sustaining phenomenon. For this reason the years from 1900 to World War I have come to be known as the Progressive Era.

THE COURSE OF REFORM

Historians have sometimes spoken of a progressive "movement." But progressivism was not a movement in any meaningful sense. There was no single

Muckraking

In this autobiographical account Charles Edward Russell, a newpaperman, describes how he got into muckraking journalism and what he thought it was all about. He never did, by the way, get back to writing music.

All America had been accustomed to laud and bepraise the makers of great fortunes. . . . Now, of a sudden, men began to discover that these great and adored fortunes had been gathered in ways that not only grazed the prison gate but imposed burdens and disadvantages upon the rest of the community. . . . In the shock of this discovery, a literature of exposition arose. . . .

Pure accident cast me, without the least desire, into the pursuit of this fashion. I had finally withdrawn from the newspaper business, and having enough money to live modestly I was bent upon carrying out a purpose long cherished [to compose music]. Upon this task I was intent when the whole business was upset with a single telegram.

One day, Mr. J. W. Midgley, who was a famous expert on railroad rates and conditions . . . let loose a flood of startling facts about the impositions practised by the owners and operators of refrigerator cars. My friend, Mr. Erman J. Ridgway . . . of *Everybody's Magazine* wired asking me to see Mr. Midgley [who] positively refused all offers to become an exposé writer. [So] Ridgway wire[d] asking me to furnish the article *Everybody's* wanted. I had not the least disposition to do so, except only that Ridgway was my friend. . . . The next thing I knew a muckrake was put into my hand and I was plunged into the midst of the game. . . .

I wrote two or three articles on the refrigerator car scandal and then went on to write a series on the methods of the Beef Trust. . . . We were all up and away, full of the pleasures of the chase . . . and all that business about poetry and music sheets forgotten. It was exhilarating sport, hunting the money octopus.

SOURCE: Charles Edward Russell, *Bare Hands and Stone Walls* (New York, Charles Scribner's Sons, 1933), 135–139.

progressive constituency, no agreed-upon agenda, no unifying organization or leadership. At different times and places, different social groups became active. People who were reformers on one issue might be conservative on another. The term *progressivism* embraces a widespread, many-sided effort after 1900 to build a better society.

A new style of popular journalism triggered much of this reform activity. During the 1890s magazines such as *Collier's* and *McClure's* had found a wide audience of urban readers. Unlike the highbrow *Atlantic Monthly* and *Harper's*, these bright new magazines, which sold for only a dime, specialized in lively and informative reporting. Almost by accident—Lincoln Steffens's article "Tweed Days in St. Louis" in the October 1902 issue of *McClure's* is credited with getting things started—editors discovered that what most interested readers was the exposure of corruption in American life.

In a series of powerful articles, Lincoln Steffens wrote about "the shame of the cities"—the corrupt ties between business and political machines. Ida M. Tarbell attacked Standard Oil, and David Graham Phillips told how money controlled the Senate. William Hard exposed industrial accidents in "Making Steel and Killing Men" (1907) and child labor in "De Kid Wot Works at Night" (1908). Hardly a sordid corner of American life escaped the scrutiny of these tireless reporters. They were moralists as well, infusing their factual accounts with personal indignation. "The sights I saw," wrote the pioneering slum investigator Jacob Riis, "gripped my heart until I felt I must tell of them, or burst, or turn anarchist."

Theodore Roosevelt, among many others, thought these journalists went too far. In a 1906 speech he compared them to the man with a muckrake in *Pilgrim's Progress* (by the seventeenth-century English preacher John Bunyan), too absorbed with raking the filth on the floor to look up and accept a celestial crown. Thus the term *muckraker* became attached to journalists who exposed the underside of American life. Their efforts were in fact health-giving. More than any other group, the muckrakers called the people to arms.

Political Reformers

Progressives framed their intentions in terms of high ideals. Their cause, pronounced Theodore Roosevelt, "is based in the eternal principles of righteousness." But in pursuit of reform, they were not all drawn to the same targets. Nor, in making their choices, were progressives indifferent to their own self-interest. In politics especially, the battles for reform reflected mixed motives of power politics and civic betterment.

In many cities the demand for good government came from local businessmen. Taxes went up, they complained, but needed services always lagged. There had to be an end, as one manufacturer said, to "the inefficiency, the sloth, the carelessness, the injustice and the graft of city administrations." The solution, argued John Patterson of the National Cash Register Company, was to get rid of old-fashioned party rule and put "municipal affairs on a strict business basis."

In 1900 a hurricane devastated Galveston, Texas, drowning 5,000 people and destroying the municipal port. Local businessmen took over and, in the process of rebuilding the city, replaced the mayor and board of aldermen with a five-member commission. The Galveston plan, although widely copied, had a serious flaw: it gave too much power to the individual commissioners. Dayton, Ohio, solved this problem by assigning policy matters to a nonpartisan commission and administrative functions to an appointed city manager. The commission-manager reform was chiefly the work of the business community and overtly a matter of the bottom line.

It was also a way of grabbing power. By making elections citywide and professionalizing city administration, municipal reformers attacked the ward politics that had favored ethnic and working-class groups. In fact, municipal reform contained a decidedly antidemocratic bias. "Ignorance should be excluded from control," said former Mayor Abram Hewitt of New York in 1901. "City business should be carried on by trained experts selected upon some other principle than popular suffrage."

Other urban progressives, however, opposed such elitism. Mayor Brand Whitlock of Toledo, Ohio, believed "that the cure for the ills of democracy was not less democracy, as so many people were always preaching, but more democracy." Whitlock's administration not only attacked municipal corruption and inefficiency, but also concerned itself with the needs of Toledo's working people. An increasing number of cities came under the leadership of such progressive mayors, including Samuel M. "Golden Rule" Jones in Toledo, Tom Johnson in Cleveland, and Mark Fagan in Jersey City. By combining popular programs and campaign magic, they won over the urban masses and challenged the rule of the machines.

The major battleground for democratic reform, however, was not the cities, but the states. Robert M. La Follette of Wisconsin led the way. Born in 1855, La Follette had followed a conventional party career as a lawyer, as district attorney, and then as congressman for three terms before breaking with the Wisconsin Republican machine in 1891, allegedly because the top party boss had tried to bribe him. La Follette became a tireless advocate of political reform, battling the Republican old guard for a decade before finally winning the governorship in 1900 on a platform of higher taxes for corporations, stricter utility and railroad regulation, and political reform.

La Follette's key proposal was a direct primary law requiring political parties to choose candidates by means of popular elections rather than in machine-run conventions. Enacted in 1903, the direct primary both expressed La Follette's political ideals and suited his particular political talents. The party regulars opposing him were insiders, more comfortable in the caucus room than out campaigning. But that was where La Follette, a superb campaigner, excelled. The direct primary gave La Follette an iron grip on the Republican party that he did not relinquish until his death twenty-five years later.

What was true of La Follette was more or less true of all successful progressive politicians. Albert B. Cummins of Iowa, Harold U'Ren of Oregon, and Hiram Johnson of California all supported democratic ideals, and all skillfuly used the direct primary as the steppingstone to political power. If they were newcomers—as Woodrow Wilson was when he left academic life to enter New Jersey politics in 1910—they showed a quick aptitude for politics and gained a solid mastery of the trade. They practiced a new kind of popular politics, which in a reform age could be a more effective route to power than the backroom techniques of the old-fashioned machine politicians.

Robert M. La Follette
La Follette was transformed into a political reformer when a Wisconsin Republican boss attempted to bribe him in 1891. As he described it in his *Autobiography*, "Out of this awful ordeal came understanding; and out of understanding came resolution. I determined that the power of this corrupt influence . . . should be broken." This photograph captures La Follette at the top of his form, taking his case in 1897 to the people of Cumberland, Wisconsin.

The Woman Progressive

Reform movements arise through a process of *recruitment*. Why do people enlist in a great cause? Each mobilized group—the progressive politicians just described, for example—is linked in some personal way to the evil crying out for correction. For middle-class women of the Progressive Era, the link was between being wives and mothers and being responsible for the social well-being of their communities.

Middle-class women had long borne the burden of humanitarian work in American cities. As voluntary investigators, they visited needy families, assessed their problems, and referred them to relief agencies.

After many years of such dedicated charity work, Josephine Shaw Lowell of New York City concluded that giving assistance to the poor was not enough. "If the working people had all they ought to have, we should not have the paupers and criminals," she declared. "It is better to save them before they go under, than to spend your life fishing them out afterward." Lowell founded the New York Consumers' League in 1890. Her goal was to improve the wages and working conditions of female clerks in the city's stores.

From these modest beginnings the league spread to other cities, and blossomed into the National Consumers' League in 1899. By then the women at its head had lost faith in voluntary action; only the state had the power to rescue poor urban families. Under the crusading Florence Kelley, formerly a chief factory inspector in Illinois, the Consumers' League became a powerful lobby for protective legislation for women and children.

Among its achievements, none was more important than the *Muller v. Oregon* decision (1908), which upheld Oregon's ten-hour workday for women workers. The Consumers' League recruited the brilliant Boston lawyer Louis D. Brandeis to defend the Oregon law before the Supreme Court. In his brief, Brandeis devoted a scant two pages to the narrow constitutional issue—whether, under its police powers, Oregon had the right to regulate women's working hours. Instead, Brandeis rested his case on data gathered by the Consumers' League showing how long hours damaged women's health and family roles. The *Muller* decision, which accepted Brandeis's reasoning, cleared the way for a wave of protective laws across the country.

Women's organizations became a mighty lobbying voice on behalf of women and children. Their victories included the first law providing public assistance for mothers with dependent children, in Illinois in 1911; the first minimum wage law for women, in Massachusetts in 1912; in many states, more effective child labor laws; and at the federal level, the Children's and Women's bureaus in the Labor Department, in 1912 and 1920, respectively. The welfare state, insofar as it arrived in America in these years, was what women progressives had made of it; they had erected a "maternalist" welfare system.

Meanwhile, other women were launching the settlement-house movement. In 1889, inspired by Toynbee Hall in the London slums, two young American women, Jane Addams and Ellen Gates Starr, established Hull House on Chicago's West Side. During the next fifteen years, scores of settlement houses sprang up in the slum neighborhoods of the nation's cities. Hull House had meeting rooms, an art gallery, clubs for children and adults, and a kindergarten. Addams herself led battles for garbage removal, playgrounds, better street lighting, and police protection. At the Henry Street Settlement in New York City, Lillian D. Wald made visiting nursing a major service.

Besides the modest good they did in the slum neighborhoods, the settlement houses also satisfied the needs of middle-class residents for meaningful lives. In a famous essay Jane Addams spoke of the "subjective necessity" of the settlement house. She meant that it was as much a response to the desire of educated young men and women to serve as it was a response to the needs of slum dwellers. Addams, for example, had grown up in a comfortable Illinois family. After college she faced an empty future, as an ornamental wife if she married, as a sheltered spinster if she did not. Hull House became her salvation, enabling her to "begin with however small a group to accomplish and to live."

Almost imperceptibly, women activists like Jane Addams and Florence Kelley breathed new life into the suffrage movement. Why should a woman who was capable of running a settlement house or lobbying a bill be denied the right to vote? If women had the right to vote, moreover, they would demand more enlightened legislation and better government. And finally, by encouraging working-class women to help themselves, women progressives got a whole new class interested in fighting for suffrage.

In 1903 social reformers founded the National Women's Trade Union League. Financed and led by wealthy supporters, the league organized women workers, played a considerable role in their strikes, and perhaps most important, helped to develop working-class leaders, such as Rose Schneiderman (see American Voices, Chapter 18, page 488) for New York garment workers and Agnes Nestor among Illinois glove workers. Athough they often resented the patronizing ways of their well-to-do patrons, trade-union women identified their cause with the broader struggle for women's rights.

In Britain, suffragists had begun to picket Parliament, assault politicians, and go on hunger strikes while in jail. Following their lead, Alice Paul, a young Quaker who had lived in Britain, applied confrontational tactics to the

Saving the Children
In the early years at Hull House, Jane Addams recalled, toddlers sometimes arrived for kindergarten tipsy from a breakfast of bread soaked in wine. To settlement-house workers, the answer to such ignorance was in child care education, and so began the program to send visiting nurses into immigrant homes. They taught mothers the proper method of caring for children—including, as this photograph shows, the daily infant bath, in a dishpan if necessary.

AMERICAN VOICES

Tracking Down Lead Poisoning

Alice Hamilton (1869–1970) studied medicine over the objections of her socially prominent family in Fort Wayne, Indiana. When she landed a job teaching pathology in Chicago in 1897, Hamilton at last had her chance to fulfill her dream of living at Jane Addams's Hull House. That experience launched her on an illustrious career as a pioneer in industrial medicine—one of the many paths to social reform opened up by settlement-house work.

Living in a working-class quarter, coming in contact with laborers and their wives, I could not fail to hear tales of the dangers that working men faced, of cases of carbon-monoxide poisoning in the great steel mills, of painters disabled by lead palsy, of pneumonia and rheumatism among the men in the stockyards. . . . At the time I am speaking of [1910] Professor Charles Henderson . . . persuaded [the governor] to appoint an Occupational Disease Commission, the first time a state had ever undertaken such a survey. . . .

One case, of colic and double wristdrop, which was discovered in the Alexian Brothers' Hospital, took me on a pretty chase. The man, a Pole, said he had worked in a sanitary-ware factory, putting enamel on bathtubs. I had not come across this work in the English or German authorities on lead poisoning, and had no idea it was a lead trade. . . . The management assured me that no lead was used in the coatings and invited me to inspect the workrooms. . . . Completely puzzled, I made a journey to the Polish quarter to see the palsied man and heard from him I had not even been in the enameling works, only the one for final touching up. The real one was far out on the Northwest Side. I found it and discovered that enameling means sprinkling a finely ground enamel over a red hot tub where it melts and flows over the surface. I learned that the air is thick with enamel dust . . . rich in red oxide of lead. A specimen . . . proved to contain as much as 20 per cent soluble lead—that is, lead that dissolves into solution in the stomach. Thus I nailed down the fact that sanitary-ware enameling is a dangerous lead trade in the United States, whatever was true of England or Germany.

SOURCE: W. Elliot Brownlee and Mary M. Brownlee, eds., *Women in the American Economy: A Documentary History* (New Haven: Yale University Press, 1976), 285–287.

American battle for woman suffrage. Rejecting the slower route of enfranchisement by the states (see Map 21.1), Paul advocated a constitutional amendment that in one stroke would give women across the country the right to vote. In 1916 Paul organized the militant National Woman's party.

The National American Woman Suffrage Association (NAWSA), from which Paul had split off, was also rejuvenated. Carrie Chapman Catt, a skilled political organizer from the New York movement, took over as national leader in 1915. Under her guidance, NAWSA brought a broad-based organization to the campaign for a federal amendment.

In the midst of this suffrage struggle something new and more fundamental began to happen. A younger generation of college-educated women, out in the world and self-supporting, refused to be hemmed in by the social constraints of women's "separate sphere." "Breaking into the Human Race" was the intention they proclaimed at a mass meeting in New York in 1914. "We intend simply to be ourselves," declared the chair Marie Jenny Howe, "not just our little female selves, but our whole big human selves."

The women at this meeting called themselves *feminists*, a term that was just coming into use. In this, its first incarnation, *feminism* meant freedom for full personal development. Thus did Charlotte Perkins Gilman, famous for her advocacy of communal kitchens as a means of liberating women from homemaking, imagine the new woman: "Here she comes, running, out of prison and off pedestal; chains off, crown off, halo off, just a live woman."

Feminists were militantly prosuffrage, but unlike their more traditional suffragist sisters, they did not stake their claim on any presumed uplifting effect of the women's vote on American politics. Rather, they demanded the right to vote

Suffragists on Parade, 1912
After 1910 the suffrage movement went into high gear. Suffragist leaders decided to demand a constitutional amendment rather than rely on gaining the vote state by state. In 1912 they served notice on both parties that they meant business and, as shown in this suffragist parade in New York, made their demands a visible part of the presidential campaign.

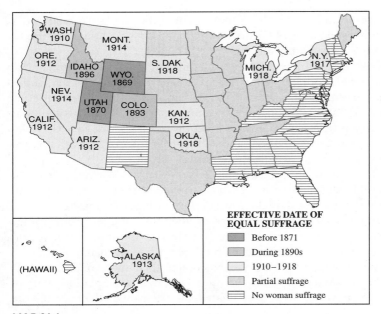

MAP 21.1

Woman Suffrage, 1869–1918

By 1909, after more than sixty years of agitation, only four lightly populated western states had granted women full voting rights. A number of
other states offered partial suffrage, limited mostly to voting for school
boards and such issues as taxes. Between 1910 and 1918, as the effort
shifted to the struggle for a constitutional amendment, eleven states (and
Alaska) joined the list granting full suffrage. The most stubborn resistance
was in the South.

because they considered themselves fully equal to men. At the point that the suffrage movement was about to triumph, it was overtaken by a larger revolution
that redefined the struggle for women's rights as a battle against all the constraints
that prevented women from achieving their potential as human beings.

Feminism brought forth a new and more radical type of woman social
progressive: Margaret Sanger. As a public health nurse in New York City,
Sanger had been repeatedly asked by immigrant women the "secret" of how
to avoid having more babies. When one of her patients died of a botched
abortion, Sanger decided to devote herself to teaching poor immigrant
women about birth control. This activity was illegal under nineteenth-century
laws that treated birth-control literature and contraceptive devices as obscene
materials. While it was easy enough for the educated middle class to evade
these laws, birth control could reach the poor only through an open campaign
of education. Undeterred by police raids or public disapproval, Sanger gave
speeches, published pamphlets, and in 1916 opened the first birth-control
clinic in the United States. If her ends were not different from Jane Ad-

dams's—both wanted to uplift the downtrodden—the means Sanger used posed a more provocative challenge to the status quo.

Urban Liberalism

Thirty minutes before quitting time on Saturday afternoon, March 25, 1911, fire broke out at the Triangle Shirtwaist Company in downtown New York City. The flames trapped the workers, mostly young immigrant women. Forty-seven leapt to their deaths; another ninety-nine never reached the windows. The tragedy caused a national furor, and led two months later to the creation of the New York State Factory Commission.

In the next four years the commission developed a remarkable program of labor reform: fifty-six laws dealing with fire hazards, unsafe machines, industrial homework, and wages and hours for women and children. The chairman of the commission was Robert F. Wagner; the vice-chairman, Alfred E. Smith. Both were Tammany Hall politicians, Democratic party leaders in the state legislature. They established the commission, participated fully in its work, and marshaled the party regulars to pass the proposals into law. All this Wagner and Smith did with the approval of the Tammany machine.

Tammany's reform role reflected something new in urban politics. Party machines increasingly recognized their limitations as social agencies in the modern industrial age. Only the state could prevent future Triangle fires, or cope with the evils of factory work and city poverty. A new generation had entered machine politics. Al Smith and Robert Wagner, men of social vision, absorbed the lessons of the Triangle investigation. They formed durable ties with such middle-class progressives as the social worker Frances Perkins, who sat on the commission as the representative of the New York Consumers' League. Historians have labeled this development *urban liberalism.*

City machines, always pragmatic, adopted urban liberalism without much of an ideological struggle. The same could not be said of trade unions, the other institution that represented American working people. The American Federation of Labor (AFL) had strongly opposed state interference in labor's affairs. Samuel Gompers preached that workers should not seek from government what they could accomplish by their own economic power and self-help. *Voluntarism,* as trade unionists called this doctrine, did not die out, but it weakened substantially during the progressive years.

In the early twentieth century the labor movement came under severe attack by the courts. In the *Loewe v. Lawlor* case (1908), the Supreme Court found a labor boycott—a call by the Hatters' Union for people not to patronize the antiunion D. E. Loewe & Company—to be a conspiracy in restraint of trade under the Sherman Act and awarded triple damages to the company. Hundreds of union members stood to lose their homes and life savings until the labor movement raised the money to pay the fines. Even worse was the employers' ability to get *injunctions*—court orders—prohibiting a union from carrying on a strike or boycott.

Only a political response could blunt these assaults on labor's economic weapons. In its "Bill of Grievances" of 1906, the AFL demanded that Congress grant unions immunity from court attack. Rebuffed, the unions decided to become more politically active, entering campaigns and giving nonpartisan support to candidates who favored their program.

Once into politics, the labor movement had difficulty denying the case for social legislation. The AFL, after all, claimed to speak for the entire working class. When muckrakers exposed exploitation of workers and middle-class progressives came forward with solutions, how could the labor movement fail to respond? Gompers served on the Triangle factory commission, and if—according to Frances Perkins—he was a less eager student than the Tammanyite members, learn he did. In state after state, organized labor joined the battle for progressive legislation and increasingly became its strongest advocate.

Conservative labor leaders offered the excuse that protective laws were for women and children, who could not defend themselves. In practice, however, trade unions became more flexible about legislative protection for men as well, especially regarding workers' compensation for industrial accidents. Between 1910 and 1917 all the industrial states enacted insurance laws covering factory injuries.

Compared to Europe, however, the United States was slow to protect workers against the hazards of modern industrial life. Health insurance and unemployment compensation, although popular in Europe, scarcely made it onto the American political agenda. Old-age pensions, which Britain adopted in 1908, got a serious hearing, only to come up against an odd barrier. The United States already had a pension system of a kind, for Civil War veterans: as many as half of all native-born men over sixty-four or their survivors were drawing benefits in the early twentieth century. It did not help, moreover, that the Republican party had shamelessly exploited veterans' pensions for partisan purposes; or that administration of the program was notoriously corrupt and laced with patronage; or finally, that easy access to veterans' benefits often reinforced fears of state-induced dependency.

Not until another generation had experienced the Great Depression would the country be ready for social insurance. A secure old age, unemployment compensation, health insurance—these human needs of a modern industrial order were beyond the reach of urban liberals in the Progressive Era.

Cultural Pluralism Embattled

Urban liberalism was driven not only by the plight of the downtrodden but by a sharpening attack on immigrants. Old-stock evangelical Protestants had long agitated for laws that would impose their moral and cultural norms on American society. After 1900 this impulse again beat strongly, expressing, in fact, one strand of progressive reform. The Anti-Saloon League, which called itself "the Protestant church in action," became a formidable force for prohibition in many states. The outlawing of liquor was related to other reform targets, for the saloon bred dirty politics and poverty. Like progressives on other fronts, prohibitionists pronounced their movement the "Revolt of Decent Citizens."

The moral-reform agenda expanded to include a new goal: restricting the immigration of southern and Eastern Europeans into the United States. La Follette's close adviser, Edward A. Ross of the University of Wisconsin, denounced the "pigsty mode of life" of immigrants. The danger, respected social scientists argued, was that the nation's Anglo-Saxon population would be "mongrelized" and its civilization swamped by "inferior" Mediterranean and Slavic cultures. Feeding on this fear, the Immigration Restriction League spearheaded a movement to end America's historic open-door policy. Like prohibition, immigration restriction was considered by its proponents to be a progressive reform.

Urban liberals thought otherwise. They bitterly resented the attacks on the worthiness of urban immigrants. Prohibition, protested one Catholic academic, was "despotic and hypocritical domination." The Tammany politician Martin McCue accused the Protestant ministry of "seeking to substitute the policeman's nightstick for the Bible."

In many ways, certainly until the Great Depression, ethnocultural issues provided a stronger basis for urban liberal politics than did economics. And because the Democrats cultivated the immigrant vote, they became destined to be the majority party once a second generation came of age. The shift from Republican domination, although not completed until the 1930s, began during the Progressive Era.

Racism and Reform

The direct primary was the flagship of progressive politics—the crucial reform, as La Follette said, for returning politics to "the people." The primary originated not in Wisconsin, however, but in the South, and by the time La Follette got his primary law in 1903, primaries were already operating in seven southern states.

In the South, however, the primary was a *white* primary. Since the Democratic nomination was tantamount to election, to be excluded from the primary meant in effect to be disfranchised. The direct primary was a reform *intended* to drive blacks out of politics.

How could democratic reform and white supremacy be thus wedded together? Because of the racism of the age. In a 1902 book on Reconstruction, Professor John W. Burgess of Columbia University denounced the Fifteenth Amendment, granting blacks the vote, as a "monstrous thing." Burgess was southern-born, but he was confident that his northern audience saw the "vast differences in political capacity" between blacks and whites, and approved of black disfranchisement. Even the Republican party offered no rebuttal. Indeed, as president-elect in 1908, William Howard Taft applauded the southern laws as necessary to "prevent entirely the possibility of domination by . . . an ignorant electorate." Taft reassured southerners that "the federal government has nothing to do with social equality."

In the North, racial tensions were on the rise. Over 200,000 blacks migrated from the South between 1900 and 1910. Their arrival in northern cities invariably sparked white resentment. Attacks on blacks became widespread. In 1908 a bloody race riot broke out in Springfield, Illinois. Equally reflective of racist sentiment was the huge success of D. W. Griffith's epic film *Birth of a Nation* (1915), which depicted Reconstruction as a moral struggle between rampaging blacks and a chivalrous Ku Klux Klan. Woodrow Wilson found the film's history "all so terribly true." His Democratic administration marked a low point for the federal government as the ultimate guarantor of equal rights: during Wilson's tenure, segregation of the U.S. civil service would have gone into effect but for an outcry among black leaders and influential white allies.

In these bleak years a core of young black professionals, mostly northern-born, began to fight back. The key figure was William Monroe Trotter, the pugnacious editor of the *Boston Guardian* and an outspoken critic of Booker T. Washington. "The policy of compromise has failed," Trotter argued. "The policy of resistance and aggression deserves a trial." In this endeavor, Trotter was joined by W. E. B. Du Bois, a Harvard-trained sociologist and author of *Souls of Black Folk*. In 1906 the two of them, having broken with Washington, called a meeting of twenty-nine supporters at Niagara Falls—but in Canada, because no hotel on the U.S. side would admit blacks. The Niagara movement, which resulted from that meeting, had an impact far beyond the scattering of members and local bodies it organized. The principles it affirmed would define the struggle for the rights of African-Americans: first, encouragement of black pride by all possible means; second, an uncompromising demand for full political and civil equality; and above all, the resolute denial "that the Negro-American assents to inferiority, is submissive under oppression and apologetic before insults."

Going against the grain, a handful of white reformers rallied to the African-American cause. Among the most devoted was Mary White Ovington, who grew up in an abolitionist family. Like Jane Addams, Ovington became a settlement-house worker, but among urban blacks in New York rather than in an immigrant Chicago neighborhood. News of the Springfield race riot of 1908 changed her life. Convinced that her duty was to fight racism, Ovington called a meeting of sympathetic white progressives, which led to the formation of the National Association for the Advancement of Colored People (NAACP) in 1909.

The Niagara movement, torn by internal disagreements, was breaking up, and most of the black activists joined the NAACP. The organization's national leadership was dominated by whites, but with one crucial exception. Du Bois became the editor of the NAACP's journal, *The Crisis*. With a passion that only a black voice could provide, Du Bois used that platform to proclaim the demand for equal rights.

In social welfare, the National Urban League became the lead organization, uniting in 1911 the many groups serving black migrants arriving in northern cities. Like the NAACP, the Urban League was interracial, including both white reformers such as Ovington and black welfare activists such as William Lewis Bulkley, a New York school principal who was the main architect of the Urban League. In the South, social welfare was very much the province of black women, whose civic activities to some degree filled the vacuum left by the disfranchisement of black men. Black women's progressivism sprang organizationally from the churches and schools, but also from the southern affiliates of the National Association of Colored Women's Clubs, which had started in 1896. And because their activities seemed unthreatening to white supremacy, black women reached across the color line and found allies and supporters among white women in the South.

Progressivism was a house of many chambers. Most were infected by the respectable racism of the age, but not all. A saving remnant of white progressives rallied to the cause of African-Americans. In the interracial NAACP and Urban League, and in such black organizations as the National Association of Colored Women's Clubs, the national institutions were formed that would lead the black struggle for a better life over the next half-century.

PROGRESSIVISM AND NATIONAL POLITICS

The gathering forces of progressivism were slow to reach the national scene. Reformers had been spurred by immediate and visible problems. Washington seemed remote from the battles they were waging in their cities and states. But in 1906 Robert La Follette moved from the governor's office in Wisconsin to the U.S. Senate. Other seasoned progressives, also ambitious for a wider stage, made the same move. By 1910 a highly vocal progressive bloc was making itself heard in both houses of Congress.

Progressivism came to national politics not via Congress, however, but via the presidency. This was partly because the White House provided a "bully pulpit"—to use Theodore Roosevelt's phrase—for mobilizing national opinion. But just as important was the twist of fate that brought Roosevelt to the White House on September 14, 1901.

The Making of a Progressive President

Except for his upper-class background, Theodore Roosevelt was cut from much the same cloth as other progressive politicians. Born in 1858, he came from a wealthy old-line New York family, attended Harvard, and might have chosen the life of a leisured man of letters. Instead, scarcely out of college, he plunged into Republican politics, and in 1882 he entered the New York State legislature. His reasons matched the high-minded motives of other budding progressives. Roosevelt always identified himself—loudly—with the cause of righteousness. But he did not scorn power and its uses. He showed contempt for the amateurism of the Mugwumps—"those political and literary hermaphrodites," he called them—and much preferred the professionalism of party politics.

Returning from the Spanish-American War the hero of San Juan Hill (see Chapter 22), Roosevelt captured the New York governorship in 1898. During his single term he clearly signaled his reformist inclinations by pushing through civil-service reform and a tax on corporate franchises. He discharged the corrupt superintendent of insurance over the Republican party's objections, and asserted his confidence in the government's capacity to improve the life of the people.

Hoping to neutralize Roosevelt, the party bosses promoted him in 1900 to a dead-end job, as William McKinley's vice-president. Roosevelt accepted reluctantly. But on September 6, 1901, an anarchist named Leon F. Czolgosz shot the president. When McKinley died eight days later, Roosevelt became president. It was a sure bet, groaned Republican boss Mark Hanna, that "that damn cowboy" would make trouble in the White House.

Roosevelt in fact moved cautiously, attending first of all to politics. He skillfully used the patronage powers of the presidency to gain control of the Republican party. But Roosevelt was also restrained by uncertainty about what reform role the federal government ought to play. At first the new president might have been described as a progressive without a cause.

Even so, Roosevelt displayed his activist bent. An ardent outdoorsman, he devoted part of his first annual message to Congress to conservation. Unlike John Muir (see Chapter 17, page 472), Roosevelt was not a preservationist devoted to defending the nation's wilderness. Rather, he wanted to *conserve* the country's resources. He was not against commercial development as long as it was regulated and mindful of the public interest. In 1902 he backed the Newlands Reclamation Act, which designated the proceeds from public land sales for irrigation in arid regions. His administration expanded the national forest reserve; upgraded the management of public lands; and to the chagrin of some Republicans, energetically prosecuted violators of federal land laws. In the cause of conservation, Roosevelt demonstrated his enthusiasm for exercising executive authority and his disdain for those who sought profit "by betraying the public."

Roosevelt showed the same determination in the face of the anthracite coal strike of 1902. Anthracite, or hard coal, was the main fuel for home heating in those days. As cold weather approached, it became urgent to settle the strike. The United Mine Workers (UMW), led by John Mitchell, were willing to submit to arbitration, but the mine operators adamantly refused to recognize the union. Advised that he had no legal grounds for intervening, the president nevertheless called both sides to a White House conference on October 1, 1902. When the operators balked, Roosevelt threatened a government takeover of the mines. He also persuaded the financier J. P. Morgan to use his considerable influence with them. At that point, the mine operators caved in. Roosevelt appointed an arbitration commission to rule on the issues, another unprecedented step. Although not especially sympathetic to organized labor, TR became infuriated by the "arrogant stupidity" of the mine owners.

"Of all the forms of tyranny the least attractive and the most vulgar is the tyranny of mere wealth," Roosevelt wrote in his autobiography. He was prepared to deploy all his presidential authority against the "tyranny" of irresponsible business.

Regulating the Marketplace

The economic issue that most troubled Roosevelt was the assault on the competitive market by big business. The drift toward large-scale enterprise had been under way for many years, as entrepreneurs sought the efficiencies of nationwide, vertically integrated firms (see Chapter 18). But, additionally, creating bigger businesses meant gaining power to control markets. Controlling markets was the motive behind the scramble to merge rival firms in the aftermath of the depression of the 1890s. These mergers—*trusts*, as they were called—greatly increased the degree of business concentration in the economy. Of the 73 largest industrial companies in 1900, 53 had not existed three years earlier. By 1910, 1 percent of the nation's manufacturers accounted for 44 percent of the nation's industrial output.

Roosevelt's uneasiness became evident as early as his first annual message to Congress, in which he referred to the "real and grave evils" of economic concentration. But what weapons could the president use in response?

The basic legal principles upholding free competition were already firmly established. Under *common law*—the body of judge-made legal precedents America had inherited from Britain—it was illegal for anyone to restrain or monopolize trade. Persons who were economically injured by such actions could sue for damages. These common-law rights had been enacted into statutory law in many states during the 1880s and then, because the problem spilled over state jurisdictions, had been incorporated into the Sherman Antitrust Act of 1890 and become part of federal law.

Neither Cleveland nor McKinley had been much inclined to enforce the Sherman Act. But the law was there to be used. Its potential rested above all on the fact that it incorporated common-law principles of unimpeachable validity. In the right hands, the Sherman Act could be a strong weapon against the abuse of economic power.

Roosevelt made his opening move in 1903 by establishing the Bureau of Corporations, empowered to investigate business practices. On the basis of evidence gathered by the bureau, the Justice Department was able to mount antitrust suits. The department had already filed such a suit in 1902 against the Northern Securities Company, a combination of the railroad systems of the Northwest. In a landmark decision, the Supreme Court ordered Northern Securities dissolved in 1904.

In the presidential election that year, Roosevelt handily defeated a weak conservative Democratic candidate, Judge Alton B. Parker. Now president in

J. Pierpont Morgan
J. P. Morgan was a giant among American financiers. He had served an apprenticeship in investment banking under his father, a leading Anglo-American banker in London. A gruff man of few words, Morgan had a genius for instilling trust and the strength of will to persuade others to follow his lead and do his bidding—qualities the great photographer Edward Steichen captured in this portrait.

his own right, Roosevelt stepped up the attack on the trusts. He took on forty-five of the nation's giant firms, including Standard Oil, American Tobacco, and Du Pont. His rhetoric rising, Roosevelt became the nation's trust-buster, a crusader against "predatory wealth."

But Roosevelt was not antibusiness. He regarded large-scale enterprise as a natural result of modern industrialism. Only firms that abused their power deserved punishment. But how would those companies be identified? Under the Sherman Act, following common-law practice, the courts decided whether an act in restraint of trade was "unreasonable," that is, actually harmed the public interest. The courts thus had the discretion to evaluate the actions of corporations on a case-by-case basis. In 1897, however, the Supreme Court repudiated this "rule of reason" in the *Trans-Missouri* case. Now, even if the impact on the market was harmless, actions that restrained or monopolized trade would automatically violate the Sherman Act.

Little noticed when it was first decided, *Trans-Missouri* placed Roosevelt in an awkward position. He had no desire to hamstring legitimate business activity, but he could not rely on the courts to distinguish between "good" and "bad" trusts. The only solution was for Roosevelt to assume that responsibility. This the president could do because it was up to him—or his attorney general—to decide whether or not to initiate antitrust prosecutions in the first place.

In November 1904, with an antitrust suit looming, the United States Steel Corporation approached Roosevelt and proposed a deal: cooperation in exchange for preferential treatment. The company would open its books to the Bureau of Corporations; if the bureau found evidence of wrongdoing, the company would be warned privately and given a chance to set matters right. Roosevelt accepted this "gentlemen's agreement" because it solved a serious dilemma for him. He could accommodate the realities of the modern industrial order while maintaining his public image as the champion against the trusts.

The railroads posed a different kind of problem for Roosevelt. As quasi-public enterprises, they had always been subject to regulation, beginning at the federal level in 1887 with the establishment of the Interstate Commerce Commission (ICC), the nation's first federal regulatory agency. Like the Sherman Act, however, railroad regulation remained pretty much a dead letter in its early years. Convinced that the railroads needed firm regulation, Roosevelt pushed through the Elkins Act of 1903, which prohibited discriminatory rebates, that is, reductions on published rates for preferred or powerful customers. Then, with the 1904 election behind him, Roosevelt launched his drive for real railroad regulation.

The central issue was government rate-setting, which the conservative Republican bloc in Congress firmly opposed. In 1906, after nearly two years of wrangling, Congress passed the Hepburn Railway Act, which empowered the ICC to set maximum rates upon complaint of a shipper, and to prescribe uniform methods of bookkeeping. But as a concession to conservatives, the courts retained broad powers to review the ICC's rate decisions.

The Hepburn Act was a triumph of Roosevelt's skills as a political operator. He had maneuvered brilliantly against determined opposition and come away with the essentials of what he wanted. Despite grumbling by Senate progressives critical of any compromise, Roosevelt was satisfied. He had achieved a landmark expansion of the government's regulatory powers over business.

The regulation of consumer products, another hallmark of progressive reform, was very much the handiwork of muckraking journalists—in particular, Samuel Hopkins Adams's riveting series of articles on the patent-medicine business in *Collier's* in 1905. For a time, industry lobbies stymied pure food and drug legislation. Then, in 1906, Upton Sinclair's novel *The Jungle* appeared. Sinclair had meant to expose labor exploitation in Chicago meat-packing plants, but his graphic descriptions of rotten meat and filthy conditions excited—and sickened—the nation. President Roosevelt weighed into the legislative battle, initiating a federal investigation of the stockyards. Within months, the Pure Food and Drug Act and the Meat Inspection Act were passed, and another administrative agency was added to the federal bureaucratic structure Roosevelt was building: the Food and Drug Administration.

During the 1904 presidential campaign Roosevelt had taken to calling his program the Square Deal. This kind of labeling was new to American politics, introducing a political style that dramatized issues, mobilized public opinion, and asserted leadership. But the Square Deal meant something of substance as well. After many years of passivity and weakness, the federal government was

Campaigning for the Square Deal
When William McKinley ran for president in 1896, he sat on his front porch in Canton, Ohio, and received delegations of voters. But Theodore Roosevelt considered the presidency a "bully pulpit" and used the office brilliantly to mobilize public opinion and assert his leadership. The preeminence of the presidency in American public life began with Roosevelt's administration. Here, at the height of his crusading powers, he stumps for the Square Deal in the 1904 election.

reclaiming the role it had abandoned after the Civil War. Now, however, the target was the new economic order. When companies misused corporate power, the government had to step in and assure ordinary Americans a "square deal."

The Fracturing of Republican Progressivism

Roosevelt was well aware that his Square Deal was built on nineteenth-century foundations. Antitrust doctrine, in particular, seemed to him inadequate in the face of a large-scale industrial order. Better, Roosevelt felt, to empower the federal government to oversee big business than to try to enforce an archaic competitive market. Roosevelt's final presidential speeches dwelt on the need for a reform agenda for the twentieth century. This was the task he bequeathed to his chosen successor, William Howard Taft.

Taft was an admirable man in many ways. An able jurist and a superb administrator, he had served Roosevelt loyally as governor-general of the Philippines and as secretary of war. He was an avowed Square Dealer. But he was not by nature a progressive politician. He disliked the give-and-take of politics, he distrusted power, and he generally deferred to Congress. In fundamental ways, moreover, Taft was conservative. He revered the processes of the law and, unlike Roosevelt, found it hard to trim his means to fit his ends.

Taft's Democratic opponent in the 1908 campaign was William Jennings Bryan. This was Bryan's last hurrah, and he made the most of it. Eloquent as ever, Bryan attacked the Republicans as the party of the "plutocrats," and outdid them in urging tougher antitrust legislation, lower tariffs, stricter railway regulation, and advanced labor legislation. Bryan's campaign moved the Democratic party into the mainstream of national progressive politics, but that was not enough to offset Taft's advantages as Roosevelt's candidate.

Taft won comfortably, and he entered the White House with a mandate to pick up where Roosevelt had left off. That, alas, was not to be.

By 1909 the ferment of reform had unsettled the Republican party. On the right, the conservatives were bracing themselves against further losses. Led by the formidable Senator Nelson W. Aldrich of Rhode Island, they were still a force to be reckoned with. On the left, progressive Republicans were rebellious. They had broad popular support—especially in the Midwest—and in Robert La Follette they had a fiery leader. The progressives felt that Roosevelt had been too easy on business, and with him gone from the White House, they intended to make up for lost time. Reconciling these conflicting forces within the Republican party would have been a daunting task for the most accomplished politician. For Taft, it spelled disaster.

First there was the tariff. Progressives considered protective tariffs a major reason why the trusts had sprung up. Although Taft had campaigned for tariff reform, he was won over by the conservative Republican bloc and ended up approving the Payne-Aldrich Tariff Act of 1909, which sheltered eastern industry from foreign competition.

Next came the Pinchot-Ballinger affair. U.S. Chief Forester Gifford Pinchot, an ardent conservationist and a chum of Roosevelt's, accused Secretary of the Interior Richard A. Ballinger of conspiring to transfer Alaskan public lands rich in natural resources to a private syndicate. When Pinchot aired the charges in January 1910, Taft fired him for insubordination. Despite Taft's strong conservationist credentials, in the eyes of the progressives he was marked for life by the Pinchot-Ballinger affair as a friend of the "interests" plundering the nation's resources.

Solemnly pledged to carry on Roosevelt's tradition, Taft found himself propelled into the conservative Republican camp, an ally of "Uncle Joe" Cannon, the dictatorial speaker of the House of Representatives. When a House revolt finally broke Cannon's power in 1910, it was regarded as a defeat for the president as well. Largely in reaction to Taft, the reformers in the Republican party turned into a distinct, organized faction. By 1910 they were calling themselves "Progressives," or in more belligerent moments, "Insurgents." Taft answered by trying to purge them in the Republican primaries that year.

The Progressives emerged from the 1910 elections stronger and angrier. In January 1911 they formed the National Progressive Republican League and began a drive to take over the Republican party. Though La Follette was their leader, the Progressives knew that their best chance to capture the presidency lay with Theodore Roosevelt.

Roosevelt, home from a year-long safari in Africa, yearned to reenter the political fray. He would have been troublesome for Taft under any circumstances. As it was, the president's handling of the Progressives fed Roosevelt's mounting sense of outrage. But Roosevelt was too loyal a party man to defy the Republican establishment, and too astute a politician not to recognize that a Republican party split would benefit the Democrats. He could be spurred into rebellion only by a true clash of principles. On the question of the trusts, just such a clash materialized.

Roosevelt had managed to reconcile public policy and economic reality during his administration by distinguishing between good and bad trusts. But this was a makeshift solution that depended on a president who was willing to stretch his powers to the limit. Taft had no such inclination. His legalistic mind rebelled at the notion that he as president should decide which trusts should be prosecuted. The Sherman Act was on the books. "We are going to enforce that law or die in the attempt," Taft promised grimly.

In its *Standard Oil* decision (1911), the Supreme Court eased Taft's problem by reasserting the common-law principle of the "rule of reason," which meant that, once again, the courts themselves would distinguish between good and bad trusts. With that burden lifted from the executive branch, Attorney General George W. Wickersham stepped up the pace of antitrust actions.

United States Steel became an immediate target. Among the charges against the Steel Trust was that it had violated the antimonopoly provision of the Sherman Act by acquiring the Tennessee Coal and Iron Company (TCI) in 1907. Roosevelt had personally approved the acquisition as a necessary step—so U.S. Steel representatives had explained it to him—to prevent a financial collapse on Wall Street. Taft's suit against U.S. Steel thus amounted to an attack on Roosevelt: he had as president arranged for U.S. Steel to circumvent the Sherman Act. Nothing was better calculated to propel Roosevelt into action than an issue that was both an affair of personal honor and a question of broad principle.

The country did not have to choose between breaking up big business and submitting to corporate rule, Roosevelt argued. There was a third way. The federal government could be empowered to oversee the nation's industrial corporations to make sure they acted in the public interest. They would be regulated by a federal trade commission as if they were natural monopolies or public utilities.

In a speech in Osawatomie, Kansas, in August 1910, Roosevelt made his case for what he called the New Nationalism. The central issue, he argued, was human welfare versus property rights. In modern society, property had to be controlled "to whatever degree the public welfare may require it." The government would become "the steward of the public welfare."

This formulation removed the restraints from Roosevelt's thinking. He took up the cause of social justice, adding to his program a federal child labor law, regulation of labor relations, and a national minimum wage for women. Most radical, perhaps, was Roosevelt's attack on the legal system. Insisting that the courts should not be making social policy, Roosevelt proposed sharp curbs on their powers, even raising the possibility of popular recall of court decisions. Beyond these specifics, the New Nationalism advanced a new political philosophy. Roosevelt was proposing a *statist* solution—an enormous expansion of the role of the federal government—to the problem of corporate power.

Early in 1912, Roosevelt announced his candidacy for the presidency and immediately swept the progressive Republicans into his camp. A bitter party battle ensued. Roosevelt won the states that held primary elections, but Taft controlled the party organizations elsewhere. Dominated by the party regulars, the Republican convention chose Taft.

Roosevelt, considering himself cheated out of the nomination, bolted from the Republicans and created a new Progressive party, soon nicknamed the "Bull Moose" party. In a crusading campaign, Roosevelt offered the New Nationalism to the people.

Woodrow Wilson and the New Freedom

While the Republicans battled among themselves, the Democrats were on the move. The scars caused by the free silver campaign of 1896 had faded, and in the 1908 campaign William Jennings Bryan had established the rejuvenated party's progressive credentials. The Democrats made dramatic gains in 1910, taking over the House of Representatives for the first time since 1892 and capturing a number of traditionally Republican governorships. After fourteen years as the party's standard-bearer, Bryan reluctantly made way for a new generation of leaders.

The ablest was Woodrow Wilson of New Jersey. Wilson was an academic, a noted political scientist, and president of Princeton University. In 1910, with no political experience, he accepted the Democratic nomination for governor of New Jersey. As governor, Wilson compiled a brilliant record: he cleaned up the boss system and passed a direct primary law, workers' compensation, and stronger regulation of railroads and utilities. Wilson went on, in a bruising battle, to win the Democratic presidential nomination in 1912.

Wilson possessed, to a fault, the moral certainty that characterized the progressive politician. A brilliant speaker, he almost instinctively assumed the mantle of righteous reform. Only gradually, however, did he hammer out, in reaction to Roosevelt's New Nationalism, a coherent reform program, which he called the New Freedom.

Wilson actually had much in common with Roosevelt. "The old time of individual competition is probably gone by," Wilson stressed. Like Roosevelt, he opposed not bigness but the abuse of economic power. Nor did Wilson think that the abuse of power could be prevented without a strong federal government. He parted company from Roosevelt over *how* government should restrain private power.

As he warmed to the debate, Wilson cast the issue in fundamental terms. "This is a struggle for emancipation," he proclaimed in October 1912. "If America is not to have free enterprise, then she can have freedom of no sort whatever." Wilson also scorned Roosevelt's social program. Welfare might be benevolent, he declared, but it also would be paternalistic and contrary to the traditions of a free people.

How, then, did Wilson propose to deal with the problem of corporate power? Court enforcement of the Sherman Act was Wilson's basic answer. His task was to figure out how to make that long-established antitrust approach work better. In this effort Wilson relied heavily on a new adviser, Louis D. Brandeis, famous as the "people's lawyer" for his public service in many progressive causes (including the landmark *Muller* case).

An expert on regulatory matters, Brandeis understood that an all-powerful trade commission was likely to end up not as defender of the public interest, but in a cozy relationship with the industries it was supposed to regulate. Nor did Brandeis believe that bigness meant efficiency. On the contrary, he argued, trusts were wasteful compared with firms that vigorously competed in a free market. The main thing was to prevent the trusts from unfairly using their power to curb free competition.

The 1912 election fell short of being a referendum on the New Nationalism versus the New Freedom. The outcome turned on a more humdrum reality: Wilson was elected because he kept the traditional Democratic vote, while the Republicans split between Roosevelt and Taft. Although he won by a landslide in the electoral college, Wilson received only 42 percent of the popular vote—115,000 fewer votes than Bryan had amassed against Taft in 1908. At best it could be said that the 1912 election signified that the American public was in the mood for reform. Only 23 percent, after all, had voted for the one candidate who stood for the status quo, President Taft. Woodrow Wilson's own reform program, however, had not received a mandate from the people.

Yet the 1912 election proved decisive in the history of national reform. The debate between Roosevelt and Wilson had brought forth, in the New Freedom, a program capable of finally resolving the crisis over corporate power that had gripped the nation for a decade. Just as important, the election created a rare legislative opportunity in Washington. Wilson became president with the Democrats in firm control of both houses of Congress, united in their eagerness to get on with the New Freedom.

Wilson chose a flanking attack on the problem of economic power. Long out of power, the Democrats were hungry for tariff reform. From the prevailing average of 40 percent, the Underwood Tariff Act of 1913 pared rates down to an average of 25 percent. Targeting especially the trust-dominated industries, Democrats confidently expected the Underwood Tariff to spur competition and reduce prices for consumers by opening protected American markets to foreign products.

Wilson's administration then turned to the nation's banking system, whose key weakness was the absence of a central reserve bank. The main function of central banks at that time was to regulate commercial banks and back them up in case they could not meet their obligations to depositors. In practice, this role had been assumed by the great New York banks, which handled the accounts of outlying banks and assisted them when they came under pressure. However, if the New York banks weakened, the entire system could collapse. This had nearly happened in 1907, when the Knickerbocker Trust Company failed and panic swept through the nation's financial markets.

The need for a reserve system became widely accepted, but the form it should take was hotly debated. Wall Street wanted a centralized system controlled by the bankers. Rural Democrats and their spokesman, Senator Carter Glass of Virginia, preferred a decentralized network of reserve banks. Progressives in both parties agreed that the essential feature should be public control over the reserve system. The bankers, whose practices were already under scrutiny by Congress, were on the defensive in this contest.

President Wilson, no expert to begin with, learned quickly and reconciled the reformers and bankers. The monumental Federal Reserve Act of 1913 gave the nation a banking system that was resistant to financial panic. The act delegated reserve functions to twelve district reserve banks, which would be controlled by their member banks. The Federal Reserve Board imposed public regulation on this regional structure. In one stroke the act strengthened the banking system and placed a measure of restraint on the "money trust."

Having dealt with tariff and banking reform, Wilson turned to the problem of corporate power. He wanted to rely on the Sherman Act, but was not sure how to make its antitrust principles more effective. Was it feasible to write strict definitions of illegal practices? Wilson finally decided that it was not. In the Clayton Antitrust Act of 1914, amending the Sherman Act, the definition of illegal practices was left flexible, subject to the test of whether the effect "substantially lessen[ed] competition or tend[ed] to create a monopoly."

As for Brandeis's advocacy of a trade commission, the problem was how much power and what functions it should have. Wilson was understandably hesitant, given his principled opposition to Roosevelt's conception of a powerful trade commission overseeing American business. Ultimately, under the 1914 law establishing it, the Federal Trade Commission (FTC) received broad powers to investigate companies and issue "cease and desist" orders against unfair trade practices that violated antitrust law. FTC decisions, however, were subject to court review, so that Wilson's entire program was situated within the original conception of antitrust enforcement. As before, it would ultimately be up to the courts to decide which business practices were illegal.

Despite a good deal of commotion, this arduous legislative process was actually an exercise in consensus building. Wilson himself had opened the debate in a conciliatory way. "The antagonism between business and government is over," he said, and the time was ripe for a program representing the "best business judgment in America." Afterward, Wilson felt he had brought the long controversy over corporate power to a successful conclusion, and in fact he had. Steering a course between Taft's conservatism and Roosevelt's radicalism, Wilson had carved out a middle way that brought to bear the powers of government without threatening the constitutional order, and that curbed abuse of corporate power without threatening the capitalist system.

On social policy, too, Wilson charted a middle way. During the 1912 campaign he had denounced Roosevelt's social program as paternalistic. The most Wilson was willing to accept was cosmetic language in the Clayton Act stating that labor and farm organizations were not illegal combinations. He rejected exempting them from antitrust prosecution.

The labor vote had grown increasingly important to the Democratic party, however. As his second presidential campaign drew nearer, Wilson lost some of his scruples about prolabor legislation. In 1915 and 1916 he championed a host of bills beneficial to American workers: a federal child labor law, the Adamson eight-hour law for railroad workers, and the landmark Seamen's Act, which eliminated age-old abuses of sailors aboard ship. Likewise, after earlier resistance, in 1916 Wilson approved the Federal Farm Loan Act, which provided the low-interest rural credit system long demanded by farmers.

Wilson encountered the same dilemma that confronted all successful progressives: the claims of moral principle versus the unyielding realities of political and economic life. Progressives were high-minded but not radical. They saw evils in the system, but they did not consider the system itself to be evil. They also prided themselves on being realists as well as moralists. So it stood to reason that Wilson, like other progressives who achieved power, would find his place at the center.

CHAPTER 21 TIMELINE

1887	Interstate Commerce Commission established
1889	Jane Addams and Ellen Gates Starr found Hull House
1890	Sherman Antitrust Act
1893	Economic depression (until 1897)
1899	National Consumers' League founded
1900	Robert M. La Follette elected Wisconsin governor First commission form of city government in Galveston, Texas
1901	President McKinley assassinated; Theodore Roosevelt succeeds United States Steel Corporation formed
1902	President Roosevelt settles national anthracite strike
1903	National Women's Trade Union League
1904	Supreme Court dissolves the Northern Securities Company
1906	Hepburn Railway Act AFL adopts Bill of Grievances Upton Sinclair's *The Jungle*
1908	*Muller v. Oregon* upholds regulation of working hours for women Federal Council of Churches founded William Howard Taft elected president
1909	NAACP formed
1910	Roosevelt announces the New Nationalism Woman suffrage movement revives; suffrage victory in Washington State
1911	*Standard Oil* decision restores "rule of reason" Triangle Shirtwaist fire
1912	Progressive party formed Woodrow Wilson elected president
1913	Federal Reserve Act Underwood Tariff
1914	Clayton Antitrust Act

CHAPTER 22

AN EMERGING WORLD POWER, 1877–1914

- The Roots of Expansion
- An American Empire
- Onto the World Stage

In 1881 Great Britain sent a new envoy to Washington. He was Sir Lionel Sackville-West, son of an earl, brother-in-law of the Tory leader Lord Denby, but otherwise distinguished only as the lover of a celebrated Spanish dancer. His well-connected friends wanted to park Sir Lionel somewhere comfortable, but out of harm's way. So they made him minister to the United States.

Twenty years later such an appointment would have been unthinkable. All the European powers had by then elevated their missions in Washington to embassies, and staffed them with top-of-the-line ambassadors. And they treated the United States, without question, as a fellow Great Power.

In Sir Lionel's day, the United States had scarcely cast a shadow on world affairs. America's army in 1881 was smaller than Bulgaria's; its navy ranked thirteenth in the world. Two decades later, however, the United States was flexing its muscles. It had just made short work of Spain in a brief but decisive war and acquired for itself an empire that stretched from Puerto Rico to the Philippines. America's standing as a rising naval power was manifest, and so was its aggressive assertion of national interest in the Caribbean and the Pacific.

The European powers could not be sure what America's role would be, since the United States retained its traditional policy of nonalignment in European affairs. But in chanceries across the Continent, the importance of the

United States was universally acknowledged, and its likely response to every event carefully assessed.

How the United States emerged onto the world stage in the years before World War I is the subject of this chapter.

THE ROOTS OF EXPANSION

In 1880 the United States had a population of 50 million, and by that measure it ranked with the great European powers. In industrial production the nation was second only to Britain and was rapidly closing the gap. Anyone who doubted the military prowess of the Americans needed only to recall the ferocity with which they had fought one another in the Civil War. The great campaigns of Lee, Sherman, and Grant had entered the military textbooks and were closely studied by army strategists everywhere.

Nor, when its vital interests were at stake, had the United States shown itself to be lacking in diplomatic vigor. The Civil War had put the United States at odds with both France and Britain. In the case of France, the issue involved the establishment in Mexico of a puppet regime under Archduke Maximilian, regarded by the United States as a threat to its security in the Southwest. When American troops under General Philip Sheridan began to mass on the Mexican border in 1867, the French military withdrew, abandoning Maximilian to a Mexican firing squad. With Britain, the thorny issue involved damages to Union shipping by the *Alabama* and other Confederate sea raiders operating from English ports. American hopes of achieving the annexation of Canada out of this dispute were dashed by Britain's grant of dominion status to Canada in 1867. But four years later, after lengthy negotiations, Britain expressed regret for its unneutral acts against the Union and agreed to the arbitration of the *Alabama* claims, settling to America's satisfaction the last outstanding diplomatic issue of the Civil War.

Diplomacy in the Gilded Age

In the years that followed, the United States lapsed into diplomatic inactivity, not out of weakness but for lack of any clear national purpose in world affairs. The business of building the nation's industrial economy absorbed Americans and turned their attention inward. And while the new international telegraphic cables provided the country with swift overseas communication after the 1860s, wide oceans still kept the world at a distance and gave Americans a sense of isolation and security.

In these circumstances, with no external threat to be seen, what was the point of maintaining a big navy? After the Civil War, the fleet gradually deteriorated. Of the 125 ships on the navy's active list, only about 25 were seaworthy at any one time. During the administration of Chester A. Arthur (1881–1885) a modest upgrading program began, commissioning new ships, raising the standards for the officer corps, and founding Naval War College. But the fleet remained small, without a unified naval command and with little more to do than maintain coastal defenses.

The conduct of diplomacy was likewise of little account. Appointment to the foreign service was mostly through the spoils system. American ministers and consular officers were a mixed lot, with many idlers and drunkards among the hard-working and competent. Domestic politics, moreover, made it difficult to develop a coherent foreign policy. Although diplomacy was an executive responsibility, the U.S. Senate jealously guarded its constitutional right to give "advice and consent" on treaties and diplomatic appointments. For its part the State Department tended to be inactive, exerting little control over either policy or its missions abroad. In remote parts of the world the American presence was often primarily religious: the intrepid missionaries bent on Christianizing the native populations of Asia, Africa, and the Pacific islands.

In the Caribbean the United States remained the dominant power, but the expansionist enthusiasms of the Civil War era subsided. Nothing came of the grandiose plans of William H. Seward, Andrew Johnson's secretary of state, nor of President Grant's efforts to purchase Santo Domingo in 1870, and the Senate regularly blocked later moves to acquire bases in Haiti, Cuba, and Venezuela. The long-cherished interest in an interoceanic canal across Central America also faded. Despite its claims of exclusive building rights, the United States stood by when a French company headed by the builder of the Suez Canal, Ferdinand de Lesseps, started to dig across the Panama isthmus in 1880. That project failed after a decade, but the reason was bankruptcy, not American opposition.

Diplomatic activity in Latin America quickened when James G. Blaine became secretary of state in 1881. He got involved in a border dispute between Mexico and Guatemala, tried to settle a war Chile was waging against Peru and Bolivia, and called the first Pan-American conference. Blaine's interventions in Latin American disputes went badly, however, and his successor canceled the Pan-American conference after Blaine left office in late 1881. This was a characteristic instance of Gilded Age diplomacy, driven partly by partisan politics and carried out without any clear sense of national purpose.

Pan-Americanism—the notion of a community of American states—took root, however, and Blaine, returning in 1889 for a second stint at the State Department, took up the plans by the outgoing Cleveland administration for a new Pan-American conference. But little came of it, except for an agency in Washington that was later named the Pan-American Union. Any Latin American goodwill won by Blaine's efforts was soon blasted by the humiliation the United States visited upon Chile because of a riot against American sailors in the port of Valparaiso in 1891. Threatened with war, Chile was forced to apologize to the United States and to pay an indemnity of $75,000.

In the Pacific, American interest centered on Hawaii. With a climate ideal for raising sugarcane, the islands had attracted American planters and investors. Nominally an independent nation, Hawaii came increasingly within the American orbit. In an 1875 treaty, Hawaiian sugar gained duty-free entry to the

American market, and the islands were declared off limits to other powers. A second treaty in 1887 granted the United States naval rights at Pearl Harbor.

When Hawaii's favored access to the American market was abruptly canceled by the McKinley Tariff of 1890, sugar planters began to plot an American takeover of Hawaii. They organized a revolt in January 1893 against Queen Liliuokalani, and quickly negotiated a treaty of annexation with the Harrison administration. Before annexation could be approved by the Senate, however, Grover Cleveland returned to the presidency and withdrew the treaty. To annex Hawaii, he declared, would violate both America's "honor and morality" and its "unbroken tradition" against acquiring territory far from the nation's shores.

Meanwhile, the American presence elsewhere in the Pacific was growing. The purchase of Alaska from imperial Russia in 1867 gave the United States not only a huge territory with vast natural resources, but an unlooked-for presence stretching across the northern Pacific. Far to the south in the Samoan islands the United States secured the right in 1878 to a coaling station in Pago Pago harbor—a key link on the route to Australia—and established an informal protectorate there.

American diplomacy in these years has been characterized as a series of incidents, not the pursuit of a foreign policy. Many things happened, but intermittently and without a plan, driven by individuals and pressure groups, not by any well-founded conception of national objectives. This was possible because, as the Englishman James Bryce remarked in 1888, America still sailed "upon a summer sea." In the stormier waters that lay ahead, a different kind of diplomacy would be required.

Economic Sources of Expansionism

America's gross national product quadrupled between 1870 and 1900, and industrial output increased even faster. But were there sufficient markets to absorb the goods flowing from America's farms and factories? America itself did constitute an enormous market. Over 90 percent of American output in the late nineteenth century was consumed at home. Even so, foreign markets were important. Roughly a fifth of the nation's agricultural output was exported, and as the industrial economy expanded, so did factory exports. Between 1880 and 1900, the industrial share of total exports jumped from 15 percent to over 30 percent.

Foreign trade was important partly for reasons of international finance. As a developing economy, the United States attracted a lot of foreign capital but invested very little abroad. The result was a heavy outflow of dollars to pay interest and dividends to foreign investors. To balance this account, the United States needed to export more goods than it imported. In fact, a favorable import-export balance was achieved in 1876. But because of its dependence on foreign capital, America had to be constantly vigilant about its export trade.

Even more important, however, was the relationship that many Americans perceived between foreign markets and the nation's social stability. In hard times, farmers took up radical politics and workers became militant strikers.

FIGURE 22.1
Balance of U.S. Imports and Exports, 1870–1914
By 1876 the United States had become a net exporting nation. The brief
reversal after 1888 aroused fears that the United States was losing its foreign markets and helped fuel the expansionist drive of the 1890s.

The problem, many thought, was that the nation's capacity to produce was
outrunning its capacity to consume. When the economy slowed, the impact
on farmers and workers was devastating, causing layoffs and farm foreclosures
across the country. The answer was to make sure that there would always be
enough buyers for America's surplus products. This meant, more than anything else, access to foreign markets.

The bulk of American exports in the late nineteenth century—over 80
percent—went to Europe and Canada. In these countries the normal instruments of diplomacy sufficed to protect the nation's economic interests. But in
Asia, Latin America, and other "backward" regions a more vigorous kind of
American intervention seemed necessary, because there the United States
found itself competing with other industrial powers.

Asia and Latin America represented only an eighth of America's export
trade in the late nineteenth century. Still, this trade was growing—it was
worth $200 million in 1900—and parts of it mattered a great deal to specific
industries, for example, the Chinese market for American textiles.

The real importance of these non-Western markets, however, was not so
much their current value as their future promise. China especially exerted a

powerful hold on the American mercantile imagination. Many felt that the China trade, although quite small, would one day be the key to American prosperity. Therefore, China and other inviting markets must not be closed to the United States.

In the mid-1880s, the pace of imperialist activity picked up. After the Berlin Conference of 1884, Africa was rapidly colonized by the European powers. In a burst of modernizing energy, Japan transformed itself into a major power. Japan easily defeated China in the Sino-Japanese War of 1894–1895, starting a scramble among the great powers, including Russia, to carve China up into spheres of influence. In Latin America, United States interests began to be challenged more aggressively by Britain, France, and Germany.

On top of all this came the Panic of 1893, setting in motion labor strikes and agrarian protests that many Americans, such as Cleveland's secretary of state, Walter Q. Gresham, took to be "symptoms of revolution." With the nation's social stability seemingly at stake, securing the markets of Latin America and Asia became an urgent necessity that inspired the expansionist diplomacy of the 1890s.

The Making of an Expansionist Foreign Policy

"Whether they will or no, Americans must now begin to look outward. The growing production of the country requires it." So wrote Captain Alfred T. Mahan, America's leading naval strategist, in his book *The Influence of Seapower upon History* (1890), which argued that first Rome and in modern times Great

Alfred T. Mahan
Mahan's theory about the influence of sea power on history came to him while he was reading Roman history in Lima, Peru, in 1885. His insight was personal as well as intellectual: embarrassed by the decrepit ships on which he served, Mahan thought the United States should have a modern fleet in which officers like himself could serve with pride (and with some hope of professional advancement).

Britain had become great empires because they had controlled the seas. From this insight Mahan developed a naval analysis that became the cornerstone of American strategic thinking.

The United States should no longer regard the oceans as barriers, Mahan argued, but as "a great highway . . . over which men pass in all directions." Traversing that highway required a robust merchant marine (America's had fallen on hard times since its heyday in the 1850s); a powerful navy to protect American commerce; and strategic overseas bases. Here technology played a role because, having converted to steam, navies required coaling stations far from home. Without such stations, Mahan warned, warships were "like land birds, unable to fly far from their own shores."

Mahan called for a canal across Central America to connect the Atlantic and the Pacific oceans. Such a canal would enable the eastern United States to "compete with Europe, on equal terms as to distance, for the markets of East Asia." The canal's approaches would need to be guarded by bases in the Caribbean Sea. And Hawaii would have to be annexed to extend American power into the Pacific.

Mahan was offering a *coherent* foreign policy, and other advocates of a powerful America flocked to him, including such coming politicians as Theodore Roosevelt and Henry Cabot Lodge. The influence of these men, few in number but strategically placed, increased during the 1890s. They pushed steadily for what Lodge called a "large policy." But mainstream politicians too accepted Mahan's underlying logic, and from the inauguration of Benjamin Harrison in 1889 onward, a surprising consistency began to emerge in the conduct of American foreign policy.

Mahan argued strongly for a battleship fleet capable of roaming the far seas and striking a decisive first blow against an enemy. In 1890 Congress appropriated funds for the first three battleships in the two-ocean fleet envisioned by Benjamin F. Tracy, Harrison's ambitious secretary of the navy. The battleship took on a special aura for those, like the young Roosevelt, who wanted to see the United States flexing its muscles. "Oh, Lord! if only the people who are ignorant about our Navy could see those great warships in all their majesty and beauty, and could realize how [well fitted they are] to uphold the honor of America!"

The incoming Cleveland administration was less spread-eagled, and by canceling Harrison's scheme for annexing Hawaii, established its antiexpansionist credentials. But after hesitating briefly, Cleveland picked up the naval program of his Republican predecessor, pressing Congress just as forcefully for more battleships (five were authorized) and making the same basic argument. The nation's commercial vitality—"free access to all markets," in the words of Cleveland's second secretary of state, Richard Olney—depended on its naval power.

While rejecting the colonialist aspects of Mahan's thinking, Cleveland absorbed the underlying strategic arguments about where America's vital interests lay. This explains the remarkable crisis that suddenly blew up in 1895 over Venezuela.

The Battleship *Oregon*
The battleship was the centerpiece of naval strategy in the industrial age and the key marker in the naval arms race among the Great Powers. Building a battleship fleet was America's ticket of entry to that race.

For years, a border dispute had simmered between Venezuela and British Guiana. Now the United States demanded that it be resolved. The European powers were carving up Africa and Asia. How could the United States be sure that the European nations did not have similar designs on Latin America? Indeed, prompted by President Cleveland, Secretary of State Olney made that point in a bristling note to London on July 25, 1895, insisting that Britain accept arbitration or face the consequences. Invoking the Monroe Doctrine, Olney intended to convey a clear message to Britain and the other European powers that the United States would brook no challenge to its vital interests in the Caribbean. (Note that these were America's vital interests, not those of Venezuela, which was not consulted during the entire dispute.)

Despite its suddenness, the pugnacious stand of the Cleveland administration was not an aberration, but a logical step in the new American foreign policy. Once the British realized that Cleveland meant business, they agreed to arbitration of the boundary dispute. Afterward, Olney remarked with satisfaction that as a great industrial nation, the United States needed "to accept [its] commanding position" and take its place "among the Powers of the earth." And other countries would have to accommodate the American need for access to "more markets and larger markets for the consumption and products of the industry and inventive genius of the American people."

The Ideology of Expansionism

As policymakers hammered out a new foreign policy, a sustaining body of ideology took shape. One source of expansionist dogma was the Social Darwinist theory that dominated the political thought of this era. If animals and plants evolved through the survival of the fittest, so did nations. "Nothing under the sun is stationary," warned the American social theorist Brooks Adams in *The Law of Civilization and Decay* (1895). "Not to advance is to recede." By this criterion, the United States had no choice; if it wanted to survive, it had to expand.

Linked to Social Darwinism was a spreading belief in the inherent superiority of the Anglo-Saxon "race." On both sides of the Atlantic, Anglo-Saxonism was in vogue. Thus did John Fiske, an American philosopher and historian, lecture the nation on its future responsibilities: "The work which the English race began when it colonized North America is destined to go on until every land on the earth's surface that is not already the seat of an old civilization shall become English in its language, in its religion, in its political habits, and to a predominant extent in the blood of its people."

Fiske entitled his lecture "Manifest Destiny." This term had been used half a century earlier to convey the sense of national mission—America's *Manifest Destiny*—to sweep aside the native American peoples and occupy the continent. In his widely read book *The Winning of the West* (1896), Theodore Roosevelt drew a parallel between the expansionism of his own time and the suppression of the Indians. It mattered little what happened to "backward peoples" because their conquest was "for the benefit of civilization and in the interests of mankind." More than historical parallels, however, linked the Manifest Destiny of the past and present.

In 1890 the U.S. Census reported the end of the westward movement on the American continent. The psychological impact of that news on Americans was profound, spawning, among other things, a new historical interpretation that stressed the importance of the frontier in shaping the nation's character. In his landmark essay setting out this thesis—"The Significance of the Frontier in American History" (1893)—the young historian Frederick Jackson Turner suggested a linkage between the closing of the frontier and overseas expansion. "He would be a rash prophet who should assert that the expansive character of American life has now entirely ceased," Turner wrote. "Movement has been its dominant fact, and, unless this training has no effect upon a people, the American energy will continually demand a wider field for its exercise." As Turner predicted, Manifest Destiny did turn outward.

Thus a strong current of ideas, deeply rooted in American experience and ideology, justified the new diplomacy of expansionism. The United States was eager to step onto the world stage. All it needed was the right occasion.

AN AMERICAN EMPIRE

Ever since Spain had lost its South American empire in the early nineteenth century, Cubans had yearned to join their mainland brothers and sisters in freedom. In February 1895 Cuban patriots rebelled and began a guerrilla war. A standoff developed; the Spaniards controlled the towns, the rebels much of the countryside. In early 1896 the newly appointed Spanish general, Valeriano Weyler, adopted a harsh policy of *reconcentration*, forcing entire populations into armed camps. Because no aggressive pursuit followed, reconcentration only inconvenienced the guerrilla fighters. The toll on civilians, however, was brutal. Out of a population of 1,600,000, as many as 200,000 may have died of starvation, exposure, or dysentery.

The Cuban Crisis

The rebel leaders recognized that their best hope was not military but political: they had to draw the United States into their struggle. A key group of exiles, the *junta*, set up shop in New York to make the case for *Cuba libre*. Their timing was perfect. William Randolph Hearst had just purchased the nearly bankrupt *New York Journal,* and he was in a hurry to build readership. Cuba was ideal for Hearst's purposes. Locked in a furious circulation war with Joseph Pulitzer's *New York World*, Hearst elevated Cuba's agony into flaming front-page headlines.

Across the country powerful sentiments stirred: humanitarian concern for the Cubans, sympathy with their aspirations for freedom, and a superpatriotism that became known as *jingoism*. Congress began calling for Cuban independence.

Cleveland, still in office when the rebellion broke out, took a cooler view of the situation. His concern was with America's vital interests, which, he told Congress, were "by no means of a wholly sentimental or philanthropic character." The Cuban civil war was disrupting the sizable trade between the two countries and destroying American investments, especially in Cuban sugar plantations. Cleveland was also worried that Spain's troubles might draw other European powers into the situation. A chronically unstable Cuba was incompatible with America's strategic interests, especially its plans for an interoceanic canal whose Caribbean approaches would have to be safeguarded.

If Spain could put down the rebellion, that was fine with Cleveland. But as Spain's impotence became clear, he urged the Spanish government to make reforms and resolve the crisis.

The McKinley administration, on taking office in March 1897, adopted much the same pragmatic line. Like Cleveland, McKinley was motivated by a conception of the United States as the dominant Caribbean power, with vital interests that had to be defended. McKinley, however, was inclined to be tougher on the Spaniards. For one thing, he was more appalled by their "uncivilized and inhumane conduct" in Cuba. And he had to contend with rising jingoism in the Republican party. But the notion, long held by historians, that McKinley was swept along against his better judgment by popular opinion and by a Republican war faction led by Theodore Roosevelt, Henry Cabot Lodge, and other aggressive advocates of a "large policy" was not true. McKinley was very much his own man. He was a skilled politician and a canny, if undramatic, president. He would not proceed until he sensed a broad national consensus for war. In particular, McKinley was sensitive to business interests fearful of disruption to an economy just recovering from depression.

The American pressure on Spain at first seemed to pay off. The conservative regime fell, and a liberal government, upon taking office in October 1897, moderated its Cuban policy. Spain recalled Weyler, limited reconcentration, and adopted an autonomy plan granting Cuba a degree of self-rule but not independence. Madrid's incapacity soon became clear, however. In January 1898, Spanish loyalists in Havana rioted against the offer of autonomy. The Cuban rebels, encouraged by the prospect of American intervention, demanded full independence.

On February 9, 1898, Hearst's *New York Journal* published a private letter of Dupuy de Lôme, the Spanish minister to the United States. In it de Lôme called President McKinley "weak" and "a bidder for the admiration of the crowd." Worse, his letter suggested that the Spanish government was not taking the American demands for reform seriously. De Lôme immediately resigned, but the damage had been done.

A week later the U.S. battleship *Maine*, at anchor in Havana harbor on a "courtesy" visit, blew up and sank, with the loss of 260 seamen. "Whole Country Thrills with the War Fever," proclaimed the *New York Journal*. From that moment onward, popular passions against Spain became a major factor in the march toward war.

But McKinley kept his head. He assumed that the sinking had been accidental: what motive could the Spanish have had for attacking the *Maine*? A naval board of inquiry, however, found that the sinking had been caused by a mine, not, as seems more likely, by an accidental explosion inside the ship. No evidence linked the Spanish to the sinking, but they had failed to protect the *Maine* from attack.

President McKinley had no stomach for the martial spirit engulfing the country. He was not swept along by the calls for blood to avenge the *Maine*. But he did have to attend to an aroused public opinion. Hesitant business leaders now also became impatient for the dispute with Spain to end. War was preferable to the unresolved Cuban crisis. On March 27 McKinley cabled to Madrid what was in effect an ultimatum: an immediate armistice for six months; abandonment of the practice of reconcentration; and, with the United States as mediator, peace negotiations with the rebels. A telegram the next day added that only Cuban independence would be regarded as a satisfactory outcome to the negotiations. Spain categorically rejected these humiliating demands.

On April 11 McKinley asked Congress for authority to intervene to end the fighting in Cuba. His motives were as he described them: "In the name of humanity, in the name of civilization, in behalf of endangered American interests which give us the right and the duty to speak and to act, the war in Cuba must stop." The War Hawks in Congress—a mixture of Republican jingoists and proindependence western Democrats—chafed under McKinley's cautious progress. But the president did not lose control, and he defeated the War Hawks on the crucial issue of recognizing the rebel republican government, which would have greatly reduced the administration's freedom of action in dealing with Spain.

The resolutions authorizing intervention in Cuba contained an amendment by Senator Henry M. Teller of Colorado disclaiming any intention by the United States of taking possession of Cuba. No European government should say that "when we go out to make battle for the liberty and freedom of Cuban patriots, that we are doing it for the purpose of aggrandizement." This had to be made clear with regard to Cuba, "whatever," Senator Teller added, "we may do as to some other islands."

Did McKinley have in mind "some other islands"? Was this really a war of aggression, secretly motivated by a desire to seize strategic territory from Spain? In a strict sense, almost certainly no. It was not *because* of expansionist ambitions that McKinley forced Spain into a corner. On the other hand, once war came McKinley saw it as an opportunity. As he wrote privately after hostilities began: "While we are conducting war and until its conclusion, we must keep all we get; when the war is over we must keep what we want." Precisely what would be forthcoming, of course, depended on the fortunes of battle.

The Spoils of War

Hostilities formally began when Spain declared war on April 24, 1898. Across the country, regiments began to form up. Theodore Roosevelt immediately resigned as assistant secretary of the navy, ordered a fancy uniform, and was commissioned lieutenant colonel in a volunteer cavalry regiment that would become famous as the Rough Riders. Raw recruits poured into makeshift bases around Tampa, Florida. Confusion reigned. Tropical uniforms did not arrive; the food was bad, the sanitation worse; and rifles were in short supply. No provision had been made for getting the troops to Cuba; the government hastily began to collect a miscellaneous fleet of yachts, lake steamers, and commercial boats. Fortunately, the small regular army was a disciplined, highly professional force, and its 28,000 seasoned troops provided a nucleus for the 200,000 civilians who had to be turned into soldiers inside of a few weeks.

The navy was in much better shape. Spain had nothing to match America's seven battleships and armored cruisers, and the ships it did have were undermanned and ill prepared for battle. The Spanish admiral, Pascual Cervera, gloomily expected that his fleet would "like Don Quixote go out to fight windmills and come back with a broken head."

On April 23, Commodore George Dewey's small Pacific fleet set sail from Hong Kong for the Philippines. Here, at this Spanish possession in the far Pacific, not in Cuba, the decisive engagement of the war took place. On May 1 Dewey cornered the Spanish fleet in Manila Bay and destroyed it. The victory produced euphoria in the United States. Immediately, part of the army being trained for the Cuban campaign was diverted to the Philippines. Manila, the Philippine capital, fell on August 13, 1898 (see Map 22.1).

With Dewey's victory, American strategic thinking clicked into place. "We hold the other side of the Pacific and the value to this country is almost beyond imagination," declared Senator Lodge. "We must on no account let the [Philippine] Islands go." President McKinley agreed, and so did his key advisers. An anchor in the western Pacific had long been coveted by naval strategists. At this time, too, the Great Powers were carving up China into spheres of influence. If American merchants wanted a place in that glittering market, the power of the United States would have to be projected into Asia.

Once the decision for a Philippine base had been made, other decisions followed almost automatically. The question of Hawaii was quickly resolved. After stalling the previous year, Hawaiian annexation went through Congress by joint resolution in July 1898. Hawaii had suddenly acquired a crucial strategic value: it was a halfway station to the Philippines. The navy pressed for a coaling base in the central Pacific; that meant Guam, a Spanish island in the Marianas. There was need also for a strategically located base in the Caribbean; that meant Puerto Rico. By July, before the assault on Cuba, the full scope of McKinley's war aims had taken shape.

The campaign in Cuba was something of an anticlimax. The Spanish fleet was bottled up in Santiago harbor, and the city itself became the key to the military campaign. Half trained and ill equipped, the American forces moving on Santiago might have been checked by a determined opponent. The Spaniards would fight to maintain their honor, but they had no stomach for a real war against the Americans.

The main battle, on July 1, occurred near Santiago on the heights commanded by San Juan Hill. Roosevelt's dismounted Rough Riders (there had been no room for horses on the transports) seized Kettle Hill. Then the frontal assault against the San Juan heights began. Four black regiments took the brunt of the fighting. White observers grudgingly credited much of the victory to the "superb gallantry" of the black soldiers. In fact, it was not quite a victory. The Spaniards, driven from their forward positions, retreated to a well-fortified second line. The exhausted Americans had suffered heavy casualties; whether they could have mounted a second assault was questionable. They were spared this test, however, by the Spanish. On July 3 Cervera's fleet in Santiago harbor made a suicidal daylight attempt to run the American blockade and was destroyed. A few days later, convinced that Santiago could not be saved, the Spanish forces surrendered.

The two nations then signed an armistice in which Spain agreed to give up Cuba and cede Puerto Rico and Guam to the United States. American forces would occupy Manila pending a peace treaty.

MAP 22.1

The Spanish-American War

The swift American victory in the Spanish-American War resulted from overwhelming naval superiority. Dewey's destruction of the Spanish fleet in Manila harbor doomed the Spaniards in the Philippines. In Cuba, American ground forces won a hard victory on San Juan Hill, for they were ill equipped and poorly supplied. With the United States in control of the seas, the Spaniards saw no choice but to give up the battle for Cuba.

Black Soldiers in a White Man's War

George W. Prioleau, the chaplain of the Ninth Cavalry regiment, expresses his bitterness against the racism experienced by black troopers in the South on their way to battle in Cuba.

Hon. H. C. Smith
Editor, *Gazette*

Dear Sir:
All the way from northwest Nebraska this regiment was greeted with cheers and hurrahs. At places where we stopped the people assembled by the thousands. While the Ninth Cavalry band would play some national air the people would raise their hats, men, women and children would wave their handkerchiefs, and the heavens would resound with their hearty cheers. . . . These demonstrations, so enthusiastically given, greeted us all the way until we reached Nashville. . . . From there until we reached Chattanooga there was not a cheer given us. . . .

    The prejudice against the Negro soldier and the Negro was great, but it was of heavenly origin to what it is in this part of Florida. . . . The southerners have made their laws and the Negroes know and obey them. They never stop to ask a white man a question. He (Negro) never thinks of disobeying. . . . Talk about fighting and freeing poor Cuba and of Spain's brutality; of Cuba's murdered thousands, and starving recon-centradoes. Is America any better than Spain? Has she not subjects in her very midst who are murdered daily without a trial of judge or jury? Has she not subjects in her own borders whose children are half-fed and half-clothed, because their father's skin is black. . . . Yet the Negro is loyal to his country's flag. . . .

    The four Negro regiments are going to help free Cuba, and they will return to their homes, some then mustered out and begin again to fight the battle of American prejudice. . . .

Yours truly,
Geo. W. Prioleau, Chaplain, Ninth Cavalry

SOURCE: *Cleveland Gazette* (May 13, 1898), reprinted in Willard B. Gatewood, *"Smoked Yankees" and the Struggle for Empire, 1898–1902* (Urbana: University of Illinois Press, 1971), 27–29.

The Imperial Experiment

The big question was the Philippines. This was an archipelago, or group, of over 7,000 islands populated—as William R. Day, McKinley's secretary of state, put it in the racist language of that era—by "eight or nine millions of absolutely ignorant and many degraded people." Not even the most avid

American expansionists advocated colonial rule over such a population: that was European-style imperialism, not the strategic bases that Mahan and his followers had in mind. Both Mahan and Lodge initially advocated keeping only Manila. It gradually became clear, however, that Manila was not defensible without the whole of Luzon, the large island on which the city is located.

McKinley and his advisers surveyed the options. One possibility was to return most of the islands to Spain, but the reputed evils of Spanish rule made that a "cowardly and dishonorable" solution. Another possibility was to partition the Philippines with one or more of the Great Powers. But as McKinley observed, to turn over valuable territory to "our commercial rivals in the Orient—that would have been bad business and discreditable."

Most plausible was the option of granting the Philippines independence. As in Cuba, Spanish rule had already stirred up a rebellion, led by the fiery patriot Emilio Aguinaldo. An arrangement might have been possible like the one being negotiated with the Cubans over Guantanamo Bay: the lease of a naval base to the Americans as the price of freedom. But after some hesitation McKinley was persuaded that "we could not leave [the Filipinos] to themselves—they were unfit for self-rule—and they would soon have anarchy and misrule over there worse than Spain's was."

As for the Spaniards, they had little choice against what they considered "the immoderate demands of a conquerer." In the Treaty of Paris they ceded the Philippines to the United States for a payment of $20 million. The treaty encountered harder going at home, and was ratified by the Senate (requiring a two-thirds majority) on February 6, 1899, with only a single vote to spare.

The narrowness of the administration's victory signaled the revival of an antiexpansionist tradition that had been briefly silenced by the patriotic passions of a nation at war. In the Senate, opponents of the treaty invoked the country's republican principles. Under the Constitution, argued the conservative Republican George F. Hoar, "no power is given to the Federal Government to acquire territory to be held and governed permanently as colonies" or "to conquer alien people and hold them in subjugation."

Leading citizens enlisted in the anti-imperialist cause, including the steelmaker Andrew Carnegie, who offered a check for $20 million to purchase the independence of the Philippines; the labor leader Samuel Gompers, who feared the competition of cheap Filipino labor; and Jane Addams, who believed that women should stand for peace. The key group, however, was a social elite of old-line Mugwump reformers such as Carl Schurz, Charles Eliot Norton, and Charles Francis Adams. In November 1898 a Boston group formed the first Anti-Imperialist League, from which blossomed a national movement over the next year.

Skillful at publicizing their cause, the anti-imperialists never managed to develop a mass following. They were an ill-assorted lot, divided in many ways, and within the Mugwump core, lacking the common touch. Nor was it easy to translate anti-imperialism into a viable political cause because the Democrats, once the treaty had been adopted, waffled over the issue. Still, if it was an accomplished fact, Philippine annexation lost the moral high ground because of the awful events that began to unfold in the Philippines.

Two days before the Senate ratified the treaty, on February 4, 1899, fighting broke out between American and Filipino patrols on the edge of Manila. Confronted by American annexation, Aguinaldo asserted his nation's independence and turned his guns on the occupying American forces.

The ensuing conflict far exceeded in ferocity the war just concluded with Spain. Fighting tenacious guerrillas, the U.S. Army resorted to the same reconcentration tactic the Spaniards had used in Cuba, moving people into towns, carrying out indiscriminate attacks outside the town limits, and burning crops and villages. In three years of warfare 4,200 Americans and many thousands of Filipinos died. The fighting ended in 1902, and Judge William Howard Taft, who had been appointed governor in 1901, set up a civilian government. He intended to make the Philippines a model of American road building and sanitary engineering.

McKinley's convincing victory over William Jennings Bryan in the 1900 election, although by no means a referendum on American expansionism, suggested popular satisfaction with America's overseas adventure. Yet a strong undercurrent of misgivings was evident. Americans had not anticipated the

Fighting the Filipinos
The United States went to war against Spain in 1898 partly out of sympathy with the Cuban struggle for independence. Yet the United States found it necessary to use the same brutal tactics to put down the Filipino struggle for independence that the Spaniards had used against the Cubans. Here the Twentieth Kansas Volunteers march through the burning village of Caloocan.

The Water Cure

In 1902, after the fighting had ceased, the U.S. Senate held hearing on the conduct of the war in the Philippines. This is the testimony of Corporal Daniel J. Evans, Twelfth Infantry, about his service on the island of Luzon.

Question: The committee would like to hear . . . whether you were the witness to any cruelties inflicted upon the natives of the Philippine Islands; and if so, under what circumstances.—*Answer*: The case I had reference to was where they gave the water cure to a native in the Ilicano Province at Ilocos Norte . . . about the month of August 1900. There were two native scouts with the American forces. They went out and brought in a couple of insurgents. . . . They tried to get from this insurgent . . . where the rest of the insurgents were at that time. . . . The first thing one of the Americans—I mean one of the scouts for the Americans—grabbed one of the men by the head and jerked his head back, and then they took a tomato can and poured water down his throat until he could hold no more. . . . Then they forced a gag into his mouth; they stood him up . . . against a post and fastened him so that he could not move. Then one man, an American soldier, who was over six feet tall, and who was very strong, too, struck this native in the pit of the stomach as hard as he could. . . . They kept that operation up for quite a time, and finally I thought the fellow was about to die, but I don't believe he was as bad as that, because finally he told them he would tell, and from that time on he was taken away, and I saw no more of him. . . .

Question: What is your observation as to the treatment of the people engaged in peaceable pursuits, as to kindness and consideration, or the reverse, from the American officers and the men?—*Answer*: They were never molested if they seemed to be peaceable natives. They would not be molested unless they showed some signs of hostility. . . . If we struck a part of the island where the natives were hostile and they would fire on our soldiers or even cut the telegraph lines, the result would be that their barrios would probably be burned.

SOURCE: Henry F. Graff, ed., *American Imperialism and the Philippine Insurrection* (Boston: Little, Brown, 1969), 80–84.

brutal methods needed to subdue the Filipino guerrillas. "We are destroying these islanders by the thousands, their villages and cities," protested the philosopher William James. "No life shall you have, we say, except as a gift from our philanthropy after your unconditional surrender to our will. . . . Could there be any more damning indictment of that whole bloated ideal termed 'modern civilization'?"

There were, moreover, disturbing constitutional issues to be resolved. Did the Constitution extend to the acquired territories? Did their inhabitants automatically become U.S. citizens? In 1901 the Supreme Court ruled negatively on both questions; these were matters for Congress to decide. A special commission appointed by McKinley recommended independence for the islands after an indefinite period of U.S. rule, during which the Filipinos would be prepared for self-government. In 1916 the Jones Act formally committed the United States to granting Philippine independence, but set no date.

The ugly business in the Philippines rubbed off some of the moralizing gloss, but left undeflected America's global aspirations. In a few years the United States had acquired the makings of a strategic overseas empire: Hawaii; Puerto Rico; Guam; the Philippines; and finally, in 1900, several of the Samoan islands that the United States had administered jointly with Germany and Britain. The United States, remarked the legal scholar John Bassett Moore in 1899, had moved "from a position of comparative freedom from entanglements into a position of what is commonly called a world power."

ONTO THE WORLD STAGE

In Europe the flexing of America's muscles against Spain caused a certain amount of consternation. At the urging of Kaiser Wilhelm II of Germany, the major powers had tried before war broke out to intercede on Spain's behalf—but tentatively, because no one was looking for trouble with the Americans. President McKinley had listened politely to the representations of their envoys on April 6, 1898, and had then, dismissively, proceeded with his war.

The decisive outcome confirmed what the Europeans already suspected. After Dewey's naval victory, the semiofficial French paper *Le Temps* observed that "what passes before our eyes is the appearance of a new power of the first order." And the London *Times* predicted, "In the future America will play a part in the general affairs of the world such as she has never played before."

A Power among Powers

The politician most ardently agreeing with the London *Times*'s vision of America's future was the man who, with the assassination of William McKinley, became president on September 14, 1901. Theodore Roosevelt was an avid student of world affairs, widely traveled and acquainted with many of the European leaders. He had no doubt about America's role in the world.

It was important, first of all, to uphold the country's honor in the community of nations. Nor should the country shrink from righteous battle. "All the great masterful races have been fighting races," Roosevelt declared. But when he spoke of war, Roosevelt had in mind actions by the "civilized" nations against "backward peoples" (such as the Filipinos whose struggle for freedom was being subdued when he entered the White House). That was why Roosevelt sympathized with European imperialism, and how he justified American dominance in the Caribbean.

As for the "civilized and orderly" policemen of the world, however, the worst thing that could happen was for them to fall to fighting among themselves. Roosevelt had an acute sense of the fragility of world peace, and he was farsighted about the chances—in this he was truly exceptional among Americans—of a catastrophic world war. He believed America was responsible for helping to maintain the balance of power.

The cornerstone of Roosevelt's thinking was Anglo-American amity. The British, increasingly isolated in world affairs, eagerly reciprocated. In the Hay-Pauncefote Agreement (1901) they gave up their treaty rights to joint participation in any Central American canal project, clearing the way for a canal under exclusive U.S. control. And two years later the last of the vexing U.S.–Canadian border disputes, this one involving British Columbia and Alaska, was settled, again to American satisfaction. No formal alliance was forthcoming, but Anglo-American friendship had been placed on such a firm basis that after 1901 the British admiralty designed its war plans on the assumption that America was "a kindred state with whom we shall never have a parricidal war."

Among nations, however, what counted was strength, not merely goodwill. Roosevelt wanted "to make all foreign powers understand that when we have adopted a line of policy we have adopted it definitely, and with the intention of backing it up with deeds as well as words." As Roosevelt famously said: "Speak softly and carry a big stick." By a "big stick" he meant above all naval power. Under Roosevelt, the battleship program went on apace. By 1904 the U.S. Navy stood fifth in the world; by 1907, it was second only to Britain's.

A canal across Panama came next on Roosevelt's agenda. With Britain's surrender of its joint rights in 1901, Roosevelt proceeded to the more troublesome task of leasing from Colombia the needed strip of land across its Panamanian province. Furious when the Colombian legislature voted down the proposed treaty, Roosevelt contemplated outright seizure of Panama, but settled on a more devious solution. Informed that an independence movement was brewing in Panama, the United States lent secret assistance that enabled the bloodless revolution against Colombia to go off on schedule. On November 7, 1903, the United States recognized Panama, and two weeks later it received a perpetually renewable lease on a canal zone. These machinations were a dirty business, but they got Roosevelt what he wanted. He never regretted the victimization of Colombia, although the United States, as a kind of conscience money, paid Colombia $25 million in 1922.

Building the canal was one of the heroic engineering feats of the century, involving a swamp-clearing project to rid the area of malaria and yellow fever,

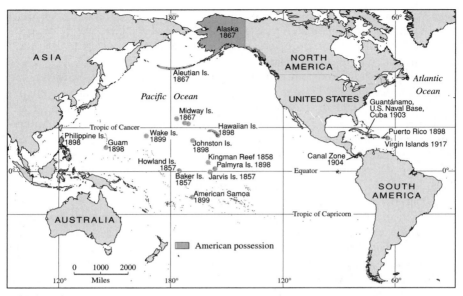

MAP 22.2
The American Empire
In 1890 Alfred T. Mahan wrote that the United States should regard the oceans as "a great highway" across which America would carry on world trade. That was precisely what resulted from the empire the United States acquired after the Spanish-American War. The Caribbean possessions, the strategically located Pacific islands, and, in 1904, the Panama Canal Zone gave the United States commercial and naval access to a wider world.

the construction of a series of great locks, and the excavation of 240 million cubic yards of earth. It took the U.S. Army Corps of Engineers eight years to finish the huge project. Opened in 1914, the Panama Canal gave the United States a commanding commercial and strategic position in the Western Hemisphere (see Map 22.2).

Next came the task of making the Caribbean basin secure. The countries there, said Secretary of State Elihu Root, had been placed "in the front yard of the United States" by the Panama Canal. Therefore, Roosevelt added, they had to "behave themselves." Believing that instability in the Caribbean invited the intervention of European powers, Roosevelt announced in 1904 that the United States would act as "policeman" of the region, stepping in, "however reluctantly, in flagrant cases . . . of wrong doing or impotence."

This policy became known as the Roosevelt Corollary to the Monroe Doctrine. It transformed what had been a broad principle of opposition against European expansionist ambitions in Latin America into an unrestricted American right to regulate Caribbean affairs. The Roosevelt Corollary was not a treaty with other states; it was a unilateral declaration sanctioned only by American power and national interest.

Under the Roosevelt Corollary the United States intervened regularly in the internal affairs of Caribbean states (see Map 22.3). In the case of Cuba, a condition of its independence had been a proviso in its constitution called the Platt amendment, which gave the United States the right to intervene if Cuba's independence or internal order was threatened. Elsewhere there was not even this semblance of legality. In 1905 American authorities took over the customs and debt management of the Dominican Republic, and similarly, Nicaragua in 1911 and Haiti in 1916. When domestic order broke down, the U.S. Marines occupied Cuba in 1906, Nicaragua in 1909, and Haiti and the Dominican Republic in later years.

The Open Door

In China, the occupying powers quickly instituted discriminatory trade regulations in their zones of control. Fearful of being frozen out of the China market, U.S. Secretary of State John Hay in 1899 sent them an "Open Door" note advancing a right of equal trade access—the Open Door—for all nations that wanted to do business in China. Even with its Philippine bases, the United States lacked real leverage and received no better than ambiguous and

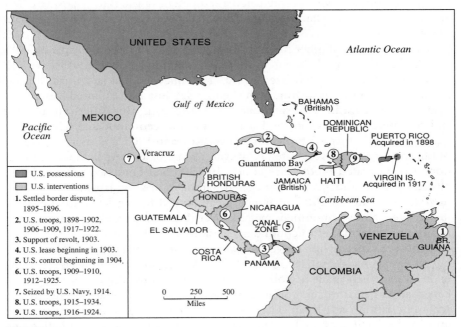

MAP 22.3
Policeman of the Caribbean
After the Spanish-American War the United States vigorously asserted its interest in the affairs of its neighbors to the south. As the record of interventions shows, the United States truly became the "policeman" of the Caribbean.

noncommital responses from the occupying powers. But Hay chose to interpret them as accepting the American Open Door position.

When a secret society of Chinese nationalists, the Boxers, rebelled against
the foreigners in 1900, the United States joined the multinational campaign to
raise the siege of the foreign legations in Peking (Beijing). America took this
opportunity to assert a second principle of the Open Door: that China would
be preserved as a "territorial and administrative entity." As long as the legal fiction of an independent China survived, so would American claims to equal
access to the China market.

The European powers had acceded to American claims to preeminence in
the Caribbean. But in the Far East Britain, Germany, France, and Russia were
strongly entrenched, and not inclined to defer to American interests. The
United States also confronted a powerful Asian nation—Japan—that had its
own vital interests. Although the Open Door was important to him, Roosevelt quickly saw in the Pacific a deadlier game of power politics that called
for American involvement.

In 1904 Japan, provoked by Russian demands for its military withdrawal
from northern Korea, suddenly attacked the Tsar's fleet at Port Arthur, Russia's
leased port in China. In a series of brilliant victories, the Japanese demolished
the Russian military forces in Asia. Anxious to restore some semblance of a
balance of power, Roosevelt mediated a settlement of the Russo-Japanese War
at Portsmouth, New Hampshire, in 1905. Japan emerged as the predominant
power in East Asia.

Contemptuous of other Asian nations, Roosevelt admired the Japanese—"a
wonderful and civilized people . . . entitled to stand in absolute equality with all
the other peoples of the civilized world." He conceded that Japan had "a paramount interest in what surrounds the Yellow Sea, just as the United States has a
paramount interest in what surrounds the Caribbean." But American strategic
and commercial interests in the Pacific had to be accommodated. The United
States approved of Japan's protectorate over Korea in 1905, and then of its claim
of full sovereignty six years later. However, a surge of anti-Asian feeling in California complicated Roosevelt's efforts. In 1906 San Francisco's school board
placed all Asian students in a segregated school, infuriating Japan. The "gentlemen's agreement" of 1907, in which Japan agreed to restrict immigration to
the United States, smoothed matters over, but the periodic resurgence of
racism in California led to continuing tensions with the Japanese.

Roosevelt meanwhile moved to balance Japan's military power by increasing American naval strength in the Pacific. American battleships visited Japan
in 1908 and then made a global tour in an impressive display of sea power.
Late that year, near the end of his administration, Roosevelt achieved a formal
accommodation with Japan. The Root-Takahira Treaty confirmed the status
quo in the Pacific, as well as the principles of free oceanic commerce and
equal trade opportunity in China.

However, William Howard Taft entered the White House in 1909 convinced that the United States had been shortchanged. He pressed for a larger

role for American bankers and investors in the Far East, especially in the railroad construction going on in China. An exponent of Dollar Diplomacy, Taft hoped that American capital would counterbalance Japanese power and pave the way for increased commercial opportunities. When the Chinese Revolution of 1911 toppled the ruling Manchu dynasty, Taft supported the Chinese Nationalists as a counterforce to the Japanese. The United States thus entered a long-term rivalry with Japan that would end in war thirty years later.

The triumphant thrust across the Pacific lost some of its luster. The United States had become embroiled in a distant struggle that promised many future liabilities, but few of the fabulous profits that had lured Americans to Asia.

Woodrow Wilson and Mexico

When Woodrow Wilson became president in 1913, he was bent on reform in American foreign policy no less than in domestic politics. Wilson did not really differ with his predecessors on the importance of economic development overseas. He applauded the "tides of commerce" that would arise from the Panama Canal. But he opposed Dollar Diplomacy, which bullied weaker countries into inequitable financial relationships and gave undue advantage to American business. It seemed to Wilson "a very perilous thing to determine the foreign policy of a nation in terms of material interest."

The United States, Wilson insisted, should conduct its foreign policy in conformity with its democratic principles. He intended to foster the "development of constitutional liberty in the world," and above all to extend it to the nation's neighbors in Latin America. In a major policy speech in October 1913 Wilson promised those nations that the United States would "never again seek one additional foot of territory by conquest." The president committed himself to advancing "human rights, national integrity, and opportunity" in Latin America. To do otherwise would make "ourselves untrue to our own traditions."

Mexico became the primary object of Wilson's ministrations. A cycle of revolutions had begun there in 1911. The dictator Porfirio Diaz was overthrown by Francisco Madero, who spoke much as Wilson did about liberty and constitutionalism. But Madero was deposed and murdered in February 1913 by one of his generals, Victoriano Huerta. Other powers quickly recognized Huerta's provisional government, but not the United States. Wilson abhorred Huerta; he called him a murderer and pledged "to force him out."

By intervening in this way, "we act in the interest of Mexico alone. . . . We are seeking to counsel Mexico for its own good." Wilson meant that he intended to put the Mexican revolution back on the constitutional path started by Madero. Wilson was not deterred by the fact that American business interests, with enormous investments in Mexico, favored Huerta.

The emergence of armed opposition in northern Mexico under Venustiano Carranza strengthened Wilson's hand. Carranza's Constitutionalist movement, ardently nationalist, had no desire for American intervention in

Carranza
Venustiano Carranza (1859–1920)
was a provincial political figure
who turned revolutionary when
the dictator Diaz intervened in his
election for the governorship of
Coahuila in 1910. Carranza proved
to be only a transitional figure because, as an old-fashioned liberal,
he opposed the statist direction the
revolution took. Before his term as
first elected president ended in
1920, he was overthrown and
killed in an ambush.

Mexican affairs. Carranza angrily rebuffed Wilson's efforts to bring about
elections through a compromise between the rebels and the Mexican government. He also vowed to fight any intrusion of U.S. troops in his country. All
he wanted from Wilson, Carranza asserted, was recognition of the Constitu-
tionalists' belligerent status, so they could purchase arms in the United States.
In exchange for vague promises to respect property rights and "fair" foreign
concessions, Carranza finally got his way in 1914. American weapons began to
flow to his troops.

When it became clear that Huerta was not about to fall, the United States
threw its own forces into the game. On the pretext of a minor insult to the
U.S. Navy, Wilson ordered the occupation of the major port of Veracruz on
April 21, 1914, an action that cost 19 American and 126 Mexican lives. At that
point the Huerta regime began to crumble. Carranza nevertheless condemned
the United States, and his forces came close to engaging the Americans. When
he entered Mexico City in triumph in August 1914, Carranza had some cause
to thank the Yankees. But if any sense of gratitude existed, it was overshadowed by the anti-Americanism inspired by Wilson's insensitivity to Mexican
pride and revolutionary zeal.

This sad chapter in Mexican-American relations had a chastening effect
on Wilson. It revealed to him the difficulties of acting on, or even living up to,
well-meant ideals amid the confusion of war, revolution, and clashing national
interests. Nor, in fact, did those ideals deter him when trouble brewed in the
Caribbean. Despite his anti-imperialist pronouncements, Wilson acted just as
his predecessors had by sending the U.S. Marines into Haiti in 1915 and into
the Dominican Republic in 1916.

The Gathering Storm in Europe

In the meantime, Europe had begun to drift toward a great world war. There were two main sources of tension. One derived from the deadly rivalry between Germany, the new military and economic superpower of Europe, and the European states threatened by its might—above all France, which had been humiliated in the Franco-Prussian War of 1870. The second danger zone was the Balkans, where the Ottoman Empire was disintegrating and where, in the midst of explosive ethnic rivalries, Austria–Hungary and Russia were maneuvering for dominance. On the basis of these conflicts an alliance system had emerged, with Germany, Austria–Hungary, and Italy (the Triple Alliance) on one side and France and Russia (the Dual Alliance) on the other.

The tensions in Europe were partially released by European imperial adventures, especially by France in Africa and by Russia in Asia. These activities placed France and Russia in opposition to imperial Britain, effectively excluding Britain from the European alliance system. Fearful of Germany, however, Britain in 1904 composed her differences with France, and the two countries reached a friendly understanding, or *entente*. When Britain came to a similar understanding with Russia in 1907, the basis was laid for the Triple Entente. A deadly confrontation between two great European power blocs became possible.

In these European quarrels Americans had no obvious stake, nor any inclination, in the words of a cautionary Senate resolution, "to depart from the traditional American foreign policy which forbids participation . . . [in] political questions which are entirely European in scope." But on becoming president, Theodore Roosevelt had taken a lively interest in European affairs, and he was eager, as the head of a great power, to make a contribution to the cause of peace there. In 1905 he got his chance.

The Anglo-French entente of the previous year had been based partly on an agreement over North Africa: the Sudan was conceded to Britain, Morocco to France. Now Germany suddenly challenged France over Morocco—a disastrous move, contrary to Germany's interest in keeping France's attention diverted from Europe. Kaiser Wilhelm turned to Roosevelt for help. Roosevelt arranged an international conference, which was held in January 1906 at Algeciras, Spain. With U.S. diplomats playing a key role, the crisis was defused. Germany got a few token concessions, but France's dominance over Morocco was sustained.

Algeciras marked, in actuality, an ominous moment at which the power blocs that would become locked in battle in 1914 first squared off against one another. But at the time it looked like a diplomatic triumph, and Roosevelt's secretary of state, Elihu Root, boasted of America's success in "preserv[ing] world peace because of the power of our detachment." Root's words prefigured how the United States would define its role among the Great Powers: it would be the apostle of peace, distinguished by its "detachment," by its lack of selfish interest in European affairs.

But opposing this internationalist impulse was the tenacious grip of America's traditional isolationism. American had applauded the international peace movement that had been launched by the Hague Peace Conference of 1899. The Permanent Court of Arbitration created by the Hague conference offered new hope for the peaceful settlement of international disputes. Both the Roosevelt and the Taft administrations negotiated arbitration treaties with other countries, pledging to submit their disputes to the Hague Court—only to see the treaties emasculated by a Senate unwilling to permit the nation's sovereignty to be compromised in any significant way. Nor was there any sequel to Roosevelt's initiative at Algeciras. It had been coolly received in the Senate and by the nation's press.

Woodrow Wilson's secretary of state, William Jennings Bryan, was a great apostle of world peace. Bryan devoted himself to negotiating a series of "cooling-off" treaties with other countries—so called because the parties agreed to wait for one year while disputed issues were submitted to a conciliation process. These bilateral agreements were admirable, but they were irrelevant to the explosive power politics of Europe. As tensions there reached the breaking point in 1914, the United States remained effectively on the sidelines.

Yet at Algeciras Roosevelt had rightly seen what the future would demand of America. So did the French writer Andre Tardieu, who remarked in 1908:

The United States is . . . a world power. . . . Its power creates for it . . . a duty—to pronounce upon all those questions that hitherto have been arranged by agreement only among European powers. . . . The United States intervenes thus in the affairs of the universe. . . . It is seated at the table where the great game is played, and it cannot leave it.

Year	Event
1867	Purchase of Alaska
1871	Settlement of *Alabama* claims
1875	Treaty brings Hawaii within U.S. orbit
1876	United States achieves favorable balance of trade
1881	Secretary of State James G. Blaine inaugurates Pan-Americanism
1889	President Benjamin Harrison begins rebuilding U.S. Navy
1890	Alfred Thayer Mahan publishes *The Influence of Seapower upon History*
1893	Annexation of Hawaii fails Frederick Jackson Turner's "The Significance of the Frontier in American History" Panic of 1893 ushers in economic depression (until 1897)
1894	Sino-Japanese war begins breakup of China into spheres of influence
1895	Venezuela crisis Cuban civil war
1898	Outbreak of Spanish-American War Hawaii annexed Anti-imperialist movement launched
1899	Treaty of Paris Guerrilla war in the Philippines Open Door policy in China
1901	Theodore Roosevelt becomes president; diplomacy of the "big stick" Hay-Pauncefote Agreement
1902	U.S. withdraws from Cuba; Platt amendment gives U.S. right of intervention
1903	U.S. recognizes Panama and receives grant of Canal Zone
1904	Roosevelt Corollary
1906	U.S. mediates Franco-German crisis over Morocco at Algeciras, Spain
1907	Gentlemen's Agreement with Japan
1908	Root-Takahira Treaty
1909	William Howard Taft becomes president; Dollar Diplomacy
1913	Woodrow Wilson asserts new principles for American diplomacy
1914	Intervention in the Mexican Revolution Panama Canal opens World War I begins

THEMATIC TIMELINE

	GOVERNMENT The Rise of the State	DIPLOMACY From Isolation to World Leadership	ECONOMY Prosperity, Depression, and War	SOCIETY Migration, Consumer Culture, and Social Change
1914	Wartime agencies expand power of the federal government	U.S. enters World War I, 1917	Shift from debtor to creditor nation Agricultural glut	Blacks migrate to northern cities
1920	Republican ascendancy Prohibition, 1920–33 Business-government partnership	Treaty of Versailles rejected by U.S. Senate, 1920 Washington Conference sets naval limits, 1922	Recession, 1920–21 Booming prosperity, 1922–29 Welfare capitalism	National Origins Act Mexican immigration increases Advertising promotes consumer culture, supports radio and news magazines
1930	Franklin D. Roosevelt becomes president, 1933 The New Deal: unprecedented government intervention in economy, social welfare, arts	Good Neighbor Policy toward Latin America, 1933 Abraham Lincoln Brigade fights in Spanish Civil War U.S. neutrality proclaimed, 1939	Great Depression, 1929–1941 Rise of labor movement	Dust Bowl migration to California and the West Indian New Deal Documentary impulse Federal patronage of the arts
1940	Government mobilizes industry for war production Rationing	U.S. enters World War II, 1941 Allies defeat Axis powers; bombing of Hiroshima, 1945	War mobilization ends depression	Rural whites and blacks migrate to war jobs in cities Civil-rights movement revitalized Film industry enlisted to aid war effort

PART 5

THE MODERN STATE AND SOCIETY

1914 – 1945

By 1914 industrialization, economic expansion abroad, and the growth of a vibrant urban culture had laid the foundations for a distinctly *modern* American society. By 1945, after two world wars and a dozen years of economic depression, the building of the new society was largely complete.

A strong national state, an essential component of modern society, came late to America. Not until the Great Depression of the 1930s and Franklin D. Roosevelt's New Deal did the country witness a dramatic growth of federal power. An even greater expansion of the state resulted from the massive mobilization necessitated by America's entry into World War II.

America's contribution to the Allied victory in World War I demonstrated the nation's potential for world leadership. Although the United States refused to join the League of Nations, its economic strength guaranteed an active role in world affairs after the war. It led the alliance that won World War II and emerged in 1945 as the dominant world power.

In this period the American economy also took on its modern contours. With the world's most productive industrial economy, the nation's businesses—increasingly large-scale corporations—played a commanding role in the international economy. Workers, however, bore the brunt of economic downturns, which fueled the dramatic growth of the labor movement in the 1930s.

Finally, the nation was transformed by demographic change and the rise of mass consumer culture. A great wave of European immigration and the movement from farms to cities gave the nation an increasingly urban tone. Internal migration was important as well, as African-Americans moved north and Dust Bowl farmers moved west in search of a better life. Advertising and the new entertainment media—movies, radio, and magazines—promoted the quest for a rising standard of living and the values of consumerism that would shape American society for the rest of the century.

CHAPTER 23

WAR AND THE AMERICAN STATE, 1914–1920

- The Great War, 1914–1918
- War on the Home Front
- An Unsettled Peace, 1919–1920

"It would be the irony of fate if my administration had to deal chiefly with foreign affairs," Woodrow Wilson told a friend early in his first term. But the United States was no longer just a regional power—it was seated at the table of the "great game" of international politics. When war broke out in Europe in August 1914, Wilson had to play his hand. For more than two years he tried to be an honest broker between the two sides. Only when Germany's resumption of unrestricted submarine attacks threatened American lives and shipping did he reluctantly ask Congress for a declaration of war.

The American decision to enter the conflict in 1917 confirmed one of the most important shifts of power in the twentieth century. Before the outbreak of the Great War in 1914, the world had been dominated by Europe; the postwar world was increasingly dominated by the United States. The historian Akira Iriye calls this broad transformation the "globalization" of America. Increasingly the United States became "involved in security, economic, and cultural affairs in all parts of the world." This development, which is usually thought to begin with World War II and its aftermath, actually started in 1917.

Related changes that shaped the country for the rest of the twentieth century also emerged at home. New federal bureaucracies had to be created to coordinate the wartime efforts of business, labor, and agriculture—a process that hastened the emergence of a national administrative state. War meant new opportunities, albeit temporary, for women and for blacks and other ethnic minorities. It also meant new divisions among Americans and new hatreds, first of Germans and Austrians and then of "Bolshevik" Reds. When the war ended, the United States was forced to confront the deep class, racial, and ethnic divisions that had surfaced during wartime mobilization.

A potent symbol of wartime mobilization was the dramatic posters Americans encountered during the nineteen months of United States participation in "the Great War." At every turn (at the movies, in schools and libraries, in shop windows and post offices, at train stations and factories) Americans were urged to do their part: "It's Up to You—Protect the Nation's Honor—Enlist Now". . . "Rivets Are Bayonets—Drive Them Home!". . . "Women! Help America's Sons Win the War: Buy U.S. Government Bonds." More than colorful reminders of a bygone era, these propaganda tools were meant to unify the American people in voluntary, self-sacrificing service to the nation. They suggest not only the increased presence of the federal government in the lives of Americans, but also the fact that in modern war, victory involved more than armies. On the home front, businessmen, workers, farmers, housewives, even children had important roles to play. The story of the United States' involvement in World War I, then, is a story of battles and diplomacy abroad and mobilization at home, all of which would have a lasting impact on the nation's future.

THE GREAT WAR, 1914–1918

When war erupted in August 1914, most Americans saw no reason to involve themselves in the struggle among Europe's imperialistic powers. No vital U.S. interests were at stake; indeed, the United States had a good relationship with both sides, and its industries benefited from providing war materiel for the combatants. Many Americans placed their faith in what historians call "U.S. exceptionalism"—the belief that their superior democratic values and institutions set their country apart from the other nations of the world and made it immune from the corruption and chaos of international struggles. Horrified by the carnage and sympathetic to the suffering, Americans nevertheless expected that they would be able to follow their president's dictum, "to be neutral in fact as well as in name."

War in Europe

Almost from the moment France, Russia, and Britain formed the Triple Entente in 1907 to counter the Triple Alliance of Germany, Austria-Hungary, and Italy (see Chapter 22), European leaders began to prepare for what they saw as an inevitable conflict. The spark that ignited the war came in Europe's perennial tinderbox, the Balkans, where Austria-Hungary and Russia competed for power and influence. Austria's seizure of the provinces of Bosnia and Herzegovina in 1908 had enraged Russia and its client, the independent state

The Landscape of War
World War I devastated the countryside: this was the battleground at Ypres in 1915. The carnage of trench warfare also scarred the soldiers who served in these surreal settings, causing the "gas neurosis," "burial-alive neurosis," and "soldiers' heart"—all symptoms of shell shock.

of Serbia. Serbian terrorists responded by recruiting Bosnians to agitate against Austrian rule. On June 28, 1914, a nineteen-year-old Bosnian student, Gavrilo Princip, assassinated Franz Ferdinand, the heir to the Austro-Hungarian throne, and his wife, the Duchess of Hohenberg, in the town of Sarajevo.

After the assassination the complex European alliance system, which had for years maintained a fragile peace, drew all the major powers into war. Austria-Hungary, blaming Serbia for the assassination, declared war on Serbia on July 28. Russia, which had a secret treaty with Serbia, mobilized its armies; Germany responded by declaring war on Russia and its ally, France, and by invading neutral Belgium. The brutality of the invasion, and Britain's commitment to Belgian neutrality, prompted Great Britain to declare war on Germany on August 4. Within a few days all the major European powers had formally entered the conflict.

The combatants were divided into two rival blocs. The Allied Powers— Great Britain; France; Japan; Russia; and, in 1915, Italy—were pitted against the Central Powers—Germany; Austria-Hungary; Turkey; and, in 1915, Bulgaria (see Map 23.1). Because the alliance system encompassed competing imperial powers, the conflict spread to parts of the world far beyond Europe, including the Middle East, Africa, and China. Its worldwide scope gave it the name the Great War, or later, World War I.

The term "Great War" also suggested the terrible devastation the conflict produced. It was the first modern war in which extensive harm was done to civilian populations. New military technology, much of it from the United States, made armies more deadly than ever before. Soldiers carried long-range, high-velocity rifles that could hit a target at 1,000 yards—a vast improvement over the 300-yard range of the rifle-musket used in the American Civil War. Another innovation was the machine gun, whose American-born inventor, Hiram Maxim, moved to Great Britain in the 1880s to follow a friend's advice: "If you want to make your fortune, invent something which will allow those fool Europeans to kill each other more quickly."

The concentrated firepower of rifles and machine guns gave troops in defensive positions a tremendous advantage. For four bloody years, between 1914 and 1918, the Allies and the Central Powers faced each other on the

MAP 23.1

Europe at the Start of World War I

In early August 1914 a complex set of interlocking alliances drew the major European powers into war. At first the United States avoided the conflict. Not until April 1917 did America enter the war on the Allied Side.

Western Front, a narrow swath of territory in Belgium and northern France crisscrossed by 25,000 miles of heavily fortified trenches, protected by deadly barbed wire. Trench warfare produced unprecedented numbers of casualties. If one side tried to break the stalemate by venturing into the "no man's land" between the trenches, its soldiers, caught in the sea of barbed wire, were mowed down by artillery fire or poison gas, first used by the Germans at Ypres in April 1915. Between February and December 1916, the French suffered 550,000 casualties and the Germans 450,000, as Germany tried to break through the French lines at Verdun. The front did not move.

The Perils of Neutrality

As the bloody stalemate continued, the United States grappled with its role in the international conflagration. Two weeks after the outbreak of war in Europe, President Woodrow Wilson made the American position clear. In a message widely printed in the newspapers, the president called on Americans to be "neutral in fact as well as in name, impartial in thought as well as in action." Wilson wanted to keep the nation out of the war partly because he believed that if America kept aloof from the quarrel, he could arbitrate—and influence—its ultimate settlement.

The nation's divided loyalties also influenced Wilson's policy. Many Americans, including Wilson, felt deep cultural ties to the Allies, especially Britain and France. Yet most Irish-Americans resented Britain's centuries-long occupation of their home country and the cancellation of Home Rule in 1914. Pro-German sentiments were also encouraged by the presence of 10 million immigrants from Germany and Austria-Hungary. Indeed, German-Americans made up one of the largest and best-established ethnic groups in the United States, and many aspects of German culture, including classical music and the German university system, were widely admired. Wilson could not easily have rallied the nation to the Allied side in 1914.

Many Americans had no strong sympathy for either side. Some progressive leaders—both Republicans and Democrats—vehemently opposed American participation in the European conflict. Newly formed pacifist groups, among them the American Union against Militarism and the Women's Peace Party, both founded in 1915, also mobilized popular opposition. Virtually the entire political left, led principally by Eugene Debs and the Socialist party, condemned the war as imperialistic. African-American leaders such as A. Philip Randolph viewed it as a conflict of the white race only. And some prominent industrialists bankrolled antiwar activities. In December 1915 Henry Ford spent almost half a million dollars to send more than a hundred men and women to Europe on a "peace ship" in an attempt to negotiate an end to the war.

All these factors mitigated against American involvement in the war, and might have kept the nation neutral if the conflict had not spread to the high seas. There the United States initially had as many arguments with Britain as with Germany. The most troublesome issue concerned neutrality rights—freedom to trade with nations on both sides of a conflict.

By the end of August 1914 the British had imposed a naval blockade on the Central Powers, hoping to cut off military supplies and starve the German people into submission. But their actions also prevented neutral nations like the United States from trading with Germany and its allies. The United States chafed at the infringement of its neutral rights but did little besides complain, largely because the spectacular increase in trade with the Allies more than made up for the lost trade with the Central Powers. American trade with Britain and France grew from $824 million in 1914 to $3.2 billion in 1916. By 1917 U.S. banks had lent the Allies $2.5 billion. In contrast, American trade with and loans to Germany totaled only $29 million and $27 million, respectively, by 1917. This imbalance in trade translated into closer U.S. ties with the Allies, despite the nation's official posture of neutrality.

To challenge British control of the seas, the German navy launched a devastating new weapon, the U-boat. On May 7, 1915, a German U-boat submerged off the coast of Ireland torpedoed the British luxury liner *Lusitania*, killing 1,198 people, 128 of them Americans. The attack on the unarmed passenger vessel incensed Americans—newspapers branded it a "mass murder"—and prompted President Wilson to send a series of strongly worded protests to Germany. The crisis continued until September 1915, when Germany announced its submarines would no longer attack passenger ships without warning.

Throughout 1915 and 1916, Wilson tried at several points to mediate an end to the European conflict through his aide, Colonel Edward House. But House concluded that neither side was interested in serious peace negotiations. The worsening tensions with Germany caused Wilson to rethink his opposition to preparedness. In the fall of 1915 he endorsed a $1 billion buildup of the army and the navy, and by 1916 armament was well under way.

Nevertheless, public opinion still ran against entering the war, a factor that profoundly shaped the election of 1916. The Republican party passed over the belligerently prowar Theodore Roosevelt in favor of Supreme Court Justice Charles Evans Hughes, a former governor of New York. The Democrats renominated Wilson, whose campaign emphasized his progressive reform record (see Chapter 21). The Democrats also picked up some votes with their widely circulated campaign slogan, "He kept us out of war." Wilson won re-election by only 600,000 popular votes and by 23 votes in the electoral college, a slim margin that limited his options in mobilizing the nation for war.

The events of early 1917 diminished Wilson's lingering hopes of staying out of the conflict. On January 31 Germany announced the resumption of unrestricted submarine warfare, a decision dictated by the impasse in the land war. In response, Wilson broke off diplomatic relations with Germany on February 3. A few weeks later, the release of the "Zimmermann telegram" moved the country closer to war. Newspapers published an intercepted communication from Germany's foreign secretary, Arthur Zimmermann, to the German minister in Mexico City, in which Zimmermann urged Mexico to join the Central Powers in the war. In return, Germany promised to help Mexico recover "the lost territory of Texas, New Mexico, and Arizona." This threat to the territorial integrity of the United States jolted both congressional and public opinion, especially in the West, where opposition to entering the war was strong. Combined with the resumption of unrestricted submarine warfare, the Zimmermann telegram inflamed anti-German sentiment.

Although the likelihood of Mexico's reconquering the border states was small, the highly explosive situation there (see Chapter 22) continued to concern American policymakers. In the final stages of the Mexican Revolution, the United States backed the Constitutionalist movement led by Venustiano Carranza. Resentful of American support for his rival, the rebel Pancho Villa orchestrated border raids that killed sixteen U.S. citizens in January 1916. In March he razed the town of Columbus, New Mexico. In response, Wilson sent troops under General John J. Pershing into Mexico to capture the elusive Villa. Carranza, strongly supported by Mexican resentment of the apparent occupation of their country, demanded that Pershing withdraw. The two governments backed off, and U.S. troops began to leave early in 1917. Carranza's government received official recognition from Washington on March 13, 1917, less than a month before the United States entered World War I.

Meanwhile, throughout March, U-boats attacked American ships without warning, sinking three on March 18 alone. On April 2, 1917, after consulting his cabinet, Wilson appeared before a special session of Congress to ask for a declaration of war. The rights of the nation had been trampled on and its trade and citizens' lives imperiled, he charged. But while U.S. self-interest shaped the decision to go to war, years of Americans' sense of their exceptionalism, coupled with the Progressive Era's zeal to right social injustices, also played a part. Believing that the United States, in sharp contrast to other nations, was uniquely high-minded in the conduct of its international affairs, many Americans could accept Wilson's claim that "America had no selfish aims: "We desire no conquest, no dominion. We seek no indemnities for ourselves, no material compensation for the sacrifices we shall freely make. We are but one of the champions of the rights of mankind." The United States would not only help to win the war, but in doing so would earn a place at the peace table where it would spread the country's democratic ideals to the rest of the world. In a memorable phrase intended to ennoble the nation's role, Wilson proposed that U.S. participation in the war would make the world "safe for democracy."

Four days after Wilson's speech, on April 6, 1917, the United States declared war on Germany. Reflecting the divided feelings of the country as a whole, the vote was far from unanimous. Six senators and fifty members of the House voted against the action, including Representative Jeannette Rankin of Montana, the first woman elected to Congress. "I want to stand by my country," she declared, "but I cannot vote for war."

Over There

In May 1917 General John J. Pershing, recently returned from his unsuccessful pursuit of Pancho Villa in Mexico, traveled to London and Paris to determine

Call to Arms
To build popular support for the war effort, the government called on artists such as Howard Chandler Christy, Charles Dana Gibson, and James Montgomery Flagg. This 1917 recruiting poster by Flagg was adapted from a June 1916 cover of *Leslie's Illustrated Weekly Newspaper*. The model was the artist.

how the United States could best support the war effort. The answer, as Marshal Joseph Joffre of France put it, was clear: "Men, men, and more men." The problem was that the United States had never maintained a large standing army in peacetime. To field a fighting force strong enough to enter a global war, the government turned to conscription. The passage of the Selective Service Act in May 1917 demonstrated the increasing impact of the state on ordinary citizens. Though draft resistance had been common during the Civil War, no major riots occurred in 1917. The selective service system worked in part because it combined central direction from Washington with local administration and civilian control, and thus did not tread on the nation's tradition of individual freedom and local autonomy. Draft registration also demonstrated the potential bureaucratic capacity of the American state. On a single day, June 5, 1917, more than 9.5 million men between the ages of twenty-one and thirty were processed for military service in their local voting precincts. By the end of the war almost 4 million men, plus a few thousand female navy clerks and army nurses, were in uniform. Another 300,000 men, called "slackers," evaded the draft, and 4,000 were classified as conscientious objectors.

Wilson chose Pershing to head the American Expeditionary Force (AEF). But the newly raised army did not have an immediate impact on the fighting. The fresh recruits had to be trained and outfitted, then wait for transport across the submarine-infested Atlantic. Initially, the nation's main contribution was to secure the safety of the seas. Aiming for safety in numbers in the face of mounting German submarine activity, the government began sending armed convoys across the Atlantic. The plan worked: no American soldiers were killed on the way to Europe, and Allied shipping losses were cut dramatically.

Meanwhile, on the Western Front, trench warfare ground on. Allied commanders pleaded for American reinforcements, but Pershing was reluctant to put his soldiers under foreign commanders. Because the AEF was not ready to fight until May 1918, the brunt of the fighting continued to fall on the French and British. Their burden increased when the Eastern Front collapsed after the Russian Revolution in November 1917. Under the Treaty of Brest-Litovsk, signed on

MAP 23.2

U.S. Participation on the Western Front, 1918

When American troops reached the European front in significant numbers in 1918, the Allied and Central powers had been grinding each other down in a war of attrition for almost four years. The influx of American troops and supplies broke the stalemate. Successful offensive maneuvers by the American Expeditionary Force included Belleau Wood, Château-Thierry, and the Meuse-Argonne campaign.

A Soldier Remembers

S̲ergeant William L. Langer, of Battery E, 1st Gas Regiment, describes the effort to work through the trenches to get to the front lines to set up devices for launching bombs at the Germans at the battle of St. Mihiel in September 1918.

There was not much activity in the trenches, certainly not enough to give reason to suppose that a large scale attack was about to start. The enemy, to be sure, kept up his Vérey lights and fired at intervals. Still, most of us were quite startled and surprised when, about 1:00 in the morning, the sky lit up behind us and the American barrage began. . . .

After depositing our loads at the position we started back for another. . . . And going back was quite a different proposition than going, for, as if by magic, the trenches had filled with men, most of them Marines . . . and troops of the 9th Infantry . . . who were to go over the top with the first wave. Those rows of cold, shivering men, equipped with grenades and with bayonets fixed, crouching in the mud of the trenches and waiting for the crucial moment, is another sight we shall never forget. . . .

We were just about to start back for the trenches [with a second load of bombs] when the Boche suddenly opened up with a concentrated bombardment of the town. Everywhere the shells were bursting. For a moment we were undecided, but then we set out on a run. . . . We reached the trenches without mishap. The first wave was just about to go over, and our machine guns had just opened a rolling barrage to precede it. For green men it was a novel experience—this stuttering breathless chatter of the machine guns behind one. The trenches were in places so congested that to get through would have been impossible had we not struck on a rather clever idea. "Heads up, men, high explosives, watch these sacks";—shouting words to that effect worked like magic and we secured an easy passage.

SOURCE: Frank Freidel, *Over There: The Story of America's First Great Overseas Crusade* (McGraw-Hill, rev. ed. 1990), 127–128.

March 3, 1918, the new Bolshevik regime under Vladimir Ilych Lenin surrendered about one-third of Russia's territories, including Russian Poland, Ukraine, the Baltic provinces, and Finland, in return for an end to hostilities.

Once hostilities with Russia had ended, the Germans launched a major offensive against the Allies on the Western Front on March 21, 1918. By May the German army had advanced to the Marne River, within 50 miles of Paris, and was attempting to subdue the city by bombardment. When Allied leaders intensified their calls for American troops, Pershing committed about 60,000 Americans to help the French repel the Germans in the battles of Château-Thierry and Belleau Wood (see Map 23.2).

American reinforcements now began to arrive in large numbers. Slowly they worked their way to the front through the clogged French transportation system. Augmented by 85,000 American troops, the Allied forces brought the German offensive to a halt in mid-July. At that point there were a million American troops in France. The counteroffensive began with a successful campaign to drive the Germans back from the Marne. In mid-September 1918, American and French troops led by General Pershing forced the Germans to retreat at Saint-Mihiel. The last major assault of the war began on September 26, when Pershing pitted over a million American soldiers against vastly outnumbered and exhausted German troops. The Meuse-Argonne campaign pushed the enemy back across the Selle River near Verdun and broke the German defenses, at a cost of over 26,000 American lives.

World War I ended on November 11, 1918, when German and Allied representatives signed an armistice in the railway car of Marshal Ferdinand Foch of France. The flood of American troops and supplies during the last six months of the war had helped secure the Allied victory. The nation's decisive contribution also signaled a shift in international power as European diplomatic and economic dominance declined and the United States emerged as a world leader.

When the war ended, about 2 million American soldiers were in France. Two-thirds of them had seen action at least briefly on the Western Front, but had escaped the horrors of sustained trench warfare that sapped the morale of Allied and German troops. During the eighteen months in which the United States fought, 48,000 American servicemen were killed in action or from wounds. Another 27,000 died from other causes, mainly the influenza epidemic that swept the world in 1918–1919. But the nation's casualties were minimal compared with the 8 million soldiers lost by the Allies and Central Powers. The French lost far more soldiers in the siege of Verdun than the United States did in the entire war.

After the armistice the war lived on in the minds of the men and women who had gone "over there." Many members of the AEF, especially those who had been spared the horror of sustained battle, experienced the war more as tourists than as soldiers. Before joining the army, most had barely traveled beyond their hometowns; for them the journey across the ocean was a monumental, once-in-a-lifetime event. Their letters described "old cathedrals, chateaux and ancient towns . . . quite wonderful . . . to eyes so accustomed to the look of the New World." In 1919 a group of former AEF officers formed the American Legion, "to preserve the memories and incidents of our association in the great war." The word *legion* captured the romantic, almost chivalric memories many veterans held of their wartime service. Only later did disillusionment over the contested legacy of World War I set in.

For African-Americans, the war experience was a bitter one. Encouraged by black leaders to enlist as a means of proving their loyalty and achieving first-class citizenship, black soldiers instead suffered continued discrimination. Placed in segregated units under white officers, they served in the most menial

A Black Veteran Returns Home
Black soldiers received segregated and unequal treatment at every stage of military service. When the war ended, black veterans faced hostility from many whites alarmed that blacks no longer "knew their place."

positions, as laborers, stevedores, and messboys. Many African-Americans emerged from the war determined to stand up for their rights, and contributed to a spirit of black militancy that characterized the early 1920s.

WAR ON THE HOME FRONT

Fighting World War I required extraordinary economic mobilization on the home front in which business, the work force, and the public all cooperated. Although the federal government did expand its power and presence during the emergency, the watchword was voluntarism. The government avoided compulsion as much as possible. Ambivalence about expanding state power, coupled with the pressures of wartime mobilization, severely damaged the impetus for progressive reforms that had characterized the prewar era. Yet even in the context of international crisis, some reformers expected that the war could serve the cause of improving American society.

Mobilization

The continuing impact of the prewar progressive reform movement was evident in the financing of the war, the cost of which would eventually mount to

$33 billion. The government paid for the war in part by using the Federal Re-
serve System established in 1913 (see Chapter 21) to expand the money supply, making it easier to borrow money. Two-thirds of the funds came from
loans, especially the popular liberty bonds. Treasury Secretary William
McAdoo encouraged the small, heavily advertised bond sales as a way of
widening support for the war and demonstrating the voluntary self-sacrifice
of the nation's virtuous citizenry. To augment the funds raised by bonds,
McAdoo rejected a sales tax in favor of an increased federal income tax. Income taxes had been instituted by Congress after the passage of the Sixteenth
Amendment to the Constitution in 1913. Now the War Revenue bills of
1917 and 1918 transformed the tax into the foremost method of federal fund
raising. The Wilson administration took a progressive approach, rejecting a tax
on all wages and salaries in favor of a tax on corporations and wealthy individuals. The excess-profits tax contained in the law passed in 1917 signaled a direct and unprecedented intrusion of the state into the workings of corporate
capitalism. By 1918 U.S. corporations were paying over $2.5 billion in excess-
profits taxes per year—more than half of all federal taxes.

The tax burden should not mask the fact that the federal government for
the most part took a collaborative rather than a coercive approach to big business during the war. To the dismay of many progressives who had hoped that
the war emergency would increase federal regulation of business, the government suspended antitrust laws to encourage cooperation and promote efficiency. For economic expertise the administration turned to those who knew
the capacities of the economy best—the nation's business leaders. Executives
flocked to Washington, where they served with federal officials on a series of
boards and agencies that sought a middle ground between total state control
of the economy and total freedom for business.

The central agency for mobilizing wartime industry was the War Industries Board (WIB), established in July 1917. In March 1918, after a fumbling
start that showed the limits of voluntarism in a national emergency, the Wilson
administration reorganized the board under the direction of Bernard Baruch,
a Wall Street financier. The WIB produced an unparalleled expansion of the
federal government's economic powers: it allocated scarce resources, gathered
economic data and statistics, controlled the flow of raw materials, ordered the
conversion from peacetime to war production, set prices, imposed efficiency
and standardization procedures, and coordinated purchasing. Though the
board had the authority to compel compliance, Baruch preferred to win voluntary cooperation by industry, often through personal intervention. Business
generally supported this governmental oversight because it coincided so well
with its own interests in improving efficiency and productivity. Despite higher
taxes, corporate profits soared, aided by the suspension of antitrust laws and
the institution of price guarantees for war work. War profits produced an economic boom that continued without interruption until 1920.

The reliance on voluntarism was best exemplified in the Food Administration, created in August 1917 and led by Stanford-trained engineer Herbert

Hoover, who proposed to "mobilize the spirit of self-denial and self-sacrifice in this country." Using the slogan "Food will win the war," Hoover encouraged farmers to expand production of wheat and other grains from 45 million acres in 1917 to 75 million in 1919. Although the Food Administration issued reams of rules and regulations for producers and retailers, at no time did the government contemplate domestic food rationing. Rather, Hoover sent women volunteers from door to door to secure housewives' cooperation in observing "wheatless" Mondays, "meatless" Tuesdays, and "porkless" Thursdays and Saturdays—a campaign that resulted in substantial voluntary conservation of food resources.

In some instances, new federal agencies took dramatic, decisive action. In the face of the severe winter of 1917–1918, which led to coal shortages in northeastern cities and industries, the Fuel Administration ordered all factories east of the Mississippi River to shut down for four days. An even more striking example of the temporary use of federal power came in December 1917. When a massive traffic snarl interfered with the transport of troops, the Railroad War Board, which coordinated the nation's sprawling transportation system, took over the railroads. Guaranteeing railroad owners a "standard return" equal to their average earnings between 1915 and 1917, the board promised that the carriers would be returned to private control no later than twenty-one months after the war. Although reformers hoped to continue this experiment in government control on behalf of labor and consumers, the government fulfilled that pledge after the armistice.

With the signing of the armistice in November 1918, the United States scrambled to dismantle wartime controls. Wilson, determined to "take the harness off," disbanded the WIB on January 1, 1919, resisting suggestions that the board would help stabilize the economy during demobilization. Like most Americans, Wilson could tolerate government planning power during an emergency but not as a permanent feature of the economy.

Although the nation's participation in the war lasted just eighteen months, it left an enduring legacy, the modern bureaucratic state. Entire industries had been organized as never before, linked to a maze of government agencies and executive departments. A modern system of income taxation had been established, with the potential for vastly increasing federal reserves. Finally, the collaboration between business and government had been mutually beneficial, teaching both partners a lesson they would put to use in the state building that occurred in the 1920s and afterward.

Besides mobilizing armies and business concerns to wage war, the federal government also needed to assure a reliable work force, especially in war industries. Acute labor shortages, caused by the demands of the draft and the abrupt decline in European immigration, as well as the urgency of war production, had enhanced workers' bargaining power. The National War Labor Board (NWLB), formed in April 1918, also helped to improve labor's position. Composed of representatives of labor, management, and the public, the NWLB established an eight-hour day for war workers, with time and a half

A Southern Migrant

*he Great Migration of southern African-Americans to the cities of the North
disrupted communities and families, but the migrants kept in touch with friends
and kin through letters and visits. While cities like Chicago offered new opportunities and experiences, as this letter indicates, migrants often found churches that provided important continuity with their southern past.*

My dear Sister: I was agreeably surprised to hear from you and to hear from
home. . . . I got here in time to attend one of the greatest revivals in the history of my life—over 500 people joined the church. . . . It was snowing some
nights and if you didnt hurry you could not get standing room. Please remember me kindly to any who ask of me. The people are rushing here by the thousands and I know if you come and rent a big house you can get all the
roomers you want. You write me exactly when you are coming. I am not
keeping house yet I am living with my brother and his wife. . . . I can get a
nice place for you to stop until you can look around and see what you want. I
am quite busy. I work in Swifts packing Co. in the sausage department. My
daughter and I work for the same company—We get $1.50 a day and we pack
so many sausages we don't have much time to play but it is a matter of a dollar with me and I feel that god made the path and I am walking therein.

Tell your husband work is plentiful here and he wont have to loaf if he
want to work. . . . Well goodbye from your sister in Christ.

SOURCE: *Journal of Negro History,* vol. 4, no. 4, 1919, p. 457.

for overtime, and endorsed equal pay for women workers. Workers were not
allowed to disrupt war production through strikes or other disturbances. In return, the NWLB supported the workers' right to organize unions, required
employers to deal with shop committees, and arbitrated labor disputes.

After years of federal hostility toward labor, the NWLB's actions brought a
welcome change in labor's status and power. From 1916 to 1919 AFL membership grew by almost a million workers, reaching over 3 million at the end
of the war. Few of the wartime gains lasted, however. Wartime inflation ate up
most of the wage hikes, and a virulent postwar antiunion movement caused a
rapid decline in union membership that lasted into the 1930s. The labor
movement did not yet have enough power to bargain on an equal basis with
business and government.

While the war emergency benefited labor, it had a special effect on workers who were traditionally excluded from many industrial jobs. For the first
time, northern factories actively recruited African-Americans, spawning the
"Great Migration" from the South. The lure of decent jobs was potent. As one

Mississippi man described his anticipation of work in the meat-packing houses of Chicago: "You could not rest in your bed at night for thoughts of *Chicago.*" Over 400,000 African-Americans relocated to northern and midwestern cities such as St. Louis, Chicago, Cleveland, and Detroit during the war. Though they encountered discrimination there as well, they found new opportunities and an escape from the repressive southern agricultural system.

Mexican-Americans in California, Texas, New Mexico, and Arizona also found new opportunities during the war. When urban growth in the Southwest exacerbated the wartime labor shortage, many Mexican-Americans left farm labor for new industrial opportunities. Continuing political instability in Mexico following the revolution encouraged many Mexicans to relocate, temporarily or permanently, across the border, a process facilitated by newly opened railroad lines. At least 100,000 Mexicans entered the United States between 1917 and 1920, often settling in segregated neighborhoods (*barrios*) in urban areas, meeting discrimination similar to that faced by African-Americans.

Women were the largest group to take advantage of wartime opportunities. White women and, to a lesser degree, black and Mexican-American women found that factory jobs usually reserved for men had been opened to them. About 1 million women joined the labor force for the first time, while many of the 8 million women who already held jobs switched from low-paying fields like domestic service to higher-paying industrial work. Americans soon got used to the sight of female streetcar conductors, train engineers, and defense workers. But everyone—including most working women—believed that those jobs would return to men after the war.

Reform and War

Supporters of woman suffrage hoped that the war would reinvigorate the reform era. The National American Woman Suffrage Association (NAWSA) continued to lobby for the proposed woman suffrage amendment to the Constitution. It also threw the support of its 2 million members behind the Wilson administration, encouraging women to do their part to win the war. Women in communities all over the country labored exhaustively to promote food conservation, to protect children and women workers, and to distribute emergency relief through organizations like the Red Cross. Many agreed with Carrie Chapman Catt, president of NAWSA, that women's patriotic service could advance the cause of woman's suffrage.

Alice Paul and the National Woman's Party (NWP) took a more militant tack. To the dismay of NAWSA leaders, NWP militants began picketing the White House in July 1917 to protest their lack of the vote. Arrested and sentenced to seven months in jail, Paul and other women prisoners went on a hunger strike, which prison authorities met with forced feeding. Public shock at the women's treatment made them martyrs, drawing attention to the cause.

The combination of suffrage militancy and NAWSA's policy of patient persuasion finally brought results. In January 1918 Woodrow Wilson withdrew his

Wartime Opportunities
Women took on new jobs during the war, working as mail carriers, police officers, drill-press operators, and farm laborers attached to the Women's Land Army. These three women clearly enjoyed the camaraderie of working in a railroad yard in 1918. When the war ended, women usually lost such employment.

opposition to a federal woman suffrage amendment. The constitutional amendment quickly passed the House, but took eighteen months to get through the Senate. Then came another year of hard work for ratification by the states. Finally, on August 26, 1920, Tennessee gave the Nineteenth Amendment the last vote it needed. The goal that had first been declared at the Seneca Falls convention in 1848 was finally achieved seventy-two years later, in large part because of women's contributions to the war effort. The suffragists had posed a simple but effective moral challenge: How could the United States fight to make the world safe for democracy while denying half its citizens the right to vote?

Throughout the mobilization period, reformers pushed for a wide range of social reforms. In the name of army efficiency, or "keeping fit to fight," the federal government launched an ambitious anti–venereal disease campaign, forcing the shutdown of "red-light" districts in cities with military training camps. With the cooperation of the YMCA and the YWCA, the government undertook a far-reaching sex education program, designed to enlighten both men and women about the dangers of sexuality and the value of "social purity." Other reformers addressed the welfare of children. The Women's Council of National Defense, a voluntary organization with federal backing, proclaimed 1918 the year of the child, conducted a nationwide growth-monitoring program, and disseminated information about child health and nutrition. From playground directors to librarians, from educators to advocates of the Americanization of immigrants, idealistic reformers proclaimed that the war was just the start of a continuing battle for social welfare.

Especially active were temperance advocates, who viewed alcoholic beverages as the key social evil. In the early twentieth century, many Americans viewed the legal prohibition of alcohol as a progressive reform, not a denial of individual freedom. Urban reformers, concerned about good government, poverty, and public morality, supported a nationwide ban on drinking. The drive for Prohibition also had substantial backing in rural communities. Many people equated liquor with all the sins of the city: prostitution, crime, immigration, machine politics, and public disorder. In addition, the churches with the greatest strength in rural areas, including the Methodists, the Baptists, and the Mormons, strongly condemned drinking. Protestants from rural areas also dominated the membership of the Anti-Saloon League, which supplanted the Women's Christian Temperance Union as the leading proponent of Prohibition early in the century.

Support for the right to drink existed primarily in the nation's heavily urbanized areas, places where immigrants had settled. Alcoholic beverages, especially beer and whiskey, played an important role in the social life of certain ethnic cultures, especially those of German-Americans and Irish-Americans. Most saloons were in working-class neighborhoods and served as gathering places for workers. Machine politicians conducted much of their business in bars. Thus many immigrants and working-class people opposed Prohibition, rightly interpreting the attack on drinking as an imposition of middle-class cultural values on them.

Although numerous states—mostly southern and midwestern states without a significant immigrant presence—already had prohibition laws, World War I soon offered the impetus for national action. Because several major breweries (Pabst and Busch, for example) had German names, beer drinking had become unpatriotic in many people's minds. To conserve food, Congress prohibited the use of foodstuffs such as hops and barley in breweries and distilleries. Finally, in December 1917, Congress passed the proposed Eighteenth Amendment, which prohibited the "manufacture, sale, or transportation of intoxicating liquors." Ratified in 1919 and effective on January 16, 1920, the Eighteenth Amendment demonstrated the widening influence of the state in matters of personal behavior.

The Eighteenth Amendment was an example of how "progressive" reform efforts could benefit from the climate of war. But despite the stimulus the Great War gave to some types of reform, for the most part it blocked rather than furthered reforms. Though many Progressives had anticipated that the stronger federal presence in wartime would lead to stronger economic controls and corporate regulation, federal agencies were quickly disbanded once the war was over, reflecting the unease most Americans felt about a strong bureaucratic state. Moreover, the wartime collaboration between government and business gave corporate leaders more influence in shaping the economy and government policy, not less.

Promoting National Unity

For the liberal reformers who so strongly believed in the possibility that the war for democracy could promote a more just society at home, perhaps the most discouraging aspect of the war was the campaign to promote what was called "One Hundred Percent Americanism," which translated into an insistence on conformity and an intolerance of dissent. Ironically, Woodrow Wilson had predicted what came to pass: "Once lead this people into war, and they'll forget there ever was such a thing as tolerance," he had warned. But the president also recognized the need to manufacture support for the war. "It is not an army we must shape and train for war, it is a nation," he acknowledged. It was this drumming up of enthusiasm that encouraged a repressive spirit hostile to reform.

In April 1917 Wilson formed the Committee on Public Information (CPI) to promote public support for the war. This government propaganda agency, headed by the journalist George Creel, became a magnet for progressive reformers and muckraking journalists. Professing high-sounding goals such as educating citizens about democracy, promoting national unity, Americanizing immigrants, and breaking down the isolation of rural life, the committee also acted as a nationalizing force by promoting the development of a common ideology.

During the war the CPI touched the lives of practically every American. It distributed 75 million pieces of patriotic literature and sponsored speeches at local movie theaters, reaching an audience estimated at more than 300 million—three times the population of the United States at the time. In its zeal, the committee often ventured into hatemongering. In early 1918, for example, it encouraged speakers to use inflammatory stories of alleged German atrocities to build support for the war effort.

As a spirit of conformity pervaded the home front, many Americans found themselves targets of suspicion. Local businesses paid for newspaper and magazine ads that asked citizens to report to the Justice Department "the man who spreads pessimistic stories, cries for peace, or belittles our efforts to win the war." Posters encouraged Americans to be on the lookout for German spies. And quasi-vigilante groups such as the American Protective League mobilized about 250,000 self-appointed agents, furnished with badges issued by the Justice Department, to spy on neighbors and co-workers.

The CPI also urged ethnic groups to give up their Old World customs in the spirit of One Hundred Percent Americanism. German-Americans bore the brunt of this campaign. In an orgy of hostility generated by propaganda about German militarism and atrocities, everything associated with Germany became suspect. German music, especially opera, was banished from the concert halls. Publishers removed pro-German references from textbooks, and many communities banned the teaching of the German language. Sauerkraut was renamed "liberty cabbage," and hamburgers were transformed into "liberty sandwiches." Though anti-German hysteria dissipated when the war ended, hostility toward the "hyphenated" American survived into the 1920s.

In law enforcement, officials tolerated little criticism of established values and institutions, as the militant suffragists picketing the White House during wartime had discovered. The main legal tools for curbing dissent were the Espionage Act of 1917 and the Sedition Act of 1918. The Espionage Act imposed stiff penalties for antiwar activities and allowed the federal government to ban treasonous materials from the mails. The postmaster general revoked the mailing privileges of groups considered to be radical, virtually shutting down their publications.

Individuals suffered as well. Because these acts defined treason and sedition loosely, they led to the conviction of more than a thousand people. The Justice Department focused particularly on socialists who criticized the war and the draft, and on radicals like the Industrial Workers of the World (see Chapter 18), whose attacks on militarism threatened to disrupt war production in the western lumber and copper industries. Socialist party leader Eugene Debs was sentenced to ten years in jail for stating that the master classes declared war while the subject classes fought the battles. (Debs was pardoned by President Warren G. Harding in 1921.) Victor Berger, a Milwaukee socialist, who had been jailed under the Espionage Act, was twice prevented from taking the seat to which he had been elected in the U.S. House of Representatives.

The courts rarely resisted these wartime excesses. In *Schenck v. United States* (1919), the Supreme Court upheld the conviction of the general secretary of the Socialist party, Charles T. Schenck, who had been convicted of mailing pamphlets urging draftees to resist induction. In a unanimous decision, Justice Oliver Wendell Holmes ruled that an act of speech uttered under circumstances that would "create a clear and present danger to the safety of the country" could be constitutionally restricted. Because of the national war emergency, then, the Court upheld limits on freedom of speech that would not have been acceptable in peacetime. Thus in wartime, the drive for conformity reigned, dashing reformers' optimistic hopes that war could be what philosopher John Dewey had called a "plastic juncture," in which the country would be more open to reason and progressive ideas.

AN UNSETTLED PEACE, 1919–1920

In January 1917 Woodrow Wilson had proposed a "peace without victory," since only a "peace among equals" could last. His goal was "not a balance of power, but a community of power; not organized rivalries, but an organized common peace." The keystone of Wilson's postwar plans was a permanent league of nations. With victory achieved, Wilson confronted the task of constructing the new moral international order. But he would first have to win over a Senate that was Republican controlled and openly hostile to the treaty he had brought home.

The Treaty of Versailles

Wilson scored an early victory when the Allies accepted his Fourteen Points as the basis for the peace negotiations that began in January 1919. In this blueprint for the postwar world, the president called for open diplomacy, "absolute freedom of navigation upon the seas," arms reduction, the removal of trade barriers, and an international commitment to territorial integrity and national self-determination. Essential to Wilson's vision was the creation of a multinational organization "for the purpose of affording mutual guarantees of political independence and territorial integrity to great and small States alike." The League of Nations became Wilson's obsession.

The Fourteen Points were imbued with the spirit of progressivism. Widely distributed as propaganda during the final months of the war, Wilson's plan proposed to extend the ideals of America—democracy, freedom, and peaceful economic expansion—to the rest of the world. The League of Nations, acting as a kind of international Federal Trade Commission, would supervise disarmament and—according to the crucial Article X of its covenant—curb unilateralism through collective military action. More grandiosely, Wilson anticipated that the League would mediate disputes between nations, preventing future wars, and thus assuring that the Great War would be "the war to end all wars." By emphasizing these lofty goals, Wilson guaranteed disappointment: his ideals for world reformation were too far-reaching to be practical or attainable.

Twenty-seven countries sent representatives to the peace conference in Versailles, near Paris. Distrustful of the new Bolshevik regime in Russia and its call for proletarian revolution, the allies deliberately excluded its representatives. Nor was Germany invited. The Big Four—Wilson, Prime Minister David Lloyd George of Great Britain, Premier Georges Clemenceau of France, and Prime Minister Vittorio Orlando of Italy—did most of the negotiating. The three European leaders sought a peace that differed radically from Wilson's plan. They wanted to punish Germany and treat themselves to the spoils of war by demanding heavy reparations. In fact, before the war ended, Britain, France, and Italy had already made secret agreements to divide up the German colonies.

It is a tribute to Wilson that he managed to influence the peace settlement as much as he did. He was able to soften some of the harshest demands for reprisal against Germany. National self-determination, a fundamental principle of Wilson's Fourteen Points, bore fruit in the creation of the independent states of Austria, Hungary, Poland, Yugoslavia, and Czechoslovakia from the defeated empires of the Central Powers. The establishment of the new nations of Finland, Estonia, Lithuania, and Latvia not only upheld the principle of self-determination, but also served Wilson's (and the Allies') desire to isolate Soviet Russia from the rest of Europe.

Wilson had less success in achieving other goals. He won only limited concessions regarding the colonial empires of the defeated powers. The old Central and Eastern European colonial empires were dismantled, only to enlarge the overseas empire of the victorious allies. Certain topics, such as freedom of the seas and free trade, never even appeared on the agenda because of Allied resistance. Finally, Wilson had only partial success in scaling back French and British demands for reparations from Germany, which eventually were set at $33 billion.

In the face of these disappointments, Wilson consoled himself with the negotiators' commitment to his proposed League of Nations. He acknowledged that the peace treaty had defects, but expressed confidence that they could be resolved by a permanent international organization dedicated to the peaceful resolution of disputes.

On June 28, 1919, representatives gathered in the Hall of Mirrors at the Palace of Versailles to sign the peace treaty. Wilson sailed home immediately after the ceremony. He came back to a public enthusiastic about a league of nations in principle. Major newspapers and the Federal Council of Churches of Christ of America supported the treaty, and even an enemy of the proposed League, Henry Cabot Lodge, acknowledged that "[T]he people of the country are very naturally fascinated by the idea of eternal preservations of the world's peace."

But when Wilson presented the treaty to the Senate on July 10, it fell far short of the two-thirds vote necessary for ratification. The rejection was not altogether surprising, for Wilson had not paid much attention to the political realities of building support for the League of Nations and the treaty in the Senate. He had failed to include a prominent Republican in the American commission that represented the United States at Versailles. Convinced of his own rectitude and ability, he had kept the negotiations firmly in his own hands. When the Senate balked at the treaty, Wilson adamantly refused to compromise. "I shall consent to nothing," he told the French ambassador. "The Senate must take its medicine."

The Senate, however, did not oblige. And despite the president's attempt to make the 1918 congressional elections a referendum for his peace plans, Americans returned a Republican majority to Congress. Wilson and the League faced stiff opposition in the Senate. Some progressive senators, who endorsed the idea of American internationalism, felt that the peace agreement was too conservative, that it served to "validate existing empires" of the victorious Allies. The "irreconcilables," including progressive senators William E. Borah of Idaho, Hiram W. Johnson of California, and Robert M. La Follette of Wisconsin, disagreed fundamentally with the premise of permanent U.S.

634   Chapter 23 • War and the American State, 1914–1920

participation in European affairs. More influential was a group of Republicans led by Senator Henry Cabot Lodge of Massachusetts. They proposed a list of amendments that focused on Article X, the section of the League covenant that called for collective security measures when a member nation was attacked. This provision, they argued, would restrict Congress's constitutional authority to declare war and would limit the freedom of the United States to pursue a unilateral foreign policy.

Wilson refused to budge, especially not to placate Lodge, his hated political rival. Hoping to mobilize support for the treaty, in September 1919 the president launched an extensive speaking tour during which he brought large audiences to tears with his impassioned defense of the treaty. But the tour had to be cut short when the ailing sixty-two-year-old president collapsed in Pueblo, Colorado, late in September. One week later, in Washington, Wilson suffered a severe stroke that paralyzed one side of his body. While his wife, Edith Bolling Galt Wilson; his physician; and the various cabinet heads oversaw the routine business of government, Wilson slowly recovered, but he was never the same again.

From his sickbed, Wilson remained inflexible in his refusal to compromise, ordering Democratic senators to vote against all Republican amendments. The treaty came up for a vote in November 1919, but was not ratified. When another attempt in March 1920 fell 7 votes short, the issue was dead. Wilson died in 1924, "as much a victim of the war," David Lloyd George noted, "as any soldier who died in the trenches."

The United States never ratified the Versailles treaty nor joined the League of Nations. Many wartime issues were only partially resolved, notably Germany's future, the fate of the colonial empires, and rising nationalist demands for self-determination. These unsolved problems played a major role in the coming of World War II; some, like the competing ethnic nationalisms in the Balkans, remain unresolved today.

Racial Strife and Labor Unrest

Wilson spent only ten days in the United States between December 1918 and June 1919. Totally preoccupied with the peacemaking process at Versailles, for more than six months he was practically an absentee president. Unfortunately, many urgent domestic issues demanded his attention, as the country grappled with the complex problems of demobilization, vainly hoping for a period of tranquility after war's disruptions.

The war years and the immediate postwar period witnessed a severe decline in race relations throughout the country. The volatile mix of black migration and raised black expectations as a result of service in World War I combined to exacerbate white racism. In the South the number of lynchings rose from forty-eight in 1917 to seventy-eight in 1919, and several African-American men were lynched while wearing military uniforms. In the North, race riots broke out in more than twenty-five cities, with one of the first and most deadly occurring in 1917 in East St. Louis, Illinois, where nine whites and more than forty blacks died in a conflict sparked by competition over jobs at a defense plant.

In the summer of 1919, the death toll from racial violence reached 120. One of the worst race riots in American history took place in Chicago in July, where five days of rioting left twenty-three blacks and fifteen whites dead. Tensions in Chicago mirrored those in other cities where violence erupted. In politics, black voters often determined the winners of close elections, thereby enraging white racists who resented black political influence. Blacks also competed with whites for jobs and scarce housing. Even before the July riot, blacks had suffered the bombing of their homes and other forms of harassment. Chicago blacks did not sit meekly by as whites destroyed their neighborhoods. They fought back, both in self-defense and for their rights as citizens. The war had an indirect effect on their actions, since many blacks had served in the armed forces. Wilson's rhetoric about democracy and self-determination had raised their expectations, too.

Workers harbored similar hopes for a better life after the war. The war years had brought them higher pay, shorter hours, and better working conditions. Soon after the armistice, however, many employers resumed their attacks on union activity, and many native-born Americans continued to identify unions with radicalism and foreigners. In addition, rapidly rising inflation—in 1919, the cost of living was 77 percent higher than its prewar level—threatened to wipe out workers' wage increases. Nevertheless, workers hoped to hold onto and perhaps even expand their wartime gains.

The result of workers' determination—and employers' resistance—was a dramatic wave of strikes. More than 4 million workers—one in every five—went on strike in 1919, a proportion never since equaled. The year began with a walkout by shipyard workers in Seattle, a strong union town. Their action spread into a general strike that crippled the city. Another hard-fought strike disrupted the steel industry when 350,000 steel workers demanded union recognition and an end to twelve-hour shifts and the seven-day workweek. And in the fall the Boston police force shocked many Americans by going on strike. Governor Calvin Coolidge of Massachusetts propelled himself into the political spotlight by declaring, "There is no right to strike against the public safety by anybody, anywhere, any time." Coolidge fired the entire police force, and the strike failed. The public supported this harsh reprisal, and Coolidge was rewarded with the Republican vice presidential nomination in 1920.

The Red Scare

A crucial factor in organized labor's failure to win many of its strikes in the postwar period was the pervasive fear of radicalism. This concern coincided with mainstream Americans' longstanding anxiety about unassimilated immigrants—an anxiety that the war had made worse. The Russian Revolution of 1917 so alarmed the Allies that Wilson sent several thousand troops to Russia in the summer of 1918 in hopes of weakening the Bolshevik regime. When the Bolsheviks founded the Third International (or Comintern) in 1919 to export communist doctrine throughout the world, American fears deepened. As domestic labor unrest increased, Americans began to see radicals everywhere. Hatred of the German Hun was quickly replaced by hostility toward the Bolshevik Reds.

Ironically, as public concern about domestic Bolshevism increased, radicals were rapidly losing members and political power. No more than 70,000 Americans belonged to either the fledgling U.S. Communist party or the Communist Labor party in 1919. Both the IWW and the Socialist party had been weakened by wartime repression and internal dissent. Yet the public and the press continued to blame almost every disturbance, especially labor conflicts, on alien radicals. "REDS DIRECTING SEATTLE STRIKE—TO TEST CHANCE FOR REVOLUTION," warned a typical newspaper headline.

Tensions mounted when a series of bombs exploded in the early spring. "The word 'radical' in 1919," the historian Robert Murray has observed, "automatically carried with it the implication of dynamite." In June a bomb detonated outside the Washington town house of the recently appointed attorney general, A. Mitchell Palmer. His family escaped unharmed, but the bomber was blown to bits. Angling for the presidential nomination, Palmer capitalized on the event, fanning fears of domestic radicalism.

In November 1919, on the second anniversary of the Russian Revolution, the attorney general staged the first of what became known as "Palmer raids." Federal agents stormed the headquarters of radical organizations, capturing such supposedly revolutionary booty as a set of blueprints for a phonograph (at first thought to be sketches for a bomb). The dragnet pulled in thousands of aliens who had committed no crime, but were suspect because of their anarchist or revolutionary beliefs or their immigrant backgrounds. Lacking the protection of U.S. citizenship, they faced deportation without formal trial or indictment. In December 1919 the U.S.S. *Buford*, nicknamed the "Soviet Ark," embarked for Finland and the Soviet state with a cargo of 294 deported radicals.

The peak of Palmer's power came with his New Year's raids in January 1920. In one night, with the greatest possible publicity, federal agents rounded up 6,000 radicals, invading private homes, union headquarters, and meeting halls, and arresting citizens and aliens alike. Palmer was riding high in his ambitions for the presidency, but then he overstepped himself. He predicted that on May Day 1920 an unnamed conspiracy would attempt to overthrow the U.S. government. State militia units and police went on twenty-four-hour alert to guard the nation against the threat of revolutionary violence, but not a single incident occurred. As the summer of 1920 passed without major labor strikes or renewed bombings, the hysteria of the Red Scare began to abate.

The wartime legacy of antiradicalism and anti-immigrant sentiment, however, persisted well into the next decade. In May 1920, at the height of the Red Scare, Nicola Sacco, a shoemaker, and Bartolomeo Vanzetti, a fish peddler, were arrested for the robbery and murder of a shoe company's paymaster in South Braintree, Massachusetts. The two men, self-proclaimed anarchists and alien draft evaders, were both armed at the time of their arrest.

Convicted in 1921, Sacco and Vanzetti sat on death row for six years while supporters appealed their verdicts. Although new evidence suggesting their innocence surfaced, Judge Webster Thayer denied a motion for a new trial. Scholars still debate the question of their guilt, but most agree that the two anarchists did not receive a fair trial, that both the evidence and procedures were tainted. Moreover, it is also clear the verdict stemmed as much from their status as radicals and immigrants as it did from evidence. As future Supreme Court jurist Felix Frankfurter said at the time, "The District Attorney invoked against them a riot of political passion and patriotic sentiment." Nevertheless, shortly before his execution in the electric chair on August 23, 1927, Vanzetti claimed triumph:

> If it had not been for these thing, I might have live out my life among scorning men. I might have die, unmarked, unknown, a failure.... Never in our full life can we hope to do such work for tolerance, for justice, for man's understanding of man, as now we do by an accident.

This oft-quoted elegy captures the eloquence and tolerance of a man caught in the last spasm of antiradicalism and fear that capped America's participation in the Great War.

That participation left other legacies as well. World War I did not have the catastrophic effect on the United States that it did on European countries. With relatively few casualties and no physical destruction at home, America emerged from the conflict stronger than ever before. Increased efficiency and technological advancements fostered exceptional industrial productivity, making the United States the envy of the rest of the world in the postwar decade. Consolidating developments that had begun with the Spanish-American War, the United States became a major international power, both economically and politically.

At home, Americans tended to view the war as a significant watershed. "Since the war" emerged as a persistent refrain used to described a wide range of changes in daily life and cultural values. In the 1920s, everything from rising divorce rates and changing sexual morality to African-American militancy and increased standardization and regimentation was attributed to the war. This was a simplistic assessment. The war—especially the nationalism that accompanied it—contributed to a climate that was inhospitable to liberal social reforms, a climate that would persist until the crisis of the Great Depression. And though mobilization was accompanied by an insistence on as much voluntarism as possible, the war emergency did leave a legacy of a stronger federal government and an enlarged bureaucracy. It also exacerbated a number of social tensions, including those involving the working class, ethnic and racial diversity, and the changing role of women. But World War I alone cannot account for the tremendous social transformations that swept American society in these years. Industrialization; immigration; urbanization; and changing patterns in work, politics, religion, leisure, and the family were under way well before 1914–1918. The war was not necessarily the cause of those massive social changes, but rather a magnifying lens that illuminated them.

CHAPTER 23 TIMELINE	
1914	Outbreak of war in Europe
	United States declares neutrality
1915	German submarine sinks *Lusitania*
1916	Woodrow Wilson reelected
	Pershing's expedition to Mexico
1917	U.S. enters World War I
	Revenue Act passed
	Selective Service Act passed
	War Industries Board established
	Suffrage militancy
	East St. Louis race riot
	Espionage Act
	Bolshevik Revolution
	Committee on Public Information
1918	Wilson proposes Fourteen Points
	Meuse-Argonne campaign
	Sedition Act
	Eugene Debs imprisoned under Sedition Act
	Armistice ends war
	U.S. troops intervene in Soviet Union
1919	Treaty of Versailles
	Chicago race riot
	Steel strike
	Red Scare and Palmer raids; *Schenck v. United States*
	American Legion founded
	League of Nations defeated in Senate
	Eighteenth Amendment (Prohibition)
	War Industries Board disbanded
1920	Nineteenth Amendment (woman suffrage)
	"Soviet Ark" sails
1924	Woodrow Wilson dies

CHAPTER 24

MODERN TIMES: THE 1920s

- Business–Government Partnership of the 1920s
- A New National Culture
- Dissenting Values and Cultural Conflict

In 1924 the sociologists Robert Lynd and Helen Merrell Lynd arrived in Muncie, Indiana, to study the life of a small American city. They observed how the citizens of Middletown (the fictional name they gave the city) made a living, maintained a home, educated their young, practiced their religion, organized community activities, and spent their leisure time. As the Lynds' fieldwork proceeded, they were struck by how much had changed over the past thirty-five years—the actual lifetime of a middle-aged Middletown resident—and decided to contrast the Muncie of the 1890s with the Muncie of the 1920s. When *Middletown* was published in 1929, this "study in modern American culture" became an unexpected best seller. Its success spoke to Americans' desire to understand the forces that were transforming their society.

The transformation to a modern society had begun with World War I. Participation in the war had made the United States a major player in the world economy; the foundations of large-scale corporate enterprise and a modern state had been firmly established. Rather than World War I, however, the 1920s were the watershed in the development of a mass national culture. Only then did the Protestant work ethic and the old values of self-denial and frugality begin to give way to the fascination with consumption, leisure, and self-realization that is the essence of modern times. In economic organization, political outlook, and cultural values, the 1920s had more in common with the United States today than with the industrializing America of the late nineteenth century.

BUSINESS-GOVERNMENT PARTNERSHIP OF THE 1920s

The business-government partnership fostered by World War I continued on an informal basis throughout the 1920s. As the *Wall Street Journal* enthusiastically proclaimed, "Never before, here or anywhere else, has a government been so completely fused with business." From 1922 to 1929 the nation's prosperity seemed to confirm the economy's ability to regulate itself with minimal government intervention. Gone, or at least submerged, was the reform impulse of the Progressive Era. Business leaders were no longer villains but respected public figures. President Warren G. Harding captured the prevailing political mood when he offered the American public "not heroics but healing, not nostrums but normalcy."

The Republican "New Era"

Except for Woodrow Wilson's two terms, the presidency had been controlled by the Republican party since 1896. When Wilson's progressive coalition floundered by 1918, the Republicans had a chance to regain the presidency. With the ailing Wilson out of the picture, in 1920 the Democrats nominated Governor James M. Cox of Ohio. Assistant Secretary of the Navy Franklin D. Roosevelt became the vice-presidential candidate. In their platforms, the Democrats called for U.S. participation in the League of Nations and a continuation of Wilson's progressivism. The Republicans, led by Warren G. Harding and Calvin Coolidge, promised a return to "normalcy," which meant a strong probusiness stance and conservative cultural values. Harding and Coolidge won in a landslide, marking the beginning of a Republican dominance that would last until 1932.

Central to what Republicans termed the "New Era" was business-government cooperation. Although Republican administrations generally opposed expanding state power to promote progressive reforms, they did use federal policy and power to assist corporations. Thus, Harding's secretary of the treasury, financier Andrew W. Mellon, engineered a tax cut that undercut the wartime Revenue Acts, benefiting wealthy individuals and corporations. The Republican-dominated Federal Trade Commission (FTC) for the most part ignored the antitrust laws rather than using federal power to police industry. In this the Commission followed the lead of the Supreme Court, which in 1920 had dismissed the long-pending antitrust case against U.S. Steel, ruling that largeness in business was not against the law as long as some competition remained.

Perhaps the best example of government-business cooperation emerged in the Department of Commerce, headed by Herbert Hoover, a believer in what historian Ellis Hawley has called the associative state. Hoover thought that with government assistance, businessmen would work in behalf of the public interest, thereby benefiting the entire country. Under Hoover, the Commerce Department expanded dramatically, offering new services like the compilation and distribution of trade and production statistics to American business. It also assisted private trade associations in their efforts to rationalize major sectors of industry and commerce by cooperating in such areas as product standardization and wage and price controls.

Unfortunately, not all government-business cooperation was as high-minded as Hoover had anticipated. President Harding was an honest man, but some of his political associates were not. When Harding died suddenly in San Francisco in August 1923, evidence of widespread fraud and corruption in his administration had just come to light. A particularly damaging scandal concerned the secret leasing of government oil reserves in Teapot Dome, Wyoming, and in Elk Hills, California, without competitive bidding. Secretary of the Interior Albert Fall was eventually convicted of taking $300,000 in bribes; he became the first cabinet officer in American history to serve a prison sentence.

After Harding's death the taciturn vice president, Calvin Coolidge, moved into the White House. In contrast to his predecessor's political cronyism and outgoing style, Coolidge personified moral rectitude. As vice president, "Silent Cal" often sat through official functions without uttering a word. A dinner partner once challenged him by saying, "Mr. Coolidge, I've made a rather sizable bet with my friends that I can get you to speak three words this evening." Responded Coolidge icily, "You lose." Although Coolidge was quiet and unimaginative, his image of unimpeachable integrity reassured voters, and he soon announced his candidacy for the presidency in 1924.

When the Democrats gathered that July in the sweltering heat of New York City, they faced a divided party. The party drew its support mainly from the South and from northern urban political machines like Tammany Hall in New York, and the two constituencies' interests often collided. They disagreed mightily over Prohibition; immigration restriction; and, most seriously, the mounting power of the racist and anti-immigrant Ku Klux Klan. The resolutions committee remained deadlocked for days over whether the party should condemn the Klan, eventually reaching a weak compromise that affirmed its general opposition to "any effort to arouse religious or racial dissension."

With this contentious background, the convention took 103 ballots to nominate John W. Davis, a Wall Street lawyer who had served as a West Virginia congressman, for the presidency. To attract rural voters, the Democrats chose as their vice-presidential candidate Governor Charles W. Bryan of Nebraska, William Jennings Bryan's brother. But the Democrats could not mount an effective challenge to their more popular and better-financed Republican rivals, whose strength came chiefly from the native-born Protestant middle class, augmented by small business people, skilled workers, farmers, northern blacks, and wealthy industrialists. Until the Democrats could overcome their sectional and cultural divisions and build an effective national organization to rival that of the Republicans, they would remain a minority party.

The 1924 campaign also featured a third-party challenge, by Senator Robert M. La Follette of Wisconsin, who ran on the Progressive party ticket. La Follette's candidacy mobilized reformers and labor leaders as well as disgruntled farmers in an effort to reinvigorate the reform movement both major parties had abandoned. The party platform called for nationalization of railroads, public ownership of utilities, and the right of Congress to overrule Supreme Court decisions. It also favored the direct election of the president by the voters rather than by indirect election through the electoral college.

The Republicans won an impressive victory. Coolidge received 15.7 million popular votes to Davis's 8.4 million and won a decisive margin in the electoral college. La Follette got almost 5 million popular votes, but he carried only Wisconsin in the electoral college. Perhaps the most significant aspect of the election was the low voter turnout. Only 52 percent of the electorate voted in 1924, compared to more than 70 percent in presidential elections of the late nineteenth century. Newly enfranchised women voters were not to blame, however; a long-term drop in voting by men, rather than apathy among women, caused the decline.

Instead of resting after their suffrage victory, women increased their political activism in the 1920s. African-American women struggled for voting rights in the Jim Crow South and pushed unsuccessfully for a federal anti-lynching law. Many women tried to break into party politics, but Democrats and Republicans granted them only token positions on party committees. Women were more influential as lobbyists. The Women's Joint Congressional Committee, a Washington-based coalition of ten major white women's organizations, including the newly formed League of Women Voters, lobbied actively for reform legislation. Its major accomplishment was the passage in 1921 of the Sheppard-Towner Federal Maternity and Infancy Act, which appropriated $1.25 million for well-baby clinics, educational programs, and visiting-nurse projects. Such major reform legislation was rare in the 1920s, however, and its success short-lived. Once politicians realized that women did not vote as a bloc, they stopped listening to the women's lobby, and in 1929 Congress cut off the program's funding.

The roadblocks women activists faced were part of a broader public antipathy to ambitious reforms. Although some states—such as New York, where an urban liberalism was coalescing under leaders like Al Smith—did enact a flurry of legislation that promoted workmen's compensation, public health programs, and conservation measures, on the national level reforms that would strengthen federal power made little headway. After years of progressive reforms and an expanded federal presence in World War I, Americans were unenthusiastic about increased taxation or more governmental bureaucracy. The Red Scare had given ammunition to opponents of reform by making it easy to claim that legislation calling for governmental activism was the first step toward Bolshevism. The general prosperity of the 1920s further hampered the reform spirit. With a

Women Get the Vote

A lice Paul, president of the Woman's Party, was a militant whose brand of feminism and reform was not shared by all women reformers. Nonetheless, this passage from her oral history captures well the widespread excitement about the opportunities the vote could bring individual women and the power it could summon for their causes in the early 1920s.

Suddenly we were regarded as having some power in the world. I mean, people were coming to you wanting *you* to get things for them. Women were coming wanting you to have them promoted in the government because they never could get the positions they thought they ought to have, and wanting to be appointed as ambassadors and everything they imagined, we could suddenly have so much power.

Congressmen began to suddenly have women secretaries; when I first went there, there was no woman secretary in all of Congress. . . . You walked into an office—all were men. . . . Everywhere—all the employees, the people earning their living by being sent to [work for] Congress were [men], because the congressmen were trying to build up votes among their constituents, who were men. . . .

[N]ormally, if a woman came there [to a committee hearing] and asked something, she was just put aside as—nobody had to pay attention to her, whether she wanted it or not.

But this time, at our first hearing after we got the vote, everybody came and said, "I represent two million women," or whatever she said she represented. *Well*, that was two million *voters* and was a totally different situation than when she came before. . . . Most of the thing the women saw in it was to get something for themselves, to come down to see if *they* could be secretaries, and *they* could be clerks of committees.

SOURCE: Ruth Barnes Moynihan, Cynthia Russett, and Laurie Crumpacker, *Second to None: A Documentary History of American Women* (University of Nebraska Press, 1993), vol. 2, pp. 150–151.

strong economy, the Republican policy of an informal partnership between business and government seemed to work and made reforms regulating corporations and the economy seem unnecessary and even harmful.

The Economy and the Heyday of Big Business

Although prosperity and the 1920s seem almost synonymous, the decade got off to a bumpy start in the transition from a wartime to a peacetime economy. In the immediate postwar years the nation suffered rampant inflation: prices jumped by a third in 1919, accompanied by feverish business activity. Federal efforts to halt inflation—through spending cuts and a contraction of the supply of credit—produced the recession of 1920–1921, the sharpest short-term downturn the United States had ever faced. Unemployment reached 10 percent. Foreign trade dropped by almost half as European nations resumed production after the disruptions of war. Prices fell dramatically—more than 20 percent—and reversed much of the wartime inflation.

The recession was short. In 1922, stimulated by an abundance of consumer products, particularly automobiles, the economy began a recovery that continued with only brief interruptions through 1929. Between 1922 and 1929 the gross national product (GNP) grew from $74.1 billion to $103.1 billion, approximately 40 percent. Per capita income rose from $641 in 1921 to $847 in 1929. Soon the federal government was recording a budget surplus. This economic expansion provided the backdrop for the partnership between business and government that flourished in the 1920s.

An abundance of new consumer products, particularly the automobile, stimulated recovery and prosperity. Manufacturing output expanded 64 percent as industries churned out cars, appliances, chemicals, electricity, radios, aircraft, and movies. Behind the growth lay new techniques of management and mass production, which brought a 40 percent increase in workers' productivity. In most industries, the demand for goods and services kept unemployment low

The Assembly Line
The success of the automobile industry contributed significantly to the prosperity of the 1920s, and mass production made automobiles affordable for ordinary citizens, not just the well to do. This photograph suggests the aptness of the phrase "rolling off the assembly line." By 1929 there were more than 23 million cars on the road.

throughout the decade. Combined with low inflation, high employment rates enhanced the spending power of many Americans, especially skilled workers and the middle class.

The economy, however, had some weaknesses. Income distribution reflected significant disparity: 5 percent of the nation's families received one-third of all income. In addition, a number of industries were unhealthy. Agriculture never fully recovered from the 1920–1921 recession. During the inflationary period of 1914–1920, farmers had borrowed heavily to finance mortgages and equipment in response to government incentives, increased demand, and rising prices. When the war ended, European countries resumed agricultural production, glutting the world market. The price of wheat dropped 40 percent as the government withdrew wartime price supports. Corn fell 32 percent and hogs 50 percent. Farmers were not the only ones whose incomes plunged. Certain "sick industries," such as coal and textiles, had also expanded in response to wartime demand, only to face overcapacity at war's end. Their troubles foreshadowed the Great Depression of the 1930s.

But despite these signs that not all was well, for the most part the nation was in a confident mood about the economy and the corporations that shaped it. Throughout the decade, business leaders enjoyed enormous popularity and respect; their reputations often surpassed those of the era's lackluster politicians. The most revered businessman of the decade was Henry Ford, whose rise from poor farm boy to corporate giant embodied both the traditional value of individualism and the triumph of mass production. Success stories like Ford's prompted President Calvin Coolidge to declare solemnly, "The man who builds a factory builds a temple. The man who works there worships there."

In this apotheosis of big business, the 1920s saw the triumph of the managerial revolution that had been reshaping American business since the late nineteenth century (see Chapter 19), as large-scale corporate organizations with bureaucratic structures of authority replaced family-run enterprises. There were more mergers in the 1920s than at any time since the heyday of business combinations in the 1880s and 1890s, with the largest number occurring in rapidly growing industries like chemicals, electrical appliances and machinery, and automobiles. By 1930 the 200 largest corporations controlled almost half the nonbanking corporate wealth in the United States. Rarely did any single corporation monopolize an entire industry; instead, *oligopolies*, in which a few large producers controlled an industry, became the norm, as in auto manufacturing, oil, and steel. The nation's financial institutions expanded and consolidated along with its corporations. Total bank assets rose dramatically as mergers between Wall Street banks enhanced New York's role as the financial center of the world. In 1929 almost half the nation's banking resources were controlled by 1 percent, or 250, of American banks.

Most Americans benefited from corporate success in the 1920s. Although unskilled African-Americans and immigrants participated far less fully in the prosperity of the decade, many members of the working class enjoyed higher wages and a better standard of living. A shorter workweek (five full days and a half-day on Saturday) and paid vacations gave many more leisure time. But despite those benefits, labor had less power in the workplace. Scientific management techniques, first introduced in 1895 by Frederick W. Taylor, but widely implemented only in the 1920s, reduced workers' control over their labor.

The 1920s were also the heyday of "welfare capitalism," a system of labor relations that stressed management's responsibility for employees' well-being. At a time when unemployment compensation and government-sponsored pensions did not exist, large corporations offered workers stock plans, health insurance, and old-age pension plans. Employee security was not, however, the primary aim of the programs, which were established mainly to deter the formation of unions. The approach reflected the conservative values of the 1920s, which placed the responsibility for economic welfare in the private sector so as to avoid government interference on the side of labor. Coupled with an aggressive drive for what corporate leaders called the *American Plan*, or an open (nonunion) shop, and with Supreme Court decisions that limited workers' ability to strike, welfare capitalism helped to erode the unions' strength. Membership dropped from 5.1 million in 1920 to 3.6 million in 1929—about 10 percent of the nonagricultural work force—and the number of strikes also fell dramatically from the level in 1919. Technology and management had combined to undermine workers' power.

Economic Expansion and Foreign Policy

The power of American corporations, so evident in their relationship with the work force, emerged also in the international arena. During the 1920s the United States was the most productive country in the world, with an enormous capacity to compete in foreign markets that eagerly desired American consumer products such as radios, telephones, automobiles, and sewing machines. The demand for U.S. capital was just as great. American investment abroad more than doubled between 1919 and 1930: by the end of the 1920s American corporations had invested $15.2 billion in foreign countries. Soon the United States became the world's largest creditor nation, reversing its pre–World War I status as a debtor and causing a dramatic shift of power in the world's capital markets.

A wide variety of American companies aggressively sought investment opportunities abroad. General Electric built new plants in Latin America, China, Japan, and Australia; Ford had major facilities throughout the British Empire. The United Fruit Company developed plantations in Costa Rica, Honduras, and Guatemala. American capital ran sugar plantations in Cuba and rubber plantations in the Philippines, Sumatra, and Malaya. Standard Oil of New Jersey led American oil companies in acquiring oil reserves in Mexico and Venezuela.

American banks supported U.S. enterprises abroad. European countries, particularly Germany, needed American capital to finance their economic recovery from World War I. Germany had to rebuild its economy and pay reparations to the Allies; Britain and France had to repay wartime loans. As late as 1930 the Allies still owed the United States $4.3 billion. American political leaders, responding to voters' disenchantment with the cost of the war, rigidly demanded payment. "They hired the money, didn't they?" President Coolidge scoffed.

European countries had difficulty repaying their debts because the United States was maintaining high protective tariffs against foreign-made goods. The Fordney–McCumber Tariff of 1922 and the Hawley–Smoot Tariff of 1930 advanced the longstanding Republican policy of protectionism and economic nationalism. Most American manufacturers favored high tariffs because they feared foreign competition would reduce their profits. But the difficulty of selling goods in the United States hindered European nations' efforts to pay off their debts in dollars.

In 1924, at the prodding of the United States, France, Great Britain, and Germany joined with the United States in a plan to promote European financial stability. The Dawes Plan, named for Charles G. Dawes, the Chicago banker who negotiated the agreement, offered Germany substantial loans from American banks and a reduction in the amount of reparations owed to the Allies. But the Dawes Plan did not provide a permanent solution, because the international economic system was inherently unstable. It depended on the flow of American capital to Germany, reparations payments from Germany to the Allies, and the repayment of the Allies' debts to the United States. If the outflow of capital from the United States were to slow or stop, the international financial structure could collapse.

American efforts to stabilize the international economy belie the common view of U.S. foreign affairs as isolationist in the interwar period—as representing a time when the United States, disillusioned after World War I, willfully retreated from involvement in the rest of the world. In fact, the United States played an active role in world affairs during this period. Expansion into new markets was fundamental to the prosperity of the 1920s. U.S. officials ardently sought a stable international order to facilitate American investments in Latin American, European, and Asian markets.

They continued the quest for peaceful ways to dominate the Western Hemisphere both economically and diplomatically, but retreated slightly from military intervention in Latin America. U.S. troops withdrew from the Dominican Republic in 1924, but remained in Nicaragua almost continuously from 1912 to 1933, and in Haiti from 1915 to 1934. Relations with Mexico remained tense, a legacy of U.S. intervention during the Mexican Revolution and of U.S. resentment over the Mexican government's efforts to wrest control of its oil and mineral deposits away from foreign owners, a policy that particularly alarmed American oil companies.

There was little popular or political support, however, for entangling diplomatic commitments to allies, European or otherwise. The United States never joined the League of Nations or the Court of International Justice (the World Court). International cooperation had to come through other forums, such as the 1921 Washington Naval Arms Conference. At that meeting, the leading naval powers—Britain, the United States, Japan, Italy, and France—agreed to halt construction of large battleships for ten years and to establish a permanent tonnage ratio of 5:5:3:1.75:1.75, respectively. By placing limits on naval expansion, policymakers hoped to encourage stability in areas like the Far East, and to protect the fragile postwar economy from an expensive arms race. A thinly veiled agenda was to contain Japan, whose expansionist tendencies in the Far East were alarming other nations.

Seven years later, in a similar spirit of international cooperation, the United States joined other nations in condemning militarism, through the Kellogg-Briand Peace Pact. Fifteen nations signed the pact in Paris in 1928; forty-eight more approved it later. The signatories agreed to "condemn recourse to war for the solution of international controversies, and renounce it as an instrument of national policy." U.S. peace groups such as the Women's International League for Peace and Freedom enthusiastically supported the pact, and the U.S. Senate ratified it 85 to 1. Yet critics complained that it lacked mechanisms for enforcement, calling it nothing more than an "international kiss."

In the end, fervent hopes and pious declarations were no cure for the massive economic, political, and territorial problems created by World War I. U.S. policymakers vacillated, as they would in the 1930s, between wanting to play a larger role in world events and fearing that treaties and responsibilities would limit their ability to act unilaterally. Their diplomatic efforts ultimately proved inadequate to the mounting crises of the interwar years.

A NEW NATIONAL CULTURE

The 1920s represented an important watershed in the development of a mass national culture. A new emphasis on leisure, consumption, and amusement characterized the era, although its benefits were more accessible to the white middle class than to minorities and other disadvantaged groups. Automobiles, paved roads, the parcel post service, movies, radios, telephones, mass-circulation magazines, brand names, chain stores—all linked mill towns in the southern Piedmont, rural outposts on the Oklahoma plains, and ethnic enclaves on the coasts in an expanding web of national experience. In fact, with the exportation of automobiles, radios, and movies to consumers throughout the world, the American experience began to be globalized.

Consumption and Advertising

In homes across the country in the 1920s, Americans sat down to a breakfast of Kellogg's corn flakes and toast from a General Electric toaster. Then they got into a Ford Model T to go about their business, perhaps shopping at one of the chain stores that had sprung up across the country, such as Safeway or A & P. In the evening the family gathered to listen to radio programs like "Great Moments in History" or to read the latest issue of the *Saturday Evening Post*; on weekends they might go to see the newest Charlie Chaplin film at the local theater. Millions of Americans, in other words, now shared the same daily experiences.

Yet participation in commercial mass culture was not universal, nor did it necessarily mean total conversion to mainstream values. The historian Lizabeth Cohen concluded that "Chicago's ethnic workers were not transformed into more Americanized, middle-class people by the objects they consumed. Buying an electric vacuum cleaner did not turn Josef Dobrowolski into *True Story*'s Jim Smith." What is more, the unequal distribution of income limited many consumers' ability to buy the enticing new products. At the height of the nation's prosperity in the 1920s, about 65 percent of families had incomes of less than $2,000 a year, which barely supported a decent standard of living. Many Americans stretched their incomes by buying on the newly devised installment plan: in 1927, two-thirds of the cars in the United States had been bought "on time." Once consumers saw how easily they could finance a car, they bought radios, refrigerators, and sewing machines on credit. "A dollar down and a dollar forever," one cynic remarked.

Many of the new products were household appliances made feasible by the rapid electrification of American homes. Such technological advances had a dramatic impact on women's lives, for despite enfranchisement and participation in the work force, the primary role for most women continued to be that of housewife. Electric appliances made housewives' chores less arduous. Plugging in an electric iron was far easier than heating an iron on the stove; using a vacuum cleaner was quicker and easier than wielding a broom and a rug beater. Paradoxically, however, the new products did not dramatically increase women's leisure time. Instead, more middle-class housewives began to do their own housework and laundry, replacing human servants with electric ones. The new gadgets also raised standards of cleanliness, encouraging women to spend more time doing household chores.

Few of the new consumer products could be considered necessities. But the advertising industry, which became big business in this period, spent billions of dollars annually to entice consumers into buying automobiles, cigarettes, radios, and refrigerators. Advertisers appealed to people's social aspirations by projecting images of successful and elegant sophisticates who smoked a certain brand of cigarette or drove a recognizable make of car. Ad writers also sold products by preying on people's insecurities, coming up with a variety of socially unacceptable "diseases," from "office hips" and "ashtray breath" to the dreaded "B.O." (body odor).

Yet, consumers were not merely passive victims of manipulative advertisers. The advertising industry recognized that the buying public made choices, and struggled to offer messages that appealed to the target audience. Nonetheless, advertising helped to make consumption a cultural ideal for most of the middle class. Character, religion, and social standing, once the main criteria for judging self-worth, became less important than the gratification of personal needs through the acquisition of more and better possessions.

No possession typified the new consumer culture better than the automobile. "Why on earth do you need to study what's changing this country?" a Muncie, Indiana, resident asked the sociologists Robert and Helen Lynd. "I can tell you what's happening in just four letters: A-U-T-O!" The showpiece of modern capitalism, the automobile revolutionized the way Americans spent their money and leisure time. In the wake of the automobile, the isolation of rural life broke down. Cars touched so many aspects of American life that the word *automobility* was coined to describe their impact on production methods, the landscape, and American values.

Mass production of cars stimulated the prosperity of the 1920s. Before the introduction of the moving assembly line in 1913, Ford workers took twelve and a half hours to put together an auto; on an assembly line, they took only ninety-three minutes. By 1927 Ford was producing a car every twenty-four seconds. Auto sales climbed from 1.5 million in 1921 to 5 million in 1929, a year in which Americans spent $2.58 billion on new and used cars. By the end of the decade Americans owned about 80 percent of the world's automobiles—an average of one car for every five people.

The success of the auto industry had a ripple effect on the American economy. In 1929, 3.7 million workers owed their jobs to the automobile, either directly or indirectly. Auto production stimulated the steel, petroleum, chemical, rubber, and glass industries. Highway construction became a billion-dollar-a-year enterprise, financed by federal subsidies and state gasoline taxes. Car ownership also spurred the growth of suburbs, contributed to real-estate speculation, and spawned the first shopping center, Country Club Plaza in Kansas City, in 1924. Not even the death of 25,000 people a year in traffic accidents—70 percent of them pedestrians—could dampen America's passion for the automobile.

The auto also changed the way Americans spent their leisure time. They took to the roads, becoming a nation of tourists. The American Automobile Association, founded in 1902, reported that in 1929 about 45 million people—almost a third of the population—took vacations by automobile, patronizing the "autocamps" and tourist cabins that were the forerunners of motels. And like movies and other products of the new mass culture, cars changed the dating patterns of young Americans. Contrary to many parents' views, sex was not invented in the backseat of a Ford, but a Model T offered more privacy and comfort than did the family living room or the front porch, and contributed to increased sexual experimentation among the young.

The Mass Media and New Patterns of Leisure

Equal in importance to the automobile in transforming American culture were the increasingly significant mass media. The movie industry probably did more than anything else to disseminate common values and attitudes. In contrast to Europe, where cinema developed as an avant-garde, highbrow art form, in America movies were part of popular culture almost from the start. They began around the turn of the century in nickelodeons, where for a nickel the mostly working-class audience could see a one-reel silent film like the spectacularly successful *The Great Train Robbery* (1903). Because the films, mostly comedies and melodramas, were silent, they could be understood by immigrants who did not speak English. Both democratic and highly lucrative, the new medium quickly became popular.

By 1910 the movie-making industry had concentrated in southern California, which had cheap land, plenty of sunshine, and varied scenery—mountains, deserts, cities, and the Pacific Ocean—within easy reach. Another attraction was Los Angeles's reputation as an antiunion town. By war's end the United States was producing 90 percent of the world's cinema. Foreign distribution of Hollywood films stimulated the market for the material culture so lavishly displayed on the screen.

As directors turned to feature films and began exhibiting them in large, ornate theaters, movies quickly outgrew their working-class audiences and began to appeal to the middle class. Early movie stars—the comedians Buster Keaton, Charlie Chaplin, and Harold Lloyd; Mary Pickford (though born in Canada, "America's Sweetheart"); and dashing leading men Douglas Fairbanks, Wallace Reid, and John Gilbert—became national idols who helped to set national trends in clothing and hairstyles. Then a new cultural icon, the flapper, burst on the scene to represent emancipated womanhood. Clara Bow, the "It" Girl ("It" represented "sex appeal"), was Hollywood's favorite flapper, a red-haired "jazz

The Flapper
The flapper phenomenon was not limited to Anglos. This 1921 photograph of a young Mexican-American woman shows how American fads and fashions reached into Hispanic communities across the country.

baby" who rose to stardom almost overnight. Decked out in short skirt and rolled-down silk stockings, the flapper wore makeup (once assumed to be a sign of sexual availability in lower-class women), smoked, and danced to jazz, flaunting her liberated lifestyle. Like so many cultural icons, the flapper represented only a tiny minority of women. Yet the movies, along with advertising, mass-marketed this symbol of women's emancipation, suggesting it was the norm.

Movies became even more powerful cultural influences with the advent of the "talkies." Warner Brothers' *The Jazz Singer* (1927), starring Al Jolson, was the first feature-length film to offer sound. Two years later all the major studios had made the transition to talkies. By the end of the 1920s the nation had almost 23,000 movie theaters, including elaborate picture palaces built by the studios in major cities. Movie attendance rose from 60 million in 1927 to 90 million in 1930. In two short decades, movies had become thoroughly entrenched as the most popular—and probably the most influential—form of urban-based mass media.

That the first talkie was *The Jazz Singer* was perhaps no coincidence. Jazz was such an important part of the new mass culture that the 1920s are often referred to as the "Jazz Age." An improvisational style whose notes were (and are) rarely written down, jazz originated in the dance halls and bordellos of New Orleans around the turn of the century. A synthesis of African-American music, such as ragtime and the blues, it also drew on African and European styles.

Most of the early jazz musicians were black, and their music undoubtedly expressed dissent and opposition to mainstream white values. As black musicians left the South, they took jazz to Chicago, New York, and other cities. Some of the best-known performers were the composer-pianist Ferdinand "Jelly Roll" Morton; the trumpeter Louis Armstrong; the singer Bessie Smith, the "Empress of the Blues"; and composer-bandleader Edward "Duke" Ellington. Phonograph records increased the appeal of jazz by capturing its spontaneity; jazz, in turn, boosted the infant recording industry. Soon this uniquely American art form had caught on in Europe, especially in France.

Besides movies and records, other forms of mass media helped to establish national standards of taste and behavior. In 1922, ten magazines claimed a circulation of at least 2.5 million, including the *Saturday Evening Post*, the *Ladies' Home Journal*, *Collier's Weekly*, and *Good Housekeeping*. *Reader's Digest*, *Time*, and the *New Yorker*, still found today in homes throughout the country, all started in the 1920s. Tabloid newspapers also became part of the national scene. Thanks to syndicated newspaper columns and features, people across the United States could read the same articles. They could also read the same books, preselected by a board of expert judges for the Book-of-the-Month Club, founded in 1926.

The newest instrument of mass culture, professional radio broadcasting, began in 1920. By 1929 about 40 percent of the nation's households owned a radio. More than 800 stations, most affiliated with the Columbia Broadcasting Service (CBS) or the National Broadcasting Company (NBC) were on the air. Unlike European networks, which were government monopolies, American radio stations operated for profit. Though the federal government licensed the stations, their revenue came primarily from advertisers and corporate sponsors.

Americans loved radio. They listened avidly to the World Series and other sports events and to variety shows sponsored by brand-name advertisers. One of the most popular radio shows of all time, "Amos 'n' Andy," premiered on NBC in 1928, featuring two white actors playing stereotypical black characters. Soon fractured phrases from "Amos 'n' Andy," such as "Check and double check," became part of everyday speech. So many people "tuned in" (another new phrase of the 1920s) that the country seemed to come to a halt during popular programs—a striking example of the pervasiveness of mass media.

The automobile and new forms of entertainment like movies and radio pointed to a new emphasis on leisure. As the workweek shrank and some workers won the right to paid vacations, Americans had more time and energy to spend on recreation. Like so much else in the 1920s, leisure became increasingly tied to consumption and mass culture. Public recreation flourished as cities and suburbs built baseball diamonds, tennis courts, swimming pools, and golf courses. Americans not only played sports, but had the time and money to watch professional athletes perform in increasingly commercialized enterprises. They could see a game in a comfortable stadium, as they had become accustomed to doing, or they could listen to it on the radio or catch highlights in the newsreel at the local movie theater.

Americans reveled vicariously in the accomplishments of the superb athletes of the 1920s. Baseball continued to be the national pastime, drawing as many as 10 million fans a year. Tarnished in 1919 by the "Black Sox" scandal, in which some Chicago White Sox players took bribes to throw the World Series, baseball bounced back with the rise of stars like Babe Ruth of the New York Yankees. African-Americans, however, had different heroes. Excluded from the white teams, black athletes like Satchel Paige played in Negro leagues formed in the 1920s.

Thanks to the media's attention, the popularity of sports figures rivaled that of movie stars. In football Red Grange of the University of Illinois was a major star, while Jack Dempsey and Gene Tunney attracted a loyal following in boxing and Bobby Jones helped to popularize golfing. Bill Tilden dominated men's tennis, while Helen Wills and Suzanne Lenglen reigned in the women's game. The decade's best-known swimmer was Gertrude Ederle, who crossed the English Channel in 1926 in just over fourteen hours.

The decade's most popular hero, however, was neither an athlete nor a movie star. On May 20, 1927, aviator Charles Lindbergh, flying the small, open-cockpit plane *The Spirit of St. Louis*, made the first successful nonstop solo flight between New York and Paris, a distance of 3,610 miles, in 33½ hours. Returning home to ticker-tape parades and effusive celebrations, he became *Time* magazine's first Man of the Year in 1928. Lindbergh captivated the nation by combining his mastery of the new technology (the airplane) with the pioneer virtues of individualism, self-reliance, and hard work. He symbolized Americans' desire to enjoy the benefits of modern industrialism without renouncing their traditional values.

DISSENTING VALUES AND CULTURAL CONFLICT

As movies, radio, advertising, and mass production industries helped to transform the country into a modern, cosmopolitan nation, many Americans welcomed them as exciting evidence of progress. But others were uneasy. Flappers dancing to jazz, youthful sexual experimentation in the back of Ford Model T's, hints of a decline in religious values—these harbingers of a new era worried more tradition-minded folk. In the nation's cities, the powerful presence of immigrants and African-Americans suggested the waning of white Protestant cultural dominance. Beneath the clichéd images of the "Roaring Twenties" were deeply felt tensions that surfaced in conflicts over immigration, religion, Prohibition, and race relations.

The Rise of Nativism

Tensions between the city and the country partially explain the decade's conflicts. As farmers struggled with severe economic problems, rural communities lost residents to the cities at an alarming rate. The 1920 census revealed the growing influence of cities. For the first time in the nation's history, city people outnumbered rural people. In 1920, 52 percent of the population lived in urban areas, compared with just 28 percent in 1870. Though the 1920 census exaggerated the extent of urbanization—its guidelines classified towns with only 2,500 people as cities—there was no mistaking the trend (see Map 24.1). By 1929, ninety-three cities had populations over 100,000. The mass media generally reflected the cosmopolitan values of these urban centers, and many old-stock Americans worried that the cities, and the immigrants who clustered there, would soon dominate the culture.

Yet the polarities between city and country should not be overstated. Rural people were affected by the same forces that influenced urban residents. Much of the new technology—especially automobiles—enhanced rural life. Country people, like their urban counterparts, were tempted by the materialistic new values proclaimed on the radio, in magazines, and in movies. Moreover, urban Americans were far from monolithic; and many urban residents—immigrant Catholics, for example—were just as alarmed about declining moral standards as rural Protestants were. A simplified urban–rural dichotomy flattens out the complexity of the decade's cultural conflicts.

These conflicts often centered on the question of growing racial and ethnic pluralism. When native-born white Protestants—both rural and city dwellers—looked at their communities in 1920, they saw a nation that had changed dramatically in only forty years. During that time more than 23 million immigrants had come to America, many of them Jews or Catholics, most

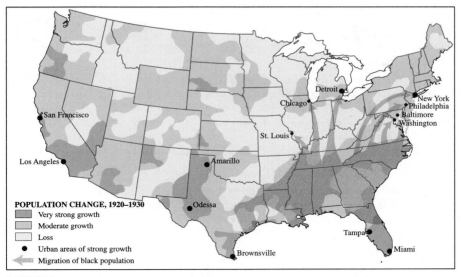

MAP 24.1
The Shift from Rural to Urban Population, 1920–1930
Despite the increasingly urban tone of modern America after 1920, regional patterns of population growth and decline were far from uniform. Cities in the South and West grew most dramatically as southern farmers moved to more promising areas with familiar climates. An important factor in the growth of northern cities, such as New York and Chicago, was the migration of southern blacks set in motion by World War I.

of peasant stock. Senator William Bruce of Maryland branded them "indigestible lumps" in the national stomach, implying that their large numbers and foreign customs could not be absorbed by mainstream society. This sentiment, termed *nativism*, was widely shared.

Nativist animosity fueled a new drive against immigration. The Chinese had been excluded in 1882, and Theodore Roosevelt had negotiated a "gentleman's agreement" to limit Japanese immigration in 1908. Yet efforts to restrict European immigration did not meet with much success until after World War I, which heightened suspicion of "hyphenated" Americans. During the Red Scare, nativists had played up the supposed association of the immigrants with radicalism and labor unrest, charging that southern and Eastern European Catholics and Jews were incapable of becoming true Americans.

In response, Congress passed an emergency bill in 1921, limiting the number of immigrants to 3 percent of each national group as represented in the 1910 census. President Woodrow Wilson refused to sign it, but the bill was reintroduced and passed under Warren Harding. In 1924 a more restrictive measure, the National Origins Act, reduced immigration until 1927 to 2 percent of each nationality's representation in the 1890 census—which included relatively small numbers of people from southeastern Europe and Russia. After 1927, the law set

AMERICAN VOICES

A Foreigner in America

A sian immigrants' experience of prejudice was much sharper than that of Euro-peans, but nonetheless Japanese immigrant Kazuo Kawai's experience echoes the problems that many young ethnic Americans in the 1920s had as they recognized that they did not belong in the old country, nor were they accepted as "One Hundred Percent Americans."

But it hurt because I couldn't say: "This is my own, my native land." What was my native land? Japan? True, I was born there. But it had seemed a queer, foreign land to me when I visited it. America? I had, until now, thought so. I had even told my father once that even in case of war between Japan and America, I would consider America as my country. In language, in thought, in ideals, in custom, in everything, I was American. But America wouldn't have me. She wouldn't recognize me in high school. She put the pictures of those of my race at the tail end of the year book. (I was a commencement speaker, so they had to put my picture near the front.) She won't let me play tennis on the courts in the city parks of Los Angeles, by city ordinance. She won't give me service when I go to a barber's shop. She won't let me own a house to live in. She won't give me a job, unless it is a menial one that no American wants. I thought I was American, but America wouldn't have me. Once I was American, but America made a foreigner out of me—Not a Japanese, but a foreigner—a foreigner to any country, for I am just as much a foreigner to Japan as to America.

SOURCE: *Stanford Survey of Race Relations* (Stanford University, 1924), Hoover Institute Archives.

a cap of 150,000 immigrants per year and continued to tie admission into the United States to a quota system that intentionally limited immigration from those regions. Japanese and Chinese immigrants were excluded entirely.

One remaining loophole in immigration law permitted unrestricted immigration from countries in the Western Hemisphere. This source became increasingly significant over the years (see Figure 24.1), as Mexicans and Central and Latin Americans crossed the border to fill jobs made available by the cutoff of immigration from Europe and Asia. Over 1 million Mexicans entered the United States between 1900 and 1930. Nativists and representatives of organized labor, who viewed Mexican immigrants as unwanted competition, lobbied Congress to close the loophole, but met with strong resistance until the 1930s and the economic devastation of the Great Depression.

Another expression of nativism in the 1920s was the revival of the Ku Klux Klan. Shortly after the premiere of *Birth of a Nation* in 1915, a group of southerners had gathered on Stone Mountain outside Atlanta to revive the racist organization. Taking as its motto "Native, white, Protestant supremacy," the modern Klan appealed to both urban and rural folk, though its largest "klaverns" were in urban areas. Spreading out from its southern base, the group found significant support in the Far West, the Southwest, and the Midwest, especially Oregon, Indiana, and Oklahoma. Unlike the Klan that was founded after the Civil War, the Klan of the 1920s did not limit its harassment to blacks; Catholics and Jews were just as likely to be its targets. Many of its tactics, however, were the same: arson, physical intimidation, and economic boycotts. The new Klan also turned to politics, succeeding in electing hundreds of Klansmen to public office. At the height of its power in 1925 the Klan had over 3 million members—including a strong contingent of women who pursued a political agenda that combined racism, nativism, and equal rights for white Protestant women.

After 1925 the Klan declined rapidly. Internal rivalries and the disclosure of rampant corruption hurt the group's image. Especially damaging was the revelation that Grand Dragon David Stephenson, the Klan's national leader,

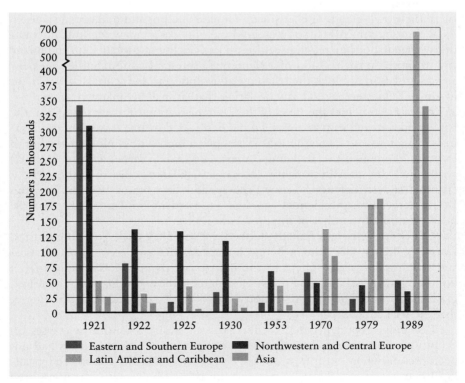

FIGURE 24.1
American Immigration after World War I
Nativism slowed the influx of immigrants after 1920, as did the dislocations brought on by depression and war in the 1930s and 1940s. Note the higher rate of non-European immigration since the 1970s.

had kidnapped and sexually assaulted his former secretary, driving her to suicide. And the passage of the National Origins Act in 1924 reduced the nativist fervor, robbing the Klan of its most potent issue.

Religious Fundamentalism and Prohibition

Other cultural tensions erupted over religion. The debate between modernist and fundamentalist Protestants, which had been simmering since the 1890s (see Chapter 20), came to a boil in the 1920s. Modernists, or liberal Protestants, tried to reconcile religion with Charles Darwin's theory of evolution and the avalanche of recent technological and scientific discoveries. Fundamentalists clung to a literal interpretation of the Bible that could not be reconciled with science. Most major Protestant denominations, especially the Baptists and the Presbyterians, experienced heated internal conflicts during the 1920s. However, the most conspicuous evangelical figures came from outside mainstream denominations. Popular preachers like Billy Sunday and Aimee Semple McPherson used revivals, storefront churches, and open-air preaching to popularize their own blends of charismatic fundamentalism and traditional values.

Religious controversy soon entered the political arena when fundamentalists, worried about increasing secularism and declining morality, turned to the law to shore up their vision of a righteous Protestant nation. Some states enacted legislation to block the teaching of evolution in the schools. In 1925, for instance, Tennessee passed a law declaring that "it shall be unlawful . . . to teach any theory that denies the story of the Divine creation of man as taught in the Bible, and to teach instead that man has descended from a lower order of animals." In a test case involving John T. Scopes, a high school biology teacher in Dayton, Tennessee, the fledgling American Civil Liberties Union (ACLU) challenged the constitutionality of that law. Clarence Darrow, the famous criminal lawyer, defended Scopes; the spellbinding orator William Jennings Bryan, three-time presidential candidate and ardent fundamentalist, was the most prominent member of the prosecution's team.

The Scopes trial was quickly dubbed the "monkey trial," referring both to Darwin's theory that human beings and primates share a common ancestor and to the circus atmosphere in the courtroom. In July 1925, more than a hundred journalists crowded the sweltering courthouse in Dayton, Tennessee, giving massive publicity to the knotty questions of faith and scientific theory that the trial addressed.

The judge rebuffed defense efforts to call expert scientific witnesses on evolution, dismissing such testimony as hearsay because the scientists had not been present when lower forms of life had evolved. Darrow countered by calling Bryan to the stand as an expert on the Bible. Under oath, Bryan asserted his belief that a "big fish" had swallowed Jonah and that God had created the world in six days. He hedged, however, about whether the "days" were literally twenty-four hours long, an inconsistency that Darrow ruthlessly exploited.

Even so, the jury took only eight minutes to delivery its verdict: guilty.

Scopes Trial
As this picture of a stall selling antievolution material in Dayton, Tennessee, suggests, the Scopes trial in 1925 became a focus of the antievolution movement. Pitting the old-time religion of rural America against modern values, the trial symbolized much of the cultural conflict of the 1920s and demonstrated the continued importance of religion to many Americans.

Though the Tennessee Supreme Court later overturned the conviction on a technicality, the reversal prevented further appeals of the case and the controversial law remained on the books more than thirty years. Historically, the trial symbolizes the conflict between the two competing value systems, cosmopolitan and traditional, that clashed in the 1920s. It suggests that despite the period's image as a frivolous and decadent time, religion continued to matter deeply to many Americans.

Like the dispute over evolution, Prohibition, the most notorious cultural debate of the 1920s, involved the power of the state to enforce social values. Americans did drink less after passage of the Eighteenth Amendment, which took effect in January of 1920 (see Chapter 23). Beer consumption declined the most, because beer was more difficult to manufacture and distribute illegally than hard liquor. But once people's willingness to flout the law became clear, this effort to legislate private morality was doomed.

More than any other issue, Prohibition gave the decade its reputation as the Roaring Twenties. In major cities, whose ethnic populations had always opposed Prohibition, noncompliance was widespread. People imitated rural moonshiners by distilling "bathtub gin." Illegal saloons called "speakeasies" sprang up everywhere—more than 30,000 of them in New York City alone. Liquor smugglers operated with ease along borders and coastlines. Organized crime, already a presence in major cities, supplied a ready-made distribution network for the bootleg liquor, using the "noble experiment," as Prohibition was called, to entrench itself more deeply in city politics. Said the decade's most notorious gangster, Al Capone, "Everybody calls me a racketeer. I call myself a businessman. When I sell liquor, it's bootlegging. When my patrons serve it on a silver tray on Lake Shore Drive, it's hospitality."

By the middle of the decade, Prohibition was clearly failing. Government appropriations for its enforcement were woefully inadequate; the few highly publicized raids hardly made a dent in the liquor trade. Forces for repeal—the "wets," as opposed to the "drys," who continued to support the Eighteenth Amendment—began the long process of gaining the necessary votes in Congress and state legislatures to amend the Constitution once more. The wets argued that Prohibition had undermined respect for the law and had seriously impinged upon individuals' liberty. The onset of the Great Depression hastened the repeal process, as politicians began to see alcohol production as a way to create jobs and prop up the faltering economy. On December 5, 1933, the Eighteenth Amendment was repealed. Ironically, drinking became more socially acceptable, though not necessarily more widespread, than it had been before the experiment began.

Intellectual Currents and Crosscurrents

The most articulate and embittered dissenters of the 1920s were writers and intellectuals disillusioned by the horrors of World War I and the crass materialism of the new consumer culture. Some artists were so repelled by what they saw as the complacent, moralistic, and anti-intellectual tone of American life that they settled in Europe—some temporarily, like the novelists Ernest Hemingway and F. Scott Fitzgerald, others permanently, like writer Gertrude Stein. Two prominent African-American artists, dancer Josephine Baker and writer Langston Hughes, sought temporary escape from racism in France. The poet T. S. Eliot, who left the United States before the war, ultimately became a British citizen. His despairing poem *The Waste Land* (1922), with its images of a fragmented civilization in ruins after the war, influenced a generation of writers. Other writers too made powerful antiwar statements, including John Dos Passos, whose first novel, *The Three Soldiers* (1921), was inspired by the war, and whose *1919* (1932), the second volume of his magnificent *USA* trilogy, railed against the obscenity of "Mr. Wilson's war." Ernest Hemingway's novels *In Our Time* (1924), *The Sun Also Rises* (1926), and *A Farewell to Arms* (1929), also powerfully described the dehumanizing consequences and the futility of war.

But the artists and writers who migrated to Europe, particularly Paris, were not simply a "lost generation" fleeing America. They were also drawn to Paris, the cultural and artistic capital of the world and a beacon of modernism. Paris, as Gertrude Stein put it, was "where the twentieth century was happening." Indeed, the *modernist* movement, which was marked by skepticism and technical experimentation in literature, art, and music, invigorated American writing both abroad and at home. Many American writers, whether they settled in Paris or remained in their home country, joined the movement, which had begun before the war as intellectuals reacted with excitement to the cultural and social changes that science, industrialization, and urbanization had brought. In the 1920s the business culture and political corruption of the Harding years caused intellectuals to cast a more critical eye on American society. One of the sharpest critics, the Baltimore journalist H. L. Mencken, directed his mordant wit against mass culture; small-town America with its guardians of public morals; and the "booboisie," his contemptuous term for the middle class. In the *American Mercury*, the journal he founded in 1922, Mencken championed writers like Sherwood Anderson, Sinclair Lewis, and Theodore Dreiser, who satirized the provincialism of American society.

The literature of the 1920s was rich and varied. Poetry enjoyed a renaissance in the works of Robert Frost, Wallace Stevens, Marianne Moore, and William Carlos Williams. Edith Wharton won a Pulitzer Prize—she was the first woman so honored—for *The Age of Innocence* (1920). Influenced by Freudian psychology, William Faulkner achieved his first critical success with *The Sound and the Fury* (1929), set in the fictional Mississippi county of Yoknapatawpha, where inhabitants clung to the values of the old agrarian South as they struggled to adjust to modern industrial capitalism. Playwright Eugene O'Neill also showed the influence of Freudian psychology in his experimental plays, including *The Hairy Ape* (1922) and *Desire under the Elms* (1924). Although both Faulkner and O'Neill went on to produce additional major works in the 1930s, the creative energy of the literary renaissance of the 1920s did not survive into the 1930s. The Great Depression, social and ideological unrest, and the rise of totalitarianism would reshape the intellectual landscape.

A different kind of cultural affirmation took place in the black community of Harlem in the 1920s. In the words of the Reverend Adam Clayton Powell, Sr., pastor of the influential Abyssinian Baptist Church, Harlem loomed as "the symbol of liberty and the Promised Land to Negroes everywhere." One aspect of this hope was the Harlem Renaissance, a movement of young writers and artists who broke with older genteel traditions of black literature to reclaim a cultural identity with African roots. Alain Locke, editor of the anthology *The New Negro* (1926), summed up the movement when he stated that, through art, "Negro life is seizing its first chances for group expression and self-determination." Authors like Claude McKay, Jean Toomer, Jessie Fauset, and Zora Neale Hurston explored the black experience and represented the "New Negro" in fiction. Countee Cullen and Langston Hughes turned to poetry, and Augusta Savage to sculpture. Their outpouring of artistic expression gave voice to the African-American struggle to find a way, as W. E. B. Du Bois put it, "to be both a Negro and an American."

The vitality of the Harlem Renaissance was short-lived. Although the NAACP's magazine *The Crisis* provided a forum for the Harlem writers, the black middle class and Harlem's intellectual elite were relatively small and could not support the group's efforts. Its major audience consisted of white intellectuals and philanthropists. The movement thus depended on white patronage for support and access to publication. During the Jazz Age, when Harlem was in vogue, publishing houses courted Harlem writers, but when the stock market crashed in 1929 their interest vanished, and the movement waned as the Depression deepened. But the legacy of the Harlem Renaissance would influence a new generation of black writers when black intellectuals rediscovered the works during the civil rights movement of the 1960s.

Although the Harlem Renaissance had little impact on the masses of African-Americans, other movements built racial pride and challenged white political and cultural hegemony. The most successful was the Universal Negro Improvement Association (UNIA), which championed black separatism under the leadership of the Jamaican-born Marcus Garvey. Based in Harlem, the UNIA was the black working class's first mass movement. At its height it

The Harlem Renaissance
The Crisis, edited by W. E. B. Du Bois, was the magazine of the National Association for the Advancement of Colored People (NAACP). This 1929 cover suggests the cultural and political awakenings associated with the Harlem Renaissance.

claimed 4 million followers, many of whom were recent migrants to northern cities. Like several nineteenth-century reformers, Marcus Garvey urged blacks to return to Africa; blacks, he reasoned, would never be treated justly in countries ruled by whites. Although he did not anticipate a massive migration, he did envision a strong black Africa which could use its power to protect blacks everywhere. Garvey's wife, Amy Jacques Garvey, appealed to black women by combining black nationalism with an emphasis on women's contributions to culture and politics.

The UNIA grew rapidly in the early 1920s. It published a newspaper called *Negro World* and undertook extensive business ventures to support black enterprise. The most ambitious project, the Black Star Line steamship company, was supposed to ferry cargo between the West Indies and the United States and take African-Americans back to Africa. Irregularities in fund raising for the project, however, led to Garvey's conviction for mail fraud in 1925, and he was sentenced to five years in prison. President Coolidge paroled him in 1927, but Garvey was deported to Jamaica. Without his charismatic leadership, the movement collapsed.

The 1928 Election

The works of the Lost Generation and the Harlem Renaissance touched only a small minority of Americans in the 1920s, but emotionally charged issues like Prohibition, fundamentalism, and nativism eventually spilled over into national politics. The Democratic party, which drew on rural Protestants in the South and the West as well as ethnic minorities in northern cities, was especially vulnerable to the cultural conflicts of the time. The 1924 Democratic national convention revealed an intensely polarized party, split between the urban machines and its rural wing.

In 1928, the urban wing held sway and succeeded in nominating New York's Governor Alfred E. Smith, a descendant of Irish immigrants and a product of Tammany Hall. Proud of his background, Smith adopted "The Sidewalks of New York" as his campaign song. His candidacy troubled many voters, however. His heavy New York accent, his brown derby, and his colorful style highlighted his urban working-class origins, and his early career in Tammany Hall suggested—incorrectly—that he was little more than a cog in the machine. Smith's stand on Prohibition—although he promised to enforce it, he wanted it repealed—alienated even more voters.

An additional handicap, however, was his religion. In 1928, most Protestants were not ready for a Catholic president. Although Smith insisted that his religion would not interfere with his duties as president, his perceived allegiance to Rome cost him the support of Democrats and Republicans alike. Protestant clergymen, who already opposed Smith because he supported the repeal of Prohibition, led the drive against him. "No Governor can kiss the papal ring and get within gunshot of the White House," declared one Methodist bishop.

Just as Smith was a new kind of presidential candidate for the Democrats, so was Herbert Hoover for the Republicans. As a professional administrator and engineer who had never before been elected to political office, Hoover embodied the new managerial and technological elite that was restructuring the nation's economic order. During his campaign, in which he gave only seven speeches, Hoover asserted that his vision of individualism and cooperative endeavor would banish poverty from the United States. That rhetoric, as well as his reputation for organizing a drive for humanitarian relief during the war, caused many voters to see him as more progressive than Smith.

Hoover won a stunning victory, receiving 58 percent of the popular vote to Smith's 41 percent, and 444 electoral votes to Smith's 87. The election reflected important underlying political changes. Despite the overwhelming loss, the Democrats' turnout increased substantially in urban areas. Smith won the industrialized states of Massachusetts and Rhode Island and carried the nation's twelve largest cities. The Democrats were on their way to fashioning a new identity as the party of the urban masses, a reorientation the New Deal completed in the 1930s.

It is unlikely that any Democratic candidate, let alone a Catholic, could have won the presidency in 1928. With a seemingly prosperous economy, national consensus on foreign policy, and strong support from the business community, the Republicans were unbeatable. Ironically, Herbert Hoover's victory would put him in the unenviable position of leading the United States when the Great Depression struck in 1929. Having claimed credit for the prosperity of the 1920s, the Republicans would not escape blame for the depression; twenty-four years would pass before a Republican won the presidency again.

But as Hoover began his presidency in early 1929, most Americans expected progress and prosperity to continue. The New Era the Republicans had touted meant more than Republican ascendancy in politics, more than business-government cooperation and a decline in the progressive reform movement. To most Americans, the New Era embodied the industrial productivity and technological advances that made consumer goods widely available, and the movies and the radio an exciting part of American life. At home and abroad the nation seemed unprecedentedly vigorous and powerful. Despite disruptive cultural conflicts and a changing workplace that was undermining workers' power, despite inequities in the racial order and in the distribution of income, the general tone was one of optimism, of faith in the modern society the country had become. That faith made the harsh realities of the Great Depression that would follow all the more shocking.

CHAPTER 24 TIMELINE

1920–1921	Recession
1920	First commercial radio broadcast Warren G. Harding elected president Census reveals shift from farms to cities Edith Wharton, *The Age of Innocence*
1921	Sheppard-Towner Act Immigration Act passed Washington Conference on Naval Disarmament
1922	Fordney-McCumber Tariff T. S. Eliot, *The Waste Land*
1923	Calvin Coolidge succeeds Harding as president
1924	Dawes Plan reduces German reparations payments Withdrawal of American troops from Nicaragua Teapot Dome scandal U.S. troops withdrawn from Dominican Republic National Origins Act passed
1925	F. Scott Fitzgerald, *The Great Gatsby* Height of Ku Klux Klan Scopes ("monkey") trial
1926	Alain Locke, *The New Negro* anthology Book-of-the-Month Club founded
1927	*The Jazz Singer:* the first "talkie" Charles Lindbergh's solo flight
1928	Herbert Hoover elected president Kellogg-Briand Pact "Amos 'n' Andy" premieres
1929	*Middletown* Ernest Hemingway, *A Farewell to Arms* William Faulkner, *The Sound and the Fury*

THE GREAT DEPRESSION

- The Coming of the Great Depression
- Hard Times
- The Social Fabric of Depression America
- Herbert Hoover and the Great Depression

Our images of the 1920s and the decade that followed are polar opposites. Flappers and movie stars, admen and stockbrokers, caught up in what F. Scott Fitzgerald called the "world's most expensive orgy"—these are our conception of the Jazz Age. The 1930s we remember in terms of bread lines and hobos, dust bowl devastation and hapless migrants piled into dilapidated jalopies. Almost all our impressions of that decade are black and white, in part because widely distributed photographs taken by Farm Security Administration photographers etched this dark visual image of depression America on the popular consciousness.

But the contrast between the flush times of the 1920s and the hard times of the 1930s is too stark. The vaunted prosperity of the 1920s was never as widespread or as deeply rooted as many believed. Though America's mass-consumption economy was the envy of the world, many people lived on its margins. Nor was every American devastated by the depression. Those with a secure job or a fixed income survived the economic downturn in relatively good shape, and some even managed to get rich. Yet few could escape the depression's wide-ranging social, political, and cultural effects. Though not every event of the 1930s should be viewed through the lens of the depression, the great economic contraction unifies the history of the decade more than any other theme.

THE COMING OF THE GREAT DEPRESSION

Booms and busts are a permanent feature of the business cycle in capitalist economies. Since the beginning of the Industrial Revolution early in the nineteenth century, the United States had experienced recessions or panics at least once every twenty years. But none was as severe as the Great Depression of the 1930s. The downturn began slowly and almost imperceptibly. After 1927, consumer spending declined and housing construction slowed. Soon inventories piled up; in 1928 manufacturers began to cut back production and lay off workers, reducing incomes and buying power and reinforcing the slowdown. By the summer of 1929 the economy was clearly in recession.

Causes of the Depression

A crisis in the stock market signaled more serious problems. By 1929 the market had become the symbol of the nation's prosperity, an icon of American business culture. The financier John J. Raskob captured this attitude in a *Ladies' Home Journal* article, "Everyone Ought to Be Rich." Invest $15 a month in sound common stocks, Raskob advised, and in twenty years the investment would grow to $80,000. Not everyone was playing the stock market, however. Only about 4 million Americans, or roughly 10 percent of the nation's households, owned stock in 1929.

Stock prices had been rising steadily since 1921, but in 1928 and 1929 they surged forward, rising on average over 40 percent. At the time, stock market activity was essentially unregulated. Margin buying in particular proceeded at a feverish pace as customers borrowed up to 75 percent of the purchase price of stocks. But then, on "Black Thursday"—October 24, 1929, and again on "Black Tuesday"—October 29—the bubble burst. On those two bleak days, more than 28 million shares changed hands in frantic trading. Overextended investors, suddenly finding themselves heavily in debt, began to sell their stocks. Waves of panic selling ensued, during which many stocks found no buyers. Practically overnight, stock values fell from a peak of $87 billion (at least on paper) to $55 billion.

The impact of what became known as the Great Crash was felt far beyond the trading floors of Wall Street. Commercial banks had invested heavily in corporate stock. What is more, speculators who had borrowed from banks to buy their stocks could not repay their loans because they could not sell their shares. Throughout the nation, bank failures multiplied. Since bank deposits were uninsured, when a bank collapsed, depositors lost all their money. The sudden loss of their life savings was a tremendous shock to the middle class, many of whom had no other resources to cope with the crisis. Besides its immediate economic impact, the crash destroyed the optimistic view of the stock market as the crowning symbol of American prosperity, precipitating a crisis of confidence that prolonged the depression.

Although the stock market crash contributed to the Great Depression, longstanding weaknesses in the economy accounted for its length and severity. Agriculture, in particular, had never recovered from the recession of

1920–1921. Farmers faced high fixed costs for equipment and mortgages, which they had incurred during the inflationary war years. When prices fell because of overproduction, many farmers defaulted on their mortgage payments, risking foreclosure. Because farmers accounted for about a fourth of the nation's gainfully employed workers in 1929, their difficulties weakened the general economic structure.

Certain basic industries also had economic setbacks during the prosperous 1920s. Textiles, facing a steady decline after the war, abandoned New England for cheaper labor in the South, but suffered still from decreased demand and overproduction. Mining and lumbering, which had expanded in response to wartime demand, confronted the same problems. And the railroad industry, damaged by stiff competition from trucks, faced shrinking passenger revenues and stagnant freight levels, worsened by inefficient management. While these older sectors of the economy faltered, newer and more successful consumer-based industries, such as chemicals, appliances, and food processing, proved not yet strong enough to lead the way to recovery.

The unequal distribution of the nation's wealth was another underlying weakness of the economy. During the 1920s the share of national income going to families in the upper- and middle-income brackets increased. The tax policies of Secretary of the Treasury Andrew Mellon contributed to a concentration of wealth by lowering personal income tax rates, eliminating the wartime excess-profits tax, and increasing deductions that favored corporations and the very affluent. In 1929, the lowest 40 percent of the population received only 12.5 percent of aggregate family income, while the top 5 percent of the population received 30 percent. Once the depression began, this skewed income distribution prevented people from spending the amount of money that was necessary to revive the economy.

The Great Depression became self-perpetuating. The more the economy contracted, the longer people expected the depression to last. The longer they expected it to last, the more afraid they became to spend or invest their money, if they had any—and spending and investing were exactly what was needed to stimulate a recovery. The economy showed some improvement in the summer of 1931, when low prices encouraged consumption, but plunged again late that fall.

The nation's banks, already weakened by the stock market crash, contributed to the worsening contraction. When agricultural prices and income fell more steeply than usual in 1930, many farmers went bankrupt, causing rural banks to fail. By December 1930, so many rural banks had defaulted on their obligations that urban banks too began to collapse. The wave of bank failures frightened depositors, who withdrew their savings, deepening the crisis.

In 1931, a change in the nation's monetary policy compounded the banks' problems. In the first phase of the depression, the Federal Reserve System had reacted cautiously. But in October 1931 the Federal Reserve Bank of New York significantly increased the *discount rate*—the interest rate charged on loans to member banks—and reduced the amount of money placed in circulation through the purchase of government securities. This miscalculation squeezed the money supply, forcing prices down and depriving businesses of funds for investment.

In the face of that money shortage, the American people could have pulled the country out of the depression only by spending faster. But because of falling prices, rising unemployment, and a troubled banking system, Americans preferred to keep their dollars, stashing them under the mattress rather than depositing them in the bank, further limiting the amount of money in circulation. Economic stagnation solidified.

The World-Wide Depression

President Hoover later blamed the severity of the depression on the international economic situation. Although domestic factors far outweighed international causes of America's protracted decline, Hoover was correct in surmising that economic problems in the rest of the world affected the United States, and vice versa. Indeed, the international economic system had been out of kilter since World War I. It functioned only as long as American banks exported enough capital to allow European countries to repay their debts and to buy U.S. manufactured goods and foodstuffs. By the late 1920s European economies were staggering under the weight of huge debts and trade imbalances with the United States, which effectively undercut their recovery from the war. By 1931 most European economies had collapsed.

In an interdependent world, the economic downturn in America had enormous repercussions. When U.S. companies cut back production, they also cut their purchases of raw materials and supplies abroad, devastating many foreign economies. When American financiers sharply reduced their foreign investment and consumers bought fewer European goods, debt repayment became even more difficult, straining the gold standard, the foundation of multilateralism in the interwar period. As European economic conditions worsened, demand for American exports fell drastically. Finally, when the Hawley-Smoot Tariff of 1930 went into effect, raising rates to all-time highs, foreign governments retaliated by imposing their own trade restrictions, further limiting the market for American goods and intensifying the world-wide depression.

No other nation was as hard hit as the United States. From the height of its prosperity before the stock market crash in 1929 to the depths of the depression in 1932 and 1933, the U.S. gross national product (GNP) was cut almost in half, declining from $103.1 billion to $58 billion in 1932. Consumption expenditures dropped by 18 percent, construction by 78 percent; private investment plummeted 88 percent, and farm income, already low, was more than halved. In this period, 9,000 banks went bankrupt or closed their doors and 100,000 businesses failed. The consumer price index (CPI) declined by 25 percent, and corporate profits fell from $10 billion to $1 billion.

Most tellingly, unemployment rose from 3.2 percent to 24.9 percent, affecting approximately 12 million workers. Statistical measures at the time were fairly crude, so the figures were probably understated. At least one in four workers was out of a job, and even those who had jobs faced wage cuts, work for which they were overqualified, or layoffs. Their stories put a human face on the almost incomprehensible dimensions of the economic downturn.

HARD TIMES

"We didn't go hungry, but we lived lean." That statement sums up the experiences of many families during the Great Depression. The vast majority of Americans were neither very rich nor very poor. For most the depression did not mean losing thousands of dollars in the stock market, or pulling children out of boarding school; nor did it mean going on relief or living in a shantytown. In a typical family in the 1930s, the husband still had a job and the wife was still a homemaker. Though life was not easy, families usually managed to "make do."

The Invisible Scar

"You could feel the depression deepen," recalled the writer Caroline Bird, "but you could not look out the window and see it." Many people never saw a bread line or a man selling apples on the corner. The depression caused a private kind of despair that often simmered behind closed doors. "I've lived in cities for many months broke, without help, too timid to get in bread lines," the writer Meridel LeSueur remembered. "A woman will shut herself up in a room until it is taken away from her, and eat a cracker a day and be as quiet as a mouse."

The depression did not create poverty, but it did extend poverty's harsh realities to more people. Hard times weighed heavily on the nation's senior citizens, many of whom faced total destitution. Formerly solid working-class and middle-class families, who strongly believed in the Horatio Alger ethic of upward mobility through hard work, suddenly found themselves floundering in a society that no longer had a place for them. Thus, the depression challenged basic American tenets of individualism and success. Yet even in the midst of pervasive unemployment, many people blamed themselves for their misfortune. This sense of damaged pride pervaded letters written to President Franklin D. Roosevelt and his wife Eleanor, summed up succinctly in one woman's plea for assistance: "Please don't think me unworthy."

Downward mobility was especially hard for middle-class Americans. An unemployed man in Pittsburgh told the journalist Lorena Hickok, "Lady, you just can't know what it's like to have to move your family out of the nice house you had in the suburbs, part paid for, down into an apartment, down into another apartment, smaller and in a worse neighborhood, down, down, down, until finally you end up in the slums."

After exhausting their savings and credit, many families faced the humiliation of going on relief. Seeking aid from state or local government hurt their pride and disrupted the traditional custom of turning to relatives, neighbors, church, and mutual-aid society in time of need. Even if families endured the demeaning process of certification for state or local relief, the amount they

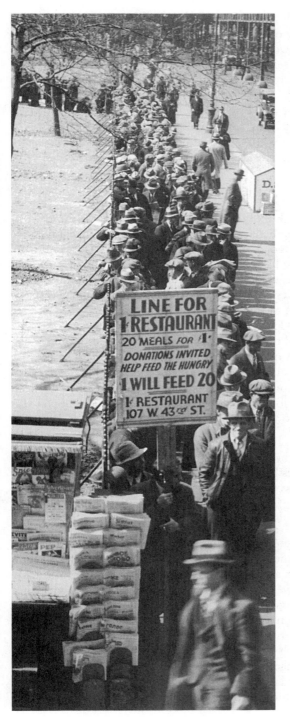

The Bread Line
Some of the most vivid images from the depression were bread lines and men selling apples on street corners. Note that all the people in this bread line are men. Women rarely appeared in bread lines, often preferring to endure private deprivation rather than violate standards of respectable behavior.

received was a pittance. In New York State, where benefits were among the highest in the nation, a family on relief received only $2.39 a week.

Such hardships left a deep wound, which Caroline Bird described as the "invisible scar." One elderly civil servant bought a plot of land outside Washington so that if the depression recurred, she would have the means to live. Virginia Durr, an Alabama civil rights activist, described another common response: "The great majority reacted by thinking money is the most important thing in the world. Get yours. And get it for your children. Nothing else matters. Not having that stark terror come at you again." For many Americans "that stark terror" of losing control over their lives was the crux of the Great Depression.

Families Face the Great Depression

Sociologists who studied family life during the 1930s found that the depression usually intensified existing behavior. If a family had been stable and cohesive before the depression, then members pulled together to overcome the new obstacles. But, if a family had shown signs of disintegration, the depression made the situation worse. On the whole, though, far more families hung together than broke apart. Men and women experienced the Great Depression differently, partly because of the gender roles that governed male and female behavior in the 1930s. From childhood men had been trained to be breadwinners; they considered themselves failures if they could no longer support their families. But while millions of men lost their jobs, few of the nation's 28 million homemakers lost their positions in the home. In contrast to men, women's sense of self-importance increased as they struggled to keep their families afloat. The sociologists Robert and Helen Lynd noticed this phenomenon in their follow-up study of Middletown (Muncie, Indiana), published in 1937:

> The men, cut adrift from their usual routine, lost much of their sense of time and dawdled helplessly and dully about the streets; while in the homes the women's world remained largely intact and the round of cooking, housecleaning, and mending became if anything more absorbing.

Even if a wife took a job when her husband lost his, she retained almost total responsibility for housework and child care. To economize, women sewed their own clothes, and canned fruits and vegetables. They bought day-old bread and heated several dishes in the oven at once to save fuel. Women who had once employed servants did their own housework. Eleanor Roosevelt described the stressful effects of the depression on these women's lives: "It means endless little economies and constant anxiety for fear of some catastrophe such as accident or illness which may completely swamp the family budget." Housewives' ability to watch every penny often made the difference in a family's survival.

Despite hard times, Americans maintained a fairly high level of consumption. As in the 1920s, households in the middle-income range—in 1935, the

A Working-Class Family Encounters the Great Depression

Although many families endured the privations of the Great Depression with equanimity, others, like Larry Van Dusen's family, experienced tremendous strains. In this passage from his oral history account to journalist Studs Terkel, he describes the pressures on male wage earners and their children.

My father led a rough life: he drank. During the Depression, he drank more. There was more conflict in the home. A lot of fathers—mine among them—had a habit of taking off. They'd go to Chicago to look for work. To Topeka. This left the family at home, waiting and hoping that the old man would find something. And there was always the Saturday night ordeal as to whether or not the old man would get home with his paycheck. Everything was sharpened and hurt more by the Depression.

Heaven would break out once in a while, and the old man would get a week's work. I remember he'd come home at night, and he'd come down the path through the trees. He always rode a bicycle. He'd stop and sometimes say hello, or give me a hug. And that smell of fresh sawdust on those carpenter overalls, and the fact that Dad was home, and there was a week's wages. . . . That's the good you remember.

And then there was always the bad part. That's when you'd see your father coming home with the toolbox on his shoulder. Or carrying it. That meant the job was over. The tools were home now, and we were back on the treadmill again.

I remember coming back home, many years afterwards. Things were better. It was after the Depression, after the war. To me, it was hardly the same house. My father turned into an angel. They weren't wealthy, but they were making it. They didn't have the acid and the recriminations and the bitterness that I had felt as a child.

SOURCE: Studs Terkel, *Hard Times* (New York: Pantheon Books, 1986), pp. 107–108.

50.2 percent of American families with an income of $500 to $1,500—did much of the buying. Several trends allowed those families to maintain their former standard of living despite pay cuts and unemployment. Between 1929 and 1935, deflation lowered the cost of living almost 20 percent. And buying on the installment plan increased in the 1930s, permitting many families to stretch their reduced incomes.

Americans spent their money differently in the depression. Telephone use and clothing sales dropped sharply, but cigarettes, movies, radio, and newspapers, once considered luxuries, became necessities. The automobile proved one of the most depression-proof items in the family budget. Though sales of new cars dropped, gasoline sales held stable, suggesting that families bought used cars or kept their old models running longer.

Another measure of the impact of the depression on family life was the change in demographic trends in the 1930s. The marriage rate fell from 10.14 per thousand persons in 1929 to 7.87 per thousand in 1932. The divorce rate decreased as well, because couples could not afford the legal expense of dissolving failed unions. And between 1930 and 1933, the birth rate, which had fallen steadily since 1800, dropped from 21.3 live births per thousand to 18.4, a dramatic 14 percent decrease. The new level, if maintained, would have produced a decline in population. Though the birth rate rose slightly after 1934, by the end of the decade it was still only 18.8. (In contrast, at the height of the baby boom following World War II, the birth rate was 25 per thousand.)

The drop in the birth rate during the Great Depression could not have happened without increased access to effective contraception. In 1936, in *United States v. One Package of Japanese Pessaries,* a federal court struck down all federal restrictions on the dissemination of contraceptive information. The decision gave doctors wide discretion in prescribing birth control for married couples, making it legal everywhere except the heavily Catholic states of Massachusetts and Connecticut. While abortion remained illegal, the number of women who underwent the procedure increased. Because many abortionists operated under unsafe or unsanitary conditions, between 8,000 and 10,000 women died each year from the illegal operations.

Margaret Sanger played a major role in encouraging the availability and popular acceptance of birth control. Sanger began her career as a public health nurse in the 1910s in the slums of New York City. At first she joined forces with socialists trying to help working-class families to control their fertility. In the 1920s and 1930s, however, she appealed to the middle class for support, identifying those families as the key to the movement's success. Sanger also courted the medical profession, pioneering the establishment of professionally staffed birth control clinics and winning the American Medical Association's endorsement of contraception in 1937. As a result of Sanger's efforts, birth control became less a feminist issue and more a medical question. And in the context of the depression, it became an economic issue as well, as financially pressed couples sought to delay or limit their childbearing while they weathered hard times.

One way for families to make ends meet was to send an additional member of the household to work. At the turn of the century, that additional member was often a child or a young, unmarried adult; in the 1930s, it was increasingly a married woman. Instead of expelling women from the work force, the depression solidified their position in it. The 1940 census reported almost 11 million women in the work force—approximately a fourth of the nation's workers—and a small increase over 1930. The number of married women employed outside the home rose 50 percent.

Working women, especially married women, encountered sharp resentment and outright discrimination in the workplace. After calculating that the number of employed women roughly equaled total unemployment in 1939, the editor Norman Cousins suggested this tongue-in-cheek remedy: "Simply fire the women, who shouldn't be working anyway, and hire the men. Presto! No unemployment. No relief rolls. No depression." Many people agreed with the idea. In a 1936 Gallup poll, asked whether wives should work when their husbands had jobs, 82 percent of those interviewed said no. Such public disapproval encouraged restrictions on women's right to work. From 1932 to 1937 the federal government would not allow a husband and wife to hold government jobs at the same time. Many states adopted laws that prohibited married women from working.

Married or not, most women worked because they had to. A sizable minority were the sole support of their families, because their husbands had left home or lost their jobs. Single, divorced, deserted, or widowed women had no husbands to support them. Moreover, women rarely took jobs away from men. "Few of the people who oppose married women's employment," observed one feminist in 1940, "seem to realize that a coal miner or steel worker cannot very well fill the jobs of nursemaids, cleaning women, or the factory and clerical jobs now filled by women." Custom, rather than law or economics, made crossovers from one field to another rare.

The division of the work force by gender gave women a small edge during the depression. Many fields with large numbers of female employees, including clerical, sales, and service and trade occupations, suffered less from economic contraction than heavy industry, which employed men almost exclusively. As a result, unemployment rates for women, although extremely high, were somewhat lower than those for men. This small bonus came at a high price, however. The jobs women held reinforced the traditional stereotypes of female work. When the depression ended, women were even more concentrated in low-paid, dead-end jobs than when it began.

White women also benefited at the expense of minority women. To make ends meet, white women willingly took jobs usually held by blacks or other minority workers—domestic service jobs, for example—and employers were quick to act on their preference for white workers. White men also took jobs once held by minority males.

During the Great Depression there were few feminist demands for equal rights, at home or on the job. On an individual basis, women's self-esteem probably rose because of the importance of their work to family survival. Most men and women, however, continued to believe that the two sexes should have fundamentally different roles and responsibilities, and that a woman's life cycle should be shaped by marriage and her husband's career.

The depression hit other family members—the nation's 21 million young people—especially hard. Though small children often escaped the sense of bitterness and failure that gripped their elders—some youngsters thought it fun to stand in a soup line—hard times made children grow up fast. About 250,000 young people became so demoralized that they took to the road as hobos and "sisters of the road," as female tramps were called. Others chose to stay in school longer: public schools were free, and they were warm in the winter. In 1930 less than half the nation's youth attended high school, compared with three-fourths in 1940, at the end of the depression. College, however, remained the privilege of a distinct minority. About 1.2 million young people, or 7.5 percent of the population between eighteen and twenty-four, attended college in the 1930s. Forty percent of them were women. After 1935 college became slightly more affordable when the National Youth Administration (NYA) gave part-time employment to more than 2 million college and high school students. The government agency also provided work for 2.6 million out-of-school youths.

College students worked hard in the 1930s; financial sacrifice encouraged seriousness of purpose. Interest in fraternities and sororities declined as many students became involved in political movements. Fueled by disillusionment with World War I, thousands of youth took the "Oxford Pledge" never to support United States involvement in a war. In 1936 the Student Strike against War drew support from several hundred thousand students across the country.

Although youths enjoyed more education in the 1930s, the depression damaged their future prospects. Studies of social mobility confirm that young men who entered their twenties during the depression era had less successful careers than those who came before or after. After extensive interviews with these youths all over the nation, the writer Maxine Davis described them as "runners, delayed at the gun," adding, "The depression years have left us with a generation robbed of time and opportunity just as the Great War left the world its heritage of a lost generation."

Popular Culture

Americans turned to popular culture to alleviate some of the trauma of the Great Depression. As the novelist Josephine Herbst observed, it provided "an almost universal liveliness that countervailed universal suffering." Mass culture flourished in the 1930s, offering not just entertainment, but commentary on the problems that beset the nation. Movies and radio served as a forum for criticizing the system—especially politicians and bankers—as well as vehicles for reaffirming traditional ideals.

Despite the closing of one-third of the country's theaters by 1933, the movie industry and its studio system flourished. Sixty percent of Americans—some 60 to 75 million people each week—flocked to the cinema, seeking solace from the pain of the depression. In the early thirties, moviegoers might enjoy or be scandalized by Mae West, who was noted for her sexual innuendos: "I used to be Snow White, but I drifted." But in response to public outcry against immorality in the movies, especially from the Protestant and Catholic churches, the industry established a means of self-censorship, the Production Code Administration. After 1934, somewhat racy films—tame by today's standards—were supplanted by sophisticated, fast-paced, screwball comedies like *It Happened One Night*, which swept the Oscars in 1934. The musical comedies of Fred Astaire and Ginger Rogers, including *Top Hat* (1935) and *The Gay*

Divorcee (1934), in which the two dancers seemed to glide effortlessly through opulent sets, were pure entertainment.

But Hollywood, which produced 5,000 films during the decade, offered much more than mere escape, with many of its movies containing complex messages that reflected a real sense of the societal crisis that engulfed the nation. The cultural historian Lawrence W. Levine has argued that depression-era films were "deeply grounded in the realities and intricacies of the Depression" and thus offer "a rich array of insights" into the period. Even if they did not deal specifically with the economic or political crisis, many films reaffirmed traditional values like democracy, individualism, and egalitarianism. They also contained criticisms—suggestions that the system was not working, or that law and order had broken down. Thus, popular gangster movies, such as *Public Enemy* (1931), with James Cagney, or *Little Caesar* (1930), starring Edward G. Robinson, can be seen as perverse Horatio Alger tales, in which the main character struggles to succeed in a harsh environment. Often these movies suggested that incompetent or corrupt politicians, police, and businessmen were as much to blame for organized crime as the gangsters themselves.

Depression-era films repeatedly portrayed politicians as cynical and corrupt. In *Washington Merry-Go-Round* (1932), lobbyists manipulated weak congressmen to undermine democratic rule. The Marx Brothers' irreverent comedies more humorously criticized authority and most everything else. In *Duck Soup* (1933), Groucho Marx played Rufus T. Firefly, president of the mythical Freedonia, who sings gleefully:

The last man nearly ruined this place,
He didn't know what to do with it.
If you think this country's bad off now,
Just wait till I get through with it.

Few filmmakers left more of a mark on the decade than Frank Capra. An Italian immigrant who personified the possibilities for success the United States offered, Capra made films that spoke to Americans' idealism. In movies like *Mr. Deeds Goes to Town* (1936) and *Mr. Smith Goes to Washington* (1939), he pitted the virtuous small town hero against corrupt urban shysters—businessmen, politicians, lobbyists, and newspaper publishers—whose machinations subverted the nation's ideals. Though the hero usually prevailed, Capra was realistic enough to suggest that the victory was not necessarily permanent, that the problems the nation faced were serious ones.

Radio occupied an increasingly important place in popular culture during the 1930s. At the beginning of the decade about 13 million households had radios; by the end, 27.5 million owned them. Listeners tuned in to daytime serials like "Ma Perkins"; picked up useful household hints on the "The Betty Crocker Hour"; or enjoyed the Big Band "swing" of Benny Goodman, Duke Ellington, and Tommy Dorsey. Weekly variety shows featured Jack Benny; George Burns and Gracie Allen; and the ventriloquist Edgar Bergen and his impudent dummy, Charlie McCarthy. And millions of listeners followed the

Mr. Smith Goes to Washington
In director Frank Capra's classic 1939 film, *Mr. Smith Goes to Washington*,
actor Jimmy Stewart plays an idealistic young senator who exposes the un-
scrupulous political machine that dominates his home state. In response,
the machine frames Senator Smith for corruption. Although he is eventually vindicated, in this scene the despairing Smith encounters the avalanche
of hostile mail generated against him by his crooked opponents.

adventures of the Lone Ranger ("Heigh-ho, Silver"), Superman, the Shadow,
and Dick Tracy.

Like movies, radio offered Americans more than escape. A running gag in
comedian Jack Benny's show was his stinginess; audiences could identify with
an unwillingness—or inability—to spend money. Even more relevant was
Benny's distrust of banks. He kept his money in an underground vault
guarded by a pet polar bear named Carmichael—presumably a more reliable
place than the nation's financial institutions.

"Amos 'n' Andy," a program whose main characters, two black men, were played by whites speaking an exaggerated black dialect, is remembered primarily for its racial stereotyping. But the exceptionally popular show also dealt with hard times, often referring explicitly to the depression. A central theme was the contrast between Amos's hard work and Andy's more carefree approach to life. Amos, tending to believe that the nation's economic crisis had been brought about by the extravagant spending of the 1920s, criticized his friend's fiscal irresponsibility. As the historian Arthur Frank Wertheim notes, "The way that the characters' hopes for monetary success were turned into business failures mirrored the lives of many Americans." Though "Amos 'n' Andy" reinforced racial stereotypes, it also reaffirmed the traditional values of "diligence, saving, and generosity."

Not all leisure time was filled by commercial entertainment. In a resurgence of traditionalism, attendance at religious services rose, and the home again became a center for pleasurable pastimes. An evening by the radio provided cheap family entertainment. Amateur photography and stamp collecting enjoyed tremendous vogues, as did the board game Monopoly. Reading aloud from books borrowed from the public library was another affordable diversion. But Americans bought books, too. Taking advantage of new manufacturing processes that made books cheaper, they made best sellers of Margaret Mitchell's *Gone with the Wind* (1936); James Hilton's *Lost Horizon* (1933); and Pearl Buck's *The Good Earth* (1932). Finally, "[t]alking was the Great Depression pastime," recalled the columnist Russell Baker. "Unlike the movies, talk was free."

THE SOCIAL FABRIC OF DEPRESSION AMERICA

Much writing about the 1930s has focused on white working-class or middle-class families caught suddenly in a downward spiral. For African-Americans, farmers, and Mexican-Americans, times had always been hard; during the 1930s they got much harder. As the poet Langston Hughes noted, "The depression brought everybody down a peg or two. And the Negroes had but few pegs to fall."

Blacks in the Depression

African-Americans had always known discrimination and limited opportunities, so they viewed the depression differently from most whites: "It didn't mean too much to him, the Great American Depression, as you call it," one man remarked. "There was no such thing. The best he could be is a janitor or a porter or shoeshine boy. It only became official when it hit the white man." The novelist and poet Maya Angelou, who grew up in Stamps, Arkansas, recalled, "The country had been in the throes of the Depression for two years before the Negroes in Stamps knew it. I think that everyone thought the Depression, like everything else, was for the white folks."

Despite the black migration to northern cities, which had begun before World War I, as late as 1940 more than 75 percent of African-Americans still lived in the South. Nearly all the farmers who were black lived in the South, their condition scarcely better than it had been at the end of Reconstruction. Only 20 percent of black farmers owned their own land; the rest toiled at the bottom of the South's exploitative agricultural system, as tenant farmers, farm hands, and sharecroppers. African-Americans rarely earned more than $200 a year. In one Louisiana parish, black women averaged only $41.67 a year picking cotton.

Throughout the 1920s, southern agriculture had suffered from falling prices and overproduction. The depression made an already desperate situation worse. Some black farmers tried to protect themselves by joining the Southern Tenant Farmers Union (STFU), which was founded in 1934. The STFU was one of the few southern groups that welcomed both blacks and whites. Landowners, however, had a stake in keeping sharecroppers from organizing, so they countered with repression and harassment. In the end the STFU could do little to reform an agricultural system that depended on a single crop, cotton.

All blacks faced harsh social and political discrimination throughout the South. In a celebrated case in Scottsboro, Alabama, in 1931, two white women who had been riding a freight train claimed to have been raped by nine black youths, all under twenty years old. The two women's stories contained many inconsistencies, and one woman later recanted. But in the South, when a white woman claimed to have been raped by a black, she was taken at her word. Two weeks later, juries composed entirely of white men found all nine defendants guilty of rape; eight were sentenced to death. (One defendant escaped the death penalty because he was a minor.) Though the U.S. Supreme Court overturned the sentences in 1932 and ordered new trials on grounds that the defendants had been denied adequate legal counsel, five of the men eventually were reconvicted and sentenced to long prison terms.

The youth of the defendants, their hasty trials, and the harsh sentences they received stirred public protest, prompting the International Labor Defense (ILD), a labor organization tied closely to the Communist party, to take over the defense. Though the Communist party had targeted the struggle against racism as a priority in the early 1930s, it was making little headway. "It's bad enough being black, why be red?" was a common reaction. White southerners resented radical groups' interference, noting that almost all those involved in the Scottsboro defense were northerners and Jews. Declared a local solicitor, "Alabama justice cannot be bought and sold with Jew money from New York."

The Scottsboro case received wide coverage in black communities across the country. Along with an increase in lynching in the early 1930s (twenty blacks were lynched in 1930, twenty-four in 1933), it gave black Americans a strong incentive to head for the North and the Midwest. Harlem, one of their main destinations, was already strained by the enormous influx of African-Americans in the 1920s. The depression only aggravated the housing shortage. Residential segregation kept blacks from moving elsewhere, so they paid excessive rents to live in deteriorating buildings where crowded living conditions fostered disease and premature death. As whites clamored for jobs traditionally held by blacks—waiters, domestic servants, elevator operators,

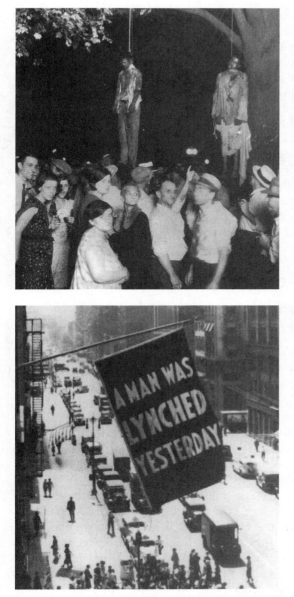

The Lynch Mob and Silent Witness

The threat of lynching remained a terrifying part of life for African-Americans in the 1930s, and not just in the South. The photograph on the top shows two young blacks who were lynched by an Indiana mob in 1930. Each day that a person was lynched, the NAACP hung a banner (bottom) outside the window of its New York office. NAACP appeals for federal antilynching legislation received little support from politicians, however.

and garbage collectors—unemployment in Harlem rose to 50 percent, twice the national rate. At the height of the depression, shelters and soup kitchens staffed by the Divine Peace Mission, under the leadership of the charismatic black religious leader Father Divine, provided 3,000 meals a day for Harlem's destitute.

In March 1935 Harlem exploded in the only major race riot of the decade. Anger about the lack of jobs, a slowdown in relief, and economic exploitation of the black community had been building for years. Although white-owned stores were entirely dependent on black trade, store owners would not employ blacks. The arrest of a black shoplifter, followed by rumors that he had been severely beaten by white police, triggered the riot. Four blacks were killed, and $2 million worth of property was damaged.

There were some signs of hope for African-Americans in the 1930s. Partly in response to the 1935 riot, but mainly in return for growing black allegiance to the Democratic party (see Chapter 26), the New Deal would channel significant amounts of relief money toward northern blacks. And the National Association for the Advancement of Colored People (NAACP) would continue to challenge the status quo of race relations. Though the call for racial justice would go largely unheeded during the depression, World War II and its aftermath would further the struggle for black equality.

Dust Bowl Migrations

A distressed agricultural sector had been one of the causes of the Great Depression. In the 1930s conditions only got worse, especially for farmers on the Great Plains. In the semiarid states of Oklahoma, Texas, New Mexico, Colorado, Arkansas, and Kansas, farmers had always risked the ravages of drought (see Chapter 17), but the years 1930–1941 witnessed the worst drought in the country's history. Low rainfall alone did not create the Dust Bowl, however. National and international market forces, like the rising demand for wheat during World War I, had caused farmers to push the farming frontier beyond its natural limits. To capture a profit, they had stripped the land of its natural vegetation, destroying the delicate ecological balance of the plains. When the rains dried up and the winds came, nothing remained to hold the soil. Huge clouds of dust rolled over the plains; streetlights blinked on as if night had fallen. Dust seeped into houses and "blackened the pillow around one's head, the dinner plates on the table, the bread dough on the back of the stove" (see Map 25.1).

The ecological disaster caused a mass exodus from the plains. Their crops ruined, their lands barren and dry, their homes foreclosed for debts they could not pay, farm families loaded their belongings into beat-up Fords. Encouraged by handbills distributed by growers that promised good jobs in California, at least 350,000 southwesterners headed west in the 1930s. Some went to metropolitan areas, but about half settled in rural areas where they worked for low wages as migratory farm laborers.

The migrants were called "Okies," whether or not they were from Oklahoma. John Steinbeck's novel *The Grapes of Wrath* (1939) immortalized them and their journey. In the novel the Joads abandon their land not only because of drought but also as a result of the transformation of American agriculture that ever since World War I had been prompting farmers to leave the land. By

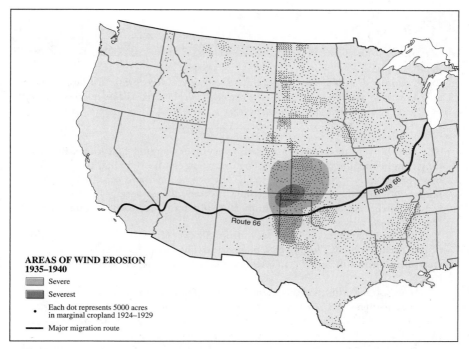

MAP 25.1

The Dust Bowl

A U.S. Weather Bureau scientist called the drought of the 1930s "the worst in the climatological history of the country." Conditions were especially severe in the southern plains, where the dramatic increases in farming on marginal land had strained production before the drought struck. Many farm families saw no choice but to follow Route 66, the highway that went west through Missouri, Oklahoma, and north Texas to California, the promised land.

the 1930s, large-scale commercialized farming had spread to the plains, where family farmers still used draft animals. In Steinbeck's novel, after the bank forecloses on the Joads' farm, a gasoline-engine tractor, the symbol of mechanized farming, plows under their crops and demolishes their home.

Though it was a powerful work, *The Grapes of Wrath* did not convey the diversity of the westward migration. Not all Okies were destitute dirt farmers; perhaps one in six was a professional, a business proprietor, or a white-collar worker. For most the drive west was fairly easy. Route 66 was a paved two-lane road: in a decent car, the journey from Oklahoma or Texas to California took only three to four days.

Before the 1930s Californians had created a different type of agriculture from that practiced in the Southwest and Midwest. Basically industrial in nature, California agriculture was large-scale, intensive, and diversified. The state's wealth came from specialty crops—citruses, grapes, potatoes—whose staggered harvests required a great deal of transient labor during short picking seasons. A

Mounting debt, plummeting prices, and widespread foreclosures led farmers to extreme measures in the early years of the depression, as this reminiscence by Harry Terrell, an Iowa farmer, makes clear.

The people were desperate. They came very near hanging that judge. Because they caught this judge foreclosing farm mortgages, and they had no other ways of stopping it. . . . They took the judge out of his court and took him to the fairgrounds and they had a rope around his neck. They were going to string him up in the old horse thief fashion. But somebody had sense enough to stop the thing before it got too far.

They had marches. . . . They came from all over the state. That was the time of the Farm Holiday. There was a picket line. The Farm Holiday movement was to hold the stuff off the market, to increase the price. It saw its violence, too.

They stopped milk wagons, dumped milk. They stopped farmers hauling their hay to market. They undertook to stop the whole agriculture process. They thought if they could block the highways and access to the packing plants, they couldn't buy these hogs at two cents a pound.

They'd say: we're gonna meet, just east of Cherokee, at the fork of the road, and so on. Now they spread it around the country that they were gonna stop everything from going through. And believe me, they stopped it. They had whatever was necessary to stop them with. Some of 'em had pitchforks. . . . You can fix the auto tire good with a pitchfork. There were blockades.

The country was getting up in arms about taking a man's property away from him. It was his livelihood. When you took a man's horses and his plow away, you denied him food, you just convicted his family to starvation. It was just that real.

SOURCE: Studs Terkel, *Hard Times* (New York: Pantheon Books, 1986), pp. 214–215.

steady supply of cheap migrant labor provided by Chinese, Mexicans, Okies, and (briefly) East Indians made this type of farming economically feasible.

The migrants had a lasting impact on California culture. At first they met outright hostility from old-time Californians—a demoralizing experience for white native-born Protestants, who were ashamed of the Okie stereotype. But they stayed, filling important roles in California's expanding economy. Soon some communities in the San Joaquin Valley—Bakersfield, Fresno, Merced, Modesto, and Stockton—took on a distinctly Okie cast, identifiable by southern-influenced evangelical religion and the growing popularity of country music.

Mexican-American Communities

The Mexican-American experience of the depression differed from that of the Dust Bowl refugees. In the depths of the depression, with fear of competition from foreign workers at a peak, perhaps a third of the Mexican-American population, most of them immigrants, returned to Mexico. A formal deportation policy instituted by the federal government was partly responsible for the exodus, but many more Mexicans left "voluntarily" when work ran out and local relief agencies refused to assist them. Racism, coupled with the proximity of Mexico, made Mexicans the only immigrants targeted for deportation during the depression.

In 1930 Los Angeles was home to 150,000 Mexican-Americans, giving it the largest concentration of Mexicans outside Mexico. Mexican-Americans spilled out of the downtown area, known as "Sonoratown," into neighborhoods, or *colonias*, in Belvedere and East Los Angeles. There mutual-aid societies, Spanish-language newspapers, and the Catholic Church fostered a sense of community. But Los Angeles lost approximately one-third of its Mexican population during the deportations of the 1930s, which separated families, disrupted children's education, and caused extreme financial hardship during the worst years of the depression. For those who remained in America, deportation was a constant threat, an unmistakable reminder of their fragile status in the United States.

Discrimination and exploitation were omnipresent in the Mexican community. The harsh experiences of migrant workers influenced a young Mexican-American named Cesar Chavez, who would become one of the twentieth century's most influential labor organizers. In the mid-1930s, Chavez's father became involved in several bitter labor struggles in the Imperial Valley. Thirty-seven major agricultural strikes occurred in California in 1933 alone, including one in the San Joaquin Valley that mobilized 18,000 cotton pickers. All these strikes failed, but they gave the young Chavez a background in labor organizing, which he would use to found a national farm workers' union in 1962.

Not all Mexican-Americans were migrant farm workers. Many worked as miners; others held industrial jobs, especially in steel mills, meat-packing plants, and refineries, where they established a vibrant tradition of labor activism. In California, Mexican-Americans also found employment in fruit- and vegetable-processing plants. Young single women especially preferred the higher-paid cannery work to domestic service, needlework, and farm labor. In plants owned by corporate giants like Del Monte, McNeill, and Libby, Mexican-American women earned around $2.50 a day, while their male counterparts received $3.50 to $4.50. Labor unions came to the canneries in 1939 with the formation of the United Cannery, Agricultural, Packing, and Allied Workers of America, an unusually democratic union in which women, the majority of the rank-and-file workers, played a leading role.

Mexican-American Poverty in Texas
In 1937 Antonia and Pablo Martinez lived in a one-room house in San
Antonio, Texas, with his parents and older brother. If either Pablo or Anto-
nia was employed in 1937, it was probably in San Antonio's pecan-shelling
industry, which depended heavily on the cheap labor of Mexican-
Americans.

Activism in the fields and factories demonstrated how a second generation, born in the United States, had turned increasingly to the struggle for political and economic justice in the United States, rather than retaining primary
allegiance to Mexico. According to the historian George Sánchez, they were
creating "their own version of Americanism without abandoning Mexican
culture." Joining American labor unions and becoming more involved in
American politics (see Chapter 26) were thus important steps in the creation
of a distinct Mexican-American ethnic identity.

HERBERT HOOVER AND THE GREAT DEPRESSION

In the presidential campaign of 1928, Herbert Hoover declared "the poorhouse is vanishing from among us." America was "nearer to the final triumph
over poverty than ever before in the history of any land." Once elected,
Hoover promised, he would preside over an era of Republican prosperity
and governmental restraint. When the stock market crashed in 1929, he

stubbornly insisted that the downturn was only temporary. Half a year later, Hoover greeted a business delegation, in June 1930, with these words: "Gentlemen, you have come sixty days too late. The Depression is over." When the country hit rock bottom in 1931 and 1932, the president finally acted, but by then it was too little, too late.

The Republican Response

Hoover's approach to the Great Depression was shaped by his priorities as secretary of commerce. Hoping to avoid coercive measures on the part of the federal government, he turned to the business community for leadership in overcoming the economic downturn. Hoover asked business executives to maintain wages and production levels voluntarily, and to work with the government to build people's confidence in the economic system.

Hoover did not rely solely on public pronouncements, however; he also used public funds and federal action to encourage recovery. Soon after the stock market crash he cut federal taxes, and called on state and local governments to increase their expenditures on public construction projects. He signed the 1929 Agricultural Marketing Act, which gave the federal government an unprecedented role in stabilizing agriculture. In 1930 and the first half of 1931, Hoover raised the federal budget for public works to $423 million, a dramatic increase in expenditures not traditionally considered to be the federal government's responsibility. Hoover also eased the international crisis by declaring a moratorium on the payment of Allied debts and reparations early in the summer of 1931. The depression continued, however. When the president asked Congress for a 33 percent tax increase to balance the budget, the ill-advised move choked investment and, to a lesser extent, consumption, contributing significantly to the continuation of the depression.

Hoover's most innovative program—one the New Deal would later draw on—was the Reconstruction Finance Corporation (RFC), approved by Congress in January 1932. Modeled on the War Finance Corporation of World War I, and developed in collaboration with the business and banking communities, the RFC was the first federal institution created to intervene directly in the economy during peacetime. To alleviate the credit crunch for business, the RFC would provide federal loans to railroads, financial institutions, banks, and insurance companies, in a strategy that has been called *pump priming*. In theory, money lent at the top of the economic structure would stimulate production, creating new jobs and increasing consumer spending. These benefits would eventually "trickle down" to the rest of the economy.

Unfortunately, the RFC lent its funds too cautiously to make a significant difference. Nonetheless, it represents a watershed in American political history and the rise of the state. When voluntary cooperation failed, the president turned to federal action to stimulate the economy. Yet Hoover's break with the past had clear limits. In many ways, his support of the RFC was just another attempt to encourage business confidence. Compared with previous chief executives—and in contrast to his popular image as a "do-nothing" president—Hoover responded to the national emergency on an unprecedented scale. But the nation's needs were also unprecedented, and Hoover's programs failed to meet them.

In particular, federal programs fell short of helping the growing ranks of the unemployed. Hoover remained adamant in his refusal to consider any plan for direct federal relief to the unemployed. Throughout his career he had believed that privately organized charities were sufficient to meet the nation's social welfare needs. During World War I he had headed the Commission for Relief of Belgium, a private group that distributed 5 million tons of food to Europe's suffering civilian population. And in 1927 he had coordinated a rescue and cleanup operation after a devastating flood of the Mississippi River left 16.5 million acres of land under water in seven states. The success of these and other predominantly voluntary responses to public emergencies had confirmed Hoover's belief that private charity, not federal aid, was the "American way" of solving social problems. He would not undermine the country's hallowed faith in individualism, even in the face of evidence that charities and state and local relief agencies could not meet the growing needs of the unemployed.

Rising Discontent

As the depression deepened, many citizens came to hate Herbert Hoover. Once the symbol of business prosperity, he became the scapegoat for the depression. "In Hoover we trusted, now we are busted," declared the hand-lettered signs carried by the down and out. New terms entered the vocabulary: *Hoovervilles* (shantytowns where people lived in packing crates and other makeshift shelters), *Hoover flags* (empty pockets turned inside out), *Hoover blankets* (newspapers). Hoover's declarations that nobody was starving, that hobos were better fed than ever before, seemed cruel and insensitive. His apparent willingness to bail out businesses and banks while leaving individuals to fend for themselves added to his reputation for cold-heartedness.

As the country entered the fourth year of depression, signs of rising discontent and rebellion emerged. Farmers were among the most vocal groups, banding together to harass the bank agents and government officers who enforced evictions and foreclosures and to protest the low prices they received for their crops. Midwestern farmers had watched the price of wheat fall from $3 a bushel in 1920 to barely 30 cents in 1932. Now they formed the Farm Holiday Association; barricaded local roads; and dumped milk, vegetables, and other farm produce in the dirt rather than accept prices that would not cover their costs. Nothing better captured the cruel irony of underconsumption and maldistribution than farmers dumping food at a time when thousands were going hungry.

Protest was not confined to rural America, however. Bitter labor strikes occurred in the depths of the depression, despite the threat that strikers would lose their jobs. In Harlan County, Kentucky, in 1931, miners struck over a 10 percent wage cut. Their union was crushed by mine owners and the National

Guard. In 1932, at Ford's River Rouge factory outside Detroit, a demonstration provoked violence from police and Ford security forces; three demonstrators were killed, and fifty more seriously injured. Later, some 40,000 people viewed the coffins under a banner charging that "Ford Gave Bullets for Bread."

In 1931 and 1932 violence broke out in the nation's cities. Groups of the unemployed battled local authorities over inadequate relief; citizens staged rent riots and hunger marches. Some of these actions were organized by the Communist party, still a tiny organization with only 12,000 members, as a challenge to the capitalist system. For example, the party helped to organize "unemployment councils" that agitated for jobs and food, and coordinated a hunger march on Washington, D.C., in 1931. Though the marches were well attended and often got results from local and federal authorities, they did not necessarily win converts to communism.

Not radicals but veterans staged the most publicized—and most tragic—protest. In the summer of 1932 the "Bonus Army," a ragtag group of about 15,000 unemployed World War I veterans, hitchhiked to Washington to demand immediate payment of their bonuses, originally scheduled

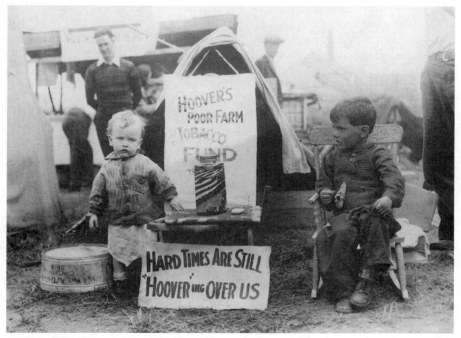

The Bonus Army
These children were camped out in the summer of 1932 on the Anacostia Flats of Washington, D.C., while their fathers lobbied Congress for early payment of World War I bonuses. Congress said no, and the U.S. Army violently disbanded the veterans' encampment.

for distribution in 1945. While their leaders lobbied Congress, the bonus army camped out in the capital. "We were heroes in 1917, but we're bums now," one veteran complained bitterly. When the marchers refused to leave their Anacostia Flats camp, Hoover called out riot troops to clear the area. Led by General Douglas MacArthur, assisted by Major Dwight D. Eisenhower and Major George S. Patton, the troops burned the encampment to the ground. In the fight that followed, more than a hundred marchers were injured. Newsreel footage captured the deeply disturbing spectacle of the U.S. Army moving against its own veterans, and Hoover's popularity plunged even lower.

The 1932 Election

Despite the evidence of discontent, the nation was not in a revolutionary mood as it approached the 1932 election. Having internalized Horatio Alger's ideal of the self-made man, many Americans initially blamed themselves rather than the system for their hardship. Despair and apathy, not anger, was the mood of most citizens. The Republicans, who could find no credible way to dump an incumbent president, unenthusiastically renominated Hoover. The Democrats turned to Governor Franklin Delano Roosevelt of New York, who won the nomination by capitalizing on that state's reputation for innovative relief and unemployment programs.

Roosevelt, born into a wealthy New York family in 1882, had attended Harvard College and Columbia Law School. He had served in the New York State legislature and as assistant secretary of the navy in the Wilson administration, a post that had earned him the vice-presidential nomination on the Democratic ticket in 1920. Roosevelt's rise to the presidency was interrupted in 1921 by an attack of polio that left both his legs paralyzed for life. But he fought back from this illness, emerging from the ordeal a stronger, more resilient man. "If you had spent two years in bed trying to wiggle your toe, after that anything would seem easy," he explained. His wife, Eleanor Roosevelt, strongly supported his return to public life, and helped to mastermind his successful campaign for the governorship of New York in 1928.

The 1932 campaign for the presidency foreshadowed little of the New Deal. Roosevelt hinted only vaguely at new approaches to the depression: "The country needs and, unless I mistake its temper, the country demands bold, persistent experimentation." He won easily, receiving 22.8 million votes to Hoover's 15.7 million. Despite the nation's economic collapse, Americans remained firmly committed to the two-party system. The Socialist party candidate, Norman Thomas, got fewer than a million votes, and the Communist party candidate, party leader William Z. Foster, drew only 100,000 votes.

The 1932 election marked a turning point in American politics, the emergence of a Democratic coalition that would dominate national politics for the next four decades. Roosevelt won the support of the Solid South, which returned to the Democratic fold after defecting in 1928 because of Al Smith's Catholicism and his views on Prohibition. Roosevelt drew substantial support in the West and in the cities, continuing a trend first noticed in 1928, when the Democrats appealed successfully to recent immigrants and urban ethnic groups. However, Roosevelt's election was hardly a mandate to re-shape American political and economic institutions. Many people voted as much against Hoover as for Roosevelt.

Having spoken, the voters had to wait until Roosevelt's inauguration in March 1933 to see him put his ideas into action. (The interval between the election and the inauguration was shortened by the Twentieth Amendment in 1933.) In the worst winter of the depression, Americans could do little but hope that things would get better. According to the most conservative esti-mates, unemployment stood at 20 to 25 percent nationwide. The rate was 50 percent in Cleveland, 60 percent in Akron, and 80 percent in Toledo—cities dependent on manufacturing jobs in industries that had basically shut down. The nation's banking system was so close to collapse, many state governors closed banks temporarily to avoid further panic.

By this time, the winter of 1932–1933, the depression had totally over-whelmed public welfare institutions. Private charity and public relief, both of whose expenditures had risen dramatically, still reached only a fraction of the needy. Hunger haunted cities and rural areas alike. When a teacher tried to send a coal miner's daughter home from school because she was weak from hunger, the girl replied, "It won't do any good . . . because this is sister's day to eat." In New York City, hospitals reported ninety-five deaths from starvation. This was the America that Roosevelt inherited when he took the oath of of-fice on March 4, 1933.

CHAPTER 25 TIMELINE

1929	Stock market crash
	Agricultural Marketing Act
1930	Midwestern drought begins
	Hawley-Smoot Tariff
1931	Scottsboro case
	Hoover declares moratorium on Allied war debts
	Miners strike in Harlan County, Kentucky
1932	Reconstruction Finance Corporation
	Bonus Army
	Height of deportation of Mexican migrant workers
	Farm Holiday Association founded
	Strike at Ford's River Rouge plant in Michigan
	Communist-led hunger marches
1933	Unemployment rises to highest level
	Franklin Delano Roosevelt becomes president
	Birth rate drops to lowest level
	The Marx Brothers in *Duck Soup*
1934	Southern Tenant Farmers Union founded
	It Happened One Night sweeps Oscars
1935	National Youth Administration
	Harlem race riot
1936	Student Strike against War
	Margaret Mitchell's *Gone with the Wind*
	Birth control legalized
1939	John Steinbeck's *The Grapes of Wrath*
	Frank Capra's *Mr. Smith Goes to Washington*

CHAPTER 26

THE NEW DEAL, 1933–1939

- The New Deal Begins, 1933–1935
- The Second New Deal, 1935–1938
- The New Deal's Impact on Society

In his bold inaugural address on March 4, 1933, President Franklin Delano Roosevelt declared, "The only thing we have to fear is fear itself." That memorable phrase rallied a nation that had already endured almost four years of the worst economic contraction in its history—with no end in sight.

His demeanor grim and purposeful, Roosevelt preached his first inaugural address like a sermon. Issuing ringing declarations of his vision of governmental activism—"This Nation asks for action, and action now"—he repeatedly compared combating the Great Depression to fighting a war. The new president was willing to ask Congress for "broad Executive power to wage a war against the emergency, as great as the power that would be given to me if we were in fact invaded by a foreign foe." He promised to "assume unhesitatingly the leadership of this great army of our people dedicated to a disciplined attack upon our common problems."

To wage this war, Roosevelt proposed the *New Deal*—a term that he first used in his acceptance speech at the Democratic National Convention in 1932, and that eventually came to stand for his administration's complex set of responses to the nation's economic collapse. In a time of major crisis, the New Deal was meant to relieve suffering and conserve the nation's political and economic institutions through unprecedented activity on the part of the national government. Its legacy would be an expanded federal presence in the economy and in the lives of ordinary citizens.

THE NEW DEAL BEGINS, 1933–1935

The Great Depression destroyed Herbert Hoover's political reputation and helped to make Roosevelt's. Although some Americans hated FDR—especially wealthy conservatives—he was immensely popular and beloved by many. Ironically, the ideological differences between Hoover and Roosevelt were not that vast. Both were committed to maintaining the nation's political and economic institutions. Both believed in the basic morality of a balanced budget and extolled the values of hard work, cooperation, and sacrifice. But Roosevelt's personal charisma, his political savvy, and his willingness to experiment made all the difference. Above all, his New Deal programs put people to work, instilling hope and restoring the nation's confidence.

Roosevelt's Style of Leadership

While the New Deal represented many things to many people, one unifying factor was the personality of its master architect, Franklin Roosevelt. A superb and pragmatic politician, Roosevelt crafted his administration's program in response to shifting political and economic conditions rather than following a set ideology or plan. He experimented with an idea; then if it did not work, he tried another. Roosevelt juggled advice in the same way. Senator Huey Long of Louisiana complained, "When I talk to him, he says 'Fine! Fine! Fine!' But Joe Robinson [the Senate majority leader] goes to see him the next day and again he says 'Fine! Fine! Fine!' Maybe he says 'Fine!' to everybody."

FDR
President Franklin Delano Roosevelt was a consummate politician who loved the adulation of a crowd. He consciously adopted a cheerful mien to keep people from feeling sorry for him because of his infirmity, knowing that he could not be a successful politician if the public pitied him.

President Roosevelt established an unusually close rapport with the American people. "Mr. Roosevelt is the only man we ever had in the White House who would understand that my boss is a son of a bitch," remarked one worker. Many ordinary citizens credited Roosevelt with the positive changes in their lives, saying, "He gave me a job" or "He saved my home." Roosevelt's masterful use of the new medium of radio, typified by the sixteen "fireside chats" he broadcast during his first two terms, fostered this personal identification. In the week after the inauguration, more than 450,000 letters, many of which addressed Roosevelt as a friend or a member of the family, poured into the White House. An average of 5,000 to 8,000 arrived weekly for the rest of the decade. One person had handled public correspondence during the Hoover administration, but a staff of fifty was required under Roosevelt.

Roosevelt's personal charisma allowed him to continue the expansion of presidential power begun in the administrations of Theodore Roosevelt and Woodrow Wilson. From the beginning Roosevelt centralized decision making in the White House; in so doing, he dramatically expanded the role of the executive branch in initiating policy, and helped to create the modern presidency. For policy formulation he turned to his talented cabinet, which included Harold Ickes at the Department of the Interior, Frances Perkins at Labor, Henry A. Wallace at Agriculture, and an old friend, Henry Morgenthau, Jr., at the Treasury. During the interregnum Roosevelt relied so heavily on the advice of the Columbia University professors Raymond Moley, Rexford Tugwell, and Adolph A. Berle, Jr., that the press dubbed them the "Brain Trust."

The Hundred Days

The first problem the new president confronted was the banking crisis. Since the stock market crash, about 9 million people had lost their savings. On the eve of the inauguration, thirty-eight states had closed their banks, and the remaining ten had restricted their hours of operation. On March 5, the day after the inauguration, the president declared a national "bank holiday"—a euphemism for closing all the banks—and called Congress into special session. Four days later Congress passed Roosevelt's proposed emergency banking bill, which permitted banks to reopen beginning on March 13—but only if a Treasury Department inspection showed they had sufficient cash reserves. The House approved the plan after only thirty-eight minutes of debate.

The Emergency Banking Act, which Roosevelt developed in consultation with banking leaders, was a conservative document that could have been proposed by Herbert Hoover. The difference was the public's reaction. On the Sunday evening before the banks reopened, Roosevelt broadcast his first fireside chat to a radio audience estimated at 60 million. In simple terms, he reassured citizens that the banks were safe, and Americans believed him. When the banks reopened on Monday morning, deposits exceeded withdrawals. "Capitalism was saved in eight days," observed Raymond Moley, who had served as Roosevelt's speechwriter in the 1932 campaign. The banking bill did its job:

though more than 4,000 banks failed in 1933—the vast majority in the months before the law took effect—only 61 closed their doors in 1934.

The Banking Act was the first of fifteen pieces of major legislation enacted by Congress in the opening months of the Roosevelt administration. This legislative session, which came to be called the "Hundred Days," remains one of the most productive ever. Congress created the Home Owners Loan Corporation to refinance home mortgages threatened by foreclosure. A second banking law, the Glass-Steagall Act, curbed speculation by separating investment banking from commercial banking, and created the Federal Deposit Insurance Corporation (FDIC), which insured deposits up to $2,500. Another act established the Civilian Conservation Corps (CCC), which sent 250,000 young men to do reforestation and conservation work. The Tennessee Valley Authority (TVA) received legislative approval for its innovative plan of government-sponsored regional development and public energy. And in a move that lifted public spirits immeasurably, Roosevelt legalized beer in April. Full repeal of Prohibition came eight months later, in December 1933.

The CCC

The Civilian Conservation Corps (CCC) was one of the most popular New Deal programs. Over ten years, it enrolled 2.75 million young Americans who worked for $1 a day on projects such as soil conservation, disaster relief, reforestation, and flood control. The CCC was limited to men, although a few camps employed out-of-work young women.

To speed economic recovery, the Roosevelt administration targeted three pressing problems: agricultural overproduction, business failures, and the need for unemployment relief. Roosevelt had long felt that a healthy farming sector was crucial to the nation's economic well-being. As he put it in 1929, "if farmers starve today, we will all starve tomorrow." Thus, he viewed the Agricultural Adjustment Act (AAA) as a key step toward the nation's recovery. The AAA established an allotment system for seven major commodities (wheat, cotton, corn, hogs, rice, tobacco, and dairy products), with cash subsidies for farmers who cut production—a tradition that continues to the present day. These benefits were financed by a tax on processing (such as the milling of wheat), which was passed on to consumers. New Deal planners hoped prices would rise in response to the federally subsidized scarcity, spurring a general recovery.

Though the AAA stabilized the agricultural sector, its benefits were distributed unevenly. Subsidies for reducing production went primarily to the owners of large and medium-sized farms, who often cut production by reducing their renters' and sharecroppers' acreage rather than their own. In the South, where many sharecroppers were black and the landowners and government administrators white, that strategy had racial overtones. As many as 200,000 black tenant farmers were displaced from their land by the AAA. Thus, New Deal agricultural policies fostered the migration of marginal farmers in the South and Midwest to northern cities and California, while they consolidated the economic and political clout of larger landholders.

The New Deal's major response to the problem of economic recovery, the National Industrial Recovery Act, launched the National Recovery Administration (NRA). The NRA established a system of industrial self-government to handle the problems of overproduction, cutthroat competition, and price instability. For each industry, a code of prices and production quotas, similar to those for farm products, was hammered out. In effect, these legally enforceable agreements suspended the antitrust laws. The codes also established minimum wages and maximum hours and outlawed child labor. One of the most far-reaching provisions, Section 7(a), guaranteed workers the right to organize and bargain collectively, "through representatives of their own choosing." These union rights dramatically spurred the growth of the labor movement in the 1930s.

General Hugh Johnson, a colorful if erratic administrator, headed the NRA. Johnson supervised negotiations for more than 600 NRA codes, ranging from large industries such as coal, cotton, and steel, to small ones such as dog food, costume jewelry, and even burlesque theaters. Trade associations, controlled by large companies, tended to dominate the code-drafting process, thus solidifying the power of large businesses at the expense of smaller enterprises. Labor had little input, and consumer interests almost none.

The early New Deal also addressed the critical problem of unemployment. In the fourth year of the depression, the total exhaustion of private and local sources of charity made some form of federal relief essential. Reluctantly,

Roosevelt moved toward federal assumption of responsibility for the unemployed. The Federal Emergency Relief Administration (FERA), set up in May 1933 under the direction of Harry Hopkins, a social worker from New York, offered federal money to the states for relief programs. FERA was designed to keep people from starving until other recovery measures took hold. In his first two hours in office, Hopkins distributed $5 million. Over the program's two-year existence, FERA spent $1 billion.

Roosevelt and his advisers maintained a strong distaste for the dole. As Hopkins worried, "I don't think anybody can go year after year, month after month, accepting relief without affecting his character in some ways unfavorably. It is probably going to undermine the independence of hundreds of thousands of families." Whenever possible, then, New Deal administrators promoted work relief over cash subsidies; they also consistently favored jobs that would not compete directly with the private sector. When the Public Works Administration (PWA), under Secretary of the Interior Harold L. Ickes, received a $3.3 billion appropriation in 1933, Ickes's cautiousness in initiating public works projects limited the agency's effectiveness. But in November 1933 Roosevelt established the Civil Works Administration (CWA), and named Harry Hopkins its head. Within thirty days the CWA had put 2.6 million men and women to work; at its peak in January 1934 it employed 4 million in jobs such as repairing bridges, building highways, constructing public buildings, and setting up community projects. The CWA, regarded as a stopgap measure to get the country through the winter of 1933–1934, lapsed the next spring after spending all its funds.

Many of these early emergency measures were deliberately inflationary. That is, they were designed to trigger price increases, which were thought necessary to stimulate recovery and halt the steep deflation. Another element of this strategy was Roosevelt's executive order of April 18, 1933, to abandon the gold standard and allow gold to rise in value like any other commodity. As the price of gold rose, administrators hoped, so too would manufactured and agricultural goods' prices. Though removing the country from the gold standard did not have much impact on the domestic economy, it did allow the Federal Reserve System to manipulate the value of the dollar in response to economic conditions, an important shift in economic power from the private to the public sector.

When an exhausted Congress recessed in June 1933, much had been accomplished. Rarely had a president so dominated a legislative session. A mass of "alphabet soup agencies," as the New Deal programs came to be known, had been created. But though they gave the impression of action, despite a slight economic upturn, they did not turn the economy around.

After the Hundred Days, with no end of the depression in sight, Roosevelt and Congress continued to pass legislation to promote recovery and restore confidence. Much of it focused on reforming business practices in order to prevent future depressions. In 1934 Congress established the Securities and Exchange Commission (SEC) to regulate the stock market and prevent insider trading, fraud, and other abuses. The Banking Act of 1935 also enhanced the federal government's role in controlling the economy and business. The act authorized the president to appoint a new Board of Governors of the Federal Reserve System, placing control of interest rates and other money market policies at the federal level rather than with regional banks. By requiring all large state banks to join the Federal Reserve System by 1942 in order to take advantage of the federal deposit insurance system, the law further encouraged centralization of the nation's banking system.

The New Deal under Attack

As Congress and the president consolidated the New Deal, their work came under attack from several quarters. Although Roosevelt billed himself as the savior of capitalism, noting that "to preserve we had to reform," his actions provoked strong hostility from many Americans. To the wealthy, Roosevelt became simply "that man," a traitor to his class. Business leaders and conservative Democrats formed the Liberty League in 1934 to lobby against the New Deal and its "reckless spending" and "socialist" reforms.

The conservative majority on the Supreme Court also disagreed with the direction of the New Deal. On Black Monday, May 27, 1935, the Supreme Court struck down the NRA in *Schechter v. United States*, ruling unanimously that the National Industrial Recovery Act represented an unconstitutional delegation of legislative power to the executive. The so-called sick-chicken case concerned a Brooklyn, New York, firm convicted of violating NRA codes by selling diseased poultry. In its decision the court also ruled that the NRA regulated commerce *within* states, while the Constitution limited federal regulation to *interstate* commerce. Roosevelt protested that the Court's narrow interpretation would return the Constitution "to the horse-and-buggy definition of interstate commerce," and worried privately that the Court might invalidate the entire New Deal.

Other citizens thought the New Deal had not gone far enough. Francis Townsend, a Long Beach, California, doctor, spoke for the nation's elderly. Many Americans feared poverty in old age because few had pension plans and many had lost their life savings in bank failures. In 1933 Townsend proposed the Old Age Revolving Pension Plan, which would have given $200 a month—a considerable sum at the time—to citizens over the age of sixty. To receive payments the elderly would have had to retire from their jobs, thus opening their positions to others, and would also have had to agree to spend the money within a month. Townsend Clubs soon sprang up across the country, particularly in the Far West.

Father Charles Coughlin also challenged Roosevelt's leadership, attracting a large following, especially in the Midwest. A parish priest in the Detroit suburb of Royal Oak, Coughlin had turned to the radio in the mid-1920s to enlarge his pastorate. In 1933 about 40 million Americans listened regularly to the Radio Priest's broadcasts. At first Coughlin supported the New Deal, but

he soon broke with Roosevelt over the president's refusal to support the nationalization of the banking system and expansion of the money supply. In
1935 Coughlin organized the National Union for Social Justice to promote
his views, billing them as an alternative to those of "Franklin Double-
Crossing Roosevelt." Because he was Canadian-born and a priest, Coughlin
was not likely to make a successful run for president, but his rapidly growing
constituency threatened to complicate the 1936 election.

The most direct threat to Roosevelt came from Senator Huey Long. In a
single term as governor of Louisiana the flamboyant Long had achieved stunning popularity. He had increased the share of state taxes paid by corporations,
and had embarked on a program of public works that included construction
of new highways, bridges, hospitals, and schools. But Long's accomplishments
came at a price: to push through his reforms, he had seized almost dictatorial
control of the state government. He maintained control over Louisiana's political machine even after his election to the U.S. Senate in 1930. Though he
supported Roosevelt in 1932, he made no secret of his own presidential
ambitions.

In 1934 Senator Long broke with the New Deal, arguing that its programs
did not go far enough. Like Coughlin, he established his own national movement, the Share Our Wealth Society, which boasted over 4 million followers
by 1935. Arguing that the unequal distribution of wealth in the United States
was the fundamental cause of the depression, Long advocated taxing 100 percent of all incomes over $1 million, and all inheritances over $5 million, and
distributing the money to the rest of the population. He knew his plan was

The Kingfish
Huey Long, the Louisiana governor and senator, was one of the
most controversial figures in American political history. He took his
nickname "Kingfish" from a character in the popular radio show
"Amos 'n' Andy." Long inspired
one of the most powerful political
novels of all time, Robert Penn
Warren's *All the King's Men,* which
won a Pulitzer Prize in 1946.

unworkable, but confided privately "When they figure that out, I'll have something new for them."

Like Coughlin, Long offered easy solutions—panaceas—to the nation's economic ills. Their extreme proposals alarmed liberals. Coughlin's rhetoric, furthermore, often had anti-Semitic overtones, and both men showed little regard for the niceties of representative government. Coughlin had actually promised to dictate if necessary to preserve democracy. And the demagogic Long had dismissed complaints about his unconstitutional interference with the Louisiana legislative process by announcing, "I'm the Constitution around here." Long's and Coughlin's ideas, and their rapid rise in popularity, suggest the depth of public dissatisfaction with the Roosevelt administration. With good reason, the president's strategists feared that Long might join forces with Coughlin and Townsend to form a third party, enabling the Republicans to win the 1936 election.

THE SECOND NEW DEAL, 1935–1938

As the depression continued and attacks on the New Deal mounted, Roosevelt and his advisers embarked on a new course which historians have labeled the Second New Deal. Unlike the First New Deal, which focused on recovery, the Second New Deal emphasized reform. Pushed to the left by the popularity of movements like Long's, as well as by signs of militancy among workers, Roosevelt, his eye fixed firmly on the 1936 election, backed legislation to increase the role of the federal government in providing for the welfare of citizens.

Legislative Accomplishments

The first beneficiary of Roosevelt's change in direction was the labor movement. The rising number of strikes in 1934—about 1,800, involving a total of 1.5 million workers—reflected the dramatic growth of rank-and-file militancy. After the Supreme Court declared the NRA unconstitutional in 1935, invalidating Section 7(a), labor representatives demanded legislation that would protect the right to organize and bargain collectively.

The Wagner Act (1935), named for its sponsor, Senator Robert F. Wagner of New York, offered a degree of protection to labor. It upheld the right of industrial workers to join a union (farm workers were not covered), and outlawed many unfair labor practices used to squelch unions, such as firing or blacklisting workers for union activities. The act also established the nonpartisan National Labor Relations Board (NLRB) to protect workers from employer coercion, supervise representation elections, and guarantee the process of collective bargaining.

The Social Security Act signed by Roosevelt on August 14, 1935, was partly a response to the political mobilization of the nation's elderly through the Townsend and Long movements. But it also reflected prodding from social reformers like Grace Abbott, head of the Children's Bureau, and Secretary of Labor Frances Perkins. The Social Security Act provided pensions for most workers in the private sector, although originally agricultural workers and domestics were not covered. Pensions were to be paid out of a federal-state fund to which both employers and employees would contribute. The act also established a joint federal-state system of unemployment compensation, funded by an unemployment tax on employers.

The Social Security Act was a milestone in the creation of the modern welfare state. With its enactment, the United States joined industrialized countries like Great Britain and Germany in providing old-age pensions and unemployment compensation to citizens. (The Roosevelt administration chose not to push for national health insurance, even though most other industrialized nations offered such protection.) The act also mandated categorical assistance to the blind, deaf, and disabled and to dependent children—the so-called deserving poor, who clearly could not support themselves. Categorical assistance programs, only a small part of the New Deal, gradually expanded over the years until they became an integral part of the American welfare system.

Roosevelt was never enthusiastic about large expenditures for social welfare programs. But in the sixth year of the depression, 10 million Americans were still out of work, creating a pressing moral and political issue for FDR and the Democrats. At this point, the Works Progress Administration (WPA) became the main federal relief agency; for the rest of the depression, it addressed the needs of the unemployed. While FERA had supplied grants to state relief programs, the WPA put relief workers directly onto the federal payroll. Between 1935 and 1943 the WPA employed 8.5 million Americans, spending $10.5 billion. The agency's employees constructed 651,087 miles of roads, 125,110 public buildings, 8,192 parks, and 853 airports, and built or repaired 124,087 bridges.

Though the WPA was an extravagant operation by the standards of the 1930s (it inspired nicknames such as "We Putter Around" and "We Poke Along"), it never reached more than a third of the nation's unemployed. The average wage of $55 a month—well below the government-defined subsistence level of $100 a month—barely enabled workers to eke out a living. In 1941, the government cut the program severely. It ended in 1943, when the economy returned to full employment during World War II.

The Revenue Act of 1935 showed Roosevelt's willingness to push for reforms that were considered too controversial earlier in his presidency. Much of the business community had already turned violently against Roosevelt in reaction to the NRA, the Social Security Act, and the Wagner Act. Wealthy conservatives quickly labeled this tax reform bill, which included federal inheritance and gift taxes, higher personal income tax rates in the top brackets, and higher corporate taxes, an attempt to "soak the rich." Roosevelt, seeking to defuse the popularity of Huey Long's Share Our Wealth plan, was just as interested in the political mileage of the tax bill as its actual results, which increased federal revenue by only $250 million a year.

As the 1936 election approached, the broad range of New Deal programs brought new voters into the Democratic coalition. Many had been personally helped by federal programs; others benefited because their interests had found new support in the federal expansion. Roosevelt could count on a potent urban-based coalition of workers, organized labor, northern blacks, farmers, white ethnic groups, Catholics, Jews, liberals, intellectuals, progressive Republicans, and middle-class families concerned about unemployment and old-age dependence. The Democrats also held on, though with some difficulty, to their traditional constituency of white southerners.

The Republicans realized that they could not compete directly with Roosevelt and his New Deal coalition. To run against the president, they chose the progressive governor of Kansas, Alfred M. Landon, who accepted the general precepts of the New Deal. Landon and the Republicans concentrated on criticizing the inefficiency and expense of many New Deal programs, stridently accusing FDR of harboring dictatorial ambitions.

Roosevelt's victory in 1936 was one of the biggest landslides in American history. The assassination of Huey Long in September 1935 had deflated the threat of a serious third-party challenge; the candidate of the combined Long-Townsend-Coughlin camp, Congressman William Lemke of North Dakota, garnered fewer than 900,000 votes (1.9 percent) for the Union party ticket. Roosevelt received 60.8 percent of the popular vote and carried every state except Maine and Vermont. The New Deal was at high tide.

Stalemate

From this high point, the New Deal soon slid into retrenchment, controversy, and stalemate. The first setback came when Roosevelt attempted to make fundamental changes in the structure of the Supreme Court. Shortly after finding the NRA unconstitutional in *Schechter v. United States*, the Court had struck down the Agricultural Adjustment Act, a coal conservation act, and New York State's minimum wage law. With the Wagner Act, the TVA, and Social Security coming up on appeal, the future of New Deal reform measures seemed in doubt.

Roosevelt's response, two weeks after his second inauguration, was to propose the addition of one new justice for each sitting justice over the age of seventy—a scheme that would have increased the number of justices from nine to fifteen. Roosevelt's opponents quickly protested that he was trying to "pack" the Court with justices who favored the New Deal. The president's proposal was also regarded as an assault on the principle of the separation of powers. But the issue became a moot one when the Supreme Court upheld several key pieces of New Deal legislation, and a series of resignations created vacancies on the Court. Within four years Roosevelt managed to reshape the Supreme Court to suit his liberal philosophy through seven new appointments, including Hugo Black, Felix Frankfurter, Stanley F. Reed, and William O. Douglas. Yet his handling of the issue was a costly blunder at a time when his second-term administration was vulnerable to the lame-duck syndrome. No one yet suspected that FDR would break with tradition by seeking a third term.

Congressional conservatives had long opposed the direction of the New Deal, but the Court-packing episode galvanized them by demonstrating that Roosevelt was no longer politically invincible. Throughout Roosevelt's second term a conservative coalition, composed mainly of southern Democrats and Republicans from rural areas, blocked or impeded social legislation. Two pieces of reform legislation that did win passage were the National Housing Act of 1937, which mandated the construction of low-cost public housing, and the Fair Labor Standards Act of 1938, which made permanent the minimum wage, maximum hours, and anti–child labor provisions in the NRA codes.

The "Roosevelt recession" of 1937–1938 dealt the most devastating blow to the president's political standing in the second term. Until that point the economy had made steady progress. From 1933 to 1937 the gross national product had grown at a yearly rate of about 10 percent, and industrial output had finally returned to 1929 levels in 1937, as did real income. Unemployment had declined from 25 percent to 14 percent—which meant that almost half the people without a job in 1933 had found one by 1937. Many Americans agreed with Senator James F. Byrnes of South Carolina that "the emergency has passed."

The steady improvement of the economy cheered Roosevelt. Basically a fiscal conservative, he had never been comfortable with large federal expenditures—which had grown from $4.8 billion in 1932 to $6.5 billion in 1934, producing deficits of about $3 billion in most years. Accordingly, Roosevelt slashed the federal budget in 1937. Between January and August, Congress cut the WPA's funding in half, causing layoffs of about 1.5 million workers. The Federal Reserve, fearing inflation, tightened credit, creating a sharp drop in the stock market. Unemployment soared to 19 percent, which meant more than 10 million workers were without jobs. Roosevelt soon found himself in the same situation that had confounded Hoover. Having taken credit for the recovery between 1933 and 1937, he had to take the blame for the recession.

Shifting gears, Roosevelt spent his way out of the downturn. Large WPA appropriations and a resumption of public works projects poured enough money into the economy to lift it out of the recession by early 1938. Roosevelt and his economic advisers were groping their way toward the general theory advanced by John Maynard Keynes, a British economist who proposed that governments use deficit spending to stimulate the economy when private spending proved insufficient. But Keynes's theory would not be widely accepted until a dramatic increase in defense spending for World War II finally ended the Great Depression.

Still struggling with attacks on the New Deal, Roosevelt decided to "purge" some of his most conservative opponents from the Democratic party as the 1938 election approached. In the spring primaries he campaigned against members of his own party who had been hostile or unsympathetic to New Deal initiatives. The purge failed abysmally and widened the liberal-conservative rift in the Democratic party. In the general election of 1938, Republicans capitalized on the "Roosevelt recession" and the backlash against the Court-packing attempt to pick up 8 seats in the Senate and 81 in the House. The party also gained 13 governorships.

Even without these political reversals, the reform impetus of the New Deal probably would not have continued. Roosevelt had always set clear limits on how far he was willing to go. His instincts were basically conservative, not revolutionary; he had wanted only to save the capitalist economic system by reforming it. The new activism of the Second New Deal was a major step beyond the informal, one-sided business-government partnership of the preceding decade—a step Roosevelt took only because the emergency of the depression had pushed him in that direction.

THE NEW DEAL'S IMPACT ON SOCIETY

Despite the limits of the New Deal, it had a tremendous impact on the nation and fundamentally altered American's relationship to their government. With an optimistic faith in using government for social purposes, New Dealers sponsored programs in the arts. It created vast projects to conserve the country's natural beauty and resources and to make them more accessible to its citizens. The broker state that emerged in the New Deal also brought the voices of more citizens—women, blacks, labor, Mexican-Americans—to the public arena, helping to promote the view that Roosevelt, and his party, represented the common people.

New Deal Constituencies

The New Deal accelerated the expansion of the federal bureaucracy that had been under way since the turn of the century. In a decade, the number of civilian government employees increased 80 percent, exceeding a million by 1940. The number of federal employees who worked in Washington grew at an even faster rate, doubling between 1929 and 1940. Power was increasingly centered in the nation's capital, not in the states. In 1939 a British observer summed up the new orientation: "Just as in 1929 the whole country was 'Wall Street conscious,' now it is 'Washington conscious.'"

The growth of the federal government increased the potential impact of its decisions (and spending) on various constituencies. And the New Deal considered a broader spectrum of the population worthy of inclusion in the political process, especially if people organized themselves into pressure groups. During the 1930s the federal government operated as a *broker state*—mediating between contending groups seeking power and benefits. Democrats recognized the importance of satisfying certain blocs of voters in order to cement their allegiance to the party. Even before the depression, they had begun to

A New Deal Activist

As an economist working for Harry Hopkins, Joe Marcus was one of thousands who formed the growing New Deal bureaucracy. Marcus's account, as told to Studs Terkel, captures some of the excitement that the New Deal generated. Marcus also suggests the way in which Roosevelt's administration expanded opportunities for Jews and other "outsiders."

I graduated college in '35. I went down to Washington and started to work in the spring of '36. The New Deal was a young man's world. Young people, if they showed any ability, got an opportunity. . . . In a few months I was made head of the department. We had a meeting with hot shots: What's to be done? I pointed out some problems: let's define what we're looking for. They immediately had me take over. . . .

The climate was exciting. You were part of a society that was on the move. You were involved in something that could make a difference. Laws could be changed. So could the conditions of people.

The idea of being involved close to the center of political life was unthinkable, just two or three years before all this happened. Unthinkable for someone like me, of lower middle-class, close to ghetto, Jewish life. Suddenly you were a significant member of society. It was not the kind of closed society you had lived in before. . . .

You were really part of something, changes could be made. Bringing *immediate* results to people who were starving. You could do something about it: that was the most important thing. . . .

We weren't thinking of remaking society. That wasn't it. I didn't buy this dream stuff. What was happening was a complete change in social attitudes at the central government level. The question was: How can you do it within this system? . . . The basic feeling—and I don't think this is just nostalgia—was one of excitement, of achievement, of happiness. Life was important, life was significant.

SOURCE: Studs Terkel, *Hard Times* (New York: Pantheon, 1986), pp. 265–266; also in the *America's History* Documents Collection, vol. 2, pp. 256–257.

build a coalition based on urban political machines and white ethnic voters. In the 1930s, organized labor, women, African-Americans, and other groups joined that coalition, receiving more attention from the Democrats and the federal government they controlled.

During the 1930s, labor relations became a legitimate arena for federal action and intervention, and organized labor claimed a place in national political life. Labor's dramatic growth in the 1930s represented one of the most important social and economic changes of the decade—an enormous contrast to its demoralized state at the end of the 1920s. Several factors encouraged the growth of the labor movement: the inadequacy of welfare capitalism in the face of the depression, New Deal legislation like the Wagner Act, the rise of the Congress of Industrial Organizations (CIO), and the growing militancy of rank-and-file workers. By the end of the decade the number of unionized workers had tripled to almost 9 million, or 23 percent of the nonfarm work force. Union strength grew rapidly in manufacturing, transportation, and mining. Organized labor won not only the battle for union recognition but for higher wages, seniority systems, and grievance procedures.

The CIO served as the cutting edge of the union movement by promoting industrial unionism—that is, organizing all the workers in an industry, both skilled and unskilled, into one union. John L. Lewis, leader of the United Mine Workers (UMW) and a founder of the CIO, was the foremost exponent of industrial unionism. Lewis began to detach himself from the American Federation of Labor (AFL), which favored organizing workers on a craft-by-craft basis, in 1935; by 1938 the break was complete.

The CIO achieved some of its momentum through the presence in its ranks of members of the Communist party. The rise of fascism in Europe had prompted the Soviet Union to mobilize support in democratic countries. In Europe and the United States, communist parties called for a "popular front," welcoming the cooperation of any group concerned about the threat of fascism

Organize
The Steelworkers' Organizing Committee was one of the most vital labor organizations contributing to the rise of the CIO. Note that the artist Ben Shahn chose a male figure to represent the American labor movement in this poster from the late 1930s. Such iconography reinforced the notion that the typical worker was male, despite the large number of women who joined the CIO.

to civil rights, organized labor, and world peace. Under the popular front, communists softened their revolutionary rhetoric and concentrated on becoming active leaders in many CIO unions. While few workers actually joined the Communist party, its influence in labor organizing in the thirties was far greater than its numbers, which in 1936 reached 40,000.

The CIO's success also stemmed from the recognition that to succeed, unions must be more inclusive. The CIO worked deliberately to attract new groups to the labor movement. Mexican-Americans and blacks found the CIO's commitment to racial justice a strong contrast to the AFL's long-established patterns of exclusion and segregation. And about 800,000 women workers also found a limited welcome in the CIO. Few blacks, Mexican-Americans, or women held leadership positions, however.

The CIO scored its first major victory in the automobile industry. On December 31, 1936, General Motors workers in Flint, Michigan, staged a sit-down strike, vowing to stay at their machines until management agreed to collective bargaining. The workers lived in the factories and machine shops for forty-four days before General Motors recognized their union, United Automobile Workers (UAW). Shortly after the CIO won another major victory, at the U.S. Steel Corporation. Despite a long history of bitter opposition to unionization (as demonstrated in the 1919 steel strike), Big Steel executives capitulated without a fight and recognized the Steel Workers Organizing Committee (SWOC) on March 2, 1937.

The victory in the steel industry was not complete, however. A group of companies known as "Little Steel" chose not to follow U.S. Steel's lead in making peace with the CIO. In response, steelworkers struck the Republic Steel Corporation plant in South Chicago. On Memorial Day, May 31, 1937, strikers and their families gathered for a holiday picnic and rally outside the plant's gates. Tension mounted, rocks were thrown, and the police fired on the crowd, killing ten protesters, all of them shot in the back. Workers in Little Steel did not win union recognition until 1941. The road to recognition for labor, even with New Deal protections, was still long and violent.

Labor's new vitality spilled over into political action. The AFL had always stood aloof from partisan politics, but the CIO quickly allied itself with the Democratic party, hoping to use its influence to elect candidates sympathetic to labor and social justice. Through Labor's Nonpartisan League, the CIO gave $770,000 to Democratic campaigns in 1936. Labor also provided solid support for Roosevelt's plan to reorganize the Supreme Court.

Despite the breakthroughs of the New Deal, the labor movement never developed into a dominant force in American life. Roosevelt never made the growth of the labor movement a high priority, and many workers remained indifferent or even hostile to unionization. And although the Wagner Act guaranteed unions a permanent place in American industrial relations, it did not revolutionize working conditions. The right to collective bargaining, rather than redistributing power in American industry, merely granted labor a measure of legitimacy. Management even found that unions could be used as a

AMERICAN VOICES

Sit-down Strike

By giving workers control of their employers' physical plant, sit-down strikes forced companies to negotiate. Bob Stinson's account of the first major sit-down strike—at General Motors in Flint, Michigan—reveals the high degree of organization and community support that characterized that forty-four-day strike.

The Flint sit-down happened Christmas eve, 1936. . . . We had guys patrol the plant, see that nobody got involved in anything they shouldn't. If anybody got careless with company property—such as sitting on an automobile cushion without putting burlap over it—he was talked to. . . .

Governor Murphy said he hoped to God he would never have to use National Guard against people. But if there was damage to property, he would do so. This was right down our alley, because we invited him to the plant and see how well we were taking care of the place.

They'd assign roles to you. When some of the guys at headquarters wanted to tell some of the guys in the plant what was cookin', I carried the message. . . .

The merchants cooperated. There'd be apples, bushels of potatoes, crates of oranges that was beginning to spoil. Some of our members were also little farmers, they come up with a couple of baskets of junk.

The soup kitchen was outside the plant. The women handled all the cooking, outside of one chef who came from New York. He had anywhere from ten to twenty women washing dishes and peeling potatoes in the strike kitchen. Mostly stews, pretty good meals. They were put in containers and hoisted up through the window. The boys in there had their own plates and cups and saucers.

SOURCE: Studs Terkel, *Hard Times* (New York: Pantheon, 1986), p. 131.

buffer against rank-and-file militancy. New Deal social welfare programs also tended to diffuse some of the pre-1937 radical spirit by channeling economic benefits to workers whether or not they belonged to unions.

Like organized workers, white women achieved new influence in the experimental climate of the New Deal, as unprecedented numbers of them were offered positions in the Roosevelt administration. Frances Perkins, the first woman named to a cabinet post, served as secretary of labor throughout Roosevelt's presidency. Molly Dewson, a social reformer turned politician, headed the Women's Division of the Democratic National Committee, where she pushed an issue-oriented program that supported New Deal reforms. Roosevelt's appointments of women included the first female director of the mint, the head of a major WPA division, and a judge on the circuit court of appeals.

Many of those women were close friends as well as professional colleagues, and cooperated in an informal network to advance feminist and reform causes.

Eleanor Roosevelt exemplified the growing prominence of women in public life. In the 1920s she had worked closely with other reformers to increase women's power in political parties, labor unions, and education. The experience proved an invaluable apprenticeship for her White House years, when her marriage to FDR developed into one of the most successful political partnerships of all time. He was the pragmatic politician, always aware of what could be done; she was the idealist, the gadfly, always pushing him— and the New Deal—to do more. Eleanor Roosevelt served as the conscience of the New Deal.

Despite the vocal support of a female political network, grave flaws still marred the treatment of women in New Deal programs. For example, a fourth of the NRA codes set a lower minimum wage for women than for men performing the same jobs. New Deal agencies like the Civil Works Administration and the Public Works Administration gave jobs almost exclusively to men: only 7 percent of CWA workers were female. And the CCC excluded women entirely, prompting critics to ask, "where is the 'she-she-she'?"

When they did hire women, New Deal programs tended to reinforce the broader society's gender and racial attitudes. Thus program administrators resisted placing women in nontraditional jobs. Under the WPA, sewing rooms became a sort of dumping ground for unemployed women. African-American and Mexican-American women, if they had access to work relief at all, often found themselves shunted into training as domestics, whose work was not covered by the Social Security and Fair Labor Standards acts.

Eleanor Roosevelt and Civil Rights
One of Eleanor Roosevelt's greatest legacies was her commitment to civil rights. For example, she publicly resigned from the Daughters of the American Revolution (DAR) in 1939 when the group refused to let the black opera singer Marian Anderson perform at Constitution Hall. Roosevelt developed an especially close working relationship with Mary McLeod Bethune of the National Youth Administration, shown here at a conference on black youth in 1939.

Just as the New Deal did not seriously challenge gender inequities, it did little to battle racial discrimination. In the 1930s, the vast majority of the American people did not regard civil rights as a legitimate area for federal intervention. Indeed, many New Deal programs reflected prevailing racist attitudes. CCC camps segregated blacks and whites, and many NRA codes did not protect black workers. Most tellingly, Franklin Roosevelt repeatedly refused to support legislation to make lynching a federal crime, claiming it would antagonize southern members of Congress whose support he needed to pass New Deal measures.

Nevertheless, blacks did receive significant benefits from New Deal relief programs directed toward the poor, regardless of their race or ethnic background. Blacks made up about 18 percent of the WPA's recipients, although they constituted only 10 percent of the population. The Resettlement Administration, established in 1935 to help small farmers buy land, and to resettle sharecroppers and tenant farmers on more productive land, fought for the rights of black tenant farmers in the South—that is, until angry southerners in Congress drastically cut its appropriations. Still, many blacks reasoned that the tangible aid from Washington outweighed the discrimination that marred many federal programs.

African-Americans were also pleased to see blacks appointed to federal office. Mary McLeod Bethune, an educator who ran the Office of Minority Affairs of the National Youth Administration, headed the "black cabinet." This informal network worked for fairer treatment of blacks by New Deal agencies, in the same way the women's network advocated feminist causes. Both groups benefited greatly from the support of Eleanor Roosevelt. The first lady's promotion of equal treatment for blacks ranks as one of her greatest legacies.

Help from the WPA and other New Deal programs, and a belief that the White House—or at least Eleanor Roosevelt—cared about their plight, caused a dramatic change in African-Americans' voting behavior. Since the Civil War blacks had voted Republican, a loyalty based on Abraham Lincoln's freeing of the slaves. As late as 1932, black voters in northern cities overwhelmingly supported Republican candidates. But in 1936, black Americans outside the South gave Roosevelt 71 percent of their votes. In Harlem, where relief dollars increased dramatically in the wake of the 1935 riot (see Chapter 25), their support was an extraordinary 81.3 percent. Black voters have remained overwhelmingly Democratic ever since.

The election of Franklin Roosevelt also had an immediate effect on Mexican-American communities, demoralized by the depression and the deportations of the Hoover years. In cities like Los Angeles and El Paso, Mexican-Americans qualified for relief more easily under New Deal guidelines, and there was more relief to go around. Even though New Deal guidelines prohibited discrimination based on an immigrant's legal status, the new climate encouraged a marked rise in requests for naturalization papers. Mexican-Americans also benefited from New Deal labor policies; for many, joining the CIO was an important stage in becoming an American. Inspired by New Deal rhetoric about economic recovery and social progress through cooperation, Mexican-Americans increasingly identified with the United States, rather than with Mexico. This shift was especially evident among American-born children of Mexican immigrants. Increasingly, participating in the political system became part of Mexican-American life. Los Angeles activist Beatrice Griffith noted, "Franklin D. Roosevelt's name was the spark that started thousands of Spanish-speaking persons to the polls." The Democrats made it clear that they welcomed Mexican-American voters and considered them an important part of the New Deal coalition.

But what about groups that did not mobilize politically or were not recognized as key participants in the New Deal coalition? The New Deal's impact on those groups and communities often depended on whether sympathetic government administrators in Washington undertook to promote their interests. Native Americans were one of the nation's most disadvantaged and most powerless minorities. The average annual income of a native American in 1934 was only $48; the unemployment rate among native Americans was three times the national average. Concerned New Deal administrators like Secretary of the Interior Harold Ickes and Commissioner of the Bureau of Indian Affairs John Collier tried to correct some of those inequities. The Indian Section of the Civilian Conservation Corps brought needed money and projects to reservations throughout the West. Indians also received benefits from FERA and CWA work relief projects.

Of far greater significance was the Indian Reorganization Act of 1934, sometimes called the "Indian New Deal." That law reversed the Dawes Severalty Act of 1887 by promoting more extensive self-government through tribal councils and constitutions. The government also abandoned the attempt to force native Americans to assimilate into mainstream society in favor of promoting cultural pluralism. The New Deal pledged to help preserve Indian languages, arts, and traditions. The problems of native Americans were so severe, however, that these changes in federal policy did little to improve their lives or reinvigorate tribal communities.

The New Deal and the Land

Concern for the land was one of the dominant motifs of the New Deal, and the shaping of the public landscape among its most visible legacies. Roosevelt brought to the presidency a love of forestry and a conservation ethic nurtured from childhood on his Hudson River estate. The expansion of federal responsibilities in the 1930s created a climate conducive to action, as did public concern heightened by the dramatic images of drought and devastation in the Dust Bowl. The New Deal resources policy stressed scientific management of the land, conservation instead of commercial development, and the aggressive use of public authority to safeguard both private and public holdings.

The most extensive New Deal environmental undertaking was the Tennessee Valley Authority. The need for dams to control flooding and erosion in the Tennessee River Basin, a seven-state area with some of the country's heaviest rainfall, had been recognized since World War I. But not until 1933 was the Tennessee Valley Authority established to develop the region's resources under public control. The TVA was the ultimate watershed demonstration area, integrating flood control, reforestation, and agricultural and industrial development, including the production of chemical fertilizers. A hydroelectric grid provided cheap electric power for the valley's residents. Admired worldwide, the TVA became one of the most popular destinations for visitors to the United States.

The Dust Bowl helped to focus attention on land management and ecological balance. Agents from the Soil Conservation Service in the Department of Agriculture taught farmers the proper technique for tilling hillsides. Government agronomists also tried to remove marginal land from cultivation, and to prevent soil erosion through better agricultural practices. One of their most widely publicized programs was the creation of the Shelterbelts, which involved the planting of 220 million trees running roughly along the 99th meridian, from Abilene, Texas, to the Canadian border. Planted as a windbreak, the trees also prevented soil erosion.

Another priority of the Roosevelt administration was helping rural Americans to stay on the land. The Rural Electrification Administration, established in 1935, brought power to farms in an attempt to improve the quality of rural life. The New Deal also encouraged urban dwellers to return to rural areas. This "back-to-the land" motif animated many New Deal projects, especially planned cooperative communities in rural areas, such as Arthurdale in West Virginia and the "Greenbelt" residential towns outside Washington, D.C.; Cincinnati; and Milwaukee.

Today, New Deal projects to conserve environment can be seen throughout the country. CCC and WPA workers built the Blue Ridge Parkway, the consummate parkway of the 1930s, which connects the Shenandoah National Park in Virginia with the Great Smoky Mountain National Park in North Carolina. In the West, government workers built the San Francisco Zoo, Berkeley's Tilden Park, and the canals of San Antonio. The CCC helped to complete the East Coast's Appalachian Trail and the West Coast's Pacific Crest Trail through the Sierras. In state parks across the country, cabins, shelters, picnic areas, lodges, and observation towers, built in a style that has been called "government rustic," are witness to the New Deal ethos of recreation coexisting with conservation.

Although the New Deal was ahead of its time in its attention to conservation, its legacy to later environmental movements is mixed. Many of the tactics used in New Deal projects—damming rivers, blasting fire roads, altering the natural landscape through the construction of buildings and shelters—are now considered intrusive. In the 1970s, the TVA came under attack for its longstanding practice of strip mining and the pollution caused by its power plants and chemical factories. Because of environmental concerns, a project as massive as the TVA probably could not be built today—an ironic comment on what was once hailed as an enlightened use of government power.

The New Deal and the Arts

In the arts, the depression had dried up traditional sources of patronage. Like most Americans, creative artists had nowhere to turn but Washington. A WPA project known as "Federal One" put unemployed artists, actors, and writers to work, but its spirit and purpose extended far beyond relief. New Deal administrators wanted to redefine the relationship between artists and the community, so that art would no longer be the exclusive province of the elite. "Art for the millions" became a popular New Deal slogan.

The Federal Art Project (FAP) gave work to many of the twentieth century's leading painters, muralists, and sculptors at a point in their careers when the lack of private patronage might have prevented them from continuing their artistic production. Under the direction of Holger Cahill, an expert on American folk art, the FAP commissioned murals for public buildings and post offices across the country. Jackson Pollock, Alice Neel, Willem de Kooning, and Louise Nevelson all received support from the FAP.

The Federal Music Project employed 15,000 musicians under the direction of Nicholas Sokoloff, the conductor of the Cleveland Symphony Orchestra. Government-sponsored orchestras toured the country, presenting free concerts of both classical and popular music. Like many New Deal programs, the Music Project emphasized American themes. The composer Aaron Copland wrote his *Billy the Kid* (1938) and *Rodeo* (1942) ballets for the WPA, basing the compositions on western folk motifs. The distinctive "American" sound and athletic dance style of these works made them immensely appealing to audiences. The federal government also employed the musicologist Charles Seeger and his wife, the composer Ruth Crawford Seeger, to catalog hundreds of American folk songs.

The former journalist Henry Alsberg headed the Federal Writers' Project (FWP), which at its height employed about 5,000 writers. Young FWP employees who later achieved fame included Saul Bellow, Ralph Ellison, Tillie Olsen, and John Cheever. The black folklorist and novelist Zora Neale Hurston finished three novels while on the Florida FWP, among them *Their Eyes Were Watching God* (1937). And Richard Wright won the 1938 *Story* magazine prize for the best tale by a WPA writer. Wright used his spare time to complete his novel *Native Son* (1940).

Of all the New Deal arts programs, the Federal Theatre Project (FTP) was the most ambitious. American drama thrived in the 1930s, the only time at which the United States had a federally supported national theater. Under the gifted direction of Hallie Flanagan, former head of Vassar College's Experimental Theater, the Theatre Project reached an audience of 25 to 30 million people in the four years of its existence. Talented directors, actors, and playwrights, including Orson Welles, John Huston, and Arthur Miller, offered their services.

The WPA arts projects were influenced by a broad artistic trend called the *documentary impulse*. Combining social relevance with distinctively American themes, this approach—which presented actual facts and events in a way that aroused the interest and emotions of the audience—characterized the artistic expression of the 1930s. The documentary, probably the decade's most distinctive genre, influenced practically every aspect of American culture: literature, photography, art, music, film, dance, theater, and radio.

The documentary impulse is evident in John Steinbeck's fiction (see Chapter 25) and in John Dos Passos's *USA* trilogy, which used actual newspaper clippings, dispatches, and headlines in its fictional story. The *March of Time* newsreels, which movie audiences saw before feature films, presented the news of the world for the pretelevision age. The filmmaker Pare Lorentz commissioned the composer Virgil Thompson to create music that set the mood for documentary movies such as *The Plow That Broke the Plains* (1936) and *The River* (1936). The new photojournalism magazines, including *Life* and *Look*, also reflected this documentary approach. And the New Deal institutionalized the trend by sending investigators like the journalist Lorena Hickok and the writer Martha Gellhorn into the field to report on the conditions of people on relief.

Finally, the federal government played a leading role in compiling the photographic record of the 1930s. The Historical Section of the Resettlement Administration had a mandate to document and photograph the American scene for the government. Through their haunting images of sharecroppers, Dust Bowl migrants, and the urban homeless, the photographers Dorothea Lange, Walker Evans, Ben Shahn, and Margaret Bourke-White permanently shaped the image of the Great Depression. The government hired photographers solely for their professional skills, not to provide them relief, as in Federal One projects. Their photographs, collected by the Historical Section, which in 1937 became part of the newly created Farm Security Administration (FSA), rank as the best visual representation of life in the United States during the depression years.

The Legacies of the New Deal

The New Deal set in motion far-reaching changes, notably the growth of a modern state of significant size. For the first time people experienced the federal government as a concrete part of everyday life. During the 1930s more than a third of the population received direct government assistance from new federal programs, including Social Security payments, farm loans, relief work, and mortgage guarantees. Furthermore, the government had made a commitment to intervene in the economy when the private sector could not guarantee economic stability. New legislation regulated the stock market, reformed the Federal Reserve system by placing more power in the hands of Washington policymakers, and brought many practices of modern corporate life under federal regulation. Thus, the New Deal accelerated the pattern begun during the Progressive Era of using federal regulation to bring order and regularity to economic life.

The New Deal also laid the foundations of America's welfare state—that is, the federal government's acceptance of primary responsibility for the individual and collective welfare of the people. But although the New Deal offered more benefits to American citizens than they had ever received before, its safety net had many holes, especially in comparison with the far more extensive welfare systems of Western Europe. The Social Security Act did not include national health care. Another serious defect of the emerging welfare system was its failure to reach a significant minority of American workers, including domestics and farm workers, for many years. And since state governments administered the programs, benefits varied widely; southern states consistently provided the lowest amounts.

To its credit, the New Deal recognized that poverty was an economic problem, not a matter of personal failure. Reformers assumed that once the depression was over, full employment and an active economy would take care of the nation's welfare needs and poverty would wither away. It did not. When later administrations confronted the persistence of inequality and unemployment, they grafted welfare programs onto the jerry-built system left over from the New Deal. Thus the American welfare system would always be marked by its birth during the crisis atmosphere of the Great Depression.

Even if the depression-era welfare system had some serious flaws, it was brilliant politics. The Democratic party courted the allegiance of citizens who benefited from New Deal programs. Organized labor aligned itself with the administration that had made it a legitimate force in modern industrial life. Blacks voted Democratic in direct relation to the economic benefits that poured into their communities. At the grass-roots level, the Women's Division of the Democratic National Committee mobilized 80,000 women who recognized what the New Deal had done for their communities. The unemployed also looked kindly on the Roosevelt administration. According to one of the earliest Gallup polls, 84 percent of those on relief voted the Democratic ticket in 1936.

But the Democratic party did not attract only the down-and-out. Roosevelt's magnetic personality and the dispersal of New Deal benefits to families throughout the social structure brought middle-class voters, many of them first- or second-generation immigrants, into the Democratic fold. Thus the New Deal completed the transformation of the Democratic party that had begun in the 1920s toward a coalition of ethnic groups, city dwellers, organized labor, blacks, and a broad cross-section of the middle class. Those voters would form the backbone of the Democratic coalition for decades to come, and would provide support for liberal reforms that extended the promise of the New Deal.

The New Deal coalition contained potentially fatal contradictions, involving mainly the issue of race. Because Roosevelt depended on the support of southern white Democrats to pass New Deal legislation, he was unwilling to challenge the economic and political marginalization of blacks in the South. At the same time, New Deal programs were changing the face of southern agriculture by undermining the sharecropping system and encouraging the migration of southern blacks to northern and western cities. Outside the South, blacks were not prevented from voting, a disparity that guaranteed that civil rights would enter the national agenda. The resulting fissures would eventually weaken the coalition that seemed so invincible at the height of Roosevelt's power.

With all its shortcomings, the New Deal nonetheless had a profound impact on the nation, all the more remarkable in light of its short duration. After 1936, the only major pieces of reform legislation passed were the National Housing Act of 1937 and the Fair Labor Standards Act of 1938. While the Supreme Court–packing scheme, the "Roosevelt recession," and the political successes of Republicans in 1938 helped to bring an end to the New Deal, the darkening international scene also played a part. As Europe moved toward war and Japan flexed its muscles in the Far East, Roosevelt became increasingly preoccupied with international relations, and placed domestic reform further and further into the background. After the United States entered the war in 1941, Roosevelt made the end of his depression program official when he announced in 1943 that it was time for "Dr. Win the War" to take the place of "Dr. New Deal." But in reality the New Deal had long ceased to propel the nation toward social reform.

CHAPTER 26 TIMELINE

1933	Banking crisis
	FDR's first fireside chat
	Emergency Banking Act
	Glass-Steagall Act establishes FDIC
	Agricultural Adjustment Act
	National Industrial Recovery Act
	Tennessee Valley Authority
	United States abandons gold standard
	Townsend Clubs
1934	Securities and Exchange Commission
	Indian Reorganization Act
1935	Supreme Court finds NRA unconstitutional
	National Union for Social Justice (Father Charles Coughlin)
	Resettlement Administration
	National Labor Relations (Wagner) Act
	Social Security Act
	Works Progress Administration
	CIO formed
1935–1939	Communist party at height of influence
1936	Supreme Court finds Agricultural Adjustment Act unconstitutional
	Roosevelt reelected
	The Plow That Broke the Plains and *The River*
	General Motors sit-down strike
1937	Memorial Day Massacre
	Supreme Court reorganization fails
1937–1938	"Roosevelt recession"
1938	Aaron Copland, *Billy the Kid*
	Fair Labor Standards Act
1939	Federal Theatre Project terminated

CHAPTER 27

THE WORLD AT WAR, 1939–1945

- The Road to War
- Mobilizing for Victory
- Life on the Home Front
- Fighting and Winning the War

Times Square, New York City, on August 15, 1945, was awash with people celebrating V-J (Victory over Japan) Day. World War II was over. Civilians and soldiers "jived in the streets and the crowd was so large that traffic was halted and sprinkler trucks were used to disperse pedestrians." The spontaneous street party seemed a fitting end to what had been the country's most popular war. For many Americans, World War II had been what one man described to journalist Studs Terkel as "an unreal period for us here at home. Those who lost nobody at the front had a pretty good time."

Americans had many reasons to view World War II as the "good war." Shocked by the Japanese attack on Pearl Harbor on December 7, 1941, they united in their determination to fight German and Japanese totalitarianism in defense of their way of life. When evidence of the grim reality of the Jewish Holocaust came to light, U.S. participation in the war seemed even more just. And despite their sacrifices, many people found the war a positive experience because it ended the devastating Great Depression, bringing full employment and prosperity. The unambiguous nature of the victory and the subsequent emergence of the United States as an unprecedentedly powerful nation further contributed to the sense of the war as one worth fighting.

But the good war had other sides. The period brought significant social disruption, accompanied by widespread anxiety about women's presence in the work force and a rise in juvenile delinquency. In a massive violation of civil liberties, over 100,000 people of Japanese ancestry were incarcerated in internment camps, victims of racially based hysteria. African-Americans served in a segregated military, and, with Chicanos, faced discrimination and violence at home. World War II also fostered the rise of a military industrial complex and unleashed the terrible potential of the atomic bomb. Finally, another enduring legacy developed out of the unresolved issues of the wartime alliance: the debilitating Cold War, which would dominate American foreign policy for decades.

THE ROAD TO WAR

The rise of fascism in Europe and Asia in the 1930s threatened the fragile peace that had prevailed since the end of World War I. When the League of Nations proved too weak to deal with the emerging crises, President Roosevelt foresaw the possibility of America's participation in another war. An internationalist at heart, he wanted the United States to play a prominent role in the international economic and political system to foster the long-term prosperity necessary for a lasting peace. Hampered at first by the pervasive isolationist sentiment in the country, by 1939 he was leading the nation toward war.

Depression Diplomacy

During the early years of the New Deal, America's involvement in international affairs, especially those in Europe, remained limited. One of Roosevelt's few diplomatic initiatives had been the formal recognition of the Soviet Union in November 1933. A second significant development was the Good Neighbor Policy, under which the United States voluntarily renounced the use of military force and armed intervention in the Western Hemisphere. At the core of this policy was the recognition that the friendship of Latin American countries was essential to the security of the United States. One practical outcome came in 1934, when Congress repealed the Platt Amendment, a relic of the Spanish-American War, which asserted the United States' right to intervene in Cuba's affairs. Indicating the limits to the Good Neighbor Policy, the U.S. Navy kept (and still maintains) a major base at Cuba's Guantanamo Bay and continued to meddle in Cuban politics. And in numerous Latin American countries, U.S. diplomats frequently resorted to economic pressure to solidify the influence of the United States and benefit its international corporations.

Roosevelt and his secretary of state, Cordell Hull, might have hoped to pursue more far-reaching diplomatic initiatives. But isolationism had been building in both Congress and the nation throughout the 1920s, a product in part of disillusionment with American participation in World War I. In 1934 Gerald P. Nye, a Republican senator from North Dakota, began a congressional investigation into the profits of munitions makers during World War I, and then widened the investigation to determine the influence of economic interests on America's decision to declare war. Nye's committee concluded that war profiteers, whom it called "merchants of death," had maneuvered the nation into World War I for financial gain.

Though most of the committee's charges were dubious or simplistic, they gave momentum to the isolationist movement, contributing to the passage of the Neutrality Act of 1935. Designed explicitly to prevent a recurrence of the events that had pulled the United States into World War I, the act imposed an embargo on arms trading with countries at war, and declared that American citizens traveled on the ships of belligerent nations at their own risk. In 1936, Congress expanded the Neutrality Act to ban loans to belligerents, and in 1937, it adopted a "cash-and-carry" provision: if a country at war wanted to purchase nonmilitary goods from the United States, it had to pay for them in cash and pick them up in its own ships.

The same year Congress explicitly reinforced earlier bans on sales of arms to Spain, where a bloody Civil War had erupted in 1936. There Francisco Franco, strongly supported by the fascist regimes in Germany and Italy, was leading a rebellion against the democratically elected republican government. Backed only by the Soviet Union and Mexico, the republicans, or Loyalists, relied heavily on volunteers from other countries, including the American Lincoln Brigade, which fought courageously and sustained heavy losses throughout the war. The governments of the United States, Great Britain, and France, despite their Loyalist sympathies, remained neutral, a policy that dismayed many American intellectuals and activists and virtually assured a fascist victory.

Aggression and Appeasement

The nation's neutrality was soon challenged by the aggressive actions of Germany, Italy, and Japan, all determined to expand their borders and their influence. The first crisis was precipitated by Japan, a country whose militaristic regime was intent on dominating the Pacific basin. In 1931 Japan occupied Manchuria, the northernmost province of China; then in 1937, it launched a full-scale invasion of China. In both instances, the League of Nations condemned Japan's action, but was helpless to stop the aggression. Japan simply served the required one-year notice of withdrawal from the League.

Japan's defiance of the League encouraged a fascist dictator half a world away. Italy's Benito Mussolini had long been unhappy with the Versailles treaty, which had not awarded Italy any formerly German or Turkish colonies. In 1935 Italy invaded Ethiopia, one of the few independent countries left in Africa. The Ethiopian emperor, Haile Selassie, appealed to the League of Nations, which condemned the invasion and imposed sanctions, but to little effect. By 1936 the Italian subjugation of Ethiopia was complete.

Not Italy, but Germany presented the gravest threat to the world order in the 1930s. There huge reparations payments, runaway inflation, fear of

communism, labor unrest, and rising unemployment fueled the rise of Adolf
Hitler and his National Socialist (Nazi) party. In 1933 Hitler became chan-
cellor of Germany, and assumed dictatorial powers. Aiming at nothing short
of world domination, as he made clear in his book *Mein Kampf* (*My Struggle*), Hitler sought to overturn the territorial settlements of the Versailles
treaty, to "restore" all the Germans of Central and Eastern Europe to a single
greater German fatherland, and to annex large areas of Eastern Europe. In
his warped vision, "inferior races" such as Jews, gypsies, and Slavs, as well as
"undesirables" such as homosexuals and the mentally impaired, would have
to make way for the "master race." In 1933 Hitler established the first concentration camp at Dachau and opened a campaign of persecution against
Jews.

Hitler's strategy for gaining territory provoked a series of crises that gave
Britain and France no alternative but to let him have his way or risk war.
British Prime Minister Neville Chamberlain was a particularly insistent proponent of what became known as "appeasement." Germany withdrew from
the League of Nations in 1933; two years later Hitler announced that he
planned to rearm the nation in violation of the Versailles treaty. No one
stopped him. In 1936 Germany reoccupied the Rhineland, a region that had
been declared a demilitarized zone under the treaty. Once again France and
Britain took no action. Later that year Hitler and Mussolini joined forces in
the Rome-Berlin Axis, a political and military alliance. When the Spanish
Civil War broke out, Germany and Italy armed the Spanish fascists. The same
year, Germany and Japan signed the Anti-Comintern Pact, a precursor to the
military alliance between Japan and the Axis that was formalized in 1940.

As persecution of German Jews and other minorities escalated, Hitler's
ambitions grew. In 1938 he sent troops to annex Austria, while at the same
time he schemed to seize part of Czechoslovakia. Because Czechoslovakia had
an alliance with France, war seemed imminent. But at the Munich Conference in September 1938, Britain and France capitulated, agreeing to let Germany annex the Sudetenland—the German-speaking border areas of
Czechoslovakia—in return for Hitler's pledge to seek no more territory.

Within six months, however, Hitler's forces had overrun the rest of
Czechoslovakia and were threatening to march into Poland. Britain and
France realized that their policy of appeasement had been disastrous, and prepared to take a stand. Then in August 1939 Hitler shocked the world by signing the Nonaggression Pact with the Soviet Union, which allowed Germany
to avoid waging war on two fronts. On September 1, 1939, German troops attacked Poland; two days later Britain and France declared war on Germany.
World War II had begun.

America and the War

Because the United States had become a major world power, whatever the
nation did would affect the course of the European conflict. Two days after

the war started, the United States officially declared its neutrality. Roosevelt made no secret of his sympathies, however. He pointedly rephrased Woodrow Wilson's declaration of 1914: "This nation will remain a neutral nation, but I cannot ask that every American remain neutral in thought as well." The overwhelming majority of Americans supported the Allies (Britain and France) over the Nazis, but most Americans did not want to be drawn into another world war.

At first, the need for American intervention seemed remote. After the German conquest of Poland in September 1939, a false calm settled over Europe. But then on April 9, 1940, Nazi tanks overran Denmark. Norway fell to the Nazi *Blitzkrieg* ("lightning war") next, and the Netherlands, Belgium, and Luxembourg soon followed. Finally, on June 22, 1940, France fell. Britain stood alone against Hitler's plans for world domination.

In America, the debate over the nation's neutrality continued. The journalist William Allen White and his Committee to Defend America by Aiding the Allies led the interventionists. Isolationists, including the aviator Charles Lindbergh, formed the America First Committee to keep the nation out of the war. They attracted the support of the Chicago *Tribune*, the Hearst newspapers, and other conservative publications.

Despite the efforts of the America First Committee, in 1940 the United States moved closer to involvement in the war. In May Roosevelt began putting the economy and the government on a defense footing by creating the National Defense Advisory Commission and the Council of National Defense. During the summer he traded fifty World War I destroyers to Great Britain in exchange for the right to build military bases on British possessions in the Atlantic, thus circumventing the nation's neutrality law by executive order. In October Congress approved a large increase in defense spending, and instituted the first peacetime draft registration and conscription in American history.

While the war expanded in Europe, Asia, North Africa, and the Middle East, the United States was preparing for the 1940 presidential election. The conflict had convinced Roosevelt that he should seek an unprecedented third term. He submitted to a "draft" at the Democratic National Convention, and despite opposition, chose the liberal secretary of agriculture Henry A. Wallace as his running mate. The Republicans nominated Wendell Willkie of Indiana, a former Democrat who supported many New Deal policies. The two parties' platforms differed only slightly. Both pledged aid to the Allies, but stopped short of calling for American participation in the war. Though Willkie's spirited campaign resulted in a closer election than those of 1932 or 1936, Roosevelt and the Democrats won 55 percent of the popular vote and a lopsided total in the electoral college.

With the election behind him, Roosevelt concentrated on persuading the American people to increase aid to Britain, whose survival he viewed as the key to American security. In November 1939 FDR had won a bitter battle in Congress to amend the Neutrality Act of 1935 to allow the Allies to buy weapons from the United States—but only on the cash-and-carry basis established for nonmilitary goods in 1937. In March 1941, with German submarines sinking British ships faster than they could be replaced, and Britain no longer able to afford to pay cash for arms, Roosevelt convinced Congress to pass the Lend-Lease Act. The legislation authorized the president to "lease, lend, or otherwise dispose of" arms and other equipment to any country whose defense was considered vital to the security of the United States. After Germany invaded the Soviet Union in June 1941 (an abandonment of the Nazi-Soviet pact of two years earlier), the United States extended lend-lease to the Soviet Union, which became part of the Allied coalition.

In his State of the Union address to Congress in January 1941, Roosevelt had connected lend-lease to the defense of democracy at home as well as in Europe. He spoke about what he called "four essential human freedoms everywhere in the world"—freedom of speech and expression, freedom of worship, freedom from want, and freedom from fear. Although Roosevelt avoided stating explicitly that America had to enter the war to protect those freedoms, he intended to justify exactly that, for he regarded United States entry in the war as inevitable. And indeed, the implementation of lend-lease marked the unofficial entrance of the United States into the European war.

The United States became even more involved in August 1941, when Roosevelt and the British prime minister, Winston Churchill, conferred secretly to discuss goals and military strategy. Their joint press release, which became known as the Atlantic Charter, provided the ideological foundation of the western cause and of the peace to follow. Like Wilson's Fourteen Points, the Charter called for economic collaboration and guarantees of political stability after the war ended, to ensure that "all men in all the lands may live out their lives in freedom from fear and want." The Charter also supported free trade, national self-determination, and the principle of collective security.

As in World War I, when Americans started supplying the Allies, Germany attacked American and Allied ships. By September 1941 Nazi submarines and American vessels were fighting an undeclared naval war in the Atlantic, unknown to the American public. Without an actual enemy attack, however, Roosevelt hesitated to ask Congress for a declaration of war.

The final provocation came not from Germany, but from Japan. Throughout the 1930s, Japanese military advances in China had upset the balance of political and economic power in the Pacific, where the United States had long enjoyed the economic benefits of the Open Door policy. After the Japanese invasion of China in 1937, Roosevelt had denounced "the present reign of terror and international lawlessness," suggesting that aggressors such as Japan be "quarantined" by peace-loving nations. Despite such rhetoric, however, the United States avoided taking a stand. During the brutal sack of Nanking in 1937 the Japanese had sunk an American gunboat, the *Panay*, in the Yangtze River. In exchange for more than $2 million in damages, the United States allowed Japan to apologize and the incident was quickly smoothed over.

Japan soon became more expansionist in its intentions, signing the Tri-Partite Pact with Germany and Italy in 1940. In the fall of 1941 Japanese troops occupied the northern part of French Indochina. The United States retaliated by effectively cutting off trade with Japan, including vital oil shipments that accounted for almost 80 percent of Japanese consumption. But in July 1941 Japanese troops occupied the rest of Indochina. Roosevelt responded by freezing Japanese assets in the United States and instituting an embargo on trade with Japan.

In September 1941 the government of Prime Minister Hideki Tojo began secret preparations for war against the United States. By November American military intelligence knew that Japan was planning an attack, but did not know where it would come. Early on Sunday morning, December 7, 1941, Japanese bombers attacked Pearl Harbor, killing more than 2,400 Americans. Eight battleships, three cruisers, three destroyers, and almost two hundred airplanes were destroyed or heavily damaged.

Although the attack was devastating, it infused the American people with a determination to fight. Pearl Harbor Day is still etched in the memories of millions of Americans who remember precisely what they were doing when they heard about the attack. The next day Roosevelt went before Congress. Calling December 7 "a date which will live in infamy," he asked for a declaration of war against Japan. The Senate voted unanimously for war, and the House concurred by a vote of 388 to 1. The lone dissenter was Jeannette Rankin of Montana, who had also opposed American entry into World War I. Three days later Germany and Italy declared war on the United States, and the United States in turn declared war on those nations.

MOBILIZING FOR VICTORY

The task of fighting a global war accelerated the growing influence of the state on all aspects of American life. A dramatic expansion of power occurred at the presidential level when Congress passed the War Powers Act of December 18, 1941, giving Roosevelt unprecedented authority over all aspects of the conduct of the war. Coordinating the changeover from civilian to war production, raising an army, and assembling the necessary work force taxed government agencies to the limit. Mobilization on such a scale demanded cooperation between business executives and political leaders in Washington, solidifying a partnership that had been growing since World War I.

Defense Mobilization

Defense mobilization had a powerful impact on the federal government's role in the economy. During the war, the federal budget expanded by a factor of ten and the national debt grew sixfold, peaking out at $258.6 billion in 1945. Along with huge federal budgets came greater acceptance of Keynesian economics— the use of fiscal policy, especially deficit spending, to stimulate economic growth. At the same time, the national government became more closely tied to its citizens' pocketbooks. The Revenue Act of 1942 continued the income tax reform that had begun during World War I by taxing not just wealthy individuals and corporations, but average citizens as well. Tax collections rose from $2.2 billion to $35.1 billion, facilitated by payroll deductions and tax withholding, instituted in 1943. This system of mass taxation, a revolutionary change in the financing of the modern state, was sold to the taxpayers as a way to express their patriotism.

The war also brought significant changes in the federal bureaucracy. The number of civilians employed by the government increased almost fourfold, to 3.8 million—a far more dramatic growth than the New Deal period had witnessed. Leadership of federal agencies also changed as the Roosevelt administration turned to business executives to replace the reformers and social activists who had staffed New Deal relief agencies in the 1930s. Those executives became known as "dollar-a-year men," because they volunteered for government service while remaining on the corporate payroll.

Many wartime agencies extended the power of the federal government. One of the most important was the War Production Board (WPB), which awarded defense contracts, evaluated military and civilian requests for scarce resources, and oversaw the conversion of industry to military production. The WPB used the carrot more often than the stick. To encourage businesses to convert to war production, the board granted generous tax write-offs for plant construction and approved contracts with cost-plus provisions, which guaranteed a profit and promised that businesses could keep the new factories after the war. As Secretary of War Henry Stimson put it, in capitalist countries at war, "you had better let business make money out of the process or business won't work."

In the interest of efficiency and maximum production, the WPB preferred to deal with major corporations rather than with small businesses. The fifty-six largest corporations got three-fourths of the war contracts; the top ten a third. This system of allocating contracts, along with the suspension of antitrust prosecution during the war, hastened the trend toward large corporate structures. In 1940 the hundred largest companies manufactured 30 percent of the nation's industrial output; by 1945 their share was 70 percent. These very large businesses would form the core of the military-industrial complex of the postwar years, which linked the federal government, corporations, and the military in an interdependent partnership (see Chapters 28 and 29).

Although not all industries could boast of freedom from *snafus* (an acronym coined during the war from the expression "*s*ituation *n*ormal, *a*ll *f*ouled *up*"), business and government compiled an impressive record. By

1945 the United States had turned out 86,000 tanks, 296,000 airplanes, 15 million rifles and machine guns, 64,000 landing craft, and 6,500 ships. Mobilization on this gigantic scale gave a tremendous boost to the economy, causing it to more than double, rising from a gross national product in 1940 of $99.7 billion to $211 billion by the end of the war. After years of depression, Americans' faith in the capitalist system was restored. But it was a transformed system that relied heavily on the federal government's participation in the economy.

An expanded state presence was also evident in the government's mobilization of a fighting force. By the end of World War II the armed forces of the United States numbered more than 15 million men and women. Draft boards had registered about 31 million men between the ages of eighteen and forty-four. More than half the men failed to meet the physical standards: many were rejected because of defective teeth and poor vision. The military also tried to screen out homosexuals, but its attempts were ineffectual. Once in the services, homosexuals found opportunities to participate in a gay subculture more extensive than that in civilian life.

Racial discrimination prevailed in the armed forces, directed mainly against the approximately 700,000 blacks who fought in all branches of the armed forces in segregated units. Though the National Association for the Advancement of Colored People (NAACP) and other civil rights groups chided the government with reminders such as "A Jim Crow army cannot fight for a free world," the military continued to segregate African-Americans and to assign them the most menial duties. In contrast, Mexican-Americans were never officially segregated. Unlike blacks, they were welcomed into combat units: seventeen Mexican-Americans won the Congressional Medal of Honor.

About 350,000 American women, both black and white, enlisted in the armed services and achieved a permanent status in the military, serving in agencies such as the WACS (Women's Army Corps) and the WAVES (Women Appointed for Volunteer Emergency Service). The armed forces limited the types of duty assigned to women, as it did with black men. Women were barred from combat, although nurses and medical personnel sometimes served close to the front lines, risking capture or death. Most of the jobs women did—clerical work, communications, and health care—reflected stereotypes of women's roles in civilian life.

Women, Workers, African-Americans, and the War Effort

When millions of citizens entered military service, the United States faced a critical labor shortage, which the War Manpower Commission sought to remedy. Well-organized government propaganda urged women into the work force. "Longing won't bring him back sooner . . . GET A WAR JOB!" one poster beckoned, and the artist Norman Rockwell's famous "Rosie the Riveter" appealed to women from the cover of the *Saturday Evening Post*.

AMERICAN VOICES

"A Loyal Negro Soldier"

A frican-Americans served in a segregated military. As shown in this letter from "A Loyal Negro Soldier" stationed in Alexandria, Virginia, wartime experiences heightened African-American militancy. This increased militancy would be one factor that prompted the postwar civil rights movement.

A few weeks after my arrival, at this camp, I went to a post exchange on my regimental area. I knew that each area has an exchange but I thought that I could make my purchase at any of them. Upon entering I could feel the place grow cold. All conversation ceased. It was then that I noticed that all the soldiers and the saleswomen were white. Not to be outdone I approached the counter and was told (even before asking for the article) that, "Negroes are not served here. This post-exchange is for white soldiers. You have one near your regiment. Buy what you want there." . . .

[Later, after protesting another example of discrimination, he was asked, "Don't you want to fight for the U.S.A. and its policies?"]

I am a soldier; I made no answer, but deep down inside I knew when I faced America's enemies I will fight for the protection of my loved ones at home.

Listen, Negro America, I am writing this article believing that it will act as a stimulant. You need awakening. . . . The [f]light on the battlefield is for your existence, not for Democracy. It is upon you that each soldier depends. In my fight my thoughts will invariably return to you who can fight for Democracy. You must do this for the soldiers because Democracy will be, and Democracy must be won at home—not on battlefields but through your bringing pressure to bear on Congress.

SOURCE: Phillip McGuire, *Taps for a Jim Crow Army: Letters from Black Soldiers in World War II* (Santa Barbara, CA: ABC-Clio, 1983), pp. 85-87.

Although the government directed its propaganda at housewives, women who were already employed gladly abandoned low-paying "women's" jobs as domestic servants or file clerks for higher-paying jobs in the defense industry. Suddenly the nation's factories were full of women working as riveters, welders, blast furnace cleaners, and drill press operators. Women made up 36 percent of the labor force in 1945, compared with 24 percent at the beginning of the war. Despite their new opportunities, women war workers faced many obstacles, including discrimination on the job. In shipyards women with the most seniority and responsibility earned $6.95 a day, while the top men made as much as $22.

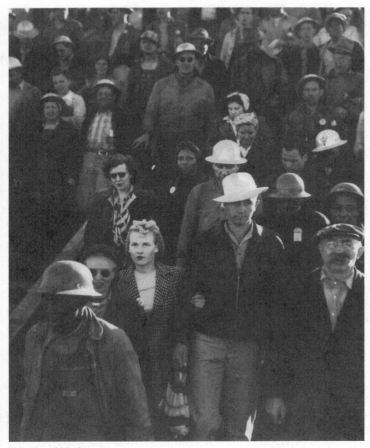

Wartime Workers
The photographer Dorothea Lange captured these shipyard construction workers coming off their shift at a factory in Richmond, California, in 1942. Note the large number of women workers and the presence of minority workers. Several of the workers prominently display their union buttons. (Courtesy of the Dorothea Lange Collection. The City of Oakland. The Oakland Museum, 1982)

When the men came home from war and the nation's plants returned to peacetime operations, Rosie the Riveter was out of a job. But many women refused to put on aprons and stay home. Though women's participation in the labor force dropped temporarily when the war ended, it rebounded steadily for the rest of the 1940s, especially among married women (see Chapter 29).

Wartime mobilization also opened up opportunities to advance the labor movement. By the end of the war almost 15 million workers—a third of the nonagricultural labor force, up from 9 million at the previous decade— belonged to unions. Organized labor responded to the war with an initial burst of patriotic unity. On December 23, 1941, representatives of the major unions made a "no-strike" pledge—though it was nonbinding—for the duration of the war. In January 1942 Roosevelt set up the National War Labor Board (NWLB), composed of representatives of labor, management, and the public. The NWLB established wages, hours, and working conditions, and had the authority to order government seizure of plants that did not comply. Forty plants were seized during the war.

During its tenure the NWLB handled 17,650 disputes affecting 12 million workers. It resolved the controversial issue of union membership through a compromise. Under the principle of maintenance of membership, new hires did not have to join a union, but those who already belonged had to maintain their membership over the life of a contract. Agitation for wage increases caused a more serious disagreement. Because managers wanted to keep production running smoothly and profitably, they were willing to pay higher wages. However, pay raises would conflict with the government's efforts to combat inflation, which drove prices up dramatically in the early war years. In 1942 the NWLB established the "Little Steel Formula," which granted a 15 percent wage increase to match the increase in the cost of living since January 1, 1941, and another 24 percent increase by 1945. Actually, incomes rose as much as 70 percent during the war because workers earned overtime pay, which was not covered by wage ceilings.

Although incomes were higher than anyone could have dreamed during the depression, many union members felt cheated as they watched corporate profits soar in relation to wages. The high point of their dissatisfaction came in 1943, when a nationwide railroad strike was narrowly averted. That year John L. Lewis led more than half a million United Mine Workers out on strike, demanding wages higher than the Little Steel Formula allowed. Though Lewis won concessions, he alienated Congress; and because he had defied the government, he became one of the most disliked public figures of the 1940s.

Congress countered Lewis's action by overriding Roosevelt's veto of the Smith-Connally Labor Act of 1943, which required a thirty-day cooling-off period before a strike, and prohibited entirely strikes in defense industries. Nevertheless, about 15,000 walkouts occurred during the war. Though less than one-tenth of 1 percent of working hours were lost to labor disputes, the public perceived the disruptions to be far more extensive. Thus labor's achievements during the war were mixed. Union membership increased dramatically, from 9 million to almost 15 million workers—a third of the non-agricultural work force. But these gains were accompanied by significant public and congressional hostility that would hamper the labor movement in the postwar years.

Just as labor sought to benefit from the war, African-Americans manifested a new mood of militancy. "A wind is rising throughout the world of free men everywhere," Eleanor Roosevelt wrote during the war, "and they will not be kept in bondage." Black leaders pointed out parallels between anti-Semitism in Germany and racial discrimination in America, and pledged themselves to a

"Double V" campaign: victory over Nazism abroad, and victory over racism and inequality at home.

Even before Pearl Harbor, black activism was on the rise. In 1940 only 240 of the nation's 100,000 aircraft workers were black, and most of them were janitors. Black leaders demanded that the government require defense contractors to integrate their work forces. When the government took no action, A. Philip Randolph, head of the Brotherhood of Sleeping Car Porters, a black union, announced plans for a "March on Washington" in the summer of 1941. Though Roosevelt was not a strong supporter of civil rights, he feared the embarrassment of a massive public protest. Even more, he worried about a disruption of the nation's war preparations.

In June 1941, in exchange for Randolph's cancellation of the march, Roosevelt issued Executive Order 8802, declaring "that there shall be no discrimination in the employment of workers in defense industries or government because of race, creed, color, or national origin." To oversee the policy, he established the Fair Employment Practices Commission (FEPC). Though this federal commitment to minority employment rights was unprecedented, it was limited in scope; for instance, it did not affect segregation in the armed forces. Moreover, the FEPC could not require compliance with its orders, and often found that the needs of defense production took precedence over fair employment practices. The committee resolved only about a third of the more than 8,000 complaints it received.

Encouraged by the ideological climate of the war years, civil rights organizations increased their membership: the NAACP grew ninefold to 450,000 by 1945. In 1942 James Farmer helped to found the Congress of Racial Equality (CORE). Unlike the NAACP, which favored lobbying and legal strategies, CORE used tactics such as demonstrations and sit-ins. In 1944 CORE forced several restaurants in Washington, D.C., to serve blacks after picketing them with signs that read "Are You for Hitler's Way or the American Way? Make Up Your Mind." These wartime developments—both federal intervention and resurgent African-American militancy—laid the groundwork for the civil rights revolution of the 1950s and 1960s.

Politics in Wartime

Although the federal government expanded dramatically during the war years, there was little attempt to use the state to promote social reform on the home front, as in World War I. An enlarged federal presence was justified only insofar as it assisted war aims.

During the early years of the war, Roosevelt rarely pressed for social and economic change, in part because he was preoccupied with the war. But he also faced political realities. The Republicans had picked up 10 seats in the Senate and 47 seats in the House in the 1940 elections, thus bolstering conservatives in Congress who sought to roll back New Deal measures. With little protest, Roosevelt agreed to drop several popular New Deal programs, including the Civilian

Conservation Corps and the National Youth Administration, which were less necessary once war mobilization brought full employment.

Later in the war, however, Roosevelt began to promise new social welfare measures. In his State of the Union address in 1944, he called for a second bill of rights, which would serve as "a new basis of security and prosperity." This extension of the New Deal identified jobs, adequate food and clothing, decent homes, medical care, and education as basic rights. But the president's commitment to them remained largely rhetorical; congressional support for this vast extension of the welfare state did not exist in 1944. Some of those rights did become realities for veterans, however. The Servicemen's Readjustment Act (1944), known as the GI Bill of Rights, provided education, job training, medical care, pensions, and mortgage loans for men and women who had served in the armed forces during the war.

Roosevelt's call for more social legislation was part of a plan to woo Democratic voters. In the 1942 election, Republicans gained seats in both houses of Congress and increased their share of state governorships. The Democrats realized they would have to work hard to maintain the strength of their coalition in 1944. Once again Roosevelt headed the ticket, concluding that the continuation of the war made a fourth term necessary. Democrats, concerned about Roosevelt's health and the need for a successor, dropped Vice-President Henry Wallace, whose outspoken support for labor, civil rights, and domestic reform was too extreme for many party leaders. In his place they chose Senator Harry S Truman of Missouri.

The Republicans nominated Governor Thomas E. Dewey of New York. Only forty-two years old, Dewey had won fame fighting organized crime as a U.S. attorney. He accepted the broad outlines of the welfare state, and was a member of the internationalist wing of the party. The 1944 election was the closest since 1916: Roosevelt received only 53.5 percent of the popular vote. The Democrats lost ground among farmers, but most ethnic groups remained solidly Democratic. The party's margin of victory came from the cities: in urban areas of more than 100,000 people the president drew 60 percent of the vote. A significant segment of this urban support came from organized labor. The CIO's Political Action Committee made substantial contributions to the party, canvassed door to door, and conducted voter registration campaigns—a role organized labor would continue to play after the war.

LIFE ON THE HOME FRONT

Although the United States did not suffer the physical devastation that ravaged much of Europe and the Pacific, the war affected the lives of those who stayed behind. Every time relatives of a loved one overseas saw the Western Union boy on his bicycle, they feared a telegram from the War Department reporting that their son, husband, or father would not be coming home. Other Americans tolerated small deprivations daily. "Don't you know there's a war on?" became the standard reply to any request that could not be fulfilled. People accepted the fact that their lives would be different "for the duration." They also accepted, however grudgingly, the increased role of the federal government in shaping their daily lives.

The War at Home

Just like the soldiers in uniform, people on the home front had a job to do. They worked on civilian defense committees, donated blood, collected old newspapers and scrap material, and served on local rationing and draft boards. About 20 million home "Victory gardens" produced 40 percent of the vegetables grown in the United States. All these endeavors were encouraged by various federal agencies, especially the Office of War Information (OWI), which strove to disseminate information and promote patriotism. Working closely with advertising agencies, the OWI urged them to link their clients' products to the "four freedoms," explaining that patriotic ads would not only sell goods, but would "invigorate, instruct and inspire [the citizen] as a functioning unit in his country's greatest effort."

Popular culture, especially the movies, reinforced the connections between the home front and troops serving overseas. Average weekly movie attendance soared to over 100 million during the war. Demand was so high that many theaters operated around the clock to accommodate defense workers on the swing and night shifts. Many movies, encouraged in part by the OWI, had patriotic themes; stars such as John Wayne, Anthony Quinn, and Spencer Tracy portrayed the heroism of American fighting men in films like *Back to Bataan* (1945), *Guadalcanal Diary* (1943), and *Thirty Seconds over Tokyo* (1945). Other movies, such as *Watch on the Rhine* (1943), warned of the danger of fascism at home and abroad, while the Academy Award–winning *Casablanca* (1943) demonstrated the heroism and patriotism of ordinary citizens. *Since You Went Away* (1943), starring Claudette Colbert as a wife who took a war job after her husband left for war, was one of many films that portrayed struggles on the home front. Newsreels accompanying the feature films kept the public up to date on the war, as did on-the-spot radio broadcasts by commentators such as Edward R. Murrow. Thus popular culture reflected America's new international responsibilities at the same time that it built up morale on the home front.

Perhaps the major source of Americans' high morale was wartime prosperity. Federal defense spending had solved the depression; unemployment had disappeared, and per capita income had risen from $691 in 1939 to $1,515 in 1945. Despite geographical dislocations and shortages of many items, about 70 percent of Americans admitted midway through the war that they had personally experienced "no real sacrifices." A Red Cross worker put it bluntly: "The war was fun for America. I'm not talking about the poor souls who lost sons and daughters. But for the rest of us, the war was a hell of a good time."

For many Americans, the major inconveniences of the war were the limitations placed on their consumption. In contrast to the largely voluntaristic approach used during World War I, federal agencies such as the Office of Price Administration subjected almost everything Americans ate, wore, or used during World War II to rationing or regulation. In response to depleted domestic gasoline supplies and a shortage of rubber, the government restricted the sale of tires, rationed gas, and imposed a nationwide speed limit of 35 miles per hour. By 1943 the amount of meat, butter, sugar, and other foods Americans could buy was also regulated. Most people cooperated with the restrictions and the complicated system of rationing points and coupons, but almost a fourth occasionally bought items on the black market, especially meat, gasoline, and cigarettes.

The war and the government affected not only what people ate, drank, and wore, but where they lived. When men volunteered for or were drafted into the armed services, their families often followed them to training bases or points of debarkation. The lure of high-paying defense jobs encouraged others to move. About 15 million Americans changed residence during the war years, half of them by moving to another state.

As a center of defense production, California was affected by wartime migration more than any other state. The western mecca welcomed nearly 3 million new residents during the war, a 53 percent growth in population. "The Second Gold Rush Hits the West," headlined the *San Francisco Chronicle* in 1943. During the war one-tenth of all federal dollars went to California, and the state turned out one-sixth of the total war production. People went where the defense jobs were—to Los Angeles, San Diego, and the San Francisco Bay area. Some towns grew practically overnight: just two years after the Kaiser Corporation opened a shipyard in Richmond, the population quadrupled.

Migration and relocation often caused strains. In many towns with defense industries, housing was scarce and public transportation inadequate. Conflicts over public space and recreation erupted between old-timers and newcomers. Of special concern were the young people the war had set adrift from traditional community restraints. Newspapers were filled with stories of "latchkey" children who stayed home alone while their mothers worked in defense plants. Adolescents were even more of a problem. Teenage girls who hung around army bases looking for a good time became known as "victory girls." In 1942 and 1943 juvenile delinquency seemed to be reaching epidemic proportions.

Another significant result of the growth of war industries was the migration of more than a million African-Americans to defense centers in California, Illinois, Michigan, Ohio, and Pennsylvania. The migrants' need for jobs and housing led to racial conflict in several cities. Early in 1942 black families encountered resistance and intimidation when they tried to move into the Sojourner Truth housing project, in the Polish community of Hamtramck near Detroit—the new home of a large number of southern migrants, both black and white. In June 1943 similar tensions erupted in Detroit itself, where a major race riot left thirty-four people dead, including twenty-five blacks. Racial conflicts broke out in forty-seven cities across the country during 1943.

Other Americans also experienced racial violence. In Los Angeles male Latinos who belonged to *pachuco* (youth) gangs dressed in "zoot suits"— broad-brimmed felt hats, pegged trousers, and clunky shoes—wore their long hair slicked down, and carried pocket knives on gold chains. The young women they hung out with favored long coats, huarache sandals, and pompadour hairdos. Blacks and some working-class white teenagers in Los Angeles, Detroit, New York, and Philadelphia also wore zoot suits as a symbol of alienation and self-assertion. To adults and to many Anglos, however, the zoot suit symbolized wartime juvenile delinquency.

In Los Angeles, white hostility toward Mexican-Americans had been smoldering for some time, and zoot-suiters soon became the targets. In July 1943 rumors that a *pachuco* gang had beaten a white sailor set off a four-day riot, during which white servicemen entered Mexican-American neighborhoods and attacked zoot-suiters, taking special pleasure in slashing their pegged pants. The attacks occurred in full view of white police officers, who did nothing to stop the violence.

Japanese Internment

Although racial confrontations and zoot-suit riots recalled the widespread racial tensions of World War I, the mood on the home front was generally calm in the 1940s. German culture and German-Americans did not come under suspicion, nor did Italian-Americans. Leftists and communists faced little repression, mainly because, after Pearl Harbor, the Soviet Union became an ally of the United States. The internment of Japanese-Americans on the West Coast was a glaring exception to this record of tolerance—the prejudice and hysteria directed at them was a reminder of the fragility of civil liberties in wartime.

California had a long history of antagonism toward both Japanese and Chinese immigrants (see Chapters 17 and 22). The Japanese-Americans, who clustered together in highly visible communities, were a small, politically impotent minority, numbering only about 112,100 in the three coastal states. Unlike German- and Italian-Americans, the Japanese stood out. "A Jap's a Jap," snapped General John DeWitt; "It makes no difference whether he is an American citizen or not." This sort of sentiment, coupled with fears of the West Coast's vulnerability to attack and the inflammatory rhetoric of newspapers and local politicians, fueled mounting demands that the region be rid of supposed Japanese spies.

In early 1942, in Executive Order 9022, Roosevelt approved a War Department plan to intern Japanese-Americans in relocation camps for the rest of the war. Despite the lack of any evidence of their disloyalty or sedition—no Japanese-American was ever charged with espionage—few public leaders opposed the plan. The announcement shocked Japanese-Americans, more than two-thirds of whom were native-born American citizens. (They were *Nisei*, children of the foreign-born *Issei*.) After being forced to sell their property and possessions at cut-rate prices, Japanese-Americans were rounded up in

Japanese Internment
A Japanese-American family arrives at its new "home" in Heart Mountain, Wyoming, after being relocated from the West Coast military zone. The average internee spent 900 days— more than two and a half years—confined behind the barbed wire, which is not visible in this picture.

temporary assembly centers and sent by the War Relocation Authority to internment camps in California, Arizona, Utah, Colorado, Wyoming, Idaho, and Arkansas—places "where nobody had lived before and no one has lived since," a historian commented.

Almost every Japanese-American in California, Oregon, and Washington was involuntarily detained for some period during World War II. Ironically, the Japanese-Americans who made up one-third of the population of Hawaii, and presumably posed a greater threat because of their numbers and proximity to Japan, were not affected. Less vulnerable to detention because of the islands' multiracial heritage, the Japanese also provided much of the unskilled labor on the islands. The Hawaiian economy simply could not function without them.

Cracks soon appeared in the relocation policy. A labor shortage in farming led the government to furlough seasonal agricultural workers from the camps as early as 1942. About 4,300 young people who had been in college when the relocation order came through were allowed to stay in school if they would transfer out of the West Coast military zone. Another route out of the camps was enlistment in the armed services. The 442d Infantry Combat Team, a segregated unit composed entirely of Nisei volunteers, served in Europe and became one of the most decorated units in the armed forces.

The Supreme Court upheld the constitutionality of internment as a legitimate exercise of power during wartime in *Hirabayashi v. United States* (1943) and in *Korematsu v. United States* (1944). It was not until 1988 that Congress decided to issue a public apology and to give $20,000 in cash to each of the 60,000 surviving internees—small restitution indeed. Though with each generation the memory of internment grows dimmer, this shameful episode has been burned into the national conscience.

FIGHTING AND WINNING THE WAR

World War II, noted the military historian John Keegan, was "the largest single event in human history." Fought on six continents at a cost of 50 million lives, it was far more global than World War I. At least 405,000 Americans were killed and 671,000 wounded in the global fighting—less than half of 1 percent of the U.S. population. In contrast, the Soviets lost as many as 21 million soldiers and civilians during the war, or about 8 percent of their population.

Wartime Aims and Strategies

The Allied coalition was composed mainly of Great Britain, the United States, and the Soviet Union; other nations, notably China and France, played lesser roles. President Franklin Roosevelt, Britain's Prime Minister Winston Churchill, and Premier Joseph Stalin of the Soviet Union took the lead in setting overall strategy. The Atlantic Charter, which Churchill and Roosevelt had drafted in August 1941, formed the basis of the Allies' vision of the postwar international order. But Stalin had not been part of that agreement, a fact that would later cause disagreements over its goals.

One way to wear down the Germans would have been to open a second front on the European continent, preferably in France. The Russians argued strongly for this strategy, because it would draw German troops away from Russian soil. In fact, the issue came up so many times that the Soviet foreign minister, Vyacheslav Molotov, was said to know only four English words: *yes, no,* and *second front.* Though Roosevelt assured Stalin informally that a second front would be opened in 1942, British opposition and the need to raise American war production to full capacity stalled the effort. At a conference in Teheran, Iran, in late November 1943, Churchill and Roosevelt agreed to open a second front within six months in return for Stalin's promise to join the fight against Japan after the war in Europe ended. Both sides kept their promises. However, the long delay in creating a second front meant that for most of the war, the Soviet Union bore the brunt of the land battle against Germany. Roosevelt and Churchill's foot-dragging angered Stalin, who was suspicious about American and British intentions. His mistrust and bitterness carried over into the Cold War that followed the Allied victory.

MAP 27.1

War in Europe

a. 1941–1943 Hitler's Germany reached its greatest extent in 1942, when Nazi forces stalled at Leningrad and Stalingrad. The tide of battle turned in the fall, when the Soviet army launched a massive counterattack at Stalingrad and Allied forces began to drive the Germans from North Africa. In 1943 the Allies invaded Sicily and the Italian mainland.

During the first six months of 1942 the military news was so bad it threatened to swamp the Grand Alliance. The Allies suffered severe defeats on land and sea in both Europe and Asia. German armies pushed deeper into Soviet territory, reaching the outskirts of Moscow and Leningrad. Simultaneously, they began an offensive in North Africa aimed at seizing the Suez Canal. At sea German submarines were crippling American convoys carrying vital supplies to Europe.

The major turning point of the war in Europe occurred in the winter of 1942–1943, when the Soviets halted the German advance in the Battle of Stalingrad. By 1944, Stalin's forces had driven the German army out of the Soviet Union. Meanwhile, the Allies launched a major offensive in North Africa, Churchill's substitute for a second front in France. Between November 1942 and May 1943 Allied troops under the leadership of General Dwight D. Eisenhower and General George S. Patton defeated Germany's crack Afrika Korps, led by General Erwin Rommel.

From Africa the Allied command moved to attack the Axis through what Churchill called its "soft underbelly": Sicily and the Italian peninsula. In July

EUROPEAN THEATER 1944–1945

- Axis Powers
- Axis occupied nations
- Allied Powers
- Neutral nations
- ← Allied advances
- ✳ Major battle

0 —— 500
Miles

b. 1944–1945 On June 6, 1944 (D-Day), the Allies finally invaded France. It would take almost a year for the Allied forces to close in on Berlin—the Soviets from the east and the Americans, British, and French from the west. Germany surrendered on May 8, 1945.

1943 Benito Mussolini's fascist regime fell, and Italy's new government joined the Allies. The Allied forces fought bitter battles against the German army during the Italian campaign, finally entering Rome in June 1944 (see Map 27.1). The last German forces in Italy did not surrender until May 1945, however.

The long-promised invasion of France came on D-Day, June 6, 1944. That morning, after an agonizing delay caused by bad weather, the largest armada ever assembled moved across the English Channel. Over the next few days, under the command of General Dwight Eisenhower, more than 1.5 million American, British, and Canadian soldiers crossed the Channel. In August Allied troops helped to liberate Paris; by September they had driven the Germans out of most of France and Belgium.

The Germans were not yet ready to give up, however. In December 1944 their forces in Belgium mounted an attack that began the Battle of the Bulge, so called because their advance made a large balloon in the Allied line on war maps. After ten days of heavy fighting in what was to be the final German offensive of the war, the Allies regained their momentum and pushed the Germans back across the Rhine River. American and British troops led the drive from the west toward Berlin, while Soviet troops advanced from the east through Poland, arriving there first. On April 30, with

Hitting the Beach at Normandy
These American reinforcements landed on the beach at Normandy two weeks after D-Day,
June 6, 1944. More than a million Allied troops came ashore during the next month. The Allies liberated Paris in August and pushed the retreating Nazi forces behind the German border
by September.

much of Berlin in rubble from intense Allied bombing, Hitler committed
suicide in his bunker. Germany surrendered on May 8, 1945, the date that
became known as V-E (Victory in Europe) Day.

When Allied troops advanced into Germany in the spring of 1945, they
came face to face with Hitler's "final solution of the Jewish question": the extermination camps where 6 million Jews had been put to death, along with
another 6 million Poles, Slavs, Gypsies, homosexuals, and other "undesirables."
Photographs of the Nazi death camps at Buchenwald, Dachau, and
Auschwitz, showing bodies stacked like cordwood and survivors so emaciated
they were barely alive, horrified the American public. But government officials could not claim that no one knew about the camps before the German
surrender. The Roosevelt administration had reliable information about the
death camps as early as November 1942.

The lack of response by the U.S. government to the systematic near annihilation of European Jewry ranks as one of the gravest failures of the Roosevelt administration. So few Jews escaped the Holocaust because the
United States and the rest of the world would not take them in. State Department policies allowed only 21,000 refugees to enter the United States
during the war. The War Refugee Board, established in 1944 with little support from the Roosevelt administration, eventually helped to save about
200,000 Jews.

An Army Nurse in Bataan

*A*rmy Nurse Juanita Redmond recounts her experiences as one of the last nurses *to remain in Bataan in the Philippines as the Japanese advanced. She was evacuated shortly before the Americans surrendered on May 6, 1942. Her description reveals both the horror of warfare and the extraordinary service performed by military nurses.*

[The bomb] landed at the hospital entrance and blew up an ammunition truck that was passing. The concussion threw me to the floor. There was a spattering of shrapnel and pebbles and earth on the tin roof. Then silence for a few minutes.

I heard the corpsmen rushing out with litters, and I pulled myself to my feet. Precious medicines were dripping to the ground from the shattered dressing carts, and I tried to salvage as much as possible.

The first casualties came in. The boys in the ammunition truck had been killed, but the two guards at the hospital gate had jumped into their foxholes. By the time they were extricated from the debris that filled up the holes they were both shell-shock cases.

There were plenty of others. . . .

Only one small section of my ward remained standing. Part of the roof had been blown into the jungle. There were mangled bodies under the ruins; a blood-stained hand stuck up through a pile of scrap; arms and legs had been ripped off and flung among the rubbish. Some of the mangled torsos were almost impossible to identify. One of the few corpsmen who had survived unhurt climbed a tree to bring down a body blown into the top branches. Blankets, mattresses, pajama tops hung in the shattered trees.

We worked wildly to get to the men who might be buried, still alive, under the mass of wreckage, tearing apart the smashed beds to reach the wounded and the dead. These men were our patients, our responsibility; I think we were all tortured by an instinctive, irrational feeling that we had failed them.

SOURCE: Judy Barrett Litoff and David C. Smith, eds., *American Women in a World at War: Contemporary Accounts from World War II* (Wilmington, Delaware: Scholarly Resource Books, 1997), pp. 85–86. Reprinted from Juanita Redmond, *I Served on Bataan* (Philadelphia: J.B. Lippincott, 1943), 106–122.

Several factors combined to inhibit U.S. action: anti-Semitism; fears of economic competition from a flood of refugees to a country just recovering from the depression; the failure of the media to grasp the magnitude of the story and to publicize it accordingly; and the failure of religious leaders, Jews and non-Jews alike, to speak out.

In justifying the American course of action, Roosevelt claimed that winning the war would be the strongest contribution America could make

MAP 27.2
War in the Pacific
a. 1941–1942   After the attack on Pearl Harbor in December 1941 the Japanese rapidly advanced in the Pacific, as far east as the Marshall and Gilbert islands and as far south as the Solomon Islands and parts of New Guinea. Japan also controlled the Philippines, much of Southeast Asia, and parts of China, including Hong Kong. American naval victories at the Coral Sea and Midway stopped further Japanese expansion.

to liberating the camps. But one cannot escape the conclusion that the United States could have done much more to lessen the Holocaust's terrible human toll.

After the victory in Europe, the Allies still had to defeat Japan. American forces bore the brunt of the fighting in the Pacific, just as the Russians had done in the land war in Europe. In the beginning of 1942 the news from the Pacific was uniformly grim. In the wake of Pearl Harbor, Japan had scored quickly with seaborne invasions of Hong Kong, Wake Island, and Guam. Japanese forces soon conquered much of Burma, Malaya, the Philippines, and the Solomon Islands, and began to threaten Australia and India. But on May 7 and 8, 1942, in the Battle of the Coral Sea, near southern New Guinea, American naval forces halted the Japanese offensive against Australia. In June, at the island of Midway, the Americans inflicted crucial damage on the Japanese fleet. With that success, the American military command, led by General Douglas MacArthur and Admiral Chester W. Nimitz, took the offensive in the Pacific. For the next eighteen months American forces advanced arduously *b. 1943–1945* Allied forces retook the islands in the Central Pacific in 1943 and 1944 and the Philippines early in 1945. The capture of Iwo Jima and Okinawa put U.S. bombers in position to attack Japan itself. The Japanese offered to surrender on August 10, after the United States dropped atomic bombs on Hiroshima and Nagasaki.

from one island to the next. In October 1944 the reconquest of the Philippines began with a victory in the Battle of Leyte Gulf, a massive naval encounter in which the Japanese lost practically their entire fleet, while the Americans suffered only minimal losses (see Map 27.2).

By early 1945, victory over Japan was in sight. The campaign in the Pacific moved slowly toward what military leaders anticipated would be a massive and costly invasion of Japan. In some of the fiercest fighting of the war, American marines won the battles for Iwo Jima and Okinawa, where they sustained more than 52,000 casualties, including 13,600 dead. The closer U.S. forces got to the Japanese home islands, the more fiercely the Japanese fought. On Iwo Jima, almost all the 21,000 Japanese died.

By mid-1945 Japan's army, navy, and air force had suffered devastating losses. American bombing of the mainland had killed about 330,000 civilians and crippled the Japanese economy. In a last-ditch effort to stem the tide, Japanese pilots began flying suicidal kamikaze missions, crashing their planes and boats into American ships. This desperate action, combined with the Japanese military leadership's refusal to surrender, suggested to military strategists that Japan would continue to fight despite overwhelming losses. American commanders grimly predicted millions of casualties in the upcoming invasion.

Planning the Postwar World

When Roosevelt, Churchill, and Stalin met in February 1945 at Yalta, a resort on the Black Sea, victory in Europe and the Pacific was in sight, but no agreement had been reached on the peace to come. Roosevelt focused on maintaining Allied unity, the key to postwar peace and stability. The fate of British colonies such as India, where an independence movement had already begun, caused friction between Roosevelt and Churchill. Some of the tensions with the Russians were resolved when, in return for additional possessions in the Pacific, Stalin agreed to enter the war against Japan within three months of the German surrender.

A more serious source of conflict was Stalin's desire for a band of Soviet-controlled satellite states to protect the Soviet Union's western border. With Soviet armies in control of much of Eastern Europe, Stalin had become increasingly inflexible on the issue of Eastern Europe, insisting that he needed friendly (that is, Soviet-dominated) governments there to provide a buffer

The Big Three at Yalta
With victory in Europe at hand, Roosevelt journeyed to Yalta, on the Black Sea, in 1945, to meet one last time with Churchill and Stalin. It was here that they discussed the problems of peace settlements. The Yalta agreement mirrored a new balance of power and set the stage for the Cold War.

zone that would guarantee the Soviet Union's national security. Roosevelt acknowledged the legitimacy of that demand but, with the Atlantic Charter's principle of self-determination in mind, hoped for democratically elected governments in Poland and the neighboring countries. Unfortunately, the two goals proved mutually exclusive.

At Yalta, Roosevelt and Churchill agreed in principle on the idea of a Soviet sphere of influence in Eastern Europe but deliberately left its dimensions vague. Stalin in return pledged to hold "free and unfettered elections" at an unspecified time. (Those elections never took place.) The compromise the three leaders reached at Yalta was open to multiple interpretations. Admiral William D. Leahy, Roosevelt's chief military aide, described the agreement as "so elastic that the Russians can stretch it all the way from Yalta to Washington without ever technically breaking it."

At Yalta the three leaders proceeded with plans to divide Germany into four zones to be controlled by the United States, Great Britain, France, and the Soviet Union. The capital city, Berlin, which lay in the middle of the Soviet zone, would also be partitioned among the four powers. The issue of German reparations remained unsettled.

The Big Three made further progress toward the establishment of an international organization in the form of the United Nations. They agreed that the Security Council of the United Nations would include the five major Allied powers—the United States, Britain, France, China, and the Soviet Union—plus six other nations elected on a rotating basis. They also decided that the permanent members of the Security Council should have veto power over decisions of the General Assembly, in which all nations would be represented. Roosevelt, Churchill, and Stalin announced that the United Nations would convene in San Francisco on April 25, 1945.

Roosevelt returned to the United States in February, visibly exhausted by his 14,000-mile trip. He neglected to inform the American public of the concessions he had made to maintain the increasingly fragile wartime alliance. When he reported to Congress on the Yalta agreements, he made an unusual acknowledgment of his physical infirmity. Referring to the heavy steel braces he wore on his legs, he asked Congress to excuse him for giving his speech while sitting down. The sixty-three-year-old president was a sick man, suffering from heart failure and high blood pressure. On April 12, 1945, during a short visit to his vacation home in Warm Springs, Georgia, Roosevelt suffered a cerebral hemorrhage and died.

When Harry Truman took over the reigns of office, he learned about the top-secret Manhattan Project, charged with developing an atomic bomb. The project, which cost $2 billion and employed 120,000 people, culminated in Los Alamos, New Mexico, where the country's top physicists assembled the first bomb. Not until the first test—at Alamogordo, New Mexico, on July 16, 1945—did scientists know that the bomb would work. A month later Truman ordered the dropping of atomic bombs on two Japanese cities, Hiroshima on August 6 and Nagasaki on August 9.

Hiroshima
This was all that remained of Hiroshima's Museum of Science and Industry on August 6, 1945. The shell of the building later became the center of a memorial to those who died in the atomic blast.

Many later questioned why the United States did not warn Japan about the attack or choose a noncivilian target; the rationale for dropping the second bomb was even less clear. Critics suggested that the fact that the Japanese were a nonwhite race facilitated the momentous decision to use the new, alarming weapon. At the time, however, the belief that Japan's military leaders would never surrender unless their country was utterly devastated convinced policymakers that they had to deploy the atom bomb. One hundred thousand people died at Hiroshima, 60,000 at Nagasaki; tens of thousands more died slowly of radiation poisoning. Japan offered to surrender on August 10, and signed a formal treaty of surrender on September 2, 1945.

Franklin Roosevelt's death and the dropping of the atomic bomb came at a critical juncture in world affairs. Many issues had been left deliberately unresolved, in hopes of keeping the wartime alliance intact through the transition to peace. But as the war ended, issues such as the fates of Poland and Germany demanded action. The resulting compromises, not all of which were fully reported to the American people, tended to promote spheres of influence as the new basis of international power, rather than the ideals of national self-determination and economic cooperation laid out in the Atlantic Charter.

Once the common enemies had been defeated, the wartime alliance became strained and then began to split apart in ways so fundamental that Roosevelt could not likely have kept it together had he lived. Perhaps the greatest legacy of World War II, then, was the Cold War that followed.

CHAPTER 27 TIMELINE

1935	Italy invades Ethiopia
1935– 1937	Neutrality Acts
1936	Rome-Berlin Axis established Japan and Germany sign Anti-Comintern Pact
1937	Japan invades China
1938	Munich agreement
1939	Nazi-Soviet Nonaggression Pact World War II breaks out in Europe
1940	Conscription reinstated
1941	Roosevelt promulgates "four freedoms" Germany invades Soviet Union Lend-Lease Act passed Fair Employment Practices Commission Atlantic Charter Japanese attack on Pearl Harbor
1942	Battles of Coral Sea and Midway Women recruited for war industries Japanese relocation
1942– 1945	Rationing
1943	Race riots in Detroit and Los Angeles Fascism falls in Italy
1944	D-Day GI Bill of Rights
1945	Germany surrenders Battles of Iwo Jima and Okinawa Yalta Conference Harry S Truman becomes president after Roosevelt's death United Nations convenes Atomic bombs dropped on Hiroshima and Nagasaki Japan surrenders

THEMATIC TIMELINE

	DIPLOMACY The Cold War Era— and After	GOVERNMENT Redefining the Role of the State	ECONOMY Rise and Fall of U.S. Economic Dominance	SOCIETY Consumerism, Social Activism, and Diversity
1945	Truman Doctrine (1947) Marshall Plan (1948) NATO founded (1949)	Truman's Fair Deal liberalism Taft-Hartley Act (1947)	Bretton Woods system established; World Bank, IMF, GATT	Urban migration Armed forces desegregated Rise of television
1950	Permanent mobilization: NSC-68 (1950) Korean War (1950–53)	Eisenhower's Modern Republicanism Warren Court activism	Rise of military-industrial complex Service sector expands	*Brown v. Board of Education* (1954) Montgomery bus boycott Growth of suburbia and the baby boom
1960	Cuban missile crisis (1962) Test ban treaty (1963) Vietnam War escalates (1965)	Great Society, War on Poverty Nixon ushers in conservative era	Kennedy-Johnson tax cut, military expenditures fuel economic growth	Shopping malls spread Student activism and youth counter culture Civil Rights Act; Voting Rights Act Revival of feminism
1970	Nixon visits China (1972)	Watergate scandal; Nixon resigns (1974) Deregulation begins under Ford and Carter	Arab oil embargo (1973–74); inflation surges Deindustrialization Income stagnation	*Roe v. Wade* (1973) New Right urges conservative agenda First Earth Day (1970) First personal computer (1977)
1980	Reagan arms buildup INF treaty (1988) Berlin Wall falls	Reagan Revolution Supreme Court conservatism	Reaganomics Budget and trade deficits soar	New Latino and Asian immigration MTV debuts AIDS epidemic
1990	War in the Persian Gulf End of Cold War U.S. peacekeeping forces in Bosnia	Democrats retrench Republican Congress shifts federal government tasks to states	Corporate downsizing NAFTA (1993) Recovery from recession	Health care crisis Information superhighway Affirmative action attacked

PART 6

AMERICA AND THE WORLD
1945 to the Present

In 1945 the United States entered an era of unprecedented international power, challenged only by the Soviet Union. The resulting conflict led to the Cold War. That bipolar struggle, which lasted until the collapse of the Soviet Union in 1991, spawned two "hot" wars, in Korea and Vietnam, fueled a debilitating nuclear arms race, and necessitated the maintenance of a large military establishment.

Government bureaucracy and power swelled in the 1950s and 1960s as Democratic presidents, especially Lyndon Johnson, dramatically expanded federal social programs. At the same time great waves of protest by African-Americans and then women, Latinos, and other groups, brought increased opportunities and progress toward legal equality for all Americans. But in the late 1970s, Republicans mounted a concerted attack on the size and role of government. In the 1980s Ronald Reagan began to whittle away at federal social programs, and in 1996 Congress terminated welfare as a federally guaranteed benefit.

In the quarter century after 1945 the growth of the military-industrial complex and the expansion of consumer culture, combined with economic dominance abroad, translated into unparalleled prosperity at home. Millions of baby-boom families flocked to new suburban developments, where they provided an expanded market for household goods and gadgets—especially television. A heady sense of unlimited progress and affluence lasted until the early 1970s, when slow growth, environmental problems, and foreign competition undermined America's economic supremacy and led to a sense of diminished expectations.

As the "old world order"—U.S. economic dominance and cold war rivalry—came to an end in the 1980s and 1990s, the outline of a "new world order" began to take shape. The United States remains the sole military superpower but shares economic leadership in a new interdependent global system. As Americans face the twenty-first century, grappling with the implications of this change will be their greatest challenge.

CHAPTER 28

COLD WAR AMERICA, 1945–1960

- The Early Cold War
- Harry Truman and the Cold War at Home
- "Modern Republicanism"

When Harry Truman arrived at the White House on April 12, 1945, after Franklin Roosevelt died, he asked the president's widow, "Is there anything I can do for you?" Eleanor Roosevelt responded, "Is there anything we can do for you? For you are the one in trouble now."

Truman inherited the presidency at one of the most perilous times in modern history. Unscathed by bombs and battles on the home front, U.S. industry and agriculture had grown rapidly during World War II. The nation wielded enormous military power as the sole possessor of the atomic bomb. The most powerful country in the world, the United States became a permanent and preeminent force in the international arena. Only the Soviet Union represented an obstacle to American *hegemony*, or dominance, in global affairs. Soon the two superpowers were locked in a Cold War of economic, political, and military rivalry, but no direct engagement on the battlefield.

Soviet-American confrontations during the postwar years had important domestic repercussions. The Cold War boosted military expenditures, fueling a growing arms race. It fostered a climate of fear and suspicion of "subversives" in government, education, and the media, who might undermine American democratic institutions. But the economic benefits of internationalism also gave rise to a period of unprecedented affluence and prosperity during which the United States enjoyed the highest standard of living in the world (see Chapter 29). That prosperity helped to continue and in some cases to expand federal power, perpetuating the New Deal state in the postwar era.

THE EARLY COLD WAR

The defeat of Germany and Japan did not bring stability to the world. Six years of devastating warfare had destroyed prewar governments and geographical boundaries, creating new power relationships that helped to dissolve colonial empires. Even before the war ended, the United States and the Soviet Union were struggling for advantage in those unstable areas; after the war they engaged in a protracted global conflict. Hailed as a battle between communism and capitalism, the Cold War was in reality a more complex power struggle covering a range of economic, strategic, and ideological issues. As each side tried to protect its own national security and way of life, its actions aroused fear in the other, contributing to a cycle of distrust and animosity that would shape U.S.-Soviet relations for decades to come.

Descent into Cold War, 1945–1946

During the war Franklin Roosevelt had worked effectively with Stalin, and had determined to continue his good relations with the Soviet Union in peacetime. In particular, he hoped that the United Nations would provide a forum for resolving postwar conflicts. Avoiding the disagreements that had doomed American membership in the League of Nations after World War I, the Senate approved America's participation in the United Nations in December 1945. Coming eight months after Roosevelt's death, the vote was in part a memorial to the late president's hopes for peace.

Shortly before his death, however, Roosevelt had been disturbed by Soviet actions in Eastern Europe. As the Soviet army drove the Germans out of Russia and back through Eastern Europe, the U.S.S.R. sponsored provisional governments in the occupied countries. At the Yalta Conference in February, both America and Britain had agreed to recognize this Soviet "sphere of influence," with the proviso that "free and unfettered elections" would be held as soon as possible. But in succeeding months the Soviets made no move to hold elections and rebuffed western attempts to reorganize the Soviet-installed governments.

When Truman assumed the presidency after Roosevelt's death, he quickly took a belligerent stance toward the Soviet Union. At a meeting held shortly after he took office, the new president berated the Soviet foreign minister, V. M. Molotov, for not honoring Stalin's agreements on Poland. Truman used what he called "tough methods" that July at the Potsdam Conference, which brought together the United States, Britain, and the Soviet Union. After learning of the successful test of America's atomic bomb, Truman "told the Russians just where they got off and generally bossed the whole meeting," recalled British Prime Minister Winston Churchill. Negotiations on critical postwar issues deadlocked, revealing serious cracks in the Grand Alliance.

The one issue that was tentatively resolved at Potsdam was the fate of occupied Germany. At Yalta the defeated German state had been divided into four zones of occupation, controlled by the United States, France, Britain, and the Soviet Union. At Potsdam the Allies agreed to disarm the country, dismantle its military production facilities, and permit the occupying powers to extract reparations from the zones they controlled. Plans for future reunification stalled, however, as the United States and the Soviet Union each worried that a united Germany would fall into the other's sphere.

In both Germany and Eastern Europe, Americans and Soviets based their actions on different perspectives on the past. Since the Soviet Union had been a victim of German aggression in both world wars, Stalin was determined to prevent the rebuilding and rearming of its traditional foe; for further protection from possible invasion, he insisted on a security zone of friendly governments in Eastern Europe. Accordingly, between 1945 and 1947 the Soviets repressed democratic parties and installed puppet governments in Poland, Hungary, Rumania, and Bulgaria. Truman, recalling Britain's disastrous appeasement of Hitler in 1938, decided that the United States had to take a hard line against Soviet expansion. "There isn't any difference in totalitarian states," he said, "Nazi, Communist, or Fascist."

As tensions over Europe divided the former allies, hopes of international cooperation in the control of atomic weapons faded as well. In the Baruch Plan, submitted to the United Nations in 1946, the United States proposed a system of international control that relied on mandatory inspection and supervision but preserved the American nuclear monopoly. The Soviets rejected the plan categorically, and worked assiduously to complete their own bomb. Meanwhile, the Truman administration pursued plans to develop nuclear energy and weapons further. Thus the failure of the Baruch Plan signaled the beginning of a frenzied nuclear arms race between the two superpowers.

Containment

As tensions mounted between the superpowers, the United States increasingly perceived Soviet expansionism as a threat to its own interests, and a new American policy, called containment, began to take shape. The most articulate and influential expression of the policy came in February 1946 from George F. Kennan. In an 8,000-word cable from his post at the U.S. Embassy in Moscow to his superiors in Washington, Kennan, who was identified only as "X," warned that the U.S.S.R. was moving "inexorably along the prescribed path, like a persistent toy automobile wound up and headed in a given direction, stopping only when it meets unanswerable force." To stop Soviet expansionism, Kennan argued, the United States should pursue a policy of "firm containment . . . at every point where [the Russians] show signs of encroaching upon the interests of a peaceful and stable world."

The emerging policy of containment crystallized in 1947 over a crisis in Greece. In the spring of 1946, several thousand local communist guerrillas, whom American advisers mistakenly believed were taking orders from Moscow, launched a full-scale civil war against the government and the British occupation authorities. In February 1947 the British informed Truman that they could no longer afford to assist anticommunists in Greece. American pol-icymakers worried that Soviet influence in Greece threatened American and European interests in the eastern Mediterranean and the Middle East, espe-cially in strategically located Turkey and the oil-rich state of Iran.

In response, the president announced what would be known as the Tru-man Doctrine. In a speech to Congress on March 12, he requested large-scale military and economic assistance to Greece and Turkey. If Greece fell to com-munism, Truman warned, the effects would be serious not only for Turkey but for the entire Middle East. This notion of an escalating communist contagion was an early version of what Dwight Eisenhower would later call the "domino theory." Not just Greece but freedom itself was at issue, Truman declared: "If we falter in our leadership, we may endanger the peace of the world—and we shall surely endanger the welfare of our own nation." Despite the open-endedness of this military commitment, Congress quickly approved Truman's request for $300 million in aid to Greece and $100 million for Turkey. The ap-propriation reversed the postwar trend toward sharp cuts in foreign spending, and marked a new level of commitment to the emerging Cold War.

During this period Secretary of State George Marshall proposed a plan to provide economic as well as military aid to Europe. In June 1947, Marshall urged the nations of Europe to work out a comprehensive recovery program and then ask the United States for aid. In Truman's words, the Marshall Plan was "the other half of the walnut" (the first half being the aggressive containment of communism). By bolstering European economies devastated by war, Marshall and Truman believed, the United States could forestall severe economic disloca-tion, which might give rise to communism. American economic self-interest was also a contributing factor; the legislation required that foreign-aid dollars be spent on U.S. goods and services. A revitalized Europe centered on a strong West German economy would provide a better market for U.S. goods.

Within Congress, however, there was significant opposition to Truman's pledge of economic aid to European economies. Republicans castigated the Marshall Plan as a huge "international W.P.A." and a "bold Socialist blue-print." But in the midst of the congressional stalemate, on February 25, 1948, came a Communist coup in Czechoslovakia. A stark reminder of the menace of Soviet expansion in Europe, the coup served to rally congressional support for the Marshall Plan. In March 1948 Congress voted overwhelmingly to ap-prove funds for the program. Like most other foreign policy initiatives of the 1940s and 1950s, the Marshall Plan won bipartisan support despite the oppo-sition of an isolationist wing of the Republican party.

Over the next four years the United States contributed nearly $13 billion to a highly successful recovery effort. Western European economies revived, and industrial production increased 64 percent, opening new opportunities for international trade. The Marshall Plan did not specifically exclude Eastern Europe or the Soviet Union, but it required that all participating nations ex-change economic information and work toward the elimination of tariffs and other trade barriers. Soviet leaders denounced those conditions as attempts to

The Marshall Plan in Action
Between 1948 and 1951 the European Recovery Program, popularly
known as the Marshall Plan after Secretary of State George C. Marshall,
contributed over $13 billion toward its objective of "restoring the confi-
dence of the European people in the economic future of their own countries and of Europe as a whole." Here a sign prominently announces that
Berlin is being rebuilt with help from the Marshall Plan.

draw Eastern Europe into the American orbit, and forbade the satellite states
of Czechoslovakia, Poland, and Hungary to participate.

The Marshall Plan accelerated American and European efforts to rebuild
and reunify the West German economy. In June 1948, after agreeing to fuse
their zones of occupation, the United States, France, and Britain initiated a
program of currency reform in West Berlin. The economic revitalization of
Berlin, located deep within the Soviet zone of occupation, alarmed Soviet policymakers, who feared a resurgent Germany aligned with the West. To forestall
that development, the Soviet Union imposed a blockade on all highway, rail,
and river traffic to West Berlin. Truman responded with an airlift: for nearly a
year American and British pilots, who had been dropping bombs on Berlin
only four years earlier, flew in 2.5 million tons of food and fuel—nearly a ton

for each resident. On May 12, 1949, Stalin lifted the blockade, which had made West Berlin a symbol of resistance to communism.

The coup in Czechoslovakia and the crisis in Berlin convinced U.S. policymakers of the need for a collective security pact. In April 1949, for the first time since the American Revolution, the United States entered into a peacetime military alliance, the North Atlantic Treaty Organization (NATO). To back up America's new stance, Truman asked Congress for $1.3 billion in military assistance to NATO, and authorized the basing of four U.S. army divisions in Western Europe. Under the NATO pact, twelve nations—the United States, Canada, Britain, France, Italy, Belgium, the Netherlands, Luxembourg, Denmark, Norway, Portugal, and Iceland—agreed that "an armed attack against one or more of them in Europe or North America shall be considered an attack against them all." In May 1949 those nations also agreed to the creation of the Federal Republic of Germany (West Germany), which joined NATO in 1955 (see Map 28.1).

MAP 28.1

Cold War Europe, 1955

In 1949 the United States sponsored the creation of the North Atlantic Treaty Organization, an alliance of ten European nations, the United States, and Canada. West Germany was formally admitted to NATO in May 1955. A few days later the Soviet Union and seven other communist nations established a rival alliance, the Warsaw Pact.

In October 1949, in response to the creation of NATO, the Soviet Union tightened its grip on Eastern Europe by creating a separate government for East Germany, which became the German Democratic Republic. The Soviets also organized an economic association, the Council for Mutual Economic Assistance (COMECON) in 1949, and a military alliance for Eastern Europe, the Warsaw Pact, in 1955. The postwar division of Europe was nearly complete.

New impetus for the policy of containment came in September 1949, when American military intelligence detected a rise in radioactivity in the atmosphere—proof that the Soviet Union had set off an atomic bomb. The American atomic monopoly, which some military and political advisers had argued would last for decades, had ended in just four years, forcing a major reassessment of the nation's foreign policy.

To devise a new diplomatic and military blueprint, Truman turned to the National Security Council (NSC), an advisory body established in 1947 to set defense and military priorities. In April 1950 the NSC delivered its report, known as NSC-68, to the president. Filled with alarmist rhetoric and exaggerated assessments of Soviet capabilities, the document made several specific recommendations, including the development of a hydrogen bomb, an advanced weapon a thousand times more destructive than the atomic bombs that had destroyed Hiroshima and Nagasaki. (The United States would explode its first hydrogen bomb in November 1952; the Soviet Union its first in 1953.) NSC-68 also supported increases in U.S. conventional forces and the establishment of a strong system of alliances. Most important, it called for increased taxes to finance "a bold and massive program of rebuilding the West's defensive potential to surpass that of the Soviet world."

Though Truman was an aggressive anticommunist, he was reluctant to commit to a major defense buildup, fearing that it would overburden the budget. But the Korean War, which began just two months after NSC-68 was completed, helped to transform the report's recommendations into reality as the Cold War became a hot war.

Containment in Asia

As mutual suspicion deepened between the United States and the Soviet Union, cold war doctrines began to influence the American position in Asia as well. American policy there was based on Asia's importance to the world economy as much as on the desire to contain communism. At first, American plans for the region centered on a revitalized China, but political instability there prompted the Truman administration to focus on developing the Japanese economy instead. After dismantling Japan's military forces and weaponry, American occupation forces under General Douglas MacArthur began the job of transforming the country into a bulwark of Asian capitalism. MacArthur drafted a democratic constitution and oversaw the rebuilding of the economy, paving the way for the restoration of Japanese sovereignty in 1951.

In China the situation was more precarious. Since the 1930s a civil war had been raging, as communist forces led by Mao Zedong (Mao Tse-tung) and Zhou Enlai (Chou En-lai) contended for power with conservative Nationalist forces under Jiang Jieshi (Chiang Kai-shek). Although dissatisfied with the corrupt and inefficient Jiang regime, officials for the Truman administration did not see Mao as a good alternative, and they resigned themselves to working with the Nationalists. Between 1945 and 1949 the United States provided more than $2 billion to Jiang's forces, but to no avail. In 1947 General Albert Wedemeyer, who had tried to work with Jiang, reported to President Truman that, until the "corrupt, reactionary, and inefficient Chinese National government" undertook "drastic political and economic reforms," the United States could not accomplish its purpose. In August 1949, when those reforms did not occur, the Truman administration cut off aid to the Nationalists, sealing their fate. The People's Republic of China was formally established on October 1, 1949, and what was left of Jiang's government fled to Taiwan.

Many Americans viewed Mao's success as a defeat for the United States. A pro-Nationalist "China lobby," supported by the powerful publisher Henry R. Luce and by Republican senators Karl Mundt of South Dakota and William S. Knowland of California, protested that under Truman's newly appointed secretary of state, Dean Acheson, the State department was responsible for the "loss of China." The China lobby's influence led to the United States's refusal to recognize what it called "Red China"; instead, the nation recognized the exiled Nationalist government in Taiwan. The United States also used its influence to block China's admission to the United Nations. For almost twenty years, U.S. administrations treated mainland China, the world's most populous country, as a diplomatic nonentity.

In Korea as in China, the seeds of cold war confrontation grew out of World War II. Both the United States and the Soviet Union had troops in Korea at the end of the war. As a result, Korea was divided at the 38th parallel into competing spheres of influence. The Soviets supported a communist government, led by Kim Il Sung, in North Korea; the United States backed a longtime Korean nationalist, Syngman Rhee, in South Korea. Soon sporadic fighting broke out along the 38th parallel, and a civil war began.

On June 25, 1950, the North Koreans launched a surprise attack across the 38th parallel (see Map 28.2, following page). The initiative for Korean reunification came from Kim Il Sung, but Stalin approved of and supported the mission (although the extent of Soviet involvement was unknown at the time). Soviet and North Korean leaders may have expected Truman to ignore this armed challenge, but the president felt that the United States must take a firm stance against the spread of communism. "There's no telling what they'll do if we don't put up a fight now," he said. Truman immediately asked the United Nations Security Council to authorize a "police action" against the invaders. Because the Soviet Union was temporarily boycotting the Security Council to protest the exclusion of the People's Republic of China from the U.N., it could not veto Truman's

MAP 28.2

The Korean War, 1950–1953
From June to September 1950
North Korean troops overran most
of the territory south of the 38th
parallel. On September 15, U.N.
forces counterattacked behind
enemy lines at Inchon and pushed
north almost to the Chinese border.
Massive Chinese intervention
forced the U.N. troops to retreat to
the 38th parallel in January 1951,
and the war was at a stalemate for
the next two years.

request. Three days after the Security Council voted to send a peacekeeping
force, Truman ordered U.S. troops to Korea.

Though fourteen other non-Communist nations sent troops, the rapidly
assembled United Nations army in Korea was overwhelmingly American. At
the request of the Security Council, President Truman named General Douglas MacArthur to head the U.N. forces. At first the North Koreans held an
overwhelming advantage, controlling practically the entire peninsula except
for the area around Pusan. But, on September 15, 1950, MacArthur launched
a surprise amphibious attack at Inchon, far behind the North Korean front
line, while U.N. forces staged a breakout from Pusan. Within two weeks the
U.N. forces controlled Seoul, the South Korean capital, and almost all the territory up to the 38th parallel.

Encouraged by this success, MacArthur sought the authority to lead his
forces across the 38th parallel and into North Korea. Truman's initial plan had
been to restore the 1945 border, but he managed to win U.N. support for the
broader goal of creating "a unified, independent and democratic Korea."
Though the Chinese government in Beijing warned repeatedly that such a
move would provoke retaliation, American officials did not heed the warnings.
MacArthur's troops crossed the 38th parallel on October 9, reaching the Chinese border at the Yalu River by the end of the month. Just after Thanksgiving,

a massive Chinese counterattack of almost 300,000 troops forced MacArthur to retreat to the 38th parallel. Then, on January 4, 1951, Communist troops reoccupied Seoul.

Two months later American forces and their allies counterattacked, regained Seoul, and pushed back to the 38th parallel. Then stalemate set in. Public support in the United States had dropped after Chinese intervention increased the likelihood of a long war. A poll revealed in early January 1951 that 66 percent of Americans thought the United States should withdraw; 49 percent felt intervening in the war had been a mistake. Given those domestic constraints and the stalemate in Korea, Truman and his advisers decided to work for a negotiated peace. They did not want to tie down large numbers of U.S. troops in Asia, far from what were considered more strategically important trouble spots in Europe and the Middle East.

MacArthur disagreed. Headstrong, arrogant, and brilliant, the general fervently believed that the nation's future lay in Asia, not Europe. Disregarding Truman's instructions, MacArthur traveled to Taiwan and urged the Nationalists to join in an attack on mainland China. He pleaded for permission to use the atomic bomb against China. In an inflammatory letter to the House minority leader, Republican Joseph J. Martin of Massachusetts, he denounced the Korean stalemate. "We must win"—MacArthur declared—"There is no substitute for victory."

Martin released MacArthur's letter on April 6, 1951, as part of a concerted Republican campaign to challenge Truman's conduct of the war. This strategy backfired. On April 11 Truman relieved MacArthur of his command in Korea and Japan, accusing him of insubordination—a decision the Joint Chiefs of Staff supported. Truman's decision was nonetheless highly unpopular. The allure of decisive victory under a charismatic military leader temporarily silenced the public's doubts about the war. Returning to tumultuous receptions in San Francisco, Chicago, and New York, the general delivered an impassioned address to a joint session of Congress. But when the shouting died down, Truman had the last word. After failing to get the Republican presidential nomination in 1952, MacArthur faded from public view.

The war dragged on for more than two years after MacArthur's dismissal. Truce talks began in Korea in July 1951, but a final armistice was not signed until July 1953. Approximately 45 percent of American casualties were sustained during this period. The final settlement left Korea divided very near the original border at the 38th parallel, with a demilitarized zone between the two countries. North Korea remained firmly allied with the Soviet Union; South Korea signed a mutual defense treaty with the United States in 1954.

The Korean War had a lasting impact on the conduct of American foreign policy. Truman had committed troops to Korea without congressional approval, arguing that he had the power to do so as commander in chief of the armed forces, and as executor of the treaty binding the United States to the United Nations. His act expanded executive power and set a precedent for other undeclared wars. The Korean War also widened American involvement in Asia, transforming containment into a truly global policy. During and after the war the United States stationed large numbers of troops in South Korea, and increased military aid to the Nationalist Chinese forces in Taiwan and to French forces fighting communist insurgents in Indochina (see Chapter 31). American foreign policy had become more global, more militarized, and more costly. Even in times of peace, the United States functioned in a state of permanent mobilization.

HARRY TRUMAN AND THE COLD WAR AT HOME

Harry S Truman brought a complex personality to the presidency. Alternately humble and cocky, he had none of Roosevelt's patrician ease, and was a distinctly unpopular president. Yet he handled affairs with an assurance and a crisp dispatch that have endeared him to later generations. "If you can't stand the heat, stay out of the kitchen," he liked to say of presidential responsibility. The major domestic issues he faced were reconversion to a peacetime economy and fears of communist infiltration and subversion—fears his administration played a part in perpetuating.

Truman Confronts Domestic Challenges

The public's main fear in 1945, that the depression would return once war production had ended, proved unfounded. Despite a drop in government spending after the war, consumer spending increased; workers had amassed substantial wartime savings and were eager to spend them. The Servicemen's Readjustment Act of 1944, popularly known as the GI Bill, also put money into the economy by providing educational and economic assistance to returning veterans. Despite some temporary dislocations as war production shifted back to civilian production and veterans entered the work force, unemployment did not soar.

But the transition was hardly troublefree. The main domestic problem was inflation. Consumers wanted to end wartime restrictions and price rationing, but Truman feared economic chaos if he lifted all controls immediately. In the summer of 1945 he eased industrial controls but retained the wartime Office of Price Administration (OPA). When he disbanded the OPA and lifted almost all the remaining controls in the following year, prices soared, producing an annual inflation rate of 18.2 percent. Rising prices and the persistence of food and other shortages irritated consumers.

The rapidly rising cost of living prompted demands for higher wages by the nation's workers. Under government-sanctioned agreements the labor movement had held the line on salary increases during the war. But after the war ended, union leaders expressed frustration. Corporate profits had doubled while real wages had declined as a result of inflation and the loss of overtime pay. Determined to make up for their war-induced sacrifices, workers mounted crippling strikes in the automobile, steel, and coal industries. General strikes

Helen Gahagan Douglas
Representative Helen Gahagan Douglas of California, a former Broadway
and film star, illustrated a 1947 speech supporting the reestablishment of
price controls by bringing a shopping basket of food to a press conference.
Douglas served in Congress from 1944 until 1950, when she was defeated in
a bid for the Senate by Representative Richard M. Nixon. In their bitterly
fought campaign Nixon linked her with communism by calling her pink.

effectively closed down business in more than a half dozen cities in 1946. By
the end of that year, 5 million workers had idled factories and mines for a total
of 107,476,000 workdays.

Truman responded dramatically. In the face of a devastating railway strike,
he used his executive authority to place the nation's railroad system under federal control, and asked Congress for the power to draft striking workers into
the army—a move that infuriated labor leaders, but pressured strikers to go
back to work. Three days later he seized control of the nation's coal mines to
end a strike by the United Mine Workers. Such actions won Truman support
from many Americans, but incurred the enmity of organized labor, an important partner in the Democratic coalition.

These domestic upheavals did not bode well for the Democrats at the
polls. In 1946 the Republicans gained control of both houses of Congress
and set about undoing New Deal social welfare measures, singling out labor
legislation as a special target. In 1947 Congress passed the Taft-Hartley Act,
a rollback of several provisions of the National Labor Relations Act, passed

in 1935. Unions especially disliked Section 14b of Taft-Hartley, which outlawed the closed shop and allowed states to pass "right-to-work" laws that
further limited unions' operations. The act also restricted unions' political
power by prohibiting use of their dues for political activity, and allowed the
president to declare an eighty-day cooling-off period in strikes that had a
national impact. Truman issued a ringing veto of the Taft-Hartley bill in
June 1947, calling it "bad for labor, bad for management, and bad for the
country." Congress easily overrode the veto, but Truman's actions countered
some of workers' hostility to his earlier antistrike activity, and kept labor in
the Democratic fold.

Most observers believed that Truman faced an impossible task in the presidential campaign of 1948. The Republicans were united, and with Thomas E.
Dewey, the politically moderate governor of New York, as their candidate
once again, they had a good chance of attracting traditional Democratic voters
(Chapter 27). To increase their appeal in the West, the Republicans nominated
Earl Warren, governor of California, for vice-president. In their platform they
promised to continue most New Deal reforms and to support a bipartisan foreign policy.

Truman, in contrast, led a party in disarray. Both the left and the right
wings of the Democratic party split off and nominated their own candidates.
Henry A. Wallace, a former New Deal liberal whom Truman had fired as secretary of commerce in 1946 because he was perceived as too "soft" on communism, ran as the candidate of the new Progressive party. Wallace advocated
increased government intervention in the economy, more power for labor
unions, and cooperation with the Soviet Union.

The other challenge to the party came from the South. At the Democratic
national convention, northern liberals such as Mayor Hubert H. Humphrey of
Minneapolis had pushed through a platform calling for the repeal of the Taft-
Hartley Act and increased federal commitment to civil rights. Southern Democrats, unwilling to tolerate federal interference in race relations, bolted the
convention and created the States' Rights party, popularly known as the Dixiecrats. They nominated Governor J. Strom Thurmond of South Carolina for
president.

Truman responded to these challenges with one of the most effective presidential campaigns ever waged. He launched a strenuous cross-country speaking tour in which he hammered away at the Republicans' support for the
antilabor Taft-Hartley Act. He also criticized Republicans for opposing legislation for housing, medical insurance, and civil rights. By combining these issues with attacks on the Soviet menace abroad, Truman began to salvage his
troubled campaign. At his rallies enthusiastic listeners shouted, "Give 'em hell,
Harry!"

Truman won a remarkable victory, receiving 49.6 percent of the vote to
Dewey's 45.1 percent. The Democrats also regained control of both houses of
Congress. Strom Thurmond carried only four southern states, and Henry Wal-
lace failed to win any electoral votes. Truman retained the support of organized

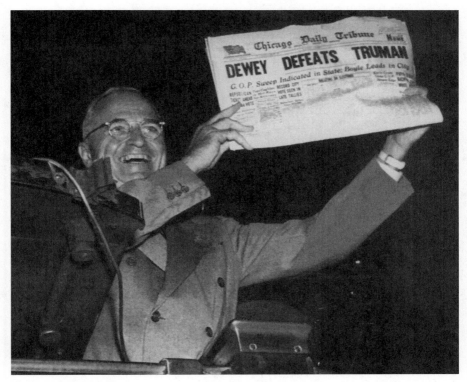

Truman Triumphant
In one of the most famous photographs in American political history, Harry S Truman gloats over an inaccurate headline in the *Chicago Tribune*. Pollsters had predicted an overwhelming victory for Thomas E. Dewey. Their primitive techniques, however, did not reflect the dramatic surge in support for Truman during the last days of the campaign.

labor. Jewish and Catholic voters in the big cities, and black voters in the North, offset his losses to the Dixiecrats. Most important, Truman appealed effectively to people like himself from the farms, towns, and small cities in the nation's heartland.

Fair Deal Liberalism

Shortly after becoming president, Truman had proposed to Congress a twenty-one-point plan for expanded federal programs based on individual "rights," including the right to a "useful and remunerative" job, controls over monopolies, good housing, "adequate medical care," "protection from the economic fears of old age," and a "good education." Later, Truman added support for civil rights and called his program the Fair Deal. Although to some extent the Fair Deal represented an extension of the New Deal's liberalism—with its faith in the positive influence of government and the use of federal power to ensure pubic welfare—it also took some new directions. Its attention to civil rights reflected the growing importance of African-Americans to the Democratic party's coalition of urban voters. And the desire to extend a high standard of living and other benefits of capitalism to an ever-greater number of citizens reflected a new liberal vision of the role of the state. Rather than rely upon extensive federal regulation of corporations and intrusive planning of the economy, as many Progressive Era and New Deal reformers had proposed, the liberals of Truman's era were more moderate. They believed that the essential role of the federal government was to manage the economy indirectly through fiscal policy. Drawing upon the Keynesian notion of using government spending to spur economic growth, they expected that welfare programs not only would provide a safety net for disadvantaged citizens but also would maintain consumer purchasing power, keeping the economy healthy.

Truman's agenda met a generally hostile Congress, despite the Democratic majority. The same conservative coalition that had blocked Roosevelt's initiatives in his second term and dismantled or cut popular New Deal programs during wartime continued to fight against Truman's proposals. Only parts of the Fair Deal won adoption: the minimum wage was raised; the Social Security program was extended to cover 10 million new workers; and Social Security benefits were increased by 75 percent. The National Housing Act of 1949 called for the construction of 810,000 units of low-income housing, but only half that number were actually built.

Interest groups successfully opposed other key items in the Fair Deal. The American Medical Association (AMA) quashed a labor-backed movement for national health insurance by denouncing it as the first step toward "socialized medicine." Catholics successfully opposed aid to education because it did not include subsidies for parochial schools. Trade associations, the National Association of Manufacturers, and other business groups also actively opposed what they called "creeping socialism." Though most corporate leaders recognized that some state involvement in the economy was necessary and even beneficial to business interests, the Fair Deal went too far, in their opinion. As a lobbyist for the National Association of Real Estate Boards explained, "In our country we prefer that government activity shall take the form of assisting and aiding private business rather than undertake great public projects of a governmental character." Through extensive lobbying and public relations campaigns, business groups agitated not only to defeat specific pieces of Fair Deal legislation but also to forestall increased taxes, antitrust activity, and other unwanted federal interference in corporate affairs. Their activities helped to block the Truman administration's efforts to mobilize popular and congressional support for dramatically enlarged federal responsibilities for economic and social welfare.

Truman's record on civil rights illustrates still other obstacles that faced the Fair Deal. Black demands for justice, which had accelerated during World War II (see Chapter 27), continued into the postwar years, spurred by symbolic victories such as Jackie Robinson's breaking through the color line in major league baseball by joining the Brooklyn Dodgers in 1947. Truman offered some support for civil rights, in part because of his desire to solidify the Democrats' hold on African-American voters as they migrated from the South, where they were effectively disfranchised, to northern and western cities. Truman was also concerned about America's image abroad, especially since the Soviet Union often compared the segregation of southern blacks with the Nazis' treatment of the Jews.

Lacking a popular mandate on the civil rights issue, Truman turned to executive action. In 1946 he appointed a National Civil Rights Commission, which in its 1947 report called for an expanded federal role in civil rights that foreshadowed much of the civil rights legislation of the 1960s. He ordered the Justice department to prepare an amicus curiae ("friend of the court") brief in the Supreme Court case of *Shelley v. Kraemer* (1948), which struck down as unconstitutional restrictive covenants that enforced residential segregation by barring home buyers of a certain race or religion. In the same year Truman signed an executive order to desegregate the armed forces. The Truman administration also proposed a federal antilynching law, federal protection of voting rights (such as an end to poll taxes), and a permanent federal agency to guarantee equal employment opportunity. A filibuster by southern conservatives blocked the legislation in Congress, however.

The outbreak of the Korean War in 1950 limited the chances of the Fair Deal being passed by diverting national attention and federal funds from domestic affairs. So did the nation's growing paranoia concerning internal subversion, the most dramatic manifestation of the Cold War's effect on American life.

The Great Fear

As American relations with the Soviet Union deteriorated, fear of communism at home fueled a widespread campaign of domestic repression. Americans often call this phenomenon McCarthyism, after Senator Joseph R. McCarthy of Wisconsin, the decade's most vocal anticommunist, but more was involved than the work of just one man. The Great Fear built on the longstanding distrust of radicals and foreigners that had exploded in the Red Scare after World War I. Worsening cold war tensions intersected with those deep-seated anxieties and with partisan politics to spawn an obsessive concern with internal subversion. Ultimately, however, few Communists were found in positions of power; far more Americans became innocent victims of false accusations and innuendos.

The roots of postwar anticommunism date back to 1938, when Congressman Martin Dies of Texas and other conservatives launched the House Committee on Un-American Activities (HUAC) to investigate alleged fascist and Communist influence in labor unions and New Deal agencies. HUAC gained heightened visibility after the war, especially after revelations in 1946 of a Soviet spy ring operating in Canada and the United States accentuated fears of Soviet subversion.

Standing up to HUAC

HUAC not only asked people about their own alleged subversive activity, but compelled them to "name names," to expose friends or colleagues with links to the Communist party or other organizations the Committee deemed disloyal. Playwright Lillian Hellman was one of a small number who refused. She explains why in a letter to HUAC in May 1952.

I am most willing to answer all questions about myself. I have nothing to hide from your Committee and there is nothing in my life of which I am ashamed. I have been advised by counsel that under the Fifth Amendment I have a constitutional privilege to decline to answer any questions about my political opinions, activities and associations, on the grounds of self-incrimination. I do not wish to claim this privilege. I am ready and willing to testify before the representatives of our Government as to my own opinions and my own actions, regardless of any risks or consequences to myself. . . .

I am not willing, now or in the future, to bring bad trouble to people who, in my past association with them, were completely innocent of any talk or any action that was disloyal or subversive. I do not like subversion or disloyalty in any form and if I had ever seen any I would have considered it my duty to have reported it to the proper authorities. But to hurt innocent people whom I knew many years ago in order to save myself is, to me, inhuman and indecent and dishonorable. I cannot and will not cut my conscience to fit this year's fashions, even though I long ago came to the conclusion that I was not a political person and could have no comfortable place in any political group.

SOURCE: Lillian Hellman, *Scoundrel Time* (Boston: Little, Brown, 1976), pp. 92–94.

In 1947 HUAC helped launch the Great Fear by holding widely publicized hearings on alleged Communist infiltration in the film industry. A group of writers and directors, soon dubbed the Hollywood Ten, went to jail for contempt of Congress when they cited the First Amendment in refusing to testify about their past associations. Hundreds of other actors, directors, and writers whose names had been mentioned in the HUAC investigation, or whose associates and friends the committee had labeled as "reds," were unable to get work, victims of an unacknowledged but very real blacklist honored by industry executives. HUAC also investigated playwrights, authors, university professors, labor activists, organizations, and government officials thought to be "left wing."

Although HUAC bore much of the responsibility for spawning the witch hunt, its effects spread far beyond the congressional committee. In March 1947 President Truman issued an executive order initiating a comprehensive investigation into the loyalty of federal employees. Following

Washington's lead, many state and local governments, universities, political organizations, churches, and businesses undertook their own antisubversion campaigns, including the requirement that employees take loyalty oaths. In the labor movement, which Communists had been active in organizing in the 1930s, charges that Soviet-led Communists were taking over American unions led to a purge of Communist members. Civil rights organizations such as the NAACP and the National Urban League also purged themselves of Communists or "fellow travelers." Thus the Great Fear was particularly devastating to the political left; accusations of guilt by association affected progressives of all stripes.

The anticommunist crusade intensified in 1948 when HUAC began an investigation of Alger Hiss, a former New Dealer and a State department official who had accompanied Franklin Roosevelt to Yalta. A former Communist, Whittaker Chambers, claimed that Hiss was a member of a secret Communist cell operating within the government and had passed him classified documents in the 1930s. Hiss categorically denied the allegations, and denied even knowing Chambers. HUAC's investigation was orchestrated by Republican Congressman Richard M. Nixon of California. Because the statute of limitations on the crime Hiss was accused of had expired, Hiss was charged instead with perjury, for lying about his Communist affiliations and acquaintance with Chambers. In early 1950 Hiss was found guilty and sentenced to five years in federal prison. Even after his death in 1996, the media continued to debate the question of his guilt or innocence.

The conviction of Hiss fueled the paranoia about a Communist conspiracy in the federal government, contributing to the meteoric rise of Senator Joseph McCarthy of Wisconsin. In February 1950, McCarthy delivered a bombshell during a speech in Wheeling, West Virginia: "I have here in my hand a list of the names of 205 men that were known to the Secretary of State as being members of the Communist Party and who nevertheless are still working and shaping the policy of the State Department."

For the next four years McCarthy became the central figure in a virulent campaign of anticommunism. Like other Republicans in the late 1940s, McCarthy leveled accusations of Communist subversion in the government to embarrass President Truman and the Democratic party. Critics who disagreed with him exposed themselves to charges of being "soft" on communism. Because McCarthy charged that his critics were themselves part of "this conspiracy so immense," few political leaders challenged him. Truman called McCarthy's charges "slander, lies, character assassination," but could do nothing to curb them. When the Republican Dwight D. Eisenhower was elected president in 1952, he refrained from publicly challenging his party's most outspoken senator.

Despite McCarthy's failure to identify a single Communist in government, a series of national and international events allowed him to retain credibility. Besides the Hiss case, the sensational 1951 espionage trial of Julius and Ethel Rosenberg fueled McCarthy's allegations. Convicted of passing atomic secrets to the Soviet Union in a highly controversial trial, the Rosenbergs were executed in 1953. (As in the case of Hiss, their convictions continue to be debated; the recent release of declassified documents from a top-secret intelligence mission has provided some new evidence of Julius Rosenberg's guilt.) The Korean War, which embroiled the United States in a frustrating fight against communism in a faraway land, also made Americans susceptible to McCarthy's claims. Blaming disloyal individuals rather than complex international factors for the problems of the Cold War undoubtedly helped many Americans make sense of a disordered world of nuclear bombs, "police actions," and other world crises.

In early 1954 McCarthy overreached himself by launching an investigation into possible subversion in the U.S. Army. When the lengthy televised hearings brought McCarthy's smear tactics and leering innuendos into the nation's living rooms, support for him declined. The end of the Korean War and the death of Stalin in 1953 also undercut public interest in McCarthy's red-hunting campaign. In December 1954 the Senate voted 67 to 22 to censure McCarthy for unbecoming conduct. He died an alcoholic three years later at the age of forty-eight, his name forever attached to a period of political repression of which he was only the most flagrant manifestation.

The Army-McCarthy Hearings
These 1954 hearings contributed to the downfall of Senator Joseph McCarthy by showing his reckless accusations, bullying tactics, and sneering innuendos to a huge television audience. Some of the most heated exchanges took place between McCarthy (right) and Joseph Welch (seated, left), the lawyer representing the army. When an exasperated Welch asked, "Have you no decency left, sir?" the audience broke into applause because someone had finally had the courage to challenge McCarthy.

"MODERN REPUBLICANISM"

In 1952, in the middle of the Korean stalemate and at the height of the Great Fear, a newly elected president, Dwight D. Eisenhower, succeeded Harry Truman, ousting the Democrats from the White House. Eisenhower set the tone for what historians have called "modern Republicanism," an updated party philosophy that emphasized a slowdown, rather than a dismantling, of federal responsibilities. Compared with their predecessors in the 1920s and their successors in the 1980s and 1990s, modern Republicans were more tolerant of government intervention in social and economic affairs, though they did seek to limit the scope of federal action. More important to the average voter than Eisenhower's political philosophy, however, was his proven leadership in trying times; he seemed the right man to guide the nation through the perils of the Cold War.

"I Like Ike": Eisenhower as President

Eisenhower's status as a war hero was his greatest political asset. Born in 1890 and raised in Abilene, Kansas, he had graduated from the U.S. Military Academy at West Point in 1915. Rising quickly through the ranks, during World War II he became Supreme Commander of Allied Forces in Europe, where he had the mammoth task of coordinating the D-Day invasion of France. To hundreds of thousands of soldiers and to the millions of civilians who followed the war on newsreels, he was simply "Ike," the best known and best liked of the nation's military leaders.

As a professional military man, Eisenhower claimed to stand "above politics." While in the army he had never voted, insisting that such political activity represented an intrusion of the military into civilian affairs. Many Democrats had hoped to make him their candidate for president in 1948 and again in 1952. But Eisenhower wanted to occupy the office as a Republican. After winning several primaries, he secured the Republican nomination and asked Senator Richard M. Nixon of California to be his running mate. Nixon, young, tirelessly partisan, and with a strong anticommunist record from his crusade against Alger Hiss, brought an aggressive campaign style as well as regional balance to the Republican ticket.

The Democrats never seriously considered renominating Harry Truman, who by 1952 was a thoroughly discredited leader. Lack of popular enthusiasm for the Korean War had dealt the most severe blow to Truman's support, but a series of scandals involving federal officials in bribery, kickback, and influence-peddling schemes had caused a public outcry about the "mess in Washington." With a certain relief the Democrats turned to Governor Adlai E. Stevenson of Illinois, who enjoyed the support of respected liberals such as Eleanor Roosevelt and of organized labor. To appease southern voters who feared Stevenson's liberal agenda, the Democrats nominated Senator John A. Sparkman of Alabama for vice-president.

Throughout the 1952 campaign Stevenson advocated New Deal and Fair Deal policies with an almost literary eloquence. But Eisenhower's artfully unpretentious speeches were more effective with voters. Eager to win the support of the broadest electorate possible, Eisenhower played down specific questions of policy. Instead, he attacked the Democrats with the "K_1C_2" formula—"Korea, Communism, and Corruption." In a campaign pledge that clinched the election, he vowed to go to Korea, with the implication that he would end the stalemated war if elected.

The Republican campaign was temporarily set back by the revelation that wealthy Californians had set up a secret "slush fund" for Richard Nixon. Eisenhower contemplated dropping Nixon from the ticket, but Nixon adroitly used a televised speech to convince voters that he had not misused campaign funds. Nixon did admit to accepting one gift—a puppy his young daughters had named Checkers. That gift he would not give back, he declared earnestly. Nixon's televised speech turned an embarrassing incident into an advantage, as sympathetic viewers flooded Republican headquarters with supportive telegrams and phone calls. Outmaneuvered, Republican leaders had no choice but to keep Nixon on the ticket. The "Checkers speech" showed how the powerful new medium of television could be used to a politician's advantage.

That November, Eisenhower won 55 percent of the popular vote, carrying all the northern and western states and four southern states. Republican candidates for Congress did not fare quite as well. They regained the Senate from the Democrats, but took the House of Representatives by a slender margin of only 4 seats. In 1954 they would lose control of both houses to the Democrats. Even though the enormously popular Eisenhower would easily win re-election over Adlai Stevenson in 1956, the Republicans would remain in the minority in Congress.

The political scientist Fred Greenstein has characterized Eisenhower's style of leadership as the "hidden-hand presidency," pointing out that the president maneuvered deftly behind the scenes while seeming not to concern himself in public with partisan questions. Seeking a middle ground between liberalism and conservatism, Eisenhower did his best to set a quieter national mood, hoping to decrease the need for federal intervention in social and economic issues.

Unlike Truman, for example, Eisenhower showed little commitment to civil rights. He was disturbed by the Supreme Court decision in *Brown v. Board of Education of Topeka* (1954), which declared racial segregation in the public schools unconstitutional (see Chapter 29), asserting, "I don't believe you can change the hearts of men with laws or decisions." Nonetheless, in 1957 the president sent federal troops to enforce the integration of Central High School in Little Rock, Arkansas. Eisenhower also signed the Civil Rights Act of 1957, a Democratic bill that created the U.S. Commission on Civil Rights to study federal policies and laws concerning race. Though the act accomplished little, it was the first national civil rights legislation to be passed since Reconstruction.

Eisenhower presided over other cautious increases in federal activity. When the Soviet Union launched the first satellite, *Sputnik*, in 1957, Eisenhower supported a U.S. space program to catch up in this new cold war competition. The National Aeronautics and Space Administration (NASA) was founded the following year. The president also persuaded Congress to appropriate additional money for college scholarships and for research and development at universities and in industry. Federal outlays for veterans' benefits, unemployment compensation, housing, and Social Security were increased, and the minimum wage was raised from 75 cents an hour to $1. The creation of the new Department of Health, Education, and Welfare (HEW) in 1953 consolidated government control of social welfare programs, confirming federal commitments in that area.

Some of the most extensive federal activity during these years was in the realm of transportation. To link the Great Lakes with the Atlantic Ocean, the United States cosponsored with Canada the construction of the St. Lawrence Seaway. Congress also passed the Interstate Highway Act of 1956, which authorized $26 billion over a ten-year period for the construction of a nationally integrated highway system. The St. Lawrence Seaway and interstate highway projects were the largest public works programs to that date, surpassing anything undertaken during the New Deal.

Thus Republicans, though they resisted the unchecked expansion of the state, did not generally cut back federal power. Only in natural resource development did the Eisenhower administration move to reduce federal activity through the relinquishment of federal offshore oil contracting to the states in 1953, and the authorization of privately financed hydroelectric dams on the Snake River in 1955. In most other matters, such as social welfare programs and defense expenditures, modern Republicanism signaled an abandonment of the traditional Republican commitment to limited government. When Eisenhower retired from public life in 1961, the federal government had become an even greater presence in everyday life than it had been when he took office.

The "New Look"

Eisenhower had earned a reputation for superb judgment in military and diplomatic affairs during his years in the armed forces. One of his first acts as president was to put that skill to use in negotiating an end to the Korean War. As he had pledged in the campaign, he visited Korea in December 1952. The final settlement was signed in July 1953, after the parties reached a compromise on the tricky issue of prisoner exchange.

Once the Korean War was settled, Eisenhower turned his attention to Europe. Stalin's death in March 1953 precipitated an intraparty struggle in the Soviet Union, which lasted until 1956, when Nikita S. Khrushchev emerged as Stalin's successor. Although Khrushchev surprised westerners by calling for "peaceful coexistence" between communist and capitalist societies, he made certain that the U.S.S.R.'s Eastern European satellites did not deviate too far from the Soviet path. When nationalists revolted in Hungary in 1956 and moved to take the country out of the Warsaw Pact, Soviet tanks moved rapidly into Budapest—an action the United States could condemn, but could not realistically resist. Soviet repression of the Hungarian revolt showed that American policymakers had few, if any, options for rolling back Soviet power in Eastern Europe, short of going to war with the U.S.S.R.

Although Eisenhower strongly opposed communism, he hoped to keep the cost of containment at a manageable level. Under his "New Look" defense policy, Eisenhower and Secretary of State John Foster Dulles decided to economize by developing a massive nuclear arsenal as an alternative to more expensive conventional forces. Nuclear weapons delivered "more bang for the buck," explained Defense Secretary Charles E. Wilson. To that end, the Eisenhower administration expanded its commitment to the hydrogen bomb, approving extensive atmospheric testing in the South Pacific and in western states such as Nevada, Colorado, and Utah. To improve the nation's defenses against an air attack from the Soviet Union, the administration made a commitment to develop the long-range bombing capabilities of the Strategic Air Command, and installed the Distant Early Warning line of radar stations in Alaska and Canada in 1958.

Those measures did little to improve the nation's security, however, as the Soviets matched the United States weapon for weapon in an escalating arms race. The Soviet Union carried out atmospheric tests of its own of hydrogen bombs between 1953 and 1958, and developed a fleet of long-range bombers. By 1958, both nations had intercontinental ballistic missiles (ICBMs). When an American nuclear submarine launched an atomic-tipped Polaris missile in 1960, Soviet engineers raced to produce an equivalent weapon. While the arms race boosted the military-industrial sectors of both nations, it debilitated their social welfare programs by funneling immense resources into soon-to-be-obsolete weapons systems.

The New Look policy also extended collective security agreements between the United States and its allies. To complement the NATO alliance in Europe, for example, Secretary of State Dulles orchestrated the creation of the Southeast Asia Treaty Organization (SEATO), which linked America and its major European allies with Australia, Pakistan, Thailand, New Zealand, and the Philippines. All told, this extensive system of defense tied the United States to more than forty other countries.

In these years U.S. policymakers tended to support stable governments, no matter how repressive, as long as they were overtly anticommunist. Some of America's staunchest allies—the Philippines, Iran, Cuba, South Vietnam, and Nicaragua—were governed by dictatorships or repressive right-wing regimes that lacked broad-based popular support. In fact, Dulles often resorted to covert interventions against governments that were, in his opinion, too closely aligned with communism. For such tasks he used the newly formed Central Intelligence Agency (CIA), which had moved beyond its original mandate of intelligence gathering into active, albeit covert, involvement in the internal affairs of foreign countries. In the 1950s the CIA successfully directed the overthrow of the governments of Iran and Guatemala and helped to install new regimes viewed as more friendly to U.S. interests.

The Emerging Third World

American leaders had devised the policy of containment in response to Soviet expansion in Eastern Europe, but they soon extended it to the new nations emerging in the Third World. Before World War II, nationalism, socialism, and religion had inspired powerful anticolonial movements; in the 1940s and 1950s those forces intensified and spread, especially in the Middle East, Africa, and the Far East. Between 1947 and 1962 the British, French, Dutch, and Belgian empires all but disintegrated. Seeking to draw the new countries into an American-led world system, U.S. policymakers encouraged the development of stable market economies in those areas. They also sought to further the ideal of national self-determination that had shaped American participation in both world wars. But given the polarities of the Cold War, both the Truman and the Eisenhower administrations often failed to recognize that indigenous nationalist or socialist movements in emerging nations had their own goals, and were not necessarily under the control of either local Communists or the Soviet Union. Their failure to appreciate the complexity of local conditions limited the effectiveness of American policy.

The Middle East, an oil-rich area that was playing an increasingly central role in strategic planning, presented one of the most complicated challenges. After World War II many Jewish survivors of Nazi extermination camps had resettled in Palestine, which was still controlled by Britain under a World War I mandate. On November 29, 1947, the U.N. General Assembly voted to partition Palestine into two states, Jewish and Arab—a decision that Egypt, Jordan, and other Arab League states resisted. On May 14, 1948, the British mandate ended and Zionist leaders of the Jewish nationalist movement proclaimed the state of Israel. President Truman quickly recognized the new state, alienating the Arabs but winning crucial support from Jewish Americans in the 1948 election.

Egypt was another site of conflict with the Arab Nations, one that reflected the way in which Third World countries became embroiled in the Cold War. When Gamal Abdel Nasser came to power in Egypt in 1954, two years after his nation won independence from Britain, he pledged to lead not just Egypt but the entire Middle East out of its dependent colonial relationship with the West through a form of pan-Arab socialism. From the Soviet Union, Nasser obtained arms and promises of economic assistance, including help in building the Aswan Dam on the Nile. Secretary of State Dulles countered with an offer of American assistance, but Nasser refused to distance himself from the Soviets, declaring Egypt's neutrality in the Cold War. Unwilling to accept this stance of nonalignment, Dulles abruptly withdrew his offer in July 1956.

A week later Nasser retaliated against the withdrawal of western financial aid by nationalizing the Suez Canal, over which Britain had retained administrative authority, and through which three-quarters of Western Europe's oil passed. After several months of fruitless negotiation, Britain and France, in alliance with Israel, attacked Egypt and retook the canal. Their attack occurred at the same time as the Soviet repression of the Hungarian revolt, placing the United States in the potentially awkward position of denouncing Soviet aggression while tolerating a similar action by its own allies. President Eisenhower and the United Nations condemned the European actions in Egypt, forcing France and Britain to pull back. Egypt retook the canal and proceeded to build the Aswan Dam with Soviet support. In the end, the Suez crisis increased Soviet influence in the Third World, intensified anti-western sentiment in Arab countries, and produced dissension among leading members of the NATO alliance.

In early 1957, in the aftermath of the Suez crisis, the president persuaded Congress to approve the Eisenhower Doctrine. Addressing concerns over declining British influence in the Middle East, the joint policy stated that American forces would assist any nation in the region "requiring such aid, against overt armed aggression from any nation controlled by International Communism." Later that year Eisenhower invoked the doctrine when he sent the U.S. Sixth Fleet to the Mediterranean to aid King Hussein of Jordan. A year later he landed 8,000 troops to back a pro–United States government in Lebanon.

The attention the Eisenhower administration paid to developments in the Middle East in the 1950s demonstrated how the desire for access to steady supplies of oil increasingly affected foreign policy. Indeed, by the late 1950s the Middle East contained about 65 percent of the world's known reserves. But more broadly, attention to the Middle East confirmed the global scope of American interests. Just as the Korean War had stretched the application of the containment policy from Europe to Asia, the Eisenhower Doctrine revealed the U.S. intention to bring the Middle East into its sphere as well.

The Impact of the Cold War at Home

While the Cold War extended to the most distant corners of the globe, it also had a devastating impact on the health of American citizens at home, some of whom became unwitting guinea pigs in the nation's nuclear weapons program. In the late 1950s, a small but growing number of citizens became concerned about the effects of radioactive fallout from aboveground bomb tests. In later years federal investigators documented a host of illnesses, deaths, and birth defects among families of veterans who had worked on weapons tests and among "down-winders"—people who lived near nuclear test sites and weapons facilities. The

Testing an Atomic Bomb
Throughout the 1950s the Atomic Energy Commission conducted above-ground tests of atomic and hydrogen bombs. Thousands of soldiers were exposed to fallout during the tests, such as this one at Yucca Flats, Nevada, in April 1952. The AEC, ignoring or suppressing medical evidence to the contrary, mounted an extensive public relations campaign to convince local residents that the tests did not endanger their health.

most shocking revelations, however, came to light in 1993, when the Department of Energy released millions of previously classified documents on human radiation experiments conducted in the late 1940s and 1950s under the auspices of the Atomic Energy Commission (AEC) and other federal agencies. Many of the subjects were irradiated without their consent or understanding.

Memories of a Cold War Childhood

The menacing threat of the atom bomb, the looming presence of the Soviet Union, and the fear of internal subversion were part of everyday life in the 1950s. In his autobiography, Born on the Fourth of July, *Ron Kovic conveys the anxiety Americans felt when the Soviets launched the satellite* Sputnik, *revealing that Americans were behind in the race to conquer outer space.*

We joined the cub scouts and marched in parades on Memorial Day. We made contingency plans for the cold war and built fallout shelters out of milk cartons. We wore spacesuits and space helmets. We made rocket ships out of cardboard boxes. And one Saturday afternoon in the basement Castiglia [a friend] and I went to Mars on the couch we had turned into a rocket ship. . . . And the whole block watched a thing called the space race begin. On a cold October night Dad and I watched the first satellite, called *Sputnik*, moving across the sky above our house like a tiny bright star. I still remember standing out there with Dad looking up in amazement at that thing moving in the sky above Massapequa. It was hard to believe that this thing, this *Sputnik*, was so high up and moving so fast around the world, again and again. Dad put his hand on my shoulder that night and without saying anything I quietly walked back inside and went to my room thinking that the Russians had beaten America into space and wondering why we couldn't even get a rocket off the pad. . . .

The Communists were all over the place back then. And if they weren't trying to beat us into outer space, Castiglia and I were certain they were infiltrating our schools, trying to take over our classes and control our minds. We were both certain that one of our teachers was a secret Communist agent and in our next secret club meeting we promised to report anything new he said during our next history class. We watched him very carefully that year.

SOURCE: Ron Kovic, *Born on the Fourth of July* (New York: Pocket Books, 1976), pp. 56–57.

The nuclear arms race affected all Americans by fostering a climate of fear and uncertainty. Bomb shelters, civil defense drills, and other survival measures provided a daily reminder of the threat of nuclear war. Eisenhower himself had second thoughts about a nuclear policy based on the premise of annihilating the enemy, even if one's own country was destroyed—the aptly named acronym MAD (Mutual Assured Destruction) policy. He also found spiraling arms expenditures a serious hindrance to balancing the federal budget, one of his chief fiscal goals. Consequently, Eisenhower tried to negotiate an arms limitation agreement with the Soviet Union. Progress along those lines was cut short, however, when on May 5, 1960, the Soviets shot down an American U-2 spy plane over their territory and captured and imprisoned its pilot, Francis Gary Powers. Eisenhower at first denied that the plane was engaged in espionage, but later admitted that he had authorized the mission and other secret flights over the U.S.S.R. In the midst of the dispute, a proposed summit meeting was canceled and Eisenhower's last chance to negotiate an arms agreement evaporated.

When Eisenhower left office in January 1961, he used his final address to warn against the growing power of what he termed the "military-industrial complex," which by then employed 3.5 million Americans. Its pervasive influence, he noted, was "felt in every city, every statehouse, every office of the Federal Government." Even though his administration had fostered the growth of the defense establishment, Eisenhower was gravely concerned about its implications for a democratic people. "We must guard against the acquisition of unwarranted influence, whether sought or unsought, by the military-industrial complex," he warned. "We must never let the weight of this combination endanger our liberties or democratic processes." With those words Dwight Eisenhower showed how well he understood the major transformations that the Cold War had wrought in the nation. The conflict between the Soviet Union and the United States not only had far-reaching international implications; it had powerful effects on domestic politics, the economy, and cultural values, and it permanently altered the contours of the modern state.

CHAPTER 28 TIMELINE

1945	Yalta and Potsdam conferences Harry S Truman succeeds Roosevelt as president End of World War II
1946	Kennan sends "long telegram" outlining containment policy Baruch Plan for international control of atomic weapons fails
1947	Taft-Hartley Act Truman Doctrine Marshall Plan
1948	Desegregation of armed forces State of Israel created Berlin airlift
1949	North Atlantic Treaty Organization (NATO) founded People's Republic of China established National Housing Act Soviet Union detonates atomic bomb; U.S. atomic monopoly ends
1950–1953	Korean War
1950	Alger Hiss convicted of perjury McCarthy presents his list of alleged Communists in government NSC-68 calls for permanent mobilization
1952	Dwight D. Eisenhower elected president U.S. detonates hydrogen bomb
1954	Army-McCarthy hearings *Brown v. Board of Education of Topeka*
1956	Crises in Hungary and Suez Interstate Highway Act
1957	Eisenhower Doctrine Eisenhower sends U.S. troops to Little Rock to ensure school integration
1958	NASA established
1959	St. Lawrence Seaway completed
1960	U-2 spy plane shot down over Soviet Union

CHAPTER 29

AFFLUENCE AND ITS
CONTRADICTIONS, 1945–1965

- The Postwar Capitalist Economy
- A Suburban Society
- American Society during the Baby Boom
- The Other America

Hula-Hoops and poodle skirts, sock hops and rock-'n'-roll, shiny cars and gleaming appliances—all signify the "fifties"—a period which really stretched from 1945 through the early 1960s. The postwar years are remembered as a time of affluence, consumerism, conformity, and stability, a time when Americans enjoyed an optimistic faith in progress and technology. It was an age of innocence, of a serene family-centered culture enshrined in television sitcoms such as "Father Knows Best."

This powerful myth, like many, has some truth to it. Certainly in the quarter-century after World War II, Americans enjoyed the highest standard of living in the world, and the fruits of a technologically advanced industrial sector. That affluence spawned a suburban culture in which many men and women turned inward to enjoy the private satisfactions of family, leisure, and consumerism.

But there were other sides to the story. Suburban prosperity often came at the expense of the vitality of cities; thus the roots of urban crises were to be found in this period. Heedless faith in technology sowed the seeds of serious environmental problems as well. Moreover, many "other Americans" did not lead lives of contentment in the suburbs. Although prosperity was more widespread than ever before, the poor, immigrants, and African-Americans had dramatically different experiences from the more affluent. Beneath the suburban calm, contradictions in women's lives, cultural rebellion among youth and intellectuals, and protests by African-Americans in the South, laid the foundations for significant social change in the future.

THE POSTWAR CAPITALIST ECONOMY

By the end of 1945, war-induced prosperity had made the United States the richest country in the world. Over the next two decades the gross national product expanded dramatically, rising from $213 billion in 1945 to more than $500 billion in 1960; in 1970 it approached $1 trillion. During this period, real wages rose steadily, and inflation remained low, providing a sense of security and progress to the majority of Americans. In the largest manufacturing industries, industrial workers won acceptance of their unions, and with it rising incomes, expanding benefits, and a growing rate of suburban home ownership. Affluence was so much a part of American culture in 1945 that a high standard of living characterized by an apparently endless array of consumer goods seemed inseparable from the basic freedoms guaranteed by the nation's political institutions. The "American way of life" became a crucial part of the cold war rhetoric the United States employed against the perceived communist menace.

This prosperity was, however, unevenly distributed. The rising standard of living was not accompanied by a redistribution of income; the top 10 percent of Americans still earned more than the lowest 50 percent. At the bottom of the economic ladder remained the permanently unemployed, the aged who subsisted on Social Security, female heads of households, and most nonwhites. In 1957 nearly one in four Americans lived below the official poverty line. Despite these limits, the period's economic expansion benefited a wider segment of society than anyone would have dreamed possible in the dark days of the depression. With economic growth underwritten by the federal government's outlays for defense and domestic programs, by exuberant consumer spending, and by the nation's powerful position in the international economy, Americans expected that abundance would be permanent, and that poverty would eventually be eradicated.

Sources of Affluence

The United States enjoyed overwhelming economic and political advantages at the end of World War II. Unlike the Soviet Union, Western Europe, and Japan, America emerged from the war physically unscathed, ready to build upon wartime mobilization to fashion postwar economic success. Manufacturers quickly applied the scientific and technological innovations that had been developed for military purposes to peacetime products, such as plastics and synthetic fibers. Consumers, released from wartime rationing and shortages, were eager to spend their $140 billion in accumulated savings. They provided a booming market for new housing and a rich array of consumer goods.

The nation also emerged from the war in an unprecedentedly powerful position internationally. The period from World War II through the late 1960s and the early 1970s witnessed the heyday of modern American capitalism. America's global economic supremacy stemmed in part from institutions created at a United Nations conference at Bretton Woods, New Hampshire, in 1944. The International Bank for Reconstruction and Development (known commonly as the World Bank) provided private loans for the reconstruction of war-torn Europe, as well as for the development of Third World countries. The International Monetary Fund (IMF), designed to stabilize the value of currencies, helped to guide the world economy after the war. Backed by the United States' money and influence, these international organizations tended to favor American-style internationalism over the economic nationalism traditional in most other countries. The result was stable prices, a flexible domestic market, a powerful American dollar, and reduced tariffs and trade barriers—all of which served the United States' global economic interests.

In addition to its global economic and political power, the United States was also a major military presence in the new world order. Defense spending was an important source of the nation's postwar prosperity. Between 1900 and 1930, except for the two years the United States fought in World War I, the country had spent less than 1 percent of its GNP for military purposes. By the early 1960s the figure was close to 10 percent, reflecting a dramatic shift in national priorities. Under the government-business partnership that President Eisenhower dubbed the military–industrial complex, the Defense department evolved into a massive bureaucracy that profoundly influenced the economy. Companies such as Boeing and Lockheed did so much business with the government that they became dependent on Defense department orders.

At the same time, science, corporate capitalism, and the federal government became increasingly intertwined. Federal money underwrote 90 percent of the cost of aviation and space research, and also subsidized the scientific instruments, automobile, and electronics industries. With the government footing part of the bill, corporations developed new products with unprecedented speed. After the Pentagon backed IBM's investment in integrated circuits in the 1960s, which were crucial to the computer revolution, the new devices went into commercial production in just three years.

The defense buildup brought mixed blessings. In positive terms, it created jobs: perhaps as many as one in seven Americans owed his or her job to the military–industrial complex in the 1960s. In the South and the West, where much of the new military activity was concentrated, dependence on defense spending was even greater (see Map 29.1, following page). But, even while increased spending put money in the pockets of millions of people, it limited the resources available for domestic needs. Critics of military spending calculated the trade-offs: the cost of a nuclear aircraft carrier and support ships equaled that of a subway system for Washington, D.C.; the money spent on one Huey helicopter matched the cost of sixty-six units of low-income housing.

Besides stimulating the economy, the expansion of the military–industrial complex hastened the concentration of power. Both the federal government and corporations became larger and more complex in these years. The predominant

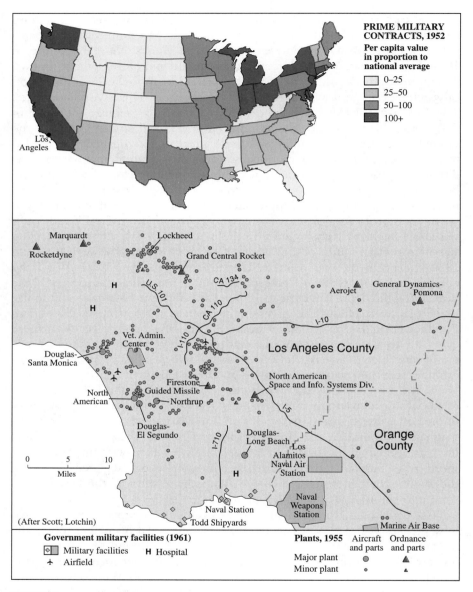

MAP 29.1

The Military-Industrial Complex in Los Angeles

The development and expansion of military facilities and defense contracting during the Cold War helped boost the populations and economies of Los Angeles and other Sun Belt cities and made the economies of some states highly dependent on defense expenditures.

trend of corporate business after 1945 continued to be the consolidation of economic and financial resources by oligopolies—a few large producers who controlled the national market, and increasingly, the world market. In 1970, for example, the top four American firms produced 91 percent of the motor vehicles sold in the domestic market.

Large firms maintained their dominance by turning to diversification. The typical corporation of the early twentieth century had produced a single line of products; its growth therefore depended on the vertical integration of related firms (see Chapter 18). After World War II, however, the most successful corporations invested heavily in research and development, produced new product lines, and moved into new markets. The Columbia Broadcasting System (CBS), for example, patented more than a hundred new devices, including a color television during the 1940s, long-playing records in the 1950s, and a video recording system in the 1960s.

Postwar managers also diversified through mergers and acquisitions, creating larger firms called *conglomerates*. International Telephone and Telegraph became a diversified conglomerate by acquiring companies in unrelated industries, including Continental Baking, Sheraton Hotels, Avis Rent-a-Car, Levitt and Sons home builders, and Hartford Fire Insurance. This pattern of corporate acquisition developed into a great wave of mergers that peaked in the 1960s.

The development of giant corporations also depended on the penetration of foreign markets. American products were considered the best in the world, and thus were widely sought after abroad. When domestic markets became saturated or recessions cut into sales, American companies adopted international strategies and turned to foreign markets. During the 1950s U.S. exports nearly doubled, producing a trade surplus of close to $5 billion in 1960, and contributing significantly to American prosperity.

The Changing World of Work

Changes in corporate structure had a powerful impact on the nature of work. Increasingly, Americans spent their workdays as part of a large bureaucracy. Since the late nineteenth century, the proportion of Americans employed in the service sector—as professionals, clerical workers, salespeople, civil servants, and other service workers—had grown steadily, while the proportion of blue-collar workers and the self-employed had declined. Industrial mobilization had temporarily halted this trend during World War II, but the growth of the service sector resumed dramatically in the postwar era to meet employers' new demands.

One of the fastest-growing groups was salaried office workers. From 1947 to 1957 the number of persons in that occupational category increased by 61 percent, while the number of factory workers decreased by 4 percent. Corporate bureaucracies also recruited increasing numbers of top executives with business-school training in information management, corporate planning, marketing, and investment. Finally, the GI Bill, which increased the public's access to college education, helped to expand the white-collar ranks.

Organization Men (and a Few Women)
The commute from home in the suburbs to corporate office in the city and back again became a week-day ritual for millions of white-collar workers in the postwar era. William H. Whyte's appropriately titled book *The Organization Man* (1956) explored the transformation of the nature of work and its impact on middle-class men who eagerly worked their way up the corporate ladder.

In the giant bureaucracies—big business, government agencies, universities, and the military—young, predominantly male college graduates used their skills to work their way up through the career ladder. To do so they had to be able to get along in a variety of situations. Corporate managers worked hard, sometimes with the assistance of the resident corporate psychologist, to become "well adjusted." Critics worried that the experience of marching off each day in gray flannel suits to work at interchangeable middle-management jobs in huge corporations was stifling men's creativity. In a best-selling book, the sociologist William Whyte painted a somber picture of "the organization man" who left home "spiritually as well as physically to take the vows of organization life."

But the popular obsession with the middle-class organization man obscured other significant changes in the postwar work force. Many of the new white-collar workers earned salaries that were lower than the total hourly wages of unionized blue-collar workers, and their jobs were as boring and repetitive as factory work. As one American Telephone and Telegraph (AT&T) operator explained in describing her routinized and carefully monitored work, "You've got a clock next to you that times every second." Millions of new service workers were blue-collar laborers who earned hourly wages toiling under factorylike conditions in laundries, restaurants, and other businesses.

Many of the new service workers were female: twice as many women worked outside the home in 1960 as in 1940. Occupational segmentation remained the norm; more than 80 percent of all working women did stereotypical "women's work" as salespersons, health-care technicians, waitresses, domestic servants, telephone operators, and secretaries. In fact, until 1964, the classified sections of most newspapers separated employment ads into columns headed "Help Wanted Male" and "Help Wanted Female." All women had limited access to the professions. Nonwhite and working-class women were largely confined to a low-paying "pink-collar" ghetto that offered jobs in restaurants, hotels, hospitals, and beauty salons. Along with these women's jobs went women's pay, which averaged 60 percent of men's in 1963.

The changing composition of the work force and the shifting nature of work posed difficult challenges for the labor movement. The postwar era witnessed the high point of organized labor and the beginning of its decline. Unions peaked in strength around the end of World War II, when they represented over 35 percent of the nonfarm work force. They remained strong and politically influential through the 1960s, despite the limits imposed by the Taft-Hartley Act in 1947 (see Chapter 28). The strength of the labor movement in this period stemmed partly from its structural unity. In 1955 Walter P. Reuther of the United Auto Workers led the Congress of Industrial Organizations (CIO) back into a formal alliance with the American Federation of Labor (AFL). That merger created a single organization, the AFL-CIO, that represented more than 90 percent of the nation's 17.5 million union members. George Meany, a New York building-trades unionist, headed the organization for the next 24 years.

New priorities shaped labor-management relations after the war. Concerned about inflation and increased levels of consumption, unions demanded higher wages as their share of postwar prosperity. The contracts they negotiated gave many workers secure and steadily rising incomes, often with a cost-of-living adjustment, or COLA. In exchange, union leaders promised labor peace and stability, that is, fewer strikes. In return for higher wages and fringe benefits, workers for the most part put aside their traditional demand for control over the pace and duration of work and allowed technologically minded managers to exert increasing control over workers' lives on the job.

One serious challenge to workers' welfare came from new technology. Long a problem for skilled workers, mechanization in the 1950s began to affect the jobs of unskilled and semiskilled factory workers as well. The Ford Motor Company, for example, introduced automatic drilling machines at a Cleveland engine plant in 1952, in the process reducing to 41 a crew that formerly numbered 117. Thousands of workers lost their jobs in steel manufacturing, coal mining, automobile assembly, and other rapidly automating industries.

With the reduction in the number of manufacturing jobs, organized labor had to look elsewhere for new recruits. Large sectors of the work force remained unorganized in the postwar era, including the lower-skilled, lower-paying service and agricultural sectors, in which workers were often black or Latino, and the female-dominated field of office work. Although unions had only minimal success in organizing these groups, they were more effective in recruiting workers in large bureaucratic organizations such as government, health care, and education. Organizers made few gains in the small, scattered service operations where many of the lowest-paid workers toiled, and could not break the hold of antiunion forces in the South. By the mid-1950s the labor movement had stalled; union membership has declined steadily ever since.

The agricultural sector also changed markedly in the postwar years, as new technologies and an expanding corporate presence transformed farm work. In 1945 the nation's farm population accounted for 17.5 percent of the total population; by 1970 it had declined to less than 5 percent. These figures represented the culmination of a long-term trend away from family farming and toward large-scale agribusiness. New technology contributed to an astonishing increase in agricultural productivity after 1945, but it also required major capital investments. Between 1940 and 1955, the cost of fuel, fertilizer, and repairs for farm machines quadrupled, and total operating costs tripled. Family farms often lacked the capital to compete with large, technologically advanced agribusiness. Many farm families left the land in these years.

Those farmers who remained managed specialized organizations that were much like small factories. They relied on industry for fertilizer, feed, seed, and pesticides and for the fuel to run an expanding array of gasoline-powered equipment. They became increasingly dependent on national and international market conditions, scientific and technological developments, and federal farm policies such as loans and subsidies. The fuller integration of farmers into the national economy, and the diminishing number of Americans who farmed for a living greatly reduced the differences between rural and urban life.

A SUBURBAN SOCIETY

As the steady decline of the family farm indicates, Americans had been gravitating toward urban areas in large numbers throughout the twentieth century. In the postwar period, the urbanization process displayed two new patterns: a shift away from older cities in the Northeast and the Midwest, and toward newer urban centers in the South and the West; and a mass defection from the cities to the suburbs. Both processes were stimulated by the dramatic growth of a car culture and the federal government's increased promotion of economic expansion.

The Building of Suburbia

At the end of World War II many cities were surrounded by pastures and working farms. Just five or ten years later they were ringed by tract housing, factories, and shopping centers. By 1960 more Americans—particularly whites—lived in suburbs than in cities.

People flocked to the suburbs in part because they offered available housing. Very little new construction had been undertaken during the depression and the war years; as a result, returning veterans and their families faced a critical housing shortage. The difficulty was partly resolved by an innovative building contractor named Arthur Levitt, who applied mass production techniques

The Suburban Boom
Hundreds of thousands of World War II veterans took advantage of low-interest loans under the G.I. Bill to purchase new homes in suburban subdivisions like this one in Los Angeles's San Fernando Valley. (Huntington Library, San Marino, California, Whittington Collection)

to home construction. Levitt's company could build 150 homes per week, a rate of one every sixteen minutes. A basic four-room house, complete with kitchen appliances and an attic that could be converted into two additional bedrooms, was priced at less than $10,000 in 1947. Other developers soon followed suit in subdivisions all over the country, hastening the exodus from the farm and central city.

Many families financed their homes with mortgages from the Federal Housing Administration (FHA) or the Veterans Administration (VA), at rates dramatically lower than those of private lenders. In 1955 the two agencies wrote 41 percent of all nonfarm mortgages. Such lending demonstrated the quiet yet revolutionary way in which the federal government was beginning to influence citizens' daily lives.

The new suburban homes—and much of the savings and loan and Veterans Administration money—were reserved almost exclusively for whites. Many communities adopted covenants prohibiting occupation "by members of other than the Caucasian Race." Though the Supreme Court had ruled restrictive covenants illegal in *Shelley v. Kraemer* (1948), the custom continued informally until the civil rights laws of the 1960s banned private discrimination.

While observers often portrayed suburbia as a homogeneous place, strong cultural and class differences often separated suburban neighborhoods. When firefighters, machine-tool makers, and sales clerks moved to the suburbs, they were far more likely to move to a modest Levittown than to an upper-middle-class suburb such as Winnetka, Illinois, or Shaker Heights, Ohio. Though most African-Americans were shut out of white suburbs, some established their own communities, such as Lincoln Heights outside Cincinnati and Kinloch near St. Louis. For many different groups of Americans, then, the suburbs offered the ultimate postwar dream of giving every child "an opportunity to grow up with grass stains on his pants."

The Automobile Culture

Automobiles and highways were essential both to suburban growth and to the development of the "Sun Belt" states of the South and the West. Rapidly expanding cities in these regions became dependent upon motor vehicles rather than upon the mass transit systems typical of the North and the Midwest. Suburbanites throughout the country needed cars to get to work and to take their children to school and piano lessons. In 1945 Americans owned 25 million cars; by 1965 the number had tripled to 75 million. As the car culture that first emerged in the 1920s expanded dramatically in the 1950s, cars—extravagant gas guzzlers with elaborate tail fins and ostentatious chrome detail—became symbols of status and success.

More cars required more highways, which were funded largely by the federal government. In 1947 Congress authorized the construction of 37,000 miles of highways; in 1956 the National Interstate and Defense Highway Act increased that commitment by another 42,500 miles. One of the largest civil engineering projects in world history, the new interstate system would link the entire country with roads at least four lanes wide. The interstate highway promoted both urban and suburban development while altering the nation's topography. It rerouted traffic through rural areas, creating artificial communities of gas stations, fast-food outlets, and motels at its cloverleaf exchanges. In urban areas, new highways cut wide swaths through old neighborhoods. Cities were soon plagued by air pollution and traffic jams, and critics complained of "autosclerosis"—a hardening of the urban arteries.

Highway construction had far-reaching effects on everyday life. Federally funded highways siphoned funding away from mass transit, contributing to an increasing dependency on the automobile. By 1960 two-thirds of Americans drove to work each day. Instead of taking a train into the city or walking to a corner grocery store, people hopped into their cars and drove to fast-growing suburban supermarkets and shopping malls. Although the first mall had appeared in the 1920s, in 1945 there were only 8; by 1960 the number had risen to almost 4,000. A 110-store complex that opened at Roosevelt Field on suburban Long Island in 1956 was conveniently situated at an expressway exit and boasted parking space for 11,000 cars. As the suburbs, highways, and the car culture transformed the nation's commercial and physical landscape, downtown retail areas and department stores declined.

Few cities are more closely identified with shopping malls, freeways, and automobiles than Los Angeles. That city, like others in the Sun Belt, witnessed remarkable growth after the war (see Map 29.2). Corporate expansion, often underwritten by the federal government's defense spending, brought new prosperity to states such as Texas, Florida, and California, while the highway system helped to integrate them into the nation's economic system and facilitate urban development. Between 1940 and 1970, Miami's metropolitan population increased by 79 percent with the addition of more than a million new residents, many of them older or retired. Cities in Texas, especially Houston and Dallas, grew as the petrochemical industry expanded after 1945. In California, the burgeoning defense industry in the Los Angeles, San Francisco, and San Diego metropolitan areas produced dramatic growth. California added 2.6 million people in the 1940s and 3.1 million more in the 1950s, until by 1970 the state claimed about a tenth of the U.S. population.

Business boosters in California and other Sun Belt states worked tirelessly to promote regional development. Local leaders lobbied for new defense contracts and installations, and successfully wooed professional sports teams like

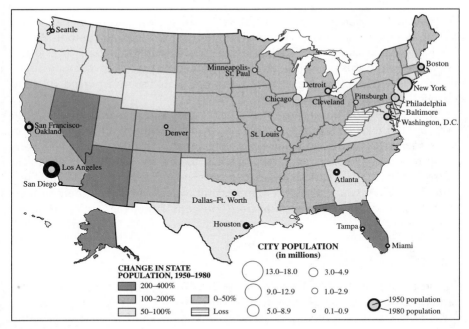

MAP 29.2

Metroplitan Growth, 1950–1980

Since the U.S. Census Bureau changed its definition of a Standard Metropolitan Statistical Area (SMSA) after 1950, it is difficult to chart urban growth precisely. This map compares the population of central cities in 1950 with population figures for the more broadly defined metropolitan areas in 1980 to illustrate the extent and geographical distribution of metropolitan growth in the postwar period.

the Brooklyn Dodgers, who relocated to Los Angeles in 1958. To attract new residents, promoters touted their region's sunny climate, attractive scenery, and relaxed lifestyles. In subsequent decades, however, the success of Sun Belt cities would create problems. Booming urban populations brought more crime and poverty, problems formerly associated with cities in the Northeast. In the West, the increasing demand for water and energy caused environmental and health problems. For example, the nuclear weapons industry, which brought jobs and income, also brought radiation contamination to residents near atomic test sites, nuclear waste facilities, and uranium mines. In the West, as elsewhere, postwar development often carried a significant social cost.

At the time, few Americans understood that trade-offs were involved in the postwar economic boom. With a strong economic position internationally and government spending to help fuel expansion at home, Americans expected an unending trajectory of progress. Their faith produced complacency—an unwillingness to look beneath the surface for the hidden implications of the forces that were transforming America.

AMERICAN SOCIETY DURING THE BABY BOOM

A term often associated with the fifties was "consensus," meaning conformity to social norms, authority, and the status quo. "Consensus" embodied the ideal that Americans could live in harmony, without social class or political conflicts. While this prevailing attitude stemmed in part from widespread affluence, it also expressed a fervent desire for stability in a period of rapid change.

In a search for tranquility—an escape from the pressures of the Cold War, the bomb, and the corporate rat race—many white middle-class Americans turned inward to the private satisfactions of home, family, and consumption. Newly married couples flocked to the suburbs, where they had more children than Americans had borne at any time since 1920. They joined the PTA, swelled church membership rosters, and raised their families in a climate of affluence, consumption, and conformity that set the tone for the period.

The Consumer Culture

In the corporate world, where work was becoming more routinized and less satisfying for both blue- and white-collar workers, consumer goods and leisure time took on growing importance as sources of meaning and pleasure. The general prosperity of the postwar period meant that even working-class families had discretionary income to spend on products such as washing machines, dryers, and the latest model car. Americans were able to stretch their rising incomes further by taking advantage of the dramatic increase in consumer credit. Between 1946 and 1958, short-term consumer credit rose from $8.4 billion to almost $45 billion. The Diners Club introduced the first credit card in 1950; by the 1970s the ubiquitous plastic credit card had revolution-ized personal and family finances.

Aggressive advertising contributed to the massive increase in consumer spending. In 1951 businesses spent more on advertising ($6.5 billion) than taxpayers did on primary and secondary education ($5 billion). The 1950s gave Americans the Marlboro man; M&M's ("They melt in your mouth, not in your hand"); the ballpoint pen that "writes under water"; and the "does she or doesn't she?" Clairol woman. Motivational researchers delved into the sub-conscious to determine what needs consumption filled and how the advertis-ing messages should be pitched. In general, the ads of the period reflected an uncritical view of American life, and suggested falsely that all Americans were white and middle class, all women were homemakers, and all families were nuclear and intact.

Consumers had more free time in which to spend their money than ever before. In 1960 the average worker put in a five-day week, with eight paid holidays a year (double the 1946 standard) plus a two-week paid vacation. Americans took to the interstate highway system by the millions, encouraging dramatic growth in motel chains, roadside restaurants, and fast-food eateries. (The first McDonald's restaurant opened in 1954 in San Bernardino, Califor-nia; the Holiday Inn motel chain started in Memphis in 1952.) Among the most popular destinations were national and state parks and Disneyland, which opened in Anaheim, California, in 1955.

Perhaps the most significant hallmark of the postwar consumer culture was television. TV quickly supplanted radio and movies as the chief diffuser of popular taste and values. By 1960, 87 percent of American families owned at least one television set. What Americans saw on television, be-sides the omnipresent commercials, was an overwhelmingly white middle-class world of nuclear families in suburban homes. "Father Knows Best," "Leave It to Beaver," "I Love Lucy," and similar sitcoms featured characters who adhered to clear-cut gender roles and plots based on small family crises that were always happily resolved by the end of the half-hour. Shows such as "The Honeymooners," starring Jackie Gleason as a Brooklyn bus driver, were rare in their treatment of working-class lives. Nonwhite char-acters appeared mainly as servants, such as Jack Benny's Rochester or the Latino gardener with the anglicized name "Frank Smith" on "Father Knows Best."

In addition to family sitcoms, Americans watched quiz shows such as "The $64,000 Question," and westerns such as "Gunsmoke"and "Bonanza" (the first TV show in color). National television coverage made professional sports into a big business with a potential far exceeding that of radio. Pro-gramming geared to children, such as "Captain Kangaroo" and Walt Disney's "Mickey Mouse Club" attracted the first generation of children to grow up glued to the tube. Although the new medium did offer some serious pro-gramming, notably live theater and documentaries, Newton Minow, head of the Federal Communications Commission, concluded in 1963 that television was "a vast wasteland." Its reassuring images of family life and postwar society, however, dovetailed with many Americans' social expectations.

The Search for Security: Religion and the Family

The dislocations of the depression and war years made Americans yearn for security and a reaffirmation of traditional values. Some of this sentiment was expressed in a renewed emphasis on religion. Church membership rose from 49 percent of the population in 1940 to 69 percent in 1960. All the major denominations shared in the growth, which was accompanied by an ecumenical movement to bring Catholics, Protestants, and Jews together. The stress on religious harmony meshed with cold war Americans' definition of themselves as a righteous people opposed to "godless communism." In 1956 Congress added "In God We Trust" to coins, and in 1954, the phrase "under God" was inserted into the Pledge of Allegiance. In the same year, President Dwight D. Eisenhower insisted that American government "makes no sense unless it is founded on a deeply felt religious faith—and I don't care what it is."

Beyond patriotism, religion also served more deep-felt needs. In his popular television program, Bishop Fulton Sheen asked, "Is life worth living?"— a question he and countless other leaders optimistically answered in the affirmative. None was more positive than Norman Vincent Peale, whose book *The Power of Positive Thinking* (1952) embodied the trend toward the therapeutic use of religion to assist men and women in coping with the stresses of modern life.

At the same time evangelical religion experienced a resurgence, most evident in the dramatic rise to popularity of the Reverend Billy Graham, who used television, radio, advertising, and print media to spread the gospel. His nondenominational Evangelistic Association, founded in 1950, was a tremendous success. Graham appealed to conservative Protestants within the major denominations. Formerly marginal churches such as the Jehovah's Witnesses and the Seventh Day Adventists also enjoyed spectacular growth in this period. Although critics suggested that middle-class interest in religion stemmed more from conformity than spirituality, the revival nonetheless spoke to Americans' search for spiritual meaning in uncertain times.

Even more dramatic testimony to the desire for stability in the postwar era was the emphasis Americans placed on the family and children. As one popular advice book put it, "The family is the center of your living. If it isn't, you've gone far astray." The families formed between 1940 and 1960 had a noteworthy demographic impact. Marriages were remarkably stable; not until the mid-1960s did the divorce rate begin to rise sharply. But the average age at marriage fell during the period, to twenty-two for men and twenty for women. In 1951 a third of all women were married by age nineteen. More important, the drop in the average age at marriage resulted in a surge of young married couples who produced a bumper crop of children. After a century and a half of declining family size, the birth rate shot up: more babies were born between 1948 and 1953 than had been born in the previous thirty years. As a result of this trend and a lengthened life expectancy due to improvements in diet, public health, and medicine, the American population rose dramatically from 140 million in 1945 to 179 million in 1960, and then to 203 million in 1970.

To rear all these baby-boom children and keep them healthy, middle-class parents increasingly relied on the advice of experts. Accepting the advice of doctors and the federal government, they had their children inoculated with the Salk polio vaccine, administered free in the nation's schools. Parents also bought millions of copies of Dr. Benjamin Spock's *Baby and Child Care*—one million in just the first year after its publication in 1946. New mothers found Spock's insistence that they abandon the rigid feeding and baby care schedules of an earlier generation liberating, though the book did not remove all their insecurities. If a mother was too protective of her children, Spock and others warned, she might hamper their adjustment to a normal adult life.

The baby boom had a broad and immediate impact on American society. It prompted a major expansion of the nation's educational system: by 1970, school expenditures were double those of the 1950 level. In addition, babies' consumer needs fueled the economy as families bought food, diapers, toys, and clothing for their expanding broods. Together with federal expenditures on national security, family spending on consumer goods fueled the unparalleled prosperity and economic growth of the 1950s and 1960s.

The parents of baby boomers experienced multiple economic and social pressures. In addition to providing for their children materially and emotionally, they were expected to adhere to rigid gender roles as a way of maintaining the family and undergirding the social order. The mass media, educators, and experts urged men to conform to a masculine ideal that emphasized their role as responsible breadwinners; women's proper place, they advised, was in the home. What Betty Friedan has called the "feminine mystique" of the 1950s—the ideal that "the highest value and the only commitment for women is the fulfillment of their own femininity"—bore a remarkable similarity to the nineteenth-century cult of true womanhood. However, the 1950s version of the cult of domesticity drew on twentieth-century science and culture, and even on Freudian psychology. Psychologists pronounced motherhood the only "normal" female sex role, and berated mothers who worked outside the home, charging that they damaged their children's development. Television, popular music, films, and advertising all reinforced that notion by depicting career women as social and sexual misfits.

Though the power of these ideas stunted the lives of many women, not all housewives were unhappy or neurotic, as Friedan would later charge in her

A Woman Encounters the Feminine Mystique

The power of the feminine mystique in the 1950s made it difficult for middle-class women who challenged the view that women's proper place was in the home. In this oral history account, "Sylvia" describes her struggle to pursue a career as an ophthalmologist.

We sat on a bench in the middle of the lobby there—I remember it looked like a train station—and he [her professor] said, "Do you plan to get pregnant or married?" I promised him I wouldn't do either. I felt like I was about ten years old. They gave me a year's trial in the research department and after that I could get a residency. Most people there, the men, had a three-year residency. I was only the second woman they'd ever accepted, and I was the only woman out of twenty men.

I had a fellowship, so when I finished with my work I'd have to go over to see how my research projects were coming along. I never, never, goofed off. These guys were watching me all the time and complaining that I wasn't doing my work. It was hard enough to be a first-year resident, where you're the bottom person who gets kicked by everybody. I had no friends. My fellow physicians were constantly telling me I should switch to obstetrics or pediatrics, I should be home having babies, that a man could earn a wonderful living for his family in my place. Finally I was at my wits' end and I called my old ophthalmology professor and told him I didn't know if I could psychologically take this for another two and a half years. He said, "You know, if you give up now I'll never be able to get another woman in there." So I went on.

SOURCE: Brett Harvey, *The Fifties: A Women's Oral History* (New York: Harper, 1993), pp. 154–155.

1963 bestseller, *The Feminine Mystique.* Many working-class women embraced their new roles as housewives; unlike their mothers and unmarried sisters, they were not compelled to take low-paid employment outside the home. But not all Americans could or did live by the norms of suburban domesticity, ideals that were out of reach of or irrelevant to many racial minorities, inner-city residents, recent immigrants, rural Americans, and homosexuals. At the height of the postwar period, more than one-third of American women held jobs outside the home. The increase in the number of working women coincided with another change of equal significance—a dramatic rise in the number of older, married middle-class women who took jobs. Once again there was a significant gap between popular culture and the reality of American lives.

How could the society of the 1950s cling so steadfastly to the domestic ideal while an increasing number of wives and mothers took jobs? Often women justified their jobs as an extension of their family responsibilities. Their paid labor allowed their families to enjoy more of the fruits of the consumer culture. Because women who took jobs outside the home still bore full responsibility for child care and household management, their families and society as a whole could avoid facing the implications of their new roles. Thus the reality of women's lives departed significantly from the cultural stereotypes glorified in advertising, sitcoms, and women's magazines. As one overburdened woman complained, she now had "two full-time jobs instead of just one—underpaid clerical worker and unpaid housekeeper."

Cultural Dissenters

Beneath the surfaces of family togetherness lay other tensions. Teenagers, especially white middle-class teenagers, had become the basis of a distinct new market that advertisers eagerly exploited. In 1956 advertisers projected an adolescent market worth $9 billion for items such as transistor radios (first introduced in 1952), clothing, and fads such as Silly Putty (1950) and Hula-Hoops (1958). Less innocuous to anxious parents were the consumer choices that teens made in books, movies, and music—choices that suggested they were rebelling against the safe and insulated suburban world their parents had worked so hard to create.

Hollywood movies played a large role in fostering and legitimizing the teenage subculture. Recognizing that young people were the largest audience for motion pictures, the studios catered to them with films such as *The Wild One* (1954), starring Marlon Brando, and *Rebel Without a Cause* (1955), starring James Dean, Natalie Wood, and Sal Mineo. "What are you rebelling against?" a waitress asked Brando in *The Wild One*. "Whattaya got?" he replied.

What really defined this generation, however, was its music. Rejecting the rigidly defined categories of traditional popular music, the teenagers of the 1950s discovered rock-'n'-roll, an amalgam of white country and western music and the black urban sound known as rhythm and blues. Young white performers such as Bill Haley, Elvis Presley, and Buddy Holly incorporated the new mixture into their own music to capitalize on the new teen market. Between 1953 and 1959, record sales increased from $213 million to $603 million, with 45-rpm rock-'n'-roll records as the driving force.

For many white youths, Elvis Presley represented the epitome of their new music. But Presley's success was based not only on his music but on his stage presence and his relationship with the audience. With his slicked-back hair, long sideburns, and tight pants, Presley cultivated a lower-class "greaser" look that proved immensely popular with teenage fans. His quivering legs, gyrating pelvis, and playful sneer drove young female fans wild; they frequently mobbed the stage, grabbing at his clothes for souvenirs.

African-Americans found Presley's success and notoriety somewhat ironic. Black musicians such as Chuck Berry had been performing similar music for

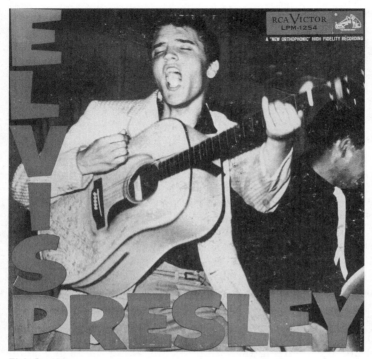

Elvis Presley
The young Elvis Presley (shown here on the cover of his first album in
1956) embodied cultural rebellion against the conservatism of adult life in
the 1950s.

years but with little commercial success among white audiences. To many, the
appropriation of black rhythm and blues by white artists was out-and-out
theft. In the long run, however, the popularity of rock-'n'-roll introduced
black performers such as Little Richard, Fats Domino, and James Brown to
white as well as black audiences.

Many white adults were appalled at the teen subculture. They saw in rock-
'n'-roll music, teen movies, and magazines such as *Mad* (introduced in 1952)
an invitation to race mixing, rebellion, and disorder. Playing on their fears, the
media featured hundreds of stories on problem teens. In 1955 a Senate sub-
committee conducted a high-profile investigation of juvenile delinquency,
blaming its origins on the popular media. Adult denunciations of the youth
culture, however, only increased its popularity among teens.

The youth rebellion was only one aspect of a broader undercurrent of
discontent with the conformist culture of the 1950s. Postwar artists, jazz musicians, and writers also expressed their alienation from mainstream society
through intensely personal, introspective art forms. In New York, Jackson
Pollock and other painters rejected the social realism of the 1930s, creating

an unconventional style that became known as abstract expressionism. Swirling and splattering paint onto giant canvases, Pollock emphasized self-expression in the act of painting, capturing the chaotic atmosphere of the nuclear age. A similar trend developed in jazz as black musicians originated a hard-driving improvisational style known as bebop. Whether the "hot" bebop of the 1940s, invented by saxophonist Charlie Parker, or the more subdued "cool" West Coast sound of the 1950s, epitomized by the trumpeter Miles Davis, postwar jazz was cerebral, intimate, and individualistic.

Black jazz musicians found eager fans not only in the African-American community, but among young white *beats* in New York and San Francisco. Beat writers and poets experimented stylistically, bringing innovation and exuberance to their works. Their messages were equally brash, as they critiqued middle-class conformity, suburban materialism, and corporate capitalism. Allen Ginsberg, in his poem *Howl* (1956), criticized the sterility of modern culture, railing against "Robot apartments! invisible suburbs! skeleton treasures! blind capitals! demonic industries!" The beats also warned against the menace of nuclear weaponry. In "Bomb" (1960), a powerful poem punctuated with lines like "Boom Boom Boom Boom," Gregory Corso called the bomb "toy of the universe."

The beats glorified spontaneity, sexual adventurism, drug use, and spirituality. In his semiautobiographical novel *On the Road* (1957), Jack Kerouac described a journey across America by his main characters—Sal Paradise and Dean Moriarity. In search of "authentic," genuine, experience, the two men often thought they found it among African-Americans or Latinos. They found black music especially exhilarating. But Kerouac's fascination with people of color could easily slip into stereotyping them as primitive. In one passage, Sal Paradise exclaimed that he walked through Denver, "wishing I were a Negro, feeling that the best the white world had offered was not enough for men, not enough life, joy, kicks, darkness, music." He wished he were a "Denver Mexican or a poor overworked Jap, anything but what I was so drearily, a white 'man' disillusioned. . . . I was only myself . . . wishing I could exchange words with the happy, true-hearted, ecstatic Negroes of America."

In his depiction of women, Kerouac also revealed the cultural biases of the society he so roundly criticized. Like other beats, he glorified sexuality, in the process often viewing women as conquests. In *On the Road*, when women became wives or mothers, they were looked upon as hindrances to the male characters' search for liberation. Almost all the well-known beat writers were male, and at least part of their rebellion focused on the circumscribed life of the organization man, on the rigid gender roles that locked men into the rat race of the breadwinner.

Important as literary innovators, the beats were also significant as outspoken social critics. Although they were apolitical—their rebellion was strictly cultural—in the 1960s they would inspire a new generation of rebels who would champion both political and cultural change.

THE OTHER AMERICA

Youth and intellectuals were not the only challengers to the status quo; many other groups lived outside the mainstream of American society. As middle-class whites flocked to the suburbs, poor and working-class migrants and immigrants, many of them nonwhite, moved into the central cities. With jobs and financial resources flowing to the suburbs, urban newcomers inherited a declining economy and a decaying environment. This "other America" remained largely invisible to affluent white suburbanites. Only in the South, where African-Americans organized to combat legal segregation, did the problem of social injustice come to the public's attention.

Postwar Immigration

Newly arrived immigrants were one of several groups that moved into the nation's cities in the postwar era. Until 1965 American immigration policy followed the restrictive quota system set up in 1924 (see Chapter 24). But during World War II and its cold war aftermath Congress slightly loosened the law for a variety of reasons. In 1948 the Displaced Persons Act admitted approximately 415,000 Europeans, but discriminated against Jews while favoring people of German origins. The Chinese Exclusion Act was repealed in 1943 in a bow to America's wartime alliance with China. And in 1952, at the height of the Cold War, the McCarran-Walter Act ended the exclusion of Japanese, Koreans, and southeast Asians from immigration and naturalization. Congress passed the measure to demonstrate to the world America's commitment to democracy. The act, however, also banned the entry of Communists and other radicals.

Foreign policy shaped immigration priorities in other ways. In 1945 Congress passed the War Brides Act, which allowed the entrance and naturalization of the wives and children of Americans who had lived abroad, mainly servicemen. Approximately 17,000 Koreans entered the United States under this law between 1950 and 1965, the vast majority of them war brides from the Korean War. Finally, in recognition of the freeing of the Philippines from American control on July 4, 1946, Filipinos received their own quota. A major increase in immigration from Asian countries, however, would not occur until after 1965 (see Chapter 30).

One of the largest groups of postwar immigrants came from Mexico. Nearly 275,000 Mexicans entered the United States in the 1950s, and almost 444,000 in the 1960s. They moved primarily to western and southwestern cities such as Los Angeles, Long Beach, El Paso, and Phoenix, where they found jobs as migrant workers or laborers in the expanding service sector. Large numbers of Mexican-Americans also settled in Chicago, Detroit, Kansas City, and Denver.

Part of the stimulus for Mexican immigration came from the reinstitution of the *bracero* program, which the Mexican and American governments had created during the labor shortages of World War II to bring temporary workers to the United States. When the Korean War produced new labor shortages, a new *bracero* program operated from 1951 to 1964. At the program's peak in 1959, 450,000 *braceros* entered the United States, and an estimated 350,000 settled permanently. But even as the federal government welcomed *braceros*, it deported those who stayed on illegally. In response to the recession of 1953–1954, which caused high unemployment throughout the nation, federal authorities deported nearly 4 million Mexicans in a program called "Operation Wetback." For a few years, the level of illegal immigration was reduced, but it rose again after the *bracero* program ended.

Another group of Spanish-speaking immigrants came from the American-controlled territory of Puerto Rico. Residents of that island had been American citizens since 1917, and thus Puerto Ricans were not subject to immigration laws. The inflow from the island increased dramatically after World War II, when mechanization of the island's sugarcane industry pushed many rural Puerto Ricans off the land. When airlines began to offer cheap direct flights between San Juan and New York City, Puerto Ricans became the first group to immigrate by air to the United States. Their massive movement, which grew from 70,000 per year in 1940 to 613,000 just twenty years later, transformed the ethnic composition of New York City. There, they faced conditions common to all recent immigrants: crowded and deteriorating housing, segregation, unemployment or restriction to menial jobs, poor schools, and the challenges of a bilingual existence.

Cuban refugees constituted the third largest group of Spanish-speaking immigrants. In the six years after Fidel Castro's seizure of power in 1959, an estimated 180,000 people fled Cuba for the United States. The Cuban refugee community grew so quickly that it turned Miami into a cosmopolitan, bilingual city almost overnight. Unlike most new immigrants, Cubans prospered, in large part because they brought with them substantial resources. Cubans differed from most other Latino immigrants in that they were predominantly middle class and politically conservative.

Migration to the City

Migration within the United States also brought people to the cities, especially African-Americans, continuing a trend that had begun during World War I (see Chapter 23). Black migration was hastened by the transformation of southern agriculture, especially its mechanization, which reduced the demand for labor. From 1930 to 1960 southern farm population fell from 16.2 million to 5.9 million.

Some of the migrants from the South settled in southern cities, where they found factory jobs. Many whites from Appalachia moved north to "hillbilly" ghettos in cities like Chicago and Cincinnati. In the most dramatic population shift, as many as 3 million black southerners headed to Chicago, New York, Washington, Detroit, Los Angeles, and other cities between 1940 and 1960.

Certain sections of Chicago seemed like the Mississippi Delta transplanted, so pervasive were the migrants. By 1960 about half the nation's black population was living outside the South, compared to only 23 percent before World War II.

In western cities, an influx of native Americans contributed to the rise in the nonwhite urban population. Congress, seeking to end federal involvement in Indian affairs, passed a resolution in 1953 authorizing a program to terminate the legal standing of native tribes and move their members off reservations and into cities. The program, which reflected the cold war preoccupation with conformity and assimilation, enjoyed strong support from mining, timber, and agricultural interests that wanted to open reservation lands for private development. But relocation proved problematic, as many Indians struggled to adjust to an urban environment and culture. Although the policy of forced termination was halted in 1958, by 1960 some 60,000 Indians had moved to the cities. Despite the program's stated goal of assimilation, most native American migrants settled together in poor urban neighborhoods alongside other nonwhite groups.

At the same time that whites were flocking to the suburbs, then, American cities saw their nonwhite populations swell. From 1950 to 1960 the nation's twelve largest cities lost 3.6 million whites and gained 4.5 million nonwhites. Tax revenues followed the more affluent whites out of the city and into the suburbs. A wealthy community such as Grosse Pointe, a suburb of Detroit, could far more easily fund first-rate schools and police than could the city of Detroit, whose tax base shrank as businesses and middle-class residents relocated to the suburbs.

By the time blacks, native Americans, and Latinos moved into the inner cities, urban America was in poor shape. Housing was a crucial problem, which city planners, politicians, and real estate developers responded to by razing blighted neighborhoods to make way for new construction. Local residents were rarely consulted about whether they wanted their neighborhoods "renewed." Urban renewal often produced grim high-rise housing projects that destroyed neighborhoods and created barren open areas vulnerable to crime. In the name of urban renewal, between 1949 and 1967, construction crews demolished almost 400,000 buildings, displacing 1.4 million people. The 575,000 units of new public housing that were built nationwide by 1964 did not begin to satisfy the need for affordable urban housing.

Increasingly, the cities became a place of last resort for the nation's poor. Unlike earlier immigrants, for whom cities had been gateways to social and economic betterment, most inner-city residents of the postwar period faced diminishing opportunities for improvement. Lured by the promise of plentiful jobs, migrants found that many employers had relocated to the suburbs. For those who needed it most, steady employment was out of reach.

Black Activism in the South

The problems of the urban poor were largely invisible to most Americans in the 1950s. But as teenagers' rebellion in musical styles and the beat generation's attack on conformity revealed currents of discontent with the cultural consensus of the period, black Americans in the South were forging a challenge to the racial status quo. Confrontations in cities like Montgomery, Alabama, and Little Rock, Arkansas, shocked white Americans, unsettling their complacency, and forcing their recognition of "other Americans" who lived outside the privileges of the affluent fifties.

Blacks who stayed in the South faced not only urban poverty but legal segregation. In most southern states in the 1950s, whites and blacks could not eat in the same rooms at restaurants and luncheonettes or use the same waiting rooms and toilets at bus and train stations. All forms of public transportation were rigidly segregated by custom or by law. Even drinking fountains were labeled "White" and "Colored."

Beginning with World War II, the National Association for the Advancement of Colored People (NAACP) redoubled its efforts to combat segregation in housing, transportation, and other areas (see Chapter 27). The first significant victory came in 1954, when the Supreme Court handed down its most far-reaching decision in *Brown v. Board of Education of Topeka*. The NAACP's chief legal counsel, Thurgood Marshall, had argued that the segregated schools mandated by the Board of Education in Topeka, Kansas, were inherently unconstitutional, because they stigmatized an entire race, denying black children the "equal protection of the laws" guaranteed by the Fourteenth Amendment. In a unanimous decision announced on May 17, 1954, the Supreme Court agreed with Marshall and overturned the longstanding "separate but equal" doctrine of *Plessy v. Ferguson* (see Chapter 19).

Over the next several years, in response to NAACP suits, the Supreme Court used the *Brown* precedent to overturn segregation in city parks, public beaches, and golf courses; in interstate and intrastate transportation; and in public housing. In the face of these Court decisions, white resistance to integration solidified. In 1956, 101 members of Congress signed the Southern Manifesto, denouncing the *Brown* decision as "a clear abuse of judicial power" and encouraging their constituents to defy it. That same year, 500,000 southerners joined White Citizens' Councils dedicated to blocking school integration and other civil rights measures. Some whites revived old tactics of violence and intimidation, swelling the ranks of the Ku Klux Klan to levels not seen since the 1920s.

In 1957, the Governor of Arkansas, Governor Orval Faubus, defied a federal court order to desegregate Little Rock's Central High School. Faubus called out the National Guard to bar nine black students who were attempting to enroll in the all-white school. After scenes of vicious mobs harassing the determined students aired on television, President Eisenhower reluctantly intervened, sending 1,000 federal troops and 10,000 nationalized members of the Arkansas National Guard to protect the students. Eisenhower thus became the first president since Reconstruction to use federal troops to enforce the rights of blacks.

Integration at Little Rock
Angry crowds taunted the nine
black students who tried to register
in 1957 at the previously all-white
Central High School in Little
Rock, Arkansas, with chants such
as "Two–four–six–eight, we ain't
gonna integrate." The court-
ordered integration proceeded only
after President Eisenhower reluctantly nationalized the Arkansas
National Guard.

White resistance to the *Brown* decision, as well as Eisenhower's hesitancy to
act in Little Rock, showed that court victories were not enough to overturn
segregation. In 1955, a new strategy, nonviolent protest, emerged from one tiny
but monumental act of defiance. On December 1, Rosa Parks, a seamstress and
a member of the NAACP in Montgomery, Alabama, refused to give up her seat
on a city bus to a white man. "I felt it was just something I had to do," Parks
stated. She was promptly arrested and charged with violating a local segregation ordinance. When the black community in Montgomery met to discuss the
proper response, they turned to the Reverend Martin Luther King, Jr., who
had become the pastor at a local church the year before. King endorsed a plan
by a Montgomery black women's organization to boycott the city's bus system
until it was integrated. For the next 381 days, members of a united black community formed carpools or walked to work. The bus company neared bankruptcy, and downtown stores saw their business decline. But not until the
Supreme Court ruled in November 1956 that bus segregation was unconstitutional did the city of Montgomery finally relent, prompting one woman boy-
cotter to proclaim, "My feets is tired, but my soul is rested."

The Montgomery bus boycott catapulted King to national prominence. In
1957, with the Reverend Ralph Abernathy and other southern black clergy,
he founded the Southern Christian Leadership Conference (SCLC), based in
Atlanta. The black church had long been the center of African-American social and cultural life. Through the SCLC it lent its moral and organizational
strength, as well as the voices of its most inspirational preachers, to the civil-
rights movement. Black churchwomen flocked to the movement, transferring
the skills they had honed through years of church work to the fight for racial
change. Soon the SCLC had joined the NAACP as one of the major advocates for racial justice. While the two groups achieved only limited victories in
the 1950s, they laid the organizational groundwork for the dynamic civil-
rights movement that would emerge in the 1960s.

The Montgomery Bus Boycott

During the Montgomery, Alabama, bus boycott of 1955, many blacks walked or—as was the case with many women who worked as maids—received rides from their white employers. Others took advantage of an informal taxi system. Yancey Martin was a college freshman on Christmas vacation when he began driving for the cause.

And so all the guys who were on my street . . . and a group of other folk whose parents had cars, we would all get up in the morning as early as we could. I mean, there were some folk out there who had to leave by six o'clock in order to get to the white lady's kitchen, and many times they were just late getting there. We'd all get up in the morning and we'd drive the route. . . . And what we had to do was we had to know the names of everybody in there or else the police would stop and try to charge you with operating an illegal jitney service. . . . But the police, when they found out what we were doing, they would patrol the bus routes just as much as we would. . . .

We saw the transportation end really kinda being the backbone of the movement because folks had to work and they had to have that little money. . . . So about four or five of us said, "Well, why do we have to go back [to college]? It's important that we get a college education, but it's important that we win this thing now that we've gotten into it. . . . I could not guarantee that my daddy would find somebody who would be able to drive that car every day like I was driving it every day. So I went on and stayed.

SOURCE: Howell Raines, *My Soul Is Rested: Movement Days in the Deep South Remembered* (New York: Penguin, 1985), pp. 58–61.

"The Fifties": The Way We Were?

For many Americans the 1950s represents the norm of American society—a time when families were close-knit and intact, children happy, and the economy flourishing. Despite the fear of nuclear annihilation, Americans were confident in the 1950s that theirs was the strongest country, both economically and morally, in the world. Changes in American family, political, and social life since then are often seen as declines from this ideal.

But perhaps the fifties were not the norm but an aberration—the result of a unique combination of circumstances that could not be sustained. In a 200-year trend toward smaller families, the postwar baby boom was certainly atypical, as was the remarkable stability of marriages. Perhaps the greatest aberration—and the reason the common view of the 1950s as the norm is so misleading—was that the nation's postwar affluence was based on international economic conditions that could not continue indefinitely. Inevitably the war-devastated economies of Japan and West Germany would rebuild, taking advantage of new technology to compete with and eventually challenge American economic supremacy. If Americans regard the economic dominance the nation enjoyed in the 1950s as the norm, any decline in that dominance will appear to be a disturbing loss of American power and economic strength, rather than a return to a more balanced state of affairs.

The stereotypes of the 1950s are misleading, if not downright false, in other ways, too. In our nostalgic memories of suburban affluence, we forget those Americans who did not share equally in the postwar American dream. Many people—displaced factory workers, destitute elderly people, female heads of households, blacks, and Latinos—watched the affluent society from the outside in the fifties, wondering why they were not permitted to share in its bounty. Not until the publication of Michael Harrington's *The Other America* in 1962 did Americans begin to realize that in the richest country in the world, more than a quarter of the population was poor.

In the turbulent decade that followed, the contrast between suburban affluence and the "other America," between the lure of the city for the poor and minorities and the grim reality of its segregated existence, and between a heightened emphasis on domesticity and widening opportunities for women, would spawn protest and change. Amid the booming prosperity of the late 1940s and 1950s, however, these fundamental social and economic contradictions were barely noticed.

CHAPTER 29 TIMELINE

1944	Bretton Woods economic conference World Bank and International Monetary Fund (IMF) founded
1946	Dr. Benjamin Spock, *Baby and Child Care*
1947	Levittown, New York, built
1948	CBS and NBC begin regular television programming
1950	Reverend Billy Graham's Evangelistic Association founded
1953–1958	Operation Wetback and Indian termination programs
1954	Polio vaccine developed by Dr. Jonas Salk *Brown v. Board of Education of Topeka, Kansas* First McDonald's opens
1955	AFL and CIO reunited Montgomery bus boycott Disneyland opens in Anaheim, California
1956	Interstate Highway Act Elvis Presley popularizes rock-'n'-roll via television Congress adds "In God We Trust" to coins
1957	Peak of postwar baby boom Jack Kerouac, *On the Road* Eisenhower sends federal troops to protect black students during school desegregation battle in Little Rock, Arkansas Southern Christian Leadership Conference founded
1958	Brooklyn Dodgers move to Los Angeles
1963	California replaces New York as the most populous state Betty Friedan, *The Feminine Mystique*

CHAPTER 30

LIBERAL REFORM AND RADICALISM, 1960-1970

- John Kennedy and the New Frontier
- The Civil-Rights Movement
- Lyndon Johnson and the Great Society
- The Continuing Struggle for Civil Rights

In his 1961 inaugural address President John Fitzgerald Kennedy challenged a "new generation of Americans" to take responsibility for the future. Kennedy exhorted, "Ask not what your country can do for you, ask what you can do for your country." Over the next decade many young Americans would respond to that sense of mission. As a civil-rights volunteer explained in 1964, "I want to do my part. There's a moral wave building among today's youth, and I intend to catch it."

Ironically, the roots of 1960s activism lay in the tranquil America of the 1950s. Postwar affluence produced a self-assured generation of young middle-class whites optimistic about their ability to cure the nation's social ills. It also reminded African-Americans of the economic and social gap between the races. In the 1960s the baby-boom generation swelled college enrollments, providing recruits for the civil-rights campaign and other student movements, including a revival of feminism. To them, the lofty cold war rhetoric of international freedom and democracy sounded hollow in the face of economic and racial injustice at home.

The sense of optimism and activism that characterized the 1960s also pervaded politics. The administrations of John F. Kennedy, and—to a much greater extent—Lyndon B. Johnson acted on an abiding faith in the positive influence of government. Johnson's "Great Society" marked the high tide of postwar liberalism, the deliberate use of federal power to spread the abundance of the postwar economy among greater numbers of people, through expanded federal programs in health care, education, and civil rights.

Liberal politicians also pursued an activist stance abroad. Seeking to protect American political and economic interests in the international arena, the Kennedy and Johnson administrations took aggressive action against communist influence in Europe, the Caribbean, and Vietnam (see Chapter 31), among other places. As time passed, however, the growing financial and political costs of that ambitious agenda hampered further progress on the domestic front, dividing the postwar liberal coalition.

JOHN KENNEDY AND THE NEW FRONTIER

Franklin Roosevelt's activist administration had expanded presidential power, heightening the public's expectations of presidential leadership during the Truman and Eisenhower administrations. By the 1960s, when American power and resources seemed limitless, many citizens looked to Washington for solutions to any and all problems, whether international, national, or local. Few presidents came to Washington more aware of these high expectations than John Kennedy, who promised a "New Frontier" of vigorous governmental activism at home and abroad.

The New Politics and Activism Abroad

The Republicans would have been happy to renominate Dwight D. Eisenhower for president in 1960, but they were prevented from doing so by the Twenty-second Amendment. Passed in 1951 by a Republican-controlled Congress to prevent a repetition of Franklin Roosevelt's four-term presidency, the amendment limited future presidents to two full terms. Thus in 1960, the Republicans turned to Vice-President Richard M. Nixon, who identified himself with Eisenhower's policies but was hampered by lukewarm support from Eisenhower. Asked whether Nixon had helped to make any major policy decisions in his administration, Eisenhower replied, "If you give me a week I might think of one."

The Democrats chose Senator John Fitzgerald Kennedy of Massachusetts to run for president, with Senate majority leader Lyndon Johnson of Texas as the vice-presidential nominee. Kennedy launched his "New Frontier" campaign with a platform calling for civil-rights legislation, health care for the elderly, aid to education, urban renewal, expanded military and space programs, and containment of communism abroad. With the country in the middle of a recession that had pushed unemployment to a postwar high, Kennedy vowed to "get American moving again."

At forty-three, Kennedy was poised to become the youngest man ever elected to the presidency, and the nation's first Catholic chief executive. Kennedy dealt with the issue of religion directly. In an address to a group of Protestant ministers in Houston he affirmed his belief in the separation of church and state and declared his political independence from the Vatican.

Turning his youth into a powerful campaign asset, Kennedy practiced what came to be called the "new politics"—an approach that emphasized

The Kennedy Magnetism
John Kennedy, the Democratic candidate for president in 1960, used his youth and personality to attract voters. Here the Massachusetts senator draws an enthusiastic crowd on a campaign stop in Elgin, Illinois.

youthful charisma, style, and personality over issues and platforms. Using the power of the media, particularly television, to reach voters directly, practitioners of the new politics relied on professional media consultants and political pollsters, with massive fund raising to pay for them. Kennedy's youth, attractiveness, and charm made for a superb television image.

A series of four televised debates between the two principal candidates—a major innovation of the 1960 campaign—showed how important the new medium of TV was becoming to political life. Nixon, far less photogenic than Kennedy, looked sallow and unshaven under the intense studio lights. Kennedy, in contrast, looked vigorous, cool, and self-confident on screen. Polls showed that television did sway its viewers' political perceptions: voters who listened to the first debate on the radio concluded that Nixon had won, whereas those who viewed it on TV judged Kennedy the winner.

Despite the edge Kennedy enjoyed in the debates, he won only the narrowest of victories, receiving 49.7 percent of the popular vote to Nixon's 49.5

percent. Kennedy had successfully appealed to the diverse elements of the Democratic coalition, attracting large numbers of Catholic and black voters and a significant sector of the middle class. The vice-presidential nominee, Lyndon Johnson, brought in southern whites. Yet only 120,000 votes separated the two candidates, and the shift of a few thousand votes in key states such as Illinois (where there were confirmed cases of voting fraud) would have reversed the outcome.

Although Kennedy's New Frontier platform had included a long list of domestic social reforms, his greatest priority as president was foreign affairs. A resolute cold warrior, Kennedy took a hard line against communist expansionism. In contrast to Eisenhower, whose cost-saving New Look program had built up the American nuclear arsenal at the expense of conventional weapons, Kennedy proposed a new policy of *flexible response*, stating that the nation must be prepared "to deter all wars, general or limited, nuclear or conventional, large or small." Congress quickly granted Kennedy's requests for increased funding, dramatically increasing the defense budget and expanding the military-industrial complex.

Flexible response measures were designed to deter direct attacks by the Soviet Union. To prepare for a new kind of warfare, evident in the wars of national liberation that had broken out in many Third World countries where inhabitants sought to overthrow colonial rulers or unpopular dictators, Kennedy adopted a new military doctrine, *counterinsurgency*. Soon U.S. Army Special Forces, called Green Berets after their distinctive headgear, were receiving intensive training in repelling the small-scale, random attacks typical of guerrilla warfare. Vietnam would soon provide a testing ground for these counterinsurgency techniques (see Chapter 31).

Another of Kennedy's projects, the Peace Corps, embodied the commitment to public service that the president had called for in his inaugural address. Thousands of young men and women, many of them recent college graduates, agreed to devote two or more years to teaching English to Filipino schoolchildren or helping African villagers obtain adequate water supplies. Embodying the idealism of the early 1960s, the Peace Corps was also a cold war weapon designed to draw Third World countries into the American orbit and away from communist influence.

For the same reason, Kennedy pushed for economic aid to developing countries. The State Department's Agency for International Development coordinated foreign aid to the Third World, including surplus agricultural products distributed to developing nations through its Food for Peace program. In Latin America, the Alliance for Progress provided funds for food, education, medicine, and other services, though it did little to enhance economic growth or improve social conditions there.

Latin America was the site of Kennedy's first major foreign policy initiative and one of his biggest failures—an effort to overthrow the new Soviet-supported regime in Cuba. The United States had long maintained a naval base at Guantánamo Bay, and had dominated the island economically and politically.

AMERICAN VOICES

A Peace Corp Volunteer

M*any Peace Corps volunteers found their projects disillusioning, but others idealistically judged the Corps to be "the greatest eye-opening, mind-stretching experience any generation of Americans has ever had." Philip A. Schaefer describes the rewarding aspects of his stint of duty in Kenya at the Uaso Nyiro Settlement.*

It is my job to assist in the difficult transformation from landless worker to successful entrepreneur. At first I thought that this would be beyond my abilities since I am a New York City "Farm boy" whose agricultural experience was previously limited to a tour of fruit and vegetable stands on the Lower East Side of New York. But . . . I soon came to realize that "Catcher" and "Fanfare" were varieties of wheat and not terms to describe the action on the baseball diamond. . . .

Dashing around on my *piki* (motorcycle) . . . with the cooperative chairman making arrangements to harvest the wheat or to purchase cattle has been hectic and exciting. But ordinary life on a settlement scheme can be pretty dreary. On Uaso Nyiro we have tried to create an exciting sense of community. We have started our own scheme newspaper, an idea which is catching on with other settlement schemes. But we are most proud of recent water show which helped to raise nearly $4,000 to bring needed water to the scheme. . . .

The people have begun to work together in the spirit of *harambee* (pulling together) as preached by *Mzee* (the old one) Jomo Kenyatta, the President of Keyna. To be a small participant in positive change is probably the most exhilarating and satisfying experience of my life. To . . . return to the wheatless streets of New York will not be entirely painless.

SOURCE: Roy Hoopes, ed., *The Peace Corps Experience* (New York: Clarkson N. Potter, Inc., 1968), p.193.

But on New Year's Day in 1959 Fidel Castro overthrew the corrupt and unpopular dictator Fulgencio Batista and called for a revolution to reshape Cuban society. When Castro began agrarian reforms and nationalized American-owned banks and industries, relations with Washington deteriorated. By early 1961 the United States had declared an embargo on all exports to Cuba, cut back on U.S. imports of Cuban sugar, and broken off diplomatic relations with the regime.

Isolated by the United States, Cuba turned increasingly toward the Soviet Union for economic and military support. Concerned about Castro's growing friendliness toward the Soviets, in early 1961 Kennedy used plans originally drawn up by the Eisenhower administration to dispatch Cuban exiles to the island to foment a counterrebellion. Though the invaders had been trained by the Central Intelligence Agency (CIA), they were ill prepared for their task and had little popular support on the island. Shortly after landing at Cuba's Bay of Pigs on April 17, the tiny force of 1,400 men was crushed by Castro's troops (see Map 30.1).

U.S.-Soviet relations, adversely affected by the Bay of Pigs invasion, deteriorated further in June 1961, when Soviet Premier Khrushchev deployed soldiers to sever East Berlin from the western sector of the German city. With congressional approval, Kennedy responded by adding 300,000 troops to the armed forces, and promptly dispatched 40,000 of them to Europe. In mid-August, to stop the rapid exodus of East Germans to the West, the Soviets ordered construction of the Berlin Wall, and East German guards began policing the border. Until it was dismantled in 1989, the Berlin Wall was the supreme symbol of the Cold War.

The climactic confrontation of the Cold War came in October 1962. After the failed Bay of Pigs invasion, the Kennedy administration increased the economic pressure on Cuba and resumed covert efforts to overthrow Castro's regime. In response, the Soviets stepped up military aid to Cuba, including the

MAP 30.1

The United States and Cuba, 1961–1962
Fidel Castro's takeover in Cuba in 1959 brought cold war tensions to the Caribbean. In 1961 the United States tried unsuccessfully to overthrow Castro's regime by supporting an invasion by Cuban exiles launched from Nicaragua. In 1962 a major confrontation with the Soviet Union occurred over Soviet missile sites in Cuba. The Soviets removed the missiles after President Kennedy ordered a naval blockade of the island, which lies just 90 miles south of Florida.

installation of defensive missiles. In early October, American reconnaissance planes photographed Soviet-built bases for intermediate-range ballistic missiles (IRBMs), which could reach targets in the United States as far as 2,200 miles away. At least some of those nuclear weapons had already been installed; more were on the way.

In a somber address televised on Monday, October 22, Kennedy confronted the Soviet Union, and announced that the United States would impose a "quarantine on all offensive military equipment" intended for Cuba. As the two superpowers went on full military alert, people around the world feared that the confrontation would end in nuclear war. Americans living within range of the missiles restocked their bomb shelters or calculated the fastest route out of town. When Khrushchev denounced the quarantine, tension mounted. But as the world held its breath, ships carrying the Soviet-made missiles turned back. After a week of tense negotiations, both Kennedy and Khrushchev made concessions: Kennedy pledged not to invade Cuba, and Khrushchev promised to dismantle the missile bases.

Although the risk of nuclear war was greater during the Cuban missile crisis than at any other time in the postwar period, it led to a slight thaw in U.S.-Soviet relations. In the words of the national security adviser, McGeorge Bundy, "having come so close to the edge, the leaders of the two governments have since taken care to keep away from the cliff." Sobered by the close brush with nuclear war, Kennedy softened his earlier cold war rhetoric and began to strive for peaceful coexistence. Soviet leaders, similarly chastened, were willing to talk. In 1963 the world's three nuclear powers—the United States, the Soviet Union, and Great Britain—agreed to ban the testing of nuclear weapons in the atmosphere, in space, and under water. Underground testing, however, was allowed to continue. The new emphasis on peaceful coexistence also led to the establishment of a Washington-to-Moscow "hot line," so that leaders of the two superpowers could contact each other quickly during potential crises.

But no matter how often American leaders talked about opening channels of communication with the Soviets, the obsession with the potential Soviet military threat to American security remained a cornerstone of U.S. policy. Nor did Soviet leaders moderate their concern over the threat they believed the United States posed to their nation's survival. The Cold War—and the escalating arms race that accompanied it—would continue for another twenty-five years.

Kennedy's Domestic Policies

The expansive vision of presidential leadership that Kennedy and his advisers brought to the White House worked less well at home than it did abroad. Hampered by the lack of a popular mandate in the 1960 election, Kennedy could not mobilize public support for the domestic component of the New Frontier. A conservative coalition of southern Democrats and western and midwestern Republicans effectively stalled most of his liberal initiatives. More important, Kennedy was not nearly as impassioned about domestic reform as he was about foreign policy.

One program that did win both popular and Congressional support was increased funding for the National Aeronautics and Space Administration (NASA), whose space program had begun in 1958. On May 5, 1961, just three months after Kennedy took office, Alan Shepard became the first American to fly in space. (The Soviet cosmonaut Yuri Gagarin had become the first person ever to enter space in April 1961.) At the height of the American public's fascination with space flight, Kennedy proposed that the nation commit itself to landing a man on the moon within a decade. To support this mission (accomplished in 1969), Kennedy persuaded Congress to greatly increase NASA's budget.

Kennedy's most striking domestic achievement was his use of modern economic theory to shape government fiscal policy. New Dealers had gradually moved away from the ideal of a balanced budget, turning instead to deliberate deficit spending to stimulate economic growth. In addition to relying on federal spending to create the desired deficit, Kennedy and his advisers proposed a reduction in income taxes. A tax cut, they argued, would produce a short-term deficit, but would put more money in the hands of taxpayers, who would spend it, creating more jobs. For a time federal expenditures would exceed federal income, but after a year or two the expanding economy would raise American incomes and generate higher tax revenues.

Congress balked at this unorthodox proposal and the measure failed to pass. But Lyndon Johnson pressed for it after Kennedy's assassination, signing it into law in February 1964. Although an economic expansion began before the effects of the tax cut could be felt, Kennedy and his economic advisers got credit for it anyway. The gross national product grew at a rate of 5 percent during the 1960s—nearly twice the rate of the Eisenhower years. Much of that growth, however, was fueled by massive defense expenditures, especially spending for the escalating Vietnam War.

Kennedy's interest in stimulating economic growth did not include a commitment to spending to meet domestic social needs. He did not entirely ignore the liberal legislative agenda of Franklin Roosevelt and Harry Truman, but on some of the issues he did choose to promote—federal aid to education, wilderness preservation, investment in mass transportation, and medical insurance for the elderly—he ran into determined congressional opposition from both Republicans and dissenters in his own party.

Some of the most significant domestic reforms of the early 1960s came not from the Kennedy administration but from the Supreme Court. Much of the Court's activism in these years was linked to Earl Warren, chief justice from 1953 to 1969. Warren had influenced his Court's most important decision, *Brown v. Board of Education* (which required desegregation of public schools), in 1954 during the Eisenhower administration (see Chapter 29). In the 1960s the Court continued to make landmark decisions. It reinforced defendants' rights in cases like *Miranda v. Arizona* (1966), which required arresting officers to notify a suspect that "he has a right to remain silent, that any statement he does make may be used in evidence against him, and that he has a right to the presence of an attorney, either retained or appointed." Tackling the issue of the reapportionment of state legislatures in *Baker v. Carr* (1962) and *Reynolds v. Sims* (1964), the Court put forth the doctrine of "one person, one vote," meaning that all citizens' votes should have equal weight, no matter where they lived. The ruling substantially increased the representation of suburban and urban areas, with their concentrations of black and Spanish-speaking residents, at the expense of rural regions. Perhaps the most controversial of the Court's decisions was *Engel v. Vitale* (1962), which banned organized prayer in public schools as a violation of the First Amendment's injunction that "Congress shall make no law respecting an establishment of religion."

In allowing the Court to take the lead on such issues, Kennedy surrendered critical opportunities to exercise presidential leadership, a failure symptomatic of his first two years in office. Despite the foreign policy crises and domestic inaction that plagued his administration, however, many political observers hoped that Kennedy was maturing as a national leader. Then tragedy struck. On November 22, 1963, as he and his wife, Jacqueline, rode through Dallas in a motorcade, Kennedy was shot. He died half an hour later. Before *Air Force One* left Dallas to take the president's body back to Washington, a grim-faced Lyndon Johnson took the oath of office as president. Two days after the assassination a nightclub owner, Jack Ruby, gunned down the accused killer, Lee Harvey Oswald, in the basement of Dallas's police headquarters. Whether Oswald, a twenty-four-year-old loner who had spent three years in the Soviet Union, had been the sole gunman became a matter of considerable controversy.

In the years that followed, Kennedy's image of buoyant youth, the collective trauma of his assassination, and the American public's sense that the nation had been robbed of a promising leader contributed to a powerful mystique that enhanced his reputation far more than his record as president deserved. Though Kennedy had exercised bold presidential leadership in foreign affairs, his flexible response program and his initiatives in Cuba and Berlin had heightened the confrontations of the superpowers in the Cold War. Moreover, his enthusiasm for foreign policy had no equivalent in domestic policy. Kennedy's proposals for educational aid, medical insurance, and other liberal reforms stalled, and his tax-cut legislation languished in Congress until after his death. But perhaps Kennedy's greatest failing was his reluctance to act on civil rights.

THE CIVIL-RIGHTS MOVEMENT

Encouraged by *Brown v. Board of Education* and other favorable civil-rights decisions, black southerners had stepped up their efforts to dismantle legal segregation in the late 1950s (see Chapter 29). In the early 1960s a younger generation of activists adopted and expanded the strategy of nonviolent action developed by the Montgomery bus boycotters, Martin Luther King, Jr., and the Southern Christian Leadership Conference (SCLC) in the 1950s. Those young people, primarily black college students, used more assertive tactics to successfully challenge segregation at lunch counters and in waiting rooms, as well as at the ballot box.

New Tactics: Sit-ins, Freedom Rides, and the March on Washington

A new phase of the civil-rights movement began in Greensboro, North Carolina, on February 1, 1960, when four black college students took seats at the "whites only" lunch counter of a local Woolworth's, determined to "sit in" until they were served. Their protest demonstrated the capricious nature of southern segregation laws. At Woolworth's, blacks could buy toothpaste, underwear, and magazines alongside whites, but not a sandwich or a cup of coffee.

Although the protesters were arrested, their sit-in tactic worked, and it quickly spread to other southern cities. A few months later Ella Baker, an SCLC administrator and a lifelong activist, helped to organize the Student Non-Violent Coordinating Committee (SNCC, pronounced "snick") to facilitate student sit-ins. By the end of the year, about 50,000 people had participated in sit-ins and other demonstrations, and 3,600 of them had been jailed. White store owners quickly realized that they would lose business if the disruptions continued. Thus, black activists and a number of white supporters succeeded in desegregating lunch counters in 126 cities throughout the South.

The success of SNCC's unorthodox tactics encouraged the Congress of Racial Equality (CORE), an interracial group founded in 1942, to organize a series of *freedom rides* on interstate bus lines throughout the South. Under the direction of executive director James Farmer, CORE targeted buses, waiting rooms, and terminal restaurants to call attention to the continuing segregation of public transportation. The activists who rode the buses, mostly young and both black and white, were brutally attacked by white mobs in Anniston, Montgomery, and Birmingham, Alabama. Governor John Patterson refused to intervene, claiming, "I cannot guarantee protection for this bunch of rabble rousers."

Although the Kennedy administration generally opposed the freedom riders' activities, films of their beating and a bus burning shown on the nightly news prompted Attorney General Robert Kennedy to send federal marshals to Alabama to restore order. Faced with Justice Department intervention against those who defied the Interstate Commerce Commission's prohibition of segregation in interstate vehicles and facilities, most southern communities quietly acceded to the pressure. And civil-rights activists learned that nonviolent protest could succeed if it provoked vicious white resistance and generated nationwide publicity. Only when forced to, apparently, would federal authorities act.

This lesson was confirmed in Birmingham, Alabama, when Martin Luther King, Jr., and the Reverend Fred Shuttlesworth called for a protest against conditions in what King called "the most segregated city in the United States." In April 1963 thousands of black demonstrators marched downtown to picket Birmingham's department stores. They were met by Eugene ("Bull") Connor, the city's commissioner of public safety, who used snarling dogs, electric cattle prods, and high-pressure fire hoses to break up the crowd. Television cameras captured the scene for the evening news.

President Kennedy, realizing that he could no longer postpone decisive action, decided to step up the federal government's role in civil rights. On June 11, 1963, Kennedy went on television to promise major legislation banning discrimination in public accommodations and empowering the Justice department to enforce desegregation. Black leaders hailed the speech as the "Second Emancipation Proclamation."

To rouse the conscience of the nation and to marshal support for Kennedy's bill, civil-rights leaders adopted a tactic A. Philip Randolph had first suggested in 1941: a massive march on Washington. Martin Luther King, Jr., of the SCLC,

Racial Violence in Birmingham

When thousands of blacks marched to downtown Birmingham, Alabama, to protest racial segregation in April 1963, they were met with fire hoses and attack dogs unleashed by Police Chief "Bull" Connor. The violence, which was televised on the national evening news, shocked many Americans and helped build sympathy for the civil-rights movement among northern whites.

Roy Wilkins of the NAACP, Whitney Young of the National Urban League, and the black socialist Bayard Rustin were the principal organizers. On August 28, 1963, about 250,000 black and white demonstrators—the largest crowd at any demonstration up to that time—gathered at the Lincoln Memorial. The march culminated in a memorable speech delivered, indeed preached, by Martin Luther King, in the evangelical style of the black church. King ended with an exclamation from an old Negro spiritual: "Free at last! Free at last! Thank God almighty, we are free at last!"

King's eloquence and the sight of blacks and whites marching solemnly together did more than any other event to make the civil-rights movement acceptable to white Americans. The March on Washington seemed to justify liberals' faith that blacks and whites could work together to promote racial harmony. It marked the climax of the nonviolent phase of the civil-rights movement, confirming King's position, especially among white liberals, as the leading spokesman for the black cause. In 1964 King won the Nobel peace prize for his leadership.

Despite the impact of the march on public opinion, however, few congressional votes were changed by the event. Southern senators continued to block Kennedy's civil-rights legislation by threatening to filibuster. Even more troubling was a new outbreak of violence by white extremists determined to oppose equality for blacks at all costs. In September 1963 a Baptist church in Birmingham was bombed, and four black Sunday school students were killed. Two months later, President Kennedy was assassinated.

Landmark Legislation

On assuming the presidency, Lyndon Johnson promptly turned the passage of civil-rights legislation into a memorial to his slain predecessor—an ironic twist in light of Kennedy's lukewarm support for the cause. The Civil Rights Act, passed finally in June 1964, was a landmark in the history of American race relations. Its keystone, Title VII, outlawed discrimination in employment on the basis of race, religion, national origin, or sex. Another section barred discrimination in public accommodations. But while the act forced the desegregation of public facilities throughout the South, including many public schools, obstacles to black voting rights remained.

In 1964, with the Civil Rights Act on the brink of passage, black organizations and churches mounted a major civil-rights campaign in Mississippi. Known as Freedom Summer, the effort drew several thousand volunteers from across the country, including many idealistic white college students. Freedom Summer workers established freedom schools for black children, conducted a major voter registration drive, and organized the Mississippi Freedom Democratic party, a political alternative to the all-white Democratic organization in Mississippi. White southerners reacted swiftly and violently to their efforts. Fifteen civil-rights workers were murdered; only about 1,200 black voters were registered that summer.

A Civil-Rights Activist Remembers

Ann Moody, a CORE activist, was one of the young African-American students involved in voter registration in the South in 1963. Already discouraged by the slow progress of voter registration, she reacted to the news of the bombing of a Birmingham, Alabama, church by challenging the civil-rights movement's commitment to passive resistance.

We were all eating and listening to the radio when the music stopped abruptly in the middle of a record. "A special news bulletin just in from Birmingham," the DJ was saying. "A church was just bombed in Birmingham, Alabama. It is believed that several Sunday-school students were killed."

Why! Why! Why! Oh God, why? Why us? Why us? I found myself asking. . . . "You know, I used to go to Sunday school when I was a little girl. . . . We were taught how merciful and forgiving you are. Mama used to tell us that you would forgive us seventy-seven times a day, and I believed in you. I bet those girls in Sunday school were being taught the same as I was when I was their age. Is that teaching wrong? Are you going to forgive their killers? You not gonna answer me, God, hmm? Well, if you don't want to talk, then listen to me.

As long as I live, I'll never be beaten by a white man again. Not like in Woolworth's. Not anymore. That's out. You know something else, God? Nonviolence is out. I have a good idea Martin Luther King is talking to you, too. If he is, tell him that nonviolence has served its purpose. Tell him that for me, God, and for a lot of other Negroes who must be thinking it today.

SOURCE: Ann Moody, *Coming of Age in Mississippi* (New York: Doubleday, 1968), 317–18.

The need for federal action to support voting rights became even clearer in March 1965, when Martin Luther King and other black leaders called for a massive march from Selma, Alabama, to the state capital in Montgomery to protest the murder of a voting rights activist. As soon as the marchers left Selma, mounted state troopers attacked them with tear gas and clubs. The scene was shown on national television that night.

Calling the episode "an American tragedy," President Johnson redoubled his efforts to persuade Congress to pass the pending voting rights legislation. In a televised speech to a joint session of Congress on March 15, quoting the best-known slogan of the civil-rights movement, "We shall overcome," he proclaimed voting rights a moral imperative.

On August 6 Congress passed the Voting Rights Act of 1965, which suspended the literacy tests and other measures most southern states used to prevent blacks from registering to vote. The act authorized the attorney general to send federal examiners to register voters in any county where less than 50 percent of the voting-age population was registered. Together with the adoption in 1964 of the Twenty-fourth Amendment to the Constitution, which outlawed the federal poll tax, and successful legal challenges to state and local poll taxes, the Voting Rights Act allowed millions of blacks to register and vote for the first time. Congress reauthorized the Voting Rights Act in 1970, 1975, and 1982.

In the South, the results were stunning. In 1960 only 20 percent of eligible blacks had been registered to vote; by 1964 the figure had risen to 39 percent, and by 1971 it was 62 percent. As Hartman Turnbow, a Mississippi farmer who risked his life to register in 1964, later declared, "It won't never go back where it was."

LYNDON JOHNSON AND THE GREAT SOCIETY

Lyndon Baines Johnson brought to the presidency far more legislative experience than any other modern president. Born in the central Texas hill country in 1908, Johnson had served in government since 1932, as congressional aide, New Deal administrator, congressman, senator, Senate majority leader, and finally vice-president. In 1964, a year after Kennedy's death, Johnson won the presidency in his own right by defeating the conservative Republican senator Barry Goldwater of Arizona. With his running mate, Senator Hubert H. Humphrey of Minnesota, Johnson achieved one of the largest margins in history, 61.1 percent of the popular vote. He used his mandate and his political experience to bring to fruition the Great Society, his name for a program to end poverty and racial injustice. The Great Society, not the much less ambitious New Frontier, would fulfill and in some cases surpass the New Deal agenda of the 1930s.

Enacting the Liberal Agenda

Like most New Deal liberals, Johnson took an expansive view of presidential leadership and the role of the federal government. The 1964 election gave him not only a popular mandate, but the filibuster-proof Senate Democratic majority he needed to push his programs forward. Johnson's first major success came in education. The Elementary and Secondary Education Act, passed in 1965, authorized $1 billion in federal funds to benefit impoverished children. The same year the Higher Education Act provided the first federal scholarships for college students. The Eighty-ninth Congress also gave Johnson enough votes to enact the federal health insurance legislation first proposed by Truman. The result was two new programs: Medicare, a health plan for the elderly funded by a surcharge on Social Security payroll taxes, and Medicaid, a health plan for the poor paid for by general tax revenues.

Although the Great Society is usually associated with programs for the disadvantaged, many of the Johnson administration's initiatives benefited a wide spectrum of Americans. Federal urban renewal and home mortgage assistance helped those who could afford to live in single-family homes or modern apartments. Medicare covered every elderly person eligible for Social Security, regardless of need. And much of the federal aid to education benefited the children of the middle class. Finally, the creation of the National Endowment for the Arts and the National Endowment for the Humanities in 1965 supported artists and historians in their efforts to understand and interpret the nation's cultural and historical heritage.

Another aspect of public welfare addressed by the Great Society was the environment. President Johnson pressed for expansion of the national park system, improvement of the nation's air and water, and increased land-use planning. At the insistence of his wife, Lady Bird Johnson, he promoted the Highway Beautification Act of 1965. His approach marked a significant break with past conservation efforts, which had tended to concentrate on maintaining natural resources and national wealth. Under Secretary of the Interior Stewart Udall, Great Society programs emphasized quality of life, battling the problem "of vanishing beauty, of increasing ugliness, of shrinking open space, and of an overall environment that is diminished daily by pollution and noise and blight."

Taking advantage of the Great Society's reform climate, liberal Democrats also brought about significant changes in immigration policy. The Immigration Act of 1965 abandoned the quota system of the 1920s that had discriminated against Asians and southern and Eastern Europeans, replacing it with more equitable numerical limits on immigration from Europe, Africa, Asia, and countries in the Western Hemisphere. Since close relatives of individuals who were already legal residents of the United States could be admitted over and above the numerical limits, the legislation led to an immigrant influx far greater than anticipated, with the heaviest volume coming from Asia and Latin America.

Perhaps the most ambitious part of Johnson's liberal agenda was the War on Poverty, based on his expectation that the Great Society could put "an end to poverty in our time." During Johnson's presidency, poor people made up about a fourth of the American population; three-fourths of them were white. They included isolated farmers and miners in Appalachia, blacks and Puerto Ricans in urban ghettos, Mexican-Americans in migrant labor camps and urban barrios, native Americans on reservations, women raising families on their own, and the abandoned and destitute elderly. As Michael Harrington had pointed out in his influential book, *The Other America* (1962), the poor were everywhere.

To reduce poverty, the Johnson administration expanded long-established social insurance, welfare, and public works programs. It broadened the Social Security program to include more workers. Social welfare expenditures increased rapidly, especially for Aid to Families with Dependent Children (AFDC), public housing, rent subsidies, and Food Stamps. As during the New Deal, these social welfare programs developed in piecemeal fashion, without central coordination.

The Great Society's showcase in the War on Poverty was the Office of Economic Opportunity (OEO), established by the omnibus Economic Opportunity Act of 1964. OEO programs produced some of the most innovative measures of the Johnson administration. Head Start provided free nursery schools to prepare disadvantaged preschoolers for kindergarten. The Job Corps, Upward Bound, and Volunteers in Service to America (VISTA), modeled on the Peace Corps, provided poor youths with training and jobs. And the Community Action Program encouraged the poor to demand "maximum feasible participation" in decisions that affected them.

Cracks in the Liberal Coalition

By the end of 1965, the Johnson administration had compiled the most impressive legislative record of liberal reforms—from civil rights to health care, from environmental concerns to food stamps—since the New Deal. It had put issues of poverty, justice, and access at the center of national political life, and had expanded the federal government's role in protecting its citizens' welfare. Yet the Great Society never quite measured up to the extravagant promises made for it; by the end of the decade, many programs were troubled and under attack.

In part, the political necessity of bowing to pressure from various interest groups hampered Great Society programs. For example, the American Medical Association (AMA) used its influence to shape the Medicare and Medicaid programs, to assure that Congress did not impose a cap on medical expenses. Its intervention produced escalating federal expenditures and contributed to skyrocketing medical costs. And Democratic-controlled urban political machines criticized VISTA and Community Action Program agents who encouraged poor people to demand the public services long withheld by unresponsive local governments. In response to such political pressure, the Johnson administration gradually phased out the Community Action Program and instead channeled spending for housing, social services, and other urban poverty programs through local municipal governments.

Another inherent problem was the limited funding of Great Society programs. The annual budget for the War on Poverty was less than $2 billion. Johnson and his advisers never considered income redistribution as the solution to poverty; they counted on enhanced education and skills to raise the income level of the poor, bringing the benefits of American capitalism to more people. Despite the limited nature of the program, the statistical decline in poverty during the 1960s suggests that the Great Society was successful on some levels. From 1963 to 1968, the proportion of Americans living below the poverty line dropped from 20 percent to 13 percent. Among African-Americans, economic advancement was even more marked. In the 1960s the black poverty rate was cut in half and millions of blacks moved into the middle class, some through federal jobs in antipoverty programs. But critics charged that the reduction in the poverty rate was due to the decade's booming economy, not to the War on

Poverty. Moreover, while the nation's overall standard of living increased, distribution of wealth was still uneven. Though the poor were better off in an absolute sense, they remained far behind the middle class in a relative sense.

Other factors also hampered the success of the Great Society. Following in the steps of Roosevelt's New Deal coalition, Kennedy and Johnson had gathered an extraordinarily diverse set of groups—middle-class and poor; white and nonwhite; Protestant, Jewish, and Catholic; urban and rural—in support of an unprecedented level of federal activism. For a brief period between 1964 and 1966 the coalition held together. But inevitably the demands of certain groups—such as blacks' demands for civil rights and the urban poors' demands for increased political power—conflicted with the interests of other Democrats, such as white southerners and northern political bosses. In the end the Democratic coalition could not sustain a consensus on the purposes of governmental activism powerful enough to resist conservatives who continued to resist expanded civil-rights and social welfare legislation.

At the same time, Democrats were plagued by disillusionment over the shortcomings of their reforms. In the early 1960s the lofty rhetoric of the New Frontier and the Great Society had raised unprecedented expectations for social change. But competition for federal largesse was keen, and the shortage of funds for the War on Poverty left many promises unfulfilled, especially after 1965, when the escalation of the Vietnam War siphoned funding away from domestic programs. In 1966 the government spent $22 billion on the Vietnam War and only $1.2 billion on the War on Poverty. Ultimately, as Martin Luther King put it, the Great Society was "shot down on the battlefields of Vietnam."

THE CONTINUING STRUGGLE FOR CIVIL RIGHTS

Just as the Great Society was plagued by internal divisions and external opposition, so too was the evolving civil-rights movement. As the struggle moved outside the South and took on the more stubborn problems of entrenched poverty and racism, black frustration and anger boiled over in a new racial militance. The rhetoric and tactics of the emerging black power movement both shattered the existing civil-rights coalition and galvanized white opposition.

Rising Militance

Once the system of legal, or de jure, segregation had fallen, the civil-rights movement turned to the more difficult task of eliminating the de facto segregation, enforced by custom, that made blacks second-class citizens throughout the nation. Outside the South, racial discrimination was less flagrant, but it was pervasive, especially in education, housing, and employment. Although the Brown decision outlawed separate schools, it did nothing to change the educational system in areas where schools were all-black or all-white because of residential segregation. Not until 1973 did federal judges begin to extend the desegregation of schools, which had begun in the South two decades earlier, to the rest of the country.

As civil-rights leaders took on the new target of northern racism, the movement fractured along generational lines. Students who had risked assault to sit in at lunch counters or to register to vote grew impatient with the gradualism of their elders. Many repudiated the nonviolent approach pursued by Martin Luther King and urged blacks to take control of their communities through more radical, and if necessary violent, means.

Some younger activists, eager for confrontation and rapid social change, questioned the very goal of integration into white society. Black separatism, espoused by earlier black leaders such as Marcus Garvey in the 1920s (see Chapter 24), was revived in the 1960s by the Nation of Islam, which had more than 10,000 members and many more sympathizers. Popularly known as the Black Muslims, the Nation of Islam was extremely hostile to whites, whom its leader Elijah Muhammad called "blue-eyed devils." Forcefully promoting their black nationalist ideology, the group stressed black pride, unity, and self-help.

The Black Muslims' most charismatic figure was Malcolm X. Born Malcolm Little in 1925, he converted to the Nation of Islam while serving time in prison for attempted burglary. A brilliant debater and spellbinding speaker, Malcolm X preached a philosophy quite different from Martin Luther King's. He advocated militant protest and separatism, though he condoned the use of violence only for self-defense and self-assertion. Hostile to the traditional civil-rights organizations, he caustically referred to the 1963 March on Washington as the "Farce on Washington."

In 1964, after a power struggle with Elijah Muhammed, Malcolm X broke with the Nation of Islam. He then made a pilgrimage to Mecca, the holiest site of traditional Islam, and toured Africa, where he embraced the liberation struggles of all colonized peoples. On his return to the United States, Malcolm X moved away from antiwhite rhetoric toward an internationalist vision of the black future. On February 21, 1965, he was assassinated while delivering a speech at the Audubon Ballroom in Harlem. Three Black Muslims were later convicted of his murder. Malcolm X's autobiography, ghostwritten by Alex Haley and published soon after his death, became one of the decade's most influential books.

Though Malcolm X's call for black cultural and political independence appealed to young black activists in SNCC and CORE, many balked at the idea of converting to Islam, preferring a secular black nationalist movement. In 1966 the SNCC leader Stokely Carmichael christened a new era in the black struggle when he called for "Black Power." Carmichael's battle cry confirmed the militant forces already present in SNCC and other civil-rights groups. In fact, by 1966 most whites had been effectively ejected from the civil-rights movement.

In the same year Huey Newton and Bobby Seale, two college students in Oakland, California, founded the Black Panthers, a militant self-defense organization dedicated to protecting local blacks from police violence. The Panthers' organization quickly spread to other cities, where members undertook a wide range of community organizing projects, including interracial efforts. But the Panthers' affinity for Third World revolutionary movements and armed struggle became their most publicized attribute. Radical black power activists were proposing a new agenda: not nonviolence but armed self-defense; not integration but separatism; not working within the system but preparing for revolution.

Among the most significant legacies of black power was the assertion of racial pride. Many young blacks insisted on the term *Afro-American* rather than *Negro*, a term they found demeaning because of its historical association with slavery and racism. Rejecting white tastes and standards, blacks wore African clothing and hairstyles and helped to awaken interest in black history, art, and literature. By the 1970s many colleges and universities were offering programs in black studies.

The new black assertiveness alarmed many white Americans. They had been willing to go along with the moderate reforms of the 1950s and early 1960s, but became wary when blacks began demanding immediate access to higher-paying jobs, housing in white neighborhoods, education in integrated schools, and increased political power. White backlash soon became a powerful force that conservative politicans in both parties quickly seized upon (see Chapter 31).

Another major reason for the erosion of white support was a wave of riots that struck the nation's cities where African-Americans had suffered economic and political marginalization for decades. Lacking education and skills, successive generations of blacks had moved out of the rural South in search of work that paid an adequate wage. In the North, many remained unemployed. Resentful of white landlords who owned the substandard housing they were forced to live in and white shopkeepers who denied them jobs in their neighborhoods, many blacks also hated police, whose violent presence in black neighborhoods seemed that of "an occupying army." Stimulated by the successes of southern blacks who had challenged whites and gotten results, young urban blacks expressed their grievances through their own brand of "direct action."

The first "long hot summer" began in July 1964 in New York City, when police shot a young black criminal suspect in Harlem. Angry youths looted and rioted there for a week. Over the next four years, the volatile issue of police brutality set off riots in dozens of cities. In August 1965 the arrest of a young black motorist in the Watts section of Los Angeles sparked six days of rioting that left thirty-four blacks dead. Ironically, Watts erupted only five days after President Johnson signed the Voting Rights Act of 1965. For many young urban blacks the legal gains of the civil-rights movement were irrelevant to their daily experience of economic exploitation. Instead of singing "We shall overcome," Watts rioters shouted "Burn, baby, burn."

The riots of 1967 were the most serious (see Map 30.2), engulfing twenty-two cities in July and August. The most devastating outbreaks occurred in

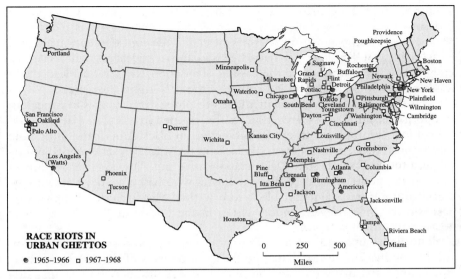

MAP 30.2
Racial Unrest in America's Cities, 1965–1968
American cities suffered through four "long hot summers" of rioting in the mid-1960s. In 1967, the worst year, riots broke out across the United States, including in the South and the West. Major riots usually did not occur in the same city two years in a row.

Newark and Detroit. Forty-three people were killed in Detroit alone, nearly all of them black, and $50 million worth of property destroyed. As in most of the riots, the arson and looting in Detroit targeted white-owned stores and property, but there was little physical violence against white people.

On July 29, 1967, President Johnson appointed a special commission to investigate the riots. The final report of the National Advisory Commission on Civil Disorders, released in March 1968, detailed the continuing inequality and racism of urban life. It also issued a warning: "Our nation is moving toward two societies, one black, one white—separate and unequal. . . . What white Americans have never fully understood—but what the Negro can never forget—is that white society is deeply implicated in the ghetto. White institutions created it, white institutions maintain it, and white society condones it."

On April 4, 1968, barely a month after the Commission on Civil Disorders released its report, Martin Luther King, Jr., was assassinated in Memphis, Tennessee, by James Earl Ray, a white ex-convict whose motive was unknown. King's death set off an explosion of urban rioting. Violence broke out in more than a hundred cities. With King's assassination the civil-rights movement lost the one leader best able to stir the conscience of white America. During the last years of his life King had moved toward a broader view of the structural problems of poverty and racism in America. In 1966 he had confronted the issue of residential segregation in a campaign for open housing in Chicago. He had also spoken out against the Vietnam War. In 1968 King was planning a poor people's campaign to raise issues of economic injustice and inequality. How successful King would have been in those endeavors will never be known. But his death marked the passing of an important national leader, and was symptomatic of the troubled course of the civil-rights movement.

The 1960s brought permanent, indeed revolutionary, changes in American race relations. Jim Crow segregation was overturned in less than a decade, and federal legislation passed to ensure protection of black Americans' most basic civil rights. The enfranchisement of blacks in the southern states ended political control by all-white state Democratic parties and allowed black candidates to enter the political arena. White candidates who had once been ardent segregationists began to court the black vote. In time Martin Luther King's greatness was recognized even among whites in the South; in 1986 his birthday became a national holiday.

Yet much remained undone. The more entrenched forms of segregation and discrimination persisted, despite the legal reforms of the 1960s. African-Americans, particularly those in the central cities, continued to make up a disproportionate number of the poor, the unemployed, and the undereducated. As the civil-rights movement gradually splintered, its agenda remained unfinished.

The Spreading Demand for Equal Rights

Despite its limitations, the black civil-rights movement provided a fresh and innovative model for social change. Although Mexican-Americans had been working actively for civil rights since the 1930s (see Chapter 25), poverty, an uncertain legal status, and language barriers made their political mobilization difficult. That situation began to change when the Mexican-American Political Association (MAPA) mobilized support for John F. Kennedy and in return Kennedy appointed several Mexican-American leaders to posts in Washington. Over the next four years, MAPA and other political organizations worked successfully to elect Mexican-American candidates to Congress: in the House, Edward Roybal of California, and Henry González and Elizo de la Garza of Texas; in the Senate, Joseph Montoya of New Mexico.

Younger Mexican-Americans quickly grew impatient with MAPA, however. The barrios of Los Angeles and other western cities produced the militant Brown Berets, modeled on the Black Panthers (who wore black berets). Rejecting the assimilationist approach of their elders, 1,500 Mexican-American students met in Denver in 1969 to hammer out a new nationalist political and cultural agenda. They proclaimed a new term, *Chicano*, to replace *Mexican-American*, and later organized a new political party, La Raza Unida ("The United Race"), to promote Chicano interests and candidates. In California and other southwestern states, students staged demonstrations and boycotts to press for bilingual education, the hiring of more Chicano teachers, and the creation of Chicano studies programs. By the 1970s dozens of such programs were offered at universities throughout the region.

Chicano strategists also pursued economic objectives. Working in the fields around Delano, California, the labor leader Cesar Chavez organized the United Farm Workers (UFW), the first union to represent migrant workers successfully. A 1965 grape pickers' strike and a nationwide boycott of table grapes brought Chavez and his union national publicity and won support from the AFL–CIO and from Senator Robert F. Kennedy of New York. Chavez soon was receiving almost as much media attention as Martin Luther King, Jr. Victory came in 1970 when California grape growers signed contracts recognizing the UFW.

North American Indians also found a model in the civil-rights movement. Native Americans, who numbered nearly 800,000 in the 1960s, were an exceedingly diverse group, divided by language, tribal history, region, and degree of integration into the mainstream of American life. But they also shared an unemployment rate ten times the national average, as well as the worst poverty, the most inadequate housing, the highest disease rates, and the least access to education of any group in the United States.

As early as World War II the National Council of American Indians had lobbied for improvement of those conditions. In the 1960s, some Indian groups became more assertive. Like the young militants in the black civil-rights movement, they challenged the accommodationist approach of their elders. Proposing a new name for themselves—native Americans—they organized protests and demonstrations to build support for their cause. In 1968 several Chipewyan from Minnesota organized the militant American Indian Movement (AIM), which drew its strength from the third of the native American population who lived in "red ghettos" in cities throughout the West.

In November 1969 AIM seized the deserted federal penitentiary on Alcatraz Island in San Francisco Bay, offering the government $24 worth of trinkets to pay for it, supposedly the sum the Dutch had paid to the native inhabitants for Manhattan Island in 1626. Their occupation of Alcatraz lasted until the summer of 1971. A year later, a thousand protesters occupied the headquarters of the Federal Bureau of Indian Affairs in Washington, D.C., to many native Americans a hated symbol of federal native American policy.

In February 1973, 200 Sioux organized by AIM leaders began an occupation of the tiny village of Wounded Knee, South Dakota, the site of an army massacre of the Sioux in 1890 (see Chapter 17). They were protesting the light sentences given to a group of white men convicted of killing a Sioux in 1972. To dramatize their cause, the protesters took eleven hostages and occupied several buildings. But when a gun battle with the FBI left one protester dead and another wounded, the seventy-one-day siege collapsed. Although the new native American activism helped to alienate many white onlookers, it did spur government action on tribal issues (see Chapter 32).

Wounded Knee Revisited
In 1973 members of the American Indian Movement staged a seventy-one-day protest at
Wounded Knee, South Dakota, the site of the 1890 massacre of 200 Sioux by U.S. soldiers.
The takeover was sparked by the murder of a local Sioux by a group of whites but quickly ex-
panded to include demands for basic reforms in federal Indian policy and tribal governance.

Civil rights, once seen as a movement exclusively for the rights of black
people, also sparked a new awareness among some predominantly white
groups. Americans of Polish, Italian, Greek, and Slavic descent, most of them
working-class and Catholic, proudly embraced their new ethnic identity.
Homosexual men and women banded together to protest legal and social oppression based on their sexual orientation. In 1969 the gay liberation movement was born in the "Stonewall riot" in New York City, when patrons of a
gay bar fought back against police harassment. The assertion of gay pride that
followed the incident drew heavily on the language and tactics of the civil-
rights movement. Activists took the new name of *gay* rather than *homosexual*;
founded advocacy groups, newspapers, and political organizations to challenge
discrimination and prejudice; and offered emotional support to those who
"came out" and publicly affirmed their homosexuality. For gays as well as
members of various ethnic and cultural groups, political activism based on
heightened group identity represented one of the most significant legacies of
the African-American struggle.

The Revival of Feminism

The black civil-rights movement also helped to reactivate feminism, a movement that had been languishing since the 1920s. Just as the abolition movement
had been the training ground for women's rights advocates in the nineteenth
century, the black struggle became an inspiration for young feminists in the

1960s. But the revival of feminism also sprang from social and demographic changes that affected women young and old. By 1970, 42.6 percent of women were working, and four out of ten working women were married. Especially significant was the growth in the number of working women with preschool children—up from 12 percent in 1950 to 30 percent in 1970. In the postwar consumer society, working mothers were becoming more accepted.

Another significant change was increased access to education for women. Immediately after World War II the percentage of college students who were women declined. The GI Bill gave men a temporary advantage in access to higher education. At the height of the baby boom, many college women dropped out of school to marry and raise families. By 1960, however, the percentage of college students who were women had risen to 35 percent; in 1970 it reached 41 percent.

The meaning of marriage was changing, too. The baby boom turned out to be only a temporary interruption of a century-long decline in the birth rate. The introduction of the birth control pill, first marketed in 1960, and the intrauterine device (IUD) helped women control their fertility. Women had fewer children, and because of an increased life expectancy (75 years in 1970—up from 54 years in 1920), they devoted proportionally fewer years to raising children. At the same time the divorce rate, which had risen slowly throughout the twentieth century, rose markedly as the states liberalized divorce laws.

As a result of these changes, traditional gender expectations were dramatically undermined. American women's lives now usually included work and marriage, often child rearing and a career, and possibly bringing up children alone after a divorce. Those changing social realities created a major constituency for the emerging women's movement of the 1960s.

During those years older, politically active professional women sought change by working through the political system. This group was galvanized in part by a report by the Presidential Commission on the Status of Women (1963), which documented the employment and educational discrimination women faced. More important than the report's rather conservative recommendations was the rudimentary nationwide network of women in public life that formed in the course of the commission's work.

Another spark that ignited the revival of feminism was Betty Friedan's best-selling book *The Feminine Mystique*, published in 1963. A pointed indictment of suburban domesticity, the book explored what Friedan called "the problem that has no name":

> As she made the beds, shopped for groceries, matched slipcover material, ate peanut butter sandwiches with her children, chauffeured Cub Scouts and Brownies, lay beside her husband at night—she was afraid to ask even of herself the silent question—"Is this all?"

Women responded enthusiastically to Friedan's book—especially white, college-educated, middle-class women. The book sold 3 million copies and was excerpted in many women's magazines. *The Feminine Mystique* gave women a vocabulary with which to express their dissatisfaction and promoted women's self-realization through employment, continuing education, and other activities outside the home.

Like so many other constituencies in postwar America, women's rights activists looked to the federal government for help. The first steps toward change had emerged in 1963, when Congress passed the Equal Pay Act, which directed that men and women be paid the same wages for doing the same job. Even more important was the Civil Rights Act of 1964, which had as great an impact on women as it did on blacks and other minorities. Title VII, which barred discrimination in employment on the basis of race, religion, national origin, or sex, eventually became a powerful tool in the fight against sex discrimination. At first, however, the Equal Employment Opportunity Commission (EEOC) avoided implementing it.

Dissatisfied with the Commission's reluctance to defend women's rights, Friedan and others founded the National Organization for Women (NOW) in 1966. Modeling itself on groups such as the NAACP, NOW aimed to be a civil-rights organization for women. "The purpose of NOW," an early statement declared, "is to take action to bring women into full participation in the mainstream of American society now, exercising all the privileges and responsibilities thereof in truly equal partnership with men." Under Friedan, who served as NOW's first president, its membership grew from 1,000 in 1967 to 15,000 in 1971. Men made up a fourth of NOW's early membership. The group is still the largest feminist organization in the United States.

Another group of new feminists, the women's liberationists, came to the women's movement through their civil-rights work. White women had made up about half the students who went south with SNCC in the Freedom Summer project of 1964. These college women developed self-confidence and organizational skills working in the South, and they found role models in older southern women like Ella Baker, Anne Braden, and Virginia Foster Durr, who were prominent in the civil-rights movement. Yet women volunteers also found they were expected to do all the cleaning and cooking at the Freedom Houses where SNCC volunteers lived. "We didn't come down here to work as a maid this summer," one complained. But the men in the movement laughed off their attempts to raise feminist issues.

After 1965 black militants made white women unwelcome in the civil-rights movement. But when these women transferred their energies to the antiwar groups that were emerging in that period (see Chapter 31), they found the New Left equally male-dominated. When the antiwar movement adopted draft resistance as a central strategy, women found themselves relegated to the role of sex objects. "Girls say yes to guys who say no" was a popular slogan. Those women who tried to raise feminist issues at conventions were shouted off the platform with jeers such as "Move on, little girl, we have more important issues to talk about here than women's liberation."

Around 1967 the contradiction between the New Left's lip service to egalitarianism and women's treatment by male leaders caused women radicals to realize that they needed their own movement. In contrast to groups such as NOW, which had traditional organizational structures and dues-paying members, these women formed loose collectives whose shifting membership often lacked any formal structure. They organized independently in five or six different cities, including Chicago, San Francisco, and New York.

Members of the women's liberation movement (or "women's lib," as it was dubbed by the somewhat hostile media) went public in 1968 in a protest at the Miss America Pageant. Their demonstration featured a "freedom trash can" into which they encouraged women to throw false eyelashes, hair curlers, brassieres, and girdles—all of which they branded as symbols of female oppression. The media quickly labeled the radical feminists "bra burners." The derisive name stuck, although no brassieres were actually burned.

Feminism on the March
The visibility of the feminist movement reached a new peak in 1970 when thousands of women in New York and other cities around the country marched to celebrate the fiftieth anniversary of woman suffrage. (© Bettye Lane)

An activity with a more lasting impact was consciousness raising—group sessions in which women shared their experiences of being female. Swapping stories about being passed over for a promotion, needing a husband's signature on a credit card application, or enduring the whistles and leers of men while walking down the street helped participants to realize that their individual problems were part of a wider pattern of oppression. The slogan "The personal is political" became a rallying cry of the movement.

By 1970, a growing convergence of interests began to blur the distinction between women's rights and women's liberation. Radical women realized that key feminist goals—child care, equal pay, and abortion rights—could best be achieved in the political arena. At the same time, more traditional activists developed a broader view of the women's movement, tentatively including divisive issues such as abortion and lesbian rights. Although the movement remained largely white and middle class, feminists were beginning to think of themselves as part of a broad, growing, and increasingly influential social crusade. Their gradual convergence would lay the foundation for more vigorous activism (see Chapter 32).

By the end of the decade, the call for moderate reform that John Kennedy had sounded in his New Frontier had been superseded by far more radical demands for political and social change. Racial and ethnic minorities were challenging racial hierarchies; women were criticizing the patriarchal family; gays were speaking out against homophobia. These challenges to the status quo set up a backlash among many white, mainstream Americans, and at the same time hampered liberal reformers' efforts to maintain their fragile coalition and implement Lyndon Johnson's Great Society. But an even more ominous fault line had emerged—one that profoundly divided the nation. The quagmire of the Vietnam War would soon challenge Americans' assumptions about their nation at home and abroad.

CHAPTER 30 TIMELINE

1960	Greensboro, North Carolina, sit-ins John F. Kennedy elected president
1961	Freedom rides Peace Corps established Bay of Pigs invasion Berlin Wall erected
1962	Michael Harrington's *The Other America* Cuban missile crisis
1963	Betty Friedan's *The Feminine Mystique* Presidential Commission on the Status of Women Report Civil-rights protest in Birmingham, Alabama March on Washington John F. Kennedy assassinated; Lyndon B. Johnson becomes president
1964	Freedom Summer Civil Rights Act Economic Opportunity Act Johnson elected president
1965	Malcolm X assassinated Voting Rights Act Immigration Act Medicare and Medicaid Elementary and Secondary Education Act Air and Water Quality acts
1966	National Organization for Women (NOW) founded Stokely Carmichael proclaims black power
1967	Height of race riots in northern cities
1968	Martin Luther King, Jr., assassinated Women's liberation movement emerges
1969	American Indian Movement seizes Alcatraz Stonewall riot begins gay liberation movement

CHAPTER 31

VIETNAM AND AMERICA, 1954–1975

- Into the Quagmire, 1945–1968
- The Challenge of Youth, 1962–1970•
- The Long Road Home, 1968–1975

In February 1969, while conducting his first mass as a Catholic Priest, James Carroll seized the opportunity to criticize the U.S. war in Vietnam. Carroll's public pronouncement against the war, delivered in a U.S. Air Force base chapel before an audience of high-ranking officers, among them his father, opened a rift in his family that never healed. Carroll's stand was not unique: he joined countless other ministers and priests who used their pulpits to condemn the war. His experience provides a dramatic example of the ruptures the Vietnam War brought to families, institutions, and the American social fabric.

Vietnam spawned a vibrant antiwar protest movement, which intersected with a broader youth movement that questioned traditional American political and cultural values. The challenges posed by youth, together with the rise of the black and Chicano power movements and explosive riots in the cities, produced a profound sense of social disorder at home. Vietnam split the Democratic party and shattered the liberal consensus. The high monetary cost of the war diverted resources from domestic uses, spelling an end to the Great Society. Beyond its domestic impact, the war wreaked extraordinary damage on the country of Vietnam and undermined U.S. credibility abroad. For the first time, average Americans began to question their assumptions about the nation's cold war objectives and the beneficence of American foreign policy.

INTO THE QUAGMIRE, 1945–1968

Like many new nations that emerged from the dissolution of European empires after World War II, Vietnam was characterized by a volatile mix of nationalist sentiment, religious and cultural conflict, economic need, and political turmoil. The rise of communism there was just one phase of the nation's larger struggle, which would eventually climax in a bloody civil war. But American policymakers viewed these events through the lens of the Cold War, interpreting them as part of an internationally inspired communist movement toward global domination. Their failure to understand the complexity of Vietnam's internal conflicts led to a long and ultimately disastrous attempt to influence the course of the war.

America in Vietnam: From Truman to Kennedy

Vietnam, which had been part of the French colony of Indochina since the late nineteenth century, had been occupied by Japan during World War II. When the Japanese surrendered in 1945, Ho Chi Minh and the Vietminh, the nationalist group that had led Vietnamese resistance to the Japanese, took advantage of the resulting power vacuum. With words drawn from the American Declaration of Independence, Ho proclaimed the establishment of the independent republic of Vietnam that September. The next year, when France rejected his claim and reasserted control over the country, an eight-year struggle that the Vietminh called the Anti-French War of Resistance ensued. Appealing to American anticolonial sentiment, Ho called on President Truman to support the struggle for Vietnamese independence. But Truman ignored his pleas and instead offered covert financial support to the French, in hopes of stabilizing the politically chaotic region and rebuilding the French economy.

By the end of the decade, cold war developments had prompted the United States to step up its assistance to the French. After the Chinese revolution of 1949, the United States became concerned that China—along with the Soviet Union—might actively support anticolonial struggles in Asia, and that newly independent countries might align themselves with the communists. At the same time, Republican charges that the Democrats had "lost" China influenced Truman to take a firmer stand against perceived communist aggression both in Korea and in Vietnam. Truman also wanted to maintain good relations with France, whose support was crucial to the success of the new NATO alliance. Finally, Indochina played a strategic role in Secretary of State Dean Acheson's plans for an integrated Pacific rim economy centered on a reindustrialized Japan.

For all these reasons, when the Soviet Union and the new Chinese leaders recognized Ho's republic early in 1950, the United States—along with Great Britain—recognized the French-installed puppet government of Bao Dai. Subsequently, both the Truman and the Eisenhower administrations provided substantial military support to the French in Vietnam. President Eisenhower argued that such aid was essential to prevent the collapse of all noncommunist governments in the area, in a chain reaction he called the domino effect: "You have a row of dominoes set up, you knock over the first one, and what will happen to the last one is the certainty that it will go over very quickly."

Despite joint French-American efforts, the Vietminh forces gained strength in northern Vietnam. In the spring of 1954, they seized the isolated administrative fortress of Dienbienphu after a fifty-six-day siege. The spectacular victory gave the Vietminh negotiating leverage in the 1954 Geneva Accords, which partitioned Vietnam temporarily at the 17th parallel (see Map 31.1) and committed France to withdraw its forces north of that line. The Accords also provided that within two years, in free elections, the voters in the two sectors would choose a unified government for the entire nation. Eight of the nine national delegations in attendance signed the agreements, but the United States refused, and instead issued a separate protocol acknowledging the agreements and promising to "refrain from the threat or use of force to disturb them."

Eisenhower had no intention of allowing a communist victory in Vietnam's upcoming election. With the help of the CIA, he made sure that a pro-American government took power in South Vietnam in June 1954, just before the accords were signed. Ngo Dinh Diem, an anticommunist Catholic who had spent eight years in the United States, returned to Vietnam as the premier of the French-backed South Vietnamese government. The next year, in a rigged election, Diem became president of an independent South Vietnam. Realizing that the popular Ho Chi Minh would easily win in both north and south, Diem then called off the reunification elections that were scheduled for 1956, a move the United States supported.

In March 1956 the last French soldiers left Saigon, the capital of South Vietnam, and the United States replaced France as the dominant foreign power in the region. American policymakers quickly asserted that a noncommunist South Vietnam was vital to U.S. security interests. In reality, Vietnam was too small a country to upset the international balance of power, and its communist movement was regional and intensely nationalistic, rather than expansionist. Nevertheless, Eisenhower and subsequent U.S. presidents persisted in viewing Vietnam as part of the cold war struggle to contain the communist threat to the free world. Between 1955 and 1961 the Eisenhower administration sent Diem an average of $200 million a year in aid and stationed approximately 675 American military advisers in Saigon. Having stepped up U.S. involvement there considerably, Eisenhower left office, passing the Vietnam situation to his successor, John F. Kennedy.

President Kennedy saw Vietnam as an ideal testing ground for the counterinsurgency techniques that formed the centerpiece of his military policy (see Chapter 30). But he first had to prop up Diem's unpopular regime, which faced a growing military threat. In December 1960, the Communist party in

MAP 31.1
The Vietnam War, 1954–1975
The Vietnam war was a guerrilla war, fought in inconclusive skirmishes rather than decisive battles. Supporters of the National Liberation Front filtered into South Vietnam along the Ho Chi Minh Trail, which wound through Laos and Cambodia. In January 1968 Viet Cong forces launched the Tet offensive, a surprise attack on several South Vietnamese cities and provincial centers shown above. American vulnerability to these attacks fueled opposition to the war.

North Vietnam organized most of Diem's opponents in South Vietnam into a revolutionary movement known as the National Liberation Front (NLF). To counter the threat, Kennedy increased the number of American military "advisers" (an elastic term that included helicopter units and special forces), raising it to more than 16,000 by November 1963. To win the "hearts and minds" of Vietnamese peasants away from the insurgents and to increase agricultural production, he also sent economic development specialists. But Kennedy refused to send combat troops to assist the South Vietnamese.

American aid did little good in South Vietnam. Diem's political inexperience and corruption, combined with his Catholicism in a predominantly Buddhist country, prevented him from creating a stable popular government. The NLF's guerrilla forces—called the Viet Cong by their opponents—made considerable headway against Diem's regime, using the revolutionary tactics of the Chinese leader Mao Zedong to blend into South Vietnam's civilian population "like fish in the water." They found a receptive audience among peasants who had been alienated by Diem's "strategic hamlet" program, which uprooted families and whole villages and moved them into barbed-wire compounds in a vain attempt to separate them from Ho Chi Minh's sympathizers.

Anti-Diem sentiment also flourished among Buddhists, who charged the government with religious persecution. Starting in May 1963, militant Buddhists staged a dramatic series of demonstrations against Diem, including several self-immolations that were recorded by American television crews. Diem's regime retaliated with raids on temples and mass arrests of Buddhist priests in August, prompting more antigovernment demonstrations.

As opposition to Diem deepened, Kennedy decided that he would have to be removed. Ambassador Henry Cabot Lodge, Jr., let it be known in Saigon that the United States would support a military coup that had "a good chance of succeeding." On November 1, 1963, Diem was driven from office and assassinated by officers in the South Vietnamese army. America's role in the coup reinforced the links between the United States and the new regime in South Vietnam, making the prospect of withdrawal from the region less acceptable to U.S. policymakers.

Less than a month later, Kennedy himself was assassinated. Although historians continue to debate whether Kennedy would have withdrawn American forces from Vietnam had he lived, his administration's actions clearly accelerated U.S. involvement. When Lyndon Johnson became president, he retained many of Kennedy's foreign policy advisers. Asserting that "I am not going to be the President who saw Southeast Asia go the way China went," he quickly declared he would maintain U.S. support for South Vietnam.

Escalation: The Johnson Years

Diem's removal did not improve the efficiency or the popularity of the government in Saigon. Secretary of Defense Robert McNamara and other top advisers argued that only a rapid, full-scale deployment of U.S. forces could prevent the imminent defeat of the South Vietnamese. But Johnson would need at least tacit congressional support, perhaps even a declaration of war, to commit U.S. forces to an offensive strategy. During the summer of 1964, the president saw his opportunity. American naval forces were conducting surveillance missions off the North Vietnamese coast, to aid amphibious attacks on the area by the South Vietnamese. When the North Vietnamese resisted the attacks, President Johnson told the nation that on two separate occasions, North Vietnamese torpedo boats had fired on American destroyers in international waters in the Gulf of Tonkin. At Johnson's request, Congress authorized him to "take all necessary measures to repel any armed attack against the forces of the United States and to prevent further aggression." On August 7 the Gulf of Tonkin resolution passed in the Senate 88 to 2 and in the House 416 to 0. Johnson's skillful representation of the unverified attack got him what he wanted—a sweeping mandate to conduct operations in Vietnam as he saw fit. The only formal approval of American intervention in Vietnam that Congress ever granted, the Tonkin resolution represented a significant expansion of presidential power.

Once congressional support was assured, and the 1964 elections had passed (see Chapter 30), the Johnson administration moved toward the Americanization of the war. The first phase of the escalation began on March 2, 1965. Operation Rolling Thunder, a protracted bombing campaign, dropped a million tons of bombs on North Vietnam between 1965 and 1968. Each B-52 sortie cost $30,000. By early 1966 the direct costs of the air war had exceeded $1.7 billion, yet the enormous expenditure of munitions continued. From 1965 to 1973 the United States dropped three times as many bombs on North Vietnam, a country roughly the size of Texas, as had fallen on all of Europe, Asia, and Africa during World War II. The several hundred captured U.S. pilots downed in the raids then became pawns in prisoner-of-war negotiations with the North Vietnamese.

To the amazement of American advisers, the bombings did not appear to impede the North's ability to wage war. The flow of troops and supplies to the south continued unabated as the North Vietnamese quickly rebuilt roads and bridges, moved munitions plants underground, and constructed networks of tunnels and shelters. Instead of destroying enemy morale and bringing the North Vietnamese to the bargaining table, Operation Rolling Thunder intensified their nationalism and will to fight. Yet the bombing continued.

A week after the launch of Operation Rolling Thunder, the United States sent its first official ground troops into combat duty. Soon U.S. Marines were skirmishing with the enemy. Beginning in the summer of 1965, combat operations shifted from a defensive stance to a search-and-destroy offense designed to uncover and kill Viet Cong forces. Fearing congressional opposition, the Johnson administration did not reveal this major change in strategy. Over the next three years the number of American troops in Vietnam grew dramatically. Although U.S. troops were accompanied by military forces from Australia, New Zealand, and South Korea, the war increasingly became an American war, fought for American aims. By 1966 more than 380,000 American soldiers were stationed in Vietnam; by 1967, 485,000; by 1968, 536,000.

The massive commitment of troops and air power threatened to destroy Vietnam's countryside. Besides the bombardment, a defoliation campaign had seriously damaged agricultural production, undercutting the economic and cultural base of Vietnamese society. After one devastating but not unusual engagement, a commanding officer reported, using the logic of the time, "It became necessary to destroy the town in order to save it." Graffiti on a plane that dropped defoliants read "Only you can prevent forests." (In later years defoliants such as Agent Orange were found to have highly toxic effects on both humans and the environment.) The destruction was not limited to North Vietnam; South Vietnam, America's ally, absorbed more than twice the bomb tonnage dropped on the north. In Saigon and other South Vietnamese cities, the influx of American soldiers and dollars distorted local economies, spread corruption and prostitution, and triggered uncontrollable inflation and black market activity.

Why did the dramatically increased American presence in Vietnam fail to turn the tide of the war? Some advisers argued that military intervention would accomplish little unless it was accompanied by reform in Saigon and increased popular support in the countryside. Other critics claimed that the United States never fully committed itself to a total victory—although what that term meant was never settled. Military strategy was inextricably tied to political considerations. For domestic reasons, policymakers often searched for an elusive "middle ground" between all-out invasion (and the possibility of sparking a nuclear exchange between the two superpowers) and the politically unacceptable alternative of disengagement. Hoping to win a war of attrition, the Johnson administration assumed that American superiority in personnel and weaponry would ultimately triumph. But that limited commitment was never enough to ensure victory, however it was defined.

The tremendous determination of the North Vietnamese was a major factor. The Viet Cong were prepared to accept limitless casualties, and to fight on for as many years as necessary. North Vietnamese strategists realized that the war did not have to be won on the battlefield, and accurately predicted that the American public would not tolerate an extended war of attrition. Time was on the Viet Cong's side, although at enormous cost to both sides.

Soldiers' Perspectives on the War in Vietnam

Approximately 2.8 million Americans served in Vietnam. At an average age of only nineteen, most of those servicemen and women were too young to vote or drink (the voting age was twenty-one until passage of the Twenty-sixth Amendment in 1971), but they were old enough to fight and die. Some were volunteers, including 7,000 women enlistees. Many others served because they were drafted. Until the nation shifted to an all-volunteer force in 1973, the draft stood as a concrete reminder of the government's impact on the lives of ordinary Americans. Blacks were drafted and died roughly in the same proportion as their share of the draft-age population (about 12 to 13 percent), although black casualty rates were significantly higher than average in the early 1960s. Even more than in other recent wars, sons of the poor and the working class shouldered a disproportionate amount of the fighting, forming an estimated 80 percent of the enlisted ranks. Young men from more affluent backgrounds were more likely to avoid combat through student deferments, medical exemptions, and appointments to National Guard and reserve units—alternatives that made Johnson's Vietnam policy more acceptable to the middle class.

At first, many draftees and enlistees shared common cold war assumptions about the need to fight communism and the superiority of the American military. However, their experience in Vietnam quickly challenged simple notions of patriotism and the inevitability of victory. In "Nam," long days of boring menial work were punctuated by brief flashes of intense fighting. "Most of the time, nothing happened," a soldier recalled, "but when something did, it happened instantaneously and without warning." Rarely were there large-scale battles, only skirmishes; rather than front lines and conquered territory, there were only daytime operations in areas the Viet Cong controlled at night.

Racism was a fact of everyday life. Because differentiating between friendly South Vietnamese and Viet Cong sympathizers was difficult, many soldiers lumped them together as "gooks." As a draftee noted of his indoctrination, "The only thing they told us about the Viet Cong was they were gooks. They were to be killed. Nobody sits around and gives you their historical and cultural background. They're the enemy. Kill, kill, kill."

Fighting under such conditions took its toll. One veteran explained that "The hardest thing to come to grips with was the fact that making it through Vietnam—surviving—is probably the only worthwhile part of the experience. It wasn't going over there and saving the world from communism or defending the country." Cynicism and bitterness were common. The pressure of waging war under such conditions drove many soldiers to seek escape in alcohol or drugs, which were cheap and readily available.

The American women who served in Vietnam shared many of these experiences. As WACs, nurses, and civilians serving with organizations such as the USO, women volunteers witnessed death and mutilation on a massive scale. Though they tried to maintain a professional distance, as a navy nurse recalled, "It's pretty damn hard not getting involved when you see a nineteen- or twenty-year-old blond kid from the Midwest or California or the East Coast screaming and dying. A piece of my heart would go with each."

The Cold War Consensus Unravels

President Kennedy and at first President Johnson as well enjoyed broad support for their conduct of foreign affairs. Both Democrats and Republicans approved Johnson's escalation of the war, and public opinion polls in 1965–1966 showed strong popular support for his policies. But in the late 1960s, public opinion began to turn against the war. In July 1967 a Gallup poll revealed that for the first time, a majority of Americans disapproved of Johnson's Vietnam policy, and believed the war had reached a stalemate.

Television had much to do with these attitudes. Vietnam was the first war in which television brought the films of the fighting directly into the nation's living rooms. By 1967 CBS and NBC were spending $5 million a year to cover the war from their Saigon bureaus. Reporters soon learned that combat footage—what they called "shooting bloody"—had a better chance of being aired than did pieces about social reform or political developments. Every night Americans watched U.S. soldiers advance steadily through the country-side and heard reporters detail staggering Viet Cong losses and minimal U.S. casualties.

Despite the glowing reports filed by the media and the administration on the progress of the war, by 1967 many administration officials had privately reached a more pessimistic conclusion. In November Secretary of Defense Robert McNamara sent a memo to the president arguing that continued es-calation "would be dangerous, costly in lives, and unsatisfactory to the Ameri-can people." Pentagon analysts confirmed McNamara's doubts, estimating that the Viet Cong could marshal 200,000 guerrillas a year, indefinitely. Despite that prognosis, however, President Johnson continued to insist that victory in Vietnam was vital to U.S. national security and prestige. Journalists, especially those who had spent time in Vietnam, soon began to warn that the Johnson

A Televised War
This harrowing scene from Saigon during the Tet offensive in 1968 depicts the head of the South Vietnamese National Police preparing to shoot a captured member of the Viet Cong. Telecast on U.S. network news, it was one of scores of disturbing images that flooded American living rooms during the Vietnam era, and helped to sway public opinion against contin-ued participation in what commentator Walter Cronkite called a "bloody experience" that would end in "stalemate."

administration suffered from a "credibility gap." The administration, they charged, was concealing important and discouraging information about the war's progress. In February 1966 television coverage of hearings by the Senate Foreign Relations Committee (chaired by J. William Fulbright, an outspoken critic of the war) raised further questions about the administration's policy.

Economic developments put Johnson and his advisers even more on the defensive. In 1966 the federal deficit was $9.8 billion; in 1967, a year the Vietnam War cost the taxpayers $27 billion, it jumped to $23 billion. Although the war consumed just 3 percent of the gross national product, its costs became more evident as the growing federal deficit nudged the inflation rate upward. But only in the summer of 1967 did Johnson ask for a 10 percent surcharge on individual and corporate incomes, an increase that Congress did not approve until 1968. By then the inflationary spiral that would plague the U.S. economy throughout the 1970s was well under way.

Another major problem facing the Johnson administration was the growing strength and visibility of the antiwar movement. As in every American military conflict, a small group of dissenters had opposed the war from the beginning; these included pacifist organizations such as the Women's International League for Peace and Freedom, as well as religious groups such as the Quakers and the Fellowship for Reconciliation. They had been joined by a new generation of peace activists represented by groups such as SANE (the National Committee for a Sane Nuclear Policy) and Physicians for Social Responsibility. These new activists were opposed to the escalating arms race in general, and to atmospheric testing in particular. They had lobbied successfully for the 1963 nuclear test-ban treaty between the United States and the Soviet Union.

Between 1963 and 1965, peace activists in both types of organization staged periodic protests, vigils, and petition- and letter-writing campaigns against U.S. involvement in the war. After the escalation of combat in the spring of 1965, various antiwar coalitions, swelled by growing numbers of students, clergy, housewives, politicians, artists, and others opposed to the war, organized several mass demonstrations in Washington, bringing out 20,000 to 30,000 people at a time. A diverse lot, participants in these rallies shared a common skepticism about the means and aims of U.S. policy. The war was morally wrong, they argued, and antithetical to American ideals; the goal of an independent, anticommunist South Vietnam was unattainable; and American military involvement in Vietnam would not help the Vietnamese people.

Some Americans felt so strongly against the war that they adopted extreme means of protest. In November 1965 Norman Morrison, a Quaker activist, set himself on fire and burned to death near the Pentagon gates, 40 yards from Defense Secretary McNamara's office. Morrison undertook his protest after reading an account by a French priest who had despaired at seeing his Vietnamese parishioners burned by the lethal incendiary substance napalm during a bombing attack. Like the priest, Morrison was torn by his inability to stop the carnage. To his wife he wrote: "Know that I love thee but must act for the children of the priest's village."

Morrison's suicide shocked the nation. Even McNamara later admitted he was horrified by this "outcry against the killing that was destroying the lives of so many Vietnamese and American youth." Three weeks later an estimated 30,000 antiwar protesters, including a large contingent of college students, converged on the White House. Over the next few years student protesters would flock to the antiwar movement, increasing its visibility and political clout. The fervor of this new generation would drive not only the antiwar movement but a youthful rebellion that challenged authority on nearly every front.

THE CHALLENGE OF YOUTH, 1962–1970

Although some of the most potent images of the 1960s show youthful protesters rebelling against the war in Vietnam, traditional values, authority, and the "system," American youth were not monolithic. Many young people, especially those in the working class, kept their distance from the more extreme expressions of rebellion. College students, whose numbers had increased dramatically in the postwar period, formed the core of those youth who challenged authority in the 1960s.

Student Activism

In June 1962 forty students from Big Ten and Ivy League universities, disturbed by the gap they perceived between the ideals they had been taught to revere and the realities in American life, met in Port Huron, Michigan, to found Students for a Democratic Society (SDS). Tom Hayden wrote their manifesto, the Port Huron Statement, which expressed their disillusionment with the consumer culture and the gulf between the prosperous and the poor. These students rejected cold war ideology and foreign policy, including but not limited to the Vietnam conflict. They castigated the bureaucracies that dominated America's corporations, political parties, and government, and blocked citizens' access to power. They called for a reinvigorated participatory politics, designating students as the major force for social change. To distinguish themselves from the "Old Left"—communists, socialists, and other left-wing sectarians of the 1930s and 1940s—the founders of SDS referred to their movement as the "New Left." Consciously adopting the activist tactics pioneered by members of the civil-rights movement, they turned to grass-roots organizing in cities and on college campuses.

The first student protests erupted in the fall of 1964 at the University of California at Berkeley after administrators banned political activity near the Telegraph Avenue entrance, where student groups had traditionally distributed leaflets and recruited volunteers. In protest, all the major student organizations, from SDS to the conservative Youth for Goldwater, formed a coalition called the Free Speech Movement (FSM) and organized a sit-in at the administration building. The university agreed to drop the ban.

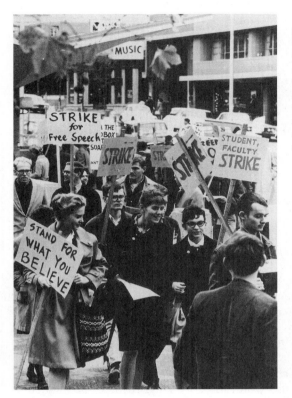

Free Speech at Berkeley, 1964
Students at the University of California's Berkeley campus protested the administration's decision to ban political activity in the school plaza. Free speech demonstrators, many of them active in the civil-rights movement, relied on the tactics and arguments that they learned in that struggle.

The FSM owed a strong debt to the civil-rights movement. Some students had just returned from Freedom Summer in Mississippi, where they were radicalized by their experience. Mario Savio spoke for many of them:

> Last summer I went to Mississippi to join the struggle there for civil rights. This fall I am engaged in another phase of the same struggle, this time in Berkeley. The two battlefields may seem quite different to some observers, but this is not the case. The same rights are at stake in both places—the right to participate as citizens in a democratic society and to struggle against the same enemy. In Mississippi an autocratic and powerful minority rules, through organized violence, to suppress the vast, virtually powerless majority. In California, the privileged minority manipulates the university bureaucracy to suppress the students' political expression.

On a deeper level Berkeley students were challenging a university that in their view had grown too big and was too far removed from the major social issues of the day. In the postwar era, the largest universities, like the largest corporations, had grown the fastest. In 1940 only two campuses in the United

States had as many as 20,000 students; by 1969 thirty-nine were that large or larger. Many students in these "multiversities" felt they were treated brusquely and impersonally. Emboldened by the Berkeley movement, students across the nation were soon protesting everything from dress codes to course requirements, from tenure decisions to academic grading.

Students also protested the universities' complicity in the problems of the ghetto. Columbia University, for example, owned substantial property in Harlem, which bordered its campus. When the university announced plans in 1968 to build a new gymnasium, which would displace local stores and housing, students tore down the fence at the construction site and took over several university buildings. Columbia officials called the police to break up the demonstration; the brutal response of New York City's Tactical Police force radicalized many more students than had originally supported the protests. As campus disturbances spread to other colleges and universities, more and more university buildings were blocked, occupied, or picketed, and classes were frequently dismissed or canceled.

Although black students participated in many protests, the student movements soon began to split along racial lines. White students focused on the antiwar movement; black students, inspired by the black power movement, demanded to study African-American history and culture. University administrators, anxious to ease campus unrest, agreed to establish Afro-American and black studies departments. By forcing the inclusion of black society and culture in the curriculum, and thus the acknowledgment of race as a key factor in American life, these students changed the way American history was taught and written. Black protesters also won university support for separate dormitories and cultural centers, to provide a sense of community for blacks residing on predominantly white campuses.

No issue provoked more impassioned and sustained protest than the Vietnam War. The highly politicized activists of the New Left, who had developed a wide-ranging critique of American society, increasingly focused on the war, and they were joined by thousands of other students in protesting American participation in the Vietnam conflict. When President Johnson escalated the war in March 1965, faculty and students at the University of Michigan organized a teach-in against the war. Abandoning their classes, they debated the political, diplomatic, and moral aspects of the nation's involvement in Vietnam. Teach-ins quickly spread to other universities as students turned from their studies to protest the war.

Many protests centered on the draft, especially after the Selective Service System abolished student deferments in January 1966. To avoid the draft, some young men enlisted in the National Guard or the reserves; others declared themselves conscientious objectors. Several thousand young men ignored their induction notices, risking prosecution for draft evasion. Others left the country, most often for Canada or Sweden. The Resistance, started at Berkeley and Stanford and widely recognized by its omega symbol, supported these draft resisters. In public demonstrations of civil disobedience, opponents of the

A Draft Resister

On October 16, 1967, Michael K. Ferber spoke at a Boston church in support of the organization Resistance's call for young men to turn in their draft cards. As the following passage makes clear, Ferber's motivation for resisting the draft went deeper than simple opposition to the Vietnam War; it incorporated many of the ideas of the New Left.

We are gathered in this church today in order to do something very simple: to say No. We have come from many different places and backgrounds and we have many different ideas about ourselves and the world, but we have come here to show that we are united to do one thing: to say No. Each of our acts of returning our draft cards is our personal No; when we put them in a single container or set fire to them from a single candle we express the simple basis of our unity. . . .

But let us not be deceived. The sun will rise tomorrow as it does every day, and when we get out of bed the world will be in pretty much the same mess it is in today. American bombers will continue to drop incendiary bombs on the Vietnamese people and American soldiers will continue to "pacify" their villages. The ghettos will continue to be rotten places to live in. Black and Mexican farm workers will continue to get miserable wages. America's schools will continue to cripple the minds and hearts of its pupils. And the American Selective Service System will continue to send young men out to the slaughter.

Today is not the End. Today is the Beginning.

SOURCE: Alexander Bloom and Wini Breines, eds., *"Takin' it to the Streets": A Sixties Reader* (New York: Oxford University Press, 1995), pp. 245–248.

war burned their draft cards, closed down induction centers, and on a few occasions broke into Selective Service offices.

As antiwar and draft protests multiplied, students realized that their universities were deeply implicated in the war effort. In some cases as much as 60 percent of a university's research budget came from government contracts, especially those of the Defense department. Protesters blocked recruiters from the Dow Chemical Company, the producer of napalm and Agent Orange. Arguing that universities should not train students for war, they demanded that the Reserve Officer Training Corps (ROTC) be removed from college campuses.

In the late 1960s student protesters joined the much larger antiwar movement of peace activists, housewives, religious leaders, and a few elected officials. After 1967 nationwide student strikes, mass demonstrations, and other organized protests became commonplace. In October 1967, more than

100,000 antiwar demonstrators marched on Washington, D.C., as part of "Stop the Draft Week." The event culminated in a "siege of the Pentagon," in which protesters clashed with police and federal marshals. Hundreds of people were arrested and several demonstrators beaten. Lyndon Johnson, who had once dismissed antiwar protesters as "nervous Nellies," rebellious children, or communist dupes, had to face the reality of large-scale public opposition to his policies.

The Rise of the Counterculture

Antiwar sentiment and protest accelerated the erosion of confidence in established American institutions and values. While the New Left took to the streets in protest, a growing number of young Americans undertook their own revolution against authority and middle-class respectability. The "hippie"—attired in ragged blue jeans, tie-dyed T-shirt, beads, and army fatigues, and wearing long, unkempt hair—symbolized the new *counterculture*, a youthful movement that glorified liberation from traditional social strictures through new music and clothing styles, spiritual exploration, and experimentation with sex and drugs.

Throughout the 1960s popular music mirrored the changing political mood. The folk singer Pete Seeger set the tone for the era with idealistic songs

Flower Children
Yale law professor Charles A. Reich celebrated the new freedom of youth in his best-selling book *The Greening of America* (1970). Reich described a new consciousness that had "emerged out of the wasteland of the Corporate State, like flowers pushing up through the concrete pavement." Counterculture hippies were also called flower children.

such as the antiwar ballad "Where Have All the Flowers Gone?" Another folk singer, Joan Baez, gained national prominence singing "We Shall Overcome" and other political anthems at mid-decade protest rallies. In 1963, the year of the Birmingham demonstrations and President Kennedy's assassination, Bob Dylan's "Blowin' in the Wind" gave voice to the impatience of those whose faith in liberalism was wearing thin.

Other winds of change in popular music came from abroad. The Beatles, four working-class youths from England, burst onto the American scene early in 1964. Their music, by turns lyrical and hard driving, was phenomenally successful, spawning a commercial and cultural phenomenon called Beatlemania. American youth's eager embrace of the Beatles deepened the generational divide begun by the advent of rock-'n'-roll in the 1950s. After the Beatles came the angrier, more rebellious, music of other British groups, notably the Rolling Stones, whose raunchy 1965 hit "(I Can't Get No) Satisfaction" signaled a new openness about sexuality, while it made fun of the consumer culture ("He can't be a man 'cause he doesn't smoke the same cigarettes as me").

Drugs intertwined with music as a crucial element of the youth culture. They were hardly new to the American scene: the beats had experimented with mind-altering drugs, and many jazz musicians had used heroin and cocaine for decades. But the recreational use of drugs—especially marijuana and the hallucinogen lysergic acid diethylamide, popularly known as LSD, or "acid"—had never been so widespread, nor so celebrated in popular music. San Francisco bands, such as the Grateful Dead and the Jefferson Airplane, and musicians like the Seattle-born guitarist Jimi Hendrix developed a musical style known as "acid rock," which was characterized by long, heavily amplified guitar solos accompanied by psychedelic lighting effects. The Beatles, whose early songs had featured conventionally romantic lyrics, turned to recording tunes such as "Lucy in the Sky with Diamonds" (1967), whose "tangerine trees and marmalade skies" celebrated the new drug culture.

For a brief time, adherents of the counterculture believed a new age was dawning. In 1967 the "world's first Human Be-In" drew 20,000 people to Golden Gate Park in San Francisco. The beat poet Allen Ginsberg "purified" the site with a Buddhist ritual, and the LSD advocate Timothy Leary, a former Harvard psychology instructor, urged the gathering to "turn on to the scene, tune in to what is happening, and drop out." That summer—dubbed the "Summer of Love"—San Francisco's Haight-Ashbury, New York's East Village, and Chicago's Uptown neighborhoods swelled with young dropouts, drifters, and teenage runaways dubbed flower children by observers. Their faith in instant love and peace quickly turned sour, however, as they suffered bad drug trips, venereal disease, loneliness, and violence. In 1967 seventeen murders and more than a hundred rapes were reported in Haight-Ashbury alone.

Meanwhile, the appeal of rock music and drugs continued to grow. In August 1969 400,000 young people journeyed to Bethel, New York, to "get

AMERICAN VOICES

A Rock Musician Remembers the Counterculture

In this selection, the rock musician Joe McDonald of Country Joe and the Fish reminisces about life in the San Francisco Bay area during the 1960s. McDonald's nostalgic account of the 1960s drugs-and-music scene suggests the ways in which values of the political left often merged with those of the counterculture.

Up until that point people had just been consuming alcohol and falling down from that. But the new idea became, "Hey, take drugs and act crazy." So everybody took drugs, different kinds of drugs, whatever kinds of drugs, whatever kinds of drugs they could find. . . .

None of this stuff was happening with any sense of danger because something magical was going on that was hard to explain then, and is still hard to explain even now. An innocence, I guess.

Ultimately, though, we found out the hard way by having our innocence smashed out of us. Lots of things happened, mainly political assassinations and the war. You can't separate the era from that, from all those caskets. Ours was an era of extremes, unbelievable extremes. And inside that era we were like this little dreamland. . . . I think back fondly on that period, but I don't romanticize it. I mean, I don't think I'd want another generation to experience the negative things we experienced—mostly I mean the war.

But there were positive things, too, that sense of community, of communication. We developed family roots that were just wonderful. I love to think about that, walking down Haight Street in San Francisco and saying hello to everybody. It was a rare moment.

SOURCE: From Joe Smith, *Off the Record: An Oral History of Popular Music,* edited by Mitchell Fink (New York: Warner Books, 1988), pp. 229–231.

high" on music, drugs, and sex at the three-day Woodstock Music and Art Fair. Despite torrential rain and numerous drug overdoses, most enjoyed the festival, which was heralded as the birth of the "Woodstock nation." A few months later, however, an outdoor concert by the Rolling Stones at Altamont Speedway near San Francisco degenerated into a near riot, leaving four dead and hundreds injured.

Some young people rejected both mainstream culture and the growing anarchy of the counterculture and headed instead for rural communes. In the mountains between Santa Cruz and San Francisco and in the valleys of Vermont, communes provided economic and sexual alternatives to the traditional nuclear family. Members grew their own food, baked their own bread, and rejected materialism and commercialism in favor of old-fashioned self-sufficiency. But the communes of the 1960s did not just look backward. Their advocacy of organic farming—growing food without chemicals or pesticides—anticipated and influenced the environmental movement that would emerge in the 1970s and 1980s (see Chapter 32).

Although the counterculture and the New Left were different movements, the distinction between them sometimes blurred. Many antiwar protesters adopted hippie clothing, experimented with drugs, and embraced the more politically oriented forms of rock music. And while most flower children professed political apathy, their antiauthoritarianism threatened many adults. Furthermore, groups such as the Youth International Party, or "Yippies," led by Abbie Hoffman and Jerry Rubin, combined political and cultural rebellion in a deliberate attempt to attract media attention. During the October 1967 March on Washington, the Yippies dressed like witches and attempted to levitate the Pentagon. To many adult observers, the antiwar movement and the counterculture had become indistinguishable.

THE LONG ROAD HOME, 1968–1975

In 1968, as Lyndon Johnson planned his reelection campaign, antiwar protests and rising battlefield casualties had begun to erode public support for a war that seemed to have no end. Moreover, since Diem's assassination in 1963, South Vietnam had undergone a confusing series of military coups and countercoups. In the spring of 1966, the Johnson administration pressured the unpopular South Vietnamese government to adopt democratic reforms, including a new constitution and popular elections. In September 1967 U.S. officials helped to elect General Nguyen Van Thieu president of South Vietnam. Thieu's regime, the administration hoped, would broaden its support at home, legitimize the South Vietnamese government in the eyes of the American public, and advance the military struggle against the communists.

1968 and Its Aftermath

The administration's hopes evaporated on January 30, 1968, when the Viet Cong unleashed a massive, well-coordinated assault on major urban areas in South Vietnam. Known as the Tet offensive, the assault was timed to coincide with the lunar new year, a festive Vietnamese holiday. Viet Cong forces struck thirty-six of the forty-four provincial capitals and five of the six major cities, including Saigon, where they raided the supposedly impregnable U.S. embassy (see Map 31.1, p. 837). In strict military terms the Tet offensive was a failure for the Viet Cong since it did not provoke the intended collapse of the South Vietnamese government. But its long-term effect was quite different. The daring attack made a mockery of official pronouncements that the United States was winning the war and swung American public opinion more strongly against the war. Just before the offensive, a Gallup poll found that 56 percent of Americans considered themselves "hawks" (supporters of the war), while only 28 percent identified with the "doves" (opponents). Three months after Tet, the doves outnumbered the hawks by 42 to 41 percent. This turnaround in public opinion did not mean that a majority of Americans supported the peace movement, however. Many who called themselves doves had simply concluded that the war was unwinnable, and were therefore opposed to it on pragmatic rather than moral grounds. As a housewife told a pollster, "I want to get out, but I don't want to give up."

The growing opposition to the war spilled over into the 1968 presidential campaign. Even before Tet, Senator Eugene J. McCarthy of Minnesota had entered the Democratic primaries as an antiwar candidate. In March, President Johnson won the early New Hampshire primary, but McCarthy received a stunning 42.2 percent of the vote. His strong showing against the president reflected profound public dissatisfaction with the course of the war—even among those who were hawks.

Johnson realized that his political support was evaporating. On March 31, and at the end of an otherwise mundane televised address, he stunned the nation by announcing that he would not seek reelection. Johnson had already reversed his policy of incremental escalation of the war. Now he called a partial bombing halt and vowed to devote his remaining months in office to the search for peace. On May 10, 1968, preliminary peace talks between the United States and North Vietnam opened in Paris.

Just four days after Johnson's withdrawal from the presidential race, Martin Luther King, Jr., was assassinated in Memphis. His death provoked riots in cities across the country, leaving forty-three people dead. Soon afterward, the student confrontation at Columbia University erupted (see page 846). The next month, a massive strike by students and labor unions toppled the French government. Student unrest seemed likely to become a world-wide phenomenon.

Then came the final painful tragedy of the year. Senator Robert Kennedy, who had entered the Democratic presidential primaries in March, had quickly become a front runner. On June 5, 1968, as he celebrated his victory in the California primary, he was shot dead by a young Palestinian who was thought to oppose Kennedy's pro-Israeli stance. Robert Kennedy's assassination shattered the dreams of many who had hoped that social change could be achieved by working through the political system. His death also weakened the Democratic party. In his brief but dramatic campaign Kennedy had excited and energized the traditional members of the New Deal coalition, including blue-collar workers and black voters, in a way that the more cerebral Eugene McCarthy, who appealed mostly to the antiwar movement, never did.

The Democratic party never fully recovered from Johnson's withdrawal and Kennedy's assassination. McCarthy's campaign limped along, while Senator George S. McGovern of South Dakota entered the Democratic race in an effort to keep the Kennedy forces together. Meanwhile, Vice-

President Hubert H. Humphrey lined up pledges from traditional Democratic constituencies—unions, urban machines, and state political organizations. Democrats found themselves on the verge of nominating not an antiwar candidate, but a public figure closely associated with Johnson's war policies.

In the end, the political divisions generated by the war consumed the Democratic party. Most of the drama occurred not in the convention hall but outside, on the streets of Chicago. Led by Jerry Rubin and Abbie Hoffman, around 10,000 protesters descended on the city, calling for an end to the war, the legalization of marijuana, and the abolition of money. To mock those inside the convention hall, they nominated a pig for president. Their stunts, geared toward maximizing their media exposure, diverted attention from the more serious and far more numerous antiwar activists who had come to Chicago as convention delegates or volunteers.

Richard J. Daley, the Democratic mayor of Chicago, who had grown increasingly angry as protesters disrupted his convention, called out the police to break up the demonstrations. Several nights of skirmishes between protesters and police culminated the evening of the nominations. In what an official report later described as a "police riot," patrolmen attacked protesters with Mace, tear gas, and clubs as demonstrators chanted, "The whole world is watching!" Television networks broadcast a film of the riot as the nominating speeches were being made, cementing a popular impression of the Democrats as the party of disorder. Inside the hall, the Democrats dispiritedly nominated Hubert H. Humphrey, who chose Senator Edmund S. Muskie of Maine as his running mate. The delegates approved a middle-of-the-road platform that endorsed continued fighting in Vietnam while the administration explored diplomatic means of ending the conflict.

The disruptive Democratic convention unleashed a backlash against antiwar protesters. The general public did not differentiate between the disruptive antics of the Yippies and the more responsible behavior of those activists who were trying to work within the system. Polls showed overwhelming support for Mayor Daley and the police.

The turmoil surrounding the New Left and the antiwar movement strengthened support for proponents of "law and order," which became a conservative catch phrase for the next several years. Indeed, many Americans, though opposed to the war, were fed up with protest and dissent. Governor George C. Wallace of Alabama, a third-party candidate, skillfully exploited their growing disapproval of the antiwar movement by making student protests and urban riots his chief campaign issues. But Wallace, who in 1963 had promised to enforce "segregation now . . . segregation tomorrow . . . and segregation forever," also exploited the mounting backlash against the civil-rights movement. Articulating the resentments of many working-class whites, he combined attacks on liberal intellectuals and government elites with strident denunciations of school desegregation and forced busing.

Hard Hats
Many construction workers (and the unions they belonged to) were vocal supporters of the
Vietnam War. Sometimes hard hats clashed with long-haired protesters during antiwar marches
and sidewalk demonstrations.

Even more than George Wallace, Richard Nixon tapped the increasingly conservative mood of the electorate. After his unsuccessful presidential campaign in 1960 and his loss in the California gubernatorial race in
1962, Nixon engineered an amazing political comeback, and in 1968 won
the Republican presidential nomination. He chose Spiro Agnew, the conservative governor of Maryland, as his running mate to attract southern
voters, especially Wallace supporters, who opposed Democratic civil-rights
legislation. Nixon pledged to represent the "quiet voice" of the "great majority of Americans, the forgotten Americans, the nonshouters, the
nondemonstrators."

Despite the Democratic debacle in Chicago, the election was a close one.
In the last weeks of the campaign, Humphrey rallied by gingerly disassociat-
ing himself from Johnson's war policies. Then, in a televised address on October 31, President Johnson announced a complete halt to the bombing of
North Vietnam. Nixon countered by intimating that he had his own plan to
end the war—although in reality no such plan existed. On election day
Nixon received 43.4 percent of the vote to Humphrey's 42.7 percent, defeating him by a scant 510,000 votes out of the 73 million that were cast. Wallace
finished with 13.5 percent of the popular vote. Though Nixon owed his
election largely to the split in the Democratic coalition, the success of his
southern strategy presaged the emergence of a new Republican majority. In

the meantime, however, the Democrats retained a majority in both houses of Congress.

The closeness of the 1968 election suggested how polarized American society had become. Nixon appealed to a segment of society that came to be known as the *silent majority*—the hardworking, nonprotesting, generally white American. Although his victory suggested a growing consensus among voters who were "unblack, unpoor, and unyoung," heated protest and controversy would persist until the war ended.

Nixon's War

Vietnam, long Lyndon Johnson's war, now became Richard Nixon's. At first Nixon sought to end the war by expanding its scope, as a means of pressuring the North Vietnamese to negotiate. But Nixon and his national security adviser, Henry Kissinger, soon realized that the public would not support such an approach. Thus, shortly after Nixon took office, he sent a letter to the North Vietnamese leaders proposing mutual troop withdrawals. In March 1969, to convince North Vietnam that the United States meant business, Nixon ordered clandestine bombing raids on neutral Cambodia, through which the North Vietnamese had been transporting supplies and reinforcements.

When the intensified bombing failed to end the war, Nixon and Kissinger adopted a policy of *Vietnamization*. On June 8, 1969, Nixon announced that 25,000 American troops would be withdrawn by August and replaced by South Vietnamese forces. As the U.S. ambassador to Vietnam, Ellsworth Bunker, noted cynically, Vietnamization was just a matter of changing "the color of the bodies." Antiwar demonstrators denounced the new policy, which protected American lives at the expense of the Vietnamese, but would not end the war. On October 15, 1969, in cities across the country, millions of Americans joined a one-day "moratorium" against the war. A month later, more than a quarter of a million people mobilized in Washington in the largest antiwar demonstration to date.

To discredit his critics Nixon denounced student demonstrators as "bums" and stated that "North Vietnam cannot defeat or humiliate the United States. Only Americans can do that." Vice-President Spiro Agnew attacked dissenters as "ideological eunuchs" and "nattering nabobs of negativism." Nixon staunchly insisted that he would not be swayed by the mounting protests against the war. During the November 1969 march on Washington the president barricaded himself in the White House and watched football on television.

On April 30, 1970, the bombing of Cambodia, which Nixon had kept secret from both the public and from Congress, culminated in an "incursion" into Cambodia by American ground forces to destroy enemy havens there. The invasion proved only a short-term setback for the North Vietnamese, who continued to boycott the Paris peace talks. More critically, the American action—along with the ongoing North Vietnamese intervention there—destabilized the country, exposing it to a takeover by the ruthless Khmer Rouge later in the 1970s.

When the *New York Times* uncovered the secret invasion of Cambodia, antiwar leaders organized a national student strike. On May 4, at Kent State University outside Cleveland, panicky National Guardsmen fired into a crowd of students at an antiwar rally. Four people were killed and eleven more wounded. Only two of those who were killed had been attending the demonstration; the other two were just passing by on their way to class. Soon afterward, National Guardsmen stormed a dormitory at Jackson State College in Mississippi, killing two black students. More than 450 colleges closed down in protest, and 80 percent of all campuses experienced some kind of disturbance. In June 1970, immediately after the Kent State slayings, a Gallup poll identified campus unrest as the issue that most troubled Americans.

At the same time, however, dissatisfaction with the war continued to spread. Congressional opposition to the war, which had been growing since the Fulbright hearings in 1966, intensified with the invasion of Cambodia. In June 1970 the Senate expressed its disapproval by voting to repeal the Gulf of Tonkin resolution, and by cutting off funding for operations in Cambodia. Even the soldiers in Vietnam were showing mounting opposition to their mission. The number of troops who refused to follow combat orders increased steadily, and thousands of U.S. soldiers deserted. Among the majority who fought on, many sewed peace symbols on their uniforms. In the heat of battle, a number of overbearing junior officers were sometimes "fragged," that is, killed or wounded in grenade attacks by their own soldiers. At home, members of a group called Vietnam Veterans against the

Kent State
The shootings by National Guardsmen of four students at Kent State University in Ohio on May 4, 1970, set off campus demonstrations and protests across the country. The protester shown here holds a placard memorializing the slain students as well as the two black students killed soon afterward at Jackson State College in Mississippi. The president of Columbia University called May 1970 "the most disastrous month . . . in the history of American higher education."

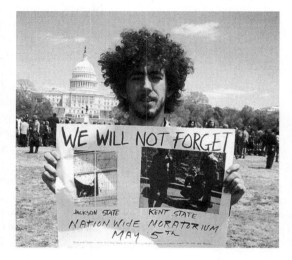

War turned in their combat medals at demonstrations outside the U.S. Capitol.

In 1971 Americans were appalled by revelations of the sheer brutality of the war when Lieutenant William L. Calley was court-martialed for atrocities committed in the village of My Lai. In March 1968 Calley and the platoon under his command had apparently murdered 350 Vietnamese villagers in retaliation for casualties sustained in an earlier engagement. The military court sentenced Calley to life in prison for his part in the massacre. Yet George Wallace and some congressional conservatives called him a hero. President Nixon had Calley's sentence reduced; he was paroled in 1974.

After a final outbreak of protest and violence following the incident at Kent State, antiwar activism began to ebb. The antiwar movement was weakened in part by internal divisions within the New Left. In the late 1960s, SDS and other antiwar groups fell victim to police harassment, and Federal Bureau of Investigation (FBI) and Central Intelligence Agency (CIA) agents infiltrated and disrupted radical organizations. After 1968 the New Left splintered into factions, its energy spent. One radical faction broke off from SDS and formed the Weathermen, a tiny band of self-styled revolutionaries who embraced terrorist tactics that alienated more moderate activists.

Nixon's Vietnamization policy also played a role in the decline of antiwar protest by dramatically reducing the number of soldiers in combat. When Nixon took office, more than 543,000 American soldiers were serving in Vietnam; by the end of 1970 there were 334,000, and two years later there were 24,200. Nixon's promise to continue troop withdrawals, end the draft, and institute an all-volunteer army by 1973 further deprived the antiwar movement of important organizing issues, particularly on college campuses. Student commitment to social causes, however, did not disappear altogether. In the early 1970s many student activists refocused their energies on issues such as feminism and environmentalism.

Détente and the End of the War

At the same time Nixon had been prosecuting the war in Vietnam, ostensibly to halt the spread of communism, he had been formulating a new policy toward the Soviet Union and China. Known as *détente* (the French word for a relaxation of tensions), Nixon's policy was to seek peaceful coexistence with the two communist powers, and to link his overtures of friendship with a plan to end the Vietnam War. In his talks with Chinese and Soviet leaders, Nixon urged them to reduce their military aid to the North Vietnamese as a means of pressuring them to the negotiating table.

A lifelong anticommunist crusader, Nixon was better able to reach out to the two communist superpowers than a Democratic president would have been. Since the Chinese revolution of 1949 the United States had refused to recognize the government of the People's Republic of China. Instead, the

State Department had recognized the Nationalist Chinese government in Taiwan. Nixon moved away from that policy, reasoning that the United States could exploit the growing rift between the People's Republic of China and the Soviet Union. In February 1972 Nixon journeyed to China in a symbolic visit that set the stage for the establishment of formal diplomatic relations, which took place in 1979.

In a similar spirit Nixon journeyed to Moscow in May 1972 to sign the first Strategic Arms Limitations Treaty (SALT I) between the United States and the Soviet Union. Although SALT I fell far short of ending the arms race, it did limit the production and deployment of intercontinental ballistic missiles (ICBMs) and antiballistic missile systems (ABMs). The treaty also signified that the United States could no longer afford the massive military spending that would have been necessary to regain the nuclear and military superiority it had enjoyed immediately following World War II. By the early 1970s, inflation, domestic dissent, and the decline in American hegemony had limited and reshaped American aims and options in international relations. Most of all, Nixon hoped that a rapprochement with the Soviets would help to resolve the prolonged crisis in Vietnam.

The Paris peace talks had been in stalemate since 1968. Though the war had been "Vietnamized," and American casualties had decreased, the South Vietnamese military proved unable to hold its own. In late 1971, as American troops withdrew from the region, communist forces stepped up their attacks on Laos, Cambodia, and South Vietnam. The next spring North Vietnamese forces launched a major new offensive against South Vietnam. In April, as the fighting intensified, Nixon ordered B-52 bombing raids against North Vietnam, and a month later he approved the mining of North Vietnamese ports.

That spring the increased combat activity and growing political pressure at home helped revive the Paris peace negotiations. Nixon hoped to undercut antiwar critics by making concessions to the North Vietnamese in the peace talks. In October Henry Kissinger and the North Vietnamese negotiator Le Duc Tho reached a cease-fire agreement calling for the withdrawal of the remaining U.S. troops; the return of all American prisoners of war; and the continued presence of North Vietnamese troops in South Vietnam. Nixon and Kissinger also promised the North Vietnamese substantial aid for postwar reconstruction. On the eve of the 1972 presidential election Kissinger announced "peace is at hand," and Nixon returned to the White House with a resounding electoral victory (see Chapter 32).

The peace initiative, however, soon stalled when the South Vietnamese rejected the provision concerning North Vietnamese troop positions, and the North declined to compromise further. With negotiations deadlocked, Nixon stepped up military action once more. From December 17 to December 30, 1972, American planes subjected civilian and military targets in Hanoi and Haiphong to the most devastating bombing of the war, referred to in the press as the Christmas bombings. Finally, on January 27, 1973, representatives of the

United States, North and South Vietnam, and the Viet Cong signed a cease-fire in Paris. But the Paris Peace Accords, which differed little from the proposal that had been rejected in October, did not fulfill Nixon's promise of "peace with honor." Basically, they mandated the unilateral withdrawal of American troops in exchange for the return of American prisoners of war from North Vietnam. For most Americans, that was enough.

Nor did the 1973 accords resolve Vietnam's civil war. Without massive U.S. military and economic aid, and with North Vietnamese guerrillas operating freely throughout the countryside, the South Vietnamese government of General Nguyen Van Thieu soon fell to the more disciplined and popular communist forces. In March 1975 North Vietnamese forces launched a final offensive. Horrified American television viewers watched as South Vietnamese officials and soldiers struggled with American embassy personnel to board the last helicopters that would fly out of Saigon before North Vietnamese troops entered the city. On April 29, 1975, Vietnam was reunited, and Saigon was renamed Ho Chi Minh City in honor of the communist leader, who had died in 1969.

The Legacy of Vietnam

Spanning nearly thirty years, the Vietnam War occupied American administrations from Truman to Nixon's successor Gerald Ford. U.S. troops fought in Vietnam for more than eleven years, from 1961 to 1973. In human terms, the nation's longest war exacted an enormous cost. Some 58,000 U.S. troops died, and another 300,000 were wounded. Even those who returned unharmed encountered a sometimes hostile or indifferent reception. Arriving home alone, with no counseling, most Vietnam veterans found the transition to civilian life abrupt and disorienting. The psychological tensions of serving in Vietnam and the difficulty of reentry sowed the seeds of what is now recognized as post-traumatic stress disorder—recurring physical and psychological problems that often lead to divorce, unemployment, and suicide. Only in the 1980s did America begin to make its peace with those who had served in the nation's most unpopular war.

In Southeast Asia, the damage was far greater. The war claimed an estimated 1.5 million Vietnamese lives and devastated the country's physical and economic infrastructure. Neighboring Laos and Cambodia also suffered, particularly Cambodia, where between 1975 and 1979 the Khmer Rouge killed an estimated 2 million Cambodians—a quarter of the population—in a brutal relocation campaign. All told, the war produced nearly 10 million refugees, many of whom immigrated to the United States. Among them were thousands of Amerasians, the offspring of American soldiers and Vietnamese women. Spurned by their fathers and by most Vietnamese, more than 30,000 Amerasians immigrated to the United States in the 1990s.

The defeat in Vietnam prompted Americans to think differently about foreign affairs, and to acknowledge the limits of U.S. power abroad. The United

States became less willing to plunge into overseas military commitments, a controversial change that conservatives dubbed the "Vietnam syndrome." In 1973 Congress declared its hostility to undeclared wars like those in Vietnam and Korea by passing the War Powers Act, which required the president to report any use of military force within forty-eight hours, and directed that hostilities must cease within sixty days without a declaration of war by Congress. On those occasions when Congress did agree to foreign intervention, as in the Persian Gulf War of 1990–1991, American leaders would insist on obtainable military objectives and careful handling of the news media—elements that had often been lacking in Vietnam. Perhaps most important, in the future, any foreign entanglement would be evaluated in terms of its potential to become "another Vietnam."

The Vietnam War also distorted American economic and social affairs. At a total price of over $150 billion, the war siphoned resources from domestic needs, added to the deficit, and fueled inflation (see Chapter 32). Lyndon Johnson's Great Society programs had been pared down, and domestic reform efforts slowed thereafter. Moreover, the war shattered the liberal consensus that had supported the Democratic coalition. Even more seriously, the conduct of the war—the lies about American successes on the battlefield, the questionable representation of events in the Gulf of Tonkin, the secret war in Cambodia—spawned a deep distrust of government among American citizens. The discrediting of liberalism, the increased cynicism toward government, and the growing social turmoil that accompanied the war would continue into the next decade, paving the way for a resurgence of the Republican party and a new mood of conservatism.

CHAPTER 31 TIMELINE

1946	War begins between French and Vietminh
1950	China and Soviet Union recognize Ho Chi Minh's government
	United States begins sending military aid to Vietnam
1954	French defeat at Dienbienphu
	Ngo Dinh Diem takes power in South Vietnam
	Geneva Accords
1960	Founding of National Liberation Front (NLF) in South Vietnam
1962	Students for a Democratic Society (SDS) founded
1963	Ngo Dinh Diem ousted in coup
1964	Gulf of Tonkin Resolution
	Free Speech Movement at Berkeley
1965	Operation Rolling Thunder
	First U.S. combat troops arrive in Vietnam
1967	Hippie counterculture's Summer of Love
1968	Tet offensive
	Martin Luther King, Jr., assassinated
	Peace talks open in Paris
	Robert F. Kennedy assassinated
	Riot at Democratic National Convention in Chicago
1969	Woodstock festival
	Vietnam moratorium
1970	Nixon orders invasion of Cambodia; renewed antiwar protests
	Kent State and Jackson State killings
	Gulf of Tonkin resolution repealed
1972	Nixon visits People's Republic of China
	SALT I with Soviet Union signed
	Christmas bombings of North Vietnam
1973	Paris Peace Accords
	War Powers Act
1975	Fall of Saigon

CHAPTER 32

THE LEAN YEARS: 1969–1980

- The Nixon Years
- Diminished Expectations and New Challenges
- Social Gridlock: Reform and Reaction in the 1970s
- Post-Watergate Politics: Failed Leadership

As the Vietnam War ended, Americans turned inward, just as they had done in the years after World Wars I and II. But the 1970s, unlike the 1920s and the 1950s, were not a time of prosperity and optimism. To many Americans, the nation's withdrawal from Vietnam represented an ignominious defeat that underscored its diminished power. In the early 1970s, growing economic problems—rising oil prices, runaway inflation, declining productivity, and stagnating incomes—compounded that sense of disillusionment, signaling the end of the nation's overwhelming economic superiority. Americans also grew disenchanted with their political leadership in the 1970s, as one public official after another, including President Richard Nixon, resigned for misconduct. In the wake of Nixon's resignation, the lackluster administrations of Presidents Gerald Ford and Jimmy Carter failed to provide the leadership necessary to cope with the nation's economic and international insecurities—a failure that fed Americans' growing skepticism about government and its capacity to improve people's lives.

Paradoxically, in the midst of this growing disaffection and skepticism, a commitment to social change persisted. Some of the social movements born in the 1960s, such as feminism and environmentalism, had their greatest impact in the 1970s. As former student radicals moved into the political mainstream, they took their struggles with them, from streets and campuses into courts, schools, workplaces, and local communities. But, like the civil-rights and antiwar movements of the 1960s, the social activism of the 1970s stirred fears and uncertainties among many Americans. Furthermore, the darkening economic climate of the new decade undercut the sense of social generosity that had characterized the 1960s, fueling a new conservatism that would become a potent political force by the decade's end.

THE NIXON YEARS

Richard Nixon set the stage for the conservative political resurgence that would influence the nation for the next several decades. His "new federalism" heralded a long-term Republican effort to trim back the Great Society and shift some federal responsibilities back to the states. At the same time, Nixon actively embraced the use of federal power—within limits—to uphold governmental responsibility for social welfare, environmental protection, and economic stability.

The Republican Domestic Agenda

In a 1968 campaign pledge to "the average American," Nixon had vowed to "reverse the flow of power and resources from the states and communities to Washington and start power and resources flowing back . . . to the people." One hallmark of this *new federalism* was the 1972 *revenue sharing* program, which distributed a portion of federal tax revenues to the states as block grants, to be spent as state officials saw fit. In later years revenue sharing would become a key Republican strategy for reducing federal social programs and federal bureaucracy.

Nixon also worked to scale down certain federal government programs that had grown dramatically during the two preceding administrations. He reduced funding for many War on Poverty programs, and dismantled the Office of Economic Opportunity altogether in 1971. Urban renewal, pollution control, and other environmental initiatives suffered when Nixon *impounded* (refused to spend) billions of dollars appropriated for them by Congress. Nixon's lack of interest in extending the gains of the civil-rights movement, as well as his effort, albeit unsuccessful, to reform the social welfare system, further exemplified the Republicans' desire to roll back the consolidation of federal power that had characterized American political life since the New Deal.

Still, with Democratic majorities in both houses of Congress, Nixon needed to be flexible in legislative matters. He agreed to the growth of major entitlement programs, such as Medicare, Medicaid, and Social Security. In 1970 he signed a bill establishing the Environmental Protection Agency (EPA), and in 1972 he approved legislation creating the Occupational Safety and Health Administration (OSHA) and the Consumer Products Safety Commission. Thus, his administration witnessed the expansion of federal power in numerous areas.

Nixon demonstrated his conservative social values most clearly in his appointments to the Supreme Court. In 1969, he nominated the conservative

Warren Burger to replace retired Chief Justice Earl Warren. After some difficulties in getting other nominees confirmed by the Senate—the nomination
of G. Harold Carswell failed in part because Carswell had participated in a
white segregationists' scheme to buy a public golf course in Florida to prevent
its integration—Nixon eventually named three other conservative justices:
Harry Blackmun, Lewis F. Powell, Jr., and William Rehnquist.

Nixon's appointees did not always hand down decisions the president approved, however. Despite attempts by the Justice department to halt further
desegregation in the face of determined white opposition, the Court ordered
busing to achieve racial balance. In 1972, it issued restrictions on the implementation of capital punishment, though it did not rule the death penalty unconstitutional. And in the controversial 1973 case *Roe v. Wade*, Justice Harry
Blackmun wrote the decision that struck down laws prohibiting abortion in
Texas and Georgia.

The 1972 Election

Nixon's reelection in 1972 was never much in doubt. In May, the threat of a
conservative third-party challenge from Alabama governor George Wallace
ended abruptly when an assailant shot Wallace, paralyzing him from the waist
down. With Wallace out of the picture, Nixon's strategy of wooing southern
white voters away from the Democrats got a boost (see Chapter 31). Nixon
also benefited from the disarray of the Democratic party. Divided over Vietnam and civil rights, the Democrats were plagued by tensions between their
newer, more liberal constituencies—women, minorities, and young adults—
and the old-line officeholders and labor union leaders who had always dominated the party. Recent changes in the party's system of selecting delegates
and candidates benefited the newer groups, and they helped to nominate Senator George McGovern of South Dakota, a noted liberal and an outspoken
opponent of the Vietnam War.

McGovern's campaign quickly ran into trouble. On learning that his running mate, Senator Thomas F. Eagleton of Missouri, had undergone elec-
troshock therapy for depression some years earlier, McGovern first supported
him and then abruptly insisted that he quit the ticket. Sargent Shriver, the former head of the Peace Corps and the Office of Economic Opportunity, replaced Eagleton. But McGovern's waffling on the matter made him appear
weak and indecisive. Moreover, he was far too liberal for many traditional
Democrats, who rejected his ill-defined proposals for welfare reform and his
call for unilateral withdrawal from Vietnam.

Nixon's campaign took full advantage of McGovern's weaknesses. Although the president had failed to end the war, his Vietnamization policy had
virtually eliminated American combat deaths by 1972. Henry Kissinger's premature declaration that "peace is at hand" raised voters' hopes for a negotiated
settlement (see Chapter 31). Not only did those initiatives rob the Democrats
of their greatest appeal—their antiwar stance—but an improving economy

further favored the Republicans. Nixon won handily, receiving nearly 61 percent of the popular vote and carrying every state except Massachusetts and the District of Columbia. Yet the president failed to kindle strong loyalty in the electorate. Only 55.7 percent of eligible voters bothered to go to the polls, and the Democrats maintained control of both houses of Congress.

Watergate

Though the Watergate scandal, one of the great constitutional crises of the twentieth century, broke in 1972, its roots lay in the early years of Nixon's first administration. Obsessed with the antiwar movement, the White House had repeatedly authorized illegal surveillance—opening mail, tapping phones, arranging break-ins—of citizens such as Daniel Ellsberg, a former Defense department analyst who had become disillusioned with the war. In 1971 Ellsberg had leaked the so-called Pentagon Papers to the *New York Times*. This secret study, commissioned by Secretary of Defense McNamara in 1967, detailed so many American blunders that, after reading it, McNamara had commented, "You know, they could hang people for what is in there." The administration had tried to get a court order to block publication of the papers. To discredit Ellsberg, White House underlings broke into his psychiatrist's office to search for damaging personal information, but the burglars failed to turn up anything embarrassing. When their break-in was revealed, the court dismissed the case against Ellsberg.

In another abuse of presidential power committed prior to the 1972 campaign, the White House had established a clandestine intelligence group, known as the "plumbers," because they were supposed to plug leaks of government information. They relied on tactics such as using the Internal Revenue Service and other government agencies to harass the administration's opponents who were named on an "enemies list" drawn up by presidential counsel John Dean. One of the plumbers' major targets was the Democratic party, whose front-running primary candidate, Senator Edmund Muskie of Maine, became the object of several of their "dirty tricks," including the distribution of phony campaign posters reading "Help Muskie in Busing More Children Now."

These secret and highly questionable activities were financed by massive illegal fund-raising efforts by Nixon's Committee to Re-Elect the President (known as CREEP). To obtain contributions from major corporations, Nixon's fund-raisers had used high-pressure tactics that included implied threats of federal tax audits and other punitive measures if companies failed to cooperate. CREEP raised over $20 million, a portion of which was used to finance the plumbers' dirty tricks, including a break-in that led to the Watergate scandal.

Early in the morning of June 17, 1972, police arrested five men carrying cameras, wiretapping equipment, and a large amount of cash, and charged them with breaking into the Democratic National Committee's headquarters

AMERICAN VOICES

Watergate Diary

Journalist Elizabeth Drew kept a diary during the Watergate crisis. This passage, written on August 5, 1974, shortly after President Nixon was forced to release some exceptionally damaging tape transcripts, explores the implications of the revelations for Americans' faith in the presidency.

For those who believed that the President was aware of, and even directed, the cover-up, it must still be a shock to *read his conversation* about it. . . .

There is an inexplicable difference between the experiences of suspecting a lie and being whacked in the face with the evidence of one. Many Americans had become accustomed to thinking of the President as a liar, and had alternately suspended belief in, scoffed at, or become enraged at his statements. But I wonder whether the enormity of his lying has sunk in yet—whether we have, or can, come to terms with the thought that so much of what he said to us was just noise, words, and that we can no longer begin by accepting any of it as the truth. This is a total reversal of the way we were brought up to think about Presidents, a departure from deeply ingrained habits. One's mind resists the thought of our President as a faithless man, capable of looking at us in utter sincerity from the other side of the television camera and telling us multiple, explicit, barefaced lies. One is torn between the idea that people must be able to have some confidence in their leaders and the idea that in this day of image manipulation a certain skepticism may serve them well. I do not think there is much comfort to be taken from the fact that eventually Nixon's lies—like Johnson's—caught up with him. It took a long time, and a great deal of damage was done meanwhile.

SOURCE: Elizabeth Drew, *Washington Journal: The Events of 1973–1974* (New York: Random House, 1974), pp. 391–392.

at the Watergate apartment complex in Washington, D.C. Two accomplices were apprehended soon afterward. Three of the men had worked in the White House or for CREEP, and four had CIA connections. Nixon later claimed that White House counsel John Dean had conducted a full investigation of the incident (no such investigation ever took place), and that "no one on the White House staff, no one in this administration, presently employed, was involved in this very bizarre incident."

Subsequent investigations revealed that shortly after the break-in, the president had ordered his chief of staff, H. R. Haldeman, to instruct the CIA to tell the FBI not to probe too deeply into connections between the White House and the burglars. When the burglars were convicted in January 1973, John Dean, with Nixon's approval, tried to buy their continued silence with $400,000 in hush money and hints of presidential pardons.

The coverup of the White House's involvement began to unravel when one of the convicted burglars began to talk. Two tenacious investigative reporters at the Washington *Post*, Carl Bernstein and Bob Woodward, exposed the attempt to hide the truth and traced it back to the White House. Reports of CREEP's "dirty tricks" and illegal fund-raising soon compounded the public's suspicions about the president. In February the Senate voted 77 to 0 to establish a select committee to investigate the widening scandal. Two months later Nixon accepted the resignations of Haldeman, Assistant Secretary of Commerce Jeb Stuart Magruder, and chief domestic adviser John Ehrlichman, all of whom had been implicated in the cover-up. He fired Dean, who had agreed to testify in the case in exchange for immunity from prosecution.

In May the Senate Watergate committee, chaired by Senator Sam Ervin of North Carolina, began holding nationally televised hearings. On June 14 Magruder testified before the committee, confessing his guilt and implicating former Attorney General John Mitchell, Dean, and others. Dean, in turn, implicated Nixon in the plot. Even more startling testimony from a Nixon aide revealed that Nixon had installed a secret taping system in the Oval Office.

The president steadfastly "stonewalled" the committee's demand that he surrender the tapes, citing executive privilege and national security. But Archibald Cox, a special prosecutor whom Nixon had appointed to investigate the case, successfully petitioned a federal court to order the president to hand the tapes over. Still Nixon refused to comply. When he ordered Attorney General Elliott Richardson to fire Cox, Richardson resigned in protest, as did the assistant attorney general. Nixon finally got the solicitor general, Robert Bork, to carry out his order, but this action backfired. The "Saturday Night Massacre" sparked public outrage and renewed demands for release of the tapes.

After receiving additional federal subpoenas the following spring, Nixon finally released a heavily edited transcript of the tapes, peppered with the words "expletive deleted." Senate Republican leader Hugh Scott called the transcripts "deplorable, disgusting, shabby, immoral." Most suspicious was an eighteen-minute gap in the tape covering a crucial meeting between Nixon, Haldeman, and Ehrlichman on June 20, 1972—three days after the break-in.

The Watergate affair moved into its final phase when on June 30 the House of Representatives voted three articles of impeachment against Richard Nixon: obstruction of justice, abuse of power, and acting to subvert the Constitution. Two days later the Supreme Court ruled unanimously that Nixon could not claim executive privilege as a justification for refusing to turn over additional tapes. Under duress, on August 5 Nixon released the unexpurgated tapes, which contained evidence that he had ordered the cover-up as early as six days after the break-in. Facing certain conviction in a Senate trial, on August 9, 1974, Nixon became the first U.S. president to resign.

The next day Vice-President Gerald Ford was sworn in as president. Ford, a former Michigan congressman and house minority leader, had replaced Vice-President Spiro Agnew in 1973 after Agnew resigned under indictment

Nixon Resigns
On August 9, 1974, Richard M. Nixon became the first American president to resign. He is shown here minutes after turning over the presidency to Gerald R. Ford. Nixon retired to his home in San Clemente, California, refusing to admit guilt for what had happened.

for accepting kickbacks on construction contracts. The transfer of power proceeded smoothly. A month later, however, Ford stunned the nation by granting Nixon a "full, free, and absolute" pardon "for all offenses he had committed or might have committed during his presidency." Ford took that action, he said, to spare the country the agony of rehashing Watergate. While Nixon retired to his estate in San Clemente, California, twenty-five members of his administration went to prison. Named only as an "unindicted co-conspirator" in their trials, Nixon refused to admit guilt for what had happened, conceding only that he had made an error in judgment.

In response to the abuses of the Nixon administration and to contain the power of what the historian Arthur M. Schlesinger, Jr., called "the imperial presidency," Congress adopted several reforms. In 1974 a strengthened Freedom of Information Act gave citizens greater access to files federal agencies had amassed on them. The Fair Campaign Practices Act of 1974 limited campaign contributions and provided for stricter accountability and public financing of presidential campaigns. Ironically, because the act allowed an unlimited number of political action committees (PACs) to donate up to $5,000 per candidate, corporations and lobbying groups found they could actually increase their influence by making multiple donations. By the end of the decade close to 3,000 PACs were playing an increasingly pivotal—and some would argue unethical—role in national elections.

Perhaps the most significant legacy of Watergate, however, was the wave of cynicism that swept the country in its wake. Beginning with Lyndon Johnson's "credibility gap" during the Vietnam War, public distrust of government had risen steadily with the disclosure of the secret bombing of Cambodia and the illegal surveillance and harassment of antiwar protesters and other political opponents. The saga of Watergate confirmed what many Americans had long suspected: that politicians were hopelessly corrupt, and that the federal government was out of control.

DIMINISHED EXPECTATIONS AND NEW CHALLENGES

Economic difficulties compounded Americans' political disillusionment. Growing international demand for natural resources, particularly oil, coupled with unstable access to foreign oil supplies, wreaked havoc with the American economy. At the same time, foreign competitors successfully expanded their share of the world market, edging out American-made products. The resulting sharp downturn in the domestic economy marked the end of America's twenty-five-year dominance of the world economy.

The Hydrocarbon Age

Until well into the twentieth century, the United States was the world's leading producer and consumer of oil. During World War II the nation had produced two-thirds of the world's oil, but by 1972 its share had fallen to only 22 percent, even though domestic production had continued to rise. By the late 1960s the United States was buying more and more of its oil on the world market to keep up with shrinking domestic reserves and growing demand.

The imported oil came primarily from the Middle East, where production had increased a stupendous 1,500 percent in the twenty-five years following World War II. The rise of nationalism and the corresponding decline of colonialism in the postwar era had encouraged the Persian Gulf nations to wrest control from the European and American oil companies that once dominated petroleum exploration and production in that region. In 1960, joining with other Third World oil-producing countries, they had formed the Organization of Petroleum Exporting Countries (OPEC). Just five of the founding countries—the Middle Eastern states of Saudi Arabia, Kuwait, Iran, and Iraq, plus Venezuela—were the source of more than 80 percent of the world's crude oil exports. During the early 1970s, when world demand climbed and oil reserves fell, they took advantage of market forces to maximize their profits. Between 1973 and 1975 OPEC deliberately raised the price of a barrel of oil from $3 to $12. By the end of the decade the price had peaked at $34 a barrel, setting off a round of furious inflation in the oil-dependent United States.

OPEC members also found that oil could be used as a weapon in global politics. In 1973 OPEC instituted an oil embargo against the United States, Western Europe, and Japan, in retaliation for their aid to Israel during the Yom Kippur War, which had begun when Egypt and Syria invaded Israel. The embargo, which lasted until 1974, forced Americans to curtail their driving or spend long hours in line at the pumps; in a matter of months, gas prices climbed 40 percent. Since the U.S. automobile industry had little to offer except "gas-guzzlers" built to run on cheap fuel, Americans turned to cheaper, more fuel-efficient foreign cars manufactured in Japan and West Germany. Soon the auto industry was in a slump, weakening the American economy.

The energy crisis was an enormous shock to the American psyche. Suddenly Americans felt like hostages to economic forces that were beyond their control. As OPEC's leaders pushed prices higher and higher, they seemed to be able to determine whether western economies would grow or stagnate. Despite an extensive public conservation campaign and a second gas shortage in 1979, caused by the Iranian revolution, Americans could not wean themselves from foreign oil. In fact, they used even more foreign oil after the energy crisis

No Gas
During the energy crisis of 1973–1974 American motorists faced widespread gasoline shortages for the first time since World War II. Although gas was not rationed, gas stations were closed on Sundays, air travel was cut by 10 percent, and a national speed limit of 55 miles per hour was imposed.

than they had before—a testimony to the enormous thirst of modern industrial and consumer societies for petroleum.

Economic Woes

While the energy crisis dealt a swift blow to the U.S. economy, other developments had equally damaging results. The high cost of the Vietnam War and the Great Society had contributed to a steadily growing federal deficit and spiraling inflation. A business downturn in 1970 had led to rising unemployment (6 percent) and declining productivity. In the industrial sector the reviving economies of West Germany and Japan over time had reduced demand for American goods worldwide. In 1955 American-made goods had accounted for 32 percent of all imports by major capitalist countries; by 1970 the proportion was only 18 percent, and it continued to decline in the 1970s. As a result, in 1971 the dollar fell to its lowest level on the world market since 1949, and the United States posted its first trade deficit in almost a century.

That year Nixon took several bold steps to turn the economy around. To stem the decline in currency and trade, he suspended the Bretton Woods system that had been set up at the United Nations monetary conference in 1944 (see Chapter 29). Once again, the dollar would fluctuate in relation to the price of an ounce of gold. The change, which effectively devalued the dollar in hopes of encouraging foreign trade, represented a frank acknowledgment that America's currency was no longer the world's strongest. Nixon also instituted wage and price controls to curb inflation, and to boost the sluggish economy he offered a "full employment" budget for 1972, including $11 billion in deficit spending.

Though these measures brought a temporary improvement in the economy, the general decline persisted. Overall economic growth, as measured by the gross national product (GNP), had averaged 4.1 percent per year in the 1960s; in the 1970s it dropped to only 2.9 percent, contributing to a noticeable decline in most Americans' standard of living. Between 1973 and the early 1980s, discretionary income per worker decreased 18 percent. At the same time, galloping inflation forced consumer prices upward, peaking at 10 percent in 1974 and over 13 percent in 1980. Housing prices, in particular, rose rapidly: the average cost of a single-family home more than doubled in the 1970s, making home ownership inaccessible to a growing segment of the working and middle classes.

Young adults faced a constricted job market in the late 1970s, as a record number of baby boomers competed for a limited number of jobs. Unemployment peaked at around 9 percent in 1975, declined briefly, then edged upward again to around 6 to 7 percent in the late 1970s. A devastating combination of inflation and unemployment—dubbed *stagflation*—bedeviled presidential administrations from Nixon to Reagan, whose remedies (such as deficit spending and tax reduction) failed to eradicate the double scourge.

American economic woes were most acute in the industrial sector, which entered a prolonged period of decline, or *deindustrialization*. Investors who had formerly bought stock in basic U.S. industries began to speculate on the stock market or put their money into mergers or foreign companies. Many U.S. firms relocated overseas, partly to take advantage of cheaper labor and production costs. By the end of the 1970s the hundred largest multinational corporations and banks were earning more than a third of their overall profits abroad.

The most dramatic consequences of deindustrialization occurred in the older industrial regions of the northeast and midwest, which came to be known as the Rust Belt. There the dominant images of American industry in the mid-twentieth century—huge factories such as Ford's River Rouge outside Detroit and the General Electric plant in Lynn, Massachusetts— were fast becoming relics. When a community's major employer closed down and left town, the devastating effect rippled through communities in America's heartland. Many workers moved to the cities of the Sun Belt, which continued the dramatic growth that began after World War II (see Chapter 29).

Deindustrialization and the changing economic conditions that provoked it posed a critical problem for the labor movement. In the heyday of labor during the 1940s and 1950s, American managers had often cooperated with unions; with profits high, there was room for accommodation. But as foreign competition cut into corporate profits in the 1970s, industry became less willing to bargain, and the labor movement's power declined. In the 1970s union membership dropped from 28 to 23 percent of the American work force. Facing strikes or labor problems, some employers simply moved their operations abroad, where they found a cheaper, more compliant work force. In a competitive global environment, labor's prospects seemed dim.

SOCIAL GRIDLOCK: REFORM AND REACTION IN THE 1970s

The nation's economic problems and growing cynicism about government led to deep public anxiety and resentment. Many Americans turned inward to private satisfactions. The journalist Tom Wolfe labeled the 1970s the "Me Decade" because of the widespread obsession with lifestyles and personal well-being, while the historian Christopher Lasch referred derisively to what he called a "culture of narcissism." Yet those labels hardly do justice to a decade in which environmentalism, feminism, lesbian and gay rights, and other social movements blossomed. Furthermore, such characterizations neglect the growing social conservatism that was in part a response to such movements. In fact, the confluence of these trends produced a pattern of shifting crosscurrents that made the 1970s a complex transitional decade.

The New Activism: Environmental and Consumer Movements

After 1970 many baby boomers left the counterculture behind and settled down to pursue careers and material goods. But these young adults sought personal fulfillment as well. In a quest for physical and spiritual well-being, millions of Americans began jogging, riding bicycles, and working out at the gym. The fitness craze coincided with a heightened environmental awareness that spurred the demand for pesticide-free foods and vegetarian cookbooks. For spiritual support, some young people embraced the self-help techniques of the human potential, or New Age, movement; others turned to religious cults such as the Hare Krishna, the Church of Scientology, and the Unification Church of Reverend Sun Myung Moon.

A few baby boomers continued to pursue the unfinished social and political agendas of the 1960s. Moving into law, education, social work, medicine, and other fields, these former radicals continued their activism on a grassroots level. Some joined the left wing of the Democratic party; others helped to establish community-based organizations, including health clinics, food co-ops, and day-care centers. On the local level, at least, the progressive spirit of the 1960s lived on.

One of the most dynamic sources of activism in the 1970s was the environmental movement. In contrast to the older generation of environmental activists, which advocated resource management and worked within the political system through organizations such as the Sierra Club (see Chapter 17), many of the new environmentalists had been 1960s-style activists. They brought their radical political sensibilities to the environmental movement, infusing it with new life. For example, they construed the search for alternative technologies (especially solar power) as a political statement against a corporate structure that was increasingly inhospitable to human-scale technology— and to humans, as well. The new activists used sit-ins and other protest tactics developed in the civil-rights and antiwar movements to mobilize mass support for specific issues or legislation.

The birth of the modern environmental movement is often dated to the publication in 1962 of Rachel Carson's *Silent Spring*, a powerful analysis of the impact of pesticides on the food chain. Other issues that galvanized public opinion included the environmental impact of industrial projects such as the Alaska pipeline and the harmful effects of chlorofluorocarbons and increased carbon dioxide levels on the earth's atmosphere. In January 1969 a huge oil spill off the coast of Santa Barbara, California, provoked an outcry, as did the discovery in 1978 that a housing development outside Niagara Falls, New York, had been built on a toxic waste site. The abnormally high rates of illness and birth defects recorded in this Love Canal neighborhood deepened public awareness of the culpability of business in generating environmental hazards. Concerned Americans also worried about the federal government's lax control of nuclear weapons plants, such as the uranium-processing plant at Fernald, Ohio, where liquid wastes were dumped into open-air storage pits.

Nuclear energy became the subject of citizen action in the 1970s, when rising prices and oil shortages pitted environmental concerns against the need for alternative energy sources. To reduce the nation's dependence on foreign oil, some politicians and utility companies began to promote the expansion of nuclear power. By January 1974, forty-two nuclear power plants were in operation,

AMERICAN VOICES

Environmental Activist

*S*am Lovejoy participated in the Clamshell Alliance, a group that used peaceful
civil disobedience in its protest against a nuclear power plant in Seabrook, New
Hampshire. His account, as given to journalist Studs Terkel, reveals the persistence
of 1960s-style political activism in the environmental movement that emerged in the
1970s.

Terkel: We are told that some issues are too complex for ordinary people, that experts . . .

Lovejoy: Bullshit. It's the best argument to delude the people. It's the
same thing we heard about the Vietnam War. If we're gonna have democracy in this country, by God, we're gonna have to start telling people the
facts. Einstein said it thirty years ago: We must take the facts of nuclear
power to the village square, and from the village square must come America's voice. . . .

[At Seabrook] We made a commitment to nonviolent civil disobedience to
stop the plant. . . .

On April 30, we brought over two thousand people to the site. The governor distrusted his state police and mobilized the National Guard. Over fourteen hundred people were arrested and locked up in the five armories for two
weeks. It created more publicity than the Clamshell Alliance had ever anticipated. The arrestees conducted workshops. The National Guard guys were
standing around, listening and participating. They're just funky people from
local towns, just like you and me. They got called off local jobs and didn't see
what the hell they were doing here, guarding a bunch of very nice people. . . .

The media is selling us on the notion of apathy and paralysis in the country. Bullshit. The movement did not die. It did the most intelligent thing it
could do: it went to find a home. It went into the community. It's working,
unnoticed, in the neighborhood. They're starting to blossom and make alliances, connections. I've been all over the country, and I have not been into
one community where I did not meet people exactly like me.

SOURCE: Studs Terkel, *American Dreams: Lost and Found* (New York: Pantheon, 1980), pp. 459–460.

and over a hundred more were planned. Suddenly, the construction of nuclear
power plants and reactors, which had gone largely unchallenged in the 1950s
and 1960s, became controversial. Community activists protested plans for new
reactors, citing inadequate evacuation plans and the unresolved problem of the
disposal of radioactive waste. In Seabrook, New Hampshire, and Shoreham,
New York, the mass protests of the Clamshell Alliance and other antinuclear

groups, reminiscent of the antiwar demonstrations of the 1960s, helped to delay or prevent the start-up of nuclear reactors.

Public fears about nuclear safety seemed to be confirmed in March 1979 when a nuclear plant at Three Mile Island near Harrisburg, Pennsylvania, came critically close to a meltdown of its central core reactor. A prompt shutdown of the plant brought the problem under control before radioactive material seeped into the environment, but as a member of the panel that investigated the accident admitted, "We were damn lucky." Ultimately, Three Mile Island caused Americans to rethink the question of whether nuclear power could be a viable solution to the nation's energy needs. Grass-roots activism, combined with public fear of the potential dangers of nuclear energy, convinced many utility companies to abandon nuclear power, despite its short-term economic advantages.

Americans' concerns about nuclear power, chemical contamination, pesticides, and other environmental issues helped to turn environmentalism into a mass movement. On the first Earth Day, April 22, 1970, 20 million citizens gathered in communities across the country to show their support for the endangered planet. Although environmentalists failed to garner support for a "Green" political party, modeled on those in European countries, they did create bipartisan support for a spate of new federal legislation. In 1969 Congress passed the National Environmental Policy Act, which required the developers of public projects to file an environmental impact statement. The next year Nixon established the Environmental Protection Agency (EPA) and signed the Clean Air Act, which toughened standards for auto emissions in order to reduce smog and air pollution. Two years later Congress banned the use of the pesticide DDT. And in 1973 the Endangered Species Act expanded the protection provided by the Endangered Animals Act of 1964, granting species such as snail darters and spotted owls protected status. Thus environmental protection joined social welfare, defense, and national security as targets of federal intervention.

The environmental movement did not go uncontested. The EPA-mandated fuel economy standards for cars, for example, provoked criticism for threatening the health of the auto industry as it struggled to keep up with foreign competitors. Corporations resented environmental regulations, but so did many of their workers, who believed that tightened standards threatened their jobs and privileged nature over human beings. "IF YOU'RE HUNGRY AND OUT OF WORK, EAT AN ENVIRONMENTALIST" read one labor union's bumper sticker. Thus, in a time of rising unemployment and deindustrialization, activists clashed head-on with proponents of economic development, full employment, and global competitiveness.

The rise of environmentalism was paralleled by a growing movement to eliminate harmful consumer products and curb dangerous practices by American corporations. The consumer protection movement had originated in the Progressive Era, with the founding of government agencies such as the Food and Drug Administration (FDA) (see Chapter 21). In the 1960s, after decades of inertia, the movement reemerged under the leadership of Ralph Nader, a young lawyer whose book *Unsafe at Any Speed* (1965) attacked General Motors for putting style ahead of safety and fuel economy in its engineering. In 1969 Nader launched a Washington-based organization that gave rise to the Public Interest Research Group, a national network of consumer groups that focused on issues ranging from product safety to consumer fraud and environmental pollution. His organization pioneered legal tactics, such as the class-action suit, which allowed people with common grievances to sue as a group. It became the model for dozens of other groups that emerged in the 1970s and afterward to combat the health hazards of smoking, unethical insurance and credit practices, and other consumer problems. With the establishment of the federal Consumer Products Safety Commission in 1972 Congress acknowledged the growing need for consumer protection.

Challenges to Tradition: The Women's Movement and Gay Rights Activism

Feminism proved the most enduring movement to emerge from the 1960s. In the next decade the women's movement grew more sophisticated, generating an array of services and organizations, from rape crisis centers and battered women's shelters to feminist health collectives and women's bookstores. In 1972 Gloria Steinem and other journalists founded *Ms.* magazine, the first consumer magazine aimed at a feminist audience. Formerly all-male bastions, such as Yale, Princeton, and the U.S. Military Academy, admitted women undergraduates for the first time, while the proportion of women attending graduate and professional schools rose markedly. Several new national women's organizations emerged, and established groups such as The National Organization for Women (NOW) continued to grow. In 1977, 20,000 women went to Houston for the first National Women's Conference. Their "National Plan of Action" represented a hard-won consensus on topics ranging from violence against women to homemakers' rights; the needs of older women; and, most controversially, abortion and other reproductive issues.

Women were also increasingly visible in politics and public life. The National Women's Political Caucus, founded in 1971, actively promoted the election of women to public office. Their success stories included Shirley Chisholm, Patricia Schroeder, and Geraldine Ferraro, all of whom served in Congress, and Ella Grasso, who won election as Connecticut's governor in 1974.

Women's political mobilization produced significant legislative and administrative gains. With the passage of Title IX of the Educational Amendments Act of 1972, which broadened the 1964 Civil Rights Act to include educational institutions, Congress prohibited colleges and universities that received federal funds from discriminating on the basis of sex, a change that particularly benefited women athletes. In 1972 Congress authorized child-care deductions for working parents; in 1974 it passed the Equal Credit Opportunity Act, which significantly improved women's access to credit.

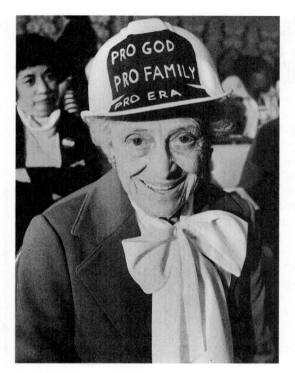

The Expanding Women's Movement
By the late 1970s the feminist movement had broadened its base, attracting women of all ages and backgrounds, such as this delegate to the 1977 National Women's Conference in Houston, Texas. As the slogan on her hat implies, though, the women's movement was already on the defensive against right-wing claims that the feminist movement was undermining traditional values. (© Bettye Lane)

The Supreme Court also significantly advanced women's rights. In several rulings the Court read a right of privacy into the Ninth and Fourteenth amendments' concept of personal liberty, to give women more control over their reproductive lives. In 1965 *Griswold v. Connecticut* had overturned state laws against the sale of contraceptive devices to married adults, a protection that was later extended to single persons. In 1973, in *Roe v. Wade*, the Court struck down Texas and Georgia statutes that allowed an abortion only if the mother's life was in danger. According to this 7–2 decision, states could no longer outlaw abortions performed during the first trimester of pregnancy.

Roe v. Wade nationalized the liberalization of state abortion laws, which had begun in New York in 1970, but also fueled the development of a powerful antiabortion movement. Charging that the rights of a fetus took precedence over a woman's right to decide whether or not to terminate a pregnancy, abortion opponents worked to circumvent or overturn *Roe v. Wade*. In 1976 they convinced Congress to deny Medicaid funds for abortions for poor women, one of the opening rounds in a protracted legislative and judicial campaign to chip away at the *Roe* decision.

Another battlefront for the women's movement was the proposed Equal Rights Amendment (ERA) to the Constitution. The ERA, first introduced in Congress in 1923 by the National Woman's party, stated in its entirety, "Equality of rights under the law shall not be denied or abridged by the United States or any State on the basis of sex." In 1970 feminists revived the amendment, which passed the House but died in the Senate. In the next session it passed both houses and was submitted to the states for ratification. But though thirty-four states quickly passed the ERA between 1972 and 1974, growing opposition by conservative groups slowed its momentum (see Map 32.1). By 1982 the amendment was dead.

The fate of the ERA and the battle over abortion rights showed that by the mid-1970s, the women's movement was beginning to weaken. Increasingly its members were divided over issues of race, class, age, and sexual orientation. For many nonwhite and working-class women, the feminist movement seemed to stand for the interests of self-seeking white career women. At the same time, the women's movement faced growing social conservatism among Americans in general. Although 63 percent of women polled in 1975 said they favored "efforts to strengthen and change women's status in society," a growing minority of both sexes expressed concern over what seemed to be revolutionary changes in women's traditional roles.

Lawyer Phyllis Schlafly, long active in conservative causes, led the antifeminist backlash. Despite the active career she had pursued while raising five

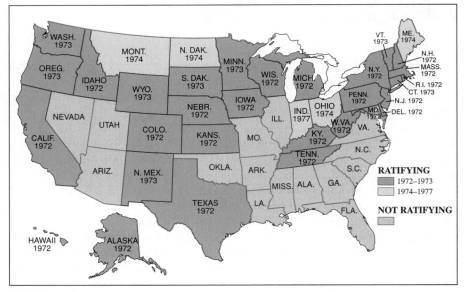

MAP 32.1
States Ratifying the Equal Rights Amendment
The Equal Rights Amendment quickly won support in 1972 and 1973 but then stalled. ERAmerica, a coalition of women's groups formed in 1976, lobbied extensively, particularly in Florida, North Carolina, and Illinois, but failed to sway the conservative legislatures in those states. Efforts to revive the ERA in the 1980s were unsuccessful.

children, Schlafly advocated traditional roles for women. Schlafly's STOP ERA organization claimed that the amendment would create a "unisex society" in which women could be drafted, homosexuals could be married, and separate toilets for men and women would be prohibited. (Feminists argued that those charges were groundless.) Alarmed, conservative women in grassroots networks mobilized, showing up at statehouses with home-baked bread and apple pies, symbols of their traditional domestic role. Their message, that women would lose more than they would gain if the ERA passed, resonated with many men and women, especially those who were troubled by the rapid pace of social change.

Although the feminist movement was on the defensive by the mid-1970s, women's lives showed no signs of returning to the patterns of the 1950s. Because of increasing economic pressures, the proportion of women in the paid work force continued to rise, from 44 percent in 1970 to 51 percent in 1980. Easier access to birth control permitted married and unmarried women to enjoy greater sexual freedom (although they also became more vulnerable to male sexual pressure). With a growing number of career options available to them, many women, particularly educated white women, stayed single or delayed marriage and child rearing. The birth rate continued its postwar decline, reaching an all-time low in the mid-1970s. At the same time, the divorce rate rose 82 percent in the 1970s, as more men and women elected to leave unhappy marriages.

Although such changes brought increased autonomy for many women, they also caused new hardships, particularly in poor and working-class families. Divorce left many women with low-paying jobs and inadequate child care. Meanwhile, more tolerant attitudes toward premarital sex, along with other social and economic factors, had contributed to rising teenage pregnancy rates. The rise in divorce and adolescent pregnancy produced a sharp increase in the number of female-headed families, contributing to the "feminization" of poverty. By 1980 women accounted for 66 percent of adults who lived below the poverty line, a development that fueled a growing wave of social reaction.

Another major focus of social activism, the gay liberation movement, achieved heightened visibility in the 1970s. Thousands of gay men and lesbians "came out," publicly proclaiming their sexual orientation. In New York's Greenwich Village, San Francisco's Castro, and other urban enclaves, growing gay communities gave rise to hundreds of new gay and lesbian clubs, churches, businesses, and political organizations. In 1973 the National Gay Task Force launched a campaign to include gay men and lesbians as a protected group under laws covering employment and housing rights. Such efforts were most successful on the local level; during the 1970s Detroit, Boston, Los Angeles, Miami, San Francisco, and other cities passed laws barring discrimination on the basis of sexual preference.

Like abortion and the ERA, gay rights came under attack from conservatives, who believed that protecting gay people's rights would encourage immoral behavior. When the Miami city council passed a measure banning discrimination against gay men and lesbians in 1977, the singer Anita Bryant led a campaign to repeal the law by popular referendum. Later that year voters overturned the measure by a 2–1 majority, prompting similar antigay campaigns around the country.

Racial Minorities

Although the civil-rights movement was in disarray by the late 1960s, in the next decade, minority group protests brought social and economic gains. Native Americans realized some of the most significant changes. In 1971 the Alaska Native Land Claims Act restored 40 million acres to Eskimos, Aleuts, and other native peoples, along with $960 million in compensation. Most important, the federal government abandoned the tribal termination program of the 1950s (see Chapter 29). Under the Indian Self-Determination Act of 1974, Congress restored the tribes' right to govern themselves and gave them authority over federal programs on their reservations (see Map 32.2).

The busing of children to achieve school desegregation proved the most disruptive social issue of the 1970s. Progress in achieving the desegregation mandated by *Brown v. Board of Education of Topeka* (see Chapter 29) had been slow. In the 1970s both the courts and the Justice department pushed for more action, not just in the South but in other parts of the country. In *Milliken v. Bradley* (1974), for example, the Supreme Court ordered cities with deeply ingrained patterns of residential segregation to use busing to integrate their classrooms. The decision sparked intense and sometimes violent opposition. In Boston in 1974–1975, the strongly Irish-Catholic working-class neighborhood of South Boston responded to the arrival of black students from Roxbury with mob action reminiscent of that in Little Rock in 1957. Threatened by court-ordered busing, many white parents transferred their children to private schools or moved to the suburbs. The resulting "white flight" exacerbated the racial imbalance busing was supposed to redress. Some black parents also opposed busing, calling instead for better schools in predominantly black neighborhoods. By the late 1970s federal courts had begun to back away from their insistence on busing to achieve racial balance.

Almost as divisive as busing was the implementation of *affirmative action* procedures—hiring and enrollment goals and recruitment and training programs designed to redress a history of discrimination against nonwhites and women in employment and education. First introduced by Lyndon Johnson's administration in 1965, affirmative action programs had expanded opportunities for blacks and Latinos. The number of black students enrolled in colleges and universities doubled between 1970 and 1977 to 1.1 million, or 9.3 percent of the total student enrollment. A small but growing number of blacks moved into white-collar professions in corporations and universities. Others found new opportunities in civil service occupations such as law enforcement or entered apprenticeships in the skilled construction trades. Latinos experienced similar gains in education and "token" advances in the job market. On the whole, however, both groups enjoyed only marginal economic improvement, since poor and working-class nonwhites bore the brunt of job loss and unemployment in the 1970s.

MAP 32.2

American Indian Reservations

Although native Americans have been able to preserve small enclaves in the northeastern states, most Indian reservations are in the West. Beginning in the 1970s, various tribes filed land claims against federal and state governments.

Nevertheless, many whites, especially men, who were feeling the economic pinch of stagflation, came to resent affirmative action programs as an infringement of their rights. In 1978 Allan Bakke, a white man, sued the University of California Medical School at Davis for rejecting him in favor of less qualified minority candidates. The Supreme Court ruling in *Bakke v. University of California* was inconclusive. Though it branded the medical school's strict quota system illegal and ordered Bakke admitted, it stated that racial factors could be considered in hiring and admission decisions, thus upholding the principle of affirmative action. But the Bakke decision was clearly a setback for proponents of affirmative action, and it prepared the way for subsequent efforts to eliminate those programs.

The activists who supported racial minorities, women, gays, consumers, and the environment had distinct agendas. However, they also had much in common. They were part of "a rights revolution"—a wide-ranging movement in the 1960s and 1970s to bring issues of social justice and welfare to the forefront of public policy. Growing out of the Great Society's liberalism, they invariably turned to the federal government for protection of individual rights and—in the case of environmentalists—the world's natural resources. The activists of this period made substantial progress in widening the notion of the federal government's responsibilities, but by the end of the 1970s their movements faced growing opposition.

The Politics of Resentment

Together with the rapidly growing antiabortion movement, the often vociferous public opposition to busing, affirmative action, gay rights ordinances, and the Equal Rights Amendment constituted a broad backlash against the social changes of the previous decade. Many Americans believed that their interests had been slighted by the rights revolution and resented a federal government that protected women who sought abortions or minorities who benefited from affirmative action. The economic changes of the 1970s, which left many working-class and middle-class Americans with lower disposable incomes, rising prices, and higher taxes, further fueled what the conservative writer Alan Crawford has termed the "politics of resentment"—a grass-roots revolt against "special-interest groups" (women, minorities, gays, and so on) and growing expenditures on social welfare. Special groups and programs, conservatives believed, robbed other Americans of educational and employment opportunities, and saddled the working and middle classes with an extra financial burden.

Although the politics of resentment most often centered on socioeconomic issues, it also took the form of local taxpayers' revolts. In 1978 California voters passed Proposition 13, a measure that reduced property taxes and eventually undercut local governments' ability to maintain schools and other essential services. Promising tax relief to middle-class homeowners and reduced funding for busing and other programs to benefit the poor—who were

An Antibusing Confrontation in Boston
Tensions over court-ordered busing ran high in Boston in 1976. When a black lawyer tried to cross the city hall plaza during an antibusing demonstration, he became another victim of Boston's climate of racial hatred and violence. This photograph by Stanley Forman for the *Boston Herald American*, showing protesters trying to impale the man with a flagstaff, won a Pulitzer Prize.

invariably viewed as nonwhite—Proposition 13 became the model for similar tax measures around the country in the late 1970s and 1980s.

The rising popularity of evangelical religion also fueled the conservative resurgence of the 1970s. Fundamentalist groups that fostered a "born-again" experience had been growing steadily since World War II, under the leadership of charismatic preachers such as Billy Graham. According to a Gallup poll conducted in 1976, some 50 million Americans—about a quarter of the population—were affiliated with evangelical movements. These groups set up their own school systems and newspapers. Through broadcasting networks, like the Christian Broadcasting Network founded by the Virginia preacher Pat Robertson, a new breed of *televangelists* such as Jerry Falwell built vast and influential electronic ministries.

As evangelicals spoke out on a broad range of issues, denouncing abortion, busing, sex education, pornography, feminism, and gay rights, they sought ways to bring their religious values to a wider public. In 1979 Jerry Falwell founded the Moral Majority, a political pressure group that promoted Christian "family values"—traditional gender roles, heterosexuality, family cohesion—and staunch anticommunism. Soon the extensive media and fund-raising networks of the Christian right became the organizational base for a larger conservative movement known as the New Right. Using computerized mass-mailing campaigns that targeted evangelical constituencies, New Right political groups mobilized thousands of followers and millions of dollars to support conservative candidates and causes.

POST-WATERGATE POLITICS: FAILED LEADERSHIP

It is not surprising that in the wake of Watergate, when many Americans became disillusioned with politics as usual, the New Right could energize voters around a new set of issues. Many citizens had become cynical about the federal government and about politicians in general. "Don't vote. It only encourages them" read one bumper sticker during the 1976 campaign. Indeed, political leaders were proving unable to deal with the rising inflation, stagnant growth, and declining productivity that plagued the U.S. economy in the 1970s. The fall of Saigon in 1975 reminded Americans of the failure of the nation's Vietnam policy. The world was changing; Americans grappled with the unsettling idea that perhaps the United States would not continue to be the all-powerful nation it had been for much of the postwar era.

Ford's Caretaker Presidency

During the two years Gerald Ford held the nation's highest office, he failed to establish his legitimacy as president. Ford's pardon of Nixon hurt his credibility as a political leader, but an even bigger problem was his handling of the economy, which was reeling from the inflation set in motion by the Vietnam War, rising oil prices, and the growing trade deficit. In 1974 the inflation rate soared to almost 12 percent, and in the following year the economy entered its deepest downturn since the Great Depression. Though many of the nation's economic problems were beyond the president's control, Ford's failure to take more vigorous action made him appear timid and powerless.

In foreign policy Ford was equally lacking in leadership. He maintained Nixon's détente initiatives by asking Henry Kissinger to stay on as secretary of state. Though Ford met with Soviet leaders hoping to hammer out the details of a SALT II (Strategic Arms Limitation Treaty) agreement, he made little progress. Ford and Kissinger also continued Nixon's policy of increasing support for the shah of Iran, ignoring the bitter opposition and antiwestern sentiment that the shah's policy of rapid modernization was provoking among the growing Muslim fundamentalist population in Iran.

Jimmy Carter: The Outsider as President

The 1976 presidential campaign was one of the blandest in years. President Ford chose as his running mate the conservative Senator Robert J. Dole of

Kansas. The Democratic choice, Jimmy Carter, Governor of Georgia, shared the ticket with Senator Walter F. Mondale of Minnesota, who had ties to the traditional Democratic constituencies of labor, liberals, blacks, and big-city machines. Avoiding issues and controversy, Carter played up his role as a Washington outsider, pledging to restore morality to government. "I will never lie to you," he earnestly told voters. Carter won the election with 50 percent of the popular vote to Ford's 48 percent.

Despite his efforts to overcome the post-Watergate climate of skepticism and apathy, Carter never became an effective leader. His outsider strategy distanced him from traditional sources of power, and he did little to heal the breach. Shying away from established Democratic leaders, Carter turned to advisers and friends who had worked with him in Georgia, none of whom had national experience. When his budget director, Bert Lance, was questioned about financial irregularities at the Atlanta bank he had headed, Carter's campaign pledge to restore integrity and morality to the government rang hollow.

Inflation was Carter's major domestic challenge. When he took office, the nation was still recovering from the severe recession of 1975–1976. Carter embarked on a fiscal policy that eroded both business and consumer confidence. Unemployment hovered between 6 and 7 percent, while inflation rose from 6.5 percent in 1977 to 13.4 percent in 1980. To counter inflation, the Federal Reserve Board raised interest rates repeatedly; in 1980 they topped 20 percent, a historic high. A deep recession finally broke the inflationary spiral in 1982, a year after Carter left office.

The Carter administration expanded the federal bureaucracy in some cases and limited its reach in others. Carter enlarged the cabinet by creating the departments of energy and education and approved new environmental protection measures, such as the $1.6 billion "Superfund" to clean up chemical pollution sites, as well as new park and forest lands in Alaska. But he continued President Nixon's efforts to reduce the scope of federal activities by reforming the civil service and deregulating the airline, trucking, and railroad industries. With deregulation, prices often dropped, but the resulting cutthroat competition drove many firms out of business and encouraged corporate consolidation. Carter also failed in his effort to decontrol oil and natural gas prices as a spur to domestic production and conservation.

Carter's attempt to provide leadership during the energy crisis also failed. He called energy conservation efforts "the moral equivalent of war," but the media reduced the phrase to "MEOW." In early 1979 a revolution in Iran raised oil prices higher, and gas lines again reminded Americans of their dependence on foreign oil. That summer Carter's approval rating dropped to 26 percent—lower than Richard Nixon's during the worst part of the Watergate scandal.

In foreign affairs, President Carter made human rights the centerpiece of his policy. He criticized the suppression of dissent in the Soviet Union—especially as it affected the right of Jewish citizens to emigrate—and withdrew economic and military aid from Argentina, Uruguay, Ethiopia, and other countries that violated human rights. Carter also established the Office of Human Rights in the State Department. Unable to change the internal policies of long-time U.S. allies who were serious violators of human rights, such as the Philippines, South Korea, and South Africa, he did manage to raise public awareness of the human rights issue, making it one future administrations would have to address.

In Latin America, Carter's most important contribution was the resolution of the lingering dispute over control of the Panama Canal. In a treaty signed on September 7, 1977, the United States agreed to turn over control of the canal to Panama on December 31, 1999. In return, the United States retained the right to send its ships through the canal in case of war, even though the canal itself would be declared neutral territory. Despite a conservative outcry that the United States was giving away more than it got, the Senate narrowly approved the treaty.

Though Carter had campaigned to free the United States from its "inordinate fear of Communism," relations with the Soviet Union soon became tense, largely because of problems surrounding arms limitation talks. Eventually the Soviet leader Leonid Brezhnev signed SALT II (1979), but hopes for Senate ratification of the treaty collapsed when the Soviet Union invaded Afghanistan that December. In retaliation for this aggression, which Carter viewed as a threat to Middle Eastern oil supplies, the United States curtailed grain sales to the U.S.S.R. and boycotted the 1980 summer Olympics in Moscow. (The Soviets returned the gesture by boycotting the 1984 summer games in Los Angeles.) When Carter left office in 1981, relations with the Soviet Union were worse than they had been when he took over.

President Carter achieved both his most stunning success and his greatest failure in the Middle East. Relations between Egypt and Israel had remained tense since the 1973 Yom Kippur War. In 1978 Carter helped to break the diplomatic stalemate by inviting Israel's prime minister Menachem Begin and Egyptian president Anwar Sadat to Camp David, the presidential retreat in Maryland. Two weeks of discussions and Carter's promise of additional foreign aid to Egypt persuaded Sadat and Begin to adopt a "framework for peace." The framework included Egypt's recognition of Israel's right to exist and Israel's return of the Sinai peninsula, which it had occupied since 1967. Transfer of the territory to Egypt took place from 1979 to 1982.

Dramatically less successful was U.S. foreign policy toward Iran. Ever since the CIA had helped to install Muhammad Reza Pahlavi on the throne in 1953, the United States had counted Iran as a faithful ally in the troubled Middle East. Overlooking the repressive tactics of Iran's CIA-trained secret police, SAVAK, Carter followed in the footsteps of previous cold war policymakers for whom access to Iranian oil reserves and the shah's consistently anticommunist stance outweighed all other considerations.

Early in 1979, however, the shah's government was overthrown and driven into exile by a revolution led by fundamentalist Muslim leader Ayatollah Ruhollah Khomeini. In late October 1979 the Carter administration admitted the deposed shah, who was suffering from incurable cancer, to the United

States for medical treatment. Though Iran's new leaders had warned that such an action would provoke retaliation, Henry Kissinger and other foreign policy leaders had argued that the United States should assist the shah, both for humanitarian reasons and in return for his years of support for American policy. In response, on November 4, 1979, fundamentalist Muslim students under Khomeini's direction seized the U.S. embassy in Teheran, taking Americans there hostage in a flagrant violation of the principle of diplomatic immunity. The hostage takers demanded that the shah be returned to Iran for trial and punishment, but the United States refused. Instead, President Carter suspended arms sales to Iran, froze Iranian assets in American banks, and threatened to deport Iranian students in the United States.

For the next fourteen months the Iranian hostage crisis paralyzed Jimmy Carter's presidency. Night after night, humiliating pictures of blindfolded hostages appeared on television newscasts. The extensive media coverage, and Carter's insistence that the safe return of the 52 hostages was his top priority, enhanced the value of the hostages to their captors. An attempt to mount a military rescue of the hostages failed miserably in April 1980, six months into the crisis, because of helicopter equipment failures in the desert. The abortive rescue mission reinforced the public's view of Carter as a bumbling and ineffective executive.

American Hostages in Iran
Images of blindfolded, handcuffed American hostages seized by Iranian militants at the American embassy in Teheran in November 1979 shocked the nation and created a foreign policy crisis that eventually cost Jimmy Carter the presidency.

The Reagan Revolution

With Carter embroiled in the hostage crisis, the Republicans gained momentum by nominating former California governor Ronald Reagan. A movie actor in the late 1930s, the 1940s, and the early 1950s, Reagan had served as president of the Screen Actors Guild and had been deeply affected by the postwar anticommunist crusade in Hollywood. He had endorsed Barry Goldwater in 1964 and had begun his own political career shortly after, serving as governor of California from 1967 to 1975. After losing a bid for the Republican nomination in 1976, Reagan secured it easily in 1980, and chose former CIA director George Bush as his running mate.

In the final months of the campaign, Carter took on an embattled and defensive tone, while Reagan remained upbeat and decisive. The Republicans benefited from superior financial resources, which allowed them to make sophisticated use of television and direct mail appeals. Reagan also had a powerful issue to exploit: the hostage stalemate. Calling the Iranians "barbarians" and "common criminals," he hinted that he would take strong action to win the hostages' return. More important, Reagan effectively appealed to the politics of resentment that flourished during the lean years of the 1970s. In a televised debate between the candidates, Reagan emphasized the economic plight of working- and middle-class Americans when he posed the rhetorical question, "Are you better off today than you were four years ago?" Battered by inflation, unemployment, and income stagnation, and resentful of the rights revolution they felt slighted them, many viewers answered no.

In November Reagan won easily, with 51 percent of the popular vote to Carter's 41 percent. The landslide also gave the Republicans control of the Senate for the first time since 1954, though the Democrats maintained their hold on the House. Voter turnout, however, was at the lowest since the 1920s: only 53 percent of those eligible to vote went to the polls. Many poor and working-class voters stayed home. Nevertheless, the election confirmed the growth in the power of the Republican party since Richard Nixon's victory in 1968.

The core of the Republican party that elected Ronald Reagan remained the upper-middle-class white Protestant voters who supported balanced budgets, disliked government activism, feared crime and communism, and believed in a strong national defense. But new groups had gravitated toward the Republican vision: southern whites disaffected by big government and black civil-rights gains; blue-collar workers, especially Catholics; young voters who identified themselves as conservatives; and residents in the West, especially those in the rapidly growing suburbs. By wooing these "Reagan Democrats," the Republican party made deep inroads into Democratic territory, eroding that party's traditional coalition of southerners, blacks, laborers, and urban ethnics.

But perhaps the most significant constituency in the Republican party was the New Right, whose emphasis on traditional values and fundamentalist Christian morality dovetailed well with conservative Republican ideology. In 1980 New Right concerns formed the basis for the party's platform, which called for a constitutional ban on abortion, voluntary prayer in public schools, and a mandatory death penalty for certain crimes. The Republicans also demanded an end to court-mandated busing, and for the first time in forty years opposed the Equal Rights Amendment. A key factor in the 1980 election, the New Right contributed to the rebirth of the Republican party under Ronald Reagan.

On January 20, 1981, at the moment Carter turned over the presidency to Ronald Reagan, the Iranian government released the American hostages. After 444 days of captivity, the hostages returned home to an ecstatic welcome, a reflection of the public's frustration over their long ordeal. While most Americans continued to maintain "We're Number One," the hostage crisis in Iran came to symbolize the loss of America's power to control world affairs. Its psychological impact was enhanced by its occurrence at the end of a decade that had witnessed Watergate, the American defeat in Vietnam, and the OPEC embargo. To a great extent, the decline in American influence had been magnified by the unusual predominance the United States had enjoyed after World War II—an advantage that could not have been expected to last forever. The return of Japan and Western Europe to economic and political power, the control of vital oil resources by Middle Eastern countries, and the industrialization of some Third World nations had widened the cast of characters on the international stage. Still, many Americans were unable to let go of the presumption of economic and political supremacy born in the postwar years. Ronald Reagan rode their frustrations to victory in 1980.

CHAPTER 32 TIMELINE	
1968	Richard Nixon elected president
1970	First Earth Day
	Environmental Protection Agency established
1971	Pentagon Papers published
1972	Revenue sharing begins
	Watergate break-in
	Congress passes Equal Rights Amendment
	Consumer Products Safety Commission established
	Nixon reelected
1973	Spiro Agnew resigns; Gerald Ford appointed vice-president
	Roe v. Wade legalizes abortion
	OPEC oil embargo begins; gas shortages
1974	*Milliken v. Bradley* mandates busing within cities
	Nixon resigns; Ford becomes president and pardons Nixon
	Freedom of Information Act strengthened
	Fair Campaign Practices Act passed
1974–1975	Busing controversy in Boston
	Economic recession
1976	Jimmy Carter elected president
1977	National Women's Conference in Houston
	Miami voters overturn a gay rights measure
1978	Carter brokers Camp David accords
	Bakke v. University of California limits affirmative action
	Exposure of the toxic waste site at Love Canal
1979	Three Mile Island nuclear accident
	Second oil crisis
	Hostages seized at American embassy in Teheran, Iran
	U.S.S.R. invades Afghanistan
1980	Superfund created to clean up chemical pollution
	Ronald Reagan elected president

CHAPTER 33

A NEW DOMESTIC AND WORLD ORDER, 1981 TO THE PRESENT

- The Reagan-Bush Years, 1981–1993
- Foreign Relations under Reagan and Bush
- An Age of Anxiety
- The Clinton Presidency: Public Life since 1993

On April 19, 1995, a truck bomb ripped apart the Federal Building in Oklahoma City, killing 168 people. Though suspicion initially focused on Middle Eastern terrorists, two years later Timothy McVeigh, an American with links to a right-wing citizens' militia group, was convicted of the crime. Resentful of big government and often sympathetic to white supremacy, men like McVeigh had been swelling the ranks of paramilitary organizations throughout the country, especially in the western states. They were extreme examples of widespread disenchantment with government, politics, and American society in general at the end of the twentieth century. Indeed, a sense of social disorder rippled through the nation and the world as the century and the millennium came to an end. With the breakup of the Soviet Union in 1991, the Cold War had ended, but new sources of conflict soon threatened world peace. In the new world order, the United States was increasingly linked to a global economy that directly affected American interest rates, consumption patterns, and job opportunities. At home, Americans grappled with racial, ethnic, and cultural conflict; crime and economic inequities; the shrinking role of the federal government; and the failure of their political leaders to solve many of the nation's pressing social problems.

THE REAGAN-BUSH YEARS, 1981–1993

George Bush's one term as president often seems indistinguishable from the two terms of his predecessor Ronald Reagan, in part because Bush followed the basic policies of the previous administration. But Bush was also over-shadowed because Reagan, while he was not a particularly capable president, possessed extraordinary charisma. First elected at sixty-nine, he was the oldest man ever to serve as president, yet he conveyed a sense of physical vigor. By capitalizing on his skills as an actor and a public speaker, and by winning the support of the emerging New Right within the Republican party, Reagan became one of the most popular presidents of the twentieth century. Distrust-ful of the federal government, both Bush and Reagan turned away from the state as a source of solutions for America's social problems, calling into ques-tion almost half a century of governmental activism. "Government is not the solution to our problem," Reagan declared, "Government is the problem."

Reaganomics

The economic and tax policies that emerged under Reagan, quickly dubbed *Reaganomics*, were based on *supply-side* economics theory. According to the

The Great Communicator
Ronald Reagan felt totally at home in front of the camera, trading stories and one-liners with audiences and the press. Commen-tator Gary Wills observed, "Reagan runs continuously in everyone's home movies of the mind. . . . He is, in the strictest sense, what Hol-lywood promoters used to call 'fabulous.'"

theory, high taxes siphoned off capital that would otherwise be invested, stimulating growth. Tax cuts would therefore promote investment, causing an economic expansion that would increase tax revenues. Together with cuts in government spending, especially on entitlement programs, tax cuts would also shrink the federal budget deficit. That, at least, was the theory. Critics charged that conservative Republicans deliberately cut taxes to force reductions in federal funding for the social programs that they abhorred.

The Economic Recovery Tax Act passed in 1981 reduced income tax rates by 25 percent over three years. The reductions were supposed to be linked to drastic cutbacks in federal expenditures. But while cuts were made in food stamps, unemployment compensation, and welfare programs such as Aid to Families with Dependent Children (AFDC), congressional resistance kept the Social Security and Medicare programs intact. The net impact of Reaganomics was to further the redistribution of income from the poor to the wealthy.

Another tenet of Reaganomics was that many federal regulations impeded economic growth and productivity. Insisting that a safety net existed for the truly needy, the administration moved to abolish or reduce federal regulation of the workplace, health care, consumer protection, and the environment. The responsibility and cost of such regulations were transferred to the states. One of the results of their policy was the deinstitutionalization of many of the mentally ill, forcing them onto the streets.

The money saved by these means—and more—was plowed into a five-year, $1.2 trillion defense buildup. This huge increase fulfilled Reagan's campaign pledge to "make America number one again." The B-1 bomber, which President Carter had canceled, was resurrected, and development of a new missile system, the MX, was begun. Reagan's most ambitious and controversial weapons plan, proposed in 1983, was the Strategic Defense Initiative (SDI), popularly known as "Star Wars." A computerized satellite and laser shield to detect and intercept incoming missiles, SDI would supposedly render nuclear war obsolete.

Reagan's programs benefited from the Federal Reserve Board's tight money policies, as well as a serendipitous drop in world oil prices, which reduced the disastrous inflation rates that had bedeviled the nation in the 1970s. Between 1980 and 1982 the inflation rate dropped from 12.4 percent to just 4 percent. Unfortunately, the Fed's tightening of the money supply also brought on the "Reagan Recession" of 1981–1982, which threw some 10 million Americans out of work. But as the recession bottomed out in early 1983, the economy began to grow, and for the rest of the decade inflation remained low. Despite rather unexceptional growth in the gross national product, the Reagan administration presided over the longest peacetime economic expansion in American history.

Reagan's Second Term

This economic growth played a role in the 1984 elections. Reagan campaigned on the theme "It's Morning in America," suggesting that a new day of prosperity and pride was dawning. The Democrats nominated former vice-president

Walter Mondale of Minnesota to run against Reagan. With strong ties to labor unions, minority groups, and party leaders, Mondale epitomized the New Deal coalition that had dominated the Democratic party since Roosevelt. To appeal to women voters, Mondale selected Representative Geraldine Ferraro of New York as his running mate—the first woman to run on a major party ticket. Nevertheless, Reagan won a landslide victory, carrying the entire nation except for Minnesota and the District of Columbia. Democrats, however, held onto the House, and in 1986 would regain control of the Senate.

A major scandal marred Reagan's second term when in 1986 news leaked out that the administration had negotiated an arms-for-hostages deal with the revolutionary government of Iran—the same government Reagan had denounced during the 1980 hostage crisis. In an attempt to gain Iran's help in freeing some American hostages held by pro-Iranian forces in Lebanon, the U.S. had covertly sold arms to Iran. Some of the profits generated by the arms sales were diverted to the Contras, counterrevolutionaries in Nicaragua, whom the administration supported over the leftist regime of the Sandinistas. The covert diversion of funds, which was both illegal and unconstitutional, seemed to have been the brainstorm of Marine Lieutenant Colonel Oliver North, a National Security Council aide at the time. One key memo linked the White House to his plan. But when Congress investigated the mounting scandal in 1986 and 1987, White House officials testified that the president knew nothing about the diversion. Ronald Reagan's defense remained simple and consistent: "I don't remember."

The scandal bore many similarities to Watergate, including the possibility that the president had acted illegally. Early in Reagan's administration, one of his critics had coined the phrase "Teflon presidency" to describe Reagan's resiliency—bad news didn't stick; it just rolled off. No matter that the president was often confused or ill informed, or that he relied heavily on close advisers, especially his wife. Even the news that Nancy Reagan was in the habit of consulting an astrologer before planning major White House events failed to shake public confidence in the president. Reagan weathered "Iran-Contragate," but the scandal did weaken his presidency.

The president proposed no bold domestic policy initiatives in his last two years in office. He had promised to place drastic limits on the federal government and to give free-market forces freer reign. Despite reordering the federal government's priorities, he failed to reduce its size or scope. And although spending for most poverty programs had been cut, Social Security and other entitlement programs remained untouched. Despite Reagan's failure to achieve his goals, his spending cuts and antigovernment rhetoric shaped the terms of political debate for the rest of the century.

One of Reagan's most significant legacies was his conservative judicial appointments. In 1981 he had nominated Sandra Day O'Connor, the first woman ever to serve on the Supreme Court. In his second term he appointed two more justices, Antonin Scalia (1986) and Anthony Kennedy (1988), both of whom were far more conservative than the moderate O'Connor. Justice William Rehnquist, a noted conservative, was elevated to chief justice in

1986. Under his leadership the Court, often by a 5–4 margin, chipped away at the Warren Court's legacy in decisions on individual liberties, affirmative action, and the rights of criminal defendants.

Ironically, though Reagan had promised to balance the budget by 1984, his most enduring legacy was the national debt, which tripled during his two terms. The huge deficit reflected the combined effects of increased military spending, tax reductions for high-income taxpayers, and Congress's refusal to approve deep cuts in domestic programs. By 1989 the national debt had climbed to $2.8 trillion—more than $11,000 for every American citizen.

The nation was also running an annual deficit in its trade with other nations. Exports had been falling since the 1970s, when American products began to encounter increasing competition in world markets. In the early 1980s a high exchange rate for dollars made U.S. goods more expensive for foreign buyers and imports more affordable for Americans. The budget and trade deficits contributed to a major shift in 1985: for the first time since 1915 the United States became a debtor rather a creditor nation. Since then, with phenomenal speed, the United States has accumulated the world's largest foreign debt.

The Bush Presidency

George Herbert Walker Bush won the Republican nomination in 1988, despite challenges from Senate minority leader Robert Dole, television evangelist Pat Robertson, and congressional representative Jack Kemp. Bush's choice for vice-president, a young conservative Indiana senator, Dan Quayle, who had used family connections to avoid service in Vietnam, added little to the ticket. In the Democratic primaries, the contest was between Governor Michael Dukakis of Massachusetts and the charismatic civil-rights leader Jesse Jackson, whose populist Rainbow Coalition had embraced the diversity of Democratic constituencies. Dukakis received the party's nomination and chose Senator Lloyd Bentsen of Texas as his running mate.

The 1988 campaign had a harsh tone: brief televised attack ads replaced meaningful discussion of the issues. The sound bite "Read My Lips: No New Taxes," drawn from George Bush's acceptance speech at the Republican convention, became the party's campaign mantra. In a television ad featuring Willie Horton, a black man convicted of murder who had killed again while on furlough from a Massachusetts prison, Republicans, pandering to voters' racist fears, charged Dukakis with being soft on crime. Dukakis, forced on the defensive, failed to mount an effective counterattack. Bush carried thirty-eight states, winning the popular vote by 53.4 percent to 45.6 percent. Only 50 percent of eligible voters went to the polls.

Though Bush did not share many of Reagan's conservative views, he failed to develop a distinctive domestic agenda. The impact of Reagan's Supreme Court nominees shaped one of the most significant domestic trends during the Bush administration—the Supreme Court's continued move away from liberal activism and toward a more conservative stance, especially on the issue of abortion. The 1989 *Webster v. Reproductive Health Services* decision permitted states to restrict abortion. The next year the Court upheld a federal regulation barring personnel at federally funded health clinics from discussing abortion with their clients. In 1992 the Court upheld a Pennsylvania law mandating informed consent and a twenty-four-hour waiting period before an abortion could be performed. But the justices also reaffirmed the "essential holding" in *Roe v. Wade*: women had a constitutional right to abortion.

In 1990 David Souter, a little known federal judge from New Hampshire, easily won confirmation to the Supreme Court. But the next year a major controversy erupted over President Bush's nomination of Clarence Thomas, a black conservative with little judicial experience. Just as Thomas's confirmation hearings were drawing to a close, a former colleague, Anita Hill, testified publicly that Thomas had sexually harassed her in the early 1980s. After widely watched and widely debated televised testimony by both Thomas and Hill before the all-male Senate Judiciary Committee, the Senate confirmed Thomas by a narrow margin. In the wake of the hearings, national polls confirmed the pervasiveness of sexual harassment on the job: four out of ten women said that they had been the object of unwanted sexual advances from men at work.

Besides developments in the Supreme Court, a key issue during Bush's four years as president was the economy. His campaign promise of a "kinder, gentler administration" was doomed by his predecessor's failed economic policies, especially the budget deficit. The Gramm-Rudman Act, passed in 1985, had mandated automatic cuts if budget targets were not met in 1991. Facing the prospect of a halt in nonessential government services and the layoff of thousands of government employees, Congress resorted to new spending cuts and one of the largest tax increases in history. Bush's failure to keep his "No New Taxes" promise earned him the enmity of Republican conservatives, which would dramatically hurt his chances for reelection in 1992.

Reagan's decision to shift the cost of many federal programs, including housing, education, public works, and social services, to state and local governments caused problems for Bush. In 1990 a recession began to erode state and local tax revenues. As incomes declined and industrial and white-collar layoffs increased, poverty and homelessness increased sharply. In 1991 unemployment approached 7 percent nationwide. To save money, state and local governments laid off workers even as demand for social services and unemployment compensation climbed.

FOREIGN RELATIONS UNDER REAGAN AND BUSH

The collapse of détente during the Carter administration, after the Soviet invasion of Afghanistan, underlay Reagan's confrontational approach to what he called the "evil empire." Backed by Republican hard-liners, and determined to reduce Communist influence in developing nations, Reagan articulated some of the harshest anti-Soviet rhetoric since the 1950s. The collapse of the Soviet Union in 1991 removed that nation as a credible threat, but new post–cold war challenges quickly appeared.

Interventions in the Third World and the End of the Cold War

Despite Reagan's rhetoric, not all his international problems involved U.S.-Soviet confrontations. In 1983, after Israel invaded Lebanon, the U.S. Embassy in Beirut was bombed by anti-Israeli Muslim fundamentalists. A second bombing killed 239 Marine peacekeepers barracked in the city. Around the world, terrorist assassins struck down Indira Gandhi in India and Anwar Sadat in Egypt. But it was the airplane hijackings and countless terrorist incidents in the Middle East that led Reagan to order air strikes against one highly visible source of terrorism, Muammar Khadafy of Libya.

The administration reserved its most concerted attention for Central America. Halting what was seen as the spread of communism in that region became an obsession. In 1983 Reagan ordered the marines to invade the tiny Caribbean island of Grenada, claiming that its Cuban-supported Communist regime posed a threat to other states in the region. Reagan's top priority, however, was to topple the leftist Sandinista government in Nicaragua. In 1981 the United States suspended aid to Nicaragua, charging that the Sandinistas were supplying arms to rebels against a repressive right-wing regime in El Salvador. At the same time, the CIA began to provide extensive covert support to the Nicaraguan opposition, the "Contras," whom Reagan called "freedom fighters." Congress, wary of the assumption of unconstitutional powers by the executive branch, responded in 1984 by passing the Boland Amendment, which banned the CIA and other intelligence agencies from providing military support to the Contras—a provision violated in the Iran-Contra affair.

Surprisingly, given Reagan's rhetoric, his second term brought a reduction in tensions with the Soviet Union. In 1985, Reagan met with the new Soviet premier, Mikhail Gorbachev, at the first superpower summit meeting since 1979. Two years later, the two leaders agreed to eliminate all intermediate-range missiles based in Europe. Although a summit in Moscow in 1988 produced no further cuts in nuclear arms, the sight of the two first families attending the Bolshoi Ballet together and strolling amiably in Red Square exemplified the thaw in the Cold War.

Under Bush's administration, even more dramatic changes abroad brought about an end to the Cold War. In 1989 the grip of communism on Eastern Europe loosened and then let go completely in a series of mostly nonviolent revolutions that climaxed in the destruction of the Berlin Wall in November. Soon the Soviet Union itself began to succumb to the forces of change. The background for these dramatic upheavals lay in the changes set in motion by Soviet president Mikhail Gorbachev after 1985. Through his policies of *glasnost* (openness) and *perestroika* (economic restructuring), Gorbachev had signaled a willingness to tolerate significant changes. But Gorbachev, who was always more popular outside his country than at home, found that to call for the dismantling of an old system was easier than to build a new system.

On August 19, 1991, alarmed Soviet military leaders seized Gorbachev and attempted unsuccessfully to oust him. The failure of the coup broke the Communist party's dominance over the Soviet Union. Lithuania had declared its independence in March 1990 and now the Baltic Republics of Latvia and Estonia followed suit. In December the Union of Soviet Socialist Republics formally dissolved itself to make way for an eleven-member Commonwealth of Independent States (CIS). Gorbachev resigned, and Boris Yeltsin, president of the new state of Russia, the largest and most populous republic, became the preeminent leader in the region.

The suddenness of the collapse of the Soviet Union and the end of the Cold War stunned America and the world. In the future, in the absence of superpower confrontations, international conflicts would arise from regional, religious, and ethnic differences. Suddenly, the United States faced unfamiliar military and diplomatic challenges.

War in the Persian Gulf, 1990–1991

The first new challenge arose in the Middle East. On August 2, 1990, Iraq, led by Saddam Hussein, invaded Kuwait, its small but oil-rich neighbor. In response, President Bush sponsored a series of resolutions in the U.N. Security Council, condemning Iraq, calling for its withdrawal, and imposing an embargo and trade sanctions. When Hussein showed no signs of yielding, Bush prodded the international organization to create a legal framework for a military offensive against the man he called "the butcher of Baghdad." In November the Security Council voted to use force if Iraq did not withdraw by January 15. In a close 52–48 vote on January 12, the U.S. Senate authorized military action. Four days later President Bush announced to the nation that "the liberation of Kuwait has begun."

The forty-two-day war was a resounding success for the United Nations' coalition forces, which were predominantly American. Under the leadership of General Colin Powell, chairman of the Joint Chiefs of Staff, and the com-

Women at War
Women played key and visible roles in the Persian Gulf War, comprising approximately 10 percent of the American troops. Increasing numbers of women are choosing to make a career out of the military, despite widespread reports of sexual harassment and other forms of discrimination.

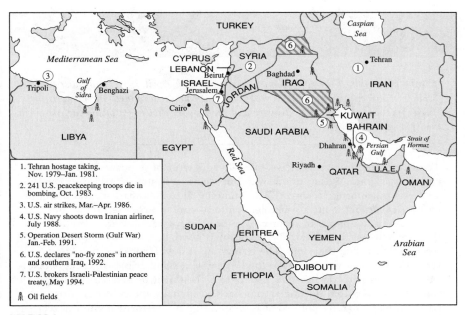

MAP 33.1
U.S. Involvement in the Middle East, 1980–1994
The United States has long played an active role in the Middle East, pursuing the twin goals of protecting Israel's security and assuring a reliable supply of low-cost oil from the Persian Gulf states. By far the largest intervention came in 1991, when, under United Nations auspices, President Bush sent 540,000 American troops to liberate Kuwait from Iraq. The United States also played a major role in the 1994 agreement allowing for Palestinian self-rule in the Gaza Strip and parts of the West Bank.

manding general, H. Norman Schwarzkopf, Operation Desert Storm opened with a month of air strikes to crush communications, destroy armaments, and pummel Iraqi ground troops. A land offensive followed. Within days thousands of Iraqi troops had fled or surrendered, and the fighting quickly ended, although Hussein remained in power (see Map 33.1).

Operation Desert Storm's success, and the amazingly low U.S. casualties (only 145 Americans were killed in action), produced a euphoric reaction at home. For many, the American victory over a vastly inferior fighting force seemed to banish the ghost of Vietnam. "By God, we've kicked the Vietnam Syndrome once and for all," Bush gloated. The president's approval rating shot up precipitously, but declined almost as quickly when a new recession showed that the easy victory had masked the country's serious economic problems.

AN AGE OF ANXIETY

Opinion polls taken in the early 1990s showed that Americans were deeply concerned about the future. They worried about crime in the streets,

AMERICAN VOICES

The Age of Anxiety

In the aftermath of the Oklahoma City bombing in April 1995, journalist Joe Klein wrote an essay for Newsweek *in which he drew connections between the shock Americans felt over the disaster and the broader challenges facing the nation in the "Nervous Nineties."*

These are the Nervous Nineties. Life—by any rational standard—is good. The economy is good. We are not at war. But we are not quite at peace, either. We are beset by amorphous threats. The bombing in Oklahoma City was a unique, discrete event, but it fits a subliminal pattern—the growing sense that our most basic assumptions of security, of rationality, of decency are more tenuous than we had ever imagined. The economy is good, but a majority (60 percent) worry about losing their jobs. The crime rate is down, but everyone knows someone who has been mugged (and 89 percent think crime is getting worse). Medicine can perform miracles, but there is the threat of new viruses . . . and some old bacteria are making a comeback. . . . Finally, the cold war is over: Russian missiles aren't pointed at Kansas City, but a terrorist bomb can turn Oklahoma City into Beruit. . . .

Not just innocence, but economic hegemony has been lost. . . . Most important, there is competition from the rest of the world. This month's *International Business* magazine predicts a "global oversupply" of *skilled* workers that will, no doubt, further depress American wages. . . . Two salaries [in the household] yield more, but also less—less time (and supervision) for children, for civic activities, for relaxation. "The dual-earner household is creating a lot more stress than people ever imagined," says the pollster Daniel Yankelovich. "And John Kennedy was wrong: a rising tide doesn't necessarily lift all boats. Right now, it seems to be lifting only yachts. The disparity in incomes is growing. That's cause for a lot of anxiety."

SOURCE: Joe Klein, "Nervous '90s," *Newsweek*, May 1, 1995, pp. 59–60.

increases in poverty and homelessness, the decline of the inner cities, illegal immigration, the environment, the failure of public schools, the unresolved abortion issue, and AIDS. But above all they worried about their own economic security, whether they would be able to keep their jobs in an era of global competition.

The Economy

One of the most salient economic trends of the past two decades has been the growing inequality in income distribution. In the 1980s, as economist Lester

Thurow noted, "all of the gains in male earnings went to the top 20 percent of the workforce and an amazing 64 percent accrued to the top 1 percent." At the same time, the pay of leading corporate executives went from "35 to 157 times that of the average production worker." America was becoming a nation of haves and have-nots. Even relatively well-advantaged Americans felt a sense of diminished expectations. Earlier generations had aspired to doing better than their parents financially; now many young adults wondered whether they could achieve even a modest middle-class lifestyle.

These diminished expectations stemmed in part from changes in the job market. By the end of the twentieth century, the average employee could typically expect to make several job shifts over the course of a lifetime. Following an established pattern, the number of minimum-wage service jobs continued to grow, while the number of union-protected manufacturing jobs was shrinking. For many—one-fifth of the labor force in 1994—part-time or temporary work was the only work that was available. Moreover, in the 1980s and 1990s the downsizing trend, in which companies deliberately shed permanent workers to cut wage costs, spread to middle management. From 1980 to 1995 IBM shrank its mostly white-collar work force from 400,000 to 220,000—a 45 percent decrease. Although most laid-off middle managers eventually found new jobs, many took a large pay cut.

These economic trends put even more pressure on women to seek paid employment. In 1994, 58.8 percent of women were in the labor force, up from 38 percent in 1962, compared with 75.1 percent of men. The traditional nuclear family of employed father, homemaker wife, and children characterized less than 15 percent of U.S. households. Although women continued to make inroads in traditionally male-dominated fields—medicine, law, law enforcement, the military, and skilled trades—one out of five held a clerical or secretarial job, the same proportion as in 1950. Women's pay lagged behind men's; among black and Latino women the gender gap was even wider than among white women.

Another major cause of diminished economic expectations was the widespread fear that American corporations were no longer competitive in the global marketplace. Americans viewed with alarm the economic success of Germany and Japan, the growing U.S. trade deficit, and the infusion of foreign workers and investment money into the United States. In order to compete, American corporations adopted new technologies, including microelectronics, biotechnology, computers, and robots, and by the late 1990s saw their competitiveness return. Bethlehem Steel, which invested $6 billion to modernize its operations, doubled its productivity between 1989 and 1997. Other firms retooled their corporate vision. In 1980–1981 the Ford Motor Company had lost $2.5 billion despite laying off 150,000 workers. In the face of this desperate situation, Ford shifted its focus from maximizing output to improving quality and consumer satisfaction, making assembly-line workers more involved in the company and its products by giving them more responsibility. The popular Ford Taurus, introduced in 1986, typified the new focus on quality.

While management struggled to improve productivity, the labor movement, hurt by downsizing, foreign competition, fear of layoffs, government hostility, and a failure to organize unskilled workers, continued to decline. By 1993, 16.6 million Americans were union members, just 15.8 percent of the work force. The Reagan administration took a tough antiunion stance from the start, breaking a nationwide strike by the Professional Air Traffic Controllers (PATCO) in 1981 and ultimately destroying the union. Reagan's action signaled to the business community that an antiunion posture was acceptable, encouraging sharp labor confrontations at Eastern Airlines, Caterpillar, and other corporations. In the mid-1990s new union leadership, a wave of union mergers, and vigorous efforts to recruit new members raised hopes that organized labor would reverse its long decline. In August 1997 the success of a dramatic strike against United Parcel Service (UPS) seemed to confirm this promise. The Teamster-backed strike won crucial concessions—union control of pensions and the conversion of part-time jobs to full-time positions with company benefits—that most observers viewed as a major victory for organized labor.

These gains for labor took place in the context of a brightening national economic picture. By the late 1990s, the United States led the world in information technology and its industries' efforts to improve manufacturing efficiency resulted in expanded productivity. In 1997, U.S. economic growth, measured at 4 percent, was among the healthiest in the world, while one of its most serious competitors in the 1980s, Japan, limped along with only a 1.1 percent growth rate. Working Americans benefited from these developments: new jobs were added to the economy at the rate of 213,000 per month in 1997. A booming stock market, which daily seemed to reach new highs, fueled the wealth and potential retirement savings of middle- and upper-class Americans. But there were downsides to the picture as well. Many stock market analysts worried that a steep drop in the stock market might create a recession. Moreover, prosperity was not equally distributed. As former Secretary of Labor Robert Reich put it, "There are still millions of people desperately trying to stay afloat. One in five children lives in poverty. Forty-four million Americans have no health insurance. The average 50-year-old without a college education hasn't seen a wage or benefit increase in 20 years. But Americans are segregated by income as never before, so it is far easier to pretend the worse off don't exist. They're out of sight."

An Increasingly Pluralistic Society

In 1996 the United States had a population of 265.5 million people, one-fourth of whom claimed African, Asian, Latino, or American Indian ancestry. Ethnic and racial diversity, always a source of conflict in American culture, became a defining theme of the 1990s, as Americans coped with racial violence, dramatically increased immigration, and widespread ethnic antagonism, especially on the part of native-born whites.

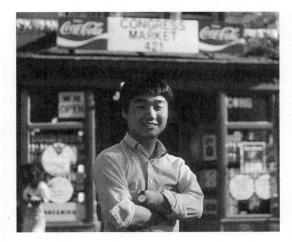

New Immigrants
In the 1980s many Korean immigrants got their start by opening small grocery stores in urban neighborhoods. Their success sometimes led to conflict with other racial groups, such as blacks and Hispanics, who were often their customers as well as competitors.

In the 1980s over 7 million immigrants entered the country, accounting for more than a third of the population growth in that decade. The greatest number of the newcomers were Latinos. Although Mexico continued to provide the largest group of Spanish-speaking immigrants, large numbers also arrived from El Salvador and the Dominican Republic. The 1986 Immigration Reform and Control Act (Simpson-Mazzoli Act), which granted amnesty to some immigrants, primarily benefited Mexicans and other Latinos who had entered the United States illegally before 1982. The second largest minority group in the United States after African-Americans and the second fastest-growing after Asians, the Latino population reached 24.3 million in 1992. Once concentrated in California, Texas, and New Mexico, Latinos now lived in urban areas throughout the country, and made up about 13 percent of the population of Florida and New York (see Map 33.2).

Asia was the other major source of new immigrants. This migration, which increased almost 108 percent from 1980 to 1990, consisted mainly of people from China, the Philippines, Vietnam, Laos, Cambodia, Korea, India, and Pakistan. More than 700,000 Indochinese refugees came to escape upheavals in Southeast Asia in the decade following the Vietnam War. The first arrivals, many of them well educated, adapted successfully to their new homeland. Later refugees lacked professional or vocational skills and took low-paying jobs where they could find them.

The new immigrants' impact on the country's social, economic, and cultural landscape has been tremendous. In many places they have created thriving ethnic communities, such as Koreatown in Los Angeles. In the 1980s tens of thousands of Jews fleeing religious and political persecution in the Soviet Union created Little Odessa in Brooklyn, New York. Ethnic restaurants and shops have sprung up across the country, while some 300 specialized periodicals serve immigrant readers.

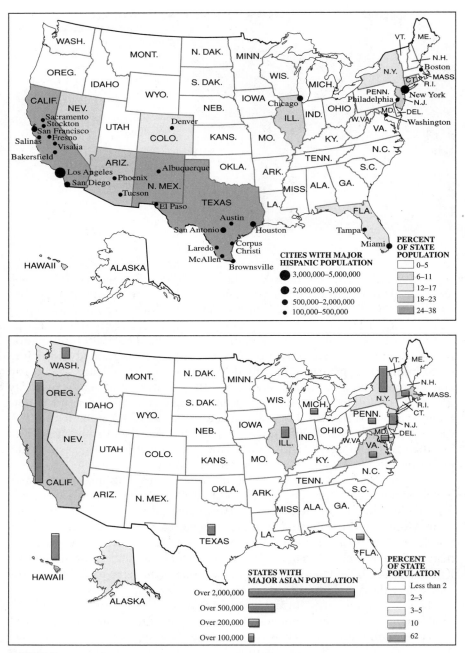

MAP 33.2

Hispanic Population and Asian-American Population, 1990
In 1990 Latinos made up almost 10 percent of the U.S. population, and Asian-Americans just under 3 percent. Demographers predict that Latinos will overtake African-Americans as the largest minority group early in the twenty-first century and that by the year 2050 only about half the U.S. population will be composed of non-Latino whites.

AMERICAN VOICES

The Undocumented Worker

*I*n *this oral history, Cuauhtémoc Mendez, an immigrant construction worker, reflects on the controversial issue of undocumented Mexican workers—an issue that
helped fuel anti-immigration sentiment in the 1980s and 1990s.*

In the United States, to get rid of all the illegals, you don't need a border or
the Immigration. Simply, if there is no work, what would the illegals do
there?. . . For the United States it is a great advantage, because Mexican labor
is very cheap. The illegal produces his product much cheaper, and they can sell
it cheaper to the American people. In this sense the illegal helps the United
States.

He also helps Mexico. All of the *mojados* bring money back. We don't take
money out of Mexico. Those of us who work in the United States help our
country more than the rich who send their Mexican money out. We support
our country.

Normally the Mexican who goes to the United States goes to work in
jobs that many Americans don't want. In the first place, it's hard work. I'm
not going to say that they can't do the work, but they don't want to work
for the same price as the Mexican. It's clear there is this contradiction, this
antipathy toward the Mexican who is there illegally. They look at the *mojados* as scabs. The Chicanos and Mexican-Americans look at us from this perspective because they think we are the reason they don't have jobs. But it's
not true. We are there at the convenience of the owners and bosses who
want cheap labor, cheaper than they can get there. It isn't our fault. We
have the necessity to work. I don't think it's a sin to subsist in another
country that offers the opportunity to live a little better than is possible for
us in Mexico.

SOURCE: Marilyn P. Davis, *Mexican Voices, American Dreams: An Oral History of Mexican Immigration to the United States*
(New York: Henry Holt and Co., 1990), p. 110.

In 1990 the immigration quota was expanded to 700,000 per year (modi-
fied in 1995 to 675,000), with priority given to skilled workers and relatives
of current residents. But by then the new immigrants had become scapegoats
for all that was wrong with the United States. Though a 1997 study by the
National Academy of Science reported that immigration has benefited the nation, adding some $10 billion a year to the economy, many American-born
workers felt threatened by immigrants. The unfounded assumption that immigrants were lured to the United States by generous public services influenced
provisions of a 1996 welfare reform act (see page 497), which severely curtailed legal immigrants' access to welfare benefits, especially food stamps. Also
in 1996 Congress enacted legislation that increased the financial requirements
for sponsors of new immigrants.

The most dramatic challenges to immigrants have emerged on the state level. In the 1980s California absorbed far more immigrants than any other state: more than a third of its population growth in that decade came from foreign immigration. In 1994 California voters overwhelmingly approved Proposition 187, a ballot initiative provocatively named "Save Our State," which barred undocumented aliens from public schools, nonemergency care at public health clinics, and all other state social services. The initiative also required law enforcement officers, school administrators, and social workers to report suspected illegal immigrants to the Immigration and Naturalization Service. Though opponents challenged the constitutionality of Proposition 187, anti-immigrant feeling soon spread to other parts of the country, becoming a hotly debated issue in the 1996 election.

Though the National Academy of Sciences report did find that "some black workers have lost their jobs to immigrants," for the most part African-Americans were not adversely affected by the new immigration. But urban African-Americans and new immigrants were forced by economic necessity and entrenched segregation patterns to fight for space in decaying, crime-ridden, ghettos, where unemployment rates sometimes hit 60 percent. Overcrowded and underfunded, inner city schools had fallen into disrepair and were unable to provide a proper education.

In April 1992 the frustration and anger of impoverished urban Americans erupted in five days of race riots in Los Angeles. The worst civil disorder since the 1960s, the violence took sixty lives and caused $850 million in damage. The riot was set off by the acquittal on all but one charge of four white Los Angeles police officers accused of using excessive force in arresting a black motorist, Rodney King, the year before. A graphic eighty-one-second amateur video showing the policemen kicking, clubbing, and beating King had not swayed the predominantly white jury. Three of the officers were later convicted on federal civil-rights charges.

The Los Angeles riot exposed the cleavages in urban neighborhoods. Trapped in the nation's inner cities, many blacks resented recent immigrants who were struggling to get ahead, and often succeeding. As a result, some blacks had targeted Korean-owned stores during the arson and looting. Latinos were also frustrated by high unemployment and crowded housing conditions. According to the Los Angeles Police Department, Latinos accounted for more than half of those arrested and a third of those killed during the rioting. Thus the riots were not simply a case of black rage at white injustice; they contained a strong element of class-based protest against the failure of the American system to address the needs of all poor people.

One of the ways federal and state governments had tried to help poor blacks and Latinos was through the establishment of affirmative action programs in government hiring, contracts, and university admissions. From the inception of affirmative action programs in 1965 and their extension in 1967 to include women, many white men had viewed them as unfair and discriminatory. But affirmative action remained official government policy until the 1990s, when white resentment deepened against the "rights revolution" (see Chapter 32) and fueled renewed debate on the issue.

The impact of affirmative action was most evident in college admissions. In 1994, the student population at the University of California, Berkeley campus was 39 percent Asian, 32 percent white, 14 percent Latino, 6 percent black, and 1 percent native American (8 percent of students did not identify their race). In 1995, under pressure from the Republican governor, Pete Wilson, the Regents of the University of California voted to scrap the university's twenty-year-old policy of affirmative action, despite protests from the faculty and from university presidents. In the November 1996 elections, the struggle over affirmative action was intensified by California's passage of Proposition 209, which banned all preference based on race or gender. As appeals worked their way through the federal courts, and black and Latino enrollments declined, the University of California actively sought new admissions criteria that would circumvent the restrictions imposed by Proposition 209.

One reason affirmative action became a political issue in the 1990s was that many, including prominent conservatives like George F. Will, William Bennett, and Patrick Buchanan, saw it as a threat to core American values. Simplistically lumping affirmative action together with multiculturalism—the attempt to represent the diversity of American society and its peoples—critics feared that all this counting by race, gender, sexual preference, and age would lead to a "balkanization," or fragmentation, of American society. Attempts to revise American history textbooks along multicultural lines aroused much anger, as did efforts by universities such as Stanford to revise college curricula to include the study of non-European cultures. Conservatives also took aim at the antiracist and antisexist regulations and speech codes that had been adopted by many colleges. Under the guise of protecting First Amendment rights, conservatives derided the attempt to regulate hate speech as politically correct (PC).

Other Culture Wars: Women and Gays

Conservative critics also targeted the women's movement. In the widely read *Backlash: The Undeclared War on American Women* (1991), the journalist Susan Faludi described a powerful reaction against the gains American women had won in the 1960s and 1970s. Spearheaded by New Right leaders and aided by the media, conservatives held the women's movement responsible for every ill afflicting modern women, from infertility to rising divorce rates; yet polls showed strong support for many feminist demands, including equal pay, reproductive rights, and a more equitable distribution of household and child-care responsibilities.

The deep national divide over abortion, one of the main issues associated with feminism, continued to polarize the country. In the 1980s and 1990s harassment and violence toward those who sought or provided abortions became common. In 1994 four workers were murdered at Boston abortion clinics. Although only a fraction of antiabortion activists supported such extreme acts, disruptive confrontational tactics had made receiving what was still a woman's legal right more dangerous.

Gay rights was another field of battle. As gays and lesbians gained legal protection against housing and job discrimination across the country, Pat Robertson, North Carolina senator Jesse Helms, and others denounced these civil-rights gains as undeserved "special rights." To conservatives, gay rights threatened America's traditional family values. In 1992 Coloradans passed a referendum (overturned by the Supreme Court in 1996) that barred local jurisdictions from passing ordinances protecting gays and lesbians. Across the nation, "gay bashing" and other forms of violence against homosexuals continued. But in 1997, when the comedian Ellen DeGeneres "came out" on national TV in both her real life and sitcom persona, "Ellen," it marked a victory for homosexuals and a blow to conservative watchdogs.

A grim backdrop to gay men's struggle against discrimination was the AIDS epidemic. Acquired immune deficiency syndrome (AIDS) was first recognized by physicians in 1981, and its cause identified as the human immunodeficiency virus (HIV). At first little government funding was directed toward AIDS research or treatment; critics charged that the lack of attention to the syndrome reflected society's antipathy toward gay men, the earliest victims of the disease. Only when heterosexuals, such as hemophiliacs who had received the virus through blood transfusions, began to be affected did AIDS begin to gain significant public attention. The death of the film star Rock

ACT UP
This poster *Untitled* (1989) by artist Keith Haring for the group ACT UP (AIDS Coalition to Unleash Power) was used to mobilize public action against the deadly disease, which would later claim Haring's life.

An Age of Anxiety

Hudson from AIDS in 1985 finally broke the barrier of public apathy. Another galvanizing moment came in 1991, when the basketball great Earvin "Magic" Johnson announced that he was HIV-positive.

As early as the mid-1980s, AIDS cases had begun to increase among heterosexuals, especially intravenous drug addicts and their sexual partners, as well as bisexuals. Women now constitute the group with the fastest-growing incidence of HIV infection. To date, more Americans have died of AIDS than were killed in the Korean and Vietnam wars combined. Between 1996 and 1997, however, deaths from AIDs in the United States dropped 19 percent. This decline—the result of new treatment strategies using a combination of drugs, or a "cocktail"—has led to cautious optimism about controlling the disease, though scientists warn that the drugs have not been effective for between 30 and 50 percent of patients.

Popular Culture and Popular Technology

Image was everything in the 1980s and 1990s—or so commentators said, pointing to rock stars Michael Jackson and Madonna, and even to President Reagan. One strong influence on popular culture was MTV, which premiered in 1981. With its creative choreography, flashy colors, and rapid cuts, it seemed perfect for a generation raised on "Sesame Street." The MTV style soon showed up in mainstream media and even political campaigns, which adapted the 30-second sound bites common on television news shows to their own purposes. The national newspaper *USA Today*, which debuted in 1982, adapted the style, featuring eye-catching graphics, color photographs, and short, easy-to-read articles. Soon more staid newspapers followed suit. At the same time, new technology, especially satellite transmission and live "mini-cam" broadcasting, reshaped the television industry. Also new was the increased availability of cable and satellite dishes. By the mid-1990s viewers could choose from well over a hundred channels, including upstarts such as Ted Turner's Cable News Network (CNN) and the Entertainment Sports Network (ESPN), an all-sports channel. Media, communications, and entertainment were big business, increasingly drawn into global financial networks, markets, and mergers.

Technology also reshaped the home in the late twentieth century. The 1980s saw the introduction of videocassette recorders (VCRs), compact disc (CD) players, cellular phones, and inexpensive fax machines. By 1993 more than three-quarters of American households had VCRs. Video was everywhere—stores, airplanes, tennis courts, operating rooms. With the introduction of camcorders, the family photo album could be supplemented by a video of a high school graduation, a marriage, or a birth.

But it was the personal computer that revolutionized both the home and office. The big breakthrough came in 1977 when the upstart Apple Computer Company offered the Apple II personal computer for $1,195—a price middle-class Americans could afford. When the Apple II became a runaway success, other companies scrambled to get into the market. IBM offered its first personal computer in the summer of 1981. Software companies such as Microsoft, whose founder, Bill Gates, is now the richest person in America, grew rapidly by providing operating systems and other software for the expanding personal computer market. In 1995, 37 percent of American households had at least one personal computer.

More than any other technological advance, the computer created the modern electronic office. Even the smallest business could keep all its records, and do all its correspondence, billing, and other business on a single desktop machine. The very concept of the office was changing as a new class of telecommuters worked at home via computer, fax machine, and electronic mail.

Today, new technologies utilizing fiberoptics, microwave relays, and satellites can transmit massive quantities of information to and from almost any place on earth, and even in outer space, via the *information superhighway*. By 1996, 40 million people in the United States alone used the Internet, and experts predict that by the year 2000 more than 250 million people in over 170 countries will have access to cyberspace. At first scientists and other professionals, who communicated with their peers through electronic mail (*E-mail*) were the primary users of the Internet. But the debut of the World Wide Web in 1991 enhanced the commercial possibilities of the Internet. The Web allowed companies, organizations, political campaigns, and even the White House to create their own "home pages," incorporating both visual and textual information. Although theoretically available to all, the glories of cyberspace are still available mostly to those who can afford them: in 1997 65 percent of Americans who used the Internet had incomes of $50,000 or more. The trend toward wiring public schools and libraries, however, should significantly increase access to the new technology.

The Environmental Movement at Twenty-five

Americans'—and increasingly the world's—love affair with technology continued to be tempered by the recognition that industrial development and economic growth had environmental consequences. On April 26, 1995, when Americans came together for the twenty-fifth anniversary of Earth Day, they had much to celebrate. The nation's rivers and waterways were cleaner; air pollution had been reduced by a third; and lead emissions from fuel, a cause of retardation in children, had been cut by an astounding 98 percent. The bald eagle and the California condor had come back from the brink of extinction. More than 6,000 communities across the country had established recycling programs.

There still was much to be done. Despite efforts to reduce urban smog, two out of five Americans lived in areas with unhealthy air. Many rivers and lakes were still unsafe for fishing and swimming. And one out of four Americans lived within 4 miles of toxic waste dumps, a trend with disproportionate effect on lower-income communities, which constituted what activists termed *environmental racism*.

In addition to addressing problems in their own communities, Americans were also becoming increasingly aware that the environment required action not just from the United States but from the global community as a whole. Three pressing environmental problems demanded international attention: the depletion of the ozone layer, acid rain, and global warming. An important precedent for international action on environmental issues was set by the Montreal Protocol (1987), in which thirty-four nations agreed to phase out ozone-damaging chlorofluorocarbons (CFCs) by 1999. In June 1992 delegates to the Earth Summit in Rio de Janeiro adopted a treaty on global warming, and in 1994 the United States joined sixty-three other countries in signing the Basel Convention, which banned the export of hazardous wastes from industrialized to developing countries. In the future, U.S. environmental policy would operate more and more within an international framework.

THE CLINTON PRESIDENCY: PUBLIC LIFE SINCE 1993

If Americans hoped to make progress on the environment, the faltering economy, and the deep social cleavages surrounding race, gender, and sexual orientation, they would need strong leadership. Yet, low voter turnout in the 1992 presidential election signaled deep dissatisfaction with the American political system. The strong showing of the independent candidate Ross Perot that year, and the early support for the conservative Republican Pat Buchanan four years later, reflected Americans' disenchantment with the two major parties. In the administration of Bill Clinton, their disaffection helped to continue the rollback of federal power begun by Reagan and Bush.

The Clinton Years

As the 1992 election campaign got under way, the economy was the overriding issue, for the recession that had begun in 1990 showed no sign of abating. Bush easily won renomination as the Republican candidate. To solidify the support of the New Right, his running mate, Dan Quayle, spoke out strongly for "family values" and other conservative social agendas. Bill Clinton, the long-time governor of Arkansas, survived charges of marital infidelity and draft dodging, as well as questions about a dubious Arkansas real estate deal called Whitewater, to win the Democratic nomination. For his running mate he chose Al Gore, a second-term senator from Tennessee. At age forty-four, Gore was a year and a half younger than Clinton, making the two men the first of the baby-boom generation to occupy the national ticket.

In the middle of the primary season, the Texas billionaire H. Ross Perot, capitalizing on voters' desire for a change from politics as usual, announced he would run as an independent candidate. Although Perot dropped out of the race on the last day of the Democratic convention, he reentered it less than five weeks before the election, adding a well-financed wild card to an unusual election year.

The Democrats mounted an effective, aggressive campaign that highlighted Clinton's plans to solve domestic problems, especially education, health care, and the economy. Gore added expertise on defense and environmental issues. Bush was hurt by the weak economy, and especially by his reneging on the "No New Taxes" pledge. On election day Clinton received 43 percent of the popular vote to Bush's 38 percent and Perot's 19 percent. Although Perot did not win a single state, his popular vote was the highest for an independent candidate since Theodore Roosevelt's in 1912. The Democrats retained control of both houses of Congress, ending twelve years of divided government. But the narrowness of Clinton's victory, and the public's perception that he did not really stand for anything, did not augur well for his ability to lead the country.

The liberals who supported Clinton hoped that a Democratic presidency could erase the Reagan-Bush legacy and oversee the creation of a new democratic social agenda. Initially, Clinton seemed to fulfill that promise. In 1993 he nominated the liberal Ruth Bader Ginsberg for a seat on the Supreme Court; she was confirmed. The president also appointed Janet Reno as attorney general—the first woman to hold that post. Other trailblazing cabinet appointments included Secretary of Health and Human Services Donna E. Shalala, and, in Clinton's second term, Secretary of State Madeline Albright. Clinton chose an African-American, Ron Brown, as secretary of commerce, and two Latinos, Henry Cisneros and Frederico Peña, to head the Department of Housing and Urban Development (HUD) and the Department of Transportation, respectively.

Clinton's early legislative and administrative record was mixed. In early 1993 he signed into law the Family and Medical Leave Act, twice vetoed by Bush, which provided workers with up to twelve weeks of unpaid leave to tend to a newborn or an adopted child or to respond to a family medical emergency. But when Clinton tried to implement a campaign promise to lift the ban on gays serving in the armed forces, he ran into such ferocious opposition that he backed off, offering a weak compromise policy—"Don't ask, don't tell, don't pursue"—instead. The solution was an ineffective palliative at best, one that called into question Clinton's willingness to stand firm on issues of principle.

By the time Clinton took office, the economy had pulled out of the 1990 recession, enabling him to focus on other economic issues, especially the opening of foreign markets to U.S. goods. In 1992 President Bush had signed the North American Free Trade Agreement (NAFTA), in which the United States, Canada, and Mexico agreed to create a free-trade zone covering all of North America. Strongly supported by the business community, NAFTA was bitterly opposed by labor unions worried about the loss of jobs to lower-paid Mexican workers, and by environmentalists concerned about the weak enforcement of antipollution laws south of the border. Nonetheless, with Clinton's support, Congress narrowly passed NAFTA in November 1993. Another major development in international trade was the revision in 1994 of the General Agreement on Tariffs and Trade (GATT), which had been created at the end of World War II. The new provisions cut tariffs on many manufactured products and for the first time established regulations protecting intellectual property such as patents; copyrights; and trademarks on software, entertainment, and pharmaceuticals.

With the recession over, crime replaced the economy as a major concern among voters. In 1993 Congress passed the Brady Handgun Violence Prevention Act, over the opposition of the National Rifle Association. A much more wide-ranging piece of legislation was the Omnibus Violent Crime Control and Prevention Act (1994), which authorized $30.2 billion for stepped-up law enforcement, crime prevention, and prison construction and administration. The act also extended the death penalty to more than fifty federal crimes, and banned the sale and possession of certain kinds of assault weapons.

Responding to the deep anxieties Americans had about their economic security, Clinton had staked his political fortunes on his campaign promise of universal health care. Though the United States spent more on health care than any other country in the world, it remained the only major industrialized country not to provide national health insurance to all. Furthermore, spiraling medical costs and rising insurance premiums had brought the health-care system to a crisis.

The president chose his wife, Hillary Rodham Clinton, to head the task force that would draft the legislation—a controversial move since no first lady had ever played a formal role in policy making. The resulting proposal was based on the idea of managed competition: market forces, not the government, would control health-care costs and expand citizen's access to health care. But even this mild form of social engineering ran into intense opposition from the well-financed pharmaceutical and insurance industries. By September 1994 congressional leaders were admitting that health reform was dead. In 1995 an estimated 40.3 million Americans—over 17 percent of the population under sixty-five—had no health insurance, and experts predicted that these statistics would climb.

Clinton seems never to have had the time to devote his full attention to pushing health reform through Congress. Three days before assuming office he had to commit his support to a missile attack President Bush had ordered on Iraq. In February foreign terrorists bombed the World Trade Center in New York City, and in April, FBI agents made a misguided assault on the Branch Davidian compound in Waco, Texas. At the White House in September, Israeli Prime Minister Yitzhak Rabin and Yasir Arafat, chairman of the Palestine Liberation Organization, signed an agreement allowing limited Palestinian self-rule in the Gaza Strip and Jericho. In October 1993, just after Clinton announced his health plan, twelve American soldiers were killed on a United Nations peacekeeping mission in Somalia. Constantly shifting from crisis to crisis, Clinton appeared to the American public to be vacillating, indecisive, and lacking in vision, especially in his handling of foreign affairs.

In the former Soviet Union, the increasing unpopularity of the Russian president Boris Yeltsin, who was trying to bring about fundamental market reforms, made American leaders less optimistic about the chances for democracy in that country. Yeltsin's harsh repression of dissent in the breakaway region of Chechnya strained Russia's already difficult relationship with the United States.

Nothing seemed more intractable than the problems that engulfed the former state of Yugoslavia, which had broken into five independent states in 1991. The province of Bosnia and Herzegovina, made up largely of Muslims and committed to a multiethnic state—Serb, Croat, and Muslim—had declared its independence in 1992. But Bosnian Serbs, supported financially and militarily by what remained of Yugoslavia, formed their own breakaway state, and began a siege of the Bosnian capital, Sarajevo. In the countryside the Serbs launched a ruthless campaign of "ethnic cleansing," driving Bosnian Muslims and Croats from their homes and into concentration camps, or shooting them to death in mass executions. More than 250,000 people were killed or reported missing after the outbreak of war in April 1992. After three years of unsuccessful efforts by the European powers to stop the carnage, President Clinton and Secretary of State Warren Christopher facilitated a peace accord in November 1995. A NATO-led peacekeeping force, backed by U.S. troops, would end the fighting, at least temporarily.

At the same time, the end of cold war superpower rivalry presented unexpected opportunities to resolve other longstanding conflicts. In Haiti, the threat of a U.S. invasion in October 1993 led to the restoration of the exiled president, Jean-Bertrand Aristide, who had been ousted by a military coup in 1991. In South Africa, the end of a fifty-year policy of racial separation was capped by the election of the rebel leader Nelson Mandela, who had spent twenty-seven years in prison for challenging apartheid, as the country's first black president in May 1994. And in a move that was seen as the symbolic end to the American experience in Vietnam, the United States established diplomatic relations with Hanoi in July 1995, two decades after the fall of Saigon.

"The Era of Big Government Is Over"

In the 1994 midterm elections, Republicans gained 52 seats in the House of Representatives, which gave them a majority in the House as well as the Senate. In the House, the centerpiece of the new Republican majority was the "Contract with America," a list of proposals that Newt Gingrich of Georgia, the new Speaker of the House, vowed would be voted on in the first 100 days of the new session. The contract included constitutional amendments to balance the budget and set term limits for congressional office; $245 billion in tax cuts for individuals, and tax incentives for small businesses; cuts in welfare and other entitlement programs; anticrime initiatives, and cutbacks in federal regulations. President Clinton, bowing to political reality, acknowledged in his State of the Union message in January 1996 that "the era of big government is over."

But the Republicans were frustrated in their commitment to cut taxes and balance the budget by the year 2002, because both practical and political considerations made many items in the budget immune to serious reductions. Interest on the national debt had to be paid. Defense spending had declined only slightly in the post–cold war world. That left Medicare and Medicaid, Social Security, and all other government programs. Since Social Security was considered untouchable, Congress looked to health care and discretionary spending for savings.

In the fall of 1995 Congress passed a budget that cut $270 billion from projected spending on Medicare, and $170 billion from spending on Medicaid over the next seven years. Other savings came from cuts in discretionary programs, including education and the environment. Clinton accepted Congress's resolve to balance the budget in seven years but, vowing to protect the nation from an "extremist" Congress, vetoed the budget itself. In the standoff that followed, nonessential departments of the government were forced to shut down twice for lack of funding, but polls showed that a majority of Americans held Congress, not the president, responsible. The budget that Clinton finally signed in April 1996 left Medicare and Social Security intact, though it did meet the Republicans' goal of cutting $23 billion from discretionary spending.

As part of the Contract with America, House Republicans were especially determined to cut welfare, a joint federal-state program that represented a fairly small part of the budget. To Republicans, the program had become a prime example of misguided government priorities. The benefits of the main welfare program, Aid for Dependent Children (AFDC), were far from generous: the average annual welfare payment to families (including Food Stamps) was $7,740, well below the established poverty line. Still, in the 1990s both Democratic and Republican statehouses sought ways to change the behavior of welfare recipients by imposing work requirements or denying benefits for additional children born to women on AFDC. In August 1996, after vetoing two Republican-authored bills, President Clinton, who had campaigned on a promise of welfare reform, signed into law the Personal Responsibility and Work Opportunity Act, a historic overhaul of federal entitlements. The 1996 law ended the federal guarantee of cash assistance to poor children by abolishing AFDC; required most adult recipients to find work within two years; set a five-year limit on payments to any one family; and gave states wide discretion in running their welfare programs.

The Republican takeover of Congress had one unintended consequence: it united the usually fractious Democrats behind the president. Unopposed in the 1996 primaries, Clinton was able to burnish his image as a moderate "New Democrat." His political fortunes were aided by the unpopularity of the Republican Congress following the government shutdowns. He also benefited from the continuing strength of the economy. Economic indicators released shortly before election day painted a promising picture. The "misery index"—a combination of the unemployment rate and inflation—was the lowest it had been in twenty-seven years.

The Republicans settled on Senate Majority Leader Bob Dole of Kansas as their presidential candidate. Acceptable to both the conservative and the moderate wings of the party, Dole had a detached campaign style that failed to generate much enthusiasm. He made a 15 percent across-the-board tax cut the centerpiece of his campaign, and selected former representative Jack Kemp, a leading proponent of supply-side economics, as his running mate.

Americans seemed to have made up their minds early about the candidates, which made for a rather desultory campaign. Clinton emphasized his success in reducing the budget deficit, raising the minimum wage to $5.15 an hour, and reforming welfare, and he took credit for the 10 million new jobs created during his first term. In November, Clinton became the first Democratic president since Franklin Roosevelt to win reelection. Voter turnout was the lowest since Calvin Coolidge won the presidency in 1924. Republicans retained control in a majority of the nation's statehouses and in the House of Representatives, and increased their majority in the Senate. Thus a key factor in Bill Clinton's second term would be the necessity, as a Democratic president working with a Republican-dominated Congress, of pursuing bipartisan policies or facing complete stalemate.

In his 1998 state of the union address, Bill Clinton outlined an impressive program of federal spending for schools, tax credits for child care, a hike in the minimum wage, and protection for the beleaguered social security system. His ability to pursue this domestic agenda was seriously compromised, however, by two crises. One revolved around an issue that had plagued him since 1992: allegations of sexual misconduct. In January 1998, attorneys representing Paula Jones, who claimed that the then governor Clinton had propositioned her when she was an Arkansas state employee, revealed that they planned to depose a former White House intern, Monica Lewinsky, about an alleged affair with President Clinton. Kenneth Starr, the independent counsel initially charged with investigating the Whitewater scandal, widened his investigation to explore whether Clinton or his aides had encouraged Lewinsky to lie in her statement. Predictably, a media frenzy—and even speculation about impeachment—ensued. Ironically, Clinton's approval rating remained exceptionally high, perhaps because Americans doubted the political motives of his attackers, and almost certainly because a strong economy kept most citizens content with the President's performance. Whatever the outcome of the investigation, the scandal detracted attention from more pressing domestic issues.

A second crisis was far more serious. The 1991 defeat of Iraq in Operation Desert Storm and the United Nation's imposition of economic sanctions left Saddam Hussein in power. In late 1997 Hussein challenged the authority of the U.N. to inspect Iraqi sites in search of hidden weapons "of mass destruction," which included nuclear, biological, and chemical warfare materials.

Domestic Terrorism
On April 19, 1995, a powerful car bomb exploded outside the Alfred P. Murrah Federal Building in Oklahoma City, killing 168 people, including nineteen children in the building's day-
care center. Antigovernment hostility was suspected as a possible motive of the two accused
bombers, Timothy McVeigh and Terry Nichols.

When Hussein ejected American members of the U.N. inspection team in
October, the United States, with limited international support, began a military buildup in the Gulf. The threatened air strike against Iraq was averted
when U.N. Secretary-General Kofi Annan went to Baghdad and brokered an
agreement that allowed Hussein to save face. The U.N. inspection teams
would have unrestricted access to all suspected weapon sites, but would be accompanied by diplomatic representatives. Although the threat of force accomplished the short term goal of permitting U.N. weapons inspectors to
continue their task, it neither assured the world that Hussein's "weapons of
mass destruction" could be discovered and destroyed nor undercut Hussein's
regime. The crisis served as a potent reminder that despite its position as the
most powerful nation in the world, the United States was limited in its ability
to achieve its foreign policy aims.

Making Sense of the Late Twentieth Century

In 1995 the *New York Times* asked readers to choose a name for the time
they were living in. Perhaps not surprisingly, the responses were fairly pes-

simistic, often including words such as *uncertainty, fragmentation*, and *disillusionment*. Reflecting the importance of new technology, one reader suggested the Silicon Age; another submitted *Kokusaika* (Japanese for "internationalization"), arguing that a non-English word would best capture the internationalization of economics, politics, culture, and society in the late twentieth century.

Indeed, the period since 1980 has brought enormous changes: the end of the four-decade Cold War; a dramatic rethinking of the role of the state in modern American life; the growing globalization of political and economic life; and a growing diversity in American culture and public affairs. The last fifteen years of the twentieth century will probably turn out to have been as important a period of realignment as the 1930s and 1940s, when the New Deal state was formed and the United States took on global responsibilities. These times are certainly as dramatic as the 1890s, when the nation completed the process of industrialization, absorbed a huge wave of immigrants, and secured an overseas empire.

Several themes from twentieth-century American history will certainly endure into the twenty-first. By the late 1990s the United States had dramatically improved its position in the world economy, but nonetheless decisions made beyond the United States continued to affect the daily lives of American workers, managers, and consumers. A startling 554-point drop in the stock market in November 1997—in part a reaction to severe economic crises in several Asian countries—served as a potent reminder of just how interconnected the global economy had become. With trade barriers falling and the Internet opening the entire world to instant communication, national boundaries and economies will become increasingly less important.

In the international political arena, the world appears to be returning to a situation in which power, both economic and military, is dispersed among a number of key players, of which the United States is the most preponderant. However, as the showdown in Iraq suggests, the nation's dominance in the new world order is offset by the limits to its power. Permanent peace in the Persian Gulf or in other hot spots will undoubtedly prove elusive.

Finally, in politics, a significant shift has occurred in the ways that Americans and their leaders seem to be thinking about government and the political system. Decisions made in the mid 1990s will probably ensure that the federal deficit will be tamed, at least temporarily, and the size of government reduced. But given all the challenges the nation will face at home and abroad, it is far too soon to declare an end to the activist American state. All that can be predicted with any assurance in that the dramatic late twentieth-century changes in domestic and world realities will shape the future of the United States and the globe in the twenty-first century and beyond.

CHAPTER 33 TIMELINE

1981	Economic Recovery Tax Act
	Sandra Day O'Connor nominated to Supreme Court
	MTV premieres
	Beginning of AIDS epidemic
1981–1982	Recession
1983	Star Wars proposed
1984	Geraldine Ferraro runs for vice-president
1985	Gramm-Rudman Act
1986	Iran-Contra scandal
	Immigration Reform and Control Act
1987	Montreal protocol
	Stock market collapse
1988	George Bush elected president
1989	*Webster v. Reproductive Health Services*
1990–1991	Persian Gulf War
1990–1992	Recession
1991	Dissolution of Soviet Union ends Cold War
	Clarence Thomas–Anita Hill hearings
1992	Los Angeles riots
	Bill Clinton elected president
1993	North American Free Trade Agreement (NAFTA) ratified
1994	Health-care reform fails
	Republicans gain control of Congress
1995	Congress passes parts of the Contract with America
	University of California Regents vote to end affirmative action
	Twenty-fifth anniversary of Earth Day
	U.S. troops enforce peace in Bosnia
1996	Personal Responsibility and Work Opportunity Act
	Bill Clinton reelected president

DOCUMENTS

THE DECLARATION OF INDEPENDENCE

The Unanimous Declaration of the Thirteen United States of America

When in the Course of human events, it becomes necessary for one people to dissolve the political bands which have connected them with another, and to assume among the Powers of the earth, the separate and equal station to which the Laws of Nature and of Nature's God entitle them, a decent respect to the opinions of mankind requires that they should declare the causes which impel them to the separation.

We hold these truths to be self-evident, that all men are created equal, that they are endowed by their Creator with certain unalienable rights, that among these are Life, Liberty, and the pursuit of Happiness. That to secure these rights, Governments are instituted among Men, deriving their just powers from the consent of the governed. That whenever any Form of Government becomes destructive of these ends, it is the Right of the People to alter or to abolish it, and to institute new Government, laying its foundation on such principles and organizing its powers in such form, as to them shall seem most likely to effect their Safety and Happiness. Prudence, indeed, will dictate that Governments long established should not be changed for light and transient causes; and accordingly all experience hath shown, that mankind are more disposed to suffer, while evils are sufferable, than to right themselves by abolishing the forms to which they are accustomed. But when a long train of abuses and usurpations, pursuing invariably the same Object evinces a design to reduce them under absolute Despotism, it is their right, it is their duty, to throw off such Government, and to provide new Guards for their future security.—Such has been the patient sufferance of these Colonies; and such is now the necessity which constrains them to alter their former Systems of Government. The history of the present King of Great Britain is a history of repeated injuries and usurpations, all having in direct object the establishment of an absolute Tyranny over these States. To prove this, let Facts be submitted to a candid world.

He has refused his Assent to Laws, the most wholesome and necessary for the public good.

He has forbidden his Governors to pass Laws of immediate and pressing importance, unless suspended in their operation till his Assent should be obtained; and, when so suspended, he has utterly neglected to attend to them.

He has refused to pass other Laws for the accommodation of large districts of people, unless those people would relinquish the right of Representation in the Legislature, a right inestimable to them and formidable to tyrants only.

He has called together legislative bodies at places unusual, uncomfortable, and distant from the depository of their public Records, for the sole purpose of fatiguing them into compliance with his measures.

He has dissolved Representative Houses repeatedly, for opposing with manly firmness his invasions on the rights of the people.

He has refused for a long time, after such dissolutions, to cause others to be elected; whereby the Legislative powers, incapable of Annihilation, have returned to the People at large for their exercise; the State remaining in the mean time exposed to all the dangers of invasion from without and convulsions within.

He has endeavoured to prevent the population of these States; for that purpose obstructing the Laws of Naturalization of Foreigners; refusing to pass others to encourage their migrations hither, and raising the conditions of new Appropriations of Lands.

He has obstructed the Administration of Justice, by refusing his Assent to Laws for establishing Judiciary powers.

He has made Judges dependent on his Will alone, for the tenure of their offices, and the amount and payment of their salaries.

He has erected a multitude of New Offices, and sent hither swarms of Officers to harass our People, and eat out their substance.

He has kept among us, in times of peace, Standing Armies without the Consent of our legislature.

He has combined with others to subject us to a jurisdiction foreign to our constitution, and unacknowledged by our laws; giving his Assent to their Acts of pretended Legislation:

For quartering large bodies of armed troops among us:

For protecting them, by a mock Trial, from Punishment for any Murders which they should commit on the Inhabitants of these States:

For cutting off our Trade with all parts of the world:

For imposing taxes on us without our Consent:

For depriving us of many cases, of the benefits of Trial by jury:

For transporting us beyond Seas to be tried for pretended offences:

For abolishing the free System of English Laws in a neighbouring Province, establishing therein an Arbitrary government, and enlarging its Boundaries so as to render it at once an example and fit instrument for introducing the same absolute rule into these Colonies:

For taking away our Charters, abolishing our most valuable Laws, and altering fundamentally the Forms of our Governments:

For suspending our own Legislatures, and declaring themselves invested with Power to legislate for us in all cases whatsoever.

He has abdicated Government here, by declaring us out of his Protection and waging War against us.

He has plundered our seas, ravaged our Coasts, burnt our towns, and destroyed the lives of our people.

He is at this time transporting large armies of foreign mercenaries to compleat the works of death, desolation, and tyranny, already begun with circumstances of Cruelty & perfidy scarcely paralleled in the most barbarous ages, and totally unworthy the Head of a civilized nation.

He has constrained our fellow Citizens taken Captive on the high Seas to bear Arms against their Country, to become the executioners of their friends and Brethren, or to fall themselves by their Hands.

He has excited domestic insurrections amongst us, and has endeavoured to bring on the inhabitants of our frontiers, the merciless Indian Savages, whose known rule of warfare, is an undistinguished destruction of all ages, sexes, and conditions.

In every stage of these Oppressions We have Petitioned for Redress in the most humble terms: Our repeated Petitions have been answered only by repeated injury. A Prince, whose character is thus marked by every act which may define a Tyrant, is unfit to be the ruler of a free people.

Nor have We been wanting in attention to our British brethren. We have warned them from time to time of attempts by their legislature to extend an unwarrantable jurisdiction over us. We have reminded them of the circumstances of our emigration and settlement here. We have appealed to their native justice and magnanimity, and we have conjured them by the ties of our common kindred to disavow these usurpations, which, would inevitably interrupt our connections and correspondence. They too have been deaf to the voice of justice and of consanguinity. We must, therefore, acquiesce in the necessity, which denounces our Separation, and hold them, as we hold the rest of mankind, Enemies in War, in Peace Friends.

We, therefore, the Representatives of the United States of America, in General Congress, Assembled, appealing to the Supreme Judge of the world for the rectitude of our intentions, do, in the Name, and by Authority of the good People of these Colonies, solemnly publish and declare, That these United Colonies are, and of Right ought to be FREE AND INDEPENDENT STATES; that they are Absolved from all Allegiance to the British Crown, and that all political connection between them and the State of Great Britain, is and ought to be totally dissolved; and that as Free and Independent States, they have full Power to levy War, conclude Peace, contract Alliances, establish Commerce, and to do all other Acts and Things which Independent States may of right do. And for the support of this Declaration, with a firm reliance on the Protection of Divine Providence, we mutually pledge to each other our Lives, our Fortunes, and our sacred Honor.

John Hancock

Button Gwinnett	George Wythe	James Wilson	Josiah Bartlett
Lyman Hall	Richard Henry Lee	Geo. Ross	Wm. Whipple
Geo. Walton	Th. Jefferson	Caesar Rodney	Saml. Adams
Wm. Hooper	Benja. Harrison	Geo. Read	John Adams
Joseph Hewes	Thos. Nelson, Jr.	Thos. M'Kean	Robt. Treat Paine
John Penn	Francis Lightfoot Lee	Wm. Floyd	Elbridge Gerry
Edward Rutledge	Carter Braxton	Phil. Livingston	Step. Hopkins
Thos. Heyward, Junr.	Robt. Morris	Frans. Lewis	William Ellery
Thomas Lynch, Junr.	Benjamin Rush	Lewis Morris	Roger Sherman
Arthur Middleton	Benja. Franklin	Richd. Stockton	Sam'el Hunington
Samuel Chase	John Morton	Jno. Witherspoon	Wm. Williams
Wm. Paca	Geo. Clymer	Fras. Hopkinson	Oliver Wolcott
Thos. Stone	Jas. Smith	John Hart	Matthew Thornton
Charles Carroll	Geo. Taylor	Abra. Clark	
of Carrollton			

THE CONSTITUTION OF THE UNITED STATES

We the People of the United States, in Order to form a more perfect Union, establish Justice, insure domestic Tranquility, provide for the common defence, promote the general Welfare, and secure the Blessings of Liberty to ourselves and our Posterity, do ordain and establish this Constitution for the United States of America.

Article I

Section 1

All legislative Powers herein granted shall be vested in a Congress of the United States, which shall consist of a Senate and a House of Representatives.

Section 2

The House of Representatives shall be composed of Members chosen every second Year by the People of the several States, and the Electors in each State shall have the Qualifications requisite for Electors of the most numerous Branch of the State Legislature.

No Person shall be a Representative who shall not have attained to the Age of twenty-five Years, and been seven Years a Citizen of the United States, and who shall not, when elected, be an Inhabitant of that State in which he shall be chosen.

Representatives and direct Taxes shall be apportioned among the several States which may be included within this Union, according to their respective Numbers, *which shall be determined by adding to the whole Number of free Persons, including those bound to Service for a Term of Years, and excluding Indians not taxed, three fifths of all other Persons.** The actual Enumeration shall be made within three Years after the first Meeting of the Congress of the United States, and within every subsequent Term of ten Years, in such Manner as they shall by Law direct. The Number of Representatives shall not exceed one for every thirty Thousand, but each State shall have at Least one Representative; and *until such enumeration shall be made, the State of New Hampshire shall be entitled to chuse three, Massachusetts eight, Rhode Island and Providence Plantations one, Connecticut five, New-York six, New Jersey four, Pennsylvania eight, Delaware one, Maryland six, Virginia ten, North Carolina five, South Carolina five, and Georgia three.*

Note: The Constitution became effective March 4, 1789. Provisions in italics have been changed by constitutional amendment.

*Changed by Section 2 of the Fourteenth Amendment.

When vacancies happen in the Representation from any State, the Executive Authority thereof shall issue Writs of Election to fill such Vacancies.

The House of Representatives shall chuse their Speaker and other Officers; and shall have the sole Power of Impeachment.

Section 3

The Senate of the United States shall be composed of two Senators from each State, *chosen by the Legislature thereof,*[†] for six Years; and each Senator shall have one Vote.

Immediately after they shall be assembled in Consequence of the first Election, they shall be divided as equally as may be into three Classes. The Seats of the Senators of the first Class shall be vacated at the Expiration of the second Year, of the second Class at the Expiration of the fourth Year, and of the third Class at the Expiration of the sixth Year, so that one-third may be chosen every second Year; *and if Vacancies happen by Resignation, or otherwise, during the Recess of the Legislature of any State, the Executive thereof may make temporary Appointments until the next Meeting of the Legislature, which shall then fill such Vacancies.*[‡]

No person shall be a Senator who shall not have attained to the Age of thirty Years, and been nine Years a Citizen of the United States, and who shall not, when elected, be an Inhabitant of that State for which he shall be chosen.

The Vice President of the United States shall be President of the Senate, but shall have no Vote, unless they be equally divided.

The Senate shall chuse their other Officers, and also a President pro tempore, in the absence of the Vice President, or when he shall exercise the Office of President of the United States.

The Senate shall have the sole Power to try all Impeachments. When sitting for that Purpose, they shall be on Oath or Affirmation. When the President of the United States is tried, the Chief Justice shall preside: And no Person shall be convicted without the Concurrence of two thirds of the Members present.

Judgment in Cases of Impeachment shall not extend further than to removal from Office, and disqualification to hold and enjoy any Office of honor, Trust or Profit under the United States: but the Party convicted shall nevertheless be liable and subject to Indictment, Trial, Judgment and Punishment, according to Law.

Section 4

The Times, Places and Manner of holding Elections for Senators and Representatives, shall be prescribed in each State by the Legislature thereof; but the Congress may at any time by Law make or alter such Regulations, except as to the Places of Chusing Senators.

The Congress shall assemble at least once in every Year, and such Meeting *shall be on the first Monday in December, unless they shall by Law appoint a different Day.*[*]

Section 5

Each House shall be the Judge of the Elections, Returns and Qualifications of its own Members, and a Majority of each shall constitute a Quorum to do Business; but a smaller number may adjourn from day to day, and may be authorized to compel the Attendance of absent Members, in such Manner, and under such Penalties, as each House may provide.

[†]Changed by Section 1 of the Seventeenth Amendment.

[‡]Changed by Clause 2 of the Seventeenth Amendment.

[*]Changed by Section 2 of the Twentieth Amendment.

Each House may determine the Rules of its Proceedings, punish its Members for disorderly Behavior, and, with the Concurrence of two thirds, expel a Member.

Each House shall keep a Journal of its Proceedings, and from time to time publish the same, excepting such Parts as may in their Judgment require Secrecy; and the Yeas and Nays of the Members of either House on any question shall, at the Desire of one-fifth of those Present, be entered on the Journal.

Neither House, during the Session of Congress, shall, without the Consent of the other, adjourn for more than three days, nor to any other Place than that in which the two Houses shall be sitting.

Section 6

The Senators and Representatives shall receive a Compensation for their Services, to be ascertained by Law, and paid out of the Treasury of the United States. They shall in all Cases, except Treason, Felony and Breach of the Peace, be privileged from Arrest during their Attendance at the Session of their respective Houses, and in going to and returning from the same; and for any Speech or Debate in either House, they shall not be questioned in any other Place.

No Senator or Representative shall, during the Time for which he was elected, be appointed to any civil Office under the Authority of the United States, which shall have been created, or the Emoluments whereof shall have been increased, during such time; and no Person holding any Office under the United States, shall be a Member of either House during his Continuance in Office.

Section 7

All Bills for raising Revenue shall originate in the House of Representatives; but the Senate may propose or concur with Amendments as on other Bills.

Every Bill which shall have passed the House of Representatives and the Senate, shall, before it becomes a Law, be presented to the President of the United States; If he approve he shall sign it, but if not he shall return it, with his Objections to that House in which it shall have originated, who shall enter the Objections at large on their Journal, and proceed to reconsider it. If after such Reconsideration two thirds of that House shall agree to pass the Bill, it shall be sent, together with the Objections, to the other House, by which it shall likewise be reconsidered, and if approved by two thirds of that House, it shall become a Law. But in all such Cases the Votes of both Houses shall be determined by Yeas and Nays, and the Names of the Persons voting for and against the Bill shall be entered on the Journal of each House respectively. If any Bill shall not be returned by the President within ten Days (Sundays excepted) after it shall have been presented to him, the Same shall be a Law, in like Manner as if he had signed it, unless the Congress by their Adjournment prevent its Return, in which Case it shall not be a Law.

Every Order, Resolution, or Vote to which the Concurrence of the Senate and the House of Representatives may be necessary (except on a question of Adjournment) shall be presented to the President of the United States; and before the Same shall take Effect, shall be approved by him, or being disapproved by him, shall be repassed by two thirds of the Senate and House of Representatives, according to the Rules and Limitations prescribed in the Case of a Bill.

Section 8

The Congress shall have Power To lay and collect Taxes, Duties, Imposts and Excises, to pay the Debts and provide for the common Defence and general Welfare of the United States; but all Duties, Imposts and Excises shall be uniform throughout the United States;

To borrow money on the credit of the United States;

To regulate Commerce with foreign Nations, and among the several States, and with the Indian Tribes;

To establish an uniform Rule of Naturalization, and uniform Laws on the subject of Bankruptcies throughout the United States;

To coin Money, regulate the Value thereof, and of foreign Coin, and fix the Standard of Weights and Measures;

To provide for the Punishment of counterfeiting the Securities and current Coin of the United States;

To establish Post Offices and post Roads;

To promote the Progress of Science and useful Arts, by securing for limited Times to Authors and Inventors the exclusive Right to their respective Writings and Discoveries;

To constitute Tribunals inferior to the supreme Court;

To define and punish Piracies and Felonies committed on the high Seas, and Offenses against the Law of Nations;

To declare War, grant Letters of Marque and Reprisal, and make Rules concerning Captures on Land and Water;

To raise and support Armies, but no Appropriation of Money to that Use shall be for a longer Term than two Years;

To provide and maintain a Navy;

To make Rules for the Government and Regulation of the land and naval Forces;

To provide for calling forth the Militia to execute the Laws of the Union, suppress Insurrections and repel Invasions;

To provide for organizing, arming, and disciplining the Militia, and for governing such Part of them as may be employed in the Service of the United States, reserving to the States respectively, the Appointment of the Officers, and the Authority of training the Militia according to the discipline prescribed by Congress;

To exercise exclusive Legislation in all Cases whatsoever, over such District (not exceeding ten Miles square) as may, by Cession of particular States, and the acceptance of Congress, become the Seat of Government of the United States, and to exercise like Authority over all Places purchased by the Consent of the Legislature of the State in which the Same shall be, for the Erection of Forts, Magazines, Arsenals, dock-Yards, and other needful Buildings;—And

To make all Laws which shall be necessary and proper for carrying into Execution the foregoing Powers, and all other Powers vested by this Constitution in the Government of the United States, or in any Department or Officer thereof.

Section 9

The Migration or Importation of such Persons as any of the States now existing shall think proper to admit, shall not be prohibited by the Congress prior to the Year one thousand eight hundred and eight but a tax or duty may be imposed on such Importation, not exceeding ten dollars for each Person.

The privilege of the Writ of Habeas Corpus shall not be suspended, unless when in Cases of Rebellion or Invasion the public Safety may require it.

No Bill of Attainder or ex post facto Law shall be passed.

No capitation, or other direct, Tax shall be laid, unless in Proportion to the Census or Enumeration herein before directed to be taken.*

No Tax or Duty shall be laid on Articles exported from any State.

---

*Changed by the Sixteenth Amendment.

No Preference shall be given by any Regulation of Commerce or Revenue to the Ports of one State over those of another: nor shall Vessels bound to, or from, one State, be obliged to enter, clear, or pay Duties in another.

No Money shall be drawn from the Treasury, but in Consequence of Appropriations made by law; and a regular Statement and Account of the Receipts and Expenditures of all public Money shall be published from time to time.

No Title of Nobility shall be granted by the United States: And no Person holding any Office of Profit or Trust under them, shall, without the Consent of the Congress, accept of any present, Emolument, Office, or Title, of any kind whatever, from any King, Prince, or foreign State.

Section 10
No State shall enter into any Treaty, Alliance, or Confederation; grant Letters of Marque and Reprisal; coin Money; emit Bills of Credit; make any Thing but gold and silver Coin a Tender in Payment of Debts; pass any Bill of Attainder, ex post facto Law, or Law impairing the Obligation of Contracts, or grant any Title of Nobility.

No State shall, without the Consent of the Congress, lay any Imposts or Duties on Imports or Exports, except what may be absolutely necessary for executing its inspection Laws: and the net Produce of all Duties and Imposts, laid by any State on Imports or Exports, shall be for the Use of the Treasury of the United States; and all such Laws shall be subject to the Revision and Control of the Congress.

No State shall, without the Consent of the Congress, lay any duty of Tonnage, keep Troops, or Ships of War in time of Peace, enter into any Agreement or Compact with another State, or with a foreign Power, or engage in War, unless actually invaded, or in such imminent Danger as will not admit of delay.

Article II

Section 1
The executive Power shall be vested in a President of the United States of America. He shall hold his Office during the Term of four Years, and, together with the Vice President, chosen for the same Term, be elected, as follows:

Each State shall appoint, in such Manner as the Legislature thereof may direct, a Number of Electors, equal to the whole Number of Senators and Representatives to which the State may be entitled in the Congress; but no Senator or Representative, or Person holding an Office of Trust or Profit under the United States, shall be appointed an Elector.

The Electors shall meet in their respective States, and vote by Ballot for two Persons, of whom one at least shall not be an Inhabitant of the same State with themselves. And they shall make a List of all the Persons voted for, and of the Number of Votes for each; which List they shall sign and certify, and transmit sealed to the Seat of the Government of the United States, directed to the President of the Senate. The President of the Senate shall, in the Presence of the Senate and House of Representatives, open all the Certificates, and the Votes shall then be counted. The Person having the greatest Number of Votes shall be the President, if such Number be a Majority of the whole Number of Electors appointed; and if there be more than one who have such Majority, and have an equal Number of Votes, then the House of Representatives shall immediately chuse by Ballot one of them for President; and if no Person have a Majority, then from the five highest on the List the said House shall in like Manner chuse the President.

But in chusing the President, the Votes shall be taken by States, the Representation from each State having one Vote; a quorum for this Purpose shall consist of a Member or Members from two thirds of the States, and a Majority of all the States shall be necessary to a Choice. In every Case, after the Choice of the President, the Person having the greatest Number of Votes of the Electors shall be the Vice President. But if there should remain two or more who have equal Votes, the Senate shall chuse from them by Ballot the Vice President. *

The Congress may determine the Time of chusing the Electors, and the Day on which they shall give their Votes; which Day shall be the same throughout the United States.

No Person except a natural born Citizen, or a Citizen of the United States, at the time of the Adoption of this Constitution, shall be eligible to the Office of President; neither shall any Person be eligible to that Office who shall not have attained to the Age of thirty five Years, and been fourteen Years a Resident within the United States.

In Case of the Removal of the President from Office, or of his Death, Resignation, or Inability to discharge the Powers and Duties of the said Office, the same shall devolve on the Vice President, *and the Congress may by Law provide for the Case of Removal, Death, Resignation, or Inability, both of the President and Vice President, declaring what Officer shall then act as President, and such Officer shall act accordingly, until the Disability be removed, or a President shall be elected.*†

The President shall, at stated Times, receive for his Services a Compensation, which shall neither be increased nor diminished during the Period for which he shall have been elected, and he shall not receive within that Period any other Emolument from the United States, or any of them.

Before he enter on the Execution of his Office, he shall take the following Oath or Affirmation:—"I do solemnly swear (or affirm) that I will faithfully execute the Office of President of the United States, and will to the best of my Ability, preserve, protect and defend the Constitution of the United States."

Section 2

The President shall be Commander in Chief of the Army and Navy of the United States, and of the Militia of the several States, when called into the actual Service of the United States; he may require the Opinion, in writing, of the principal Officer in each of the executive Departments, upon any Subject relating to the Duties of their respective Offices, and he shall have Power to Grant Reprieves and Pardons for Offences against the United States, except in Cases of Impeachment.

He shall have Power, by and with the Advice and Consent of the Senate, to make Treaties, provided two thirds of the Senators present concur; and he shall nominate, and by and with the Advice and Consent of the Senate, shall appoint Ambassadors, other public Ministers and Consuls, Judges of the supreme Court, and all other Officers of the United States, whose Appointments are not herein otherwise provided for, and which shall be established by Law: but the Congress may by Law vest the Appointment of such inferior Officers, as they think proper, in the President alone, in the Courts of Law, or in the Heads of Departments.

The President shall have Power to fill up all Vacancies that may happen during the Recess of the Senate, by granting Commissions which shall expire at the End of their next Session.

---

*Superseded by the Twelfth Amendment.

†Modified by the Twenty-Fifth Amendment.

Section 3

He shall from time to time give to the Congress Information of the State of the Union, and recommend to their Consideration such Measures as he shall judge necessary and expedient; he may, on extraordinary Occasions, convene both Houses, or either of them, and in Case of Disagreement between them, with Respect to the Time of Adjournment, he may adjourn them to such Time as he shall think proper; he shall receive Ambassadors and other public Ministers; he shall take Care that the Laws be faithfully executed, and shall Commission all the Officers of the United States.

Section 4

The President, Vice President and all civil Officers of the United States, shall be removed from Office on Impeachment for, and Conviction of, Treason, Bribery, or other high Crimes and Misdemeanors.

Article III

Section 1

The judicial Power of the United States, shall be vested in one supreme Court, and in such inferior Courts as the Congress may from time to time ordain and establish. The Judges, both of the supreme and inferior Courts, shall hold their Offices during good Behaviour, and shall, at stated Times, receive for their Services a Compensation, which shall not be diminished during their Continuance in Office.

Section 2

The judicial Power shall extend to all Cases, in Law and Equity, arising under this Constitution, the Laws of the United States, and Treaties made, or which shall be made, under their Authority;—to all Cases affecting Ambassadors, other public Ministers and Consuls;—to all Cases of admiralty and maritime Jurisdiction;—to Controversies to which the United States shall be a Party;—to Controversies between two or more States;—between a State and Citizens of another State;*—between Citizens of different States;—between Citizens of the same State claiming Lands under Grants of different States, and between a State, or the Citizens thereof, and foreign States, Citizens or Subjects.

In all Cases affecting Ambassadors, other public Ministers and Consuls, and those in which a State shall be Party, the supreme Court shall have original Jurisdiction. In all the other Cases before mentioned, the supreme Court shall have appellate Jurisdiction, both as to Law and Fact, with such Exceptions, and under such Regulations as the Congress shall make.

The trial of all Crimes, except in Cases of Impeachment, shall be by Jury; and such Trial shall be held in the State where said Crimes shall have been committed; but when not committed within any State, the Trial shall be at such Place or Places as the Congress may by Law have directed.

Section 3

Treason against the United States, shall consist only in levying War against them, or in adhering to their Enemies, giving them Aid and Comfort. No Person shall be convicted of Treason unless on the Testimony of two Witnesses to the same overt Act, or on Confession in open Court.

*Restricted by the Eleventh Amendment.

The Congress shall have Power to declare the Punishment of Treason, but no Attainder of Treason shall work Corruption of Blood, or Forefeiture except during the Life of the Person attainted.

Article IV

Section 1
Full Faith and Credit shall be given in each State to the public Acts, Records, and judicial Proceedings of every other State. And the Congress may by general Laws prescribe the Manner in which such Acts, Records, and Proceedings shall be proved, and the Effect thereof.

Section 2
The Citizens of each State shall be entitled to all Privileges and Immunities of Citizens in the several States.

A Person charged in any State with Treason, Felony, or other Crime, who shall flee from Justice, and be found in another State, shall on demand of the executive Authority of the State from which he fled, be delivered up, to be removed to the State having Jurisdiction of the Crime.

No Person held to Service or Labour in one State, under the Laws thereof, escaping into another, shall, in Consequence of any Law or Regulation therein, be discharged from such Service or Labour, but shall be delivered up on Claim of the Party to whom such Service or Labour may be due.*

Section 3
New States may be admitted by the Congress into this Union; but no new State shall be formed or erected within the Jurisdiction of any other State; nor any State be formed by the Junction of two or more States, or parts of States, without the Consent of the Legislatures of the States concerned as well as of the Congress.

The Congress shall have Power to dispose of and make all needful Rules and Regulations respecting the Territory or other Property belonging to the United States; and nothing in this Constitution shall be so construed as to Prejudice any Claims of the United States, or of any particular State.

Section 4
The United States shall guarantee to every State in this Union a Republican Form of Government, and shall protect each of them against Invasion; and on Application of the Legislature, or of the Executive (when the Legislature cannot be convened) against domestic Violence.

Article V

The Congress, whenever two thirds of both Houses shall deem it necessary, shall propose Amendments to this Constitution, or, on the Application of the Legislatures of two thirds of the several States, shall call a Convention for proposing Amendments, which, in either Case, shall be valid to all Intents and Purposes, as Part of this Constitution, when ratified by the Legislatures of three fourths of the several States, or by Conventions in three fourths thereof, as the one or the other Mode of Ratification

---

*Superseded by the Twelfth Amendment.

may be proposed by the Congress; Provided that no Amendment which may be made prior to the Year One thousand eight hundred and eight shall in any Manner affect the first and fourth Clauses in the Ninth Section of the first Article; and that no State, without its Consent, shall be deprived of its equal Suffrage in the Senate.

Article VI

All Debts contracted and Engagements entered into, before the Adoption of this Constitution, shall be as valid against the United States under this Constitution, as under the Confederation.

This Constitution, and the Laws of the United States which shall be made in Pursuance thereof; and all Treaties made, or which shall be made, under the Authority of the United States, shall be the supreme Law of the Land; and the Judges in every State shall be bound thereby, any Thing in the Constitution or Laws of any State to the Contrary notwithstanding.

The Senators and Representatives before mentioned, and the Members of the several State Legislatures, and all executive and judicial Officers, both of the United States and of the several States, shall be bound by Oath or Affirmation, to support this Constitution; but no religious Test shall ever be required as a Qualification to any Office or public Trust under the United States.

Article VII

The Ratification of the Conventions of nine States shall be sufficient for the Establishment of this Constitution between the States so ratifying the Same.

Done in Convention by the Unanimous Consent of the States present the Seventeenth Day of September in the Year of our Lord one thousand seven hundred and Eighty seven and of the Independence of the United States of America the Twelfth. In Witness whereof We have hereunto subscribed our Names.

Go.Washington
President and deputy from Virginia

New Hampshire
John Langdon
Nicholas Gilman

Massachusetts
Nathaniel Gorham
Rufus King

Connecticut
Wm. Saml. Johnson
Roger Sherman

New York
Alexander Hamilton

New Jersey
Wil. Livingston
David Brearley
Wm. Paterson
Jona. Dayton

Pennsylvania
B. Franklin
Thomas Mifflin
Robt. Morris
Geo. Clymer
Thos. FitzSimons
Jared Ingersoll
James Wilson
Gouv. Morris

Delaware
Geo. Read
Gunning Bedford jun
John Dickenson
Richard Bassett
Jaco. Broom

Maryland
James McHenry
Dan. of St. Thos. Jenifer
Danl. Carroll

Virginia
John Blair
James Madison, Jr.

North Carolina
Wm. Blount
Richd. Dobbs Spaight
Hu Williamson

South Carolina
J. Rutledge
Charles Cotesworth Pickney
Pierce Butler

Georgia
William Few
Abr. Baldwin

AMENDMENTS TO THE CONSTITUTION

Amendment I [1791]*

Congress shall make no law respecting an establishment of religion, or prohibiting the free exercise thereof; or abridging the freedom of speech, or of the press; or the right of the people peaceably to assemble, and to petition the Government for a redress of grievances.

Amendment II [1791]

A well regulated Militia, being necessary to the security of a free State, the right of the people to keep and bear Arms shall not be infringed.

Amendment III [1791]

No Soldier shall, in time of peace, be quartered in any house, without the consent of the Owner, nor in time of war, but in a manner to be prescribed by law.

Amendment IV [1791]

The right of the people to be secure in their persons, houses, papers, and effects, against unreasonable searches and seizures, shall not be violated, and no Warrants shall issue, but upon probable cause, supported by Oath or affirmation, and particularly describing the place to be searched, and the persons or things to be seized.

Amendment V [1791]

No person shall be held to answer for a capital or otherwise infamous crime, unless on a presentment or indictment of a Grand Jury, except in cases arising in the land or naval forces, or in the Militia, when in actual service in time of War or public danger; nor shall any person be subject for the same offence to be twice put in jeopardy of life or limb; nor shall be compelled in any criminal case to be a witness against himself, nor be deprived of life, liberty, or property, without due process of law; nor shall private property be taken for public use, without just compensation.

Amendment VI [1791]

In all criminal prosecutions, the accused shall enjoy the right to a speedy and public trial, by an impartial jury of the State and district wherein the crime shall have been committed, which district shall have been previously ascertained by law, and to be informed of the nature and cause of the accusation; to be confronted with the witnesses against him; to have compulsory process for obtaining witnesses in his favor, and to have the Assistance of Counsel for his defence.

---

*The dates in brackets indicate when the amendments were ratified.

Amendment VII [1791]

In suits at common law, where the value in controversy shall exceed twenty dollars, the right of trail by jury shall be preserved, and no fact tried by a jury, shall be otherwise reexamined in any Court of the United States, than according to the Rules of the common law.

Amendment VIII [1791]

Excessive bail shall not be required, nor excessive fines imposed, nor cruel and unusual punishments inflicted.

Amendment IX [1791]

The enumeration in the Constitution, of certain rights, shall not be construed to deny or disparage others retained by the people.

Amendment X [1791]

The powers not delegated to the United States by the Constitution, nor prohibited by it to the States, are reserved to the States respectively, or to the people.

Amendment XI [1798]

The Judicial power of the United States shall not be construed to extend to any suit in law or equity, commenced or prosecuted against one of the United States by Citizens of another State, or by Citizens or subjects of any foreign state.

Amendment XII [1804]

The Electors shall meet in their respective States and vote by ballot for President and Vice-President, one of whom, at least, shall not be an inhabitant of the same State with themselves; they shall name in their ballots the person voted for as President, and in distinct ballots the person voted for as Vice-President, and they shall make distinct lists of all persons voted for as President, and of all persons voted for as Vice-President, and of the number of votes for each, which lists they shall sign and certify, and transmit sealed to the seat of the government of the United States, directed to the President of the Senate;—the President of the Senate shall, in the presence of the Senate and House of Representatives, open all the certificates and the votes shall then be counted;—The person having the greatest number of votes for President, shall be the President, if such number be a majority of the whole number of Electors appointed; and if no person have such majority, then from the persons having the highest numbers not exceeding three on the list of those voted for as President, the House of Representatives shall choose immediately, by ballot, the President. But in choosing the President, the votes shall be taken by States, the representation from each State having one vote; a quorum for this purpose shall consist of a member or members from two-thirds of the States, and a majority of all the States shall be necessary to a choice. And if the House of Representatives shall not choose a President whenever the right of choice shall devolve upon them, before *the fourth day of March* next following, then the Vice-President shall act as President, as in the case of the death or other constitutional disability of the President.*—The person having the greatest number of votes as Vice-President, shall be the Vice-President, if such number be a majority of the whole number of Electors appointed, and if no person have a majority, then from the two highest numbers on the list, the Senate shall choose the Vice-President; a quorum for the purpose shall consist of two-thirds of the whole number of Senators, and a majority of the whole number shall be necessary to a choice. But no person constitutionally ineligible to the office of President shall be eligible to that of Vice-President of the United States.

Amendment XIII [1865]

Section 1
Neither slavery nor involuntary servitude, except as a punishment for crime whereof the party shall have been duly convicted, shall exist within the United States, or any place subject to their jurisdiction.

Section 2
Congress shall have power to enforce this article by appropriate legislation.

Amendment XIV [1868]

Section 1
All persons born or naturalized in the United States, and subject to the jurisdiction thereof, are citizens of the United States and of the State wherein they reside. No State shall make or enforce any law which shall abridge the privileges or immunities of citizens of the United States; nor shall any State deprive any person of life, liberty, or property, without due process of law; nor deny to any person within its jurisdiction the equal protection of the laws.

Section 2
Representatives shall be apportioned among the several States according to their respective numbers, counting the whole number of persons in each State, excluding Indians not taxed. But when the right to vote at any election for the choice of electors for President and Vice-President of the United States, Representatives in Congress, the Executive and Judicial officers of a State, or the members of the Legislature thereof, is denied to any of the male inhabitants of such State, being twenty-one years of age, and citizens of the United States, or in any way abridged, except for participation in rebellion, or other crime, the basis of representation therein shall be reduced in the proportion which the number of such male citizens shall bear to the whole number of male citizens twenty-one years of age in such State.

Section 3
No person shall be a Senator or Representative in Congress, or elector of President and Vice-President, or hold any office, civil or military, under the United States, or

---

*Superseded by Section 3 of the Twentieth Amendment.

under any State, who, having previously taken an oath, as a member of Congress, or as an officer of the United States, or as a member of any State legislature, or as an executive or judicial officer of any State, to support the Constitution of the United States, shall have engaged in insurrection or rebellion against the same, or given aid or comfort to the enemies thereof. Congress may by a vote of two-thirds of each house, remove such disability.

Section 4
The validity of the public debt of the United States, authorized by law, including debts incurred for payment of pensions and bounties for services in suppressing insurrection or rebellion, shall not be questioned. But neither the United States nor any State shall assume or pay any debt or obligation incurred in aid of insurrection or rebellion against the United States, or any claim for the loss or emancipation of any slave; but all such debts, obligations and claims shall be held illegal and void.

Section 5
The Congress shall have power to enforce, by appropriate legislation, the provisions of this article.

Amendment XV [1870]

Section 1
The right of citizens of the United States to vote shall not be denied or abridged by the United States or by any State on account of race, color, or previous condition of servitude—

Section 2
The Congress shall have power to enforce this article by appropriate legislation.

Amendment XVI [1913]

The Congress shall have power to lay and collect taxes on incomes, from whatever source derived, without apportionment among the several States, and without regard to any census or enumeration.

Amendment XVII [1913]

The Senate of the United States shall be composed of two Senators from each State, elected by the people thereof, for six years; and each Senator shall have one vote. The electors in each State shall have the qualifications requisite for electors of the most numerous branch of the State legislatures.

When vacancies happen in the representation of any State in the Senate, the executive authority of such State shall issue writs of election to fill such vacancies: *Provided*, That the legislature of any State may empower the executive thereof to make temporary appointments until the people fill the vacancies by election as the legislature may direct.

This amendment shall not be so construed as to affect the election or term of any Senator chosen before it becomes valid as part of the Constitution.

Amendment XVIII [1919]

Section 1
After one year from the ratification of this article the manufacture, sale, or transportation of intoxicating liquors within, the importation thereof into, or the exportation thereof from the United States and all territory subject to the jurisdiction hereof for beverage purposes hereby prohibited.

Section 2
The Congress and the several States shall have concurrent power to enforce this article by appropriate legislation.

Section 3
This article shall be inoperative unless it shall have been ratified as an amendment to the Constitution by the legislatures of the several States, as provided by the Constitution, within seven years from the date of submission hereof to the States by the Congress.*

Amendment XIX [1920]

The right of citizens of the United States to vote shall not be denied or abridged by the United States or by any State on account of sex.

Congress shall have power to enforce this article by appropriate legislation.

Amendment XX [1933]

Section 1
The terms of the President and Vice-President shall end at noon on the 20th day of January, and the terms of Senators and Representatives at noon on the 3d day of January, of the years in which such terms would have ended if this article had not been ratified; and the terms of their successors shall then begin.

Section 2
The Congress shall assemble at least once in every year, and such meeting shall begin at noon on the 3d day of January, unless they shall by law appoint a different day.

Section 3
If, at the time fixed for the beginning of the term of the President, the President elect shall have died, the Vice-President elect shall become President. If a President shall not have been chosen before the time fixed for the beginning of his term, or if the President elect shall have failed to qualify, then the Vice-President elect shall act as President until a President shall have qualified; and the Congress may by law provide for the case wherein neither a President elect nor a Vice-President elect shall have qualified, declaring who shall then act as President, or the manner in which one who is to act shall be selected, and such person shall act accordingly until a President or Vice-President shall have qualified.

---

*Repealed by Section 1 of the Twenty-First Amendment.

Section 4

The Congress may by law provide for the case of the death of any of the persons from whom the House of Representatives may choose a President whenever the right of choice shall have devolved upon them, and for the case of the death of any of the persons from whom the Senate may choose a Vice-President whenever the right of choice shall have devolved upon them.

Section 5

Sections 1 and 2 shall take effect on the 15th day of October following the ratification of this article.

Section 6

This article shall be inoperative unless it shall have been ratified as an amendment to the Constitution by the legislatures of three-fourths of the several States within seven years from the date of its submission.

Amendment XXI [1933]

Section 1

The eighteenth article of amendment to the Constitution of the United States is hereby repealed.

Section 2

The transportation or importation into any State, Territory, or possession of the United States for delivery or use therein of intoxicating liquors, in violation of the laws thereof, is hereby prohibited.

Section 3

This article shall be inoperative unless it shall have been ratified as an amendment to the Constitution by conventions in the several States, as provided in the Constitution, within seven years from the date of submission hereof to the States by the Congress.

Amendment XXII [1951]

Section 1

No person shall be elected to the office of President more than twice, and no person who has held the office of President, or acted as President, for more than two years of a term to which some other person was elected President shall be elected to the office of the President more than once. But this Article shall not apply to any person holding the office of President when this Article was proposed by the Congress, and shall not prevent any person who may be holding the office of President, or acting as President, during the term within which this Article becomes operative from holding the office of the President or acting as President during the remainder of such term.

Section 2

This article shall be inoperative unless it shall have been ratified as an amendment to the Constitution by the legislatures of three-fourths of the several States within seven years from the date of its submission to the States by the Congress.

Amendment XXIII [1961]

Section 1
The District constituting the seat of Government of the United States shall appoint in such manner as the Congress may direct:

A number of electors of President and Vice-President equal to the whole number of Senators and Representatives in Congress to which the District would be entitled if it were a State, but in no event more than the least populous State; they shall be in addition to those appointed by the States, but they shall be considered, for the purposes of the election of President and Vice-President, to be electors appointed by a State; and they shall meet in the District and perform such duties as provided by the twelfth article of amendment.

Section 2
The Congress shall have power to enforce this article by appropriate legislation.

Amendment XXIV [1964]

Section 1
The right of citizens of the United States to vote in any primary or other election for President or Vice-President, for electors for President or Vice-President, or for Senator or Representative in Congress, shall not be denied or abridged by the United States or any State by reason of failure to pay any poll tax or other tax.

Section 2
The Congress shall have power to enforce this article by appropriate legislation.

Amendment XXV [1967]

Section 1
In case of the removal of the President from office or of his death or resignation, the Vice-President shall become President.

Section 2
Whenever there is a vacancy in the office of the Vice-President, the President shall nominate a Vice-President who shall take office upon confirmation by a majority vote of both houses of Congress.

Section 3
Whenever the President transmits to the President pro tempore of the Senate and the Speaker of the House of Representatives his written declaration that he is unable to discharge the powers and duties of his office, and until he transmits to them a written declaration to the contrary, such powers and duties shall be discharged by the Vice-President as Acting President.

Section 4
Whenever the Vice-President and a majority of either the principal officers of the executive departments or of such other body as Congress may by law provide, transmit

to the President pro tempore of the Senate and the Speaker of the House of Representatives their written declaration that the President is unable to discharge the powers and duties of his office, the Vice-President shall immediately assume the powers and duties of the office as Acting President.

Thereafter, when the President transmits to the President pro tempore of the Senate and the Speaker of the House of Representatives his written declaration that no inability exists, he shall resume the powers and duties of his office unless the Vice-President and a majority of either the principal officers of the executive department or of such other body as Congress may by law provide, transmit within four days to the President pro tempore of the Senate and the Speaker of the House of Representatives their written declaration that the President is unable to discharge the powers and duties of his office. Thereupon Congress shall decide the issue, assembling within forty-eight hours for that purpose if not in session. If the Congress, within twenty-one days after receipt of the latter written declaration, or, if Congress is not in session, within twenty-one days after Congress is required to assemble, determines by two-thirds vote of both Houses that the President is unable to discharge the powers and duties of his office, the Vice-President shall continue to discharge the same as Acting President; otherwise, the President shall resume the powers and duties of his office.

Amendment XXVI [1971]

Section 1
The right of citizens of the United States, who are eighteen years of age or older, to vote shall not be denied or abridged by the United States or by any state on account of age.

Section 2
The Congress shall have power to enforce this article by appropriate legislation.

Amendment XXVII [1992]

No law varying the compensation for services of the Senators and Representatives, shall take effect, until an election of Representatives shall have intervened.

APPENDIX

TERRITORIAL EXPANSION

Territory	Date Acquired	Square Miles	How Acquired
Original states and territories	1783	888,685	Treaty of Paris
Louisiana Purchase	1803	827,192	Purchased from France
Florida	1819	72,003	Adams–Onís Treaty
Texas	1845	390,143	Annexation of independent country
Oregon	1846	285,580	Oregon Boundary Treaty
Mexican cession	1848	529,017	Treaty of Guadalupe Hidalgo
Gadsden Purchase	1853	29,640	Purchased from Mexico
Midway Islands	1867	2	Annexation of uninhabited islands
Alaska	1867	589,757	Purchased from Russia
Hawaii	1898	6,450	Annexation of independent country
Wake Island	1898	3	Annexation of uninhabited island
Puerto Rico	1899	3,435	Treaty of Paris
Guam	1899	212	Treaty of Paris
The Philippines	1899–1946	115,600	Treaty of Paris; granted independence
American Samoa	1900	76	Treaty with Germany and Great Britain
Panama Canal Zone	1904–1978	553	Hay–Bunau-Varilla Treaty
U.S. Virgin Islands	1917	133	Purchased from Denmark
Trust Territory of the Pacific Islands★	1947	717	United Nations Trusteeship

★A number of these islands have recently been granted independence: Federated States of Micronesia, 1990; Marshall Islands, 1991; Palau, 1994.

THE LABOR FORCE

(thousands of workers)

Year	Agricul-ture	Mining	Manufac-turing	Construc-tion	Trade	Other	Total
1810	1,950	11	75	—	—	294	2,330
1840	3,570	32	500	290	350	918	5,660
1850	4,520	102	1,200	410	530	1,488	8,250
1860	5,880	176	1,530	520	890	2,114	11,110
1870	6,790	180	2,470	780	1,310	1,400	12,930
1880	8,920	280	3,290	900	1,930	2,070	17,390
1890	9,960	440	4,390	1,510	2,960	4,060	23,320
1900	11,680	637	5,895	1,665	3,970	5,223	29,070
1910	11,770	1,068	8,332	1,949	5,320	9,041	37,480
1920	10,790	1,180	11,190	1,233	5,845	11,372	41,610
1930	10,560	1,009	9,884	1,988	8,122	17,267	48,830
1940	9,575	925	11,309	1,876	9,328	23,277	56,290
1950	7,870	901	15,648	3,029	12,152	25,870	65,470
1960	5,970	709	17,145	3,640	14,051	32,545	74,060
1970	3,463	516	20,746	4,818	15,008	34,127	78,678
1980	3,364	979	21,942	6,215	20,191	46,612	99,303
1990	3,186	730	21,184	7,696	24,269	60,849	117,914
1994	3,409	669	20,157	7,493	25,699	65,633	123,060

SOURCE: *Historical Statistics of the United States, Colonial Times to 1970* (1975), 139; *Statistical Abstract of the United States*, 1995, Table 653.

Changing Labor Patterns

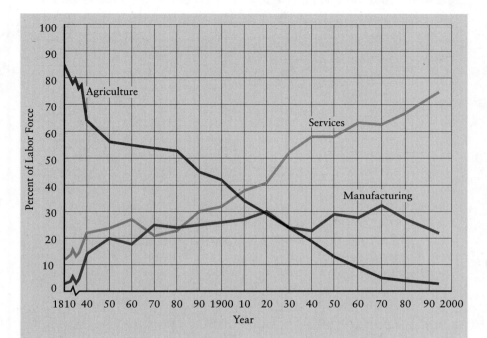

AMERICAN POPULATION

Year	Population	Percent Increase	Year	Population	Percent Increase
1610	350	—	1810	7,239,881	36.4
1620	2,300	557.1	1820	9,638,453	33.1
1630	4,600	100.0	1830	12,866,020	33.5
1640	26,600	478.3	1840	17,069,453	32.7
1650	50,400	90.8	1850	23,191,876	35.9
1660	75,100	49.0	1860	31,443,321	35.6
1670	111,900	49.0	1870	39,818,449	26.6
1680	151,500	35.4	1880	50,155,783	26.0
1690	210,400	38.9	1890	62,947,714	25.5
1700	250,900	19.2	1900	75,994,575	20.7
1710	331,700	32.2	1910	91,972,266	21.0
1720	466,200	40.5	1920	105,710,620	14.9
1730	629,400	35.0	1930	122,775,046	16.1
1740	905,600	43.9	1940	131,669,275	7.2
1750	1,170,800	29.3	1950	150,697,361	14.5
1760	1,593,600	36.1	1960	179,323,175	19.0
1770	2,148,100	34.8	1970	203,235,298	13.3
1780	2,780,400	29.4	1980	226,545,805	11.5
1790	3,929,214	41.3	1990	248,709,873	9.8
1800	5,308,483	35.1	1993	259,383,000	4.3

Note: These figures largely ignore the native American population. Census takers never made any effort to count the native American population that lived outside their political jurisdictions and compiled only casual and incomplete enumerations of those living within their jurisdictions until 1890. In that year the federal government attempted a full count of the Indian population: the Census found 125,719 Indians in 1890, compared with only 12,543 in 1870 and 33,985 in 1880.

SOURCE: *Historical Statistics of the United States, Colonial Times to 1970* (1975); *Statistical Abstract of the United States,* 1995.

SUGGESTED READINGS

CHAPTER 16

The starting point for the study of Reconstruction is Eric Foner's major synthesis, *Reconstruction: America's Unfinished Revolution, 1863–1877* (1988), which is also available in a shorter version. Two older surveys that provide useful introductions are John Hope Franklin, *Reconstruction: After the Civil War* (1961), and Kenneth M. Stampp, *The Era of Reconstruction* (1965). *Black Reconstruction in America* (1935), by the black activist and scholar W. E. B. Du Bois, deserves attention as the first book to challenge traditional racist interpretations of Reconstruction as carpetbagger rule unjustly imposed on the defeated South by Radical Republicans.

Presidential Reconstruction

For important studies of presidential efforts to rebuild the Union, see the books on Abraham Lincoln listed in Chapter 15 and the following works on Andrew Johnson: Albert Castel, *The Presidency of Andrew Johnson* (1979); Eric L. McKitrick, *Andrew Johnson and Reconstruction* (1960); and James Sefton, *Andrew Johnson and the Uses of Constitutional Power* (1979). On the Radical resistance to presidential Reconstruction, see James M. McPherson, *The Struggle for Equality: Abolitionists and the Negro in the Civil War and Reconstruction* (1965). Books that focus on Congress include LaWanda Cox and John H. Cox, *Politics, Principle, and Prejudice, 1865–1867* (1963); David Donald, *The Politics of Reconstruction, 1863–1867* (1965); and William B. Brock, *An American Crisis: Congress and Reconstruction, 1865–1867* (1963). For insight into developments in the South, see Dan T. Carter, *When the War Was Over: The Failure of Self-Reconstruction in the South, 1865–1867* (1985). Michael Perman, *Reunion without Compromise: The South and Reconstruction, 1865–1868* (1973), stresses the South's handling of Johnson. On the freedmen, Willie Lee Rose, *Rehearsal for Reconstruction: The Port Royal Experiment* (1964); Peter Kolchin, *First Freedom: The Responses of Alabama's Blacks to Emancipation and Reconstruction* (1972); Leon F. Litwack, *Been in the Storm So Long: The Aftermath of Slavery* (1979); Ira Berlin et al., *Freedom: A Documentary History of Emancipation, 1861–1867: The Wartime Genesis of Free Labor* (1990); Berlin et al., *Slaves No More: Three Essays on Emancipation and the Civil War* (1992); Julie Saville, *The Work of Reconstruction: From Slave to Wage Laborer in South Carolina, 1860–1870* (1994). Jacqueline Jones, *Labor of Love, Labor of Sorrow: Black Women, Work, and the Family from Slavery to the Present* (1985), is a pioneering work on the impact of emancipation on black women.

Radical Reconstruction

For Congress's role in radical Reconstruction, see Michael Les Benedict, *A Compromise of Principle: Congressional Republicans and Reconstruction* (1974), and Hans L. Trefousse, *Impeachment of a President: Andrew Johnson, the Blacks, and Reconstruction* (1975). William S. McFeely, *Grant: A Biography* (1981), deftly explains the politics of Reconstruction. Also helpful is Brooks D. Simpson, *Let Us Have Peace: Ulysses S. Grant and the Politics of War and Reconstruction, 1861–1868* (1991). State studies of Reconstruction include Richard Lowe, *Republicans and Reconstruction in Virginia, 1856–1870* (1991), and Otto Olsen, ed., *Reconstruction and Redemption in the South* (1980). The best account of carpetbaggers is Richard N. Current, *Those Terrible Carpetbaggers: A Reinterpretation* (1988). On blacks during radical Reconstruction, see Joel Williamson, *After Slavery: The Negro in South Carolina during Reconstruction, 1861–1877* (1965); Robert Cruden, *The Negro in Reconstruction* (1969); Thomas Holt, *Black over White: Negro Political Leadership in South Carolina during Reconstruction* (1977); Barry A. Crouch, *The Freedmen's Bureau and Black Texans* (1992). Other studies covering southern race relations over a longer time span include John Blassingame, *Black New Orleans, 1860–1880* (1973); Howard N. Rabinowitz, *Race Relations in the Urban South, 1865–1890* (1977); Barbara Fields, *Slavery and Freedom on the Middle Ground: Maryland during the Nineteenth Century* (1985); and Jonathan M. Bryant, *How Curious a Land: Conflict and Change in Greene County, Georgia, 1850–1885* (1996).

Redemption

The most thorough study of the Ku Klux Klan is Allen W. Trelease, *White Terror: The Ku Klux Klan Conspiracy and Southern Reconstruction* (1972). To survey Reconstruction politics in the South, consult Michael Perman, *The Road to Redemption: Southern Politics, 1869–1879* (1984). On politics in the North, see Eugene H. Berwanger, *The West and Reconstruction* (1981); James Mohr, ed., *The Radical Republicans in the North: State Politics during Reconstruction* (1976); and William Gillette, *Retreat from Reconstruction, 1863–1879* (1979). The emergence of the sharecropping system is explored in Roger L. Ransom and Richard Sutch, *One Kind of Freedom: The Economic Consequences of Emancipation* (1977); Jay Mandle, *The Roots of Black Poverty: The Southern Plantation Economy after the Civil War* (1978); Gavin Wright, *Old South, New South: Revolutions in the Southern Economy since the Civil War* (1986); Edward Royce, *The Origins of Southern Sharecropping* (1993); Harold Woodman, *New South, New Law: The Legal Foundations of Credit and Labor Relations in the Postbellum Agricultural South* (1995). On yeomen farmers, consult Steven Hahn, *The Roots of Southern Populism: Yeoman Farmers and the Transformation of the Georgia Upcountry, 1850–1890* (1983). For the impact of Reconstruction on the national state, see Morton Keller, *Affairs of State: Public Life in Late Nineteenth-Century America* (1977), and Richard F. Bensel, *Yankee Leviathan: The Origins of Central State Authority in America, 1859–1877* (1990). On political corruption, see Mark W. Summers, *The Era of Good Stealings* (1993). On the Compromise of 1877, see C. Vann Woodward's classic *Reunion and Reaction* (1956), and K. I. Polakoff, *The Politics of Inertia: The Election of 1876 and the End of Reconstruction* (1973).

CHAPTER 17

Western history has become a bitterly contested ground in recent years. The fountainhead of the voluminous traditional scholarship is Frederick Jackson Turner's famous essay "The Significance of the Frontier in American History" (1893), reprinted in Ray A. Billington, ed., *Frontier and Section: Selected Essays of Frederick Jackson Turner* (1961). The "new" western history is critical of Turnerian scholarship for being "Eurocentric"—for seeing western history only through the eyes of frontiersmen and settlers—and for masking the rapacious and environmentally destructive underside of western settlement. Patricia N. Limerick's skillfully argued *The Legacy of Conquest: The Unbroken Past of the American West* (1987) opened the debate. Richard White, *"It's Your Misfortune and None of My Own": A New History of the American West* (1991), provides the fullest synthesis of the new scholarship. For an authoritative, balanced treatment of the main themes of western history, see the essays in Clyde A. Milner II et al., *The Oxford History of the American West* (1994). On women's experience—another primary concern of the new western history—the starting point is Susan Armitage and Elizabeth Jameson, eds., *The Women's West* (1987). There are incisive environmental essays in Donald Worster, *Under Western Skies: Nature and History in the American West* (1992).

The Great Plains

The classic book, stressing the settlers' adaptation to climate and environment, is Walter P. Webb, *The Great Plains* (1931). Robert M. Utley, *The Indian Frontier of the American West, 1846–1890* (1984), is a good introduction; Robert H. Lowie, *Indians of the Great Plains* (1954), is a classic anthropological study. On the religious life of the Plains Indians, see Howard L. Harrod, *Renewing the World: Plains Indians Religion and Morality* (1987). The assault on Indian culture is told in Fredrick E. Hoxie, *A Final Promise: The Campaign to Assimilate the Indians, 1880–1920* (1984). On phases of plains settlement see Oscar Winther, *The Transportation Frontier: The Trans-Mississippi West, 1865–1890* (1964); Lewis Atherton, *The Cattle Kings* (1964); Gilbert Fite, *The Farmer's Frontier, 1865–1900* (1966); and Mary W. M. Hargreaves, *Dry-Farming in the Northern Great Plains* (1954). Ecological impact is subtly probed in Frieda Knobloch, *The Culture of Wilderness: Agriculture as Colonization in the American West* (1996). The peopling of the plains can be explored in Craig Miner, *West of Wichita: Settling the High Plains of Kansas, 1865–1890* (1986); Frederick C. Luebke, ed., *Ethnicity and the Great Plains* (1980); Nell Irvin Painter, *Exodusters: Black Migration to Kansas after Reconstruction* (1976); Julie Roy Jeffrey, *Frontier Women: The Trans-Mississippi West, 1840–1880*; Deborah Fink, *Agrarian Women: Wives and Mothers in Rural Nebraska, 1880–1940* (1992); and Elaine Lindgren, *Land in Her Own Name: Women as Homesteaders in North Dakota* (1991). On the integration of the plains economy with the wider world, an especially rich book is William Cronon, *Nature's Metropolis: Chicago and the Great West* (1991). Richard Slotkin, *The Fatal Environment: The Myth of the Frontier in the Age of Industrialization, 1800–1890* (1985), deals with the process by which Americans translated the hard realities of conquering the West into a national mythology.

The Far West

The best book on western mining is Rodman Paul, *Mining Frontiers of the Far West: 1848–1880s* (1963). An important case study of women in a mining town is Paula Petrik, *Women and Family on the Rocky Mountain Frontier: Helena, Monotana, 1865–1900* (1987). On western miners the standard book is Mark Wyman, *Hard Rock Epic: Western Miners and the Industrial Revolution, 1860–1910* (1979); and on the western labor movement, an important new interpretation is David Brundage, *The Making of Western Working-Class Radicalism: Denver's Organized Workers, 1878–1905* (1994). Two valuable regional histories are Carlos A. Schwantes, *The Pacific Northwest: An Interpretive History* (1989), and David Alan Johnson, *Founding the Far West: California, Oregon, and Nevada* (1992). A very imaginative recent treatment of the New Mexico peasantry is Sarah Deutsch, *No Separate Refuge* (1987). On Hispanic Texas an important book is David Montejano, *Anglos and Mexicans in the Making of Texas* (1987). Important local studies of laboring Hispanics and their communities are Mario T. Garcia, *Desert Immigrants: The Mexicans of El Paso, 1880–1920* (1981), and Richard Griswold del Castillo, *The Los Angeles Barrio, 1850–1890* (1979). On the Asian migration to America, the best introduction is Ronald Takaki, *Strangers from a Different Shore: A History of Asian Americans* (1989), which can be supplemented with Gunther Barth, *Bitter Strength: A History of the Chinese in the United States, 1850–1870* (1964), and Sucheng Chan, *This Bittersweet Soil: The Chinese in California Agriculture, 1860–1910* (1986). Labor's opposition to the Chinese is skillfully treated in Alexander Saxton, *The Indispensable Enemy: Labor and the Anti-Chinese Movement in California* (1971). Kevin Starr, *California and the American Dream, 1850–1915* (1973), provides a comprehensive account of the emergence of a distinctive California culture.

CHAPTER 18

The most useful introduction to the economic history of this period is Edward C. Kirkland, *Industry Comes of Age, 1860–1897* (1961). A more sophisticated analysis can be found in W. Elliot Brownlee, *Dynamics of Ascent* (rev. ed., 1979). For essays on many of the topics covered in this chapter, consult Glenn Porter, ed., *Encyclopedia of American Economic History* (3 vols., 1980).

Industrial Capitalism Triumphant

On railroads a convenient introduction is John F. Stover, *American Railroads* (1970). The growth of the railroads as an integrated system has been treated in George R. Taylor and Irene D. Neu, *The American Railway Network, 1861–1890* (1956). Julius Grodinsky, *Jay Gould: His Business Career, 1867–1892* (1957), is a complex study demonstrating the contributions this railroad buccaneer made to the transportation system. Books such as Grodinsky's have gone a long way to resurrect Gilded Age businessmen from the debunking tradition first set forth with great power in Matthew Josephson, *Robber Barons: Great American Fortunes* (1934). Peter Temin, *Iron and Steel in the Nineteenth Century* (1964), is the best treatment of that industry. Joseph F. Wall, *Andrew Carnegie* (1970), is the definitive biography of the great steelmaker. Equally definitive on the oil king is Allan Nevins, *A Study in Power: John D. Rockefeller* (2 vols., 1953). On the development of mass production the key book is David A. Hounsell, *From the American System to Mass Production, 1800–1932* (1984). Alfred D. Chandler, *The Visible Hand: The Managerial Revolution in American Business* (1977), is not an easy book but will amply repay the labors of interested students.

On the New South the standard work has long been C. Vann Woodward, *Origins of the New South, 1877–1913* (1951). Equally essential as a modern reconsideration is Edward L. Ayers, *The Promise of the New South: Life after Reconstruction* (1992). A brilliant reinterpretation of the causes of the South's economic retardation is Gavin

Wright, *Old South, New South: Revolutions in the Southern Economy since the Civil War* (1986). Jacqueline Jones, *The Dispossessed: America's Underclasses from the Civil War to the Present* (1992), contains an excellent treatment of southern labor.

The World of Work

To understand the impact of industrialism on American workers, three collections of essays make the best starting points: Herbert G. Gutman, *Work, Culture and Society in Industrializing America* (1976); Michael S. Frisch and Daniel J. Walkowitz, eds., *Working-Class America: Essays on Labor, Community and American Society* (1983); and Leon Fink, *In Search of the Working Class* (1994). On the introduction of Taylorism, the most useful book is Daniel Nelson, *Managers and Workers: Origins of the New Factory System* (2d ed., 1995). The impact of Taylorism on American workers is treated with insight in David Montgomery, *The Fall of the House of Labor: The Workplace, the State, and American Labor Activism, 1865–1925* (1987).

Two valuable collections of essays on immigrant workers are Richard Ehrlich, ed., *Immigrants in Industrial America* (1977), and Dirk Hoerder, ed., *American Labor and Immigration History, 1877–1920: Recent European Research* (1983). John Bodnar, *Immigration and Industrialization: Ethnicity in an American Mill Town* (1977), is an important case study of a single community. On women workers the best introduction is Alice Kessler-Harris, *Out to Work* (1982). Ava Baron, ed., *Work Engendered: Toward a New History of American Labor* (1991), is a rich collection of essays that apply gender analysis to the history of working people. On black workers useful introductions are William H. Harris, *The Harder We Run: Black Workers Since the Civil War* (1982), and Philip S. Foner, *Organized Labor and the Black Worker* (1974). Walter Licht, *Getting Work: Philadelphia, 1840–1950* (1992), is a pioneering history of a labor market in operation.

The Labor Movement

The standard book on the struggle between labor reform and trade unionism is Gerald N. Grob, *Workers and Utopia, 1865–1900* (1961). For the Knights of Labor, it should be supplemented by Leon Fink, *Workingmen's Democracy: The Knights of Labor and American Politics* (1983), which captures the cultural dimensions of labor reform not seen by earlier historians. The place of labor in the political environment is the subject of David Montgomery, *Citizen Worker* (1993). Paul Krause, *The Battle for Homestead, 1880–1892* (1992), puts the great strike in a larger social context. The most recent survey, incorporating much of the latest scholarship, is Bruce Laurie, *Artisans into Workers: Labor in Nineteenth Century America* (1989).

The founder of the AFL is the subject of a lively brief biography by Harold Livesay, *Samuel Gompers and Organized Labor in America* (1978). Among the many books on individual unions, Robert Christie, *Empire in Wood* (1956), best reveals the way pure-and-simple unionism worked out in practice. On industrial conflict, the most vivid book is Robert V. Bruce, *1877: Year of Violence* (1959). The best book on the IWW is Melvyn Dubofsky, *We Shall Be All* (1969). On socialism, David Shannon, *The Socialist Party of America* (1955), remains the standard account. There is, however, a fine biography of that party's leader that supersedes previous studies: Nick Salvatore, *Eugene V. Debs: Citizen and Socialist* (1982). A dimension of American radicalism long neglected has received sensitive attention in Mari Jo Buhle, *Women and American Socialism, 1870–1920* (1982).

CHAPTER 19

The best introductions to American politics in the late nineteenth century are John A. Garraty, *The New Commonwealth, 1877–1890* (1968), and R. Hal Williams, *Years of Decision: American Politics in the 1890s* (1978). More detailed and comprehensive is Morton Keller, *Affairs of State: Public Life in Late Nineteenth-Century America* (1977). Joel L. Silbey, *The American Political Nation, 1838–1893* (1991), focuses on the party system and political behavior.

The Politics of the Status Quo, 1877–1893

Various aspects of national politics are discussed in Robert D. Marcus, *Grand Old Party: Political Structure in the Gilded Age* (1971); J. Rogers Hollingsworth, *The Whirligig of Politics: The Democracy of Cleveland and Bryan* (1963); H. Wayne Morgan, *From Hayes to McKinley: National Party Politics, 1877–1896* (1969); and David J. Rothman, *Politics and Power: The Senate, 1869–1901* (1966). On the development of public administration, see Leonard D. White, *The Republican Era, 1869–1901* (1958), and Stephen Skowronek, *Building a New American State: The Expansion of National Administrative Capacities* (1982).

The ideological basis for conservative national politics is fully treated in Sidney Fine, *Laissez Faire and the General Welfare State, 1865–1901* (1956); Robert G. McCloskey, *American Conservatism in the Age of Enterprise* (1951); and the opening section of Morton J. Horwitz, *The Transformation of American Law, 1870–1960* (1992). On the popular sources of political participation, see especially Michael E. McGerr, *The Decline of Popular Politics: The American North, 1865–1928* (1986), and Paul Kleppner, *The Third Electoral Party System, 1853–1892: Parties, Voters, and Political Cultures* (1979). On the Mugwump reformers, see John G. Sproat, *The "Best Men": Liberal Reformers in the Gilded Age* (1965); and Ari Hoogenboom, *Outlawing the Spoils: The Civil Service Reform Movement, 1865–1883* (1961). The existence of a women's political culture in the late nineteenth century can be traced in Carl N. Degler, *At Odds: Women and the Family from the Revolution to the Present* (1979). A valuable book setting the stage is Ellen Carol Du Bois, *Feminism and Suffrage: The Emergence of an Independent Women's Movement in America, 1848–1869* (1978).

The Crisis of American Politics: The 1890s

The most recent synthesis on Populism is Robert C. McMath, *American Populism* (1993). Richard D. Hofstadter, *The Age of Reform* (1955), stresses the darker side of Populism, in which intolerance and paranoia figure heavily. Hofstadter's thesis, which once dominated debate among historians, has given way to a much more positive assessment. The key book here is Lawrence Goodwyn, *Democratic Promise: The Populist Moment in America* (1976), which argues that Populism was a broadly based radical response to industrial capitalism. Peter H. Argesinger, *The Limits of Agrarian Radicalism: Western Politics and American Politics* (1995), stresses the capacity of the political status quo to frustrate western Populism. Two stimulating books that follow the history of Populism into the twentieth century are Grant McConnell, *The Decline of Agrarian Democracy* (1953), which focuses on farm organizations, and Michael Kazin, *The Populist Persuasion* (1995), which describes how the language of Populism entered the discourse of mainstream American politics.

The money question is elucidated in Walter Nugent, *Money and American Society, 1865–1880* (1968), and Allan Weinstein, *Prelude to Populism: Origins of the Silver Issue* (1970). On the politics of the 1890s, see especially Robert F. Durden, *Climax of Populism: The Election of 1896* (1965), and Paul W. Glad, *McKinley, Bryan, and the People* (1964).

Race and Politics in the South

On southern politics the seminal book for the post-Reconstruction period is C. Vann Woodward, *Origins of the New South, 1877–1913* (1951), which still defines the terms of discussion among historians. The most far-reaching revision is Edward L. Ayers, *The Promise of the New South* (1992). Complementary books on the social basis of southern politics are Dwight B. Billings, *Planters and the Making of "New South": North Carolina, 1865–1900* (1979), and Paul Escott, *Many Excellent People: Power and Privilege in North Carolina, 1850–1900* (1985).

The classic book on segregation is C. Vann Woodward, *The Strange Career of Jim Crow* (2d ed., 1968), but it should be supplemented by Howard N. Rabinowitz, *Race Relations in the Urban South, 1865–1890* (1978). A powerful analysis of southern racism, stressing its psychosocial roots, is Joel Williamson, *A Rage for Order: Black/White Relations in the American South since Emancipation* (1986). Disfranchisement is treated with great analytic sophistication in J. Morgan Kousser, *The Shaping of Southern Politics: Suffrage Restriction and the Establishment of the One-Party South, 1880–1910* (1974), and as an aspect of progressivism in Jack Temple Kirby, *Darkness at the Dawning: Race and Reform in the Progressive South* (1972). August Meier, *Negro Thought in America, 1880–1915* (1963), is a key analysis of black accommodation and protest. The preeminent exponent of accommodation is the subject of a superb two-volume biography by Louis B. Harlan, *Booker T. Washington: The Making of a Black Leader* (1973) and *Wizard of Tuskegee* (1983); and equally fine on Washington's main critic is David Levering Lewis, *W. E. B. Du Bois: Biography of a Race 1868–1919* (1993).

CHAPTER 20

Useful introductions to urban history are Charles N. Glaab and A. Theodore Brown, *A History of Urban America* (1967), and Arthur M. Schlesinger, *The Rise of the City* (1936), a pioneering study; and Blake McKelvey, *The Urbanization of America, 1860–1915* (1963). A sampling of the innovative scholarship that opened new historical paths can be found in Stephan Thernstrom and Richard Sennett, eds., *Nineteenth-Century Cities: Essays in the New Urban History* (1969).

Urbanization

Allan Pred, *Spatial Dynamics of U.S. Urban Growth, 1800–1914* (1971), traces the patterns in which cities grew. On the revolution in urban transit, see the pioneering book by Sam B. Warner, *Streetcar Suburbs: The Process of Growth in Boston, 1870–1900* (1962). In a subsequent work, *The Private City: Philadelphia in Three Periods* (1968), Warner broadened his analysis to show how private decision making shaped the character of the American city. Innovations in urban construction are treated in Carl Condit,

American Building Art: Nineteenth Century (1969) and *Chicago School of Architecture* (1964); Robert C. Twombly, *Louis Sullivan* (1986); Alan Trachtenberg, *The Brooklyn Bridge* (1965); and Harold L. Platt, *The Electric City: Energy and the Growth of the Chicago Area, 1880–1930* (1991). The problems of meeting basic human needs are treated in Jon C. Teaford, *The Unheralded Triumph: City Government in America, 1870–1900* (1984); Eric H. Monkkonen, *Police in Urban America, 1860–1920* (1981); and David B. Tyack, *The One Best System: A History of American Urban Education* (1974). The struggle to re-shape the chaotic nineteenth-century city can be explored in John D. Fairchild, *The Mysteries of the Great City: The Politics of Urban Design, 1877–1937* (1993); William H. Wilson, *The City Beautiful Movement in Kansas City* (1964); and David Schuyler, *The New Urban Landscape: The Redefinition of City Form in Nineteenth-Century America* (1986).

City People

Among the leading books on immigrants and the city are Moses Rischin, *The Promised City: New York's Jews, 1870–1914* (1962); Joseph Barton, *Peasants and Strangers: Italians, Rumanians, and Slovaks in an American City, 1890–1950* (1975); and Humbert S. Nelli, *The Italians in Chicago, 1860–1920* (1970). On blacks in the city, see Gilbert Osofsky, *Harlem: The Making of a Ghetto, 1890–1930* (1966); Allan H. Spear, *Black Chicago, 1860–1920* (1966); and Kenneth L. Kusmer, *A Ghetto Takes Shape: Black Cleveland, 1870–1930* (1976). David C. Hammack, *Power and Society: Greater New York at the Turn of the Century* (1982), is a sophisticated treatment that places the party ma-chine in the larger context of municipal power politics. The encounter of Protes-tantism with the city is treated in Henry F. May, *Protestant Churches and Urban America* (1949); Aaron I. Abell, *The Urban Impact on American Protestantism* (1943); and William G. McLoughlin, *Modern Revivalism* (1959). On the Catholic Church, see Robert D. Cross, *The Emergence of Liberal Catholicism in America* (1958). Aspects of an emerging city culture are studied in Gunther Barth, *City People: The Rise of Modern City Culture in Nineteenth-Century America* (1982); Susan Porter Benson, *Counter Cultures: Sales-women, Managers, and Customers in American Department Stores, 1890–1940* (1986); John F. Kasson, *Amusing the Million: Coney Island at the Turn of the Century* (1978); Timothy J. Gilfoyle, *City of Eros: New York City, Prostitution and the Commercialization of Sex, 1790–1920* (1991); Kathy Peiss, *Cheap Amusements: Working Women and Leisure in Turn-of-the-Century New York* (1986); and David Nasaw, *Going Out: The Rise and Fall of Pub-lic Amusements* (1993). George Chauncey, *Gay New York: Gender, Urban Culture, and the Making of the Gay New York World, 1890–1940* (1994), reveals a terrain hitherto invisi-ble to the historian.

Upper Class/Middle Class

Urban social mobility is the focus of Stephan Thernstrom, *The Other Bostonians: Poverty and Progress in an American City, 1880–1970* (1973), which also contains a useful sum-mary of mobility research on other cities. On the social elite see Frederic C. Jaher, *The Urban Establishment: Upper Strata in Boston, New York, Charleston, Chicago, and Los Angeles* (1982). Two recent books greatly advance our understanding of the urban middle class: Stuart S. Blumin, *The Emergence of the Middle Class: Social Experience in the American City, 1760–1900* (1989), and Olivier Zunz, *Making Corporate America, 1870–1920* (1990).

Aspects of middle-class life are revealed in Margaret Marsh, *Suburban Lives* (1990); Gwendolyn Wright, *Moralism and the Model Home: Domestic Architecture and Cultural Conflict in Chicago, 1873–1913* (1980); Susan Strasser, *Never Done: A History of American Housework* (1983); John F. Kasson, *Rudeness and Civility: Manners in Nineteenth-Century America* (1990); and, on the entry of immigrants into the middle class, Andrew R. Heinze, *Adapting to Abundance: Jewish Immigrants, Mass Consumption, and the Search for American Identity* (1990). Contemporary notions of sexuality are skillfully captured in John S. Haller and Robin M. Haller, *The Physician and Sexuality in Victorian America* (1980). Whether those views actually applied to the private world of the middle class is strongly questioned in Karen Lystra, *The Searching Heart: Women, Men, and Romantic Love in Nineteenth-Century America* (1989). Control over reproduction is fully explored in Janet Farrell Brodie, *Contraception and Abortion in Nineteenth-Century America* (1994). On the fostering of high culture in the American city, see Daniel M. Fox, *Engines of Culture: Philanthropy and Art Museums* (1963). The best introduction to intellectual currents in the emerging urban society is Alan Trachtenberg, *The Incorporation of America: Culture and Society, 1865–1893* (1983).

CHAPTER 21

The most recent survey of the Progressive Era is John Milton Cooper, *Pivotal Decades: The United States, 1900–1920* (1990). Two older but still serviceable narrative accounts are George E. Mowry, *The Era of Theodore Roosevelt, 1900–1912* (1958), and Arthur S. Link, *Woodrow Wilson and the Progressive Era, 1910–1917* (1954). A highly influential interpretation of progressive reform that is worth reading despite its disputed central arguments is Richard Hofstadter, *Age of Reform* (1955). Robert H. Wiebe, *The Search for Order, 1877–1920* (1967), places progressive reform in a broader context of organizational development. On the debate over progressivism as a movement, see Daniel Rodgers, "In Search of Progressivism," *Reviews in American History* 10 (1982).

The Course of Reform

The progressive mind has been studied from many different angles. The religious underpinnings are stressed in Robert M. Crunden, *Ministers of Reform: The Progressives' Achievement in American Civilization, 1889–1920* (1982). In *The New Radicalism in America, 1889–1963* (1965), Christopher Lasch sees progressivism as a form of cultural revolt. Most useful on political thinkers is Charles Forcey, *The Crossroads of Liberalism: Croly, Weyl, Lippmann, and the Progressive Era* (1961). A provocative study set in an international context is James T. Kloppenberg, *Uncertain Victory: Social Democracy and Progressivism in European and American Thought, 1870–1920* (1986). On the journalists, see David M. Chalmers, *The Social and Political Ideas of the Muckrakers* (1964), and Harold S. Wilson, *McClure's Magazine and the Muckrakers* (1970).

Political reform has been the subject of a voluminous literature. Wisconsin progressivism can be studied in David P. Thelen, *The New Citizenship: Origins of Progressivism in Wisconsin, 1885–1900* (1972). Important progressives are discussed in Spencer C. Olin, *California's Prodigal Son: Hiram Johnson and the Progressive Movement* (1968), and Richard Lowitt, *George W. Norris: The Making of a Progressive* (1963). On city reform, see Bradley R. Rice, *Progressive Cities: The Commission Government Movement* (1972);

Jack Tager, *The Intellectual as Urban Reformer: Brand Whitlock and the Progressive Movement* (1968); and Melvin G. Holli, *Reform in Detroit: Hazen S. Pingree and Urban Politics* (1969).

The best treatment of the settlement-house movement is Allen F. Davis, *Spearheads of Reform* (1967). Allen F. Davis, *American Heroine: Jane Addams* (1973); George Martin, *Madame Secretary: Frances Perkins* (1976); and Kathryn Kish Sklar, *Florence Kelley and the Nation's Work: The Rise of Women's Political Culture* (1995), deal with leading woman progressives. The connection to working women is effectively treated in Nancy S. Dye, *As Equals and Sisters: Feminism, the Labor Movement, and the Women's Trade Union League of New York* (1980). Women garment workers, the key labor constituency for women progressives, are studied with great skill and insight in Susan A. Glenn, *Daughters of the Shtetl: Life and Labor in the Immigrant Generation* (1990). Two path-breaking books on the origins of American feminism are Rosalind Rosenberg, *Beyond Separate Spheres: The Intellectual Origins of Modern Feminism* (1982), and Nancy F. Cott, *The Grounding of Modern Feminism* (1987). The leading social reformer to spring from feminism is treated in Ellen Chesler, *Woman of Valor: Margaret Sanger and the Birth Control Movement* (1992).

On urban liberalism, the standard book is John D. Buenker, *Urban Liberalism and Progressive Reform* (1973). The relationship to organized labor can be followed in Irwin Yellowitz, *Labor and the Progressive Movement in New York State* (1965). Two important recent books by historical sociologists treat the halting progress toward the welfare state: Theda Skocpol, *Protecting Soldiers and Mothers* (1992), and, in a comparison of the United States with Canada and Britain, Ann Shola Orloff, *The Politics of Pensions* (1993). The most comprehensive survey is Morton Keller, *Regulating a New Society: Public Policy and Social Change In America, 1900–1933* (1994). On the South, see Dewey Grantham, *Southern Progressivism* (1983); on southern black women as social reformers, see Glenda Elizabeth Gilmore, *Gender amd Jim Crow: Women and the Politics of White Supremacy in North Carolina, 1869–1920* (1996); and on the racial conservatism of social progressives, see Elizabeth Lasch-Quinn, *Black Neighbors: Race and the Limits of Reform in the American Settlement-House Movement* (1993). The revival of black protest is vigorously described in Stephen R. Fox, *The Guardian of Boston: William Monroe Trotter* (1971), and in David Levering Lewis, *W. E. B. Du Bois: Biography of a Race, 1868–1919* (1993).

Progressivism and National Politics

National progressivism is best approached through its leading figures. John Milton Cooper, *The Warrior and the Priest* (1983), is a provocative joint biography of Roosevelt and Wilson that emphasizes their shared world view. Lewis S. Gould, *The Presidency of Theodore Roosevelt* (1991), provides a useful synthesis. Aspects of national progressive politics can be followed in James Penick, *Progressive Politics and Conservation: The Ballinger-Pinchot Affair* (1968); James Holt, *Congressional Insurgents and the Party System* (1969); and David Sarasohn, *The Party of Reform: The Democrats in the Progressive Era* (1989). Naomi Lamoreaux, *The Great Merger Movement in American Business, 1895–1904* (1985), offers a sophisticated modern analysis of trust activity, and Thomas K. McCraw, ed., *Regulation in Perspective* (1981), contains valuable interpretive essays on the problems of trust regulation. A comprehensive rethinking of the progressive struggle to fashion a regulatory policy for big business is offered in Martin J. Sklar, *The Corporate Reconstruction of American Capitalism, 1890–1916: The Market, the Law, and Politics* (1988).

CHAPTER 22

Two useful surveys of late nineteenth-century diplomatic history are Foster R. Dulles, *Prelude to World Power, 1865–1900* (1965), and Charles S. Campbell, *The Transformation of American Foreign Relations, 1865–1900* (1976). Invaluable as a historiographical guide is Robert L. Beisner, *From the Old Diplomacy to the New, 1865–1900* (2d ed., 1986).

The Roots of Expansionism

Standard works on the preexpansionist era are David M. Pletcher, *The Awkward Years: American Foreign Relations under Garfield and Arthur* (1963), and Milton Plesur, *America's Outward Thrust: Approaches to American Foreign Affairs, 1865–1890* (1971). Walter LaFeber's highly influential *The New Empire, 1860–1898* (1963) places economic interest—especially the need for overseas markets—at the center of scholarly debate over the sources of American expansionism. On American business overseas the definitive work is Myra Wilkins, *The Emergence of the Multinational Enterprise: American Business Abroad from the Colonial Era to 1914* (1970). Other important books dealing with aspects of American expansionism are David Healy, *U.S. Expansionism: The Imperialist Urge in the 1890s* (1970); Robert Seager, *Alfred Thayer Mahan* (1977); Michael Hunt, *Ideology and U.S. Foreign Policy* (1987); Mark R. Shulman, *Navalism and the Emergence of American Sea Power, 1882–1893* (1995); and Kenneth J. Hagan, *This People's Navy: The Making of American Seapower* (1991).

An American Empire

On the war with Spain, see John Offner, *An Unwanted War: The Diplomacy of the United States and Spain over Cuba, 1895–1898* (1988); David S. Trask, *The War with Spain in 1898* (1981); Frank Freidel, *A Splendid Little War* (1958); and Lewis Gould, *The Spanish-American War and President McKinley* (1982), which emphasizes McKinley's strong leadership. Ernest R. May, *Imperial Democracy: The Emergence of America as a Great Power* (1961), exemplifies the earlier view that McKinley was a weak figure driven to war by jingoistic pressures. On the Philippines, see Richard E. Welch, *Response to Imperialism: The United States and the Philippine-American War, 1898–1903* (1979), and, for the subsequent history, Peter Stanley, *A Nation in the Making: The Philippines and the United States, 1899–1921* (1974). Robert L. Beisner, *Twelve against Empire: The Anti-Imperialists, 1898–1900* (1968), remains the best book on that subject.

Onto the World Stage

On the European context a useful introduction can be found in the early chapters of Felix Gilbert, *The End of the European Era, 1890 to the Present* (4th ed., 1991). For a stimulating interpretation, see L. C. B. Seaman, *From Vienna to Versailles* (1955). On American relations with Britain the standard work is Bradford Perkins, *The Great Rapprochement: England and the United States, 1895–1914* (1968). On Roosevelt's diplomacy the starting point remains Howard K. Beale, *Theodore Roosevelt and the Rise of America to World Power* (1956). There are keen insights into the diplomatic views of both Roosevelt and Wilson in John Milton Cooper, *The Warrior and the Priest* (1983).

On the thrust into the Caribbean, see Walter LaFeber, *The Panama Canal* (1979); Richard Lael, *Arrogant Diplomacy: U.S. Policy toward Colombia, 1903–1922* (1987); David Healy, *Drive to Hegemony: The United States in the Caribbean, 1898–1917* (1988); and Thomas D. Schoonover, *The United States in Central America, 1860–1911* (1991). America's Asian involvements are treated in Thomas J. McCormick, *China Market: America's Quest for Informal Empire, 1893–1901* (1967); Michael H. Hunt, *The Making of a Special Relationship: The United States and China to 1914* (1983); and Akira Iriye, *Pacific Estrangement: Japanese and American Expansion, 1897–1911* (1972). On the Mexican involvement, see John S. D. Eisenhower, *Intervention! The United States and the Mexican Revolution* (1993). There is a lively and critical analysis of Wilson's misguided policies in Robert E. Quirk, *An Affair of Honor: Woodrow Wilson and the Occupation of Veracruz* (1962). The revolution as experienced by the Mexicans is brilliantly depicted in John Womack, *Zapata and the Mexican Revolution* (1968).

CHAPTER 23

Ronald Schaffer, *America in the Great War* (1991), and David M. Kennedy, *Over Here* (1980), provide comprehensive overviews of the period. A less scholarly, but highly readable account is Meirion and Susie Harries, *The Last Days of Innocence* (1997). On the links between the Progressive Era and the war, see Neil A. Wynn, *From Progressivism to Prosperity* (1986); John A. Thompson, *Reformers and War* (1987); John F. McClymer, *War and Welfare* (1980); and Robert M. Crunden, *Ministers of Reform* (1982). Ellis W. Hawley, *The Great War and the Search for a Modern Order, 1917–1933* (1979), stresses the continuities between the war years and the 1920s.

The Great War, 1914–1918

On America's entry into World War I, see John Coogan, *The End to Neutrality* (1981); Ross Gregory, *The Origins of American Intervention in the First World War* (1971); and Thomas A. Bailey and Paul Ryan, *The Lusitania Disaster* (1975). There is a large body of material on the policies and personality of Woodrow Wilson, beginning with Arthur Link's five-volume biography (1947–1965) and his *Woodrow Wilson: Revolution, War and Peace* (1979). Other studies of Wilson include August Hecksher, *Woodrow Wilson* (1991); Kendrick Clements, *The Presidency of Woodrow Wilson* (1992); Robert Ferrell, *Woodrow Wilson and World War I* (1985); Arthur S. Link, ed., *Woodrow Wilson and a Revolutionary World* (1982); and John Milton Cooper, Jr., *The Warrior and the Priest: Woodrow Wilson and Theodore Roosevelt* (1983).

On American participation in the war, Russell Weigley, *The American Way of War* (1973), and Edward M. Coffman, *The War to End All Wars* (1968) provide useful introductions. They can be supplemented by Laurence Stallings, *The Doughboys* (1963), and A. E. Barbeau and Florette Henri, *The Unknown Soldiers: Black Troops in World War I* (1974). John Whiteclay Chambers II, *To Raise an Army* (1987), covers the draft. Allan Brandt, *No Magic Bullet* (1985), discusses anti–venereal disease campaigns. Mary E. Odem, *Delinquent Daughters* (1995), provides a discussion of the attempt to control sexuality during the war years. On Prohibition, see Joseph R. Gusfield, *Symbolic Crusade* (1963); James H. Timberlake, *Prohibition and the Progressive Movement* (1963); and K. Austin Ker, *Organized for Prohibition* (1985).

War on the Home Front

Robert D. Cuff, *The War Industries Board* (1973), provides an excellent case study of mobilization for war. Lawrence E. Gelfand, ed., *Herbert Hoover* (1979), includes several essays on Hoover's role in food conservation. See also Stephen Skowronek, *Building a New American State* (1982); Charles Gilbert, *American Financing of World War I* (1970); and David F. Noble, *America by Design* (1977). Valerie Jean Conner, *The National War Labor Board* (1983), covers federal policies toward labor, and Melvyn Dubofsky, *The State and Labor in Modern America* (1994), offers a valuable discussion of the "positive state" and labor during the war.

Maurine Greenwald, *Women, War, and Work* (1980), and Barbara Steinson, *American Women's Activism in World War I* (1982), provide good overviews of women's wartime experiences. Ellen Carol Du Bois, *Harriet Stanton Blatch and the Winning of Woman's Suffrage* (1997); Eleanor Flexner, *Century of Struggle* (1959); and Christine A. Lunardini, *From Equal Suffrage to Equal Rights: Alice Paul and the National Woman's Party, 1910–1928* (1986), cover the final stages of the woman suffrage campaign. On the peace movement, see C. Roland Marchand, *The American Peace Movement and Social Reform, 1898–1918* (1973); Charles Chatfield, *For Peace and Justice* (1971); and Charles DeBenedetti, *Origins of the Modern Peace Movement* (1978).

Efforts to promote national unity are covered in Stephen Vaughan, *Holding Fast the Inner Lines: Democracy, Nationalism, and the CPI* (1980); William J. Breen, *Uncle Sam at Home* (1984); Paul L. Murphy, *World War I and the Origins of Civil Liberties* (1979); William Preston, Jr., *Aliens and Dissenters* (1963); and Frederick Luebke, *Bonds of Loyalty: German-Americans and World War I* (1974). On free speech, see Richard Polenberg, *Fighting Faiths: The Abrams Case, the Supreme Court, and Free Speech* (1987), as well as Zechariah Chaffee, Jr.'s, classic *Free Speech in the United States* (1941). For the experiences of Mexican-Americans, see Rodolfo Acuña, *Occupied America* (1980), George Sánchez, *Becoming Mexican American* (1993); Ricardo Romo, *History of a Barrio: East Los Angeles* (1977); and Wayne Cornelius, *Building the Cactus Curtain* (1980).

An Unsettled Peace, 1919–1920

On Wilson's diplomacy, see Thomas Knock, *To End All Wars* (1992); Lloyd Ambrosius, *Woodrow Wilson and the American Diplomatic Tradition* (1987); Arthur Walworth, *Wilson and the Peacemakers* (1986); and N. Gordon Levin, Jr., *Woodrow Wilson and World Politics* (1968). For more on Versailles and the League of Nations, see Ralph A. Stone, *The Irreconcilables* (1970), and Arno J. Mayer, *Politics and Diplomacy of Peacemaking* (1967). See also William Widenor, *Henry Cabot Lodge and the Search for an American Foreign Policy* (1980). On American intervention in Russia, see George F. Kennan, *The Decision to Intervene* (1958); John L. Gaddis, *Russia, The Soviet Union, and the United States* (1978); and Peter Filene, *Americans and the Soviet Experiment, 1917–1933* (1967).

Robert K. Murray, *The Red Scare* (1955), summarizes the antiradicalism of the postwar period. See also James Weinstein, *The Decline of Socialism in America, 1912–1923* (1967); and John Higham, *Strangers in the Land* (1955). David Brody, *Labor in Crisis* (1965), describes the steel strike of 1919; for a more general overview, see David Montgomery, *The Fall of the House of Labor* (1987). On race relations, see Joe William Trotter, Jr., ed., *The Great Migration in Historical Perspective* (1991); James R. Grossman, *Land of Hope: Chicago, Black Southerners, and the Great Migration* (1989); William M. Tuttle, Jr.,

Race Riot (1970); Jacqueline Jones, *Labor of Love, Labor of Sorrow* (1985); Robert V. Haynes, *A Night of Violence: The Houston Riot of 1917* (1976); and Elliot M. Rudwick, *Race Riot at East St. Louis, July 2, 1917* (1964). An invaluable primary source is Chicago Commission on Race Relations, *The Negro in Chicago* (1922). For an introduction to the Sacco and Vanzetti case, see Louis Joughin and Edmund Morgan, *The Legacy of Sacco and Vanzetti* (1948), and Roberta Strauss Feuerlicht, *Justice Crucified* (1977).

CHAPTER 24

General overviews of the 1920s are provided by Lynn Dumenil, *The Modern Temper* (1994); Ellis Hawley, *The Great War and the Search for a Modern Order, 1917–1933* (1979); William Leuchtenburg, *The Perils of Prosperity*, 2d ed. (1995); and Frederick Lewis Allen, *Only Yesterday* (1931). Ann Douglas, *Terrible Honesty: Mongrel Manhattan in the 1920s* (1995), uses New York City to look broadly at culture in the 1920s. Robert S. Lynd and Helen Merrell Lynd, *Middletown* (1929), remains a superb study of American life and values in the 1920s.

Business–Government Partnership of the 1920s

Discussion of corporate developments can be found in Alfred Chandler, *The Visible Hand* (1977), and James Gilbert, *Designing the Industrial State* (1972). Irving Bernstein, *The Lean Years* (1960); David Brody, *Workers in Industrial America* (1980); Dana Frank, *Purchasing Power: Consumer Organizing, Gender, and the Seattle Labor Movement, 1919–1929* (1994); and David Montgomery, *The Fall of the House of Labor* (1987), cover labor developments.

The domestic and international aspects of the economy are treated in Jim Potter, *The American Economy between the Wars* (1974); Mira Wilkins, *The Maturing of Multinational Enterprise* (1974); and Emily Rosenberg, *Spreading the American Dream* (1982). Interpretations of foreign policy include Akira Iriye, *The Globalizing of America, 1913–1945* (1993); Warren Cohen, *Empire without Tears* (1987); William Appleman Williams, *The Tragedy of American Diplomacy* (1962); and Walter LaFeber, *Inevitable Revolutions* (1983).

General introductions to politics in the 1920s can be found in John D. Hicks, *Republican Ascendancy* (1960); David Burner, *The Politics of Provincialism* (1967); and Robert Murray, *The Politics of Normalcy* (1973). Alan Dawley, *Struggles for Justice* (1991), analyzes the fate of reform. Biographies of the decade's major political figures include Donald McCoy, *Calvin Coolidge* (1967); David Burner, *Herbert Hoover* (1979); Joan Hoff Wilson, *Herbert Hoover* (1975); and Paula Elder, *Governor Alfred E. Smith* (1983). On women in politics, see J. Stanley Lemons, *The Woman Citizen* (1973); Clarke A. Chambers, *Seedtime of Reform* (1963); Nancy Cott, *The Grounding of Modern Feminism* (1987); and Elisabeth Israels Perry, *Belle Moskowitz* (1987).

A New National Culture

Daniel Boorstin, *The Americans: The Democratic Experience* (1973); David Nasaw, *Going Out: The Rise and Fall of Public Amusements* (1993); and essays in Catherine L. Covert and John D. Stevens, eds., *Mass Media between the Wars* (1984), provide excellent introductions to the emerging mass culture. On movies, see Robert Sklar, *Movie-Made America* (1975); Lary May, *Screening Out the Past* (1980); Lewis A. Erenberg, *Steppin' Out* (1981); David Stenn, *Clara Bow, Runnin' Wild* (1988); and Sumiko Higashi, *Virgins,*

Vamps and Flappers (1978). Erik Barnouw, *A Tower in Babel* (1966); Susan Douglas, *Inventing American Broadcasting* (1987); and Philip Rosen, *The Modern Stentors* (1980), discuss radio. See also Melvin Patrick Ely, *The Adventures of Amos 'n' Andy* (1991), and Claude E. Fischer, *America Calling: A Social History of the Telephone to 1940* (1992). Stewart Ewen, *Captains of Consciousness* (1976); Daniel Pope, *The Making of Modern Advertising* (1983); Roland Marchand, *Advertising the American Dream* (1985); Vincent Vinikas, *Soft Soap, Hard Sell* (1992); and T. J. Jackson Lears, *Fables of Abundance* (1994), cover advertising. Paula Fass, *The Damned and the Beautiful* (1977), and Beth L. Bailey, *From Front Porch to Back Seat* (1988), cover youth, while Susan Strasser, *Never Done* (1982), and Ruth Schwartz Cowan, *More Work for Mother* (1983), discuss white middle-class women. Lizabeth Cohen, *Making a New Deal* (1990), suggests how working-class communities adapted mass culture for their purposes. Joan Shelley Rubin describes the middle class in *The Making of Middlebrow Culture* (1992).

The impact of the automobile on modern American life is documented by James Flink, *The Car Culture* (1975) and *The Automobile Age* (1988), and by Clay McShane, *Down the Asphalt Path: The Automobile and the American City* (1994), and Virginia Scharff, *Taking the Wheel* (1991). For sports, see Allen Guttmann, *A Whole New Ball Game* (1988); Harvey Green, *Fit for America* (1986); and Susan Cahn, *Coming on Strong: Gender and Sexuality in 20th Century Women's Sport* (1994). The Negro Leagues are covered in Robert W. Peterson, *Only the Ball Was White* (1970), and Donn Rogosin, *Invisible Men* (1985).

Dissenting Values and Cultural Conflict

Paul Carter, *Another Part of the Twenties* (1977), outlines the decade's deeply felt cultural controversies. Background on rural and urban life is provided by Don Kirschner, *City and Country* (1970); Zane Miller, *The Urbanization of America* (1973); and Jon Teaford, *The Twentieth-Century American City* (1986). John Higham, *Strangers in the Land* (1955), describes immigration restriction and nativism. Richard K. Tucker, *The Dragon and the Cross* (1991), and Leonard Moore, *Citizen Klansmen* (1991), cover the Klan's rise and fall, while Kathleen M. Blee, *Women of the Klan* (1991), and Nancy MacLean, *Behind the Mask of Chivalry* (1994), offer provocative discussions of racism and gender in the 1920s. See also Kenneth Jackson, *The Ku Klux Klan in the City, 1915–1930* (1965). George M. Marsden, *Fundamentalism and American Culture* (1980), and William G. McLoughlin, *Fundamentalism in American Culture* (1983), cover religion. Lawrence W. Levine, *Defender of the Faith* (1965), traces the last years of William Jennings Bryan's career. Robert Crunden, *From Self to Society, 1919–1941* (1972); Roderick Nash, *The Nervous Generation* (1969); Frederick J. Hoffman, *The 20s* (1962); and Daniel Singal, ed., *Modernist Culture in America* (1991), cover key intellectual developments. On the Harlem Renaissance see Jervis Anderson, *This Was Harlem, 1900–1950* (1982); Nathan Huggins, *Harlem Renaissance* (1971); and Gloria T. Hull, *Color, Sex, and Poetry: Three Women Writers of the Harlem Renaissance* (1987); see also Burton Peretti, *The Creation of Jazz* (1992). Judith Stein, *The World of Marcus Garvey* (1985), and Theodore Vincent, *Black Power and the Garvey Movement* (1970), describe Marcus Garvey. On prohibition, see Andrew Sinclair, *Prohibition* (1962); Joseph R. Gusfield, *Symbolic Crusade* (1963); and Norman Clark, *Deliver Us from Evil* (1976). The 1928 election is covered in David Burner, *The Politics of Provincialism* (1967); Oscar Handlin, *Al Smith and His America* (1958); Kristi Andersen, *The Creation of a Democratic Majority, 1928–1936* (1979); and Allan J. Lichtman's quantitative study, *Prejudice and the Old Politics* (1979).

CHAPTER 25

Useful overviews of the Great Depression are T. H. Watkins, *The Great Depression: America in the 1930s* (1993); John A. Garraty, *The Great Depression* (1987); and Robert S. McElvaine, *The Great Depression, 1929–1941* (1984).

The Coming of the Great Depression

Historians and economists continue to debate the causes of the Great Depression. See John Kenneth Galbraith, *The Great Crash* (1954); Milton Friedman and Anna Schwartz, *The Great Contraction, 1929–1933* (1965); Charles Kindelberger, *The World in Depression* (1974); Peter Temin, *Did Monetary Forces Cause the Great Depression?* (1976); and Michael Bernstein, *The Great Depression* (1988).

Hard Times

A wealth of material brings the voices of the 1930s to life. The Federal Writers' Project, *These Are Our Lives* (1939); Tom Terrill and Jerrold Hirsch, eds., *Such as Us: Southern Voices of the Thirties* (1978); and Ann Banks, ed., *First-Person America* (1980), all draw on oral histories collected by the Works Progress Administration during the 1930s. See also Richard Lowitt and Maurine Beasley, eds., *One-Third of a Nation: Lorena Hickock Reports the Great Depression* (1981), and Robert S. McElvaine, ed., *Down and Out in the Great Depression* (1983), for firsthand accounts. Evocative secondary sources include Studs Terkel, *Hard Times: An Oral History of the Great Depression* (1970); Irving Bernstein, *The Lean Years* (1960); and Caroline Bird, *The Invisible Scar* (1966).

Descriptions of family life in the 1930s include Robert and Helen Lynd, *Middletown in Transition* (1937); Mirra Komarovsky, *The Unemployed Man and His Family* (1940); and Roger Angell, *The Family Encounters the Depression* (1936). Russell Baker's autobiography, *Growing Up* (1982), provides an often humorous description of family life in the 1930s. Glen H. Elder, Jr., *Children of the Great Depression* (1974), and John A. Clausen, *American Lives: Looking Back at the Children of the Great Depression* (1993), look at the long-term effects. For more on youth, see Maxine Davis, *The Lost Generation* (1936); Eileen Eagan, *Class, Culture, and the Classroom* (1981); Beth L. Bailey, *From Front Porch to Back Seat* (1988); and John Modell, *Into One's Own: From Youth to Adulthood, 1920–1975* (1989).

Frederick Lewis Allen, *Since Yesterday* (1939), provides an impressionistic overview of popular culture in the 1930s. See also the essays in Lawrence W. Levine, *The Unpredictable Past* (1993). Specific studies of movies and Hollywood include Robert Sklar, *Movie-Made America* (2d ed., 1987); Andrew Bergman, *We're in the Money* (1971); Molly Haskell, *From Reverence to Rape: The Treatment of Women in the Movies* (2d ed., 1987); and Thomas Schatz, *The Genius of the System: Hollywood Film Making in the Studio Era* (1988). On radio, see Arthur Frank Wertheim, *Radio Comedy* (1979).

Material on women in the 1930s can be found in Susan Ware, *Holding Their Own* (1982); Winifred Wandersee, *Women's Work and Family Values, 1920–1940* (1981); and Lois Scharf, *To Work and to Wed* (1981). For the special dimensions of white rural women's lives, see Margaret Hagood, *Mothers of the South* (1939). Jeane Westin, *Making Do: How Women Survived the '30s* (1976), is a lively account drawn from interviews. The birth control movement is surveyed in Linda Gordon, *Woman's Body, Woman's Right* (2d ed., 1990); James Reed, *From Private Vice to Public Virtue* (1978); Estelle Freedman and John D'Emilio, *Intimate Matters: A History of Sexuality in America* (1988); and Ellen Chesler, *Woman of Valor: Margaret Sanger and the Birth Control Movement in America* (1992).

The Social Fabric of Depression America

Developments in the black community during the 1930s are covered in Cheryl Lyn Greenberg, *"Or Does It Explode?": Harlem in the Great Depression* (1991); Gilbert Osofsky, *Harlem: The Making of a Ghetto* (1966); Gunnar Myrdal, *An American Dilemma* (1944); David Lewis, *When Harlem Was in Vogue* (1981); Jervis Anderson, *This Was Harlem, 1900–1950* (1982); and Robert Weisbrot, *Father Divine and the Struggle for Racial Equality* (1983). James Goodman, *Stories of Scottsboro* (1994), and Dan T. Carter, *Scottsboro* (1969), cover that case. Donald Grubbs, *Cry from Cotton* (1971), tells the story of the Southern Tenant Farmers Union. Robin D. G. Kelley, *Hammer and Hoe* (1990), is an excellent account of Alabama communists during the Great Depression. Donald Worster, *Dust Bowl* (1979), evokes the plains during the "Dirty Thirties," as does Ann Marie Low's memoir, *Dust Bowl Diary* (1984). James N. Gregory, *American Exodus: The Dust Bowl Migration and Okie Culture in California* (1989), treats the experiences of migrants in and their impact on California culture and the economy.

On the experiences of Mexican-Americans during the 1930s see Mario T. Garcia, *Mexican Americans: Leadership, Ideology, and Identity, 1930–1960* (1989); Devra Weber, *Dark Sweat, White Gold: California Farm Workers, Cotton, and the New Deal* (1994); and Mario T. Garcia, *Memories of Chicano History: The Life and Narrative of Bert Corona* (1994). George J. Sánchez, *Becoming Mexican American* (1993), examines Chicano Los Angeles from 1900 to 1945. See also Carey McWilliams, *North from Mexico* (1948), and Richard A. Garcia, *The Rise of the Mexican-American Middle Class* (1990). For Mexican-American women's lives, see Vicki Ruiz, *Cannery Women, Cannery Lives: Mexican Women, Unionization, and the California Food Processing Industry, 1930–1950* (1987), and Patricia Zavella, *Women's Work and Chicano Families* (1987).

Herbert Hoover and the Great Depression

Hoover's response to the depression is chronicled in Alfred Romasco, *The Poverty of Abundance* (1965), and Jordan Schwartz, *The Interregnum of Despair* (1970). See also David Burner, *Herbert Hoover* (1978); Joan Hoff Wilson, *Herbert Hoover: Forgotten Progressive* (1975); and William Barber, *Herbert Hoover, the Economists, and American Economic Policy, 1921–1933* (1986). Eliot Rosen, *Hoover, Roosevelt, and the Brain Trust* (1977), treats the transition between the two administrations, as does Frank Freidel, *Launching the New Deal* (1973). On the 1932 election and the beginnings of the New Deal coalition, see David Burner, *The Politics of Provincialism* (1967); Samuel Lubell, *The Future of American Politics* (1952); and John Allswang, *The New Deal in American Politics* (1978).

CHAPTER 26

Comprehensive introductions to the New Deal include Robert S. McElvaine, *The Great Depression* (1984); Anthony J. Badger, *The New Deal* (1989); William E. Leuchtenburg, *Franklin D. Roosevelt and the New Deal* (1963); Barry Karl, *The Uneasy State* (1983); John A. Garraty, *The Great Depression* (1987); Roger Biles, *A New Deal for the American People* (1991); and Harvard Sitkoff, ed., *Fifty Years Later: The New Deal Evaluated* (1985).

The New Deal Begins, 1933–1935

The New Deal has inspired a voluminous bibliography. Frank Freidel, *Launching the New Deal* (1973), covers the first hundred days in detail. Monographs include Bernard Bellush, *The Failure of the NRA* (1975); Thomas K. McCraw, *TVA and the Power Fight* (1970); John Salmond, *The Civilian Conservation Corps* (1967); Roy Lubove, *The Struggle for Social Security* (1968); Susan Kennedy, *The Banking Crisis of 1933* (1973); Michael Parrish, *Securities Regulation and the New Deal* (1970); Mark Leff, *The Limits of Symbolic Reform: The New Deal and Taxation, 1933–1939* (1984); James Olson, *Saving Capitalism: The Reconstruction Finance Corporation and the New Deal, 1933–1940* (1988); and Bonnie Fox Schwartz, *The Civilian Works Administration, 1933–1934* (1984). Ellis Hawley, *The New Deal and the Problem of Monopoly* (1966), provides a stimulating account of economic policy. Agricultural developments are covered in Theodore Saloutos, *The American Farmer and the New Deal* (1982); Paul Mertz, *The New Deal and Southern Rural Poverty* (1978); and Sidney Baldwin, *Poverty and Politics: The Rise and Decline of the Farm Security Administration* (1968). Greg Mitchell, *The Campaign of the Century* (1992), describes Upton Sinclair's campaign for the California governorship, and Alan Brinkley, *Voices of Protest* (1982), covers the Coughlin and Long movements. See also Leo Ribuffo, *The Old Christian Right* (1983).

The Second New Deal, 1935–1938

Roosevelt's second term has drawn far less attention than has the 1933–1936 period. James MacGregor Burns, *Roosevelt* (1956), provides an overview, as does Barry Karl, *The Uneasy State* (1983). Alan Brinkley, *The End of Reform* (1995), discusses the New Deal and liberalism between 1937 and 1945. The growing opposition to the New Deal is treated in James T. Patterson, *Congressional Conservatism and the New Deal* (1967); Richard Polenberg, *Reorganizing Roosevelt's Government* (1966); and Barry Karl, *Executive Reorganization and Reform in the New Deal* (1963).

The New Deal's Impact on Society

Katie Louchheim, ed., *The Making of the New Deal: The Insiders Speak* (1983), provides an engaging introduction to some of the men and women who shaped the New Deal. See also Peter Irons, *New Deal Lawyers* (1982), and Jordan A. Schwartz, *The New Dealers* (1993). On women in the New Deal, see Susan Ware, *Beyond Suffrage* (1981). Blanche Cook, *Eleanor Roosevelt* (1991), takes the story to 1933; see also Lois Scharf, *Eleanor Roosevelt* (1987). George Martin, *Madam Secretary* (1976), covers the career of Frances Perkins.

On minorities and the New Deal, see Harvard Sitkoff, *A New Deal for Blacks* (1978); John B. Kirby, *Black Americans in the Roosevelt Era* (1980); Robert Zangrando, *The NAACP Crusade against Lynching, 1909–1950* (1980); and Nancy J. Weiss, *Farewell to the Party of Lincoln* (1983). George J. Sánchez, *Becoming Mexican American: Ethnicity, Culture and Identity in Chicano Los Angeles, 1900–1945* (1993), describes the politicization of Mexican-Americans in the 1930s.

Irving Bernstein, *The Turbulent Years* (1970), and *A Caring Society: The New Deal, the Worker, and the Great Depression* (1985), chronicle the story of the labor movement through 1941. Additional studies include Peter Friedlander, *The Emergence of a UAW Local* (1975); Melvin Dubofsky and Warren Van Tine, *John L. Lewis* (1977); Sidney Fine, *Sit-Down: The General Motors Strike of 1936–1937* (1969); David Brody, *Workers in Industrializing America* (1980); Ronald Schatz, *The Electrical Workers* (1983); Bruce Nelson, *Workers on the Waterfront* (1988); and Lizabeth Cohen, *Making a New Deal* (1990). Steven Fraser, *Labor Will Rule* (1991), is a fine biography of Sidney Hillman.

On Indian policy see Donald Parman, *Navajoes and the New Deal* (1976); Laurence Hauptman, *The Iroquois and the New Deal* (1981); and Laurence C. Kelly, *The Assault on Assimilation: John Collier and the Origins of Indian Policy Reform* (1983). For material on rural electrification, see D. Clayton Brown, *Electricity for Rural America* (1980), and Marquis Childs, *The Farmer Takes a Hand* (1952).

The creation of the New Deal's welfare system is treated in James T. Patterson, *America's Struggle against Poverty* (1981), which carries the story through 1980. Linda Gordon, *Pitied but Not Entitled* (1994), looks at single mothers and the history of welfare. See also Michael Katz, *In the Shadow of the Poorhouse* (1986); John Garraty, *Unemployment in History* (1978); and Otis Graham, *Towards a Planned Society* (1976). For the enduring impact of Franklin Roosevelt on the political system, see William Leuchtenburg, *In the Shadow of FDR* (1983).

The various New Deal programs have found historians in Jerry Mangione, *The Dream and the Deal: The Federal Writers' Project, 1935–1943* (1972); Monty Penkower, *The Federal Writers' Project* (1977); Richard McKinzie, *The New Deal for Artists* (1973); and Jane DeHart Mathews, *The Federal Theater, 1935–1939* (1967). Marlene Park and Gerald Markowitz, *Democratic Vistas* (1984), surveys New Deal murals and art. General studies of cultural expression include William Stott, *Documentary Expression and Thirties America* (1973), and Richard Pells, *Radical Visions and American Dreams* (1973). See also Karen Becker Ohrn, *Dorothea Lange and the Documentary Tradition* (1980), and F. Jack Hurley, *Portrait of a Decade: Roy Stryker and the Development of Documentary Photography in the Thirties* (1972).

Daniel Aaron, *Writers on the Left* (1961), provides an overview of literary currents in the decade. Material on the relationship between intellectuals and the Communist party can be found in Harvey Klehr, *The Heyday of American Communism* (1984), and Irving Howe and Lewis Coser, *The American Communist Party* (1957). Warren Susman provides a provocative analysis of culture and commitment in the 1930s in *Culture as History* (1984).

CHAPTER 27

John Morton Blum, *V Was for Victory* (1976); William O'Neill, *A Democracy at War* (1993); Michael C. C. Adams, *The Best War Ever* (1994); Richard Polenberg, *War and Society* (1972); and Geoffrey Perret, *Days of Sadness, Years of Triumph* (1973), offer good introductions to American politics and culture during the war years. A valuable collection of articles is Lewis A. Erenberg and Susan E. Hirsch, eds., *The War In American Culture* (1996). A powerful and provocative oral history of the war is Studs Terkel, *The Good War: An Oral History of World War Two* (1984). John Keegan, *The Second World War* (1990), offers the best one-volume account of the battlefront aspects.

The Road to War

Depression and wartime diplomacy are covered in Robert Dallek, *Franklin D. Roosevelt and American Foreign Policy, 1932–1945* (1979); Akira Iriye, *The Globalizing of America, 1913–1945* (1993); Robert Divine, *The Reluctant Belligerent* (2d ed., 1979); Arnold Offner, *American Appeasement* (1976); and David Schmitz, *The United States and*

Fascist Italy, 1922–1940 (1988). On American isolationism, see Wayne Cole, *Roosevelt and the Isolationists, 1932–1945* (1983). Warren T. Kimball, *The Juggler* (1991), provides an overview of Roosevelt's wartime leadership. Roberta Wohlstetter, *Pearl Harbor* (1962), and Gordon W. Prange, *At Dawn We Slept* (1981), describe the events that led to American entry.

Mobilizing for Victory

Gerald T. White, *Billions for Defense* (1980), and Harold G. Vatter, *The U.S. Economy in World War II* (1985), discuss America's economic mobilization. Alan Winkler, *The Politics of Propaganda* (1978), covers the Office of War Information. On labor's role during war, see George Lipsitz, *Rainbow at Midnight* (1994), and Nelson Lichtenstein, *Labor's War at Home* (1982). Michael S. Sherry, *In the Shadow of War* (1995), provides an account of the World War II origins of the militarization of the United States. For more on politics in wartime, see James McGregor Burns, *Roosevelt: The Soldier of Freedom* (1970), and Alan Brinkley, *The End of Reform* (1995).

Women's roles in wartime are covered by Susan Hartmann, *The Home Front and Beyond* (1982); Leila J. Rupp, *Mobilizing Women for War* (1978); D'Ann Campbell, *Women at War with America* (1984); Ruth Milkman, *Gender at Work* (1987); and Sherna B. Gluck, *Rosie the Riveter Revisited* (1987). Judy Barrett Litoff and David C. Smith, *We're in This War, Too* (1994), includes letters from American women in uniform.

Life on the Home Front

William M. Tuttle, Jr., *"Daddy's Gone to War"* (1993), describes World War II from the perspective of the nation's children. Alan Clive, *State of War* (1979), provides a case study of Michigan during the war; Marilynn S. Johnson, *The Second Gold Rush* (1993), describes Oakland and the East Bay. See also Gerald D. Nash, *The American West Transformed* (1985), and Marc Scott Miller, *The Irony of Victory: World War II and Lowell, Massachusetts* (1988). Clayton R. Koppes and Gregory D. Black, *Hollywood Goes to War* (1987), covers the film industry. The experience of black Americans is treated in Albert Russell Buchanan, *Black Americans in World War II* (1977), and Neil Wynn, *The Afro-American and the Second World War* (1975). On racial tensions, see Dominic Capeci, Jr., *Race Relations in Wartime Detroit* (1984), and Mauricio Mazan, *The Zoot Suit Riots* (1984). August Meier and Elliott Rudwick, *CORE* (1973), describes the founding of an important civil-rights organization. Richard Dalfiume, *Desegregation of the U.S. Armed Forces* (1969), covers black soldiers in the military, and Phillip McGuire, comp., *Taps for a Jim Crow Army* (1993), offers a collection of letters from black soldiers. Alan Berube, *Coming Out under Fire* (1990), is an oral history of gay men and lesbians in the military. Two accounts of Japanese relocation are Audre Girdner and Anne Loftus, *The Great Betrayal* (1969), and Roger Daniels, *Prisoners without Trial* (1993). See also John Tateishi, ed., *And Justice for All: An Oral History of the Japanese-American Detention Camps* (1984), and Peter Irons, *Justice at War: The Story of the Japanese-American Internment Cases* (1983). Valerie Matsumoto, *Farming the Home Place* (1993), describes a Japanese-American community in California from 1919 to 1982.

Fighting and Winning the War

Extensive material chronicles the American military experience during World War II. Albert Russell Buchanan, *The United States and World War II* (1962), and Russell F. Weigley, *The American Way of War* (1973), provide overviews. Cornelius Ryan, *The Last Battle* (1966); John Toland, *The Last Hundred Days* (1966); and Stephen Ambrose, *D-Day, June 6, 1944* (1994), describe the end of the fighting in Europe. David S. Wyman, *The Abandonment of the Jews* (1984), describes the lack of American response to the Holocaust from 1941 to 1945. On the Far East, see John W. Dower, *War without Mercy* (1986); Ronald H. Spector, *Eagle against the Sun* (1984); and John Toland, *Rising Sun* (1970). See Geoffrey Perret, *Old Soldiers Never Die* (1996), on General Douglas MacArthur.

American diplomacy and the strategy of the Grand Alliance are surveyed in Lloyd Gardner, *Spheres of Influence* (1993). The relationship between the wartime conferences and the onset of the Cold War are treated in Walter LaFeber, *America, Russia, and the Cold War* (7th ed., 1993); Stephen Ambrose, *Rise to Globalism* (7th ed., 1993); John L. Gaddis, *The United States and the Origins of the Cold War* (1972); and Herbert Feis, *Between War and Peace* (1960). Richard Rhodes, *The Making of the Atomic Bomb* (1987); McGeorge Bundy, *Danger and Survival* (1988); and Martin Sherwin, *A World Destroyed* (1975), provide compelling accounts of the development of the bomb. See also Gar Alperowitz, *The Decision to Use the Atomic Bomb* (1995); Ronald Takaki, *Hiroshima* (1995); Gregg Herken, *The Winning Weapon* (1980); John Hersey, *Hiroshima* (2d ed., 1985); and Robert Jay Lifton and Greg Mitchell, *Hiroshima in America: Fifty Years of Denial* (1995).

CHAPTER 28

General works on the politics and diplomacy of the cold war era include William Chafe, *The Unfinished Journey* (3d ed., 1995); Paul Boyer, *Promises to Keep* (1995); and James T. Patterson, *Grand Expectations: The United States, 1945–1974* (1996).

The Early Cold War

The best overviews of the Cold War are Walter LaFeber, *America, Russia, and the Cold War, 1945–1990* (7th ed., 1992); Stephen Ambrose, *Rise to Globalism* (7th ed., 1993); and Thomas G. Paterson, *On Every Front* (rev. ed., 1992). Melvyn P. Leffler presents a masterful and exhaustive synthesis of Truman's foreign policy in *A Preponderance of Power* (1992). For critical views of American aims, see H. W. Brands, *The Devil We Knew* (1993); and Richard Ned Lebow and Janice Gross Stein, *We All Lost the Cold War* (1994). John Lewis Gaddis, *Strategies of Containment* (1982), blames the Cold War on both the United States and the Soviet Union, although his more recent works, *The Long Peace* (1987) and *The United States and the End of the Cold War* (1992), are more sympathetic to American policy making. For international perspectives on the Cold War, see Melvyn P. Leffler and David S. Painter, eds., *Origins of the Cold War* (1994); Thomas J. McCormick, *America's Half-Century* (1989); and Warren I. Cohen, *America in the Age of Soviet Power* (1993).

For collective accounts of key policymakers, see Walter Isaacson and Evan Thomas, *The Wise Men* (1986), and Donald R. Mcloy, *The Making of the American Establishment* (1992).

McGeorge Bundy, *Danger and Survival* (1989); Martin J. Sherwin, *A World Destroyed* (1975); and Gar Alperovitz, *Atomic Diplomacy* (2d ed., 1994), cover the impact of atomic weapons on American policy. For general discussions of America and nuclear weapons, see Paul Boyer, *By the Bomb's Early Light* (1985); Richard G. Hewlett and Jack Hall, *Atoms for Peace and War, 1953–1961* (1989); Howard Ball, *Justice Downwind* (1986); and Lawrence S. Wittner, *One World or None* (1993).

For developments in Asia, Akira Iriye, *The Cold War in Asia* (1974), is a good start-ing point. See also William Borden, *The Pacific Alliance* (1984), and Warren I. Cohen, *America's Response to China* (2d ed., 1980). There is an abundance of scholarship on the Korean War, including Callum McDonald, *Korea* (1987); Burton Kaufman, *The Korean War* (1986); and Bruce Cumings, *Liberation and the Emergence of Separate Regions, 1945–1947* (1981) and *The Roaring of the Cataract, 1945–1950* (1990). Sergei N. Goncharov et al., *Uncertain Partners* (1994), uses newly released Soviet and Chinese documents to analyze the role of those countries in the war.

Harry Truman and the Cold War at Home

Harry Truman, in his *Memoirs* (1952–1962), tells his own story. See also two recent bi-ographies, Alonzo Hamby, *Man of the People* (1995), and Robert Ferrell, *Harry S. Tru-man* (1994). General accounts of the Truman presidency can be found in Robert J. Donovan, *Tumultuous Years* (1982); Alonzo Hamby, *Beyond the New Deal* (1973); and William Pemberton, *Harry S. Truman* (1989). Critical perspectives are presented in Barton J. Bernstein, ed., *Politics and Policies of the Truman Administration* (1970), and Michael J. Lacey, ed., *The Truman Presidency* (1989).

The literature on McCarthyism is voluminous. Two recent overviews are Richard Fried, *Nightmare in Red* (1990), and Stephen J. Whitfield, *The Culture of the Cold War* (1991). David Caute, *The Great Fear* (1978), provides another introduction, which can be supplemented by Victor Navasky, *Naming Names* (1980). Two biographies of Mc-Carthy are Thomas C. Reeves, *The Life and Times of Joe McCarthy* (1982), and David Oshinsky, *A Conspiracy So Immense* (1983). Robert Griffith, *The Politics of Fear* (1970), and Richard Fried, *Men against McCarthy* (1976), look at the politics involved.

Allen Weinstein, *Perjury* (1978), covers the still-debated Hiss case. Walter and Miriam Schneir, *Invitation to an Inquest* (1965), and Ronald Radosh and Joyce Milton, *The Rosenberg File* (1983), cover the Rosenberg case. Griffin Fariello, ed., *Red Scare* (1995), provides a compelling oral history of McCarthyism, and Eric Bentley, ed., *Thirty Years of Treason* (1971), collects excerpts from testimony before the House Com-mittee on Un-American Activities.

"Modern Republicanism"

Two standard overviews of the Eisenhower administration, Herbert S. Parmet, *Eisen-hower and the American Crusades* (1972), and Charles C. Alexander, *Holding the Line* (1975), can be supplemented by Fred I. Greenstein, *The Hidden-Hand Presidency* (1982), and Stephen Ambrose, *Eisenhower the President* (1984). Blanche Wiesen Cook, *The Declassified Eisenhower* (1981), contrasts the covert activities of the administration with its public image. On specific aspects of the Eisenhower administration, see Jeff Broadwater, *Seeing Red: Eisenhower and the Anti-Communist Crusade* (1992), and Robert F. Burk, *The Eisenhower Administration and Black Civil Rights* (1984).

For the complex foreign policy of the 1950s, consult Walter LaFeber, *America, Russia, and the Cold War* (1996), and Thomas J. McCormick, *America's Half-Century*. Other overviews are provided in Robert Divine, *Eisenhower and the Cold War* (1981), and Ronald Steel, *Pax Americana* (1967). An excellent book on the CIA is Victor Marchetti and John D. Marks, *The CIA and the Cult of Intelligence* (1974). For the links among economics, corporations, and the defense industry, see Mira Wilkins, *The Maturing of Multinational Enterprise* (1974); Richard Barnet and Ronald Muller, *Global Reach* (1974); and Paul Hammond, *Organizing for Defense* (1971). Gabriel Kolko, *Confronting the Third World, 1945–1980* (1988), offers a highly critical view of U.S. policy. On American involvement in the Middle East, see Bruce Kuniholm, *The Origins of the Cold War in the Near East* (1980), and Michael Stoff, *Oil, War, and American Security* (1980). On Latin America, see Peter H. Smith, *Talons of the Eagle: Dynamics of U.S.–Latin American Relations* (1996), and Stephen Rabe, *Eisenhower and Latin America* (1988).

On specific policy situations in the 1950s, see Robert Divine, *Blowing in the Wind: The Nuclear Test Ban Debate, 1954–1960* (1978); Robert Stookey, *America and the Arab States* (1975); and John Snetsinger, *Truman, the Jewish Role, and the Creation of Israel* (1974). Steven Z. Freiberger, *Dawn over Suez* (1992), and Diane B. Kunz, *The Economic Diplomacy of the Suez Crisis* (1991), examine the Suez crisis of 1956.

CHAPTER 29

General introductions to postwar society include Paul Boyer, *Promises to Keep* (1995); William Chafe, *The Unfinished Journey* (3d ed., 1995); James T. Patterson, *Grand Expectations: The United States, 1945–1974* (1996); and David Halberstam, *The Fifties* (1993).

The Postwar Capitalist Economy

For overviews on the economic changes of the postwar period, see W. Elliot Brownlee, *Dynamics of Ascent* (1979), and David P. Calleo, *The Imperious Economy* (1982). Robert Kuttner, *The End of Laissez-Faire* (1991), provides ample background on the Bretton Woods system. Herman P. Miller, *Rich Man, Poor Man* (1971), and Gabriel Kolko, *Wealth and Power in America* (1962), discuss inequality in income distribution. Michael Harrington, *The Other America* (1962), documents the persistence of poverty in the postwar era, as does Harry M. Caudill, *Night Comes to the Cumberlands* (1963). Michael B. Katz, *In the Shadow of the Poorhouse* (1986), and James Patterson, *America's Struggle against Poverty, 1900–1980* (1981), offer longer-term perspectives. John Kenneth Galbraith, *The Affluent Society* (1958) and *The New Industrial State* (1967), shaped much of the public discussion of the economy in the period.

John L. Shover, *First Majority—Last Minority* (1976), analyzes the transformation of rural life in America. David Brody, *Workers in Industrial America* (1980); James R. Green, *The World of the Worker* (1980); and Robert Zeiger, *American Workers, American Unions, 1920–1985* (1994), provide overviews of labor in the twentieth century. On the impact of technology and automation, see Elting E. Morison, *From Know-how to Nowhere* (1974), and David F. Noble, *Forces of Production* (1984). Harry Braverman, *Labor and Monopoly Capital* (1974), looks at the degradation of work from a Marxist perspective.

The most influential study of the new middle class remains David Reisman et al., *The Lonely Crowd* (1950). See also William H. Whyte, *The Organization Man* (1956), and the work of C. Wright Mills, especially *White Collar* (1951) and *The Power Elite* (1956).

Alfred D. Chandler, *The Visible Hand* (1977), is the definitive history of American corporate structure and strategy. Myra Wilkin, *The Maturing of Multinational Enterprise* (1974), and Richard J. Barnet and Ronald E. Muller, *Global Reach* (1974), describe American business abroad. See also Robert Sobel, *The Age of Giant Corporations* (1972), and Barry Bluestein and Bennett Harrison, *The Deindustrialization of America* (1982).

A Suburban Society

The best overviews of urbanization in the South and the West are Carl Abbott, *The New Urban America* (1981), and Richard Bernard and Bradley Rice, eds., *Sunbelt Cities* (1983). Mark H. Rose, *Interstate* (1979), describes the politics of building the highway system. On the development of suburbs, see Kenneth Jackson, *Crabgrass Frontier* (1985); Jon C. Teaford, *City and Suburb* (1979); Robert Fishman, *Bourgeois Utopias* (1987); and Zane Miller, *Suburb* (1981).

American Society during the Baby Boom

Books that highlight the social and cultural history of the 1950s include Elaine Tyler May, *Homeward Bound* (1988); Larry May, ed., *Recasting America* (1989); Douglas T. Miller and Marion Nowak, *The Fifties* (1977); and Stephen Whitfield, *The Culture of the Cold War* (1991).

For popular culture, George Lipsitz, *Time Passages* (1991) and *Rainbow at Midnight* (2d ed., 1994), look at working-class culture and rock-'n'-roll. Eric Barnouw, *Tube of Plenty* (2d. ed., 1982), chronicles the impact of television and Karal Ann Marling, *As Seen on TV* (1994), challenges many assumptions about television and culture. Other treatments of the mass media include James L. Baughman, *The Republic of Mass Culture* (1992), and Nora Sayre, *Running Time* (1982). Vance Packard's influential unmasking of the advertising industry, *The Hidden Persuaders* (1957), can be supplemented by Stephen Fox, *The Mirror Makers* (1984). Daniel Horowitz's biography, *Vance Packard* (1994), provides valuable insights into intellectuals and the consumer culture.

Richard Easterlin, *American Baby Boom in Historical Perspective* (1962) and *Birth and Future* (1980), analyze the demographic changes, as does Landon Y. Jones, *Great Expectations* (1980). Jane S. Smith, *Patenting the Sun* (1990), looks at Salk's development of the polio vaccine. Diane Ravitch describes education from 1945 to 1980 in *The Troubled Crusade* (1983).

Elaine May's *Homeward Bound* (1990) is the classic introduction to postwar family life, providing a historical corollary to Betty Friedan's *Feminine Mystique* (1963), but see also Joanne Meyerowitz, ed., *Not June Cleaver* (1994), and Wini Breines, *Young, White, and Miserable* (1992). Alice Kessler-Harris, *Out to Work* (1982), surveys women's role in the work force.

Youth culture is the subject of William Graeber's *Coming of Age in Buffalo* (1990). James Gilbert, *A Cycle of Outrage* (1986), looks at juvenile delinquency in the 1950s. Peter Guralnick, *Last Train to Memphis* (1994), is the definitive biography of Elvis Presley's early years. Discussions of cultural dissent in the 1950s can be found in Bruce Cook, *The Beat Generation* (1971), and Dan Wakefield, *New York in the Fifties* (1992).

The Other America

Reed Ueda, *Postwar Immigrant America* (1994), and David Reimers, *Still the Open Door* (1985), examine new trends in immigration since 1945. Nicholas Lemann examines postwar black migration in *The Promised Land* (1991), while Jacqueline Jones compares black and white urban migrants in *The Dispossessed* (1992). Donald Fixico, *Termination and Relocation* (1986), looks at federal native American policy from 1945 to 1970.

Jon C. Teaford, *Rough Road to Renaissance* (1990); John Mollenkopf, *The Contested City* (1983); and Kenneth Fox, *Metropolitan America* (1985), offer the most complete accounts of postwar urban development. Herbert Gans, *The Urban Villagers* (1962), tells the story of a Boston Italian community displaced by urban renewal.

Richard Kluger, *Simple Justice* (1975), and Mark Tushnet, *The NAACP's Legal Strategy against Segregated Education* (1987), analyze the *Brown* decision, while Anthony Lewis, *Portrait of a Decade* (1964), covers southern reaction to the decision. J. Harvey Wilkinson III continues the story of the Supreme Court and integration through the 1970s in *From Brown to Bakke* (1979). Taylor Branch, *Parting the Waters: America in the King Years, 1954–1963* (1988), provides a good account of Martin Luther King's early years and of the importance of black churches to the civil-rights movement. Henry Hampton and Steve Fayer provide an oral history of the movement in *Voices of Freedom* (1990).

CHAPTER 30

Among the best surveys of the 1960s are David Steigerwald, *The Sixties and the End of Modern America* (1995); David Chalmers, *And Crooked Places Made Straight* (1991); David Farber, *The Age of Great Dreams* (1994); Todd Gitlin, *The Sixties* (1987); and Allen J. Matusow, *The Unraveling of America* (1984). Overviews of American foreign policy in the 1960s include Stephen Ambrose, *Rise to Globalism* (7th ed., 1993); Walter LaFeber, *America, Russia, and the Cold War* (7th ed., 1992); and Diane Kunz, ed., *The Diplomacy of the Crucial Decade* (1994).

John Kennedy and the New Frontier

Among the best general accounts of the Kennedy years are Richard Reeves, *President Kennedy* (1993); James Giglio, *The Presidency of JFK* (1991); and David Burner, *JFK and a New Generation* (1988). Critical views appear in David Halberstam, *The Best and the Brightest* (1972); Henry Fairlie, *The Kennedy Promise* (1973); and Garry Wills, *The Kennedy Imprisonment* (1980).

On foreign policy, see Michael Beschloss, *The Crisis Years: Kennedy and Khrushchev, 1960–1963* (1990); Thomas Paterson, *Kennedy's Quest for Victory* (1989); and Richard Walton, *Cold War and Counterrevolution* (1972). James Nathan, *The Cuban Missile Crisis Revisited* (1992); Raymond Garthoff, *Reflections on the Cuban Missile Crisis* (1989); and Thomas Paterson, *Contesting Castro* (1994), assess the Cuban missile crisis. On U.S. relations with the Third World, see John L. S. Girling, *America and the Third World* (1980), and Samuel Baily, *The United States and the Development of South America, 1945–1975* (1977). Gerald T. Rice, *The Bold Experiment* (1985), and Karen Schwarz, *What You Can Do for Your Country* (1991), cover the Peace Corps.

Kennedy's domestic policies are treated in the general works on his presidency noted above. On the Warren Court, see Bernard Schwartz, *Super Chief* (1983). Earl Warren was the chief author of the Warren Report (1964), investigating the Kennedy assassination. More recently, Gerald Posner, *Case Closed* (1993), provides the most definitive treatment of that event.

The Civil-Rights Movement

Robert Weisbrot, *Freedom Bound* (1990), and Harvard Sitkoff, *The Struggle for Black Equality* (2d ed., 1993), offer comprehensive overviews. Two fine oral histories of the civil-rights movement are Howell Raines, *My Soul Is Rested* (1977), and Henry Hampton and Steve Fayer, *Voices of Freedom* (1990). Local accounts of grass-roots organizing include William H. Chafe's superb study of Greensboro, North Carolina, *Civilities and Civil Rights* (1980), and two recent studies of Mississippi: John Dittmer, *Local People* (1994), and Charles M. Payne, *I've Got the Light of Freedom* (1995). The role of women in the civil-rights movement is examined in Vicki L. Crawford et al., *Women in the Civil Rights Movement* (1990). On federal policy making, see Hugh Davis Graham, *Civil Rights and the Presidency* (1992), and Mark Stern, *Calculating Visions* (1992). Martin Luther King, Jr., told his own story in *Why We Can't Wait* (1964). His biographers include David Garrow, *Bearing the Cross* (1986), and Taylor Branch, *Parting the Waters* (1988).

Lyndon Johnson and the Great Society

Lyndon Johnson's account of his presidency can be found in *The Vantage Point* (1971). Doris Kearns, *Lyndon Johnson and the American Dream* (1976), and Merle Miller, *Lyndon* (1980), are based on extensive conversations with LBJ. Other accounts of Johnson's career include Robert A. Caro, *The Path to Power* (1982) and *Means of Ascent* (1989); Robert Dallek in *Lone Star Rising* (1991); and Joseph A. Califano, Jr., *The Triumph and Tragedy of Lyndon Johnson* (1991).

A major synthesis of the Great Society is Irwin Unger, *The Best of Intentions* (1996). Michael Harrington called attention to poverty in *The Other America* (1962), and later critiqued the War on Poverty in *The New American Poverty* (1984). Charles Murray's conservative viewpoint in *Losing Ground: American Social Policy, 1950–1980* (1983) can be balanced by Michael Katz's liberal perspective in *The Undeserving Poor* (1989).

The Continuing Struggle for Civil Rights

Major texts of the black power movement include Stokely Carmichael and Charles Hamilton, *Black Power* (1967); James Baldwin, *The Fire Next Time* (1963); and Eldridge Cleaver, *Soul on Ice* (1968). *The Autobiography of Malcolm X* (cowritten with Alex Haley, 1965) has become a literary classic. William L. Van Deburg, *New Day in Babylon* (1992), provides a general historical account of the black power movement. Hugh Pearson in *The Shadow of the Panther* (1994) looks at Huey Newton and the Black Panthers, as does the former Black Panther Elaine Brown in *A Taste of Power* (1992).

Report of the National Advisory Commission on Civil Disorders (1968) analyzes the decade's major race riots. Sidney Fine's book on the Detroit riot, *Violence in the Model*

City (1989), provides the most thorough historical treatment of race rioting in this period.

Carlos Muñoz, Jr., *Youth, Identity and Power* (1989), and Juan Gomez-Quiñones, *Chicano Politics* (1990), examine the rise of the Chicano movement in the 1960s. Peter Matthiessen, *In the Spirit of Crazy Horse* (1983), and Vine DeLoria, Jr., *Behind the Trail of Broken Treaties* (1974) and *Custer Died for Your Sins* (1969), convey the new Indian assertiveness. John D'Emilio, *Sexual Politics, Sexual Communities* (1983), describes the emergence of gay identity between 1940 and 1970, while Martin Duberman, *Stonewall* (1993), looks at the birth of the gay movement in the late 1960s.

Jo Freeman, *The Politics of Women's Liberation* (1975); Barbara Deckard, *The Women's Movement* (1975); and Judith Hole and Ellen Levine, *The Rebirth of Feminism* (1971), chronicle the revival of feminism in the 1960s and 1970s. Sara Evans, *Personal Politics* (1979), traces the roots of feminism in the civil-rights movement and the New Left, while Alice Echols, *Daring to Be Bad* (1989), examines radical feminism. General histories of women's activism in the 1960s include Cynthia Harrison, *On Account of Sex* (1988); Leila J. Rupp and Verta Taylor, *Survival in the Doldrums* (1987); and Susan M. Hartmann, *From Margin to Mainstream* (1989).

Important feminist works of the period include Robin Morgan, ed., *Sisterhood Is Powerful* (1970); Kate Millett, *Sexual Politics* (1970); Germaine Greer, *The Female Eunuch* (1972); and Susan Brownmiller, *Against Our Will: Men, Women, and Rape* (1975).

CHAPTER 31

Among the best general accounts of the Vietnam War are George Herring, *America's Longest War* (2d ed., 1986); Stanley Karnow, *Vietnam* (rev. ed., 1991); Gary R. Hess, *Vietnam and the United States* (1990); and Marilyn Young, *The Vietnam Wars, 1945–1990* (1991). Guenter Lewy offers a controversial defense of American involvement in *America in Vietnam* (1978).

Into the Quagmire, 1945–1968

The origins of American involvement in Vietnam are covered in Loren Baritz, *Backfire* (1985); Larry Berman, *Planning a Tragedy* (1982) and *Lyndon Johnson's War* (1989); Lloyd Gardner, *Approaching Vietnam* (1988); Conrad Gibbons, *The U.S. Government and the Vietnam War* (1986–1989); David Halberstam, *The Best and the Brightest* (1972) and *The Making of a Quagmire* (rev. ed., 1987); and Brian VanDeMark, *Into the Quagmire* (1991). A fascinating insight into Vietnam policy making in the 1960s can be found in Neil Sheehan, *The Pentagon Papers* (1971). Secretary of Defense Robert McNamara offers an insider's view and a belated apologia in *In Retrospect* (1995). James C. Thompson, *Rolling Thunder* (1980), and John Galloway, *The Gulf of Tonkin Resolution* (1970), cover specific topics. Eric Bergerud, *Dynamics of Defeat* (1991), examines the military aspects of the war, and Daniel Hallin, *The Uncensored War* (1986), and Clarence R. Wyatt, *Paper Soldiers* (1993), look at the role of the media. Frances FitzGerald, *Fire in the Lake* (1972), discusses the war in the context of South Vietnamese society.

For a sense of what the war felt like to the soldiers who fought it, see Mark Baker, *Nam* (1982); Philip Caputo, *Rumor of War* (1977); Gloria Emerson, *Winners and Losers* (1976); Michael Herr, *Dispatches* (1977); Tim O'Brien, *If I Die in a Combat Zone* (1973); Bernard Edelman, ed., *Dear America: Letters Home from Vietnam*; and Ron

Kovic, *Born on the Fourth of July* (1976). Wallace Terry, *Bloods* (1984), surveys the experiences of black veterans, and Keith Walker, *A Piece of My Heart* (1985), introduces the often forgotten stories of the women who served in Vietnam. Lawrence Baskir and William A. Strauss, *Chance and Circumstance* (1978), explains who was drafted and why. Christian G. Appy offers a class analysis of the Vietnam experience in *Working-Class War* (1993). Neil Sheehan surveys the entire Vietnam experience through the life of the career soldier John Paul Vann in *A Bright and Shining Lie* (1988).

The Challenge of Youth, 1962–1970

On the student activism of the 1960s, see Kenneth Keniston, *The Uncommitted* (1965) and *Young Radicals* (1969); Daniel Bell and Irving Kristol, *Confrontation* (1969); and Nathan Glazer, *Remembering the Answers* (1970). On student revolt, see, W. J. Rorabaugh, *Berkeley at War* (1989); Seymour Lipset and Sheldon Wolin, eds., *The Berkeley Student Revolt* (1965); Jerry Avorn, *Up against the Ivy Wall* (1968); Kirkpatrick Sale, *SDS* (1973); Wini Breines, *Community and Organization in the New Left, 1962–1968* (1982); and James Miller, *Democracy Is in the Streets* (1987). Terry Anderson, *The Movement and the Sixties* (1994), and Irwin Unger, *The Movement: A History of the American New Left* (1974), provide general accounts of 1960s activism. Todd Gitlin, *The Whole World Is Watching* (1980), discusses the impact of the mass media on the New Left.

The definitive book on the antiwar movement is Charles DeBenedetti, with Charles Chatfield, *An American Ordeal* (1990). Nancy Zaroulis and Gerald Sullivan, *Who Spoke Up* (1984), examine the role of the New Left in the antiwar movement, while Melvin Small and William D. Hoover, eds., *Give Peace a Chance* (1992), is an anthology of recent work. An eloquent account of one man's embrace of the movement is James Carroll, *An American Requiem* (1996).

Morris Dickstein, *Gates of Eden* (1977), is an excellent account of cultural developments in the 1960s. Todd Gitlin, *The Sixties* (1987), also treats the counterculture extensively. Other sources include Theodore Roszak, *The Making of a Counter-Culture* (1969), and Charles Reich, *The Greening of America* (1970). Gerald Howard, ed., *The Sixties* (1982), is a good anthology of the decade's art, politics, and culture, and *Takin' It to the Streets*, edited by Alexander Bloom and Wini Breines (1995), is an excellent collection of documents. Philip Norman, *Shout! The Beatles in Their Generation* (1981), and Jon Weiner, *Come Together: John Lennon in His Times* (1984), cover developments in popular music. Tom Wolfe, *Electric Kool-Aid Acid Test* (1965), describes the antics of Ken Kesey and his Merry Pranksters, key players in the counterculture. Joan Didion, *Slouching toward Bethlehem* (1968) and *The White Album* (1979), explore some of the darker side of the hippie phenomenon. David Farber, *The Age of Great Dreams* (1994), and David Farber, ed., *The Sixties* (1994), an anthology of articles, provide excellent insights into the Vietnam era.

The Long Road Home

The Tet offensive is the subject of Don Oberdoffer, *Tet!* (1971), whereas the domestic events of 1968 are covered in David Caute, *The Year of the Barricades* (1968); David Farber, *Chicago '68* (1988); and Lewis Chester, Godfrey Hodgson, and Bruce Page, *An American Melodrama* (1970). Norman Mailer provides a contemporary view of the conventions in *Miami and the Siege of Chicago* (1968). Dan Carter, *The Politics of Rage*

(1996), examines the political career of George Wallace, while Kevin Phillips, *The Emerging Republican Majority* (1969), and Richard Scammon and Ben J. Wattenberg, *The Real Majority* (1970), describe the voters Richard Nixon tried to reach. Theodore H. White, *The Making of the President—1968* (1969), covers the divisive election of 1968.

Robert S. Litwak, *Détente and the Nixon Doctrine* (1984); Seymour Hersh, *The Price of Power* (1983); and Tad Szulc, *The Illusion of Peace* (1978), are overviews of Nixon's foreign policy. On his Vietnam policy see the general works on Vietnam listed above, as well as the highly critical study by William Shawcross, *Sideshow: Kissinger, Nixon, and the Destruction of Cambodia* (1979). An account of the My Lai massacre can be found in Seymour Hersh, *Cover-Up* (1972). Frank Snepp, *Decent Interval* (1977), examines the Paris peace process. Robert Jay Lifton, *Home from the War* (1973); Paul Starr, *The Discarded Army* (1973); and Lawrence Baskir and William A. Strauss, *Chance and Circumstance* (1978), discuss the problems of returning Vietnam veterans.

CHAPTER 32

A definitive scholarly history of the 1970s has yet to be written. Peter N. Carroll's popular history, *It Seemed Like Nothing Happened* (1982), provides a general overview of the period, as do the chapters on the 1970s in Paul Boyer, *Promises to Keep* (1995), and William H. Chafe, *The Unfinished Journey* (1995).

The Nixon Years

Jonathan Schell, *The Time of Illusion* (1976), offers an insightful discussion of the Nixon administration. Herbert Parmet, *Richard Nixon and His America* (1990), and Stephen Ambrose's three-volume *Nixon* (1987, 1991) are two of many biographies. Kim McQuaid, *The Anxious Years* (1989), is an overview of the Nixon era. See also William Safire, *Before the Fall* (1975); Leonard Silk, *Nixonomics* (1972); and Garry Wills, *Nixon Agonistes* (rev. ed., 1990).

Stanley Kutler, *The Wars of Watergate* (1990); Anthony Lukas, *Nightmare* (1976); and Theodore H. White, *Breach of Faith* (1975), are comprehensive accounts of the Watergate scandal. See also Carl Bernstein and Bob Woodward, *All the President's Men* (1974) and *The Final Days* (1976). John Dean, *Blind Ambition* (1976), is the best account by a participant; see also H. R. Haldeman, *The Ends of Power* (1978), and Richard M. Nixon, *RN: The Memoirs of Richard Nixon* (1978). Arthur M. Schlesinger, Jr., *The Imperial Presidency* (1973), analyzes the changes in the presidency that provided a backdrop for the Watergate affair.

Lowered Expectations and New Challenges

Barry Commoner, *The Closing Circle* (1971) and *The Poverty of Power* (1976), and Robert Heilbroner, *An Inquiry into the Human Prospect* (1974), cogently assess the origins of the energy crisis and the prospects for the future. See also Lester C. Thurow, *The Zero-Sum Society* (1980), and Robert Stobaugh and Daniel Yergin, *Energy Fu*̄ (1980). Daniel Yergin, *The Prize* (1991); John M. Blair, *The Control of Oil* (197̄ J. C. Hurewitz, ed., *Oil, the Arab-Israeli Dispute, and the Industrial World* (̄ OPEC developments.

General introductions to the economic developments of the decade are Barry Bluestone and Bennett Harrison, *The Deindustrialization of America* (1982); Richard J. Barnet and Ronald E. Muller, *Global Reach* (1974); Richard J. Barnet, *The Lean Years* (1980); John P. Hoerr, *And the Wolf Finally Came: The Decline of the Steel Industry* (1988); Robert Calleo, *The Imperious Economy* (1982); and Gardner Means et al., *The Roots of Inflation* (1975).

Social Gridlock: Reform and Reaction in the 1970s

Tom Wolfe gave the decade its name in "The Me Decade and the Third Great Awakening," *New York Magazine* (August 23, 1976). Influential books include Christopher Lasch, *The Culture of Narcissism* (1978), and Gail Sheehy, *Passages* (1976).

For a general overview of the environmental movement, see Samuel P. Hays, *Beauty, Health, and Permanence* (1987). Roderick Nash provides a history of environmental ethics in *The Rights of Nature* (1989). Books that were influential in shaping public awareness of ecological issues include Rachel Carson, *Silent Spring* (1962); Paul R. Ehrlich, *The Population Bomb* (1968); Frances Moore Lappé, *Diet for a Small Planet* (1971); and Philip Slater, *Earthwalk* (1974). Charles McCarry chronicles Ralph Nader's crusade for consumer protection in *Citizen Nader* (1972).

On women and feminism in the 1970s, see Alice Echols, *Daring to Be Bad* (1989); Susan M. Hartmann, *From Margin to Mainstream* (1989); and Winifred D. Wandersee, *On the Move* (1988). Donald G. Mathews and Jane S. De Hart analyze the struggle over the ERA in *Sex, Gender, and the Politics of ERA* (1990), while Carol Felsenthal examines the life of the ERA opponent Phyllis Schlafly in *The Sweetheart of the Silent Majority* (1981). David Garrow, *Liberty and Sexuality* (1994), is an in-depth examination of the 1973 abortion decision. On the abortion debate, see Faye Ginsberg, *Contested Lives* (1989), and Kristen Luker, *Abortion and the Politics of Motherhood* (1984).

Leigh W. Rutledge surveys the gay and lesbian movement in *The Gay Decades* (1992). Thomas Byrne Edsall with Mary D. Edsall, *Chain Reaction: The Impact of Race, Rights and Taxes on American Politics* (1991), examines some of the divisive social issues of the 1970s. Stanley Aronowitz, *False Promises* (1973); Richard Krickus, *Pursuing the American Dream* (1976); and Michael Novak, *The Rise of the Unmeltable Ethnics* (1977), describe the concerns of the white ethnic middle class. J. Anthony Lukas, *Common Ground* (1985), tells the story of the Boston busing crisis. Nathan Glazer, *Affirmative Discrimination* (1975); Thomas Sowell, *Race and Economics* (1975); and Allan P. Sindler, *Bakke, Defunis, and Minority Admissions* (1978), treat affirmative action.

Alan Crawford, *Thunder on the Right* (1980), and Peter Steinfels, *The Neo-Conservatives* (1979), survey the new conservatism. John Woodridge, *The Evangelicals* (1975), and Quentin J. Schultze, *Televangelism and American Culture* (1991), analyze the rise of evangelical religion. On the political role of the Christian right, see Michael Liensch, *Redeeming America* (1993).

Post-Watergate Politics: Failed Leadership

Much of the material on post-Watergate politics has been provided by journalists rather than historians. James Cannon, *Time and Chance: Gerald Ford's Appointment with History* (1993), and John Osborne, *White House Watch: The Ford Years* (1977), cover the ^ord presidency. See also A. James Reichley, *Conservatives in an Age of Change: The*

Nixon and Ford Administrations (1981). Jules Witcover, *Marathon* (1977), describes the pursuit of the presidency in 1976.

Generally unfavorable portraits of the Carter presidency are found in Burton Kaufman, *The Presidency of James Earl Carter, Jr.* (1993); Robert Shogan, *Promises to Keep* (1977); Haynes Johnson, *In the Absence of Power* (1980); and Clark Mollenhoff, *The President Who Failed* (1980). See also Erwin Hargrove, *Jimmy Carter as President* (1989), and Charles Jones, *The Trusteeship Presidency* (1988). James Wooten, *Dasher* (1978), and Betty Glad, *Jimmy Carter* (1980), are competent biographies. See also Jimmy Carter's presidential memoirs, *Keeping Faith* (rev. ed., 1995). James Fallows, *National Defense* (1981), provides an incisive overview of defense developments. See also A. Glenn Mower, Jr., *Human Rights and American Foreign Policy: The Carter and Reagan Experiences* (1987). Gary Sick, *All Fall Down* (1986), provides an account of the Iranian hostage crisis, and Jack Germond, *Blue Smoke and Mirrors* (1981), examines the presidential election of 1980.

CHAPTER 33

Few historians have turned their attention to the period after 1980, leaving the field to journalists, economists, and political scientists. The Bureau of the Census offers a fine introduction to the period in its *Statistical Abstract of the United States* (114th ed., 1994). Essays on important issues are available in the *Congressional Quarterly Researcher.* Indexes to newspapers and periodicals identify stories on major events.

The Reagan-Bush Years, 1981–1993

Haynes Johnson, *Sleepwalking through History* (1991), provides an excellent overview of America in the Reagan years. See also Robert Dallek, *Ronald Reagan* (1982); Michael Rogin, *Ronald Reagan* (1987); and Lou Cannon, *President Reagan* (1991). On electoral politics, see Jack W. Germond and Jules Witcover, *Wake Us When It's Over* (1985), and Frances Fox Piven and Richard Cloward, *Why Americans Don't Vote* (1988).

On Reaganomics, George Gilder's *Wealth and Poverty* (1981) represents the views held by many in the Reagan administration, but David Stockman's memoir, *The Triumph of Politics* (1986), is more revealing. See also Benjamin Friedman, *Day of Reckoning* (1988).

On the Bush administration, see James A. Baker, *The Politics of Diplomacy* (1995); Barbara Bush, *Barbara Bush: A Memoir* (1994); and Stephen R. Graubard, *Mr. Bush's War* (1992). For an insider's critical account of the Bush White House, see Charles Kolb, *White House Daze* (1994). On politics, see E. J. Dionne, *Why Americans Hate Politics* (1992); William Greider, *Who Will Tell the People?* (1992); and Kevin Phillips, *The Politics of Rich and Poor* (1990).

Foreign Relations under Reagan and Bush

For foreign policy, Stephen Ambrose, *Rise to Globalism* (7th ed., 1993), provides a comprehensive overview of the Reagan and Bush years. The Iran-Contra scandal is covered in Jane Hunter et al., *The Iran-Contra Connection* (1987). Good introductions to the United States and Central and South America include Walter LaFeber, *Inevitable Revolutions* (1984); Abraham F. Lowenthal, *Partners in Conflict: The United St*

Latin America (1987); and Kenneth Coleman and George C. Herring, eds., *The Central America Crisis* (1985).

The emergence of a new world order has provoked commentary from economists, journalists, and historians, including Paul Kennedy, *The Rise and Fall of the Great Powers* (1987); Joseph Nye, *Bound to Lead: The Changing Nature of American Power* (1990); Robert Kuttner, *The End of Laissez Faire: National Purpose and the Global Economy after the Cold War* (1991); and Henry R. Nau, *The Myth of America's Decline* (1990). Bernard Gwertzman and Michael T. Kaufman, eds., *The Collapse of Communism* (1990), reviews the events of 1989 through articles published in the *New York Times*. See also Michael Beschloss and Strobe Talbott, *At the Highest Levels: The Inside Story of the End of the Cold War* (1994). H. Norman Schwartzkopf's autobiography, *It Doesn't Take a Hero* (1992), recounts the Gulf War, as does former chairman of the Joint Chiefs of Staff Colin Powell in *My American Journey* (1995).

An Age of Anxiety

Paul Krugman, *Peddling Prosperity* (1994), and Jeffrey Madrick, *The End of Affluence* (1995), provide overviews of economic trends since the 1970s. Lester C. Thurow offers an insightful analysis of the world economic changes accompanying the collapse of communism in *The Future of Capitalism* (1996). For overviews of U.S. competitiveness in the global marketplace, see Hedrick Smith, *Rethinking America* (1995); Lester Thurow, *Head to Head: The Coming Economic Battle among Japan, Europe, and America* (1992); and Robert B. Reich, *The Work of Nations* (1991). Books that address the growing inequality in American life include William J. Wilson, *The Truly Disadvantaged* (1987); Michael Katz, *The Undeserving Poor* (1989); Nicholas Lemann, *The Promised Land* (1989); and Linda Gordon, *Pitied but Not Entitled: Single Mothers and the History of Welfare* (1994). A lively work that provides statistics on America's world standing on a variety of social and economic measures is Andrew L. Shapiro, *We're Number One* (1992).

On the problems of women, work, and families, see Hilda Scott, *Working Your Way to the Bottom* (1985); Arlie Hochschild, *The Second* (1989); and Juliet Schor, *The Overworked American* (1991). For feminism and its critics, see Susan Faludi, *Backlash* (1991). Toni Morrison, ed., *Race-ing Justice, En-gendering Power* (1992), covers the Clarence Thomas–Anita Hill hearings.

David Reimers, *Still the Golden Door* (2d ed., 1992), covers immigration policy in the postwar period. Linda Chavez, *Out of the Barrio* (1991), discusses Hispanic assimilation, while Ronald Takaki, *Strangers from a Different Shore* (1989), covers Asian-Americans, and Julian Simon, *The Economic Consequences of Immigration* (1989), assesses the economic implication of immigration. Various analyses of the 1992 racial uprising in Los Angeles are provided in Haki R. Madhubuti, ed., *Why L.A. Happened* (1993).

Randy Shilts, *And the Band Played On* (1987), is a controversial critique of inaction in the early years of the AIDS epidemic. See also Elinor Burkett, *The Gravest Show on Earth* (1995). Allan Bloom, *The Closing of the American Mind* (1987), and E. D. Hirsch, Jr., *Cultural Literacy* (1988), deal with issues of curriculum, learning, and literacy. Lawrence W. Levine, *The Opening of the American Mind* (1996), challenges many of their assumptions. For differing views on affirmative action, see Stephen L. Carter, *Reflections of an Affirmative Action Baby* (1991), and Gertrude Ezorsky, *Racism and Justice* (1991). For the story of Bill Gates and Microsoft, see Steven Manes, *Gates* (1993); James Wallace, *Hard Drive* (1992); and Gates's own *The Road Ahead* (1995).

Gregg Easterbrook provides a general overview of the environment in *A Moment on the Earth* (1995). Al Gore, *Earth in the Balance* (1992), reports on how well or poorly the world is doing on environmental awareness. Daniel Yergin, *The Prize* (1991), chronicles how oil dominates modern life, with both economic and environmental consequences.

The Clinton Presidency: Public Life since 1993

For an excellent overview of Clinton's first year, see Elizabeth Drew, *Finding His Voice* (1994). Other sources include Bob Woodward, *The Agenda* (1994); Roger Morris, *Promises of Change* (1996); and Richard Cohen, *Changing the Guard* (1993). James B. Stewart, *Blood Sport* (1996), analyzes the Whitewater scandal. On the Republican agenda, see Newt Gingrich, *To Renew America* (1995).

CREDITS

Illustrations

Project; **p. 659** Corbis-Bettmann; **p. 662** Henry Lee Moon Library and Civil Rights Archive of the NAACP.

Chapter 25   p. 671 Franklin D. Roosevelt Library, Hyde Park, NY; **p. 678** MOMA–Film Stills Archive; **p. 681** (top) UPI/Corbis-Bettmann; (bottom) Schomburg Center for Research in Black Culture, The New York Public Library. Astor, Lenox, and Tilden Foundations; **p. 686** University of Texas, The Institute of Texan Cultures, The *San Antonio Light* Collection; **p. 689** Corbis-Bettmann.

Chapter 26   p. 694 AP/Wide World Photos; **p. 696** Library of Congress; **p. 700** UPI/Corbis-Bettmann; **p. 707** Ben Shahn, *Steel Workers Organizing Committee* Poster, 1930s, Library of Congress; **p. 710** AP/Wide World Photos.

Chapter 27   p. 729 Courtesy of the Dorothea Lange Collection, The City of Oakland, The Oakland Museum 1982; **p. 736** Myron Davos, *Life Magazine* © Time Warner, Inc; **p. 740** UPI/Corbis-Bettmann; **p. 744** Franklin D. Roosevelt Library, Hyde Park, NY (Photographed by US Army Signal Corps); **p. 746** UPI/Corbis-Bettmann.

Chapter 28   p. 754 UPI/Corbis-Bettmann; **p. 761** Carl Albert Center Congressional Archives, University of Oklahoma; **p. 763** UPI/Corbis-Bettmann; **p. 768** Robert Phillips/ Black Star; **p. 775** FPG International.

Chapter 29   p. 784 Photo by Dan Weiner, Courtesy Sandra Weiner; **p. 787** The Huntington Library, San Marino, California (Whittington Collection); **p. 796** © 1956 BMG Music; **p. 802** AP/Wide World Photos.

Chapter 30   p. 808 AP/Wide World Photos; **p. 816** Charles Moore/Black Star; **p. 828** UPI/Corbis-Bettmann; **p. 831** Bettye Lane.

Chapter 31   p. 842 AP/Wide World Photos; **p. 845** Bancroft Library, University of California, Berkeley; **p. 848** Paul Fusco/Magnum; **p. 854** Burt Glinn/Magnum; **p. 856** Michael Abramson/Black Star.

Chapter 32   p. 868 Dennis Brack/Black Star; **p. 870** Tony Korody/Sygma; **p. 877** Bettye Lane; **p. 880** Stanley Forman; **p. 887** Mingam/Gamma Liaison.

Chapter 33   p. 892 Rick Rickman/Matrix; **p. 898** Luc Delahaye/SIPA Press; **p. 903** Kay Chernush/The Image Bank; **p. 908** Estate of Keith Haring; **p. 917** Sygma.

Text

Chapter 17   p. 455 H. Arnold Barton, ed., *Letters from the Promised Land* (University of Minnesota Press, 1975). Copyright © 1975 by the University of Minnesota Press.

Chapter 18   p. 488 Rose Schneiderman, *All for One* (1967), reprinted in Irving Howe and Kenneth Libo, eds., *How We Lived* (New York: New American Library, 1979). Reprinted with permission. **p. 490** Jerold S. Auerbach, ed., *American Labor: The Twentieth Century* (Indianapolis: The Bobbs-Merrill Company, Inc., 1969). Reprinted by permission.

Chapter 20   **p. 540** Irving Howe and Kenneth Libo, eds., *How We Lived* (New York: New American Library, 1979). Reprinted with permission.

Chapter 21   **p. 556** Reprinted with the permission of Scribner, a Division of Simon & Schuster from *Bare Hands and Stone Walls* by Charles Edward Russell. Copyright ©1933 by Charles Edward Russell, renewed 1961. **p. 562** W. Elliot Brownlee and Mary M. Brownlee, eds., *Women in the American Economy: A Documentary History* (New Haven: Yale University Press, 1976). Copyright © 1976 by Yale University Press.

Chapter 23   **p. 621** Frank Freidel, *Over There: The Story of America's First Great Overseas Crusade*, rev. ed. (New York: McGraw-Hill, 1990). Reproduced with permission of The McGraw-Hill Companies.

Chapter 24   **p. 643** Reprinted from *Second to None: A Documentary History of American Women, Volume II: From 1865 to the Present*, edited by Ruth Barnes Moynihan, Cynthia Russett and Laurie Crumpacker by permission of the University of Nebraska Press. © 1993 by the University of Nebraska Press.

Chapter 25   **pp. 673, 684** From *Hard Times* by Studs Terkel. Copyright © 1970 by Studs Terkel. Reprinted by permission of Pantheon Books, a division of Random House, Inc. **p. 677** Burt Kalmar and Harry Ruby, *Freedonia Hymn*. Copyright © 1933 by Famous Music Corporation. Reprinted by permission.

Chapter 26   **pp. 706, 709** From *Hard Times* by Studs Terkel. Copyright © 1970 by Studs Terkel. Reprinted by permission of Pantheon Books, a division of Random House, Inc.

Chapter 27   **p. 728** Copyright © 1993, from *Taps for a Jim Crow Army: Letters from Black Soldiers in World War II*, by Phillip McGuire, editor. Reprinted with permission of The University Press of Kentucky. **p. 741** Judy Barret Litoff and David C. Smith, eds., *American Women in a World at War: Contemporary Accounts from World War II* (Wilmington: Scholarly Resource Books, 1997). Reprinted from Juanita Redmond, *I Served on Bataan* (Philadelphia: J. B. Lippincott Co., 1943).

Chapter 28   **p. 766** Lillian Hellman, *Scoundrel Time* (Boston: Little, Brown and Co., 1976). Reprinted by permission. **p. 776** Ron Kovic, *Born on the Fourth of July* (New York: McGraw-Hill, 1976). Reprinted by permission of McGraw-Hill, Inc.

Chapter 29   **p. 794** Brett Harvey, *The Fifties: A Women's Oral History* (New York: Harper-Collins, 1993). Reprinted by permission of Brett Harvey. **p. 803** Reprinted by permission of The Putnam Publishing Group from *My Soul Is Rested* by Howell Raines. Copyright © 1977 by Howell Raines.

Chapter 30   **p. 810** Roy Hoopes, ed., *The Peace Corps Experience* (New York: Clarkson N. Potter, Inc., 1968). Reprinted by permission. **p. 400** From *Coming of Age in Mississippi* by Anne Moody. Copyright © 1968 by Anne Moody. Used by permission of Doubleday, a division of Bantam Doubleday Dell Publishing Group, Inc.

Chapter 31   **p. 847** Alexander Bloom and Wini Breindes, eds., *"Takin' it to the Streets": A Sixties Reader* (Oxford University Press, 1995). Reprinted by permission. **p. 850** Joe Smith, *Off* *the Record: An Oral History of Popular Music,* edited by Mitchell Fink (New York: Warner Books, 1988). Reprinted by permission.

Chapter 32   **p. 866** From *Washington Journal: The Events of 1973-1974* by Elizabeth Drew. Copyright © 1974 by Elizabeth Drew. Reprinted by permission of Random House. **p. 874** From *American Dreams: Lost and Found* by Studs Terkel. Copyright © 1980 by Studs Terkel. Reprinted by permission of Pantheon Books, a division of Random House, Inc.

Chapter 33   **p. 900** From *Newsweek,* May 1, 1995. © 1995, Newsweek, Inc. All rights reserved. Reprinted by permission. **p. 905** From *Mexican Voices, American Dreams* by Marilyn P. Davis, © 1990 by Marilyn P. Davis. Reprinted by permission of Henry Holt and Company, Inc.

INDEX

Note: Italic letters following page numbers refer to figures *(f)*, illustrations *(i)*, maps *(m)*, and tables *(t)*.

Abbott, Grace, 702
Abbott, Jacob, 553
Abernathy, Ralph, 802
abortion, 674
  Supreme Court decisions
    1989–1992, 896
    Roe decision (1973), 864, 877, 896
  violence against people seeking or providing,
    907–908
abstract expressionism, 797
Abyssinian Baptist Church (New York City), 661
Acheson, Dean, 757, 835
"Acres of Diamonds" (Conwell), 550
activism. *See also* antiwar movement (1960s–1970s)
  1960s, 806, 844–848
  1970s, 872–884
    antibusing movement, 880, 880*i*, 882
    antinuclear movement, 873–875
    environmental movement, 873–875
    native Americans, 880
    resentment, politics of, 883–884
    women's movement, 876–879, 877*i*
ACT UP, 908*i*
Adams, Brooks, 590
Adams, Charles Francis, Jr., 512, 597
Adams, Samuel Hopkins, 573
Addams, Jane, 560, 561*i*, 597
adolescence, 554. *See also* young people
advertising (advertising industry), 481, 649, 791
AFDC (Aid to Families with Dependent Children),
  820, 915
affirmative action, 882, 906–907
affluence. *See* prosperity
Afghanistan, 886
AFL (American Federation of Labor), 496, 565, 566,
  626, 707, 785
AFL-CIO (American Federation of Labor-Congress
  of Industrial Organizations), 785
Africa, colonization of, 587
African-Americans. *See* blacks
agencies and executive departments, federal. *See* federal agencies and executive departments
Agency for International Development, 809
Agent Orange, 840
Age of Innocence, The (Wharton), 661
Agnew, Spiro, 854, 855, 867–868
agribusiness, 786
Agricultural Adjustment Act (AAA; 1933), 697,
  703
Agricultural Marketing Act (1929), 687
agriculture. *See also* farmers; *and specific crops*
  in 1920s, 645

in 1930s, Agricultural Adjustment Act (AAA;
  1933), 697
  1945–1970, 786
  dry farming, 458
  Great Depression and, 667–668, 680, 682
    California, 683–684
  homesteading in the Great Plains and, 454–458
  sharecropping, 441*i*, 441–442
  in the South, 481, 697
Aguinaldo, Emilio, 597, 598
AIDS (acquired immune deficiency syndrome),
  908–909
Aid to Families with Dependent Children (AFDC),
  820, 915
Alabama, 431, 440, 483
Alabama (warship), 583
Alaska, 585
Alaska Native Land Claims Act (1971), 880
Alcatraz Island, AIM occupation of (1969–1971),
  827
alcohol consumption. *See also* prohibition
  ethnocultural conflict over, 510
Aldrich, Nelson W., 575
Algeciras conference (1906), 607, 608
Albright, Madeline, 912
Alliance for Progress, 809
Allied Powers, in World War I, 614
All the King's Men (Warren), 700*i*
Alsberg, Henry, 714
Amalgamated Association of Iron and Steel Workers,
  497
America First Committee, 723
American Automobile Association, 650
American Civil Liberties Union (ACLU), 658
American Commonwealth, The (Bryce), 502
American Equal Rights Association, 431
American Expeditionary Force (AEF), 620–622,
  621*m*
American Federation of Labor (AFL), 496, 565, 566,
  626, 707, 785
American Indian Movement (AIM), 827, 828*i*
Americanism, 541
American Legion, 622
American Medical Association (AMA), 674, 764,
  821
American Mercury (journal), 661
American Plan, 646
American Protective League, 630
American Railway Union (ARU), 498
American Woman's Home, The (Beecher), 552
Ames, Adelbert, 440
"Amos 'n' Andy" (radio program), 653, 679
amusement parks, 543
anarchists, 496
Angelou, Maya, 679